AF473741

BONUS:

GRAFFITI CREATION

Because of the bad reputation of subway graffiti, graffiti art has been stereotyped as illegal and unpopular. As a matter of fact, many graffiti artists are commissioned to create works. Besides, for most graffiti artists starting up, they prefer to practise drawing in their sketchbook for a long time before they actually put works on walls. This chapter introduces basic knowledge and general making process of graffiti tags, stencil graffiti, and wheatpaste graffiti to those craving to create graffiti works of their own.

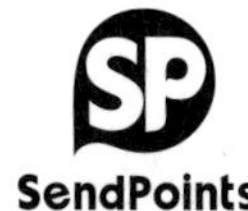

SendPoints

GRAFFITI ALL THROUGH MY LIFE

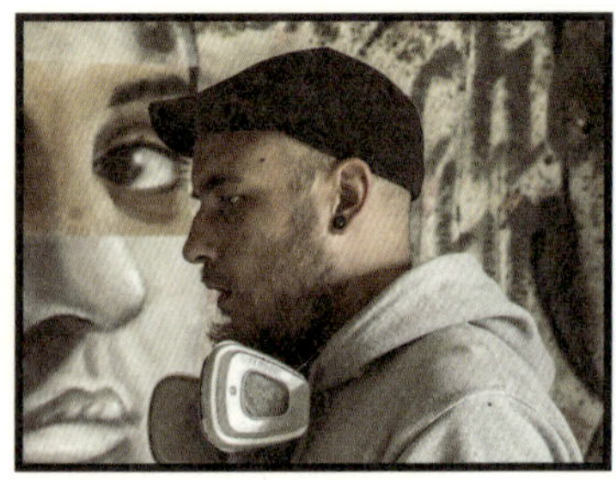

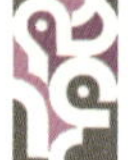

Asier
street artist @Spain
asier.com.es

I can recall a memory when I was 8 years old. My teacher asked my parents to come over and told them I had problems with "space": when my teacher gave me a sheet of paper, I didn't draw on the whole surface; instead, I just drew on a small corner of the entire sheet. Years later, I was on the road of a street artist, and was surrounded by artist friends who had so many seemingly weird little habits when they created arts. Every time I think of this 8-year-old memory, I know this is where my exploration of the possibilities of art begins. This "space" problem that once troubled my parents turned out to be a good beginning of my life story, because I could never live without art from then on.

Madrid is a city full of joy and celebration. Street arts are everywhere. The first time I got to know about graffiti was from the neighborhood I resided in. Active and energetic kid as I was, I stopped to read carefully the tags by graffiti writers. I was amazed by their bold and reckless creative tags. I knew I was charmed, with no chance of getting away. Actually, not just me, teenagers like me were obsessed with this form of art, or vandalism as some people see it. At school, the senior students would secretly sketch their graffiti tags on the margins of their books, and their notebooks had more notes for tags than schoolwork. I guess this is the original black book[1] for these future writers.

[1] Black book, also known as "piece book," is a graffiti artist's sketchbook.

My whole teenager time was soaked in street arts, and at the end of high school, I finally owned my first spray cans. Like most writers, I just tagged around my name "ASIER," a name unique enough among Spanish names. Vandalism as it is, tagging is no doubt the realest and most authentic graffiti form. It is about the recognition of the identity writers choose for themselves. I hung around the city and discovered that elaborate works, especially portraits or characters, drew most of the pedestrian attention. The idea of getting people to stop and watch excited me, for it reminded me of the stop-and-watch kid I used to be. I wish my works could charm the audience the way I was charmed.

With a concept or message in mind, I will study first the walls or the surfaces I am going to paint, and how my work can integrate into the environment by observing the colors of the area, the shapes, etc. Then, I would design the image on computer or simply hand paint and then digitalize it to determine which colors to use. After all these preliminary works, I start to paint on walls. To paint on walls, wearing a mask is always a must, because spray paints are toxic. If it is windy in the street, I might wear it less often. After days of hard work, your piece is finally done, but whether it is a legal or illegal piece, it risks being intervened, for it is street art after all and it belongs to the street and it is up to the street how it evolves over time. Thanks to the social network, street artists can save the moment when the piece is freshly made, and share it around the world.

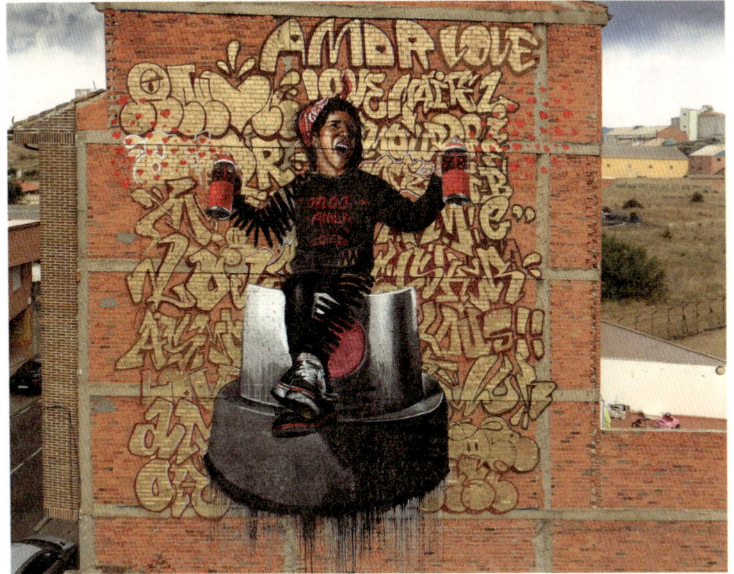

We are living in a world of chaos, competition, wars, social issues, food security, etc. We are overloaded with the dark side of life sometimes. However, painting is like therapy. The problems and concerns that bother me will find a way out whenever I am indulging in painting. Everything that happens in the world could be an inspiration. Some so sad, some so irritating, some so ridiculous, the emotional experience drives me to go outside and paint. All through the years, graffiti have grown in me. It becomes my identity, my innate drive, and my voice. And, it will keep motivating me to go further.

GRAFFITI EQUIPMENT

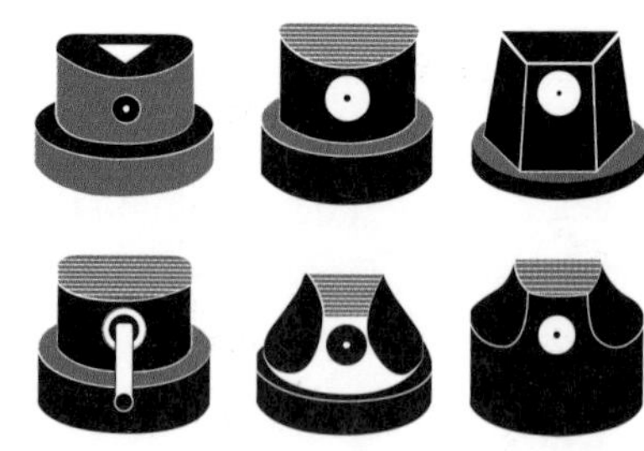
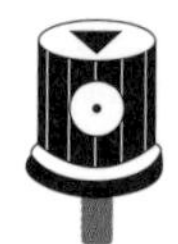
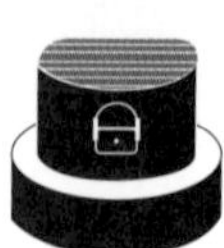
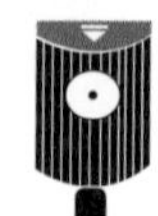
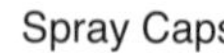

Spray Caps

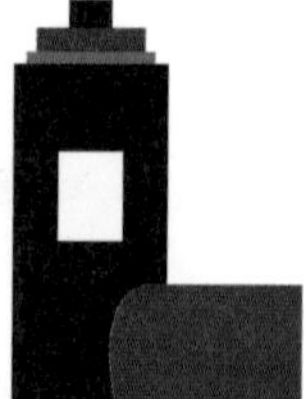
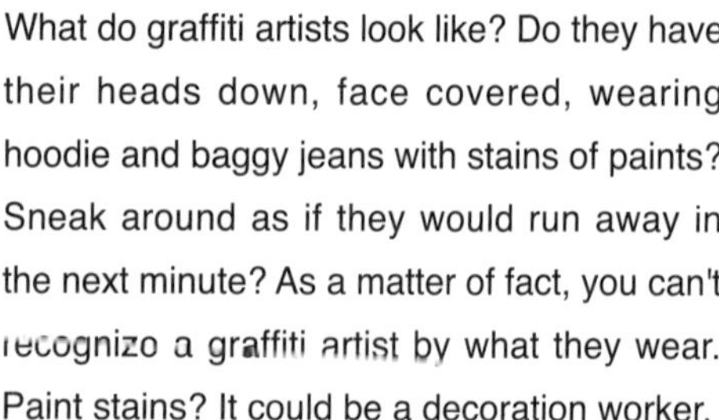

Spray Cans

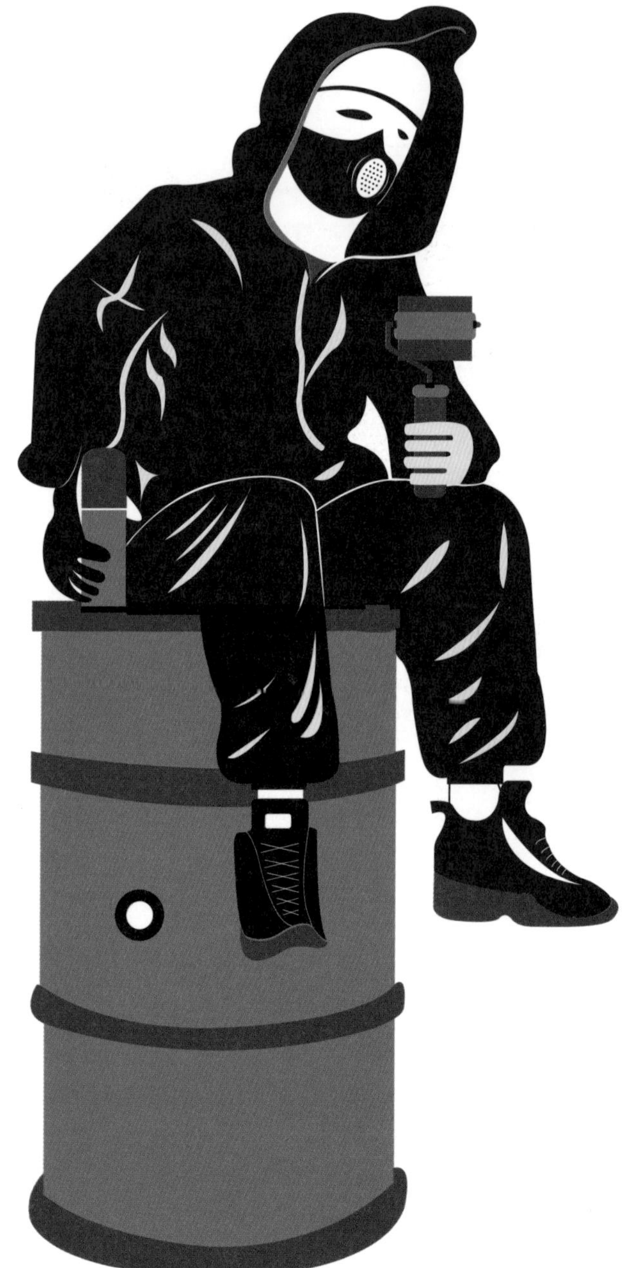

What do graffiti artists look like? Do they have their heads down, face covered, wearing hoodie and baggy jeans with stains of paints? Sneak around as if they would run away in the next minute? As a matter of fact, you can't recognize a graffiti artist by what they wear. Paint stains? It could be a decoration worker.

The one way you can tell whether they are street artists is when they are doing their work, using a bunch of tools and equipment. The most noticeable would be the respirator and gloves they wear, and all kinds of painting supplies and tools, including spray cans, caps, and brushes. As more and more artists are taking commissions to paint large-scale walls, a scissor lift and/or boom lift are often seen at the scene.

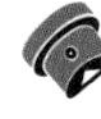
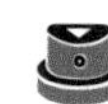
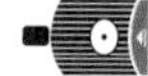

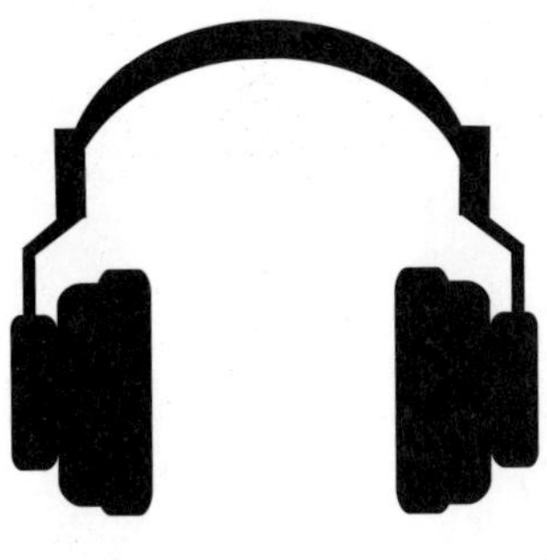

Headset

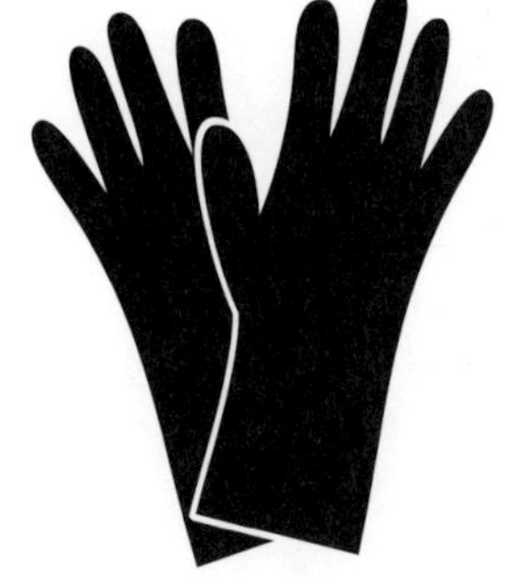

Latex Gloves

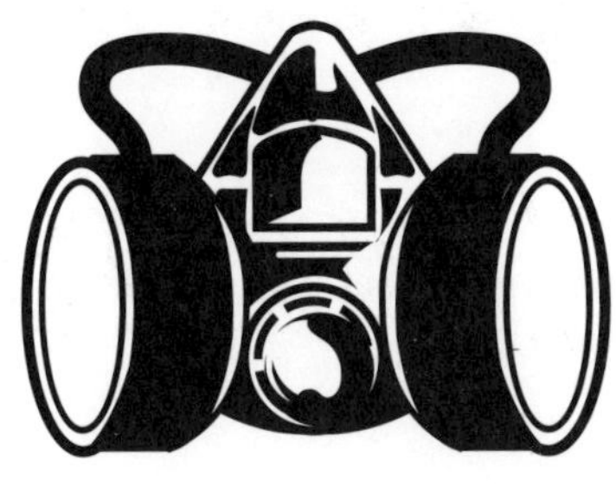

Respirator

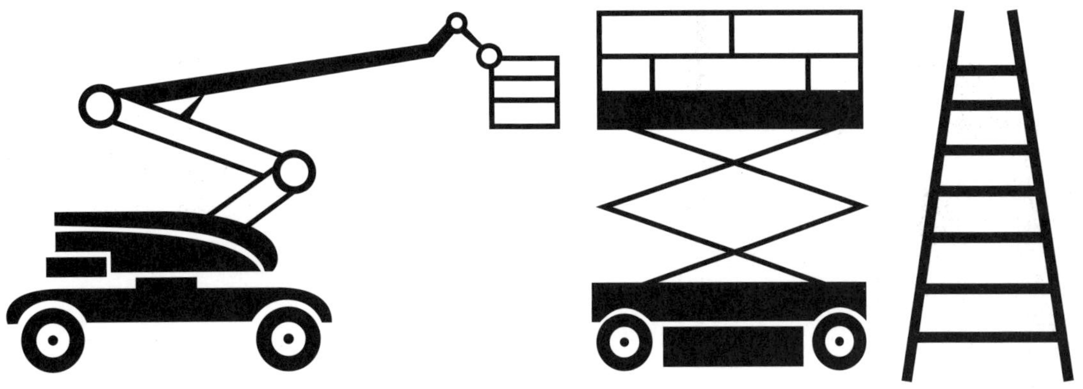

Boom Lift

Scissor Lift

Ladder

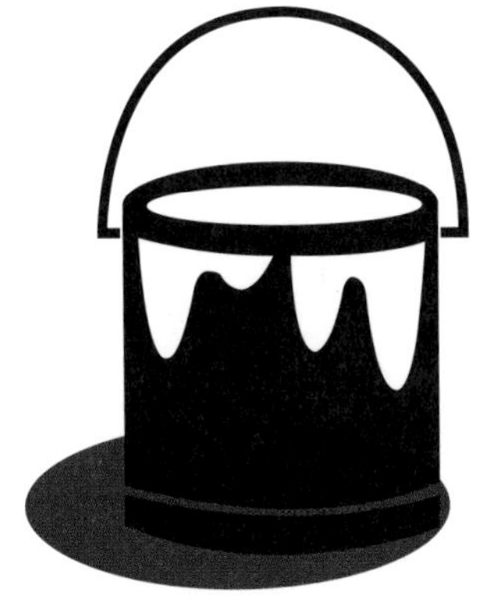

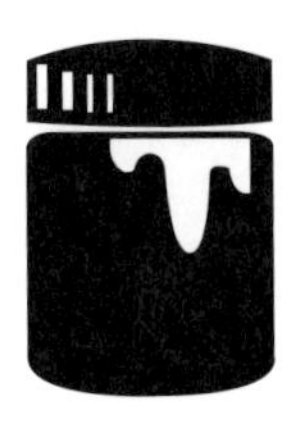

Acrylic Paint

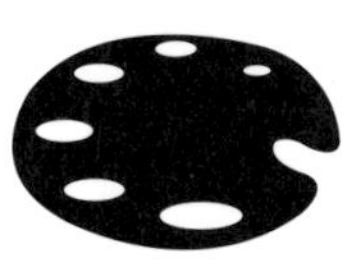

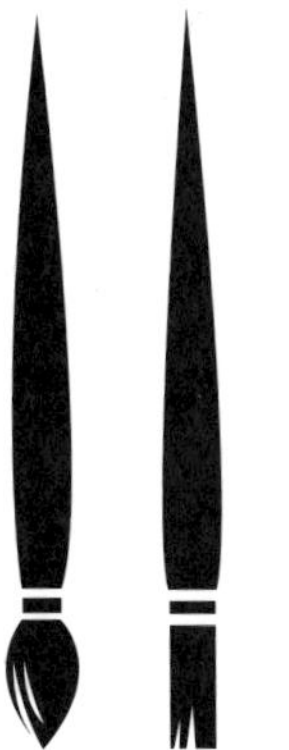

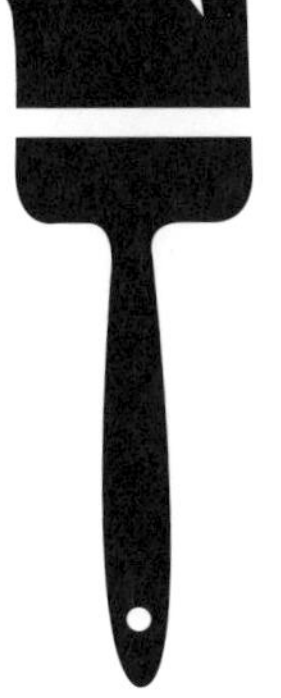

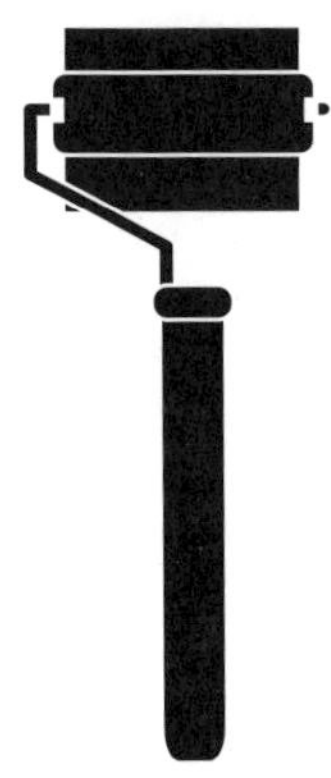

Paint Bucket

Color Palette

Paint Brushes

Roller Brush

HOW TO CREATE A GRAFFITI TAG

A graffiti tag is a signature a graffiti writer chooses for himself. It could be anything including name initials, favorite color, middle name, a neighborhood name plus a number, and an abbreviation of a word. Usually, a tag comprises of more or less five letters which look and sound awesome together. Now graffiti tag is more than a tag. It could be referred to an artistic style that has integral characteristics.

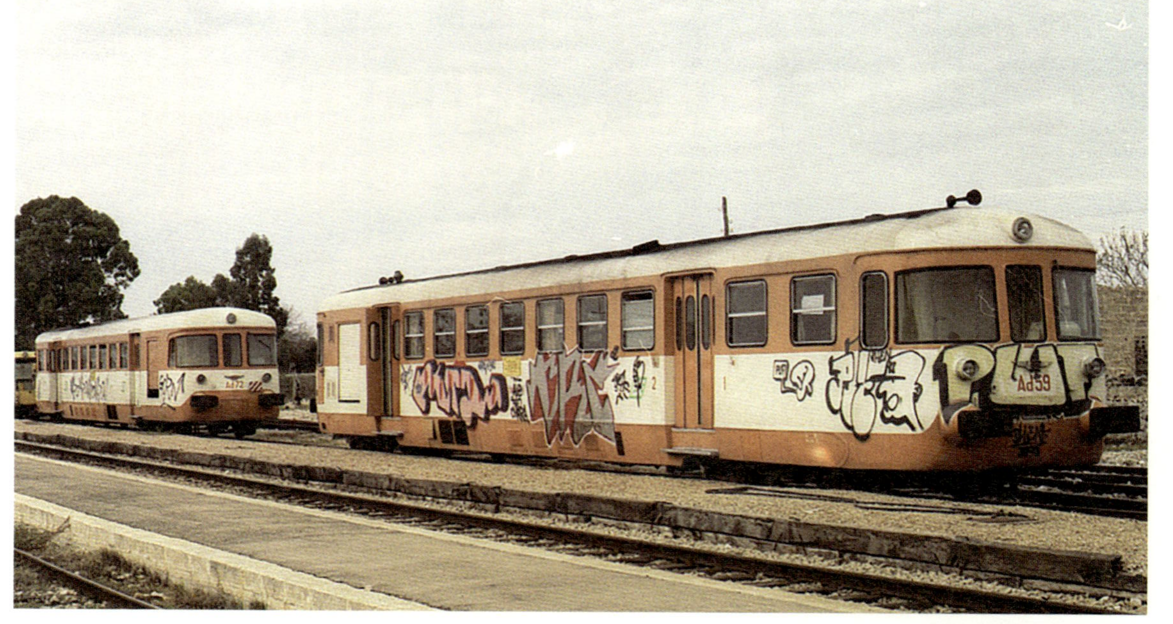

Photo/ Phil Richards (Flickr)

SPRAY CAN

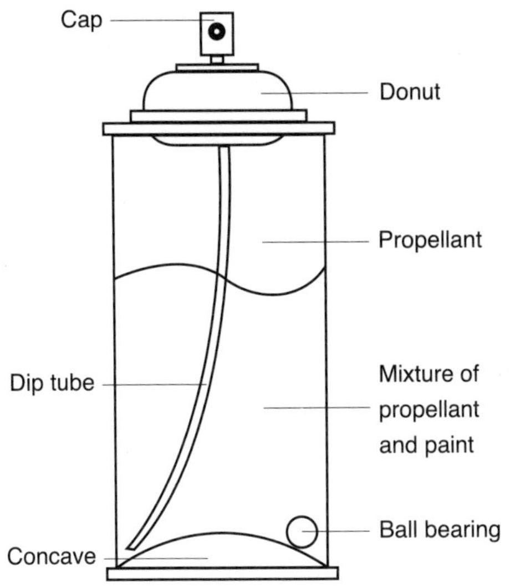

Cap—regulating the diameter and quantity of paint that gets off the can.
Donut—a circle on the top of the can, usually indicating the color.
Propellant—a liquefied gas. When the valve is open, the reduced pressure of propellant enables the forming of a gas layer which pushes out the mixture of paint and propellant through the dip tube.
Paint—oil-based paint, or acrylic paint
Ball Bearing—mixing the spray paint and the propellant.
Concave—balancing out internal pressure and stabilize the body of the can.

Usage: Shake the spray can hard enough to make sure the paint and the propellant are well mixed.

SPRAY CAP

Thin Cap—producing thin lines, which are good for painting small areas, fine details, light shading, and highlights.
Standard Cap—producing a medium line width, and used for general purpose, mostly filling and outlining.
Fat Cap—used for painting larger areas and filling in quickly.
Soft Cap—used for stencils, highlights, hazes, shadings and other effects.
Stencil Cap—producing extremely thin lines.
Calligraphy Cap—producing a calligraphy pen or marker type of squared-off lines.
Needle Cap—producing spatter effects or patterns with its short tube projecting out of its discharge area.

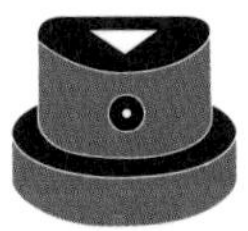
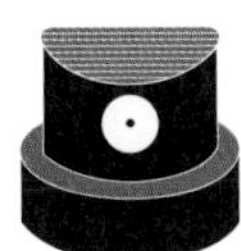
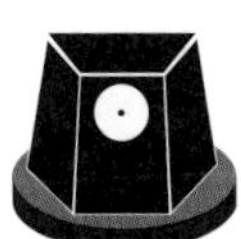

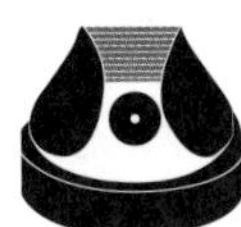
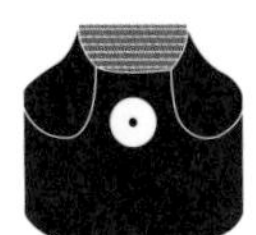
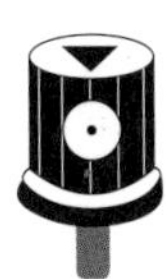
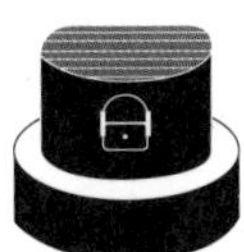
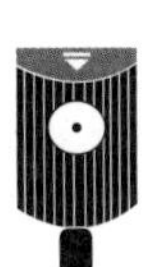

STYLE

Distinctive styles of tag lettering are found in different regions of the US. Below are the most common tag styles.

PHILADELPHIA STYLE

Slender

NEW YORK STYLE

Curvy and Angular

LOS ANGELES STYLE

Square

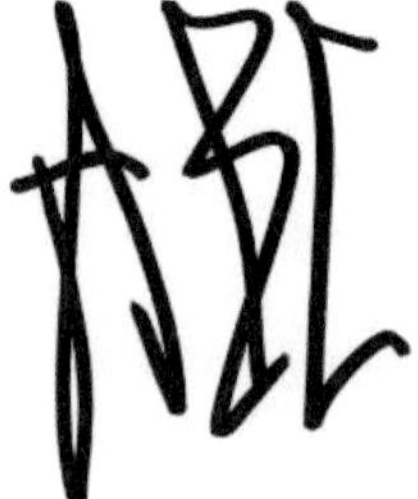

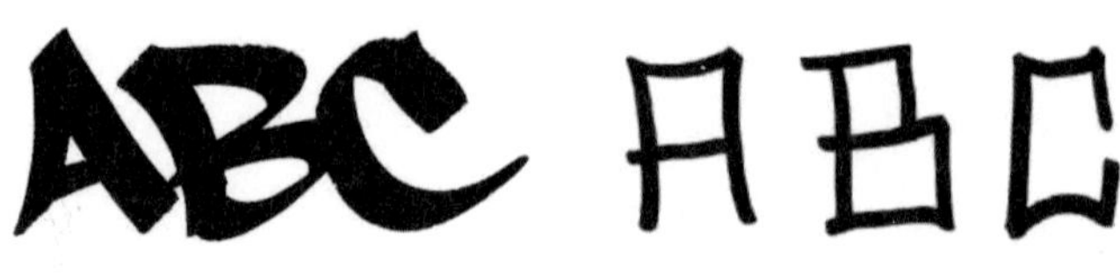

ORNAMENT

Some decorative elements will be added to a tag, such as a star, a heart, a halo, an arrow, an underline, or a simple character. These elements help complete the composition of a tag, but make it illegible even more for the audience.

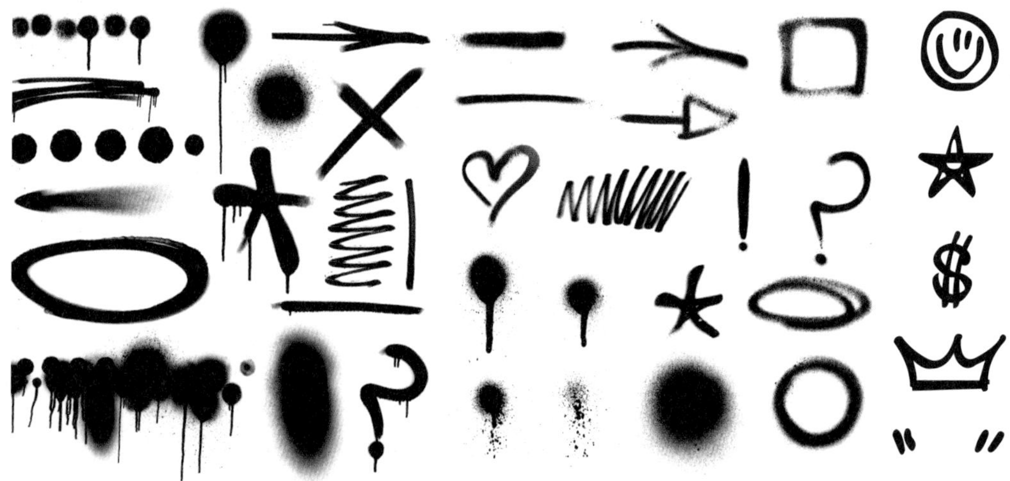

Photo/ Freepik

LAYOUT

Tags, no matter how complicated they appear to be, follow some sort of layout patterns. The letters and ornaments will be arranged in a compact way.

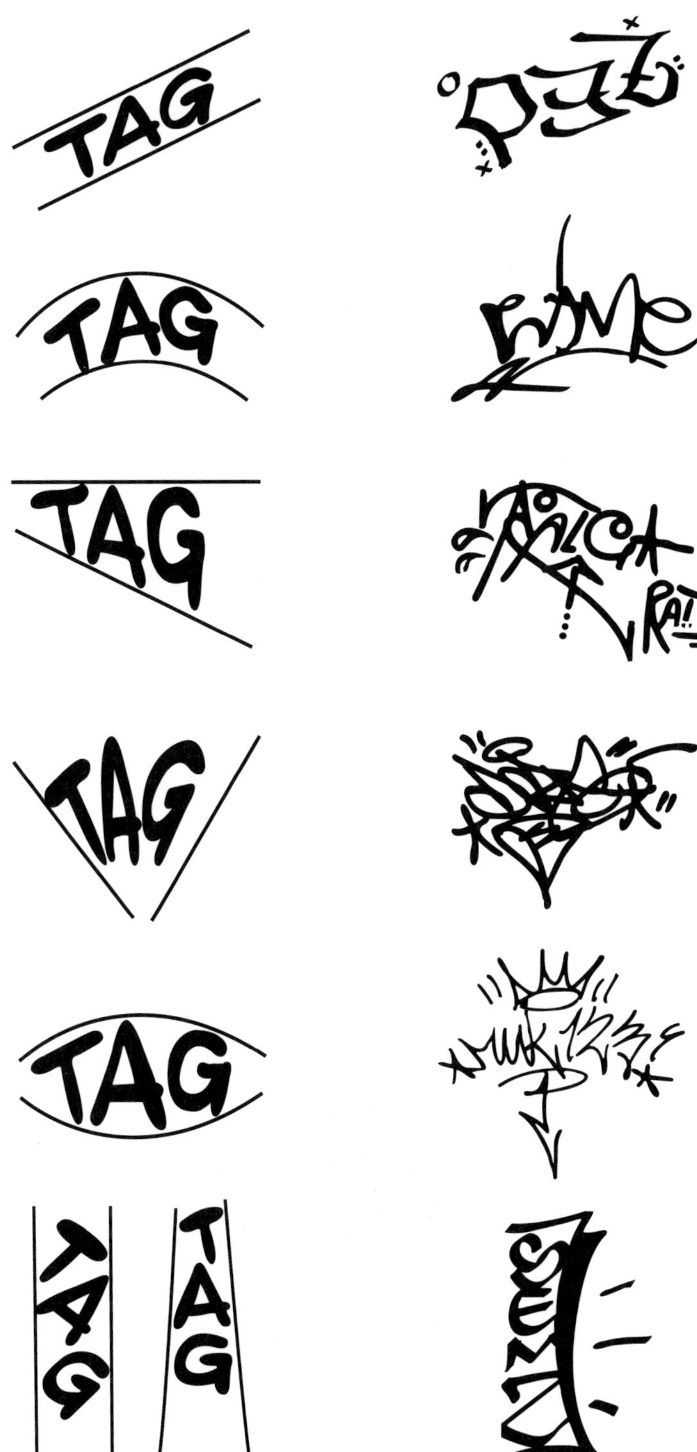

HOW TO CREATE STENCIL GRAFFITI

TOOLS & MATERIALS

spray paints/roller brush
caps
marker pen
respirator mask
latex gloves
paper/plastic sheet
utility knife
tape or spray adhesive

STENCIL PARTS

Positive Space—the cutout part where the paint goes through onto the surface.

Negative Space—the part of the stencil that does not get sprayed.

Bridge—holds other parts together and keep the stencil from falling apart.

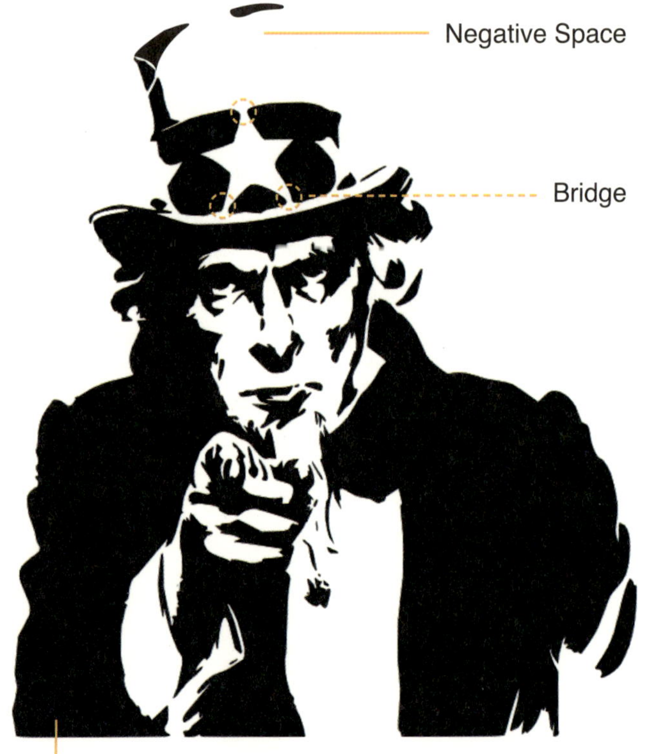

STENCILING PROCEDURE

1.

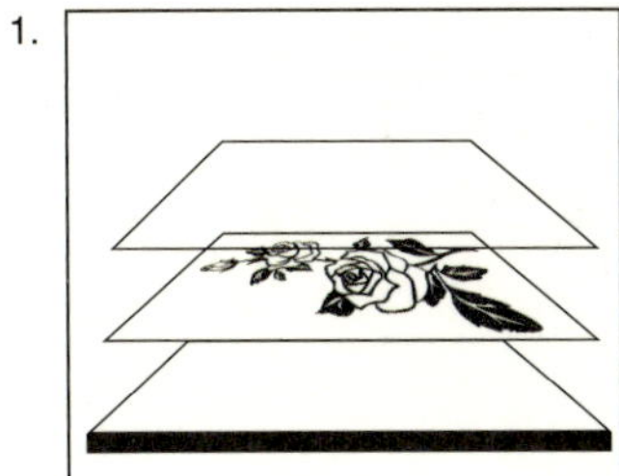

Place your design on the craft cutting board, and put a plastic sheet on top of it.

2.

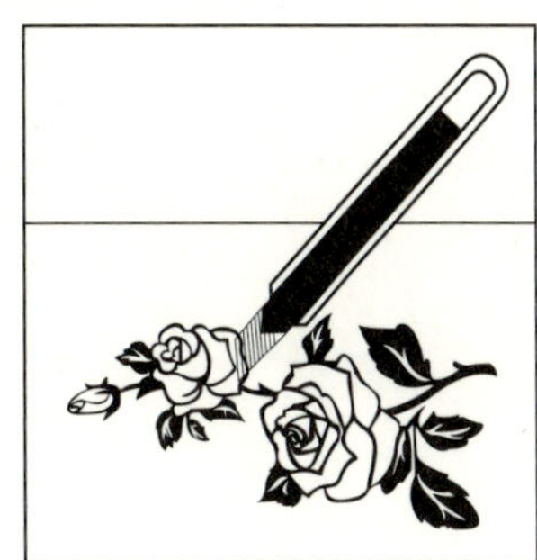

Use a knife to cut out two designated coloring parts respectively on two pieces of stencils.

3.

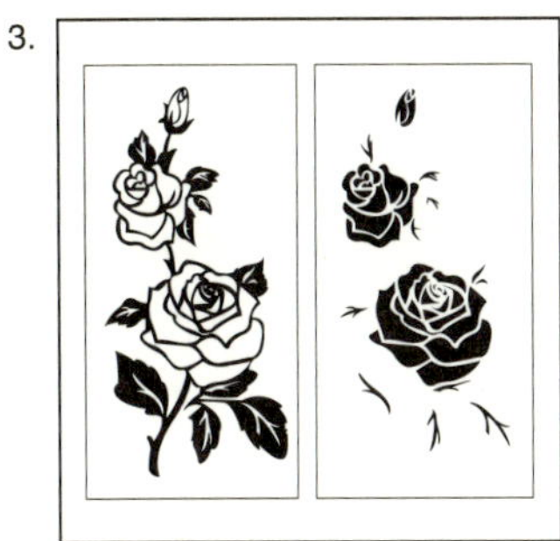

Then you have two pieces of stencils, with the black color indicating the positive spaces.

4.

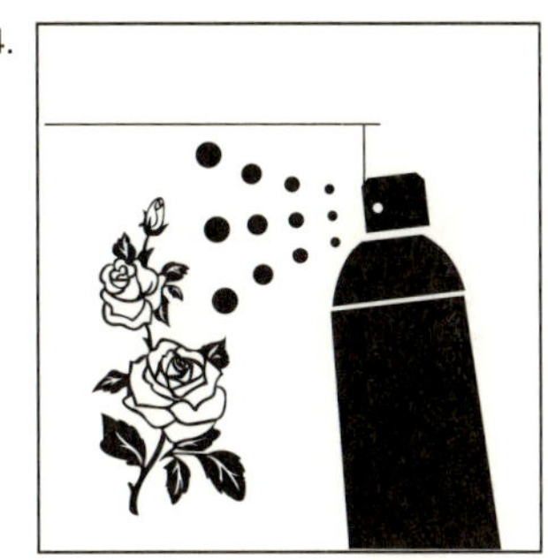

Put the first layer of stencil on the surface, and spray the black color through it.

5.

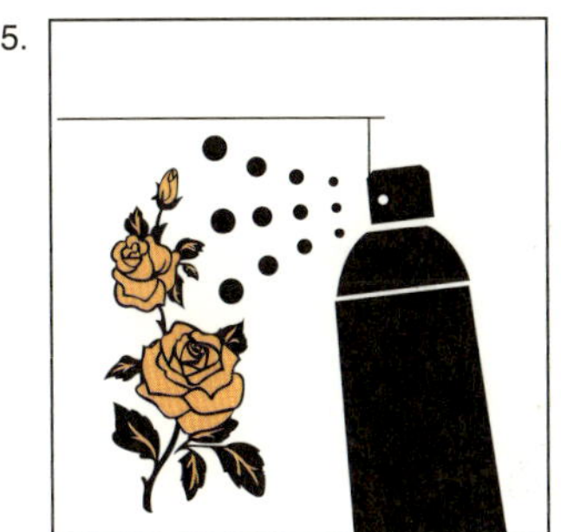

Do that again with the second layer using another color.

6.

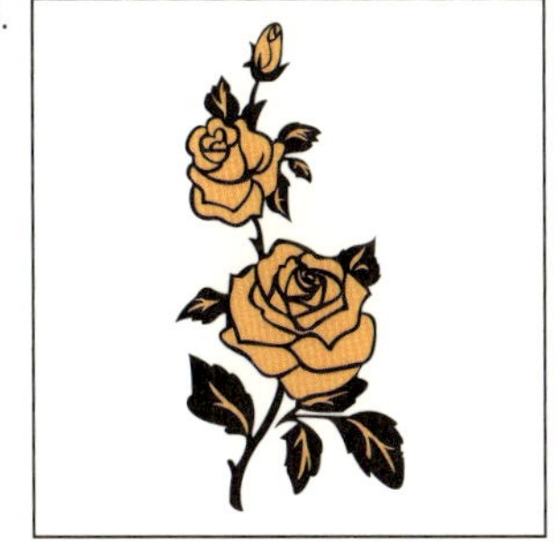

There you have it.

STENCILING TIPS

1. When spraying paints, keep moving your hands to avoid too much paint.
2. Spray paints by shoulder leading the arm and wrist.
3. Use a pencil, brush, or stick to press the stencil closely to the surface to make the shape of the image clear.

HOW TO MAKE A WHEATPASTE POSTER

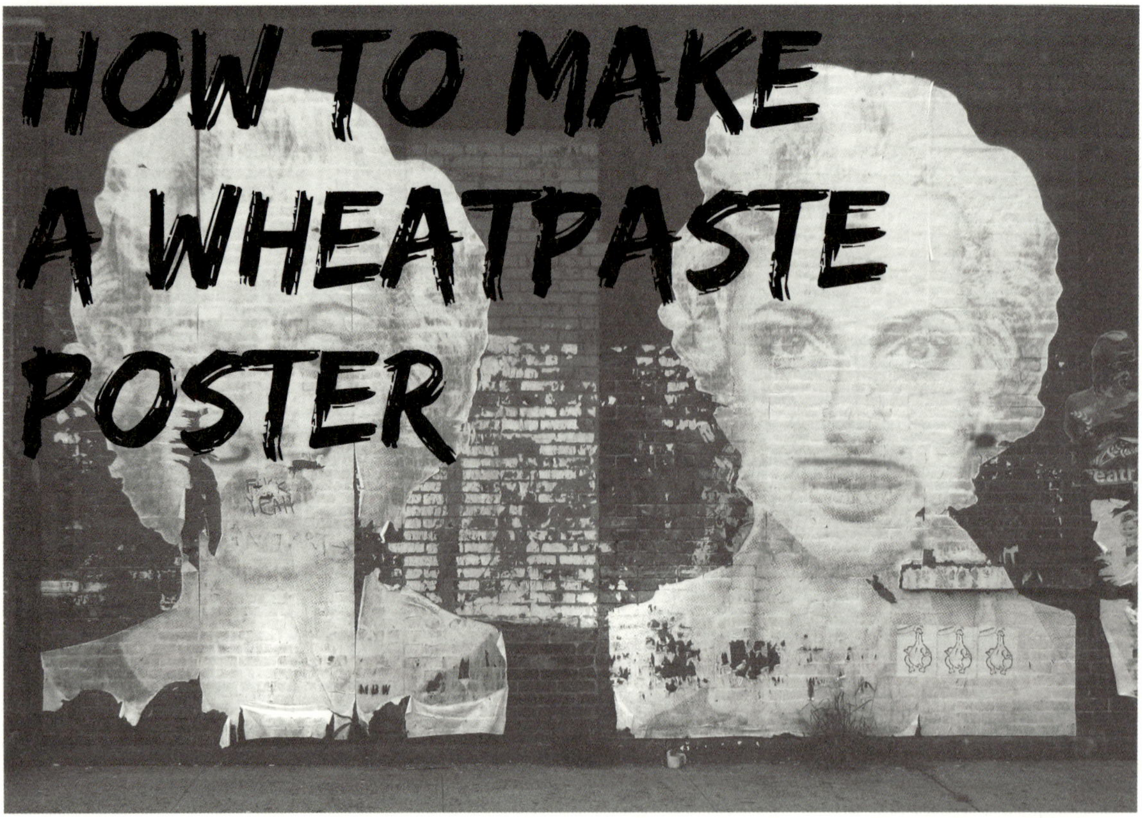

Photo/ Lauren Manning (Flickr)

MAKING THE WHEAT PASTE

Ingredients: whole wheat flour, water, a pot for boiling water, a container

Steps:

1. Add water to pot and heat up until it boils up.
2. Pour wheat flour into the pot and stir until there are no clumps in the mixture.
3. Turn off the heat when the mixture becomes smooth and glue-like.
4. Pour the paste into a container and use it as soon as possible.

*The referential flour to water ratio is 1:4.

Ingredients:

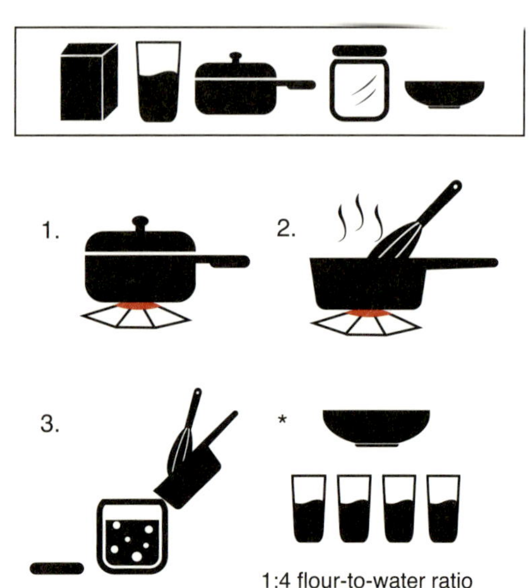

Ingredients:

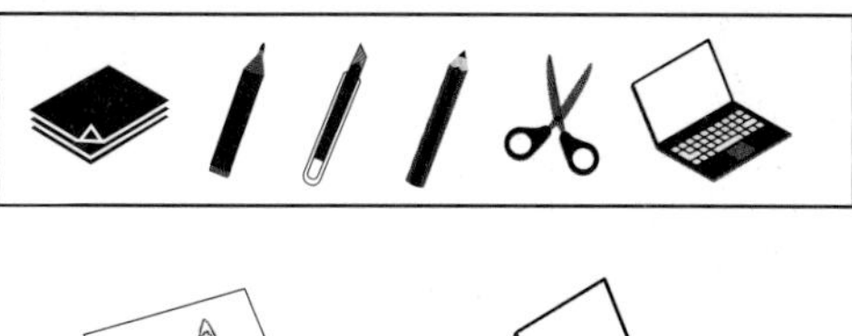

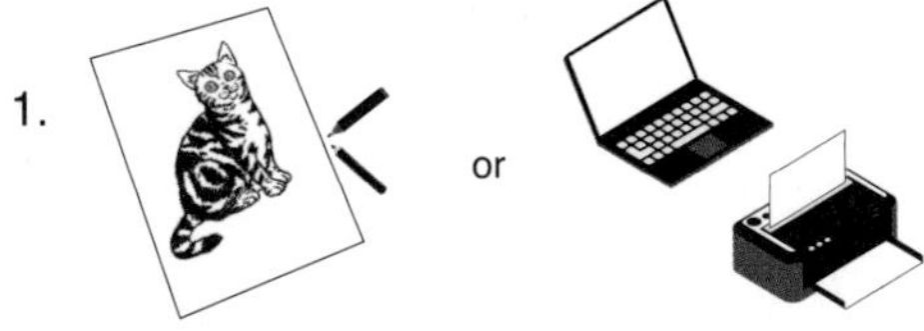

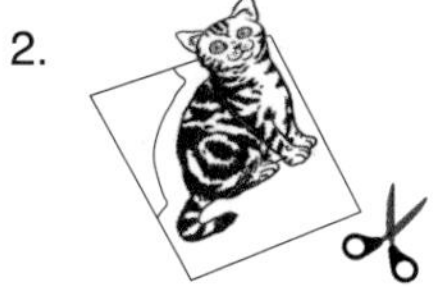

MAKING A POSTER

Ingredients: paper, oil-based marker pens, scissor/utility knife

Steps:

1. Create your image on paper, or design it on computer and print it out.
2. Cut out the design with scissors or a utility knife.

PASTING THE POSTER

Tools: a bucket or container holding your wheat paste, paint brush or roller brush

Steps:

1. Find a smooth or semi-smooth wall surface, and prepare the surface by applying a layer of wheat paste.
2. Place your artwork on top of the wet surface.
3. Apply a layer of wheat paste on top of the artwork until it is soaked. And let it dry for a few hours.
4. The final look.

*Warning: Be aware of the legal risks of placing street art on public/private property.

Tools:

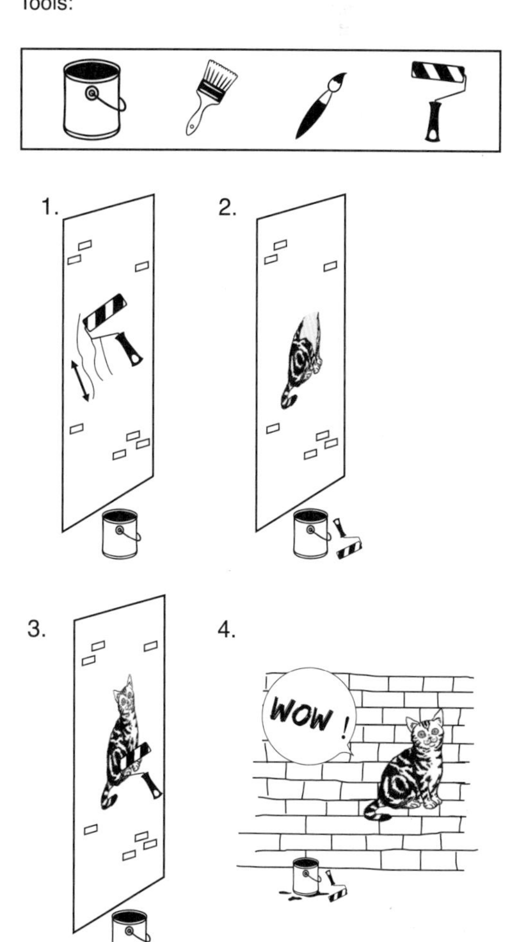

WORKS IN PROGRESS

Artist/ Pipsqueak Was Here!!!
©Millen von Ende

Heartlane
@Hengelo, The Netherlands 2017

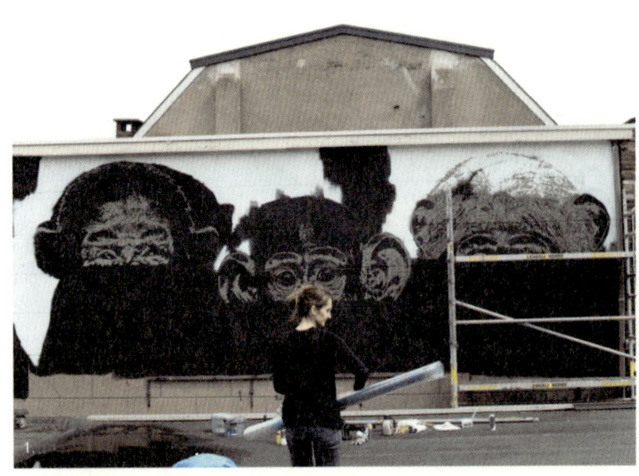

1.

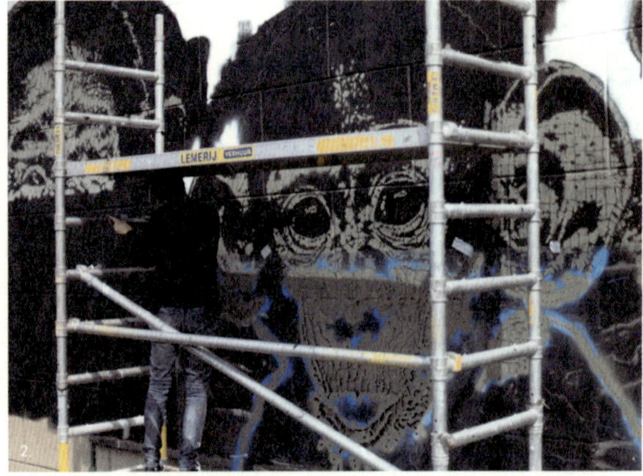

2.

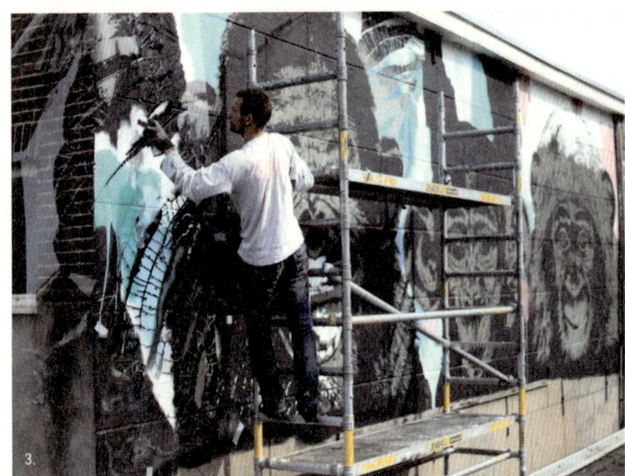

3.

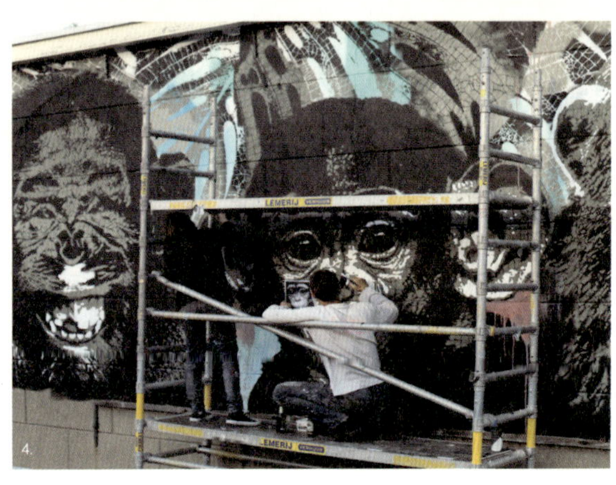

4.

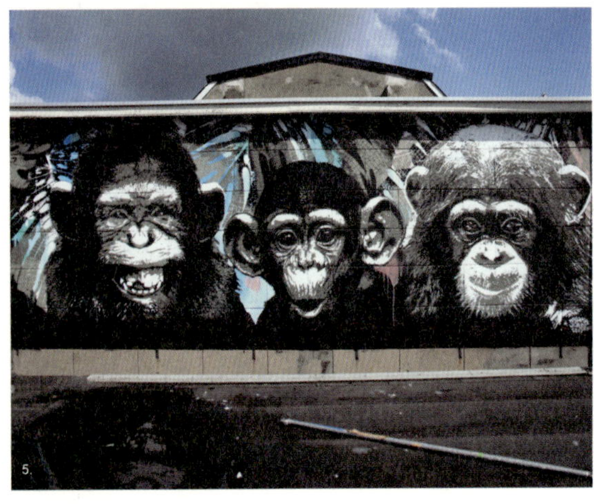

5.

1, 2. Paint the wall with black and white as the underpainting, and apply the upper half pieces of stencil to the right place, spray the grey color through it. Do the same to the lower part.

3. Add more details in the background by applying a tinge of cyan first, and then attach a new layer of stencil, spray black color to create the pattern of leave veins.

4. Compare the piece with the original design, and use a paint brush to add details.

5. The final piece.

A small piece of stenciled work is easy to make, but if you use more than one layer, or make it a large-scale piece, this would be another thing. Normally, artists will cut the whole large stencil into a few smaller pieces. But a new problem arises: How can you place the pieces so that they are seamlessly connected to one another? In most cases, artists use tape to stick them together. Sometimes, two X marks will be made on both the wall surface and the stencil, so if the stencil moves, it is easy to adjust it at once.

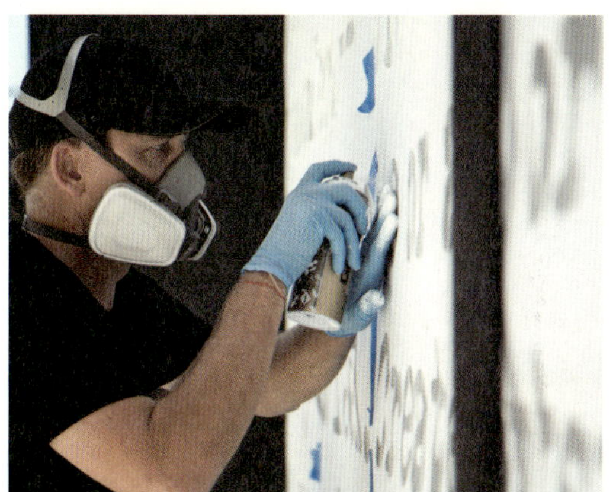

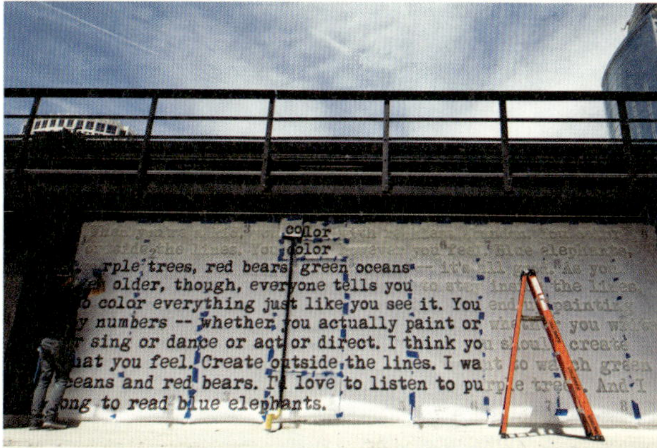

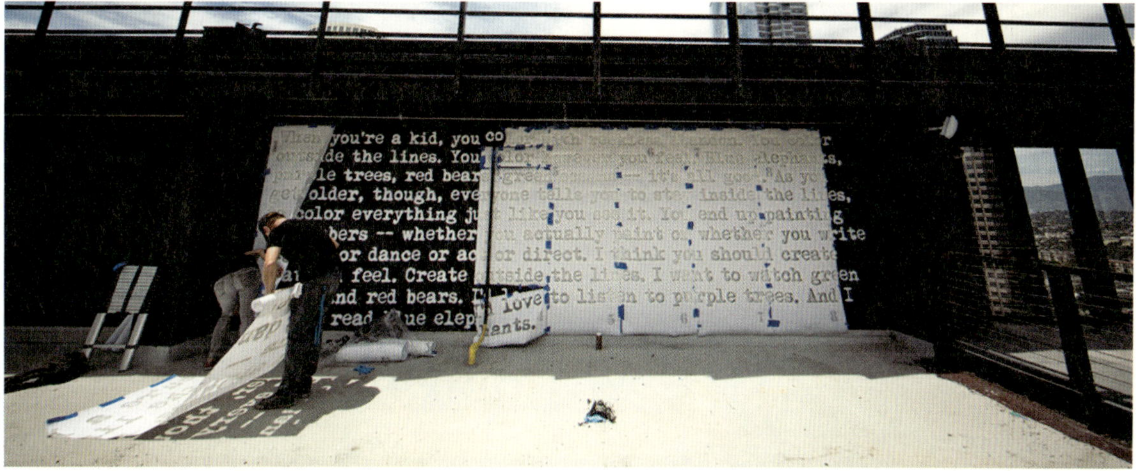

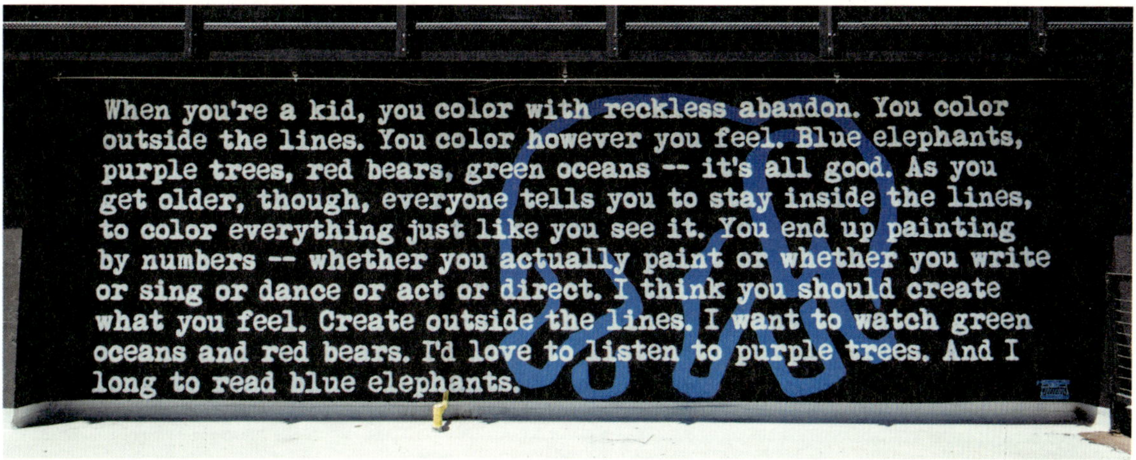

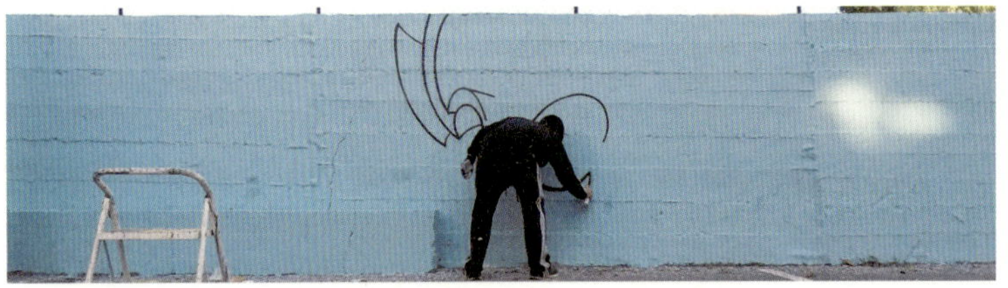

Andrea Antoni, born in Monfalcone in 1980, is a freelance graphic designer, graffiti writer, street artist and active blogger. He has painted graffiti since 1997 under the tag name "Style1". He is now one of the founders of the High Field Visual Team , and a member of the TDK collective of Milan, CBS in Los Angeles and MT in Milan.

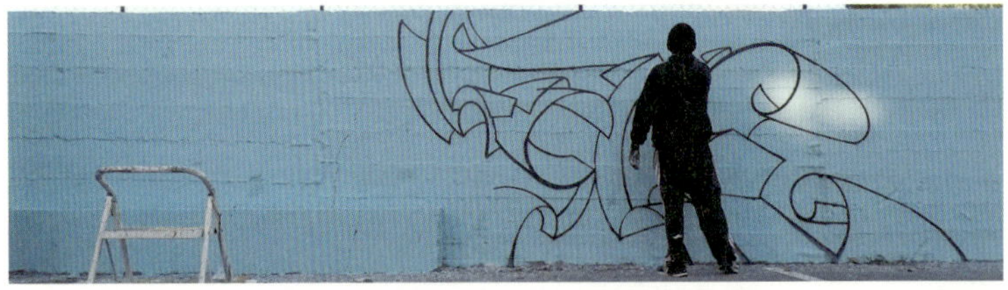

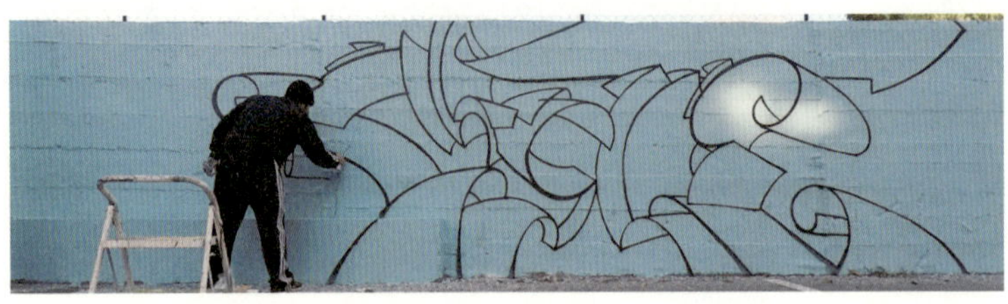

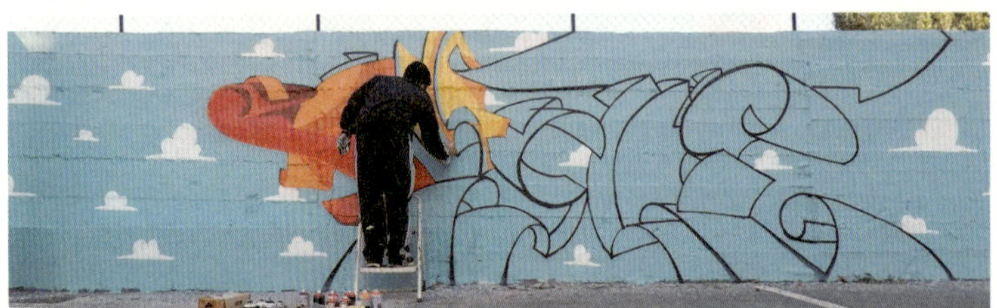

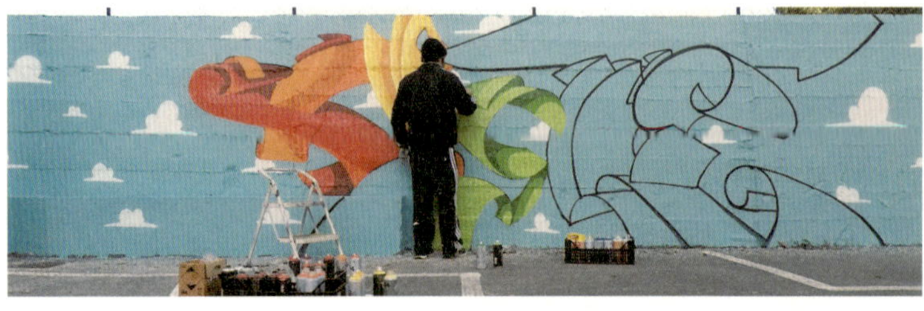

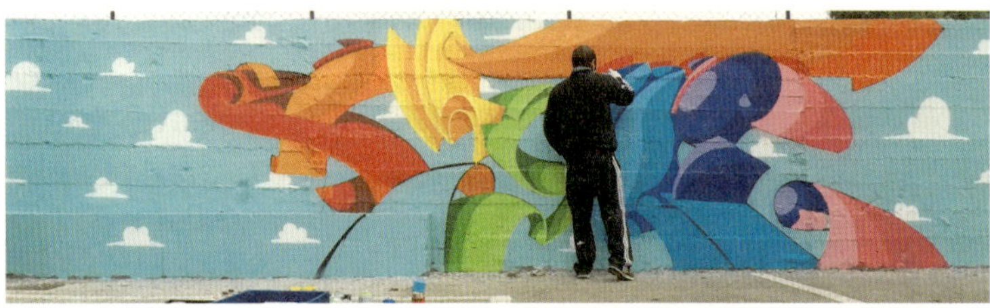

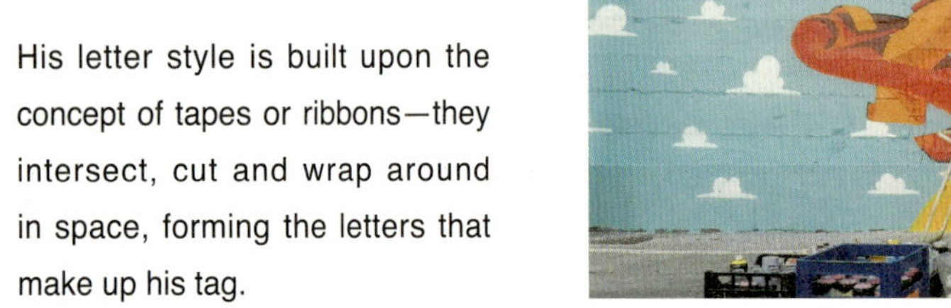

His letter style is built upon the concept of tapes or ribbons—they intersect, cut and wrap around in space, forming the letters that make up his tag.

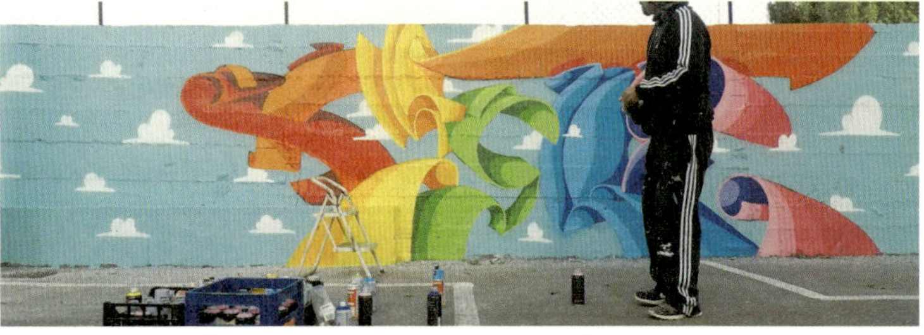

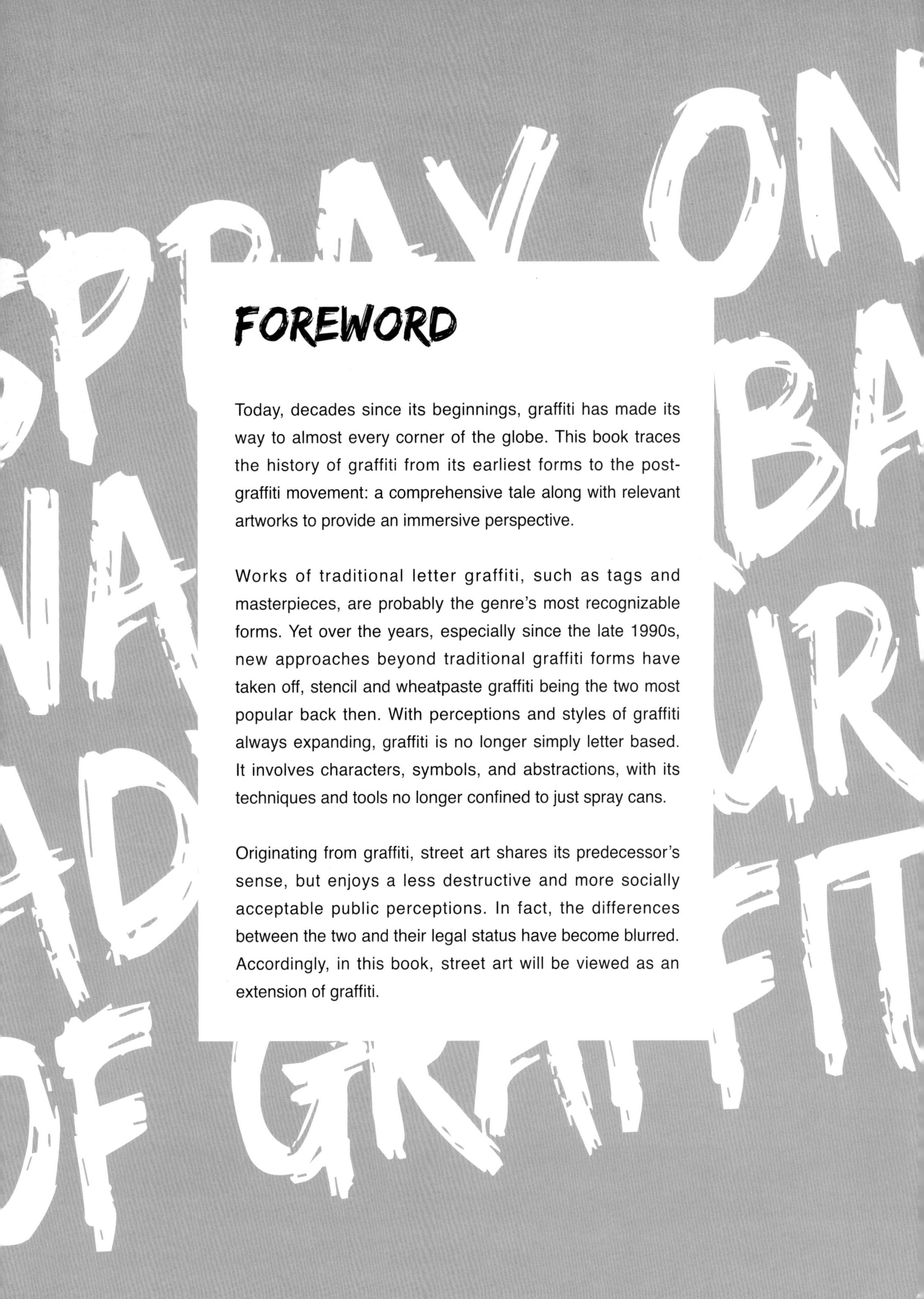

FOREWORD

Today, decades since its beginnings, graffiti has made its way to almost every corner of the globe. This book traces the history of graffiti from its earliest forms to the post-graffiti movement: a comprehensive tale along with relevant artworks to provide an immersive perspective.

Works of traditional letter graffiti, such as tags and masterpieces, are probably the genre's most recognizable forms. Yet over the years, especially since the late 1990s, new approaches beyond traditional graffiti forms have taken off, stencil and wheatpaste graffiti being the two most popular back then. With perceptions and styles of graffiti always expanding, graffiti is no longer simply letter based. It involves characters, symbols, and abstractions, with its techniques and tools no longer confined to just spray cans.

Originating from graffiti, street art shares its predecessor's sense, but enjoys a less destructive and more socially acceptable public perceptions. In fact, the differences between the two and their legal status have become blurred. Accordingly, in this book, street art will be viewed as an extension of graffiti.

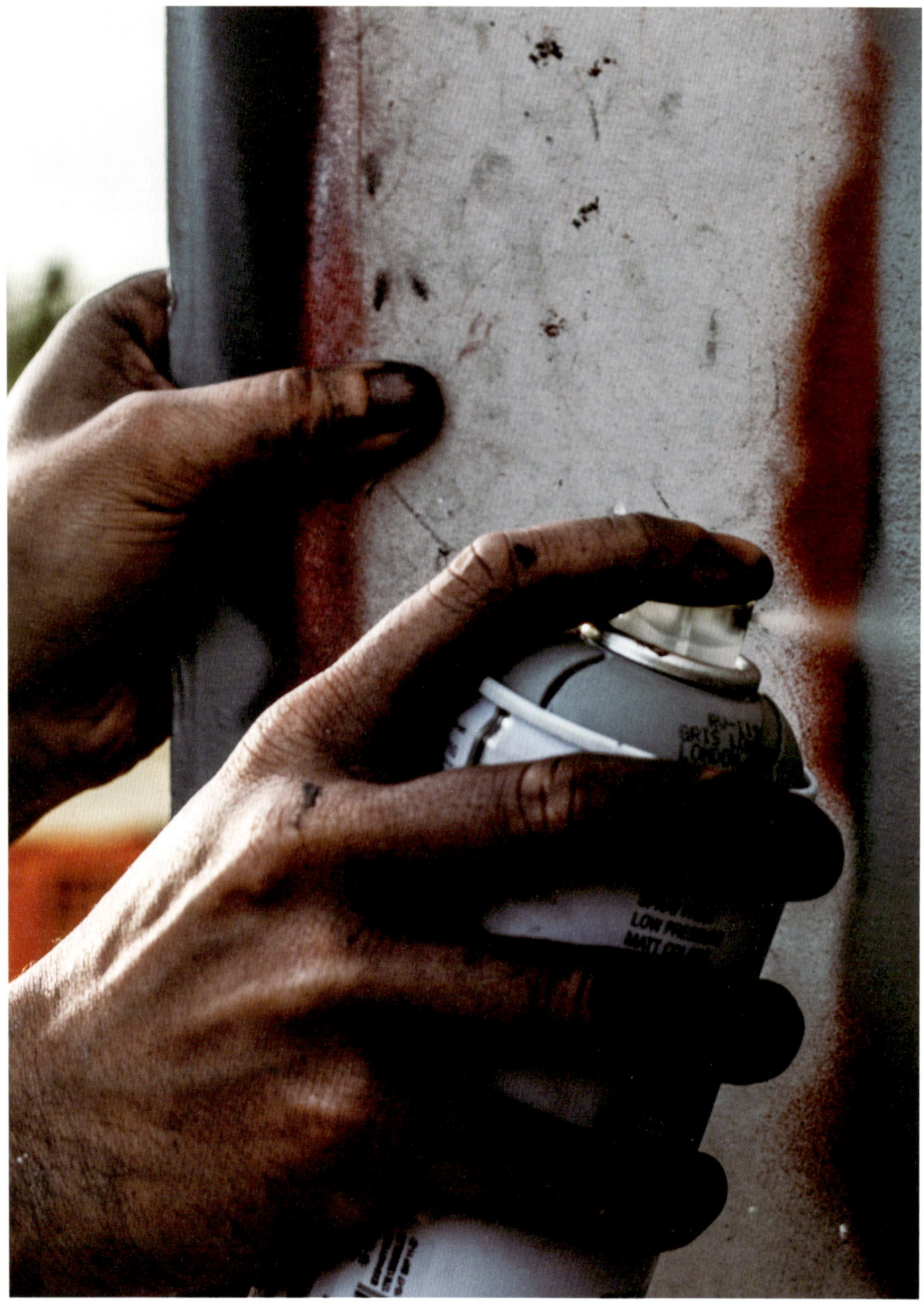

Photo/ SAMINA

CONTENTS

BONUS : GRAFFITI CREATION..................1

1.TEXT-BASED GRAFFITI....................020

2.STENCIL GRAFFITI...........................054

3.WHEATPASTE GRAFFITI...................084

4.CONTEMPORARY GRAFFITI STYLES....102

TEXT-BASED GRAFFITI

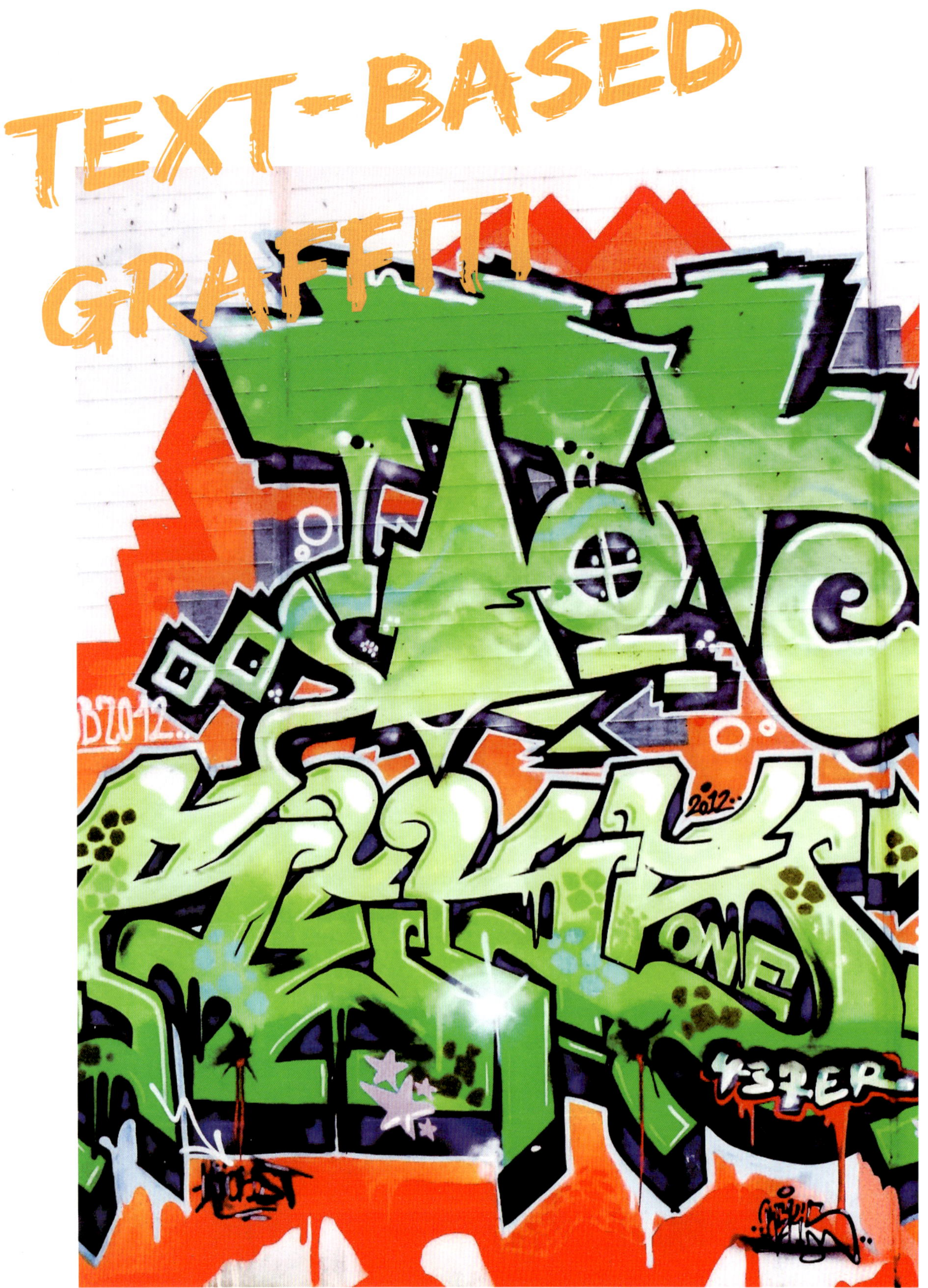

Photo/ Pixabay

TEXT-BASED GRAFFITI

Sauntering about modern cities, if attentive enough you can always find traces of graffiti on traffic signs, lampposts, curbs, notice boards, and street corners. Though aping the shapes of English letters and appearing to mirror certain writing patterns, they remain barely legible. These are tags: the earliest form of modern graffiti, and scrawled mostly with marker pens or spray cans. Based on tags, derivative forms—masterpiece, bubble letter, block letter, and Wildstyle—were developed. Because this kind of graffiti is characterized as text-based, in this chapter we categorize them all as Text-based Graffiti.

WHAT IS GRAFFITI?

Graffiti, if we trace it back to the first scratch on a cave wall, has been around for thousands of years. But obviously the ancient, anthropological sense of graffiti is different from what people normally perceive in the genre now, which is more street-related, carefree, and even rebellious. Therefore, before we proceed to introduce the styles of graffiti, we need to clarify what graffiti is.

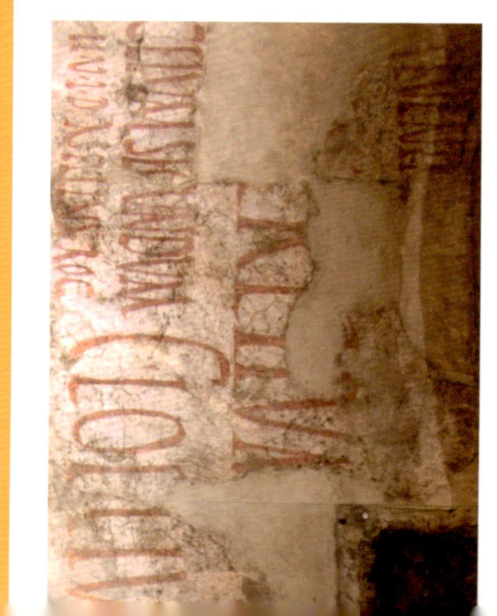

Getting to know the origin and evolution of the word "graffiti" helps us understand its connotations. The word comes from the Italian word *graffiato*, meaning to scratch, cut, or paint. Based on this basic idea, graffiti may refer to any graphic applied to the surface of a wall. Mindless scribbles, however, are just too far away from the modern style of graffiti. Taking a closer look, what if there are purposes behind the drawing? And yes, we find graffiti in ancient Greece and Rome believed to serve certain purposes. In the ruins of Ephesus, a graffiti is found near a stone walkway, showing the drawing of a foot, a hand, a heart, and a number. It is believed to be a unique advertisement for prostitution. Ancient Rome also keeps plenty of graffiti. Graffiti preserved in Pompeii include Latin curses, magic spells, declarations of love, political slogans, and literary quotes. The function of public notifications on walls has already stood out.

Ancient ad for a brothel in the city of Ephesus.

Photo/ Meredith P. (Flickr)

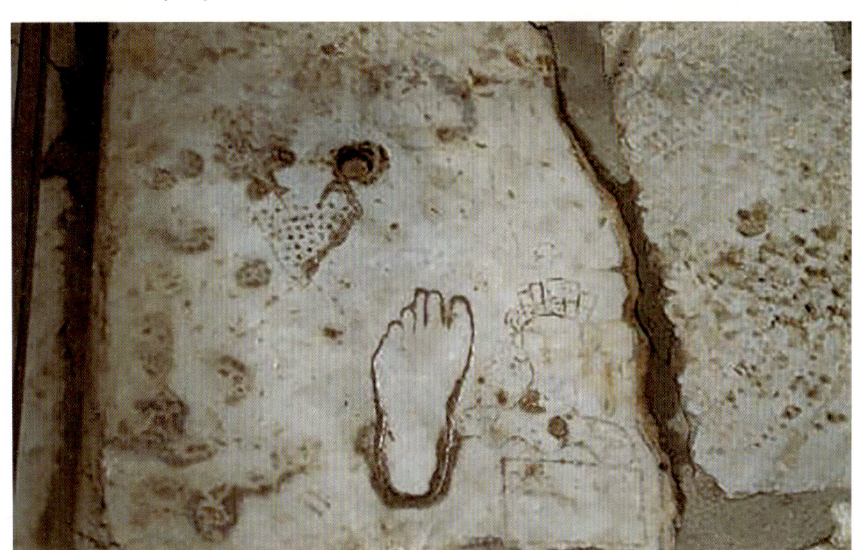

Graffiti on the wall in Pompeii.

Author/ Amadalvarez

Photo/ Wikimedia Commons

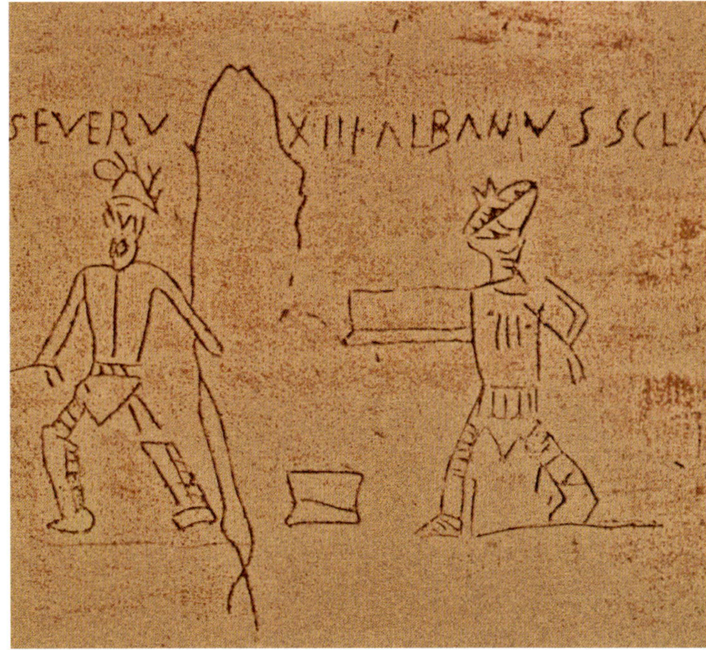

Scribe drawing of two gladiators found in Pompeii.

Author/ Mediatus

Photo/ Wikimedia Commons

But art may also have no purpose. This fascinating ancient graffiti found in the Cueva de las Manos, Argentina, is made by holding the left hand against the stone and blowing paint through a bone tube. Mayan ruins also offer a treasure of graffiti traces.

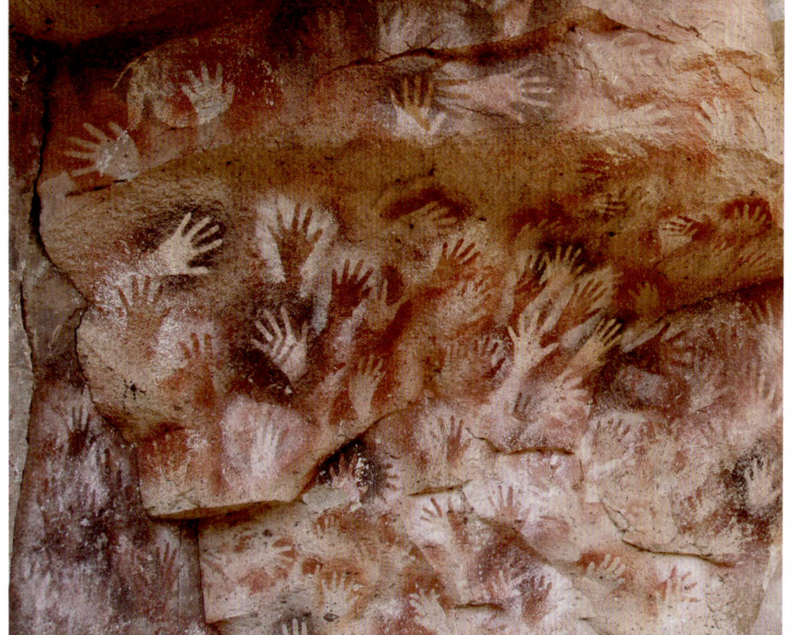

Hands at the Cuevas de las Manos, Argentina. Manos, Argentina.

Author/ Mariano
Photo/ Wikimedia Commons

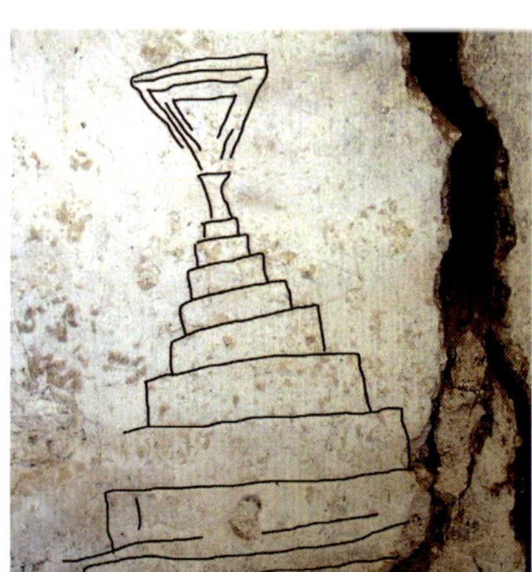

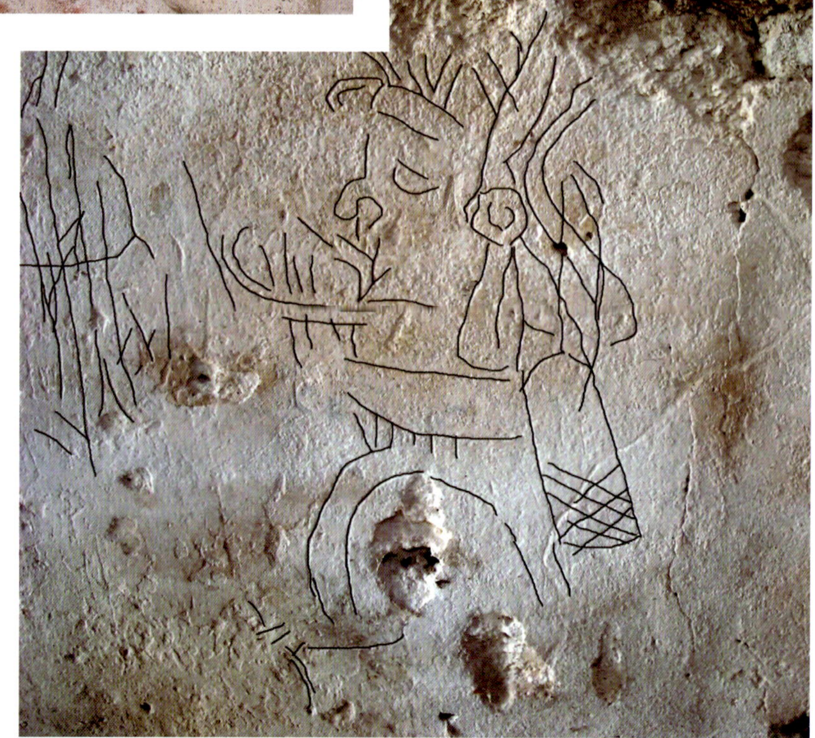

Graffiti at La Blanca, Petén,Guatemala with lines digitally overdrawn in black for visibility.

Author/ Simon Burchell
Photo/ Wikimedia Commons

During the Second World War, the Nazis tried to provoke hatred towards the Jews by drawing political slogans and the swastika on walls. Among American soldiers and their allies fighting against the Nazis, a graffiti including the phrase "Kilroy was here" and a cartoon character suddenly caught on, appearing whenever the army was stationed, encamped, or visited.

So far, the various connotations of graffiti have been explained. Graffiti may refer to random drawings, to a form that serves political and commercial purposes, or to a form of art. Corresponding to modern graffiti, they are all graffiti painted on streets, walls, and trains, commissioned works of a clothing brand, or works exhibited in an art gallery. But since when is graffiti also a form of vandalism? This leads to the subway graffiti developed in the US during the 1960s.

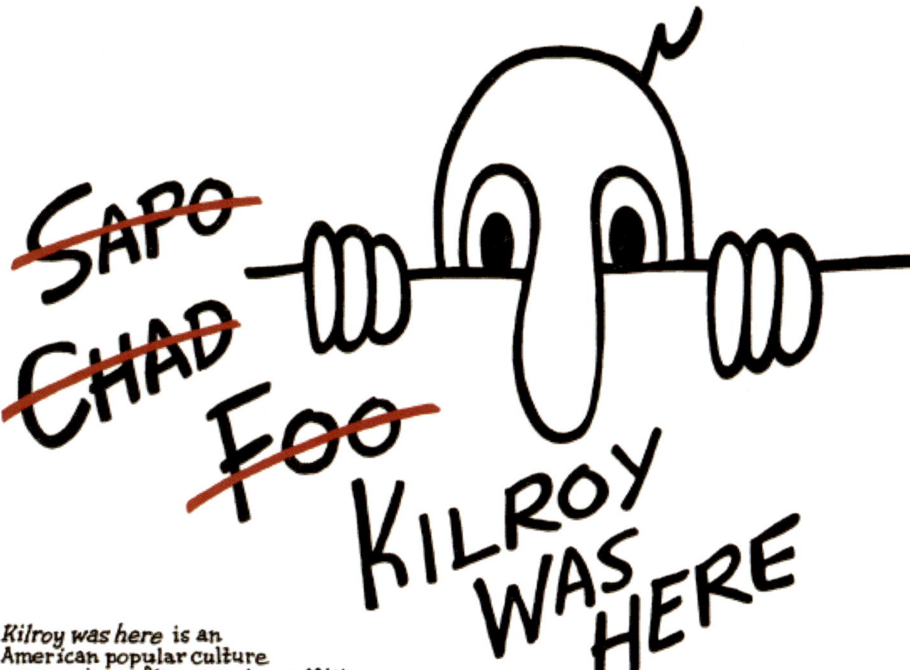

Kilroy was here is an American popular culture expression, often seen in graffiti. The distinctive doodle of "Kilroy" peeking over a wall also appears in other cultures, but the character is not named *Kilroy*, but *Foo* — as in *Foo was here*.

In the United Kingdom, such graffiti is known as a "chad." In Chile, the graphic is known as a "sapo" (toad).

The phrase appears to have originated through United States servicemen, who would draw the doodle and text on the walls where they were stationed or encamped.

One theory identifies James J. Kilroy, an American shipyard inspector, as the man behind the signature. During World War II, he worked at the Bethlehem Steel Shipyard in Quincy, Massachusetts, where he claimed to have used the phrase to mark rivets he had checked. Later, the phrase would be found in places that no graffiti artist could have reached (inside sealed hull spaces, for example), which fed the mythical significance of the phrase.

An American pop culture "Kilroy was here" expression has its equivalents in Australia, the UK, and Chile, with "Kilroy" replaced respectively by "Foo,""Chad," and "Sapo."

Author/ Greg Williams

Photo/ Wikimedia Commons

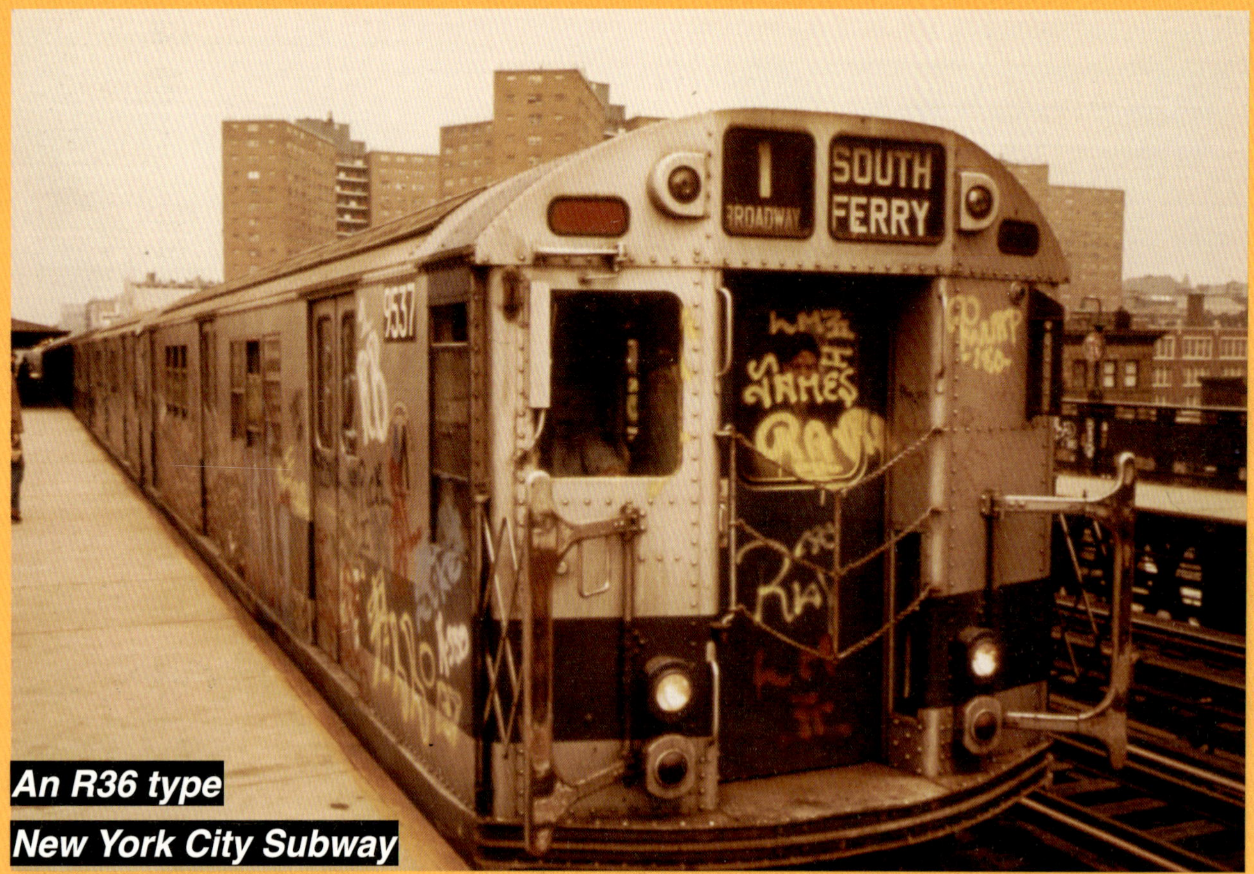

An R36 type New York City Subway car leading a 1 train, September 1973.

Author/ Erik Calonius
Photo/ The National Archives Catalog

SUBWAY GRAFFITI

Mid-to-late 1960s: Modern Graffiti

Modern graffiti originated in Philadelphia, Pennsylvania during the 1960s, when Cornbread, Cool Earl, and other practitioners tagged their names all over the city. Darryl McCray, namely Cornbread, is credited with being the first modern graffiti artist. It is said that he got his nickname from a cook at a youth detention center where McCray kept asking the cook for cornbread instead of stale white bread. No cornbread was ever served to him there, but the name "Cornbread" led him to fame. Before social media swept the world, such a deed was enough to make him notorious. Exposed to the public and enjoying fame that few had known pushed him to go bolder. No longer confined to ordinary street walls, he left his tag in tricky places—the Jackson 5's plane, police cars, and most audacious of all, the body of an elephant. The wind of change was influencing every teenager eager for fame and recognition. After Cornbread, the tags of Cool Earl, Kool Klepto Kidd, and Kair began spreading across the city.

Graffiti Pier, officially named Pier 124, is a historical site in Philadelphia. Located along the Delaware River, it was originally an old coal mining pier and was shut down in 1991. With the machinery and train racks removed, the abandoned site attracted many graffiti artists thereafter.

Photo/ Pixabay

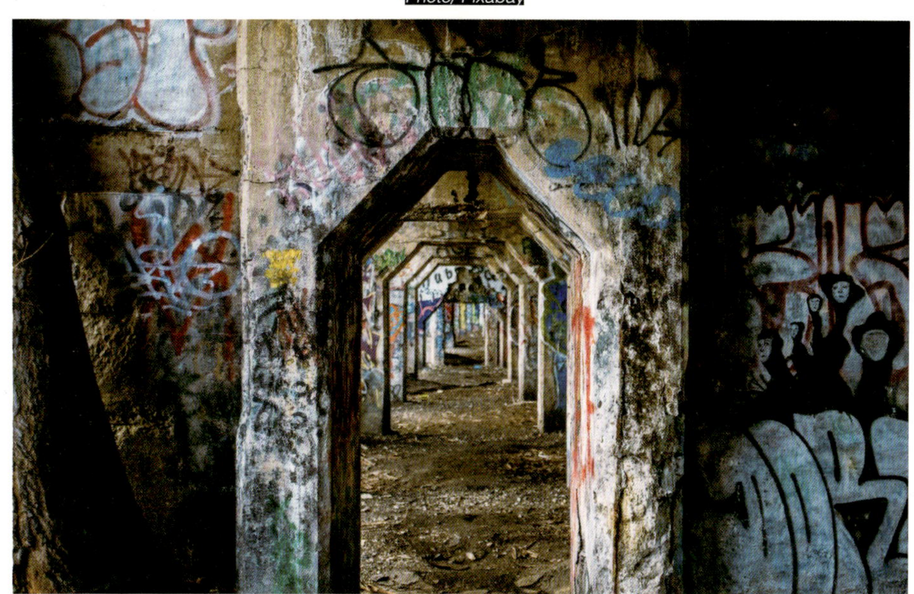

Late 1960s to 1970s:
the rise and development of subway graffiti

Since the late 1960s, Manhattan, Brooklyn, and the Bronx gave rise to graffiti writers consecutively. TAKI 183 was one of the representatives of this period. "TAKI 183" was the alias of a kid from Washington Heights. It comes from his given name, Demetrius, and his residential street number. At the time, he was a foot messenger. By taking the subway, he was able to tag all of New York city. In 1971, The New York Times published an article titled "'Taki 183' Spawns Pen Pals." This article sparked the public curiosity of graffiti writers. TAKI 183 became the first one to be recognized outside the graffiti world. At that moment, JULIO 204, FRANK 207, and JOE 136 were also poised to become some of the earliest influential writers.

During the early 1970s, subway trains appeared to be tagged inside out, with the moving trains proving to be the best way to expedite the spread of writers' tags. Writers from five boroughs of New York quickly became aware of each other, and subway tagging became increasingly competitive. Because the trains stayed in the station for only a few minutes every time, writers had to use the "bombing" method: finishing a piece of graffiti in a very short time, so as to save time to run from railway police. To make the tags more noticeable and unique, writers enhanced them with stars, clouds, outlines, and other designs. The realization of different nozzle widths of spray cans led to the development of graffiti techniques. The tag scale was also becoming wilder: spanning the entire height of a subway car. A large-scale, elaborate piece is termed a "masterpiece." Usually, it involves at least three colors, color transitions, shade and three-dimensional effect. TRACY 168, STAY HIGH 149, PHASE 2, and JUNIOR 161 were active writers during this period.

A "SLAVE" piece by LEE FABUL OUS FIVE on a late 70's IRT express.

Photo/ JJ & Special K (Flickr

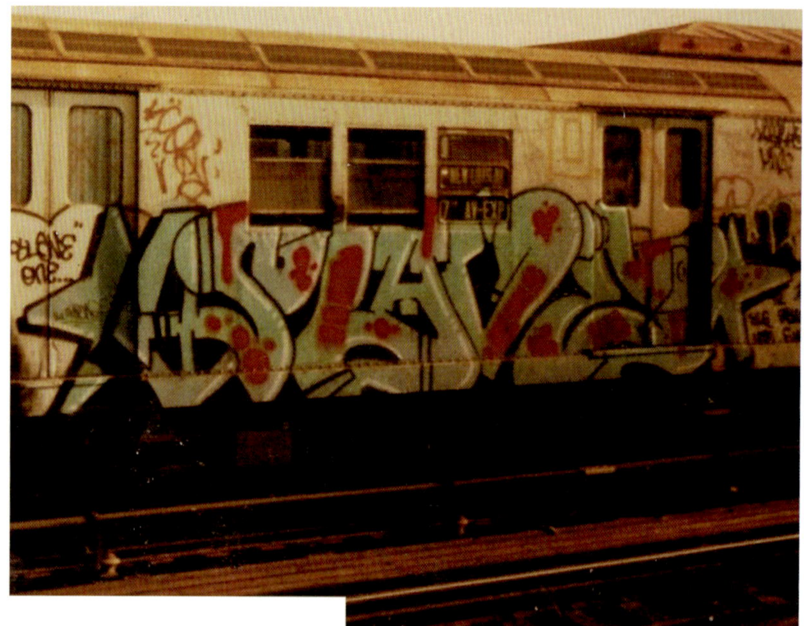

The competitive atmosphere of subway graffiti set off the actual development of style. In 1972, TOPCAT 126 created the broadway style of tagging, which featured long, slender letters with platforms on the bottoms of the stems. The broadway style later evolved into block letters. In 1973, PHASE 2 developed bubble letters, also known as softie. Based on the original tags, arrows, curls, connections, and twists were added to adorn letters. The development of tagging styles prompted the graffiti writers to rethink the structure and combination, which led to the emergence of unreadable Wildstyle graffiti.

Graffiti writer CLIFF's tag during the early 1970s.

Photo/ JJ & Special K (Flickr)

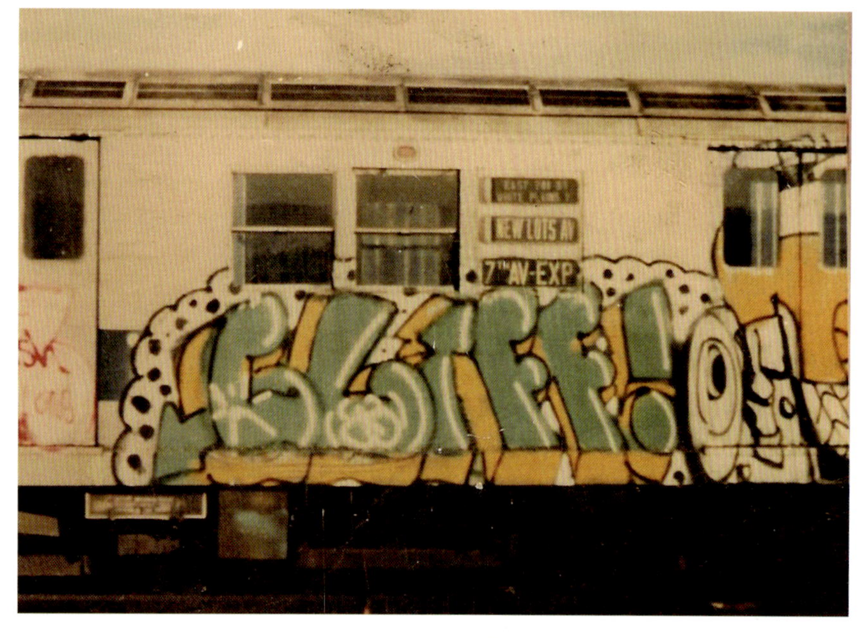

A piece "WORM 2" wascreated by Part One on a IRT express train during the late 1970s .

Photo/ JJ & Special K (Flickr)

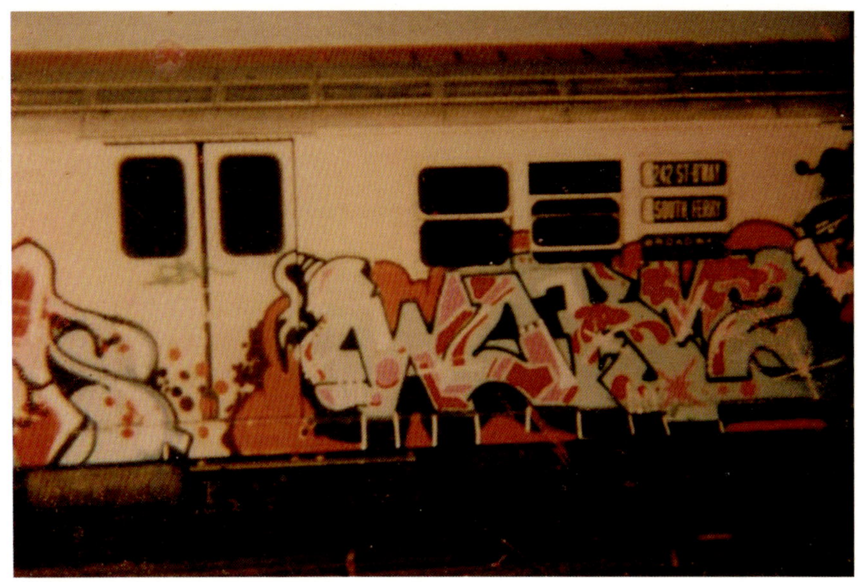

In 1972, sociologist Hugo Martinez founded the United Graffiti Artists, with COCO 144 taking the CEO post. Graffiti works were brought into formal art galleries and exhibited as a form of art. The release of the article titled "The Graffiti 'Hit' Parade," by journalist Richard Goldstein, and the book *The Faith of Graffiti* attracted loads of public attention towards graffiti world.

In 1974, BLADE, among others, started to create masterpieces on entire trains. Graffiti like this, covering the entire visible surface of a train car, is called "whole car." At this time "throw-up," a quick piece consisting of only a basic outline and fills, caught on. Graffiti crews and writers were competing to do the best throw-up. From 1975 to 1977, New York City was broke, so the transit system was poorly maintained, which led to the heaviest bombing in history. In 1977, the crave for creativity bloomed again. Style wars between crews such as CIA, TDS, and MAFIA were peaking once again.

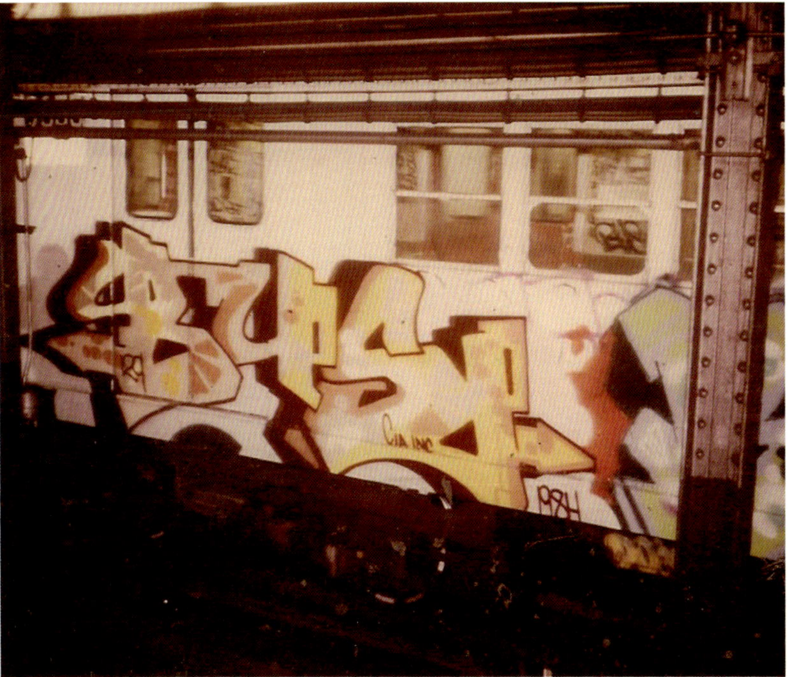

A "BUS" piece by CIA on the IRT express trains during early 1980s.

Photo/ JJ & Special K (Flickr)

1980s: the decline of subway graffiti

During the early-to-mid 1980s, graffiti culture deteriorated dramatically, partly due to a decline in greater society in general. The drug trade grew furious, and the street became an increasingly tense place. Legislation was passed to restrict writing activity. Graffiti removal was more frequent and effective. Many writers started to quit and consider other creative paths. Writers that stayed became aggressive and territorial. During the late 1980s, the MTA initiated the Clean Train Movement. By 1989, the last train with large amounts of graffiti on it was taken off the lines. Subway graffiti is not dead, but no longer thrive.

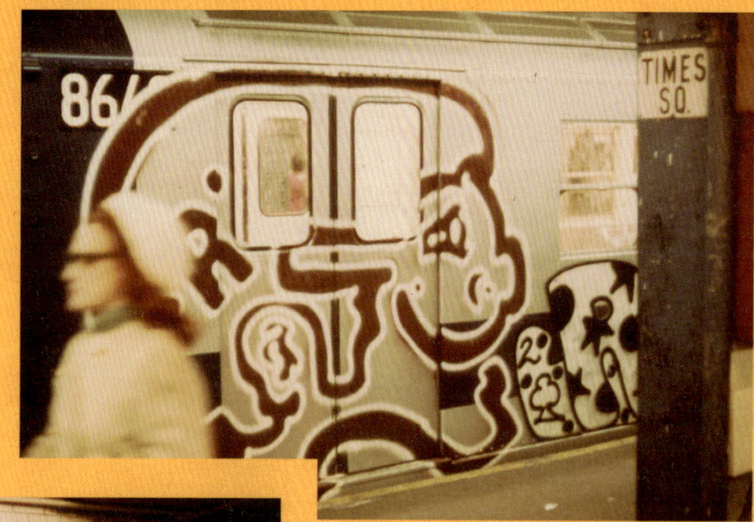

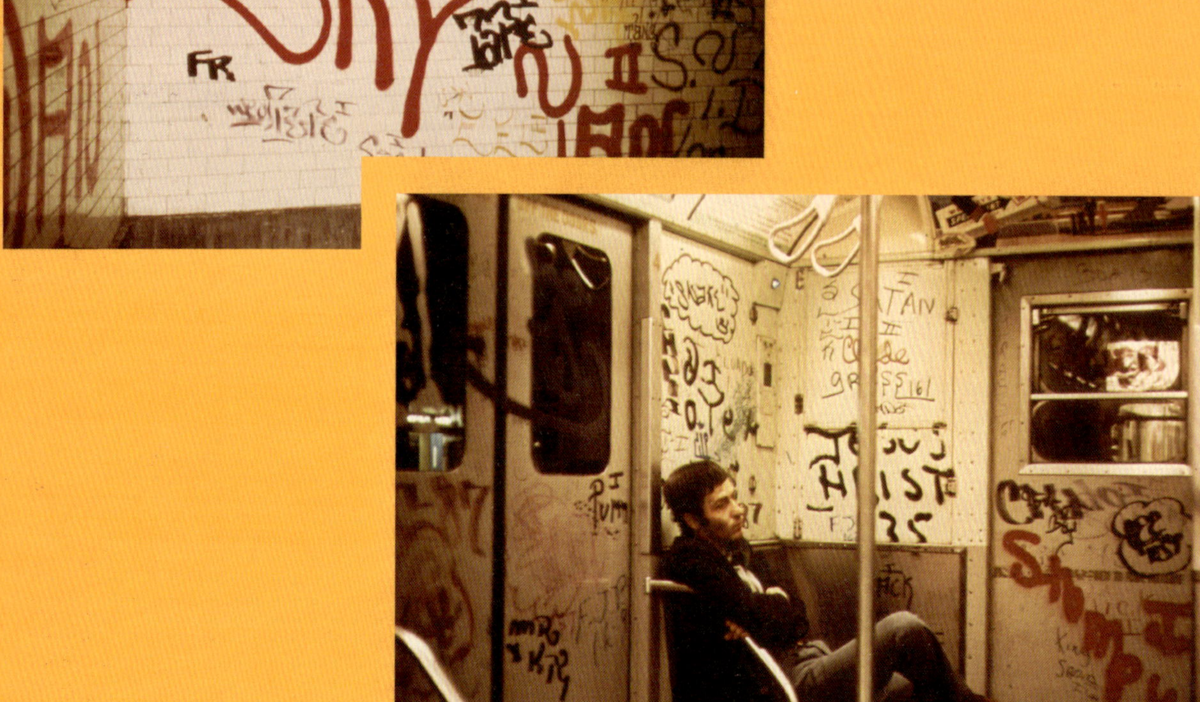

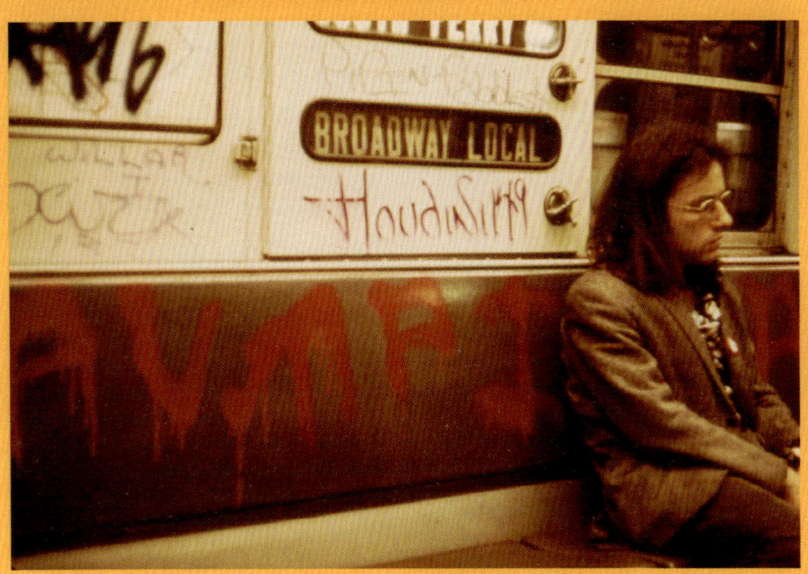

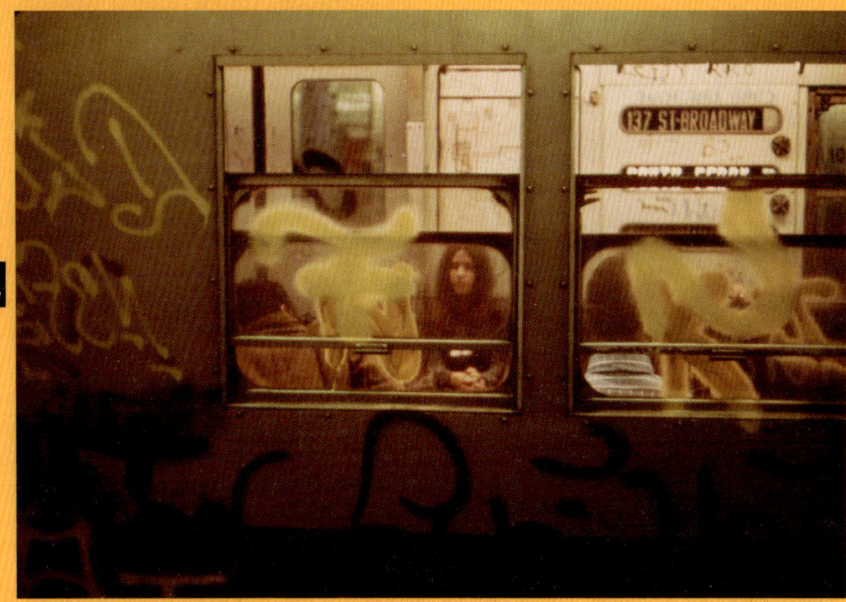

Spray-painted subway trains in New York during the 1970s.

Photo/ The U.S. National Archives

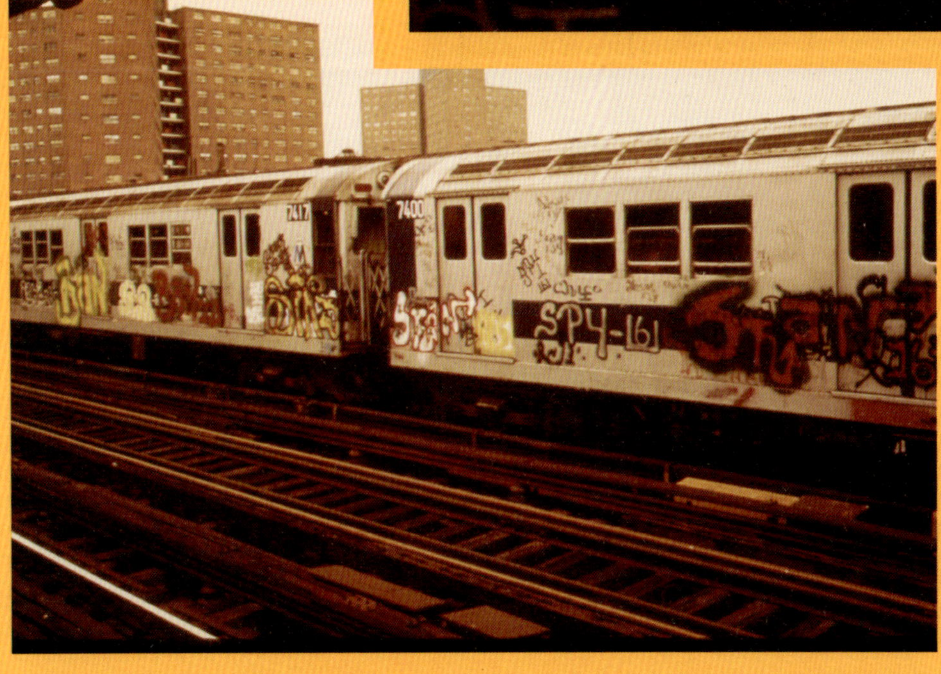

THE WORLD IS SPEEDING, WE ARE INDULGING

The 1960s witnessed dramatic changes in human history. The big events happening during this time were so profound that we are still affected. Sprite was released by Coca-Cola, the DNA genetic code was deciphered, the Vietnam War broke out, John F. Kennedy took office, Adolf Eichmann was hanged in Israel, the Rolling Stones made their debut, the Cuban Missile Crisis started, the term "personal computer" was first mentioned, "equal pay for equal work" was enacted, the Beatles rose to fame, and Neil Armstrong stepped on the Moon... Every single event was powerful enough to shape the world we have today. Yet it is when we look back that we know how significant these events were.

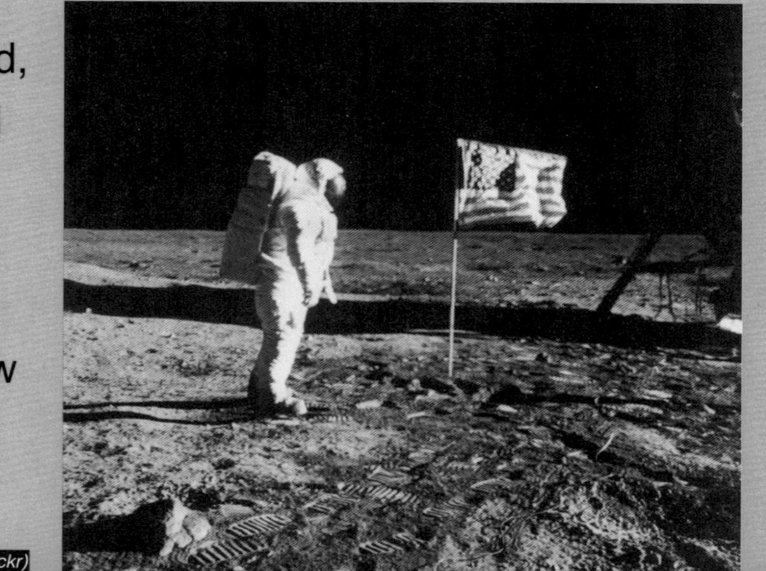

Photo/ Tullio Saba (Flickr)

During the years of WWII, something grew wild and uncontrollable like a tumor inside the heads of both sides. Truths were based on concepts instead of facts. Crazy people cannot tolerate anyone having different understanding of truths. The bloodshot eyes, the firearms that kept recoiling back and forth, the desperate yelling of pain, the bullets that traversed through the veins... One down, two down, fighting to the death. The wars not only consumed the wartime supplies squeezed out of common people, but the beautiful imagination of humanity. Evil is not just a word; it is deeds done by empty heads. In the name of justice, both sides were drained to skins. Twenty years after that, the world were still gasping for breath. Everything seemed back on track, but under the surface is the cautious hearts overwhelmed by the speeding world.

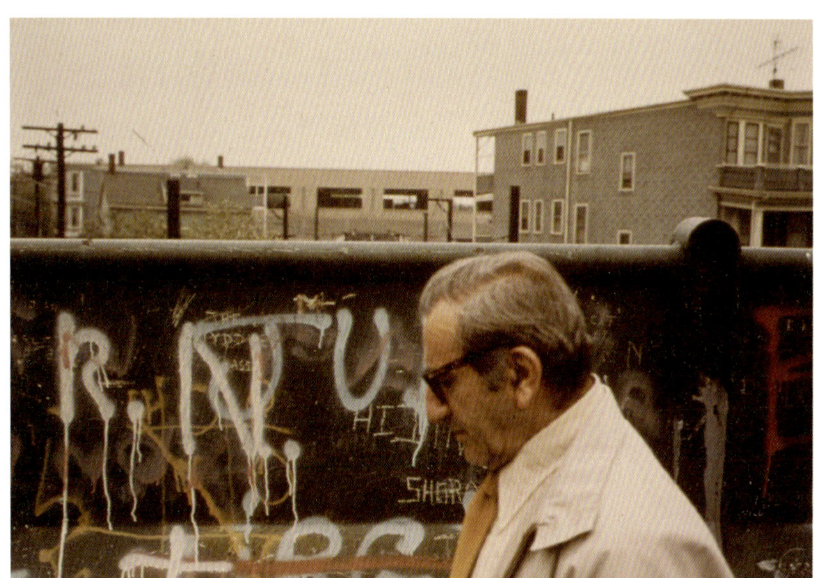

Photo/ The U.S. National Archives

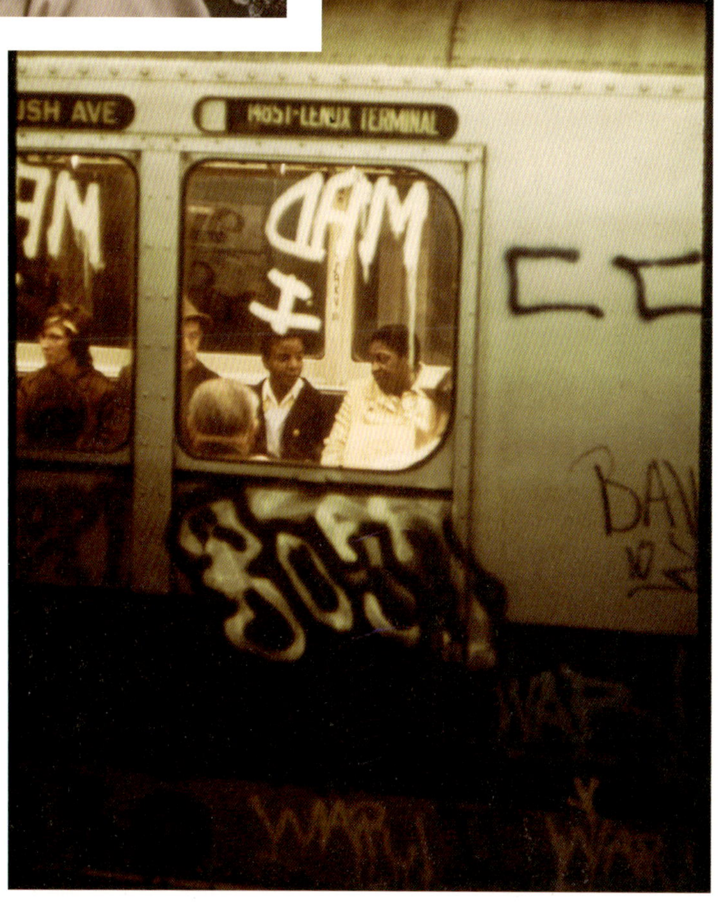

Photo/ The U.S. National Archives

Sixties teenagers, born after WWII, formed a unique generation eager to explore, to create, and even to fail. They blamed war on their parents, on capitalism and on the Establishment. Yet the young envisioned a bright future with millions of possibilities. Their timid parents and the post-war youth appeared to be going on different roads. Growing up was uncool of youth. Big events were unimportant. Grooving with one's friends was all that matters.

Time needs to be killed, especially when you have an empty lot. An immigrant kid calling himself "TAKI 183" imitated his predecessor JULIO 204 in tagging as many places as possible. When his tagging spread throughout the whole city, he started to be introduced as "this is him," and was credited with the title of "king." The bias and prejudice usually towards an immigrant melted away in the world of graffiti. He gained recognition for what he did for the genre. For him, time doomed to pass and the uncertainty of the future ahead would not be wasted in the world of graffiti.

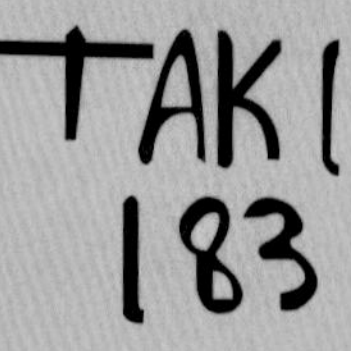

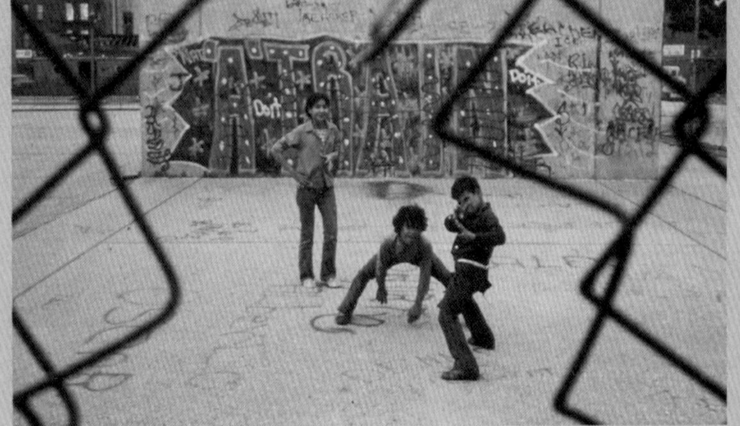

Photo/ The U.S. National Archives

The wave of graffiti tagging triggered teenagers' desires for self expression. The innocence and recklessness of young people go against their parents' compromises with and hopelessness towards life. If the young didn't leave something on walls, trains, or other public places, who was to hear them at a time with no social media? Big events were so big that they attracted attention once they happened. They were known only on TV shows, on radio broadcasts, but not in teens' real lives. The increasingly fierce gangsters and severe migration conflicts creeping up the neighborhood were real.

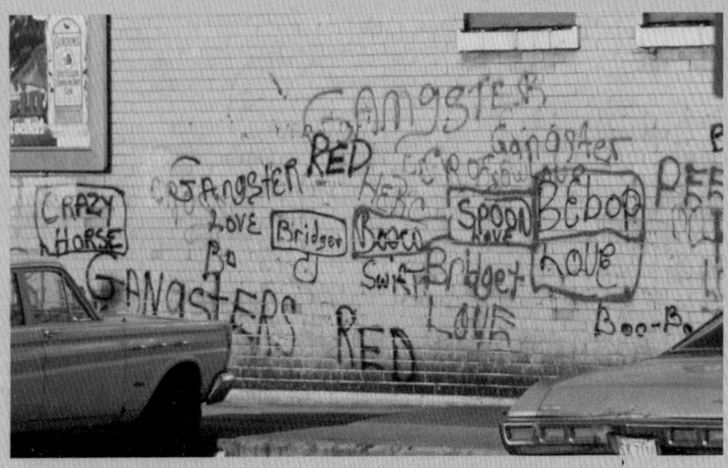

Photo/ The U.S. National Archives

Some graffiti writers even joined several gangs to avoid being attacked during the 1970s. Picture on the right shows Latin Kings graffiti of the King Master along with the initials "L" and "K" on the sides.

Author/ Foadddy23
Photo/ Wikimedia

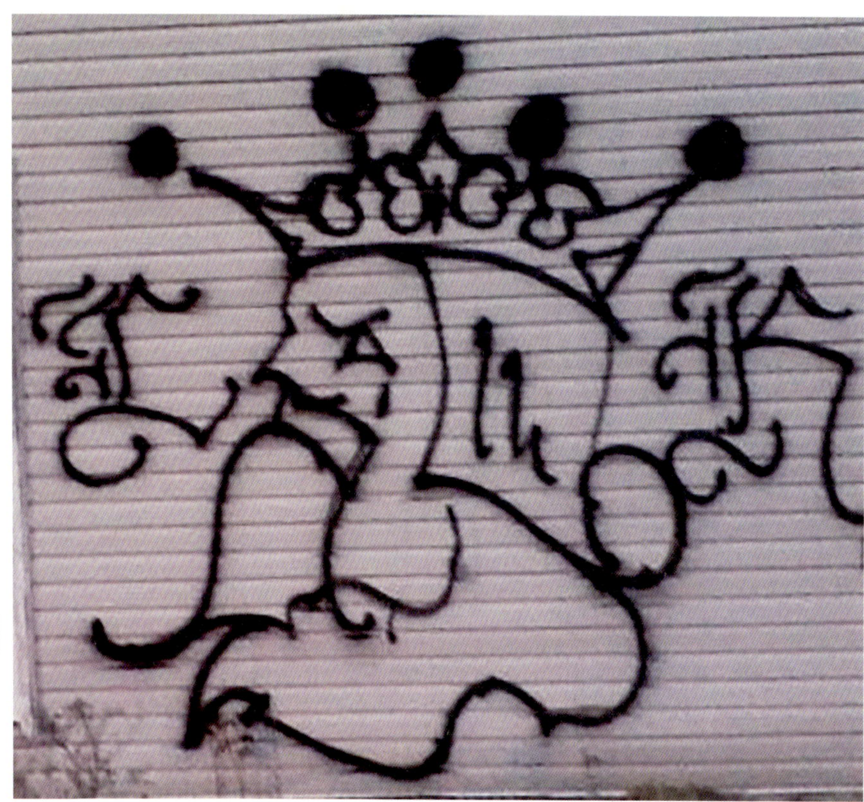

However, graffiti is graffiti on its own terms. Because of the anonymity of graffiti, regardless of your color, race, height, and social status, your works is the only way that you win other writers' recognition and respect. Dealing with police and gangsters, some writers stuck around, while some left. But it is no doubt that graffiti writers and their followers created their own culture, a culture for the young to express their inner world.

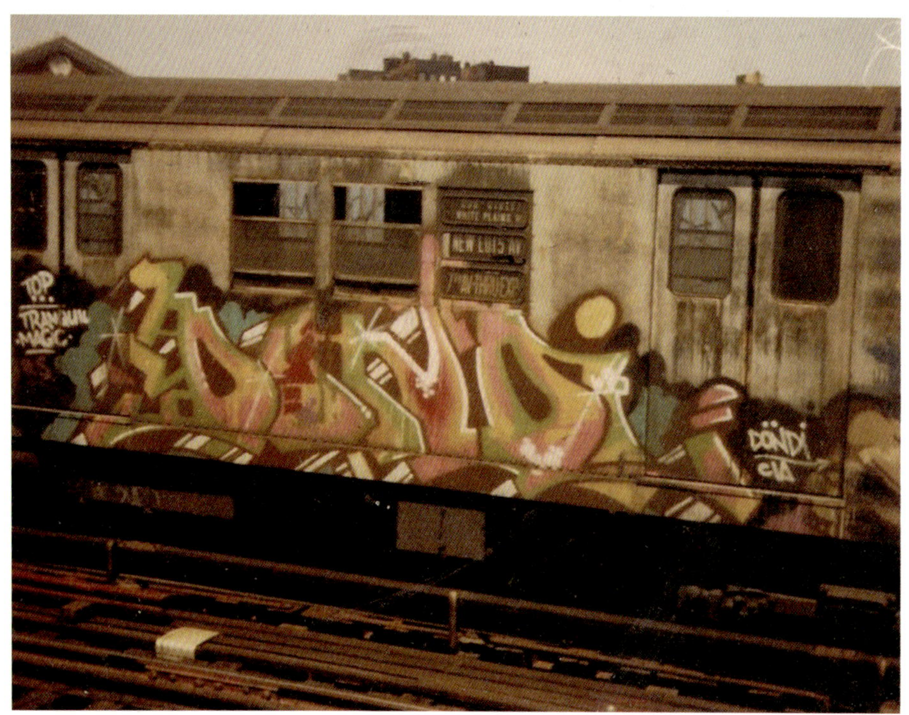

Photo/ JJ & Special K

GRAFFITI LETTER STYLE

Bubble Letter

Bubble letter is a style of graffiti lettering originally created by PHASE 2 and is often used for throw-ups. The letters are circular and often partially overlap each other, creating an image that seems to bubble up. Bubble letters are done mostly in two colors, where the outline and fill-in are sprayed in different hues to create contrast. But as the style developed, sometimes characters and more exuberant effects were added.

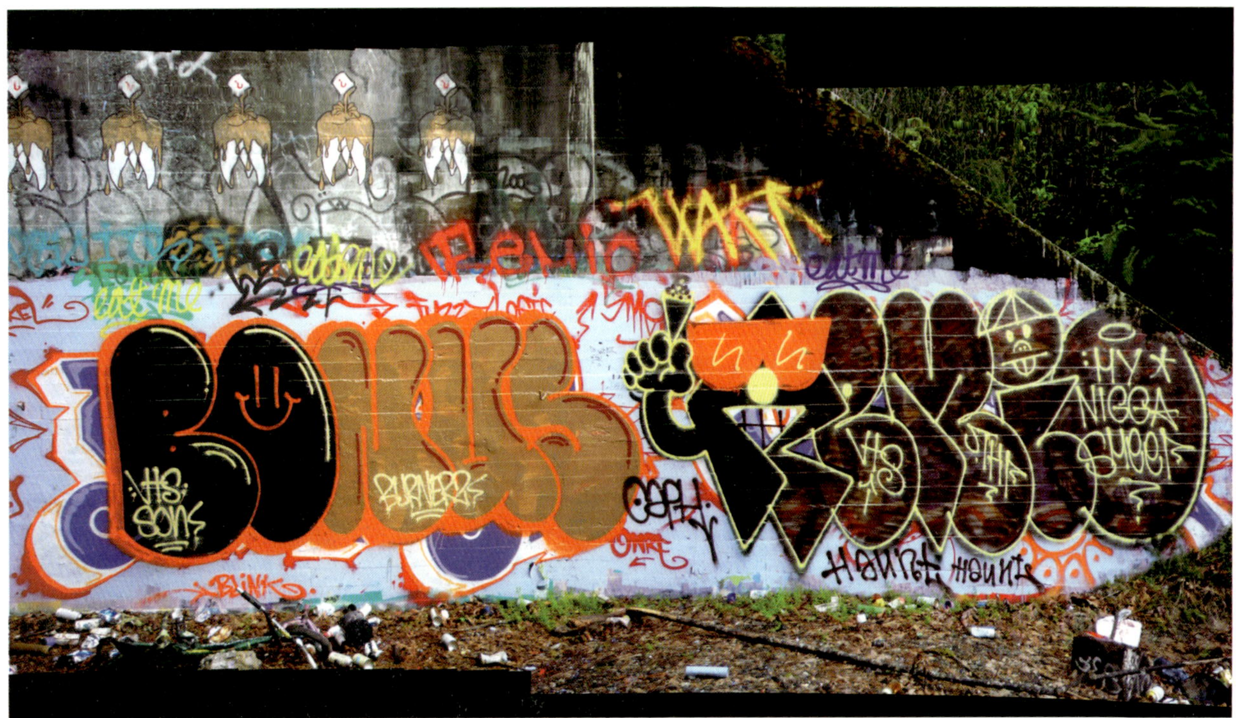

Photo/ Jason Taellious (Flickr)

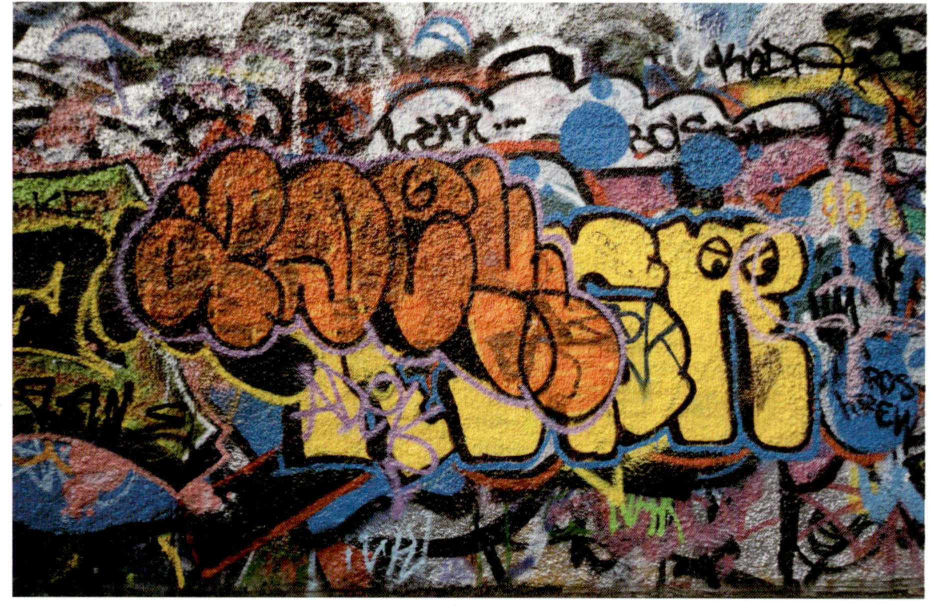

Photo/ William Murphy (Flickr)

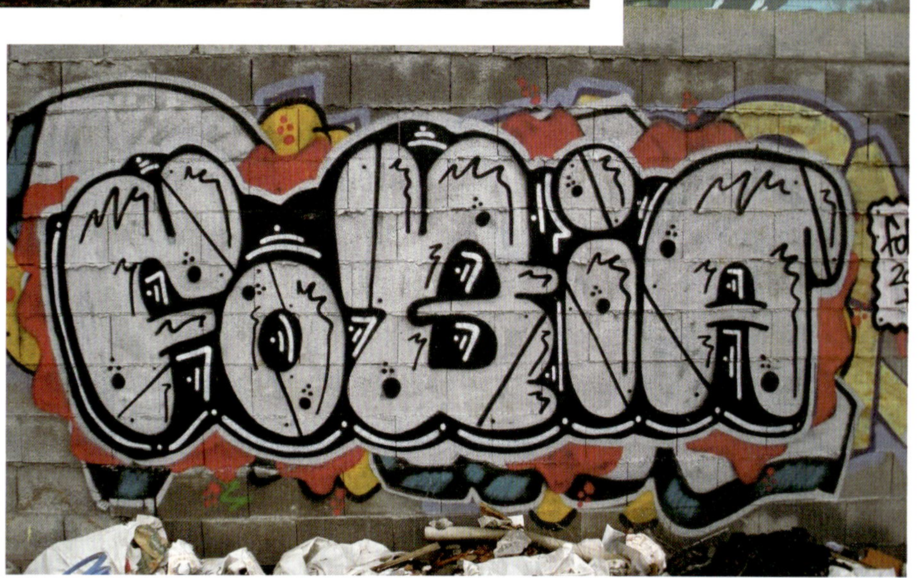

Author/ Zarateman

Photo/ Wikimedia Commons

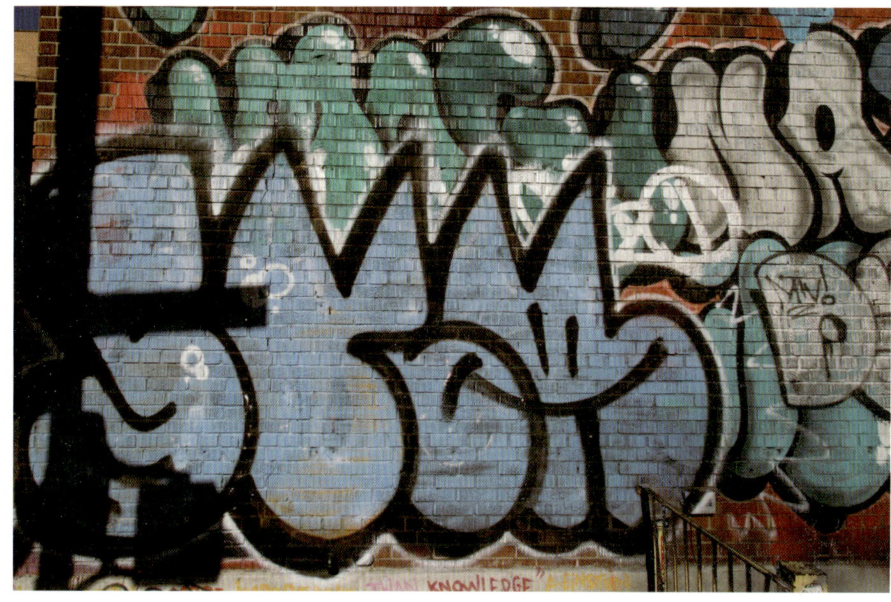

Author/ George Hodan

Photo/ Public Domain Pictures

Block Letter

In graffiti terms, block letter is often known as "straight," "blockbuster," and sometimes as "simple." This graffiti style is featured with square and rectangular edges. Blockbuster, referred to as "block graffiti" or "whole car," was mainly invented for maximum coverage in painting trains and smaller walls. BLADE is credited with having invented this style. Because of its solid lines, this form is mostly used to convey strong messages.

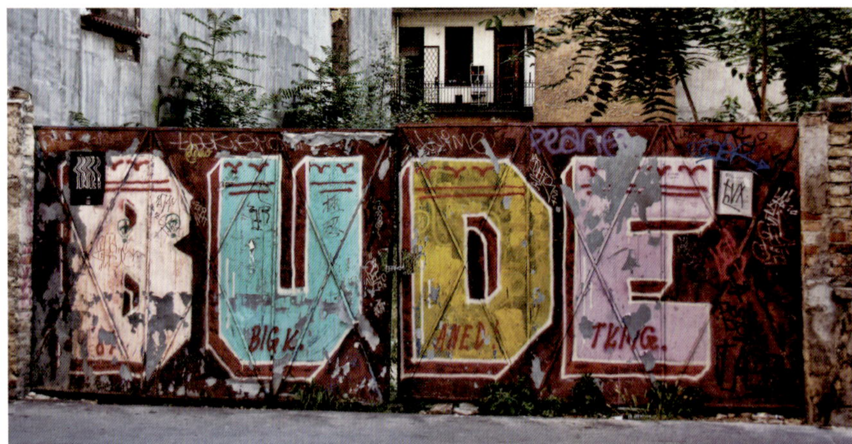

Photo/ Pixabay

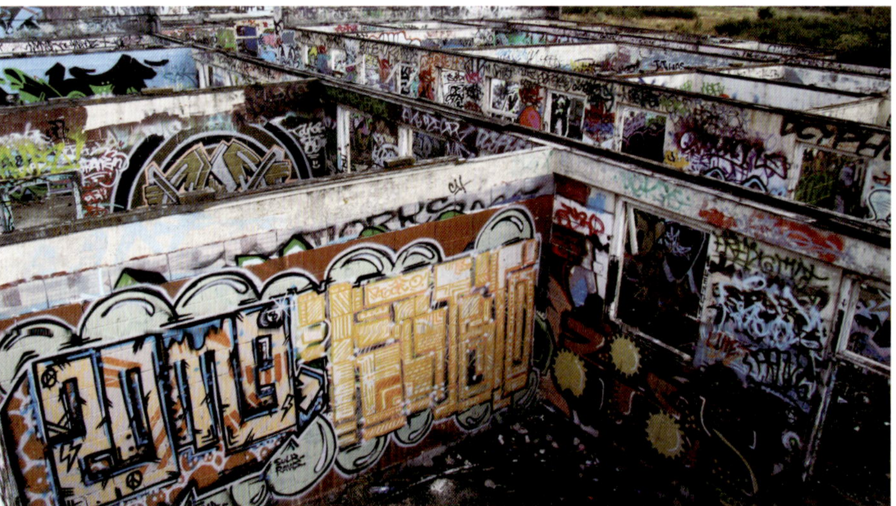

Photo/ NCSphotography (Flickr)

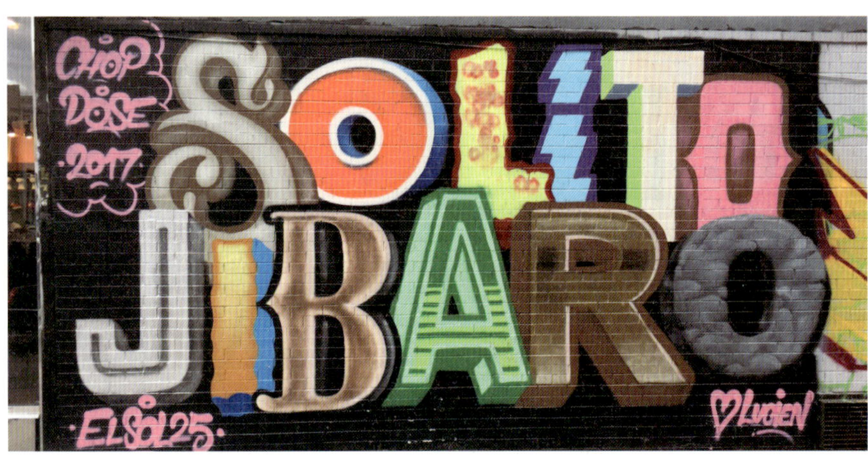

Artist/ El Sol 25

Wildstyle Letter

Wildstyle graffiti is a form featuring letters so stylized as to be rendered in an undecipherable manner. These pieces are often harder to read for non-graffiti artists. The letters often interlock, connecting and sometimes three dimensional. They may include arrows, spikes, and other decorative elements, depending on the technique used. Wildstyle is said to be the Queen discipline of New York graffiti, the purest lettering style and deserving of the most consideration.

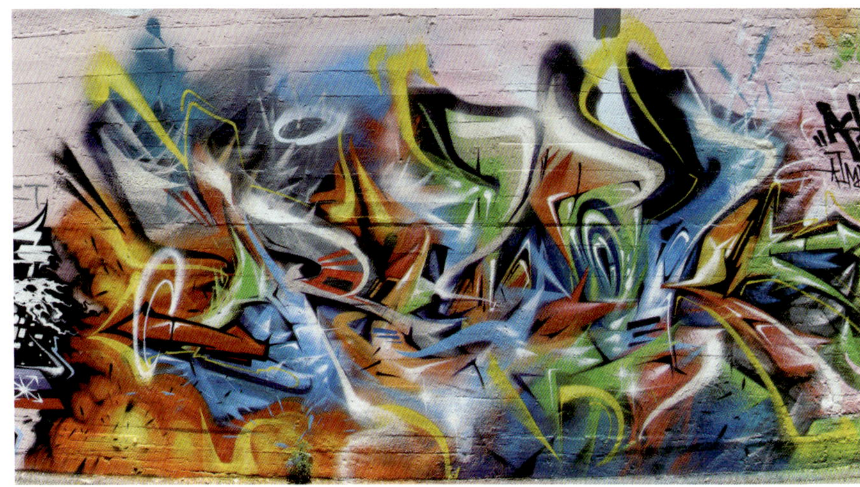

Photo/ A Syn (Flickr)

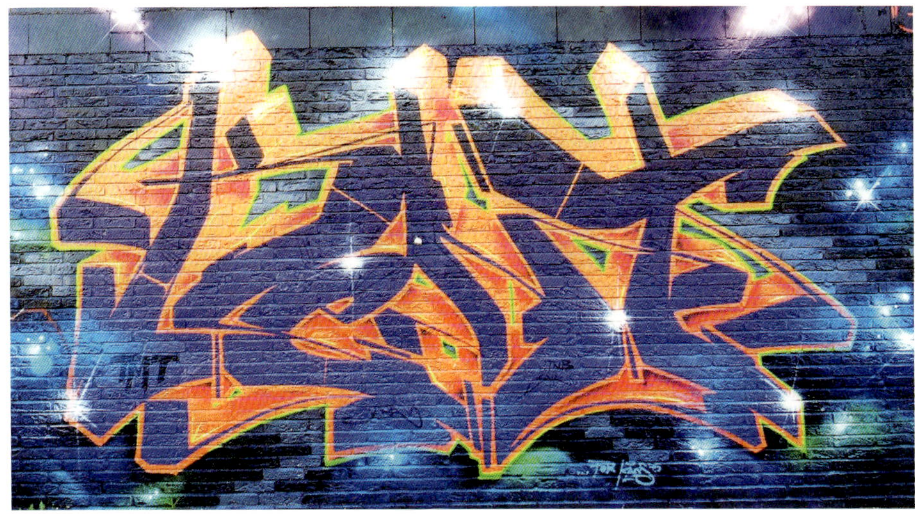

Photo/ Pixabay

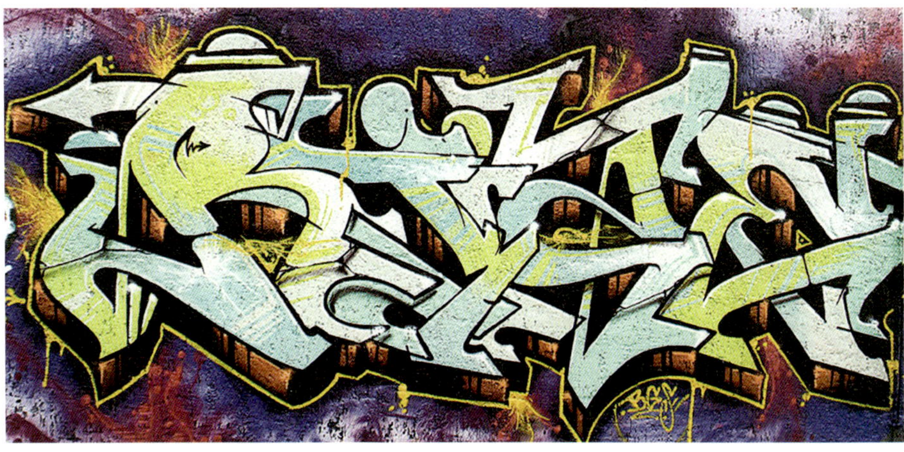

Photo/ Px4u by Team Cu29 (Flickr)

GRAFFITI SLANG

Writer
A graffiti artist.

Crew
A loosely organized group of writers.

Head
A writer who has much skill and a high reputation among other writers.

King/Queen
A respected writer among others.

Angel
Late respected graffiti artist.

Toy
Unskilled writer or poor work .

Get up
To develop your reputation.

Bomb
To cover an area with tags or throw-ups.

Burn
To beat a competitor with a style.

Dress up
To completely write all over a specific area.

Slam
To paint an extremely conspicuous or dangerous location.

Soak up
To consider other pieces for inspiration.

Bite
To steal another artist's style.

Buff
To remove painted graffiti.

Rack
To steal, usually paints or markers.

Slash
To put a line through, or tag over, others' graffiti.

Tag
A writer's signature with marker or spray paint.

Throw-up
Usually quickly done bubble letters or very simple pieces using only two colors for outlines and fills.

One-liner
A tag, throw-up, or bomb written in one constant motion.

Roller/Blockbuster
An large-scale piece created with a paint roller instead of aerosol.

Hollow
A piece of graffiti that contains no fill.

Piece/Masterpiece
A large, complex, and labor-intensive graffiti painting.

Back to back
A piece covering a wall from end to end.

Landmark
A piece that stays for at least 5 years.

Dub

A piece executed in silver or chrome paint.

Inside

A piece done inside trains.

Underside

A tag or signature painted on the under carriage of passenger trains.

Window down

A piece painted below the window borders of a train.

Top to bottom

A piece that covers the whole height of the car.

End to end/e2e

A piece covering a train car from one side to another.

Whole car/train

A piece covering a whole car.

Married couple

Two simultaneous whole cars painted next to each other.

Heaven spot

A piece painted in hard-to-reach places.

Ghost

A mark left after paint or ink has been unsuccessfully buffed.

Legal

A graffiti piece made with permission.

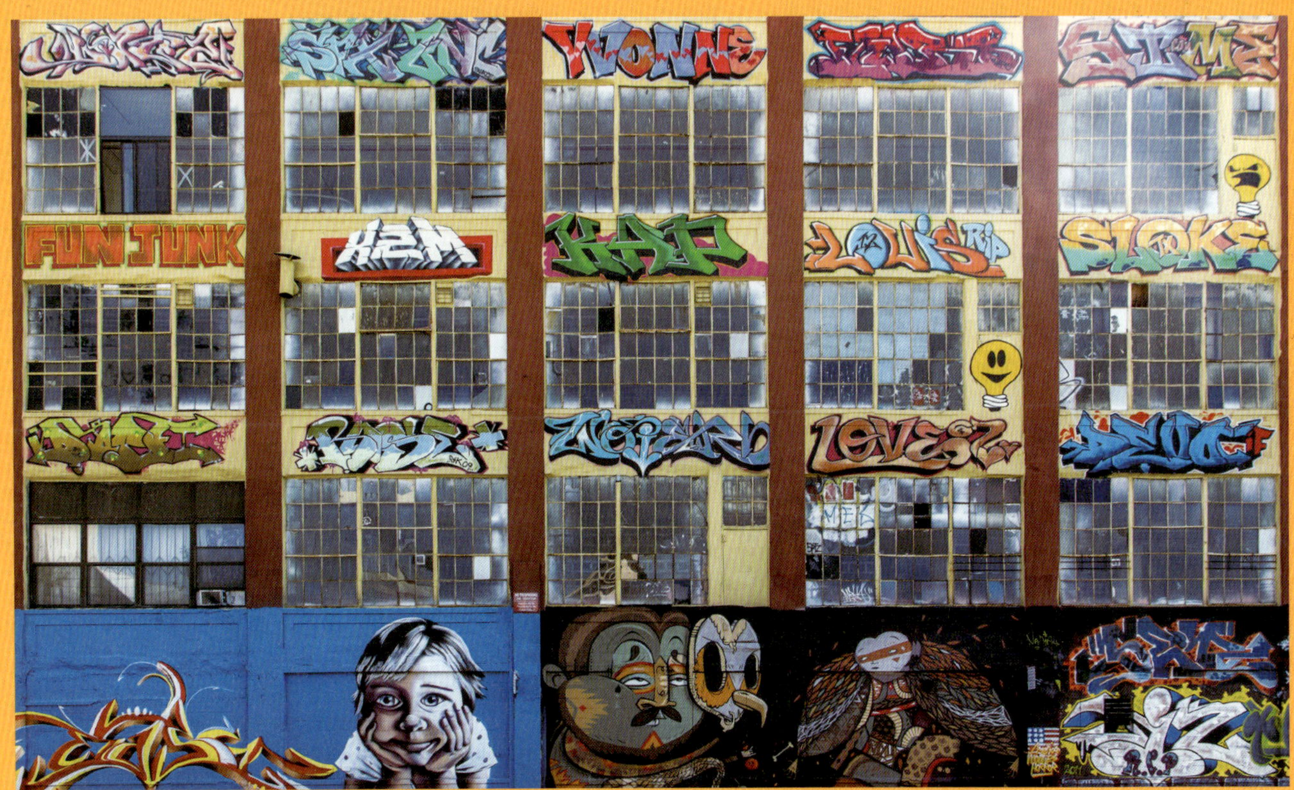

5 Pointz, short for 5 Pointz Aerosol Art Center, Inc., is considered the Mecca of premiere graffiti, exhibiting outdoor arts on the walls of a 200,000-square-foot factory building in Long Island City, New York. However, it was fully demolished by November 2014, regardless of constant protest and petition.

Author/ P.Lindgren

Photo/ Wikimedia Commons

Trang Khoa is a street artist from Ho Chi Minh City, Vietnam, and he is now the founder of Wallovers and a member of the Three Flare Krew (TFK). His masterpieces of graffiti have all these interconnected strokes of wildstyle letters, and the highlights of the letter edges make every letter appear to be 3-dimensional. Because of his experience of being an illustrator, his works are full of delicate details of touches.

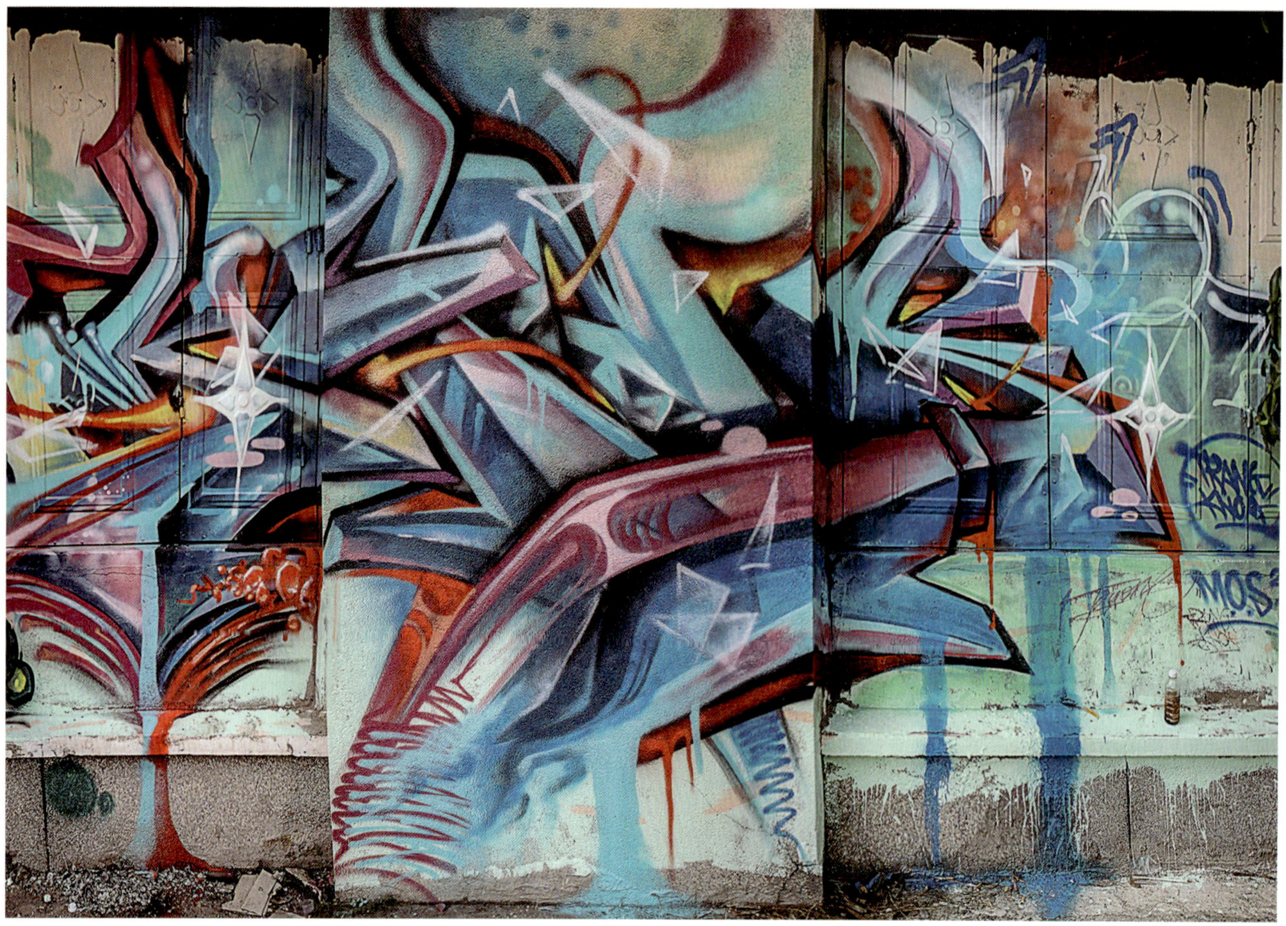

@Ho Chi Minh City, Vietnam 2017

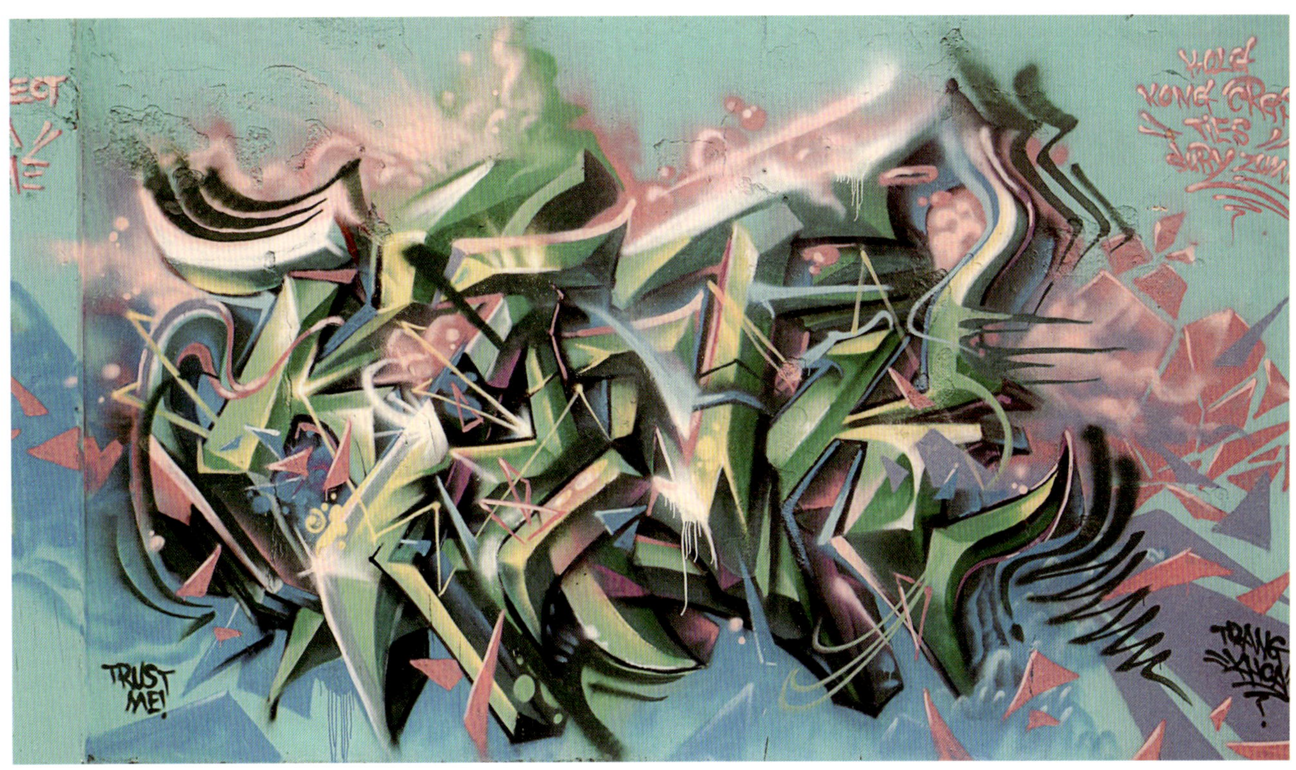

@Ho Chi Minh City, Vietnam 2017

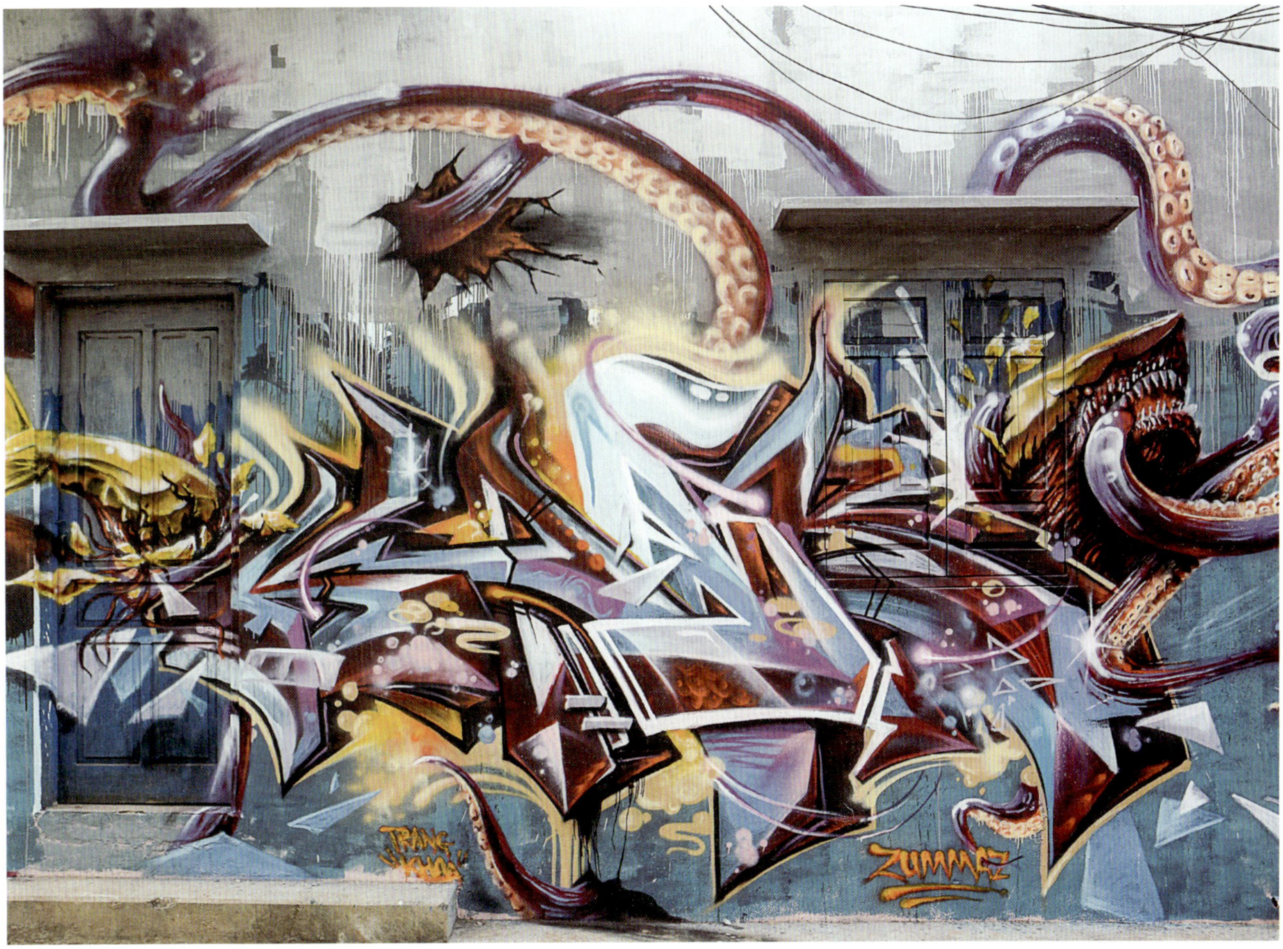

@Pleiku City, Vietnam 2017

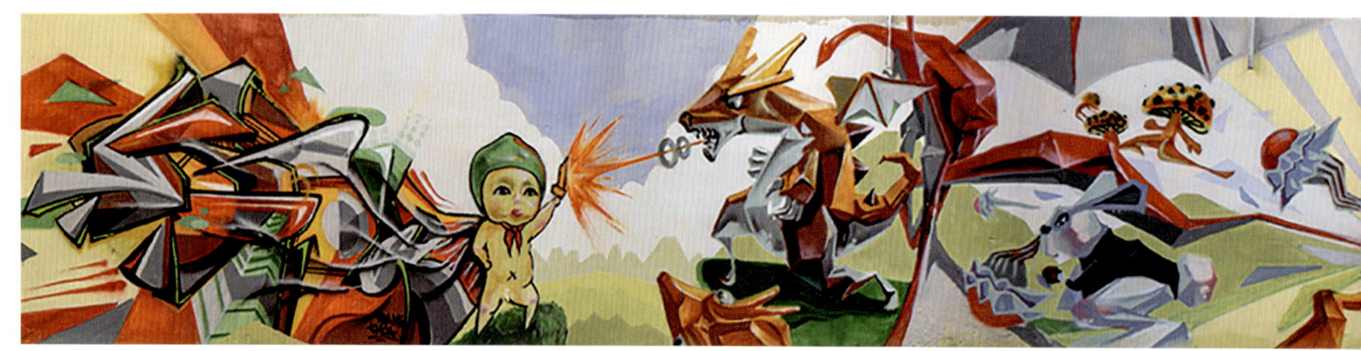

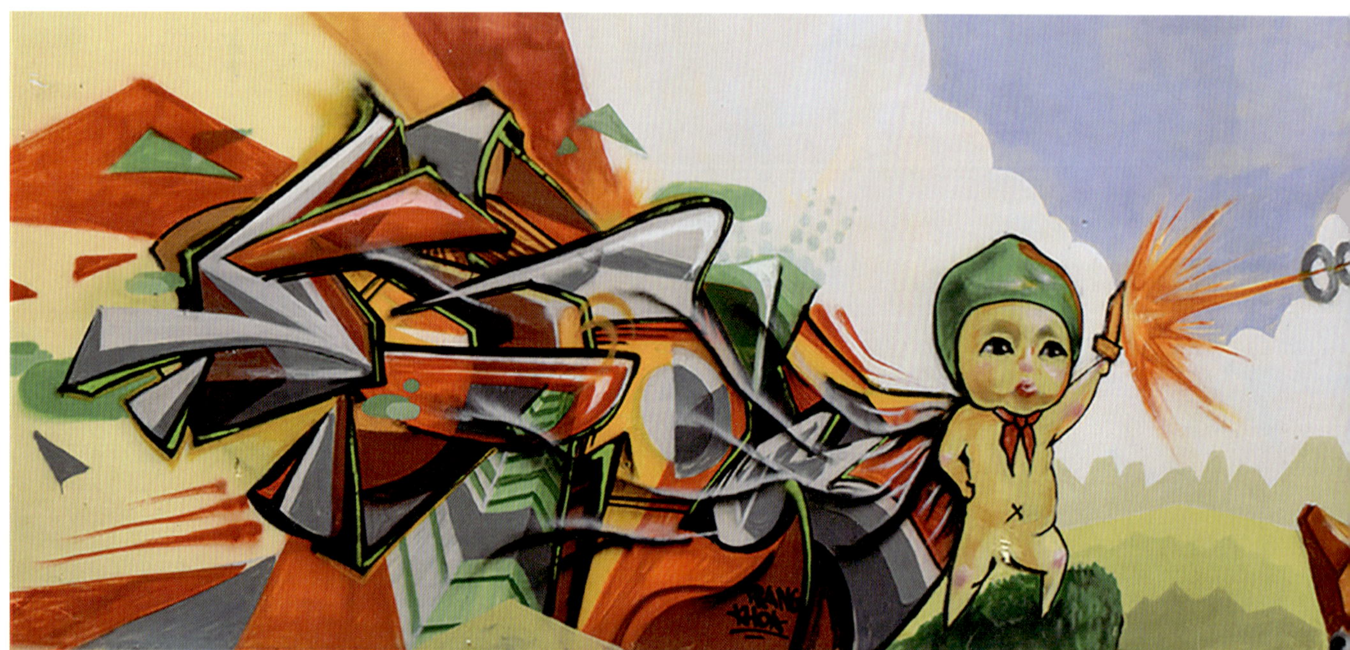

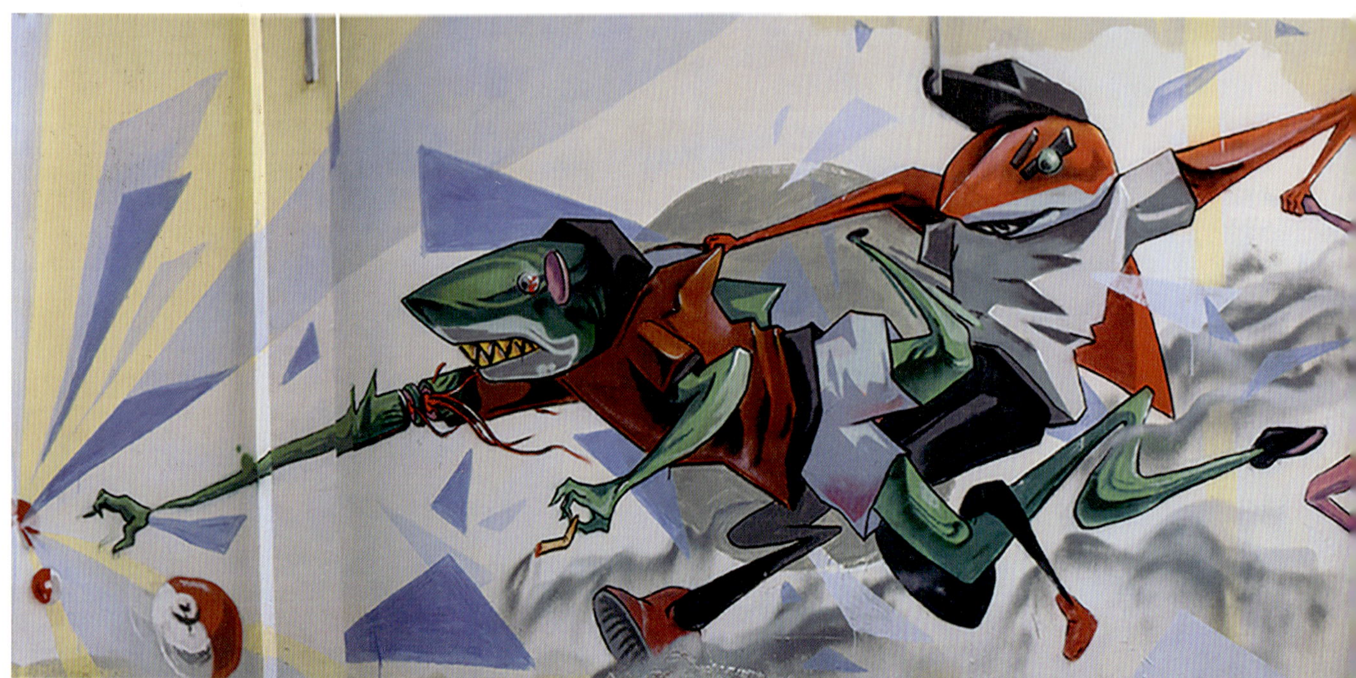

The Little Dream
@Ho Chi Minh City, Vietnam 2016

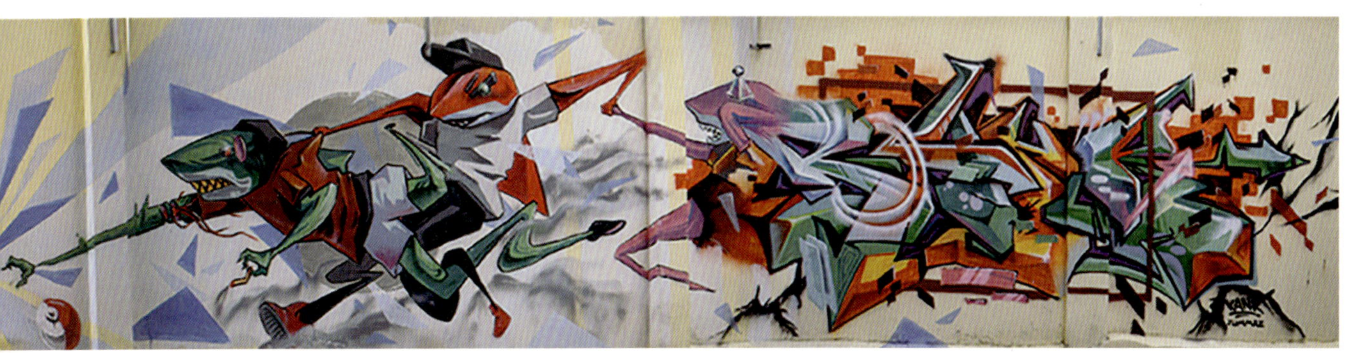

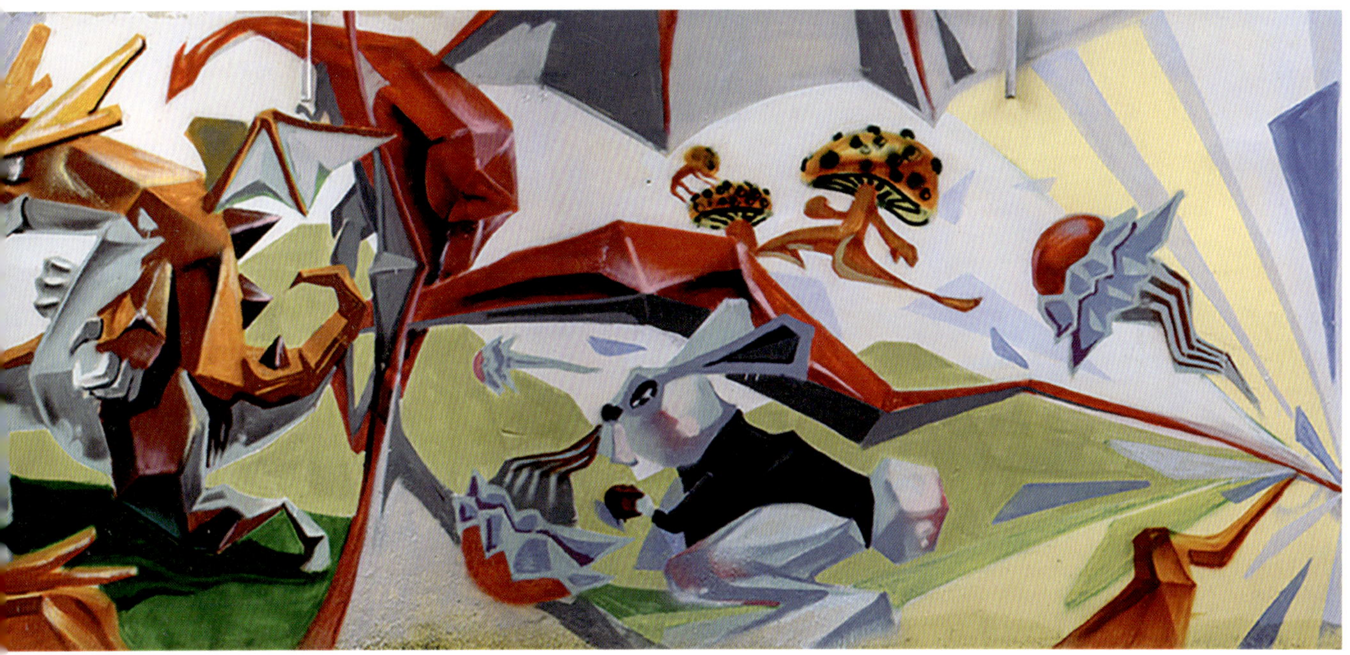

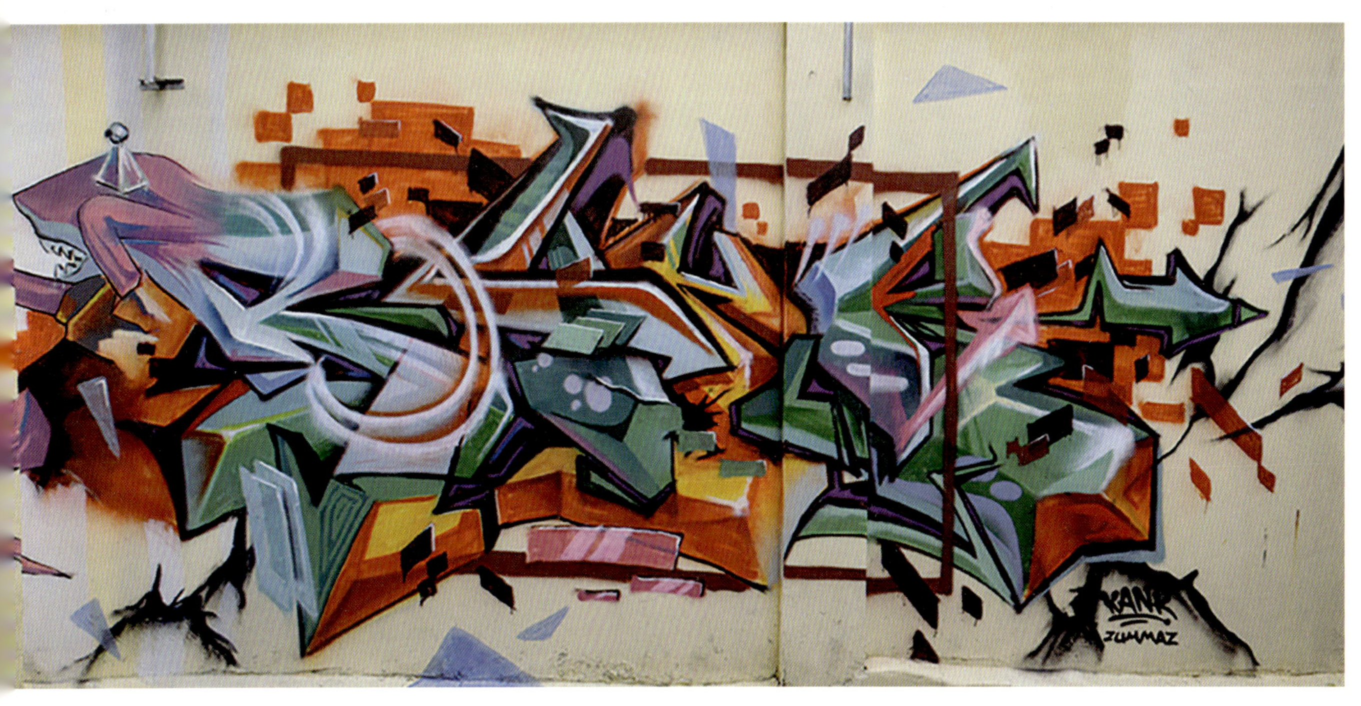

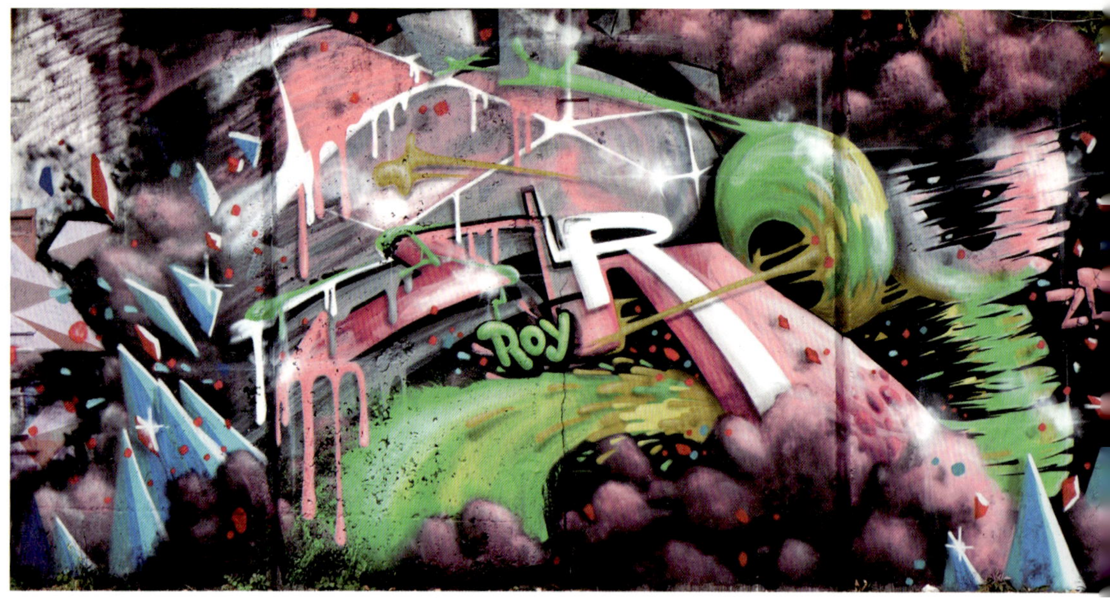
Roy

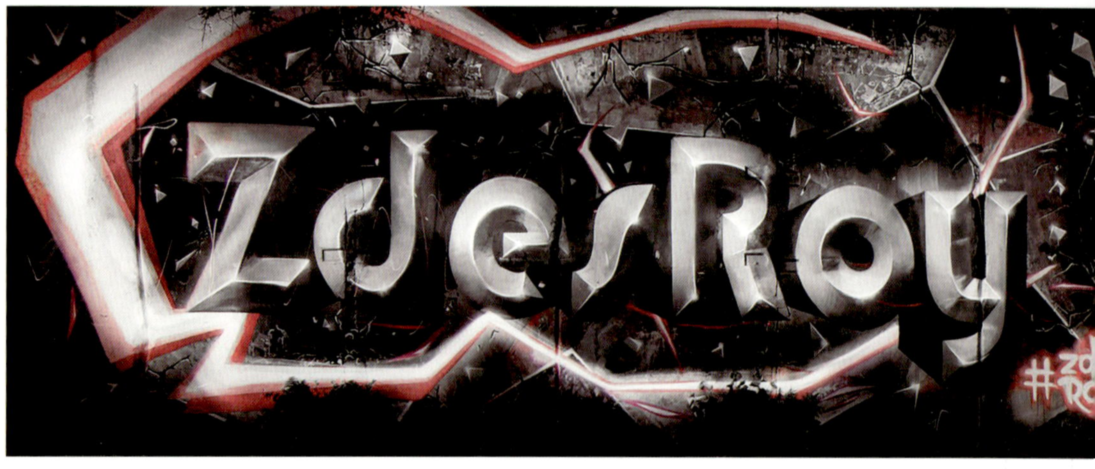
ZdesRoy

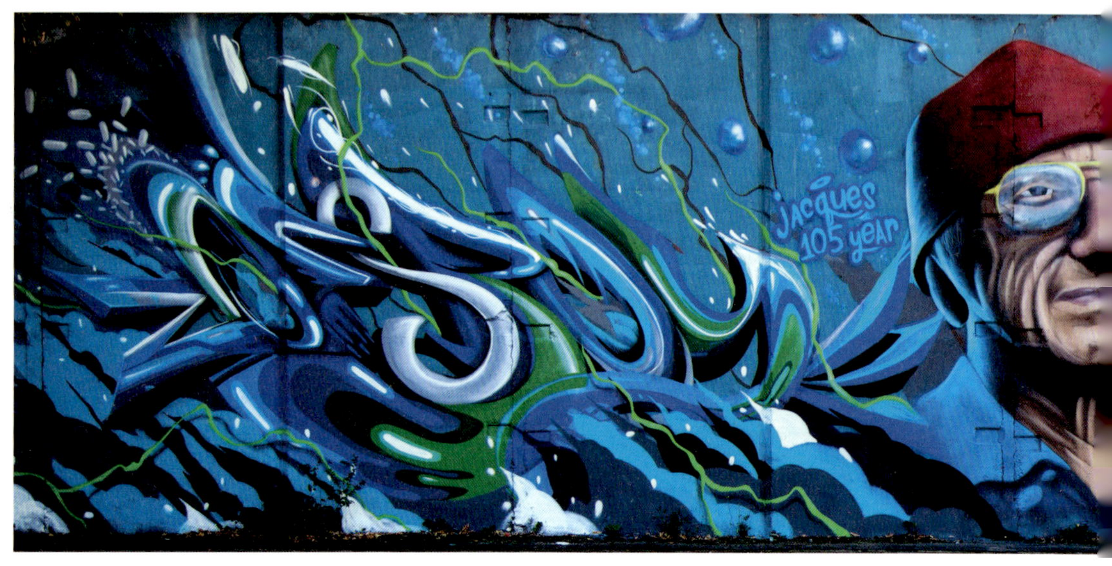
Jacques
105 year

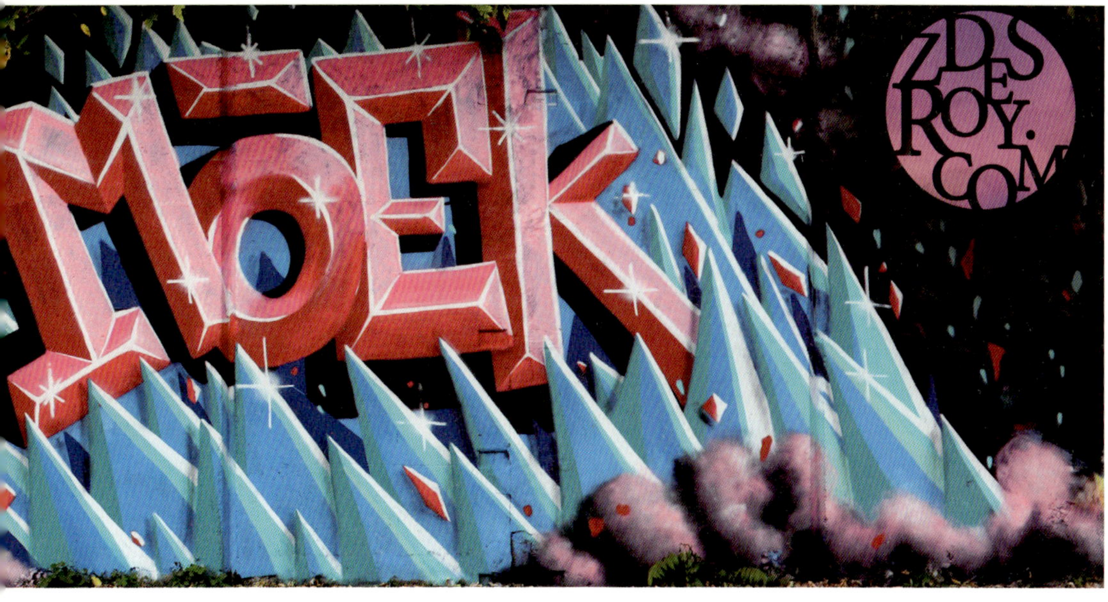

Collaboration with Moek
@Dnipro, Ukraine 2014

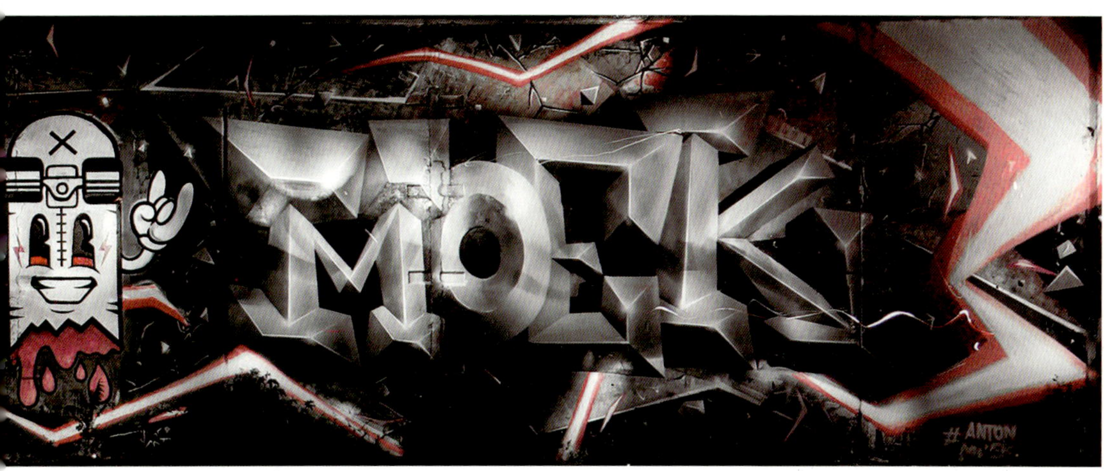

Collaboration with Moek
@Munich, Germany 2015

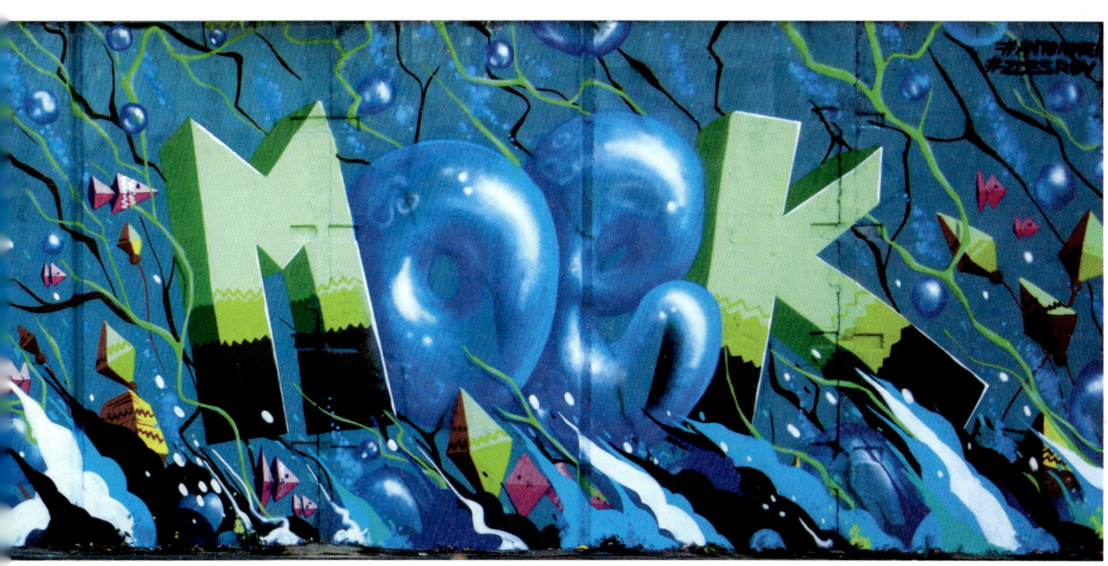

Collaboration with Moek
@Dnipro, Ukraine 2015 ©Anton Dmitriev

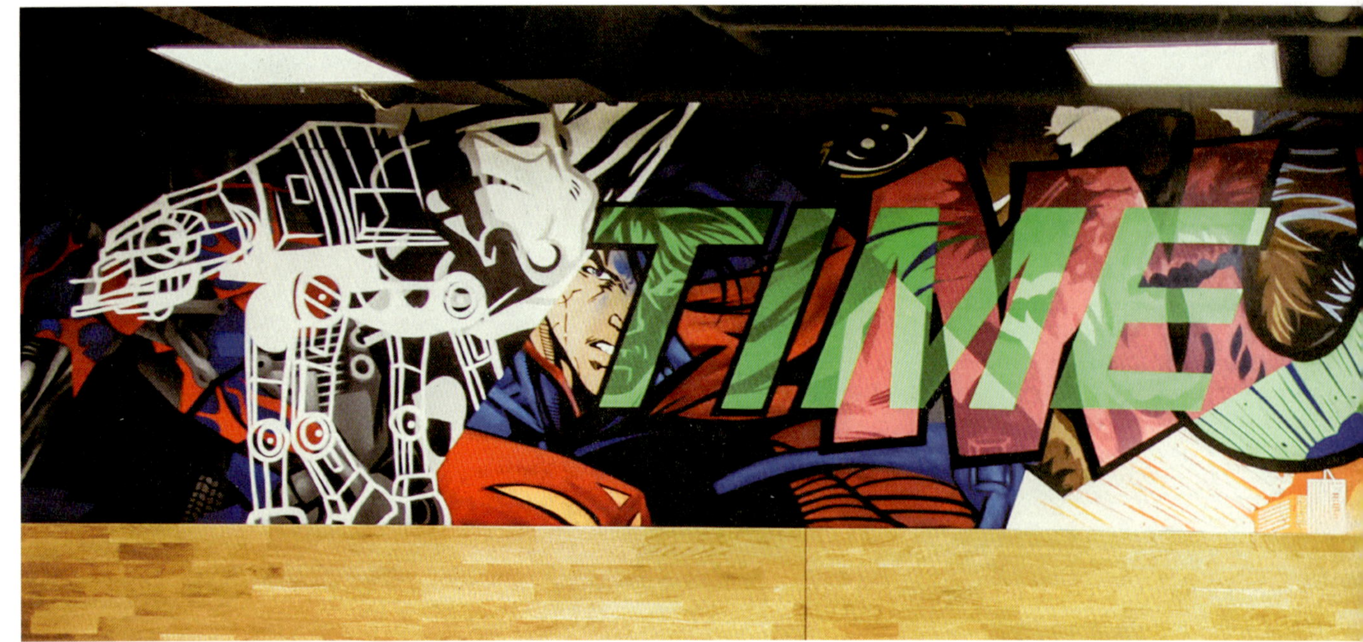

Artist/ Zdes Roy

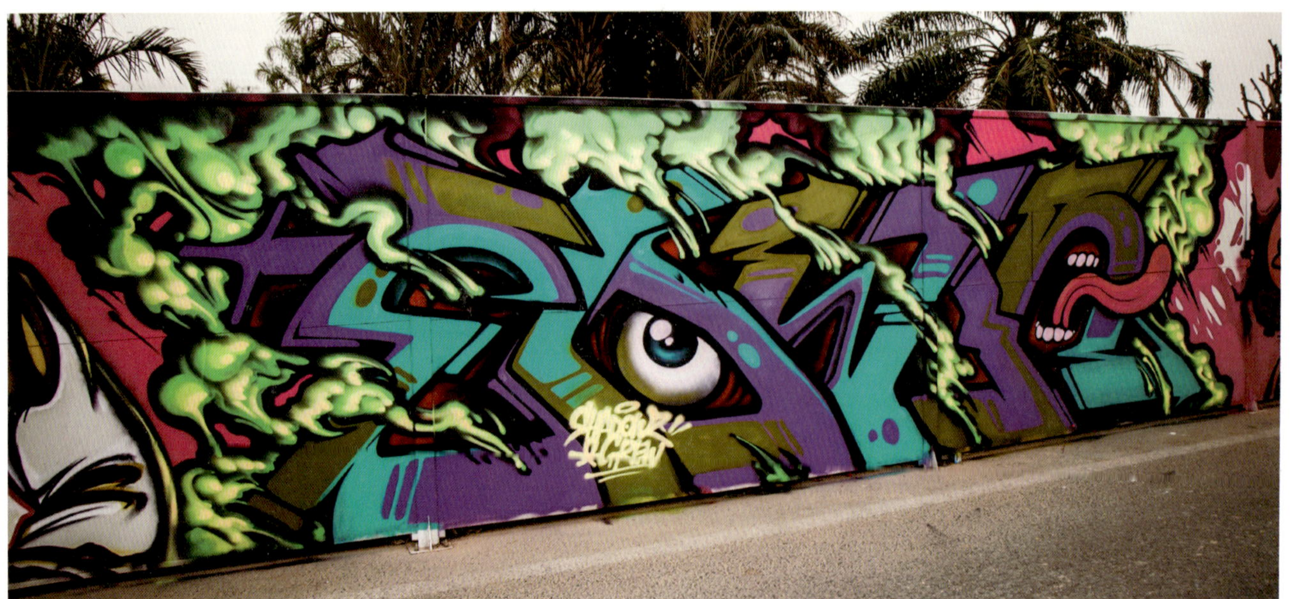

Artist/ Edwin Yang

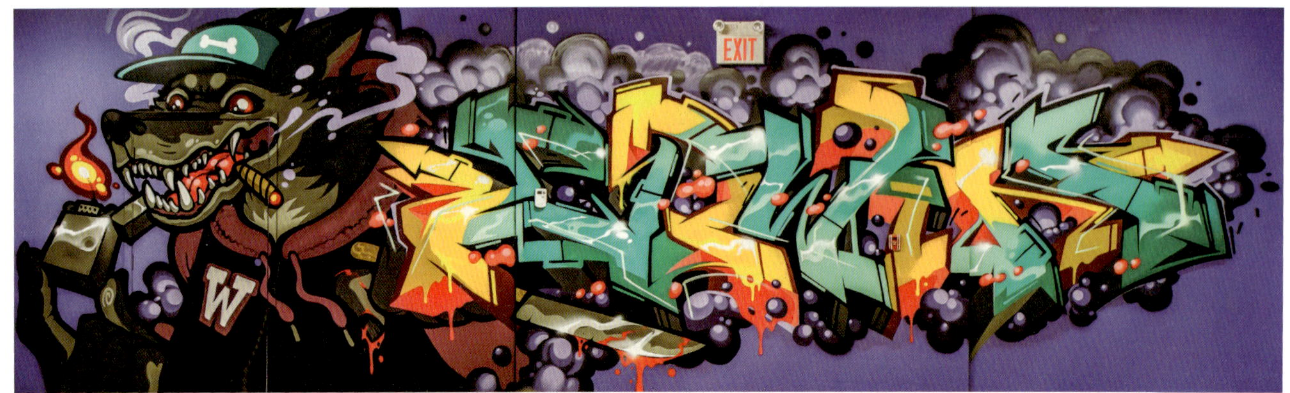

Artist/ Edwin Yang

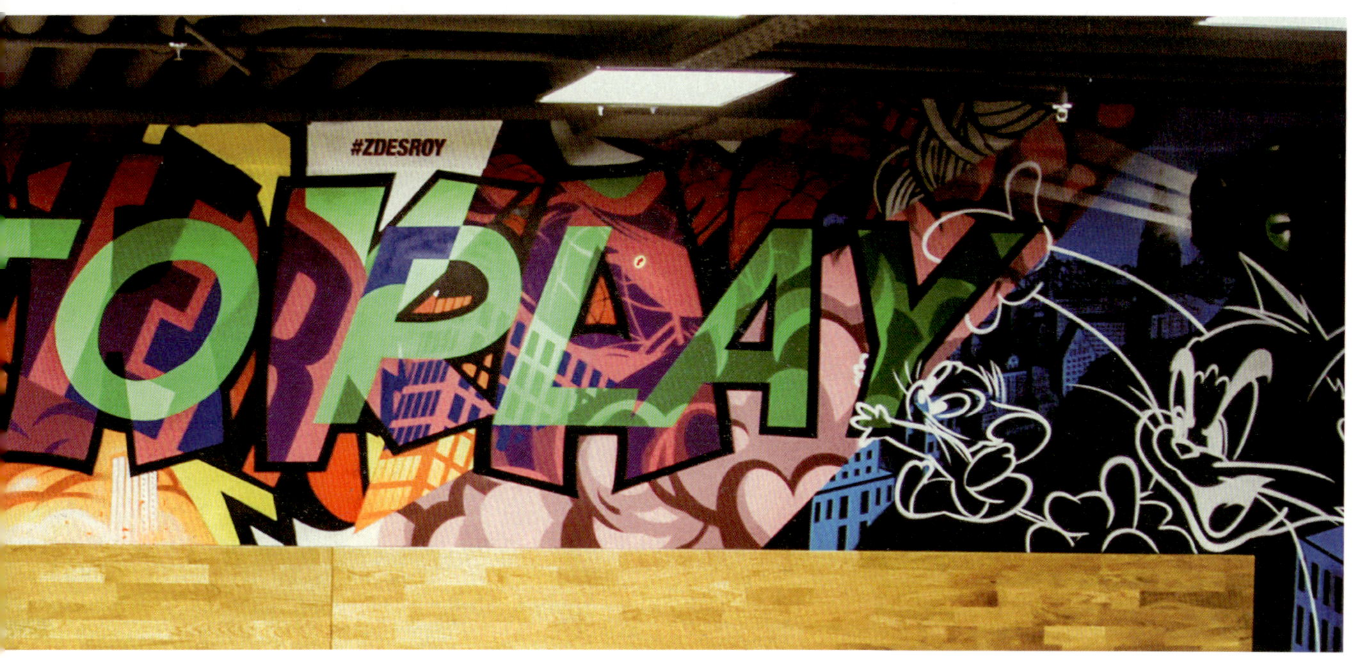

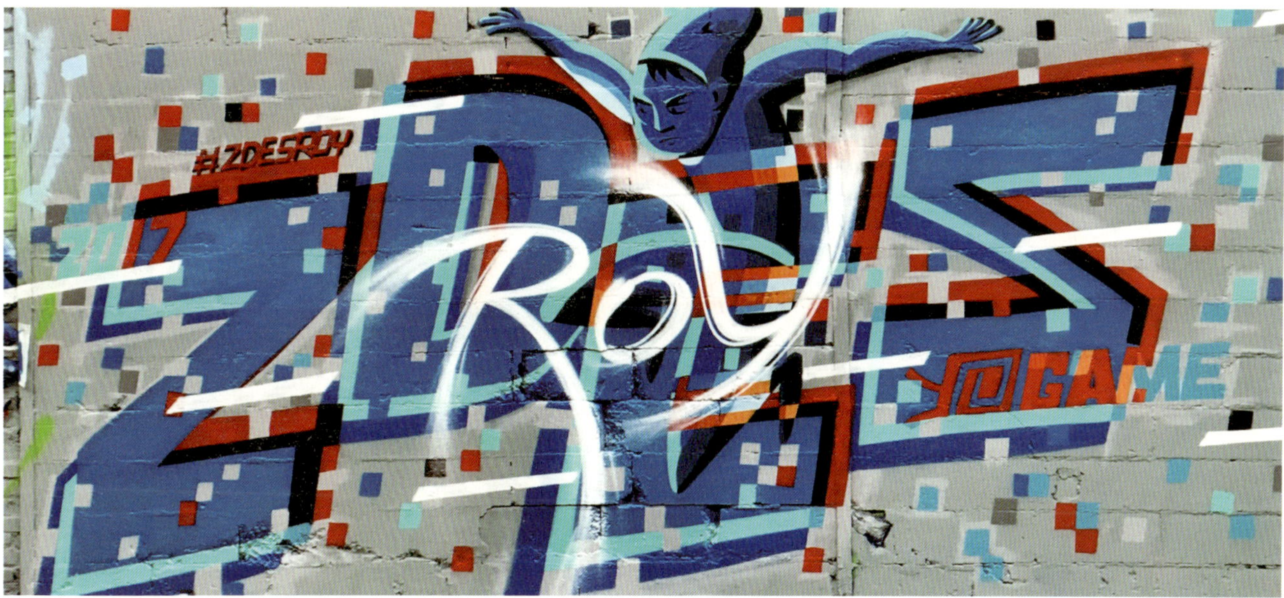

Artist/ Zdes Roy

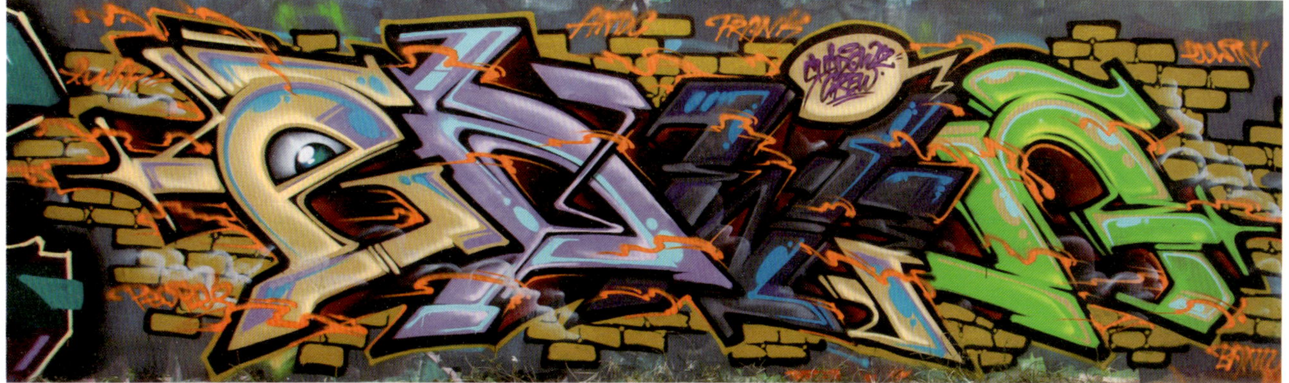

Artist/ Edwin Yang

Artist/ Mr. Zero

In 1994, having drawn all through his childhood, Mr. Zero sprayed his first comic character on a wall in his hometown in Hungary. Taking his artistic development more and more seriously, he created a unique picture-and-character language that earned him national and European recognition.

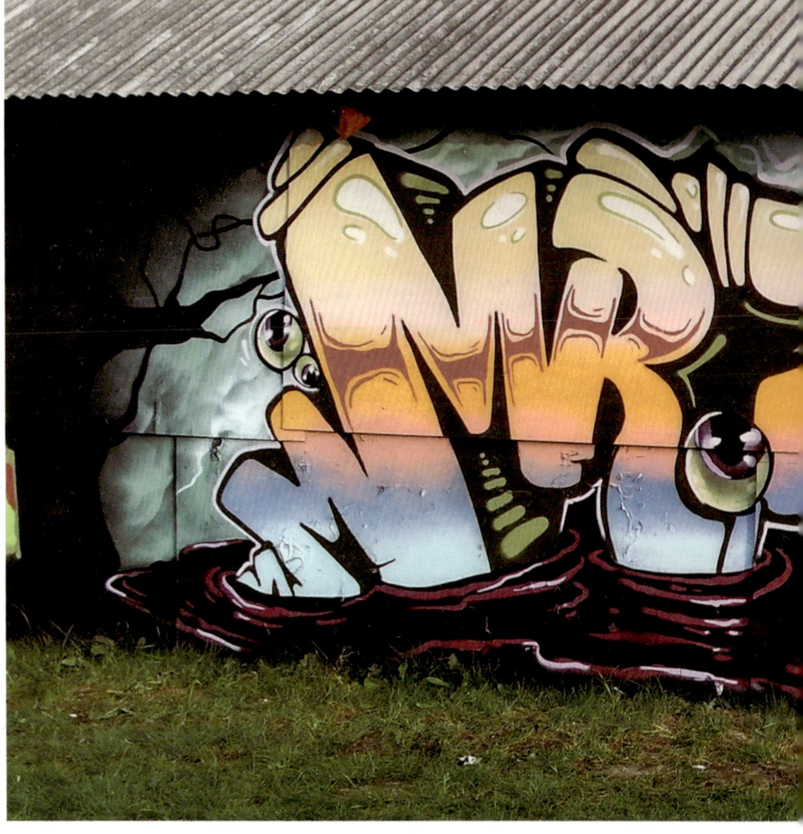

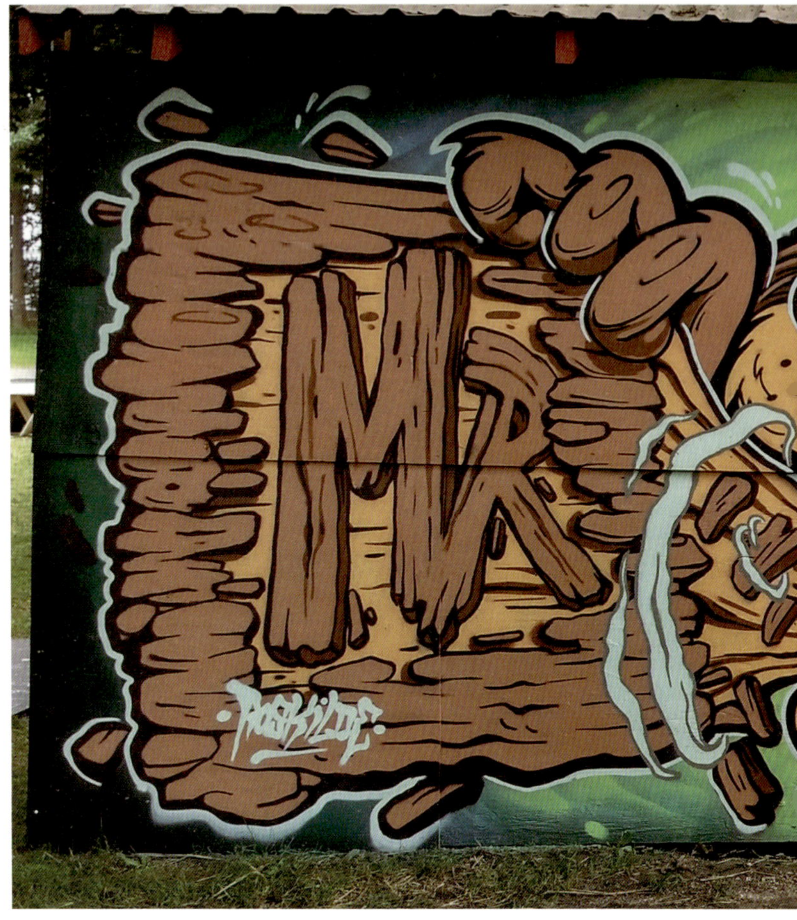

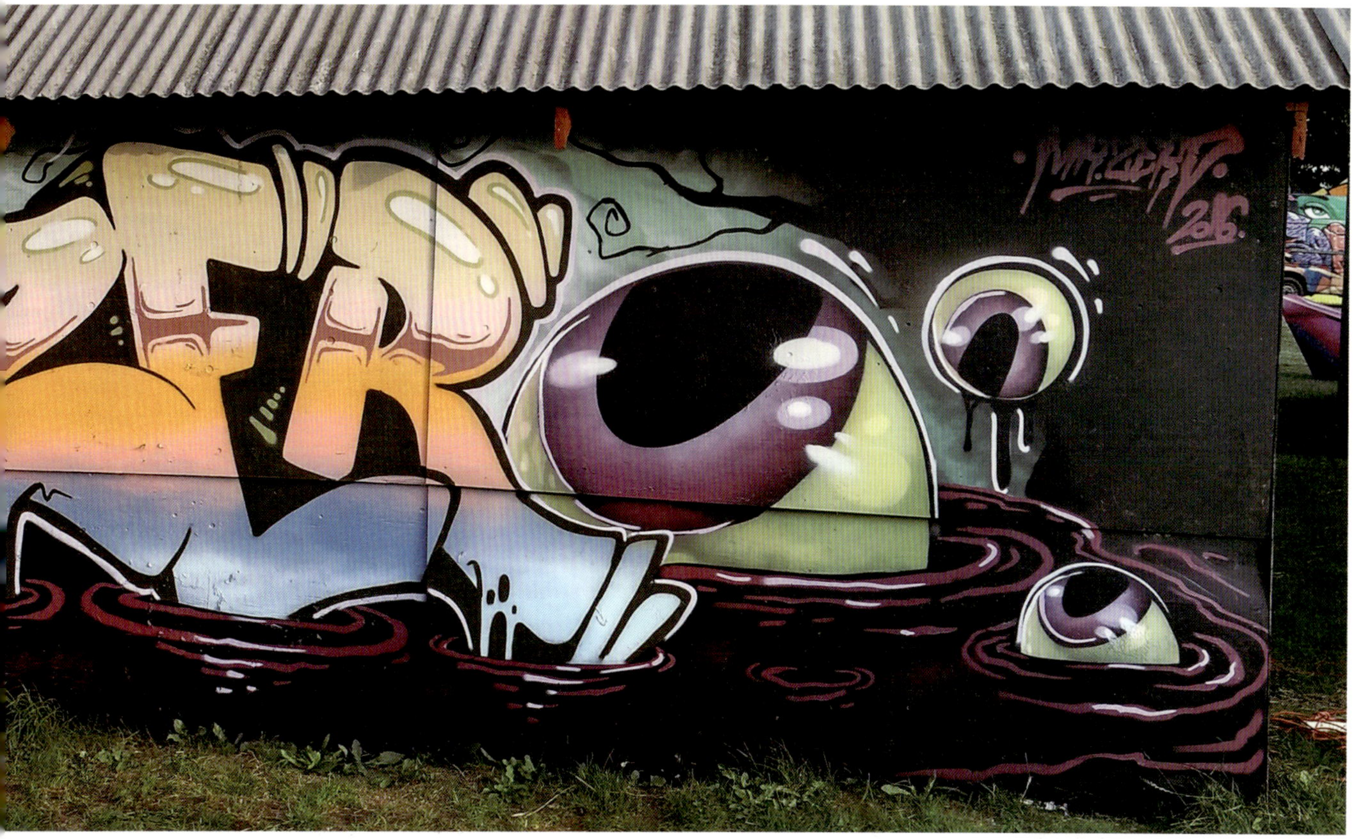

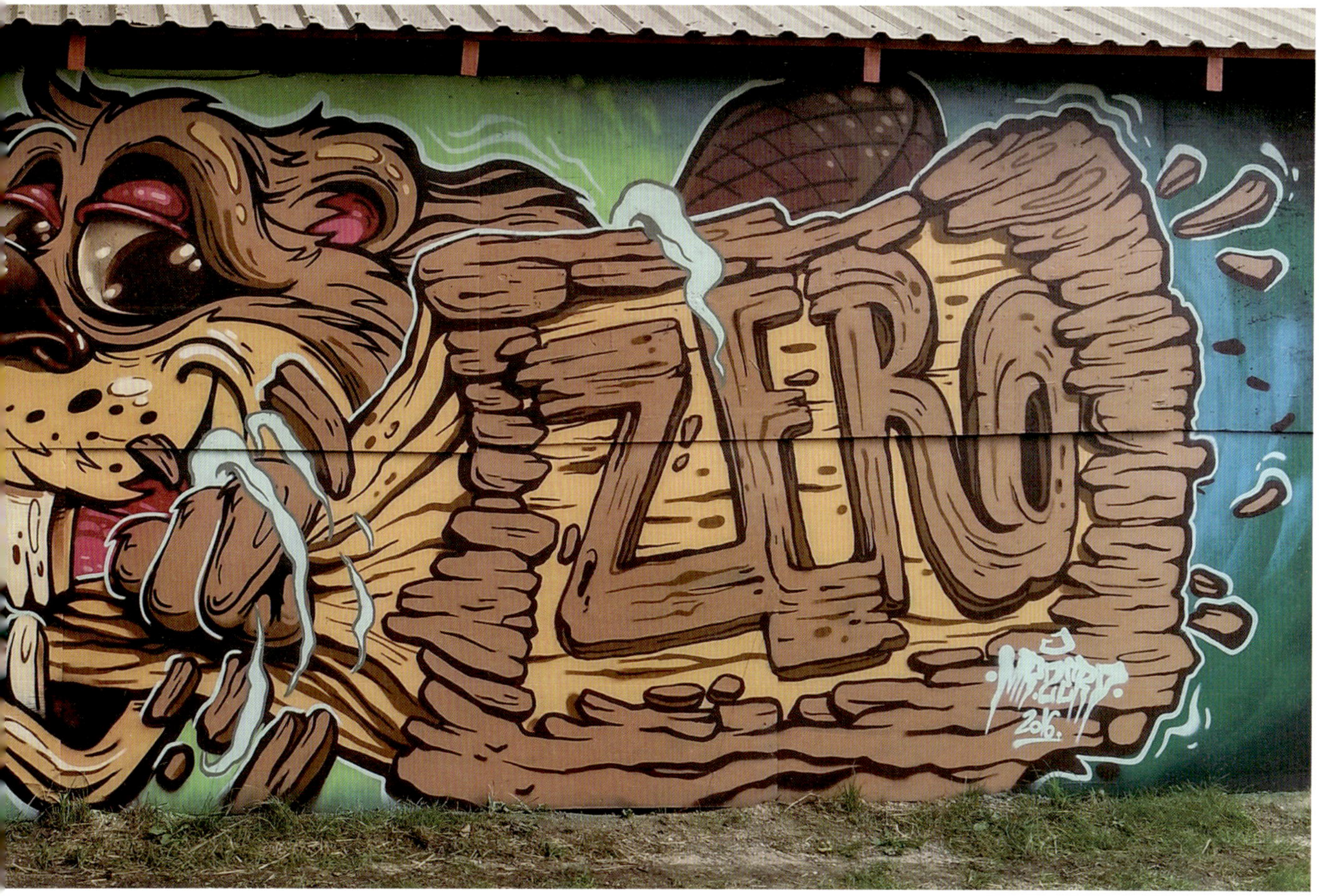

Artist/ Edwin Yang

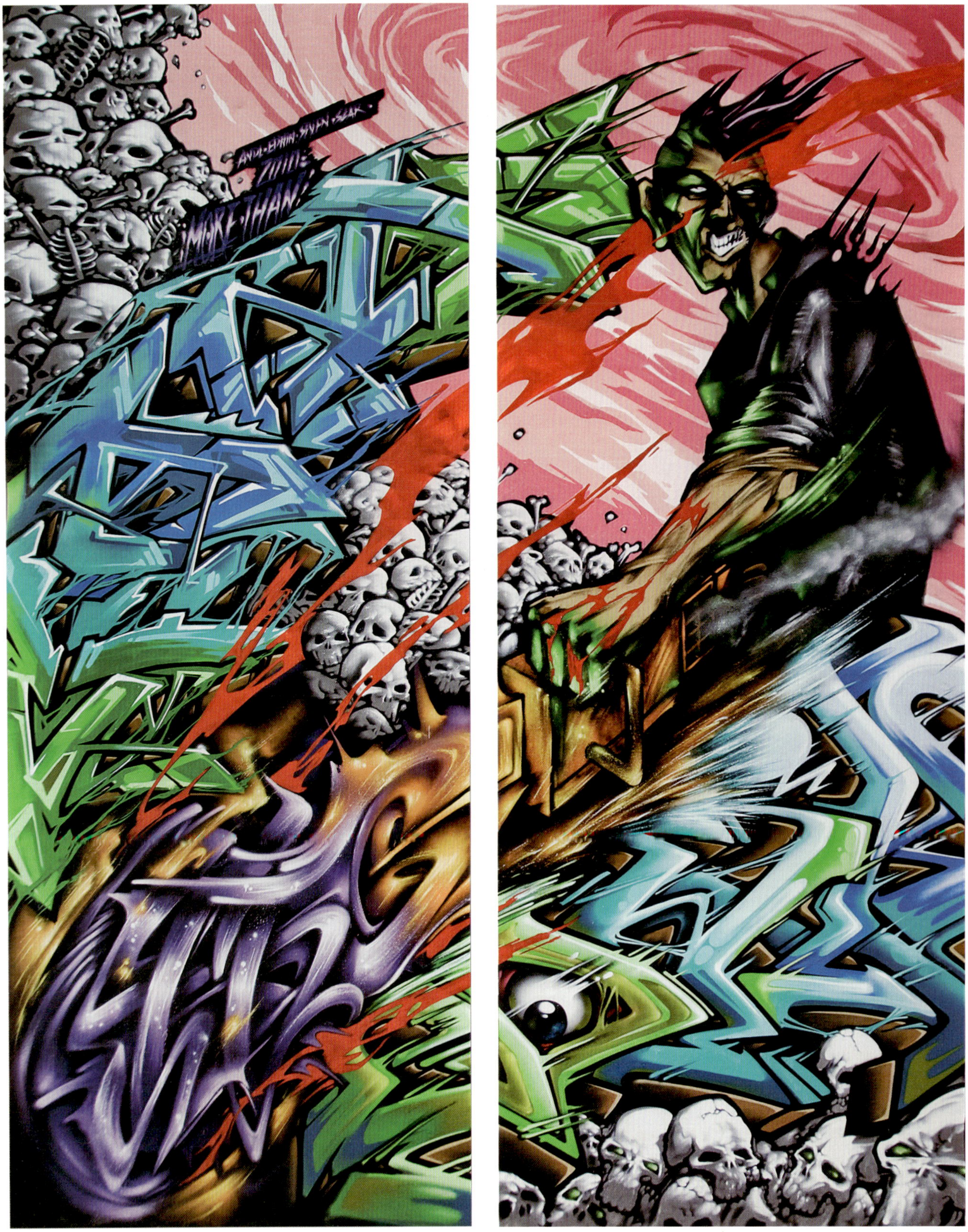

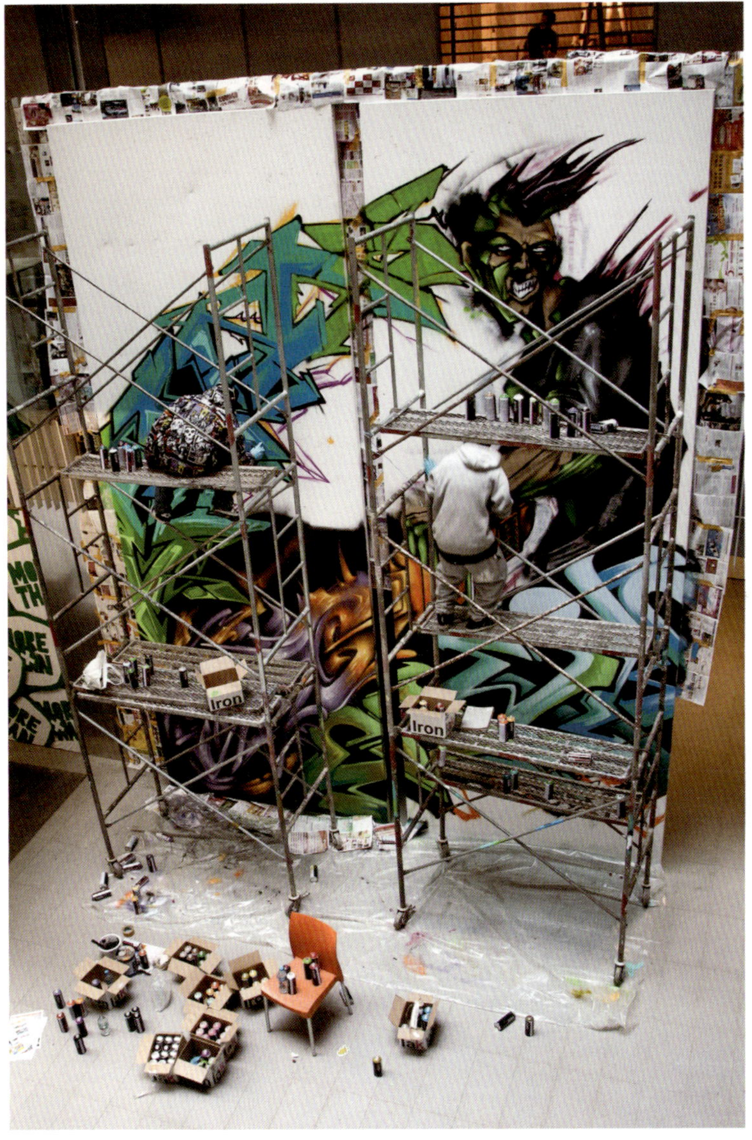

This giant canvas work is part of the MTD Exhibition Project held in 2010. The art activity was named "More Than." Over a hundred artists from East Asia and Europe were invited. With the theme of environmental protection in mind, artist Edwin Yang combined skull elements and wildstyle letters to create a bloody horror picture, suggesting that the environment is deeply related to the existence of human beings.

Collaboration with ABS-Crew
@Toronto, Canada 2010

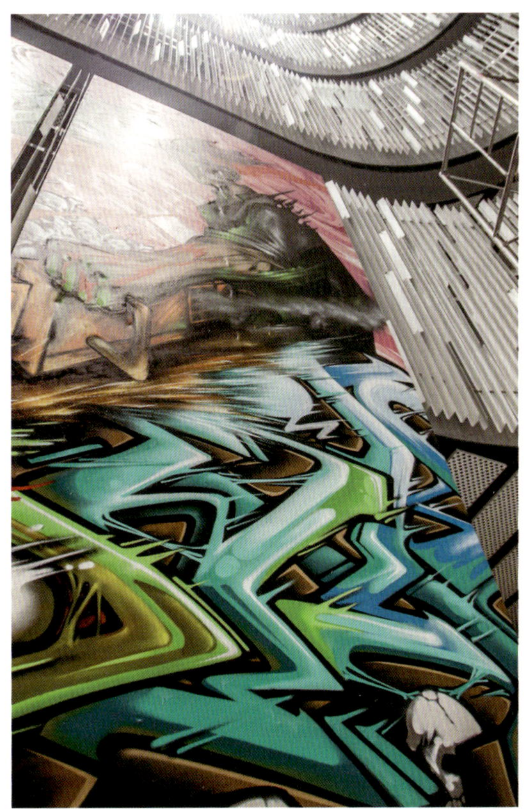

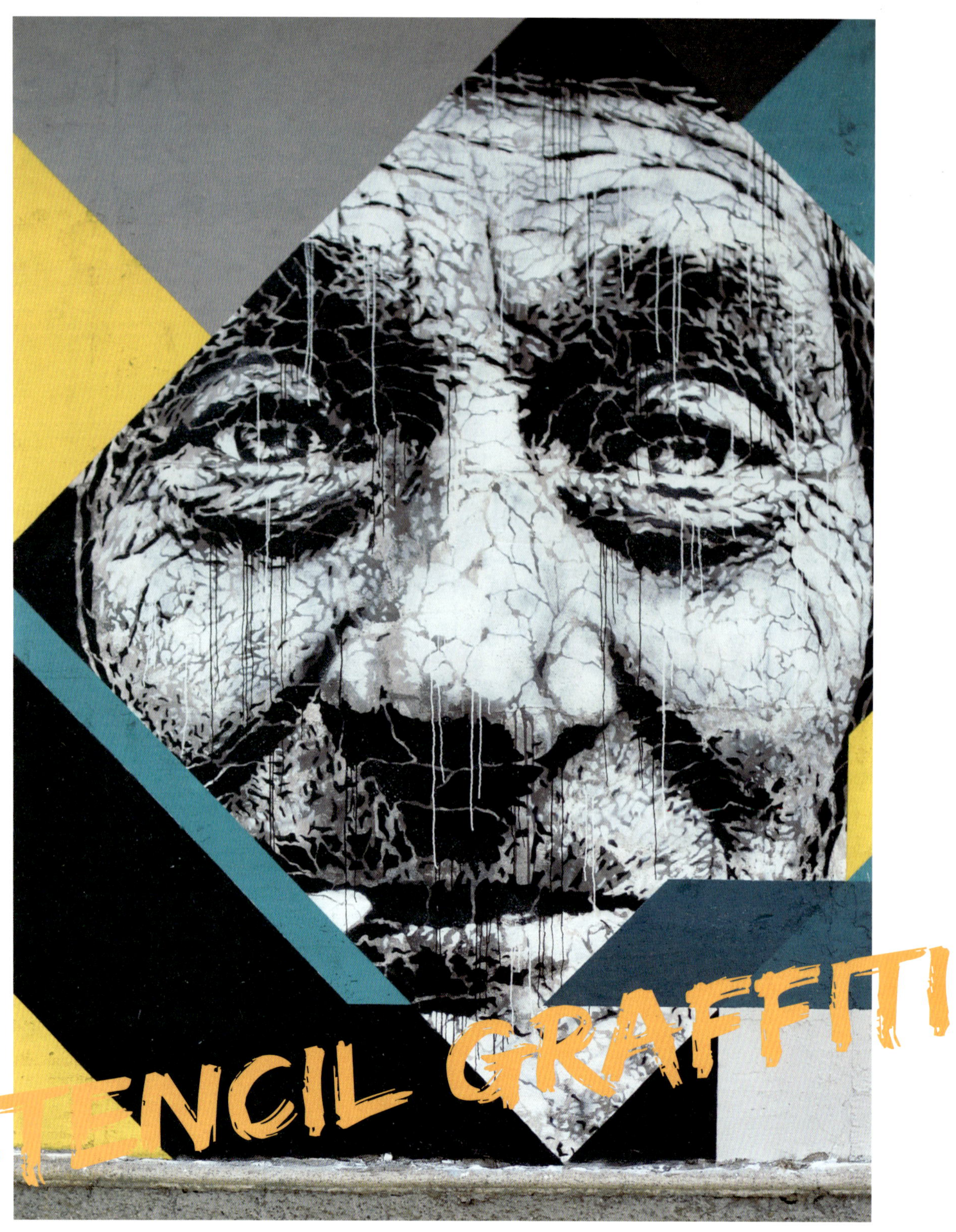

Artist/ SAMINA

STENCIL GRAFFITI

Ever since British graffiti artist Banksy created works that received extensive recognition from the public and achieved huge success in the world, stencil graffiti has been related to humorous sarcasm of social issues, and a wave of creating stencil graffiti has risen. In fact, stenciling has been around for at least hundreds of years. Its convenience and re-usability were rediscovered by some street artists during the 1960s who became the pioneers of stencil graffiti. Combined with spray paints, stencil graffiti conveys a sense of roughness that mirrors the chaotic, restless character of the street.

THE ART OF STENCIL

Stenciling is a simple, common technique. The earliest stencil application was found in Paleolithic caves of France and Spain, when hands were used as stencils. Although there is no evidence showing the specific origin of this technique, how it spread outwards, and how it was used in production and reproduction, it is no doubt that stenciling has been used in printing, cloth making, painting, decoration, and many more fields.

Water Pattern (late 19th century)

Photo/ Wikipedia Commons

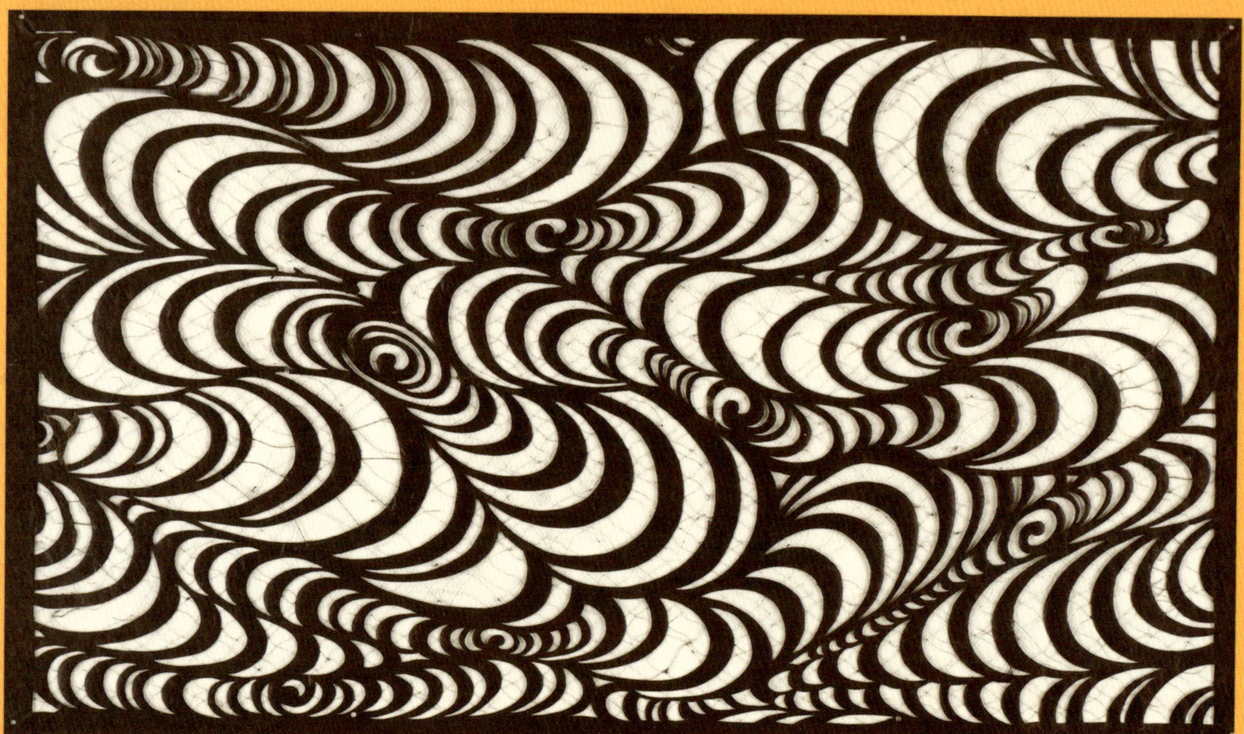

Katagami

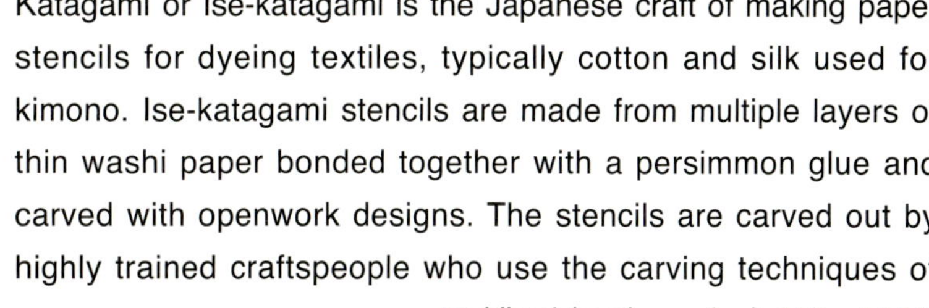

Katagami or Ise-katagami is the Japanese craft of making paper stencils for dyeing textiles, typically cotton and silk used for kimono. Ise-katagami stencils are made from multiple layers of thin washi paper bonded together with a persimmon glue and carved with openwork designs. The stencils are carved out by highly trained craftspeople who use the carving techniques of tsukibori (push carving), kiribori (drill carving), shimabori (stripe carving), and dogubori (tool punching). Each method involves a unique type of carving knife and pattern. Because the designs can be extremely intricate, Katagami art is rather fragile.

Bracken Fronds and Water (late 19th ceåntury)

Photo/ Wikipedia Commons

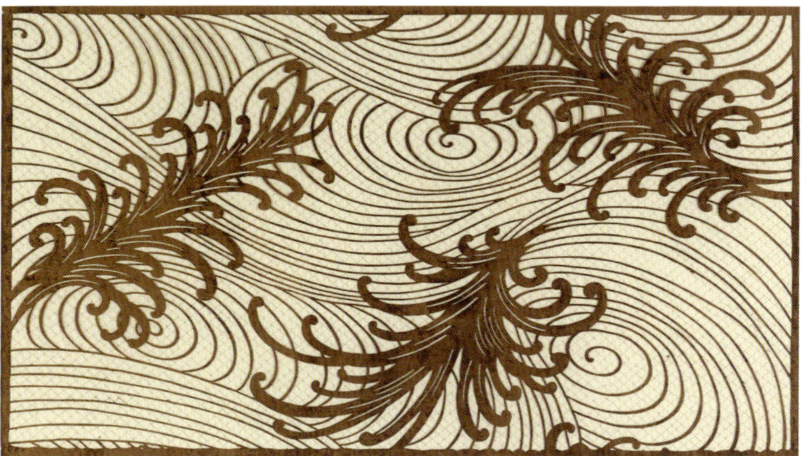

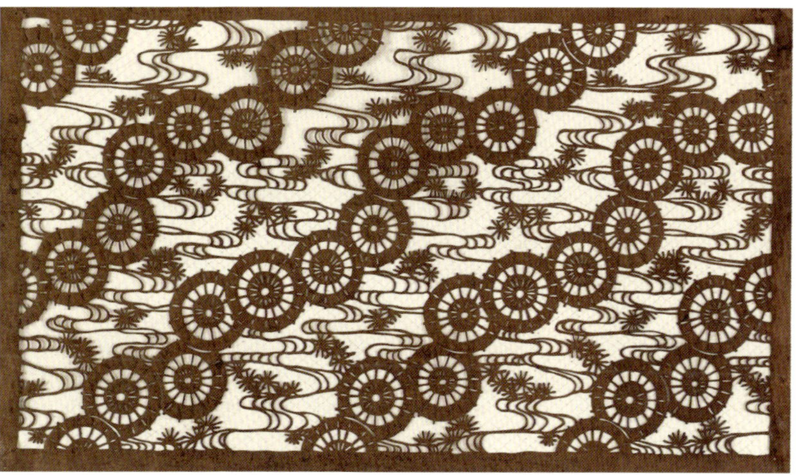

Umbrellas, Water and Pine Needle Clusters (late 19th century)

Photo/ Wikipedia Commons

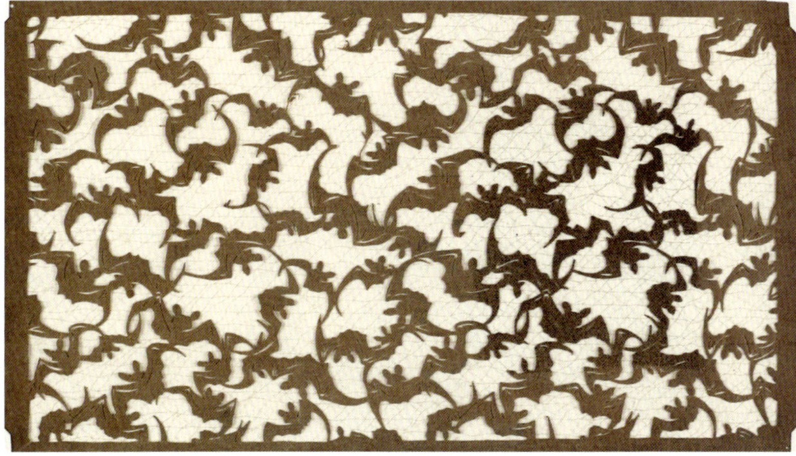

Flying Bats (1780–1830)

Photo/ Wikipedia Commons

Pochoir

The use of stencils to Europe began in the 1500s and reached its peak in the mass production of items such as playing cards, postcards, fabric, and wallpaper. In the middle of the 19th century, Japanese prints spurred the refined use of stencils, which then culminated in the development of pochoir. Pochoir, the French word for "stencil," is a stencil-based technique employed in printmaking to add colors to pre-existing prints. It was most popular from the late 19th century through the 1930s, with its center of activity in Paris. Pochoir was primarily used to create prints devoted to fashion, patterns, and architectural design and is most often associated with Art Nouveau and Art Deco. In its heyday during the early 20th century, there were as many as 30 graphic design studios in France, each employing up to 600 workers. Pochoir begins with the analysis of the composition, including color tones and densities, of a color image. Pochoir is both labor and time intensive, making it an expensive and slow process of printmaking. Stencils created by the découpeur with a straight-edged knife would be passed on to the coloristes, who then applied the pigments using a variety of brushes and methods of paint application to create the finished pochoir print.

Japanese stencil print around 1890.

Author/ Lengwiler
Photo/ Wikipedia Commons

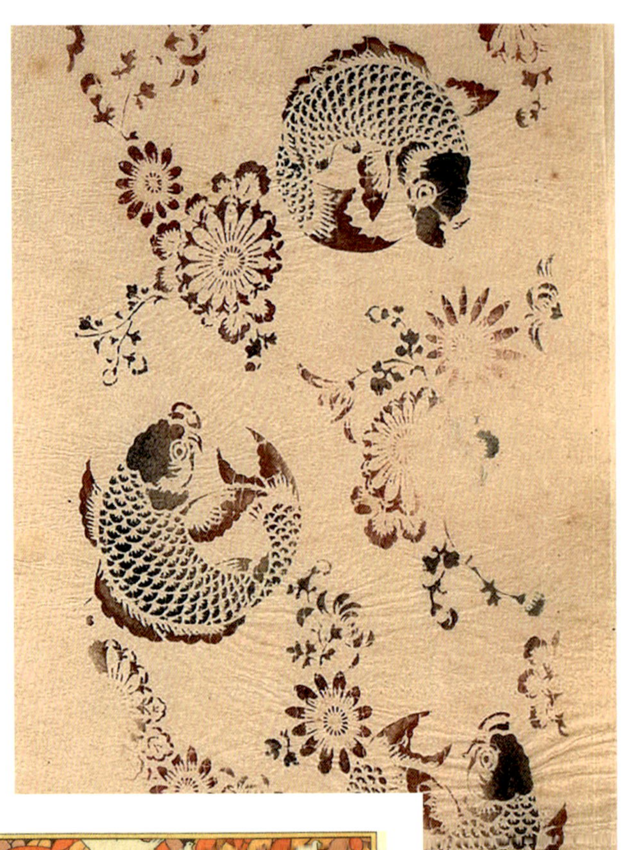

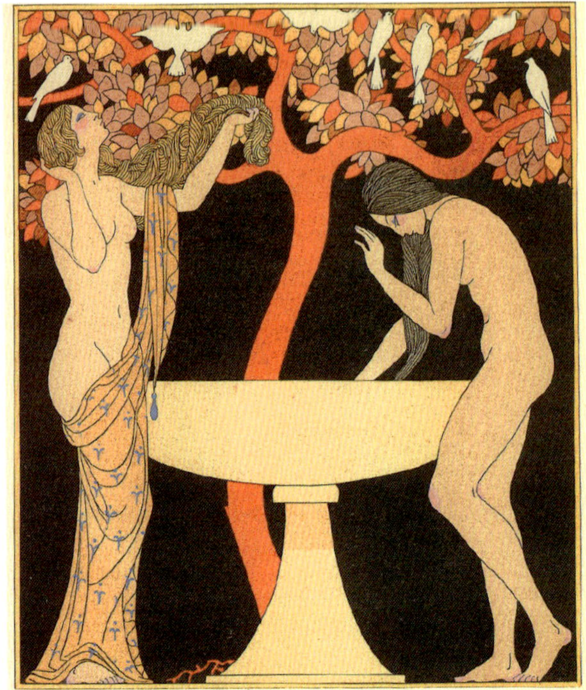

Untitled pochoir from the 1922 edition of Songs of Bilitis.

Artist/ George Barbier
Photo/ Wikipedia Commons

Decorative Stenciling

During the early 20th century, a multitude of stencil patterns were developed from Renaissance, Art Nouveau, Art Deco, and Arts and Crafts styles. They were used widely in public buildings, churches, and modest homes. However, as mass-produced wallpapers became accessible, stenciling fell out of public decorating consciousness until the late 1970s and early 1980s, when its effectiveness was rediscovered.

Photo/ Open Library, ID: OL6711848M

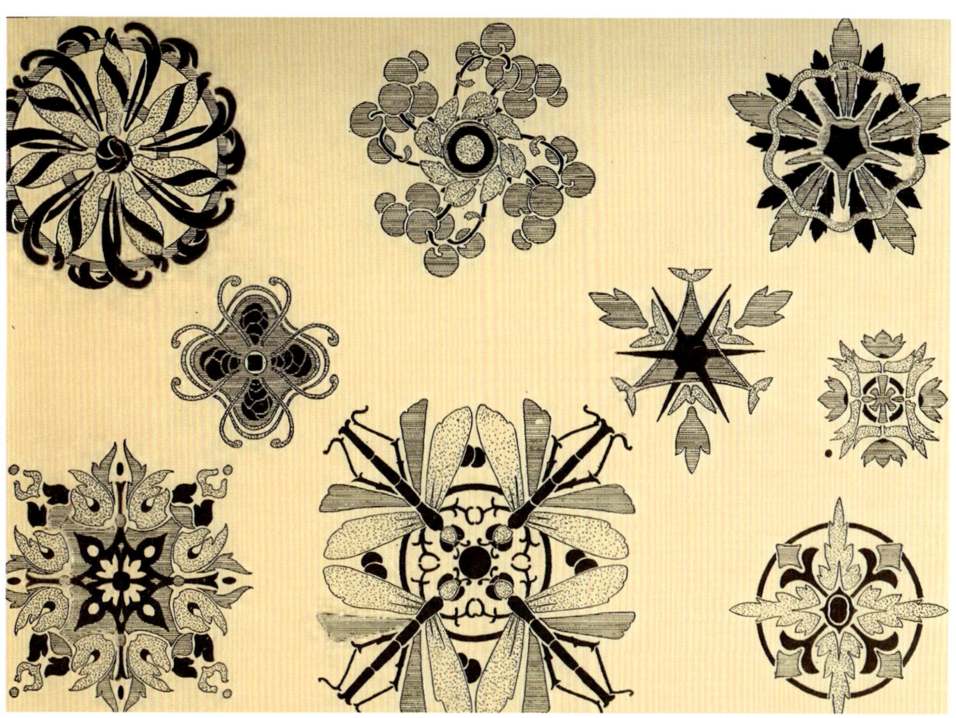

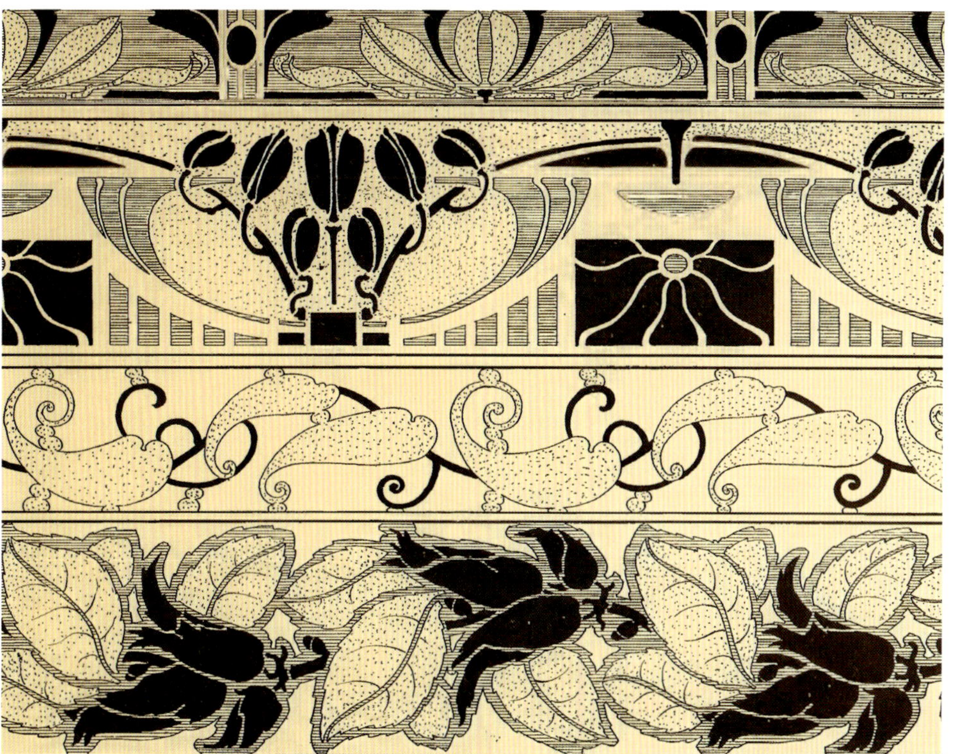

STENCIL GRAFFITI

Stenciling, as a printing method, a step of the kimono-making process, and an interior decorating tool, has demonstrated its convenience, flexibility, and availability for hundreds of years. However, the use of stencils in graffiti dates back only to the second half of the 20th century. During the Second World War, stencils were used to mark military equipment and direct the way to stations in war-torn towns. After the war, stencils were employed by common European people to express their standpoints in protests. Making these early stencils was risking being caught, but stencil graffiti was so quick to finish that a few seconds of brushing or spraying largely decreased the odds. Stenciling was recognized as a way of public expression, yet was still far from becoming an artistic expression.

Photo/ Wikimedia Commons

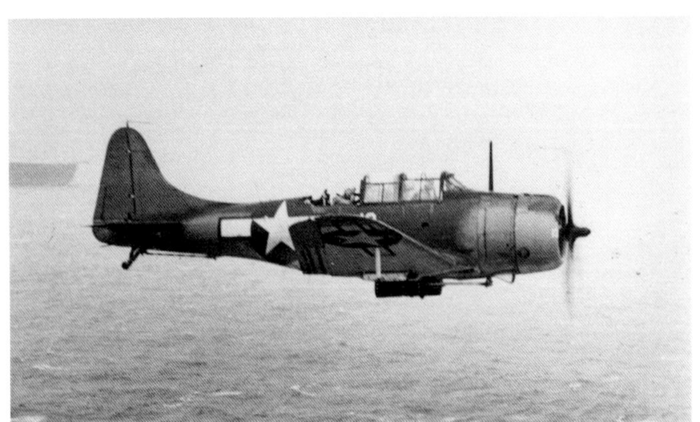

During the 1960s, stencils were imported to the US. It was a time when controversial issues provoked the concerns and distrust towards government and society, especially the middle and lower-class. Meanwhile, some punk rock bands emerged with music that communicated these concerns. To promote their songs, the bands stenciled the titles and slogans on the walls and streets where they performed. Before long, the first man of stencil graffiti in a real sense came out. In 1968, John Fekner began to present his works in public. He was the first among his fellow artists to apply stenciling in urban art. His works are straight, short, yet ironic. Within a few words, his opinions on certain matters were clearly conveyed in a teasing way. Sadly, except for the French artist Ernest Pignon-Ernest, this period did not see many noticeable figures in this field.

Artist/ John Fekner

Photo/ Wikipedia Commons

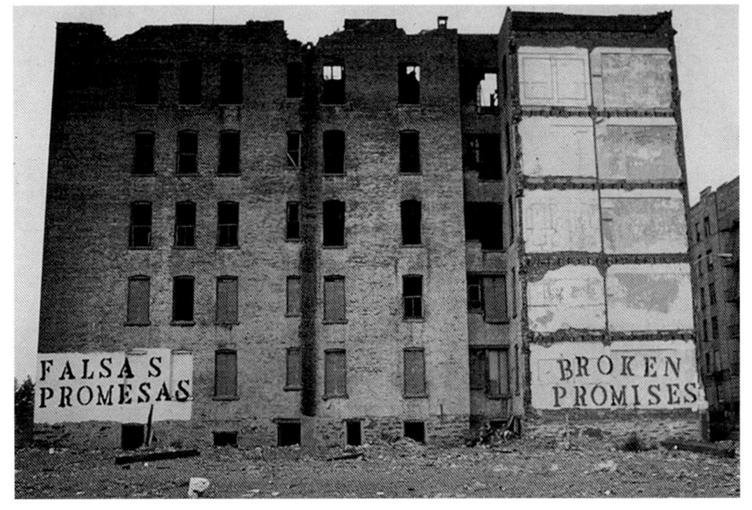

Things changed in the 1980s. French artist Blek le Rat began making stencil graffiti of rats all over Paris. Blek le Rat is the pseudonym of Xavier Prou. He paid a visit to New York when he was a student, and the scene of underground graffiti made an indelible imprint in his mind. After he was back to Paris, he dived into the field of graffiti and determined to make his name within it. He chose the image of rats for his stencils because the word "rat" is a anagram of "art," and the rat symbolizes a city invader who can go wherever it wants. Blek le Rat is often credited as the father of stencil graffiti, for he pushed this art form to a level no longer confined to pure words, such as those of John Fekner.

Artist/ Blek le Rat

Photo/ Lord Jim (Flickr)

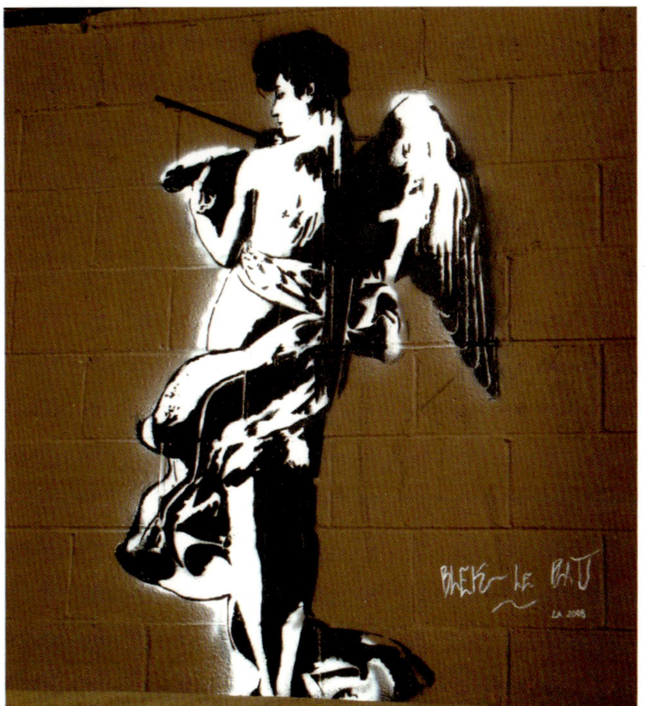

Artist/ Blek le Rat

Photo/ Kevin Collins (Flickr)

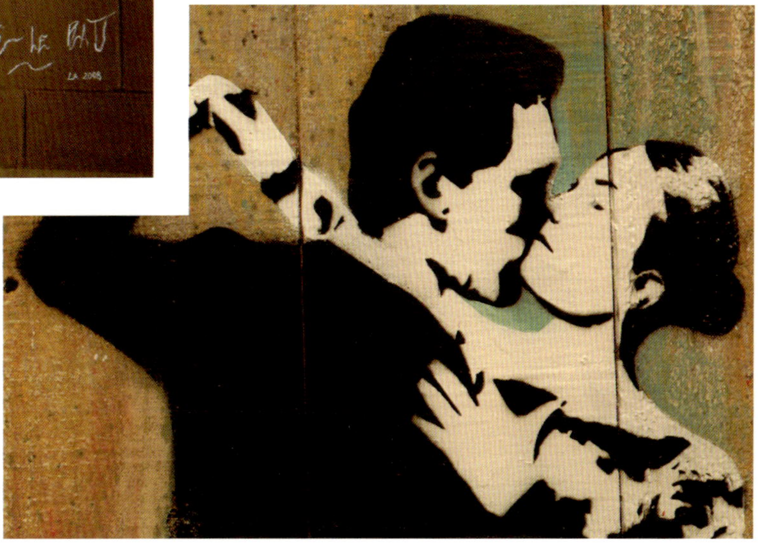

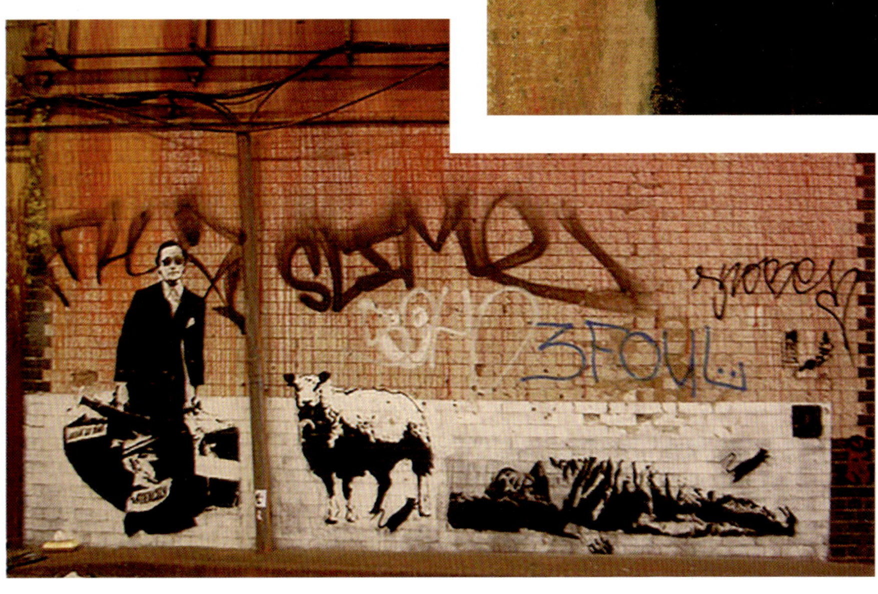

Artist/ Blek le Rat

Photo/ bixentro (Flickr)

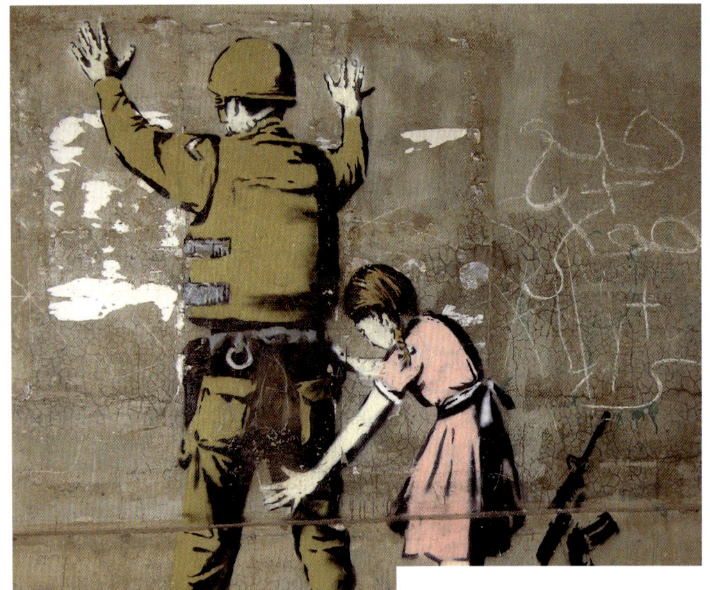

Artist/ Banksy
Photographer/ Pawel Ryszawa
Photo/ Wikipedia Commons

In 1990s, an artist who truly brought stencil graffiti to the public emerged. Banksy, a British graffiti artist and political activist, was active as a member of the DryBreadZ Crew around Bristol. Since the 21st century, Banksy has focused on creating stencil graffiti. Allegedly, he attributes this to his experience when running away from police officers and hiding beneath a dump truck. There he noticed a stenciled number and realized how quickly it could be done by using stencils. So he started to using this technique. Banksy's works are often centered on anti-war, anti-capitalism, and anti-establishment themes, with rats, apes, the elderly, children, policemen, and soldiers as subjects. In 2006, Christina Aguilera brought two works of Banksy's for an excessively high price. Although Banksy might not have intended so, his works gained huge commercial success and even gave rise to the Banksy effect. For the last twenty years, Banksy has been incessantly active: holding solo exhibitions, directing the film *Exit Through the Gift Shop*, and constantly creating stencil graffiti. He is no doubt the representative of the stencil graffiti scene as we understand it today.

Artist/ Banksy
Photo/ Tom Thai (Flickr)

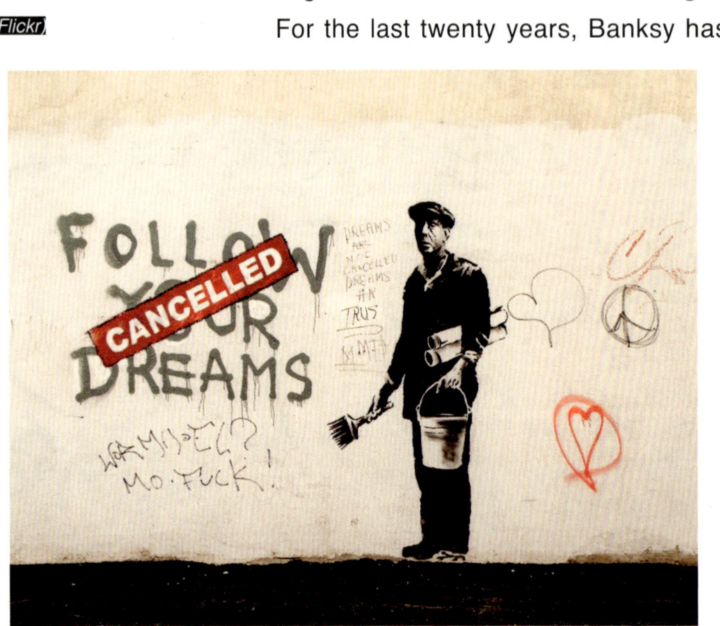

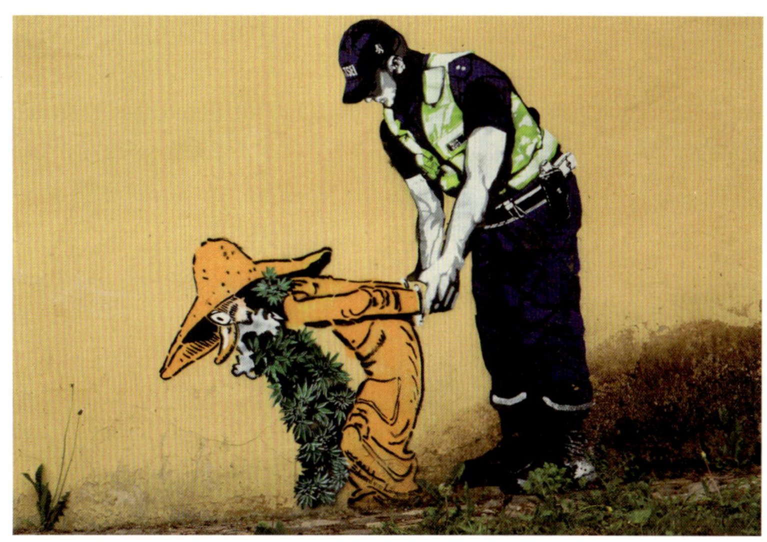

Artist/ Edward von Lõngus
Photographer/ Ivo Kruusamägi
Photo/ Wikipedia Commons

Banksy revealed the amazing possibilities of stencil graffiti to a large number of artists, including Dolk, Pøbel, Evol, SAMINA, Sten & Lex, Above, and Edward von Lõngus. They extensively added variety to this field. When stencils are pressed against a surface, no matter how closely and tightly, there will be gaps. And because spray paint is vaporous, when removing the stencil, the edge of the work appears fuzzy and smudged. This distinctive effect makes stencil graffiti rough enough to integrate with the casual, versatile, authentic, and public nature of street art. No matter how diverse stencil graffiti becomes, the messages and humor of stencil graffiti are always its most alluring charm.

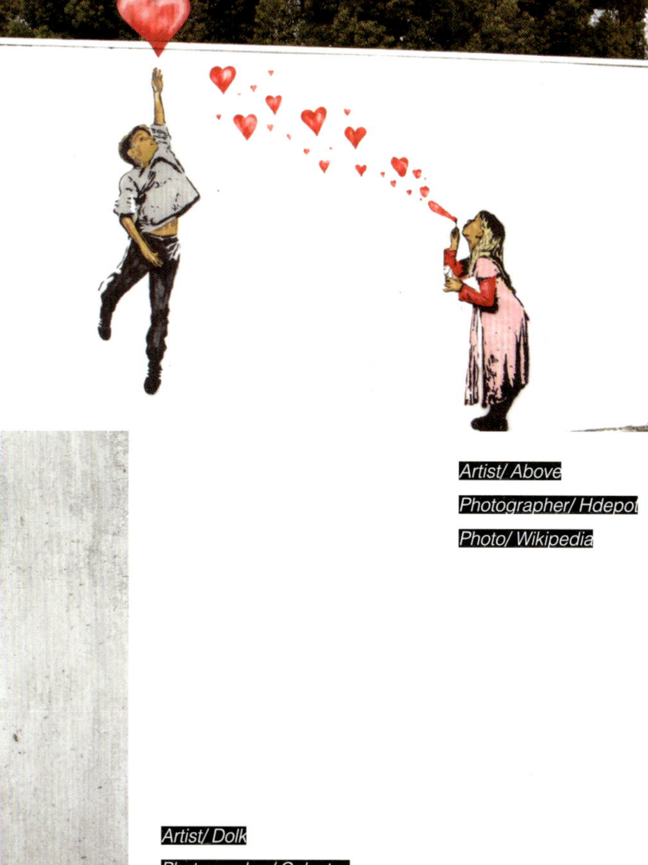

Artist/ Above
Photographer/ Hdepot
Photo/ Wikipedia

Artist/ Dolk
Photographer/ Gulosten
Photo/ Wikipedia Commons

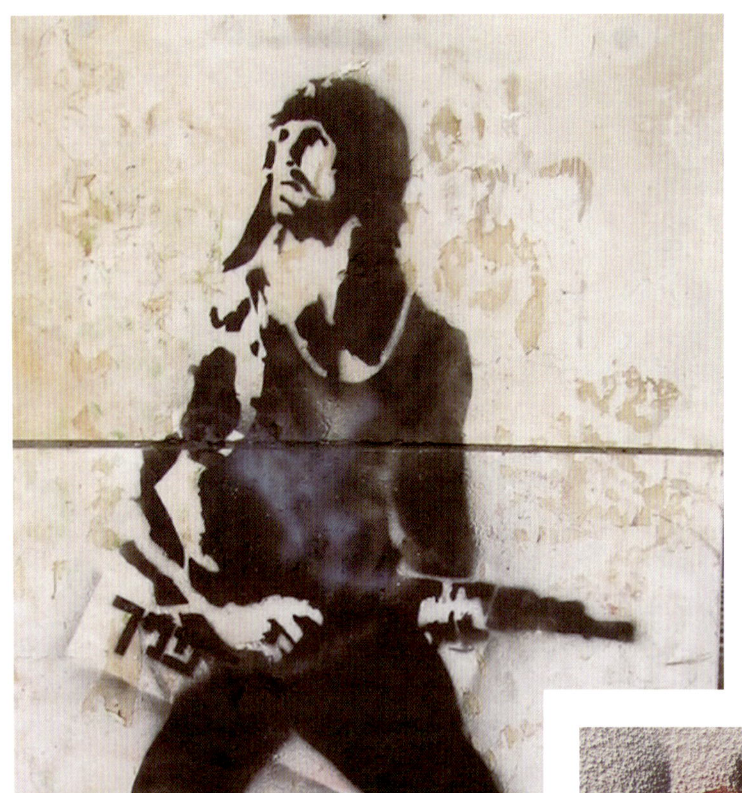

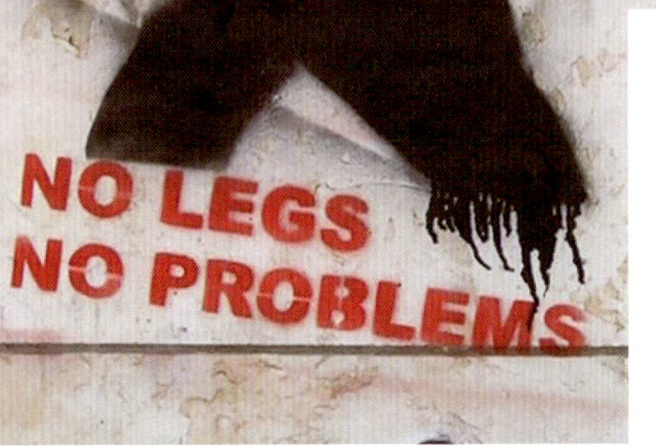

Photo/ Pablo Matamoros (Flickr)

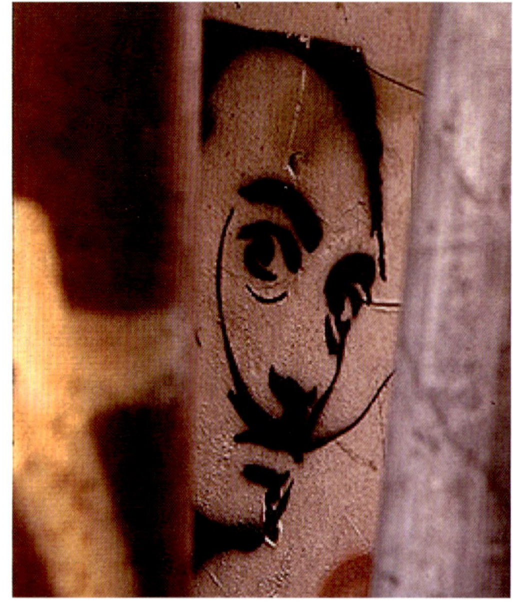

Photo/ Pablo Matamoros (Flickr)

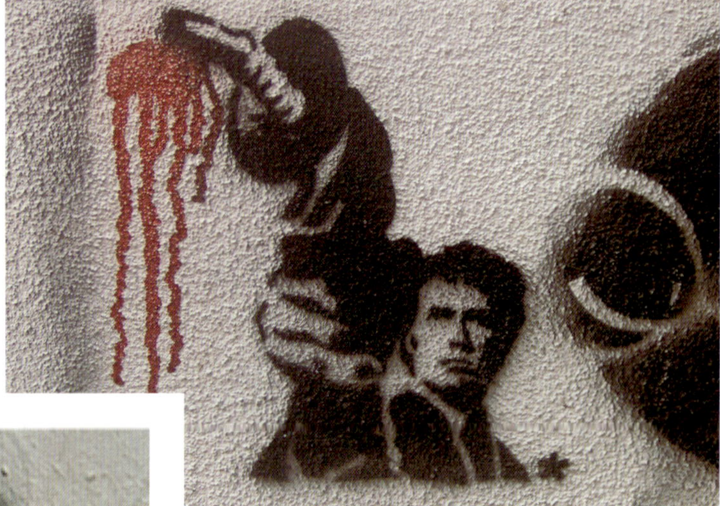

Photographer/ Twayna Mayne

Photo/ Wikimedia Commons

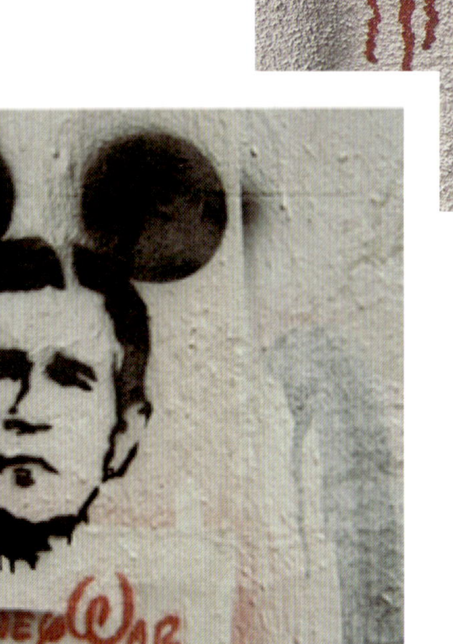

Photographer/ Gonzaurio

Photo/ Wikimedia Commons

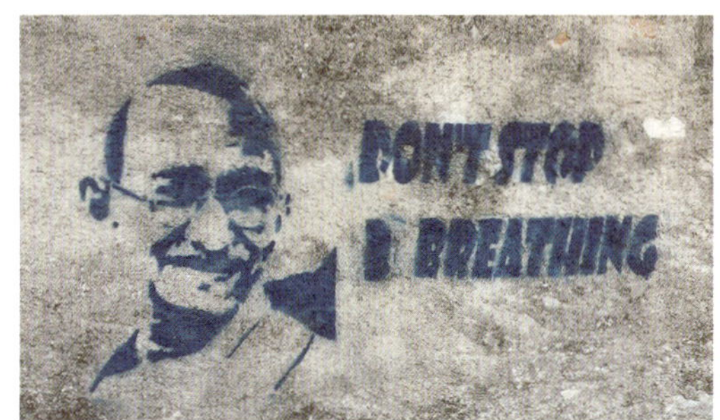

Photo/ Pixabay

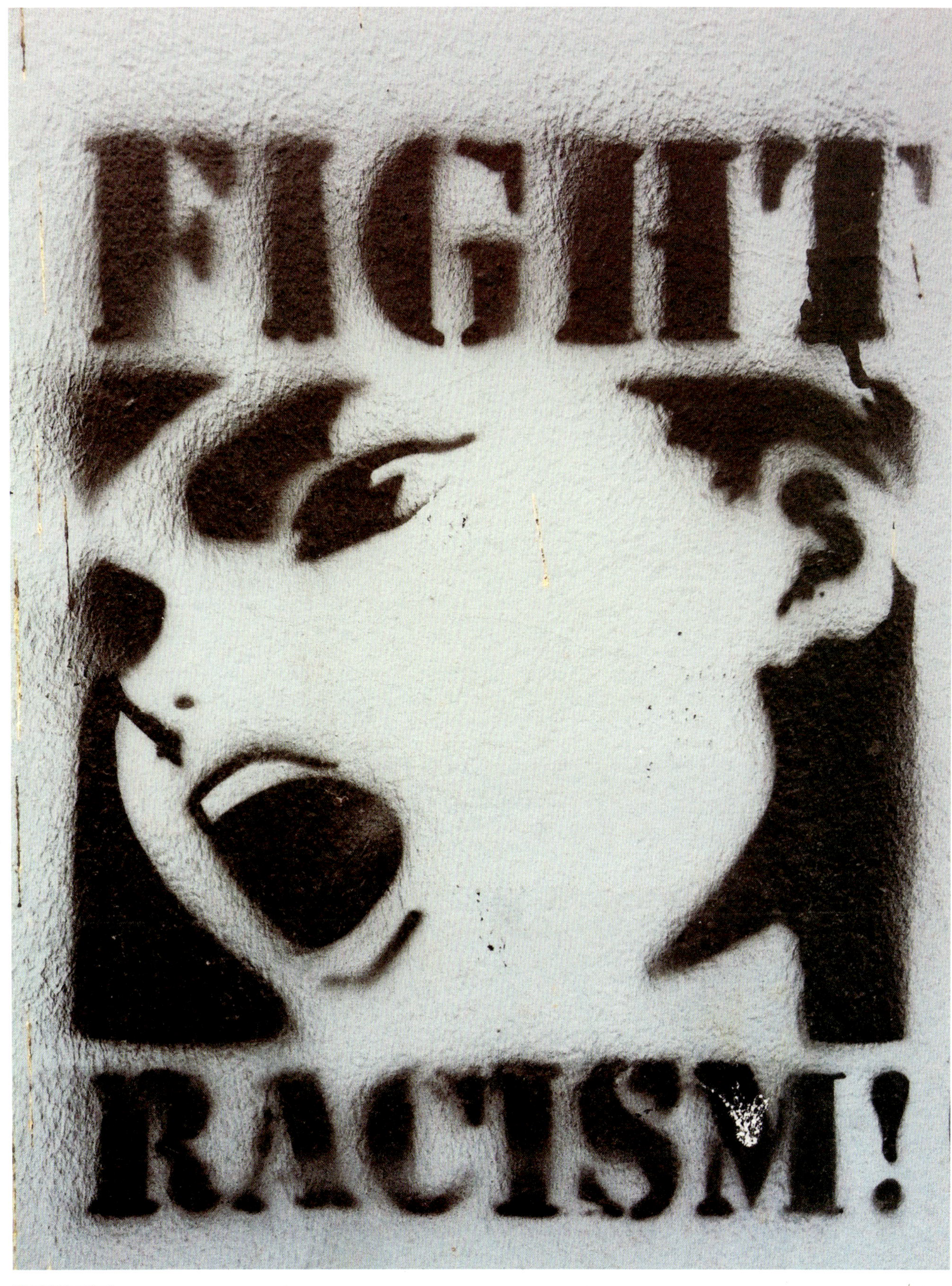

Photo/ Max Pixel

IF EXHIBITED IN GALLERIES, IS IT STILL GRAFFITI?

No TV

Artist/ John Fekner

Photo/ Wikipedia Commons

@New York, USA 1980

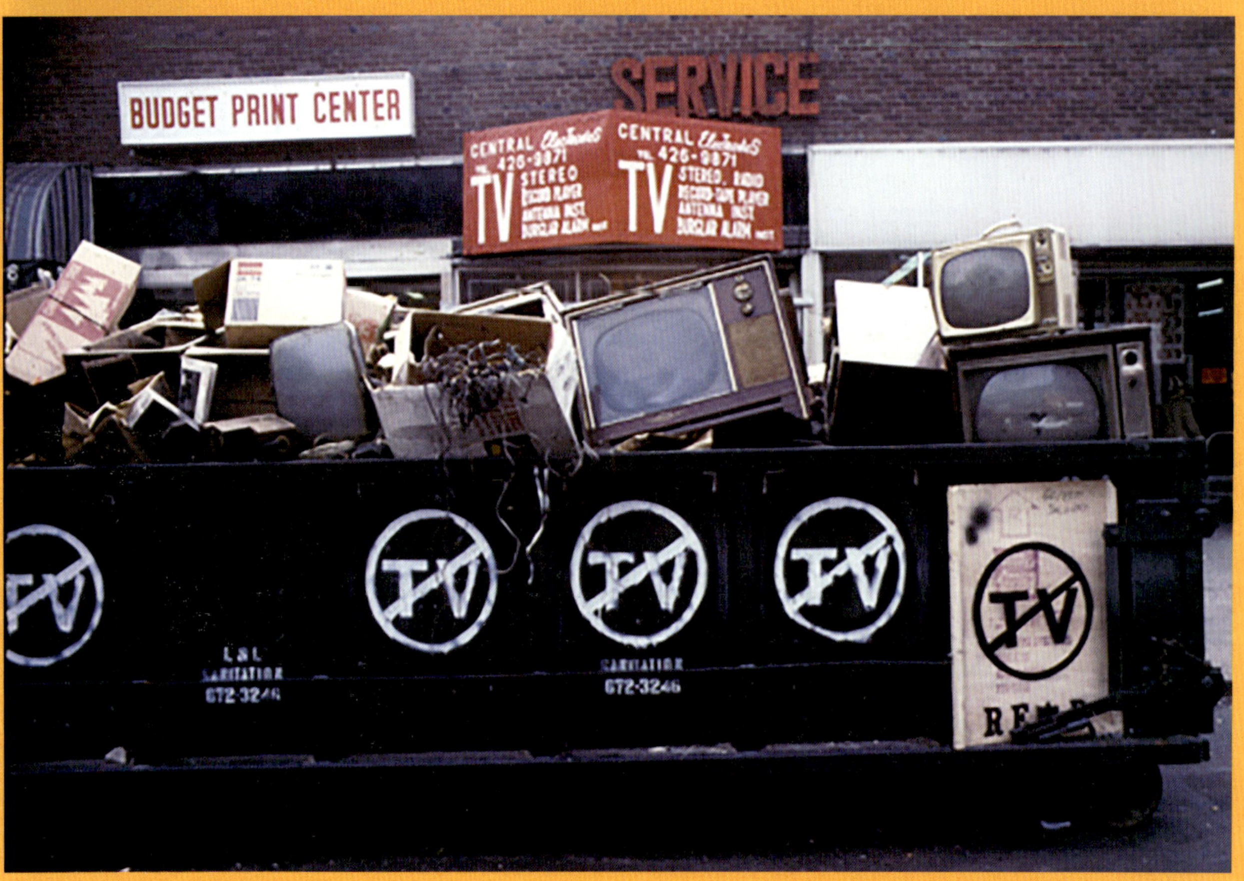

Graffiti was born on the streets, whose raw energy inspired its aesthetic. It is well acknowledged that as a unique art form, graffiti has distinctive characteristics and historical background. As early as in the 1970s, graffiti work, mainly tagging, was exhibited in art galleries. Entering the 21st century, because of globalization and Internet development, graffiti art has garnered more and more attention. That the works of England-based artist Banksy were sold for surprising high prices highlighted the commercial value of the art form. Many graffiti artists have been employed or collaborated with enterprises and galleries to create works for them. Some critics have argued this is a way of selling out, contradicting the spirit of graffiti. However, back to graffiti the art itself: What features define graffiti?

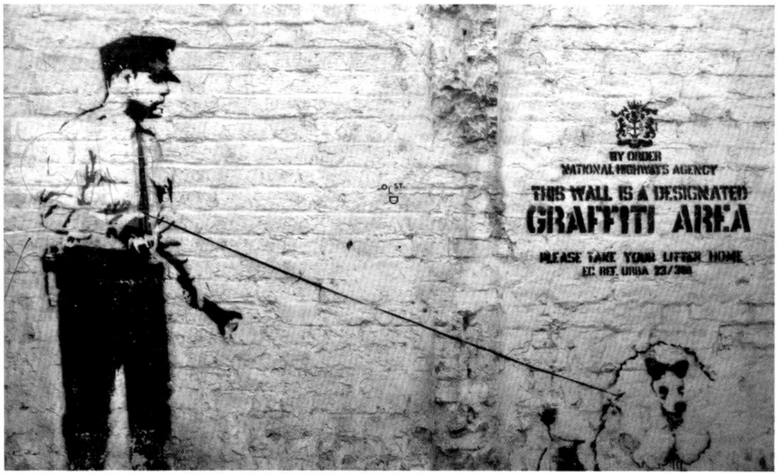

The first and most obvious feature of graffiti is its artistic style, such as that used in early tags. Second, graffiti is public. Anyone, regardless of gender, color, nationality, or age, can view graffiti as long as that person can walk down a street. The third attribute of graffiti is its interactivity, ranging from wildstyle tagging to large-scale outdoor painting. Art is not necessarily understandable or reasonable. As long as the work arouses some sort of emotional experience from viewers—leading them to observe, imagine, and think—that is an interaction. Remember that early tags were intentionally illegible so they could be deciphered only between insiders. Last but not least, graffiti is doomed to be ephemeral. During the era of subway graffiti, graffiti was made without permission, and thus illegally. The tags on trains were buffed off in days, if not immediately. Besides, graffiti writers and crews were competing with one another, and putting works on top of others was common. Nowadays, even though artists are employed to paint, their works are likely to be torn out with the rapidly changing urban landscapes, as buildings are torn down and new ones rise up.

Photo/ Berit Watkin (Flickr)

The public and interactive attributes of graffiti determine that the form should be made only for the street and stays on the streets. However, the strong style of graffiti enables it to combine with commercial brands and help advertise the brands' identities. To support themselves and their families, it is understandable that artists profit from this collaboration. But as long as the graffiti work is created for the streets, no matter where it will end up, it is graffiti to the core.

INTERVIEW WITH WRDSMTH

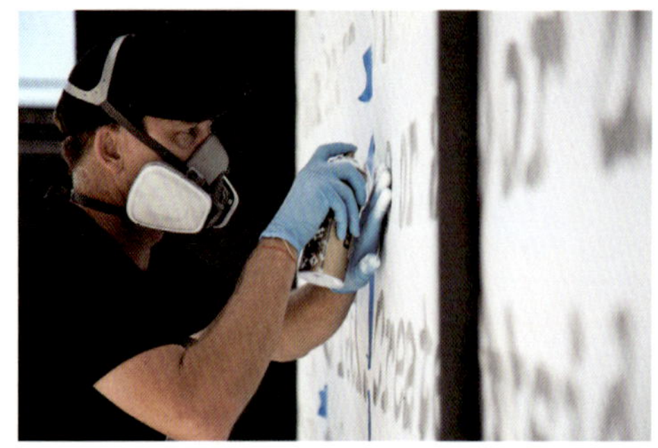

Artist/ WRDSMTH

Q1: Could you tell us a little about how you went from being a copywriter, a writer, and now to being a street artist? What prompted you to go through these transitions?

I am a writer, first and foremost. I just love to write and I do it in many different mediums. I've written scripts, short films, worked in documentary TV, and I am a published author. In 2013, I had a very good year creatively, but that means I was sitting in front of the computer for long stretches every day. So much so, I realized I needed an active hobby—something that got me out/about, but something that was also creatively fulfilling. The answer was street art.

Q2: How did you come up with the idea of making a stencil image of a vintage typewriter with a wheatpaste page and words on it? What was your initial intention?

When I was toying with the notion of trying my hand at street art, I knew it would need to be word-based in order to satisfy the writer in me. When I thought "word-based," I immediately saw an image of a typewriter with the words coming out of it. And when I realized the typewriter could/would be painted and the page wheatpasted, I really got excited about what I felt was a simple, yet indelible idea.

Q3: The way you create line breaks within a sentence is so poetic. For street art works, it creates both a visual effect and an emotional effect. Did you apply some knowledge of poetry, or it just naturally happen to be?

It was natural. With my WRDs, I emulate how I talk and how I place emphasis on words and thoughts when I speak. I liken it to an actor who delivers lines, but does it in the most compelling manner possible.

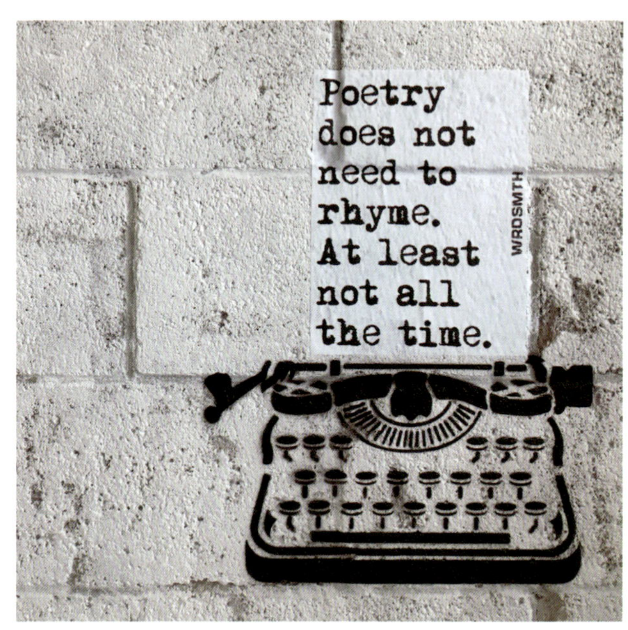

Q4: I think one of the reasons why so many people can resonate with your works, especially the text, is your style of writing. It is mostly short, warm, and conversational. Is this your writing style, as a published author, or just for the street art works?

It is my style. I am a firm believer in less is more and I always strive to craft sentences and thoughts utilizing words that affect. WRDSMTH is such a merger of worlds for me and the freedom to present my work to the world exactly as I want it to be is awesome and the fact that my work is resonating with so many is intoxicating.

Q5: Apart from the love notes and motivational words, you show great love for the city of Los Angeles. What about the City of Angels attracts you?

I moved to Los Angeles from Chicago solely for career reasons and I thought I'd hate it. However, the city completely surprised me. There's so much awesomeness that makes LA a unique creative hub. Part of that is the film industry, but there's also countless musicians and singers and dancers and artists that bring an energy to every area and every day. LA is definitely home for me now.

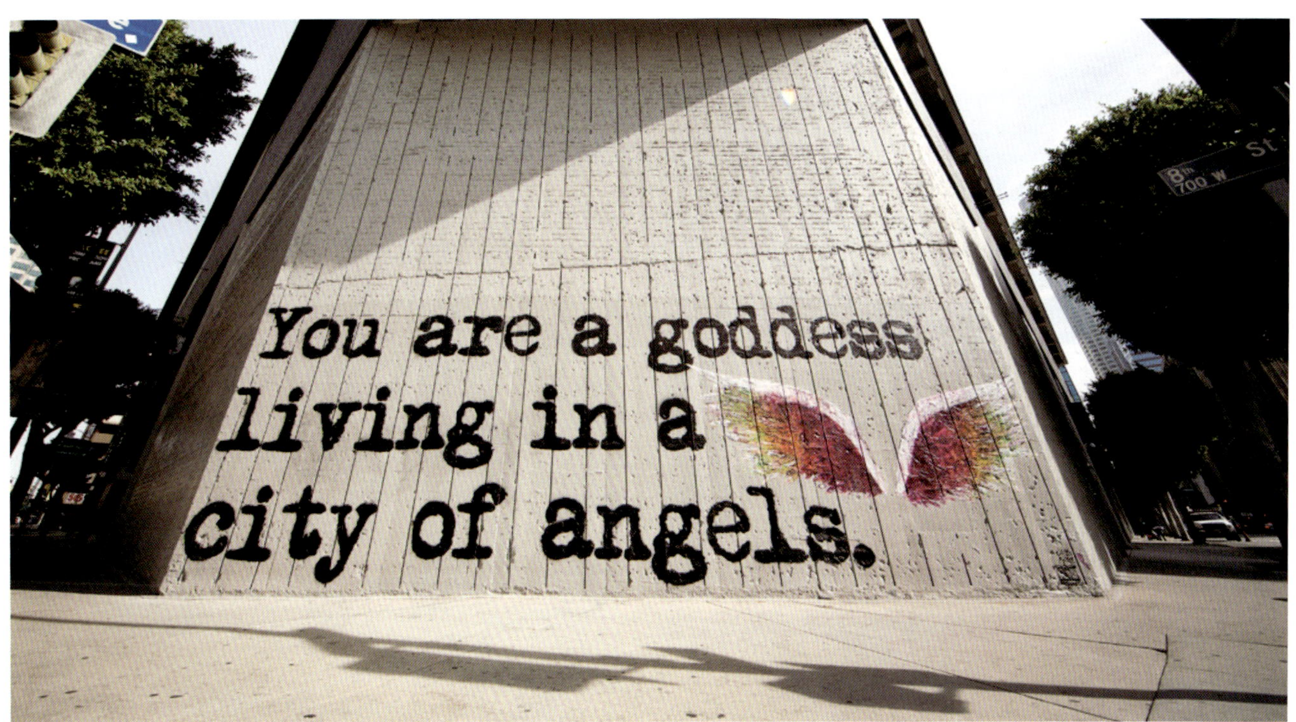

Q6: You once said you never considered yourself as an artist of the paint and brush variety. But here you are, doing things like an artist with all these spray paint cans, working desk, and spotted clothes. Did you learn everything about art all by yourself? Were there any difficulties in the process?

The caveat missing from that quote is, "at first." Now, four years later, I am an artist and now realize I always was. I surprised myself with what was inside me waiting to be released. I learned a lot along the way by myself and I learned a lot from others. The art community is so supportive and encouraging. Any questions I had were often answered by artists who inspired me long before I started WRDSMTHing. And there are always difficulties encountered with any endeavor, however the desire to "aspire to inspire others" fuels my creative fire and keeps me going even on the toughest days.

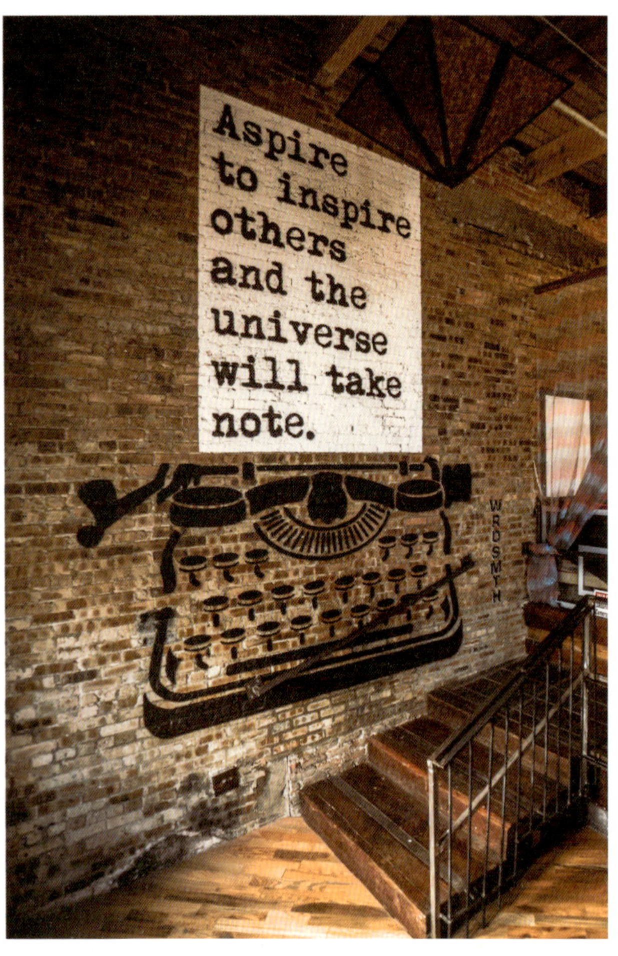

Q7: Why are you keeping your true identity from the public while revealing yourself to your fans?

I'm not obsessed with my anonymity, but the mystery definitely works in my favor. People love wondering, "Who's putting up these pieces in the middle of night all over the world?" and I like that. Having said that, if someone comes to a gallery show or an event, I have no problem shaking their hand and introducing myself. They sought me out, and I like to reward anyone present for their support.

Q8: I read another interview about you that says you rise early in the morning when the street is still quiet and dark and hit the street to paint and paste, and you feel like a crime fighter. Why is putting up street art an action of "fighting crime"? What kind of crimes?

It's just a fun metaphor I came up with. I grew up on comic books and liken street artists to superheroes because cities are often filled with many different artists working under different names and styles in the quiet of the night.

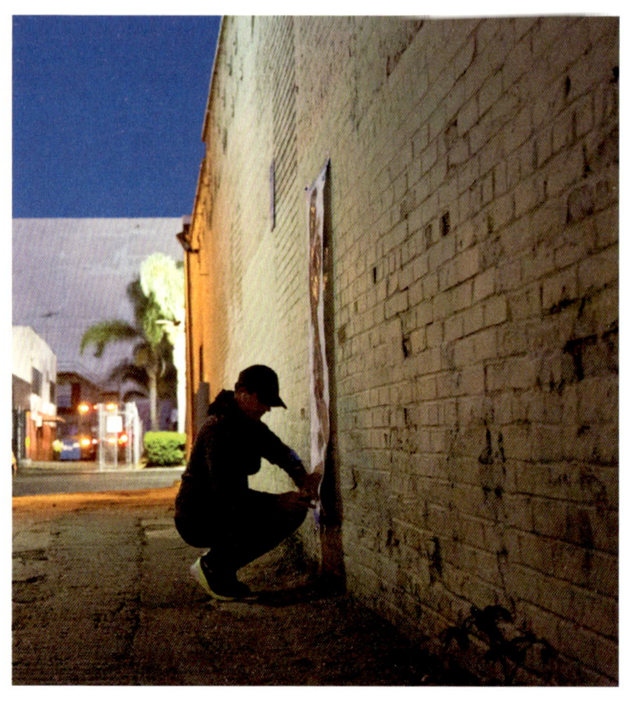

Q9: The words you wrote are inspirational from the first read, and I believe you must have received much positive feedback from the public. But just like the quotes from Chicken Soup for the Soul, do you think people are already fed up with these words which, however lovely they are, might be lame and can only motivate people for a while and that's it?

To an extent, maybe. I think it depends on the person. Musicians produce beautiful songs that people get sick of, but then look at The Beatles—who ever tires of their work? I don't. There are street artists who have made a career out of the replication of a single image or idea. While the image of the typewriter stays the same, my words constantly change. Even my "greatest hits" are treated differently over time in size, design, and added imagery. I can't please everyone all the time, but I also don't think I'm a one-trick pony.

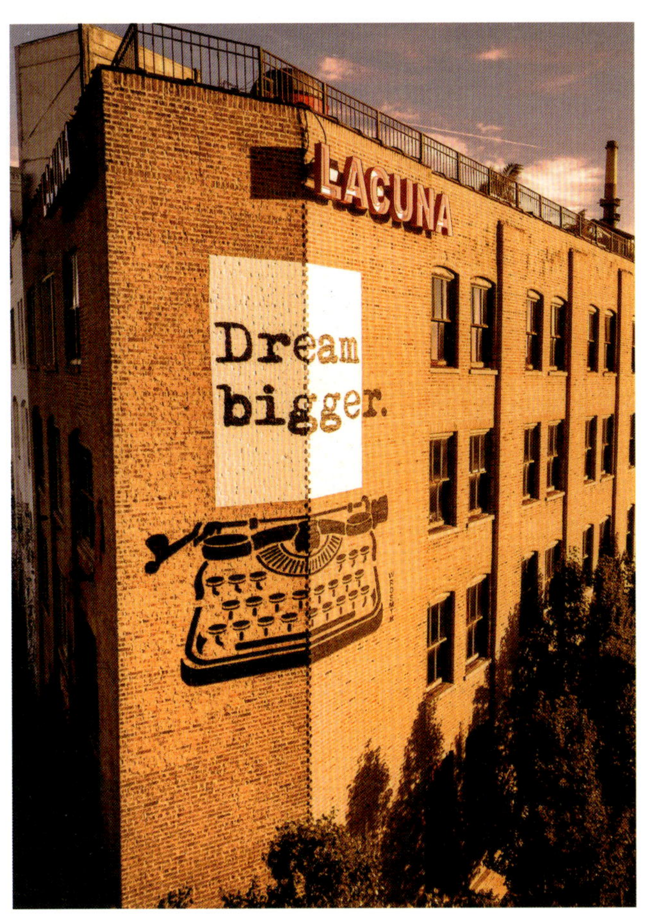

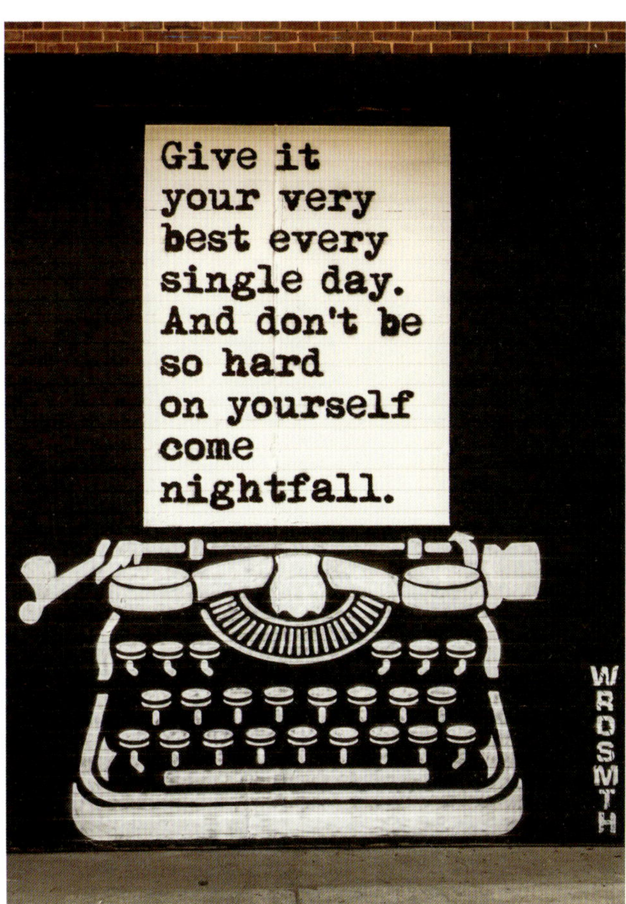

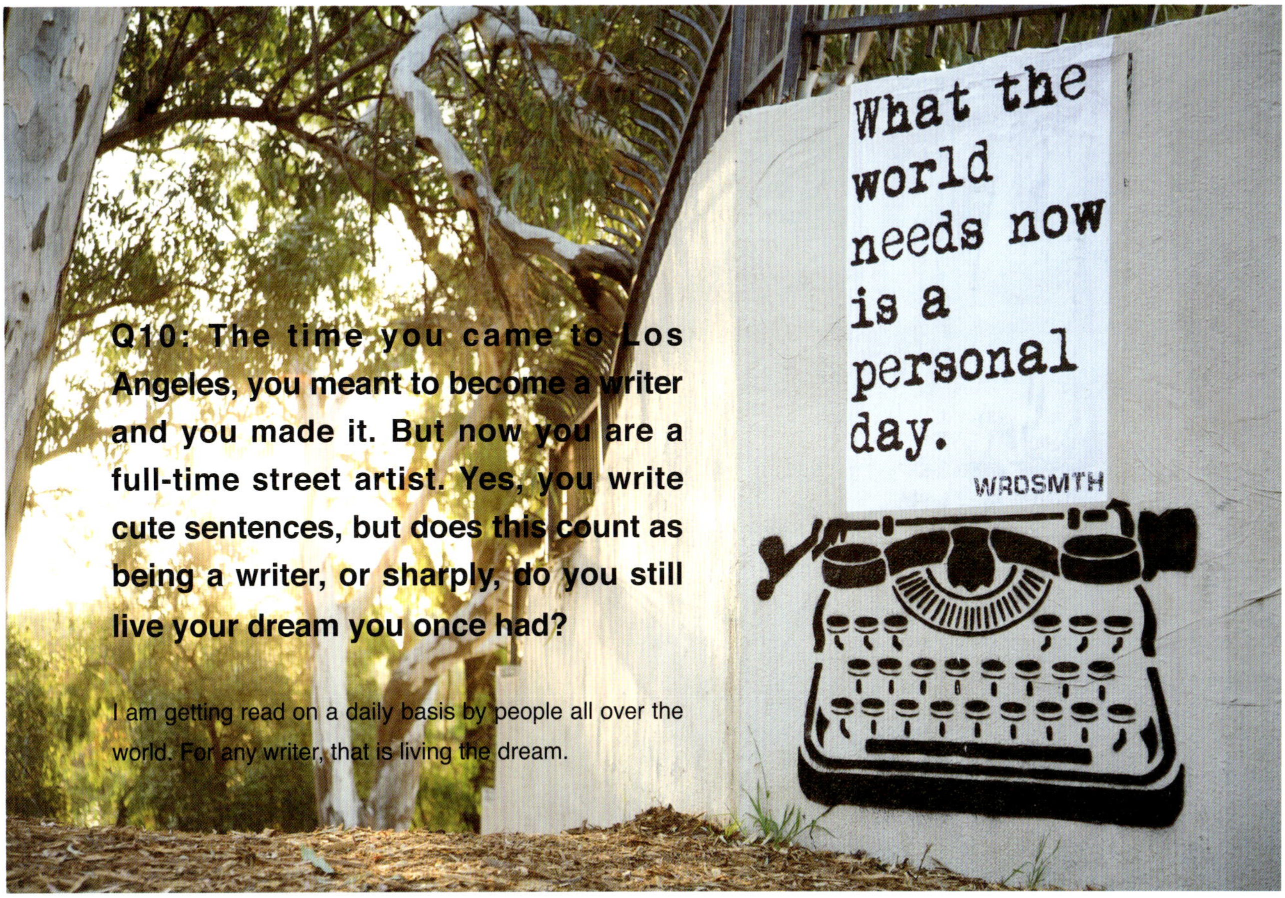

Q10: The time you came to Los Angeles, you meant to become a writer and you made it. But now you are a full-time street artist. Yes, you write cute sentences, but does this count as being a writer, or sharply, do you still live your dream you once had?

I am getting read on a daily basis by people all over the world. For any writer, that is living the dream.

INTERVIEW WITH SAMINA

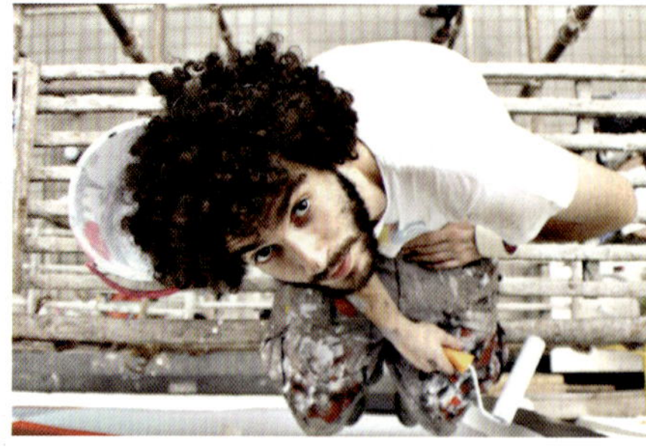

Artist/ SAMINA @Lisbon, Portugal

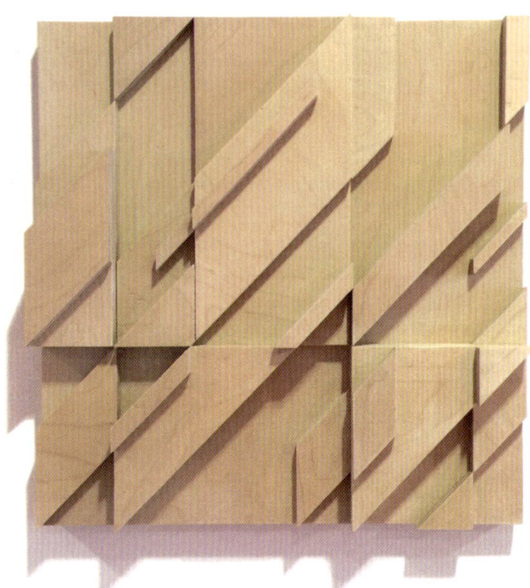

Q1: Street art comprises of various forms, but among them, you chose to dig into the art of stencil. How did it all start?

As a kid I always loved graffiti and all kinds of street art interventions. When I was 13 or 14, I was super into sticker art. Names like D*Face, Shepard Fairey, Flying Förtress, Orticanoodles, Zibe, etc. were my references. My goal was to spread as many stickers as possible. I wasn't particularly good at lettering, neither at drawing characters, so when I found that I could make the same images with stencils in a short time as convenient and fast as spreading stickers. I then fell in love with the technique and started to take my skills to the next level, so I could have bigger and better results with it.

Q2: You used to spread stickers around the streets as a teenager. What was the city scene like?

I'm from a small village, and at that time I was studying in Setúbal, a city 15 km away that always had a strong graffiti scene. Back then, probably influenced by what was happening around the world, the local writers also started to do a lot of paste-ups on the streets and I was definitely influenced by all that.

Q3: Your works appear to be a combination of stenciling and geometric shapes. Those geometric elements are arranged in a way that produces a graphically spatial effect which resembles that of architecture. What kind of visual image or impression you try to achieve?

I studied architecture and that definitely gave me a lot that I still bring to my work today. The local context is really important for me. Not so much as a theme but more in a spatial way. I have to know exactly where I'm working and what the architectural context of the wall is. Maybe because of all that I'll try to integrate my paintings in a way that it can merge with the environment.

Q4: Stencil art on the street is often referred to stencil graffiti which is less complicated and has a smaller scale. What intrigued you to make large pieces of stencil art? What are the skills required for large pieces?

It's true that stenciling is a technique based on an image with a simple aesthetic that you can reproduce and repeat easily lots of times. But that is the technical point of view I think. I always looked to the stencil as a technique that is more than that. Once you master the basics of the technique, you will feel that it's not that complicated to adapt small scales to bigger ones. The thing is that you need to determine what kind of scale you will work on. Once you make the choice, you can adapt your drawing to it. For example, if you are going to paint a 5-meter high stencil, it may be more powerful if you add more detail to it. In my way of doing it, I just have to find a better balance between the details and the real size of the stencil.

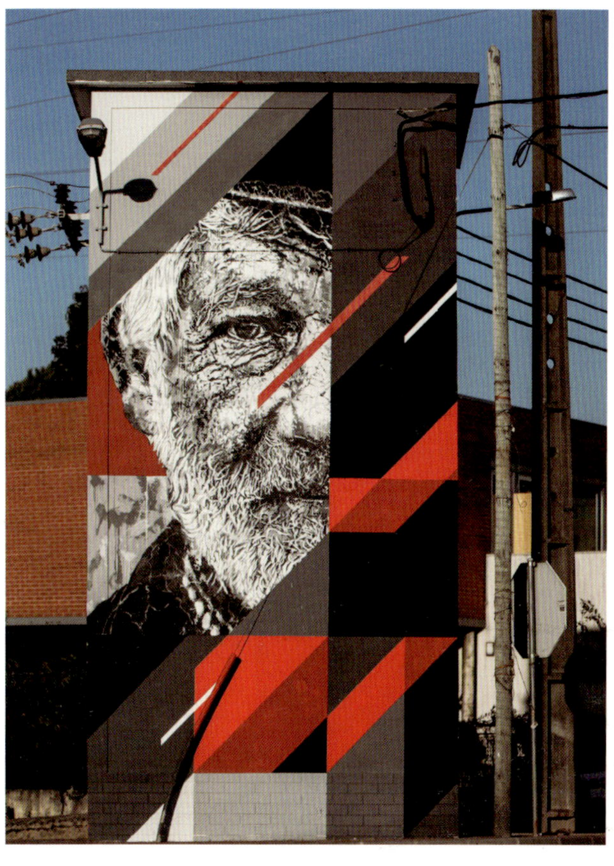

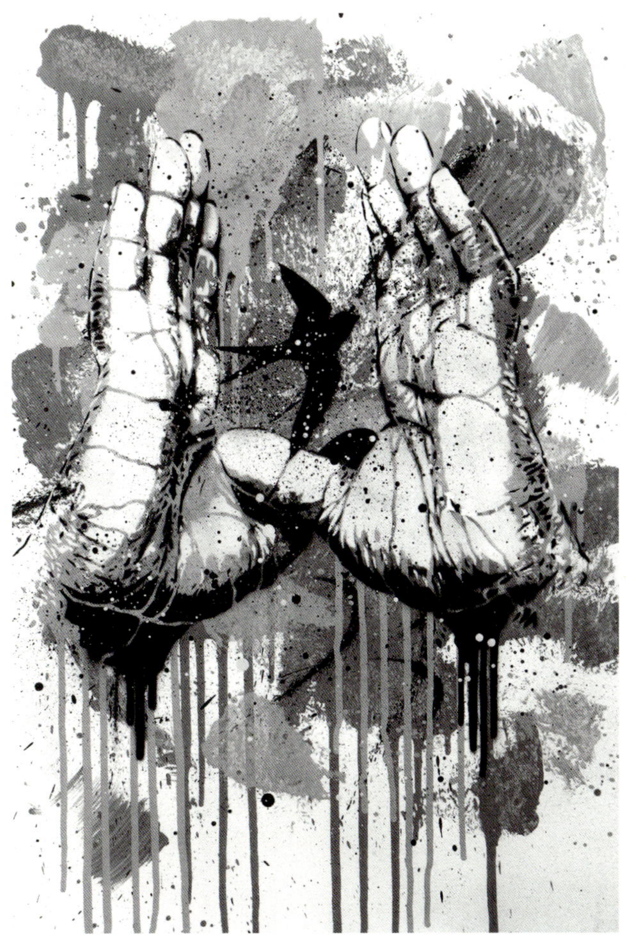

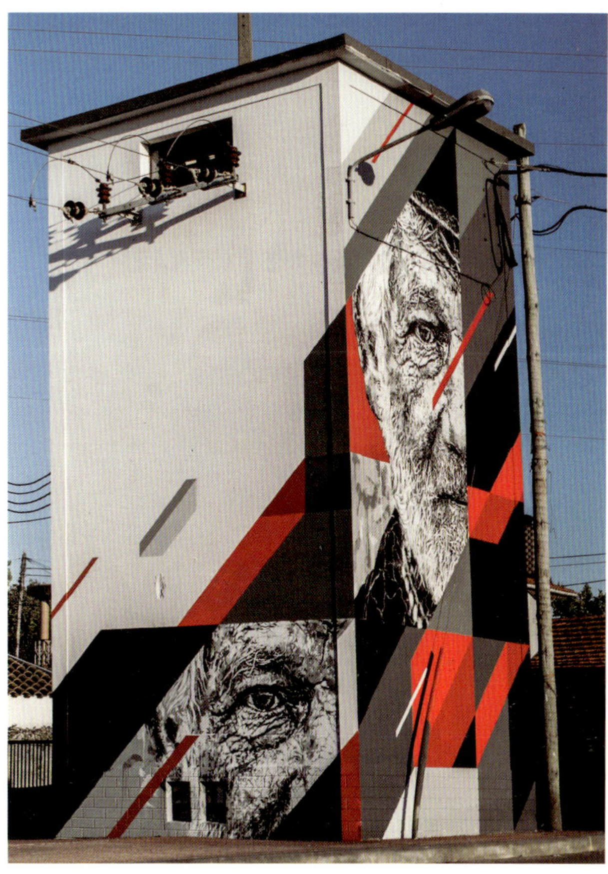

@Estarreja, Portugal 2016
©Mistaker Maker / Miguel Oliveira

Q5: At a close-up look, the white paints of your woks drip down, which is not the effect you design on paper. Did you come up with this idea and did it deliberately when working on the walls, or just too much paint?

It's totally on purpose. Stencil can be too bi-dimensional and look too flat sometimes. I was always attracted to dripping paint textures, so adding dripping and splatter to a stencil can give more expression to the painting. That's also what makes a stencil differ from one another. Even if I'm repeating the same I get different feelings.

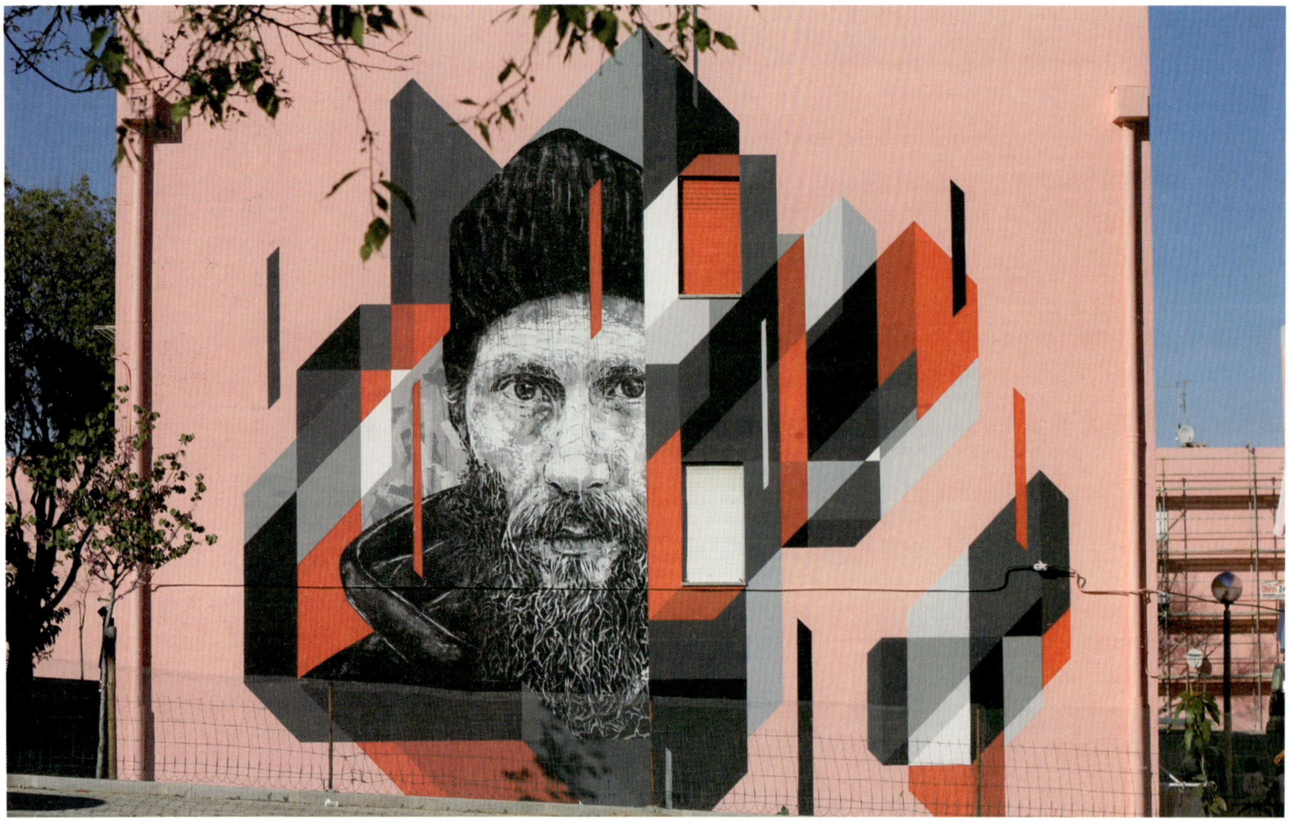

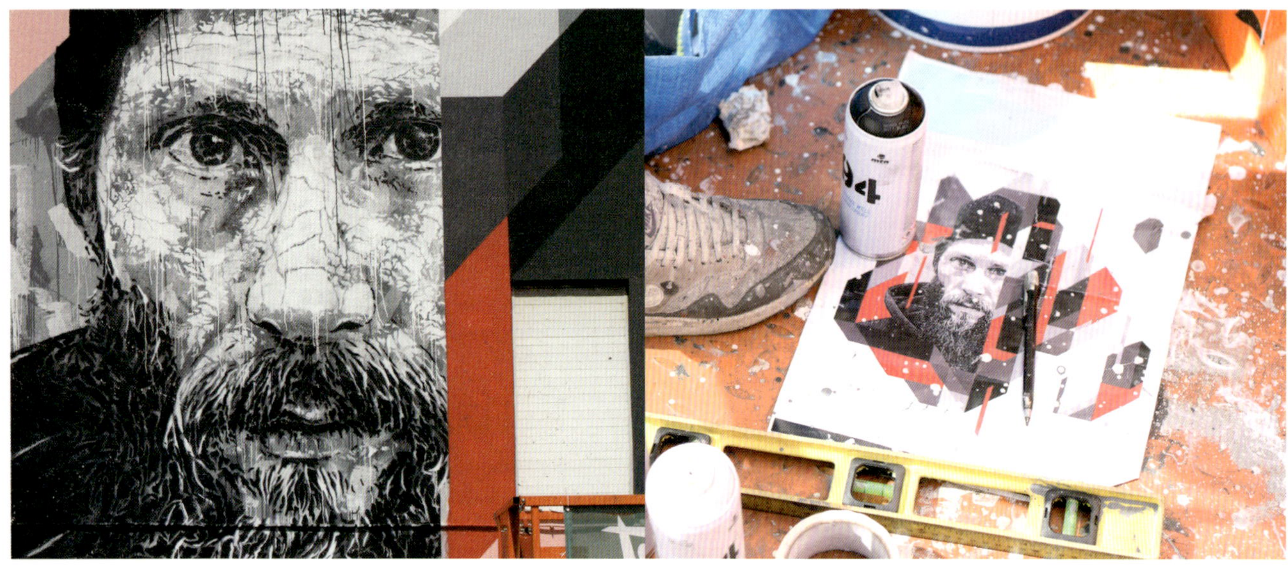

@Setúbal, Portugal 2017
©Tiago Durães Fotografia Digital

Q6: For most common people, stenciling does not require that much skill. Some of the famous works of Banksy reinforce this idea: although his works are of black humor and profoundly meaningful, his skill seems not hard to master. What do you think about it?

To most people, stenciling seems like the easiest way to make a cool design. They also think that it's super simple because you can paint an image on a wall really quick. What they don't know is how much work it takes before it actually goes on the wall. Today you can find lots of tutorials teaching you how to create a stencil, and that's a good way to learn the basics and the mechanics of the technique.

The problem is if you just follow a tutorial you will get the stencil that is generated by a computer. It will be the same stencil as everyone else who followed the same tutorial. It won't be unique. When I started stenciling, YouTube didn't exist. This allowed me to learn the basics the hard way—by looking at other stencils and doing a ton of experiments. Once you learn the mechanics you have an infinite number of ways of doing the stencil, so you can look for the aesthetic you like the most. It can be realistic, colourful, detailed, depending on what you are looking for.

If we look carefully at Banksy's stencils, we can see that even with less detailed or simplest shapes, there is an impeccable notion of what's being done. There is a perfect idea of how many shapes he needs to have a perfect image definition in order to express the idea he wants. He even has to create shapes where they in fact don't exist in the original image. He also knows what kind of aesthetic he wants. The stencils are totally the results of his hand drawing, not from any digital stencil generator. You are only putting this question exactly because you can almost automatically recognize his stencils. His style, combined with his strong message and black humor, makes his work awesome.

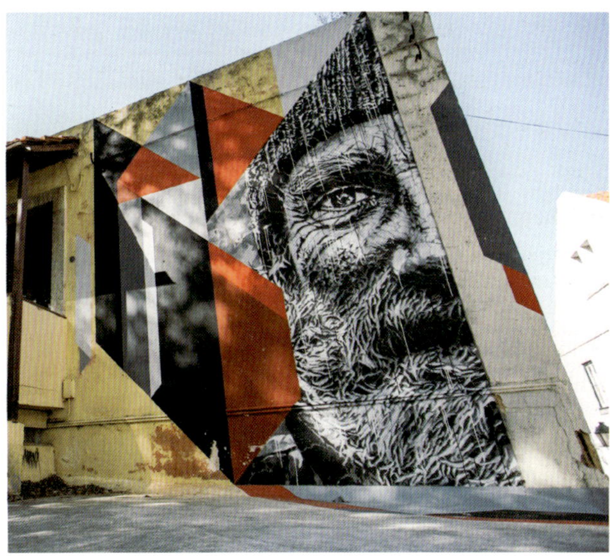

@Cascais, Portugal 2015
©Mistaker Maker / Rui Gaiola

Q7: The cutting shapes of your stencils are very delicate. They are like small pieces patched together to form the contrast of light and shade. How did this design come to you?

The base of a stencil is the shadow part of an image. Usually that's enough to define an image, but after some time, it didn't feel like enough to me. I worked with multi-layered stencils a few times, but once I discovered my way of doing two-layer stencils, it felt really right.

Drawing a stencil can take a lot of time. Usually, the more you add layers to it, the more it looks real, which is something I never really wanted to do. Stencils have a specific aesthetic I've always loved, so I always want to keep that feeling.

My stencils are based on 3 layers of colors: one for shadows, one for lights and one that exists in between. (On a black and white stencil, that would be grey.) If you paint the middle layer with the same grey, each repetition of the same stencil will look the same. You would also need to cut that layer, which would mean more time spent on cutting. I discovered that if I paint the grey layer with acrylic paint and rollers directly on a wall, I can put as many greys as I want on it, making it unique each time. This technique allows me to work with a 3-layered look, when actually I only have to create two.

Q8: What is your general creation procedure, from preparation to practically working on walls?

First and foremost, I need to know about the wall and its surroundings. Then I decide what kind of image to use. My work is all about facial expressions, sometimes even more so than the person I'm portraying. Sometimes it makes sense to paint a local. Other times it's more about finding the perfect expression that speaks with the locals in some way. Once I have the image I can make a sketch of the piece, so I can know the future size of the stencil. Then I draw the stencil for the estimated size, I print and cut it. From there I go to the wall and start working based on the previous layout plan.

Q9: Some argue that street art is environmental, and it has to be merged into the environment. What do think of this argument?

I have mixed feelings. I believe we can never forget the specific architectural and social environment the wall we're painting lives in. The same wall in a different country would be a different wall. There is always an urban and social context. However, this does not mean that the theme of the painting has to be directly connected with the local history. Moreover, painting something out of context with the place itself should be a conscious act. It must be intentional which in turn will probably provide meaning. For instance, draw a sea in the middle of a desert can be an extremely strong action, exactly because of its decontextualization. I believe your painting has to connect with your composition, bear in mind that your canvas isn't just the wall, but also its surroundings.

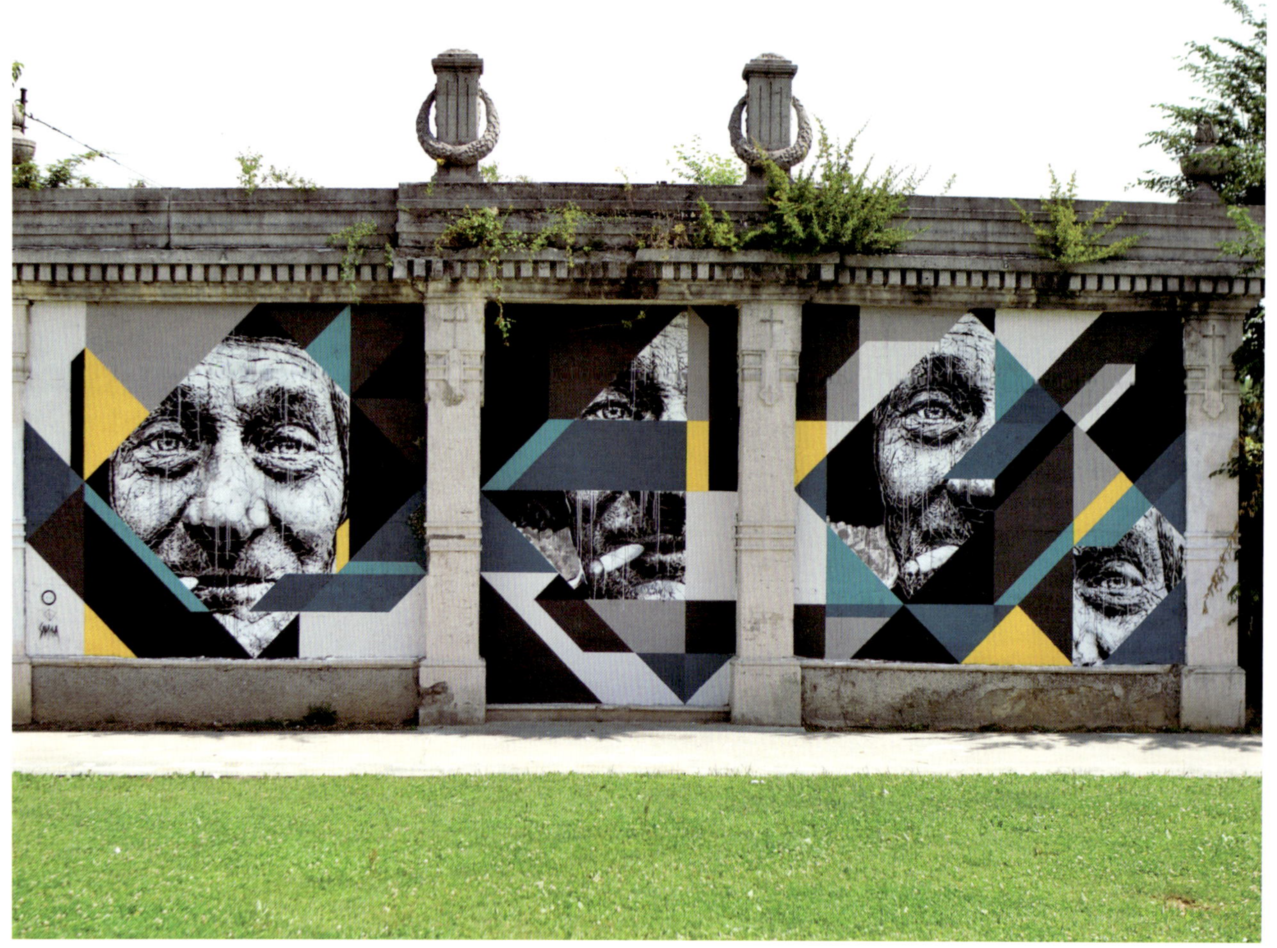

@Bérgamo, Italy 2015
©Pigmenti

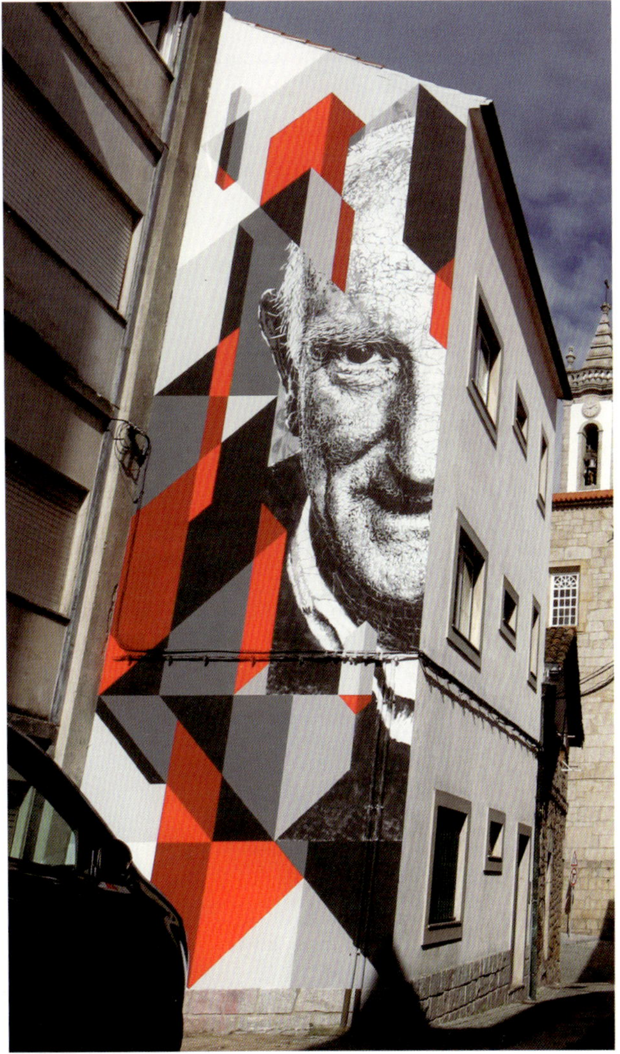

@Covilhã, Portugal 2015
©WOOL / Pedro Seixo Rodrigues

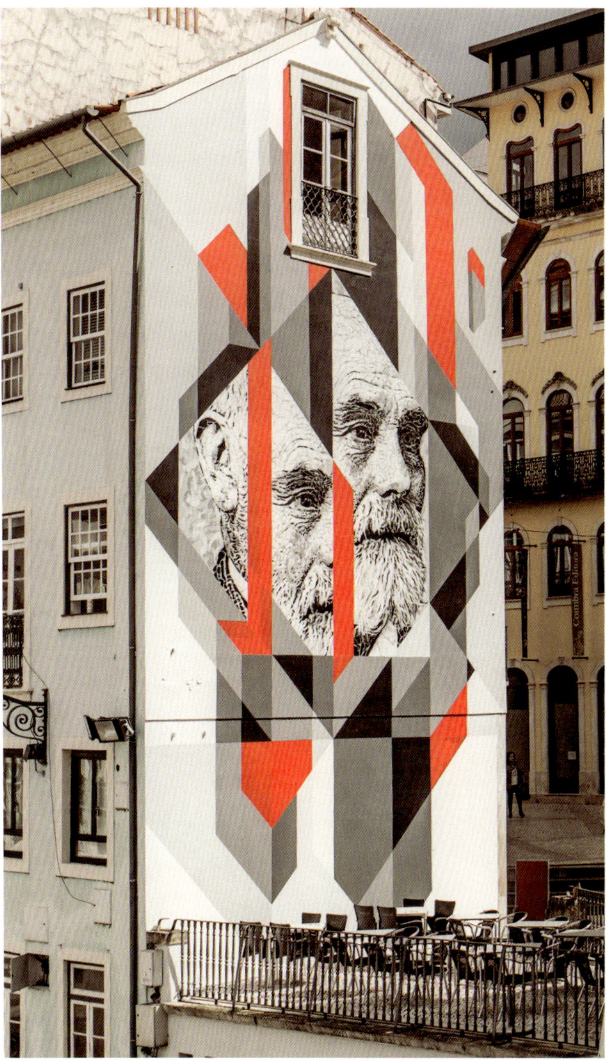

@Coimbra, Portugal 2016
©Mistaker Maker / Miguel Oliveira

Q10: Street artist is a profession a lot of young people long for. All the traveling, meeting new people, and realizing the creative ideas on your mind are appealing. But what do you dislike most being a street artist? Are there any stereotypes of street artists that you would like to clarify?

That is actually one of the stereotypes. Not all artists travel a lot, or earn a lot of money. It's an amazing thing to travel, meeting new people through your work while being paid for it. However it is rarely that simple, and it takes a lot of work and a lot of sacrifice too.

When younger artists approach me about becoming street artists, the best advice I can give is that if it comes naturally to you, do it. Don't do it because of the hype and the dream of travelling around the world and earning lots of money. Do it for your art and naturally good ideas will come. I always wanted to paint and do my own work and, naturally, it became my profession. That does not mean I didn't work hard for it.

I think it's not easy as a freelancer of any kind to sometimes have work and not be paid. But nowadays, I believe one of the worst things about being a street artist is the growing financial interest in it. The interest itself is not bad, but it gradually becomes all that matters, going to the point of organizing festivals and painting murals just for the buzz it will generate and not for the art or the people. It's not always easy, but I cannot complain at all. I'm happy I get to do what I love and, at least for the time being, live by my passion.

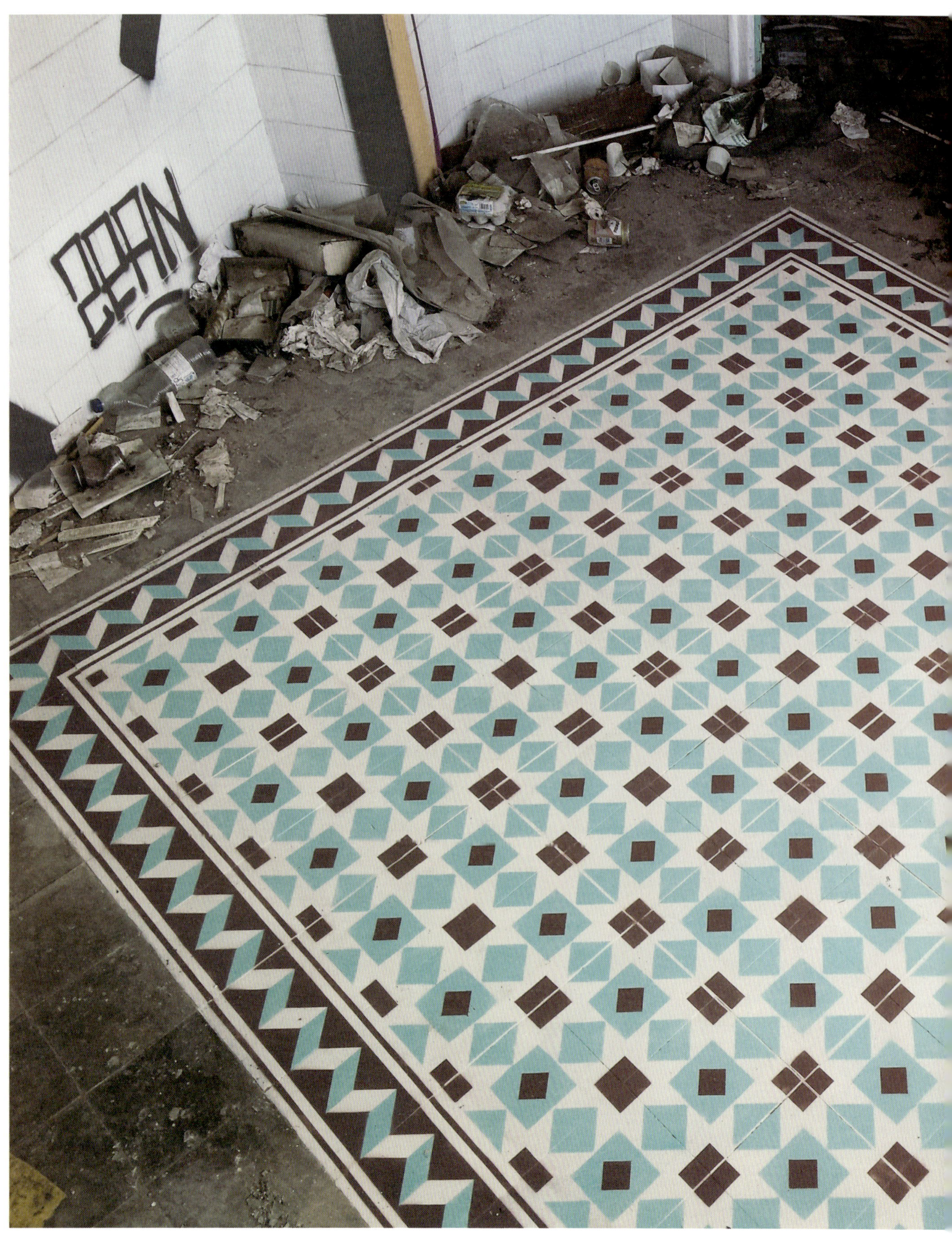

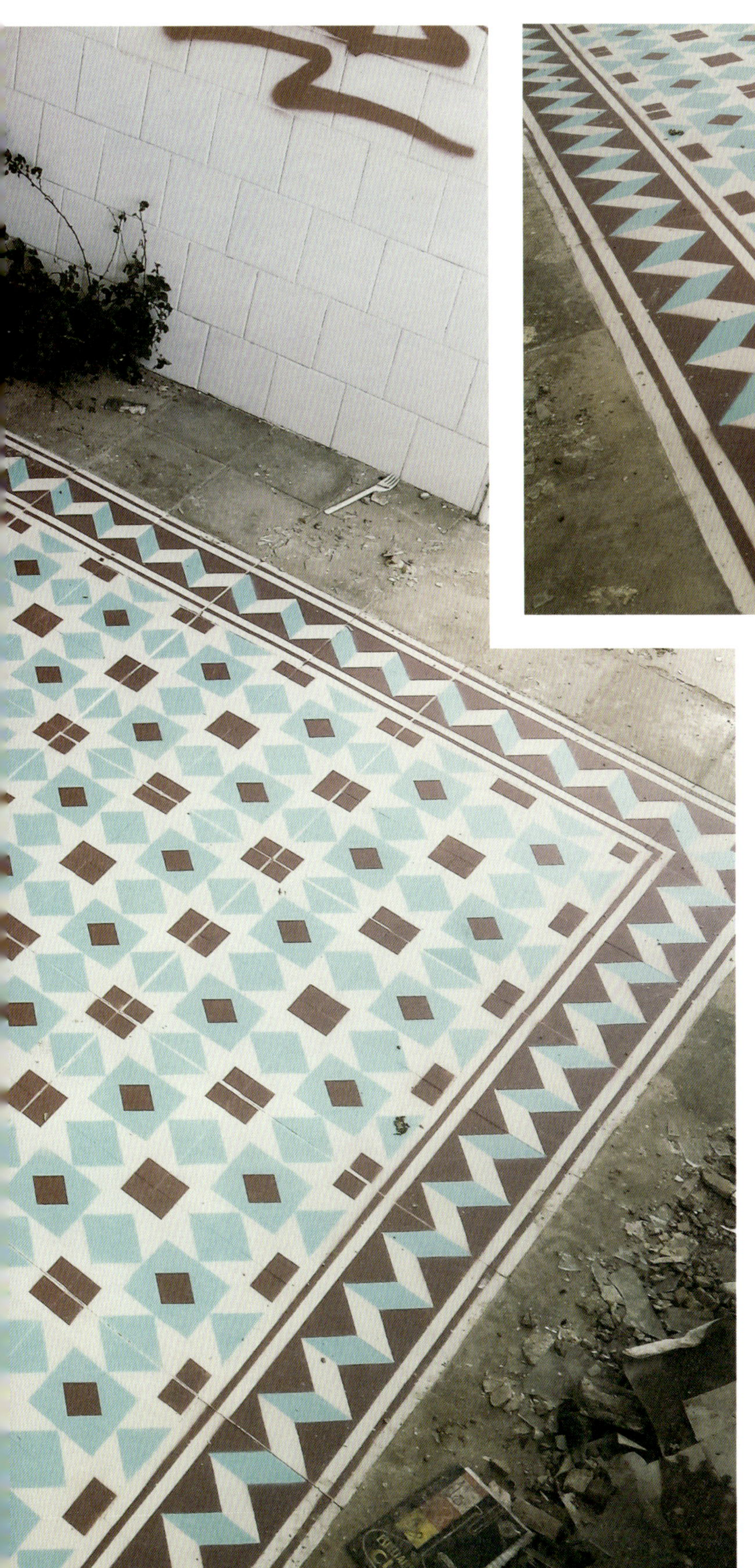

Javier de Riba is a Catalan designer and artist born in Barcelona. He develops graphics and communication projects with a focus on sustainability and humane treatment. For Javier de Riba, hydraulic mosaic tiles are family memories in many Catalan homes. He locates abandoned and grey floors and applies patterns to them. With his interventions, he tries to question the value of the spaces. He proposes a slough-off skin that changes the perception of the entire environment.

Amada
@Barcelona, Spain 2016

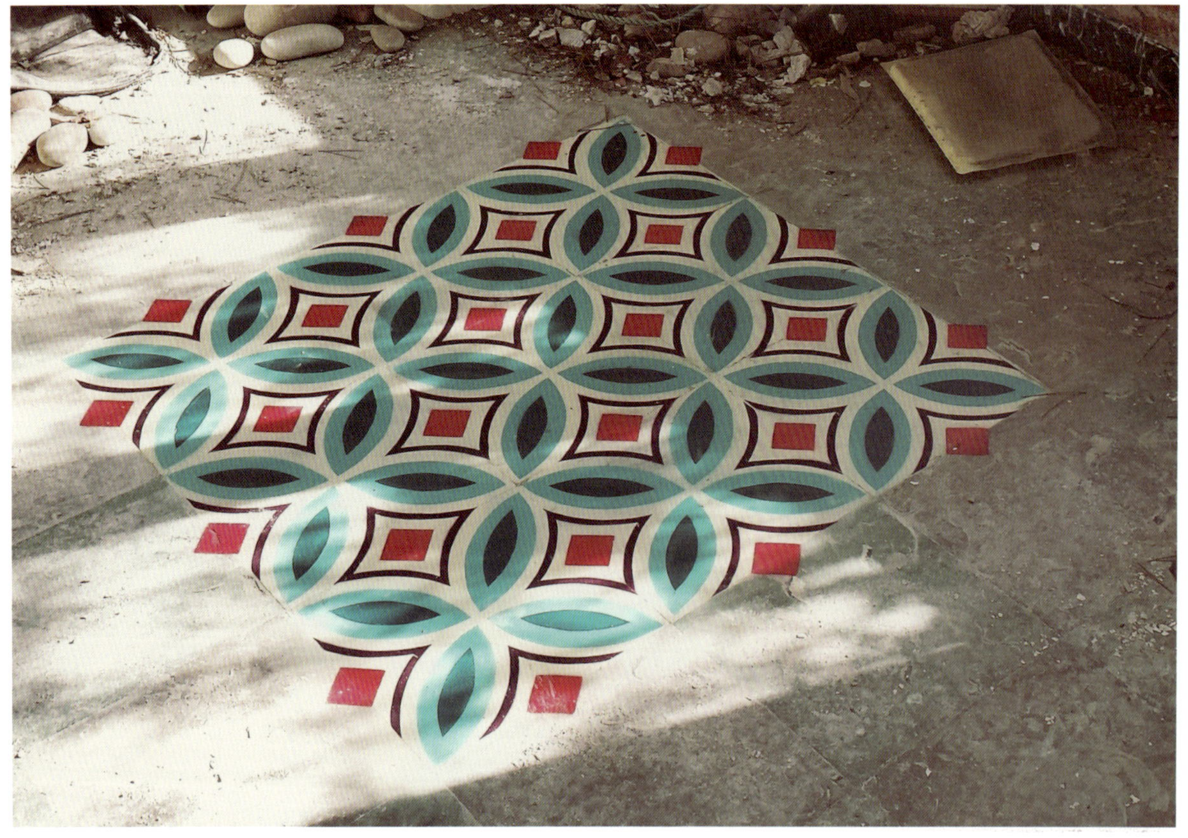

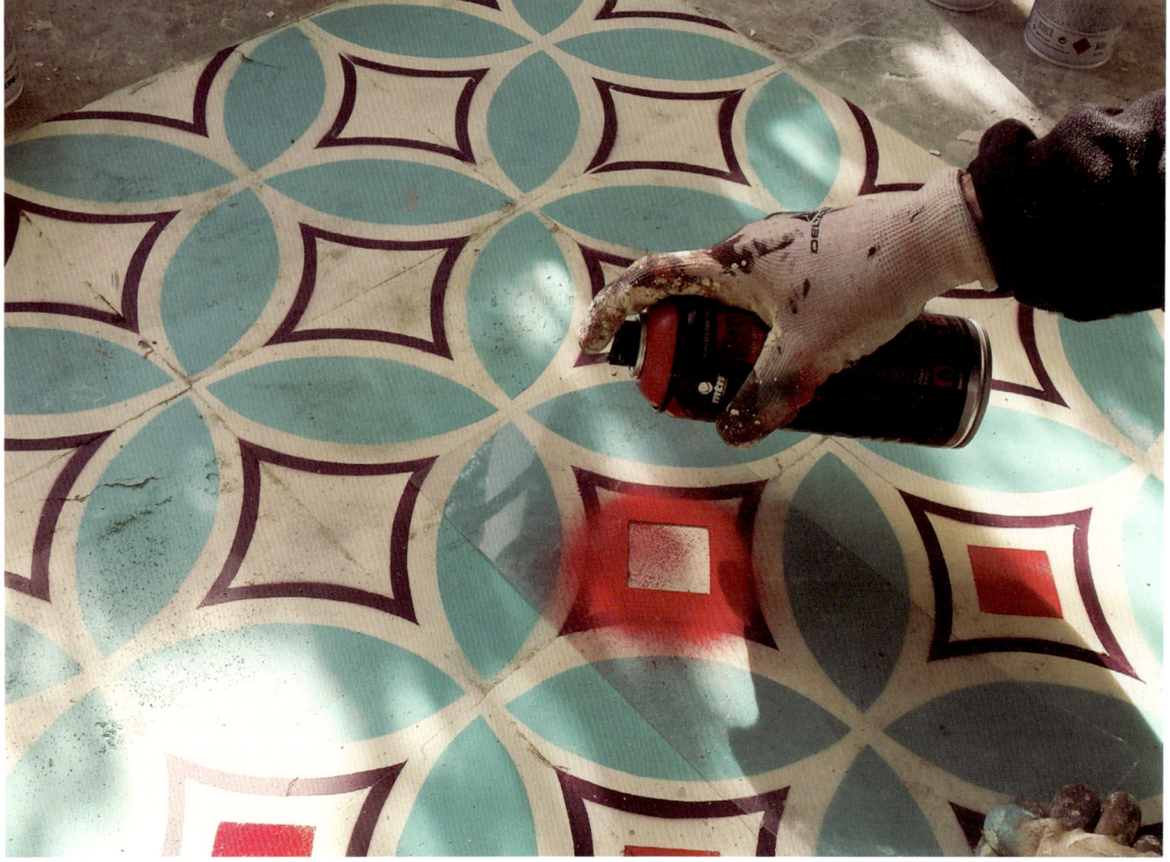

Bungalow
@Tarragona, Spain 2015

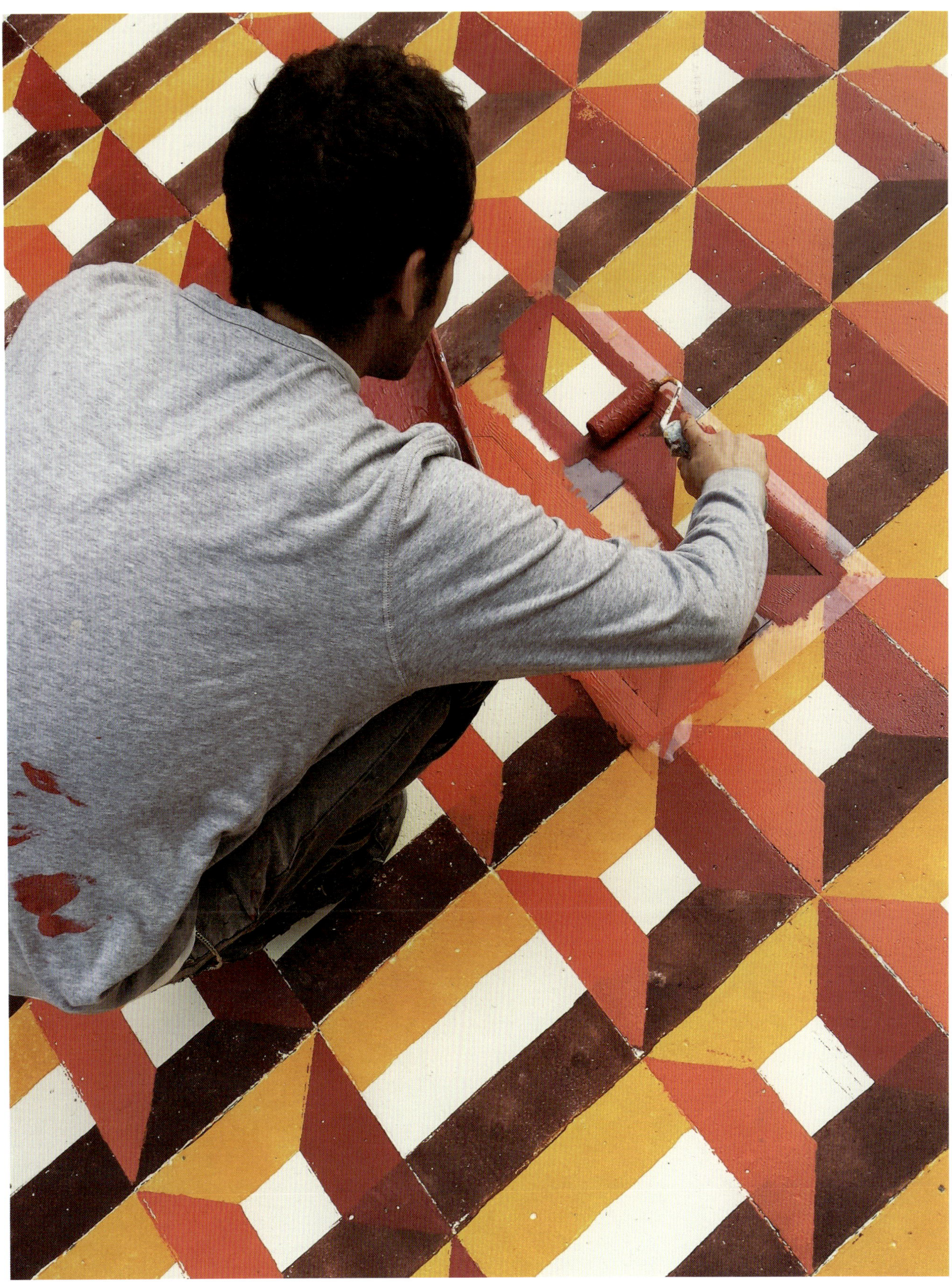

Break
@Barcelona, Spain 2015

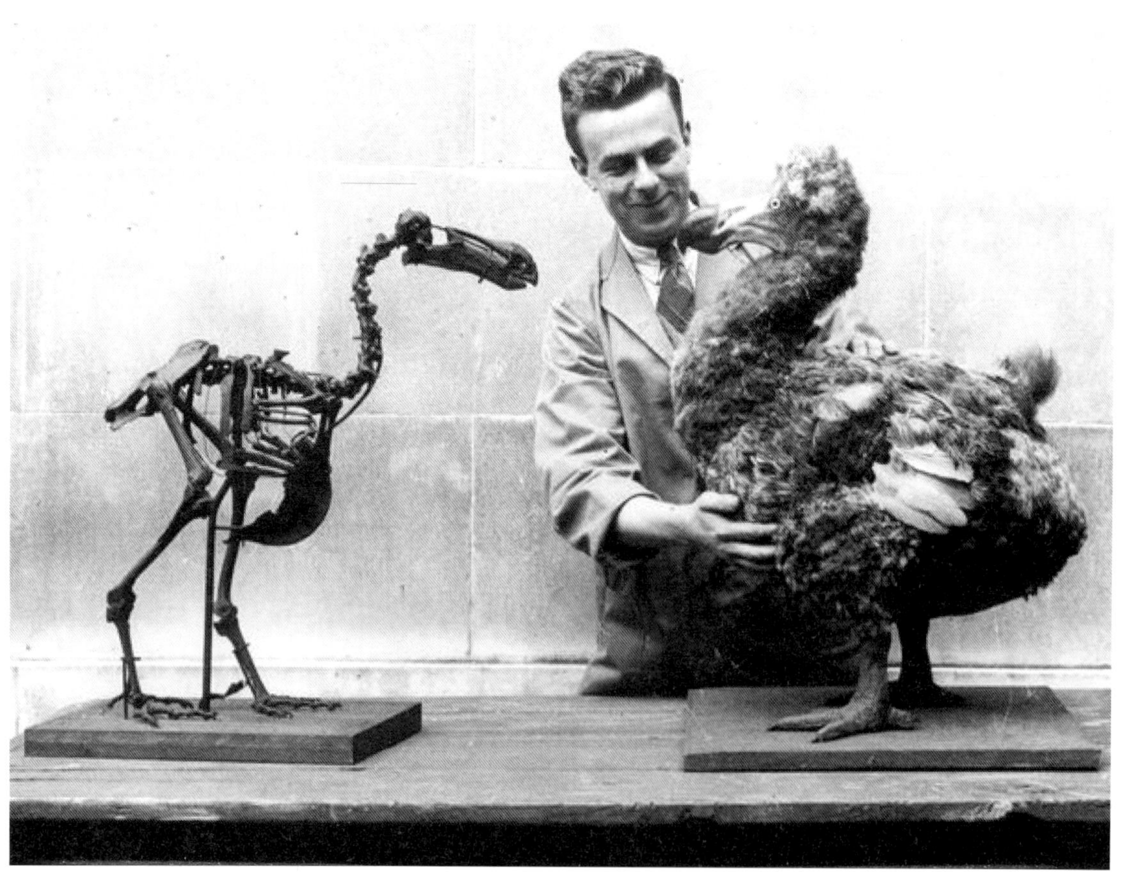

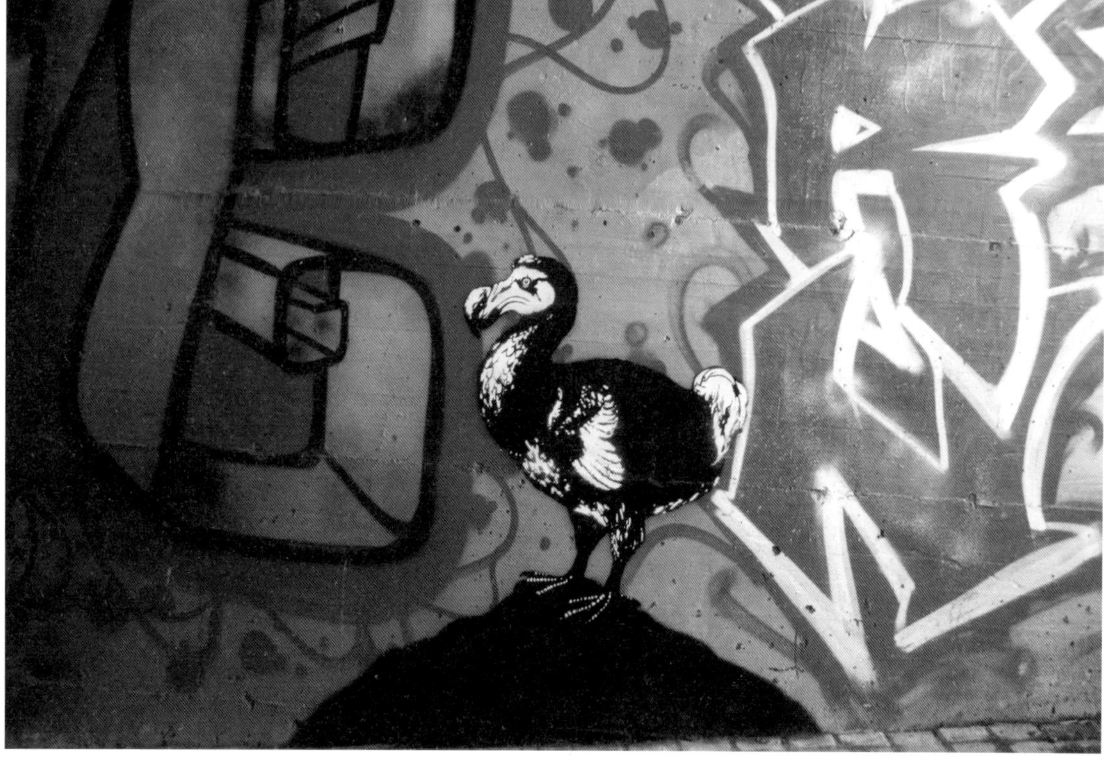

"Dodo Expansion" is a long-term personal street project started around 2013. The subject is the dodo, which became extinct long ago and now has become a symbol of colonization's destructive effects. Matteo Pietra used an almost one-to-one stencil-to-object ratio with a real dodo. The colors used are black and white, which create a sharp image that immediately captures the attention of passers-by .

Dodo Expansion
@La Spezia, Italy 2013

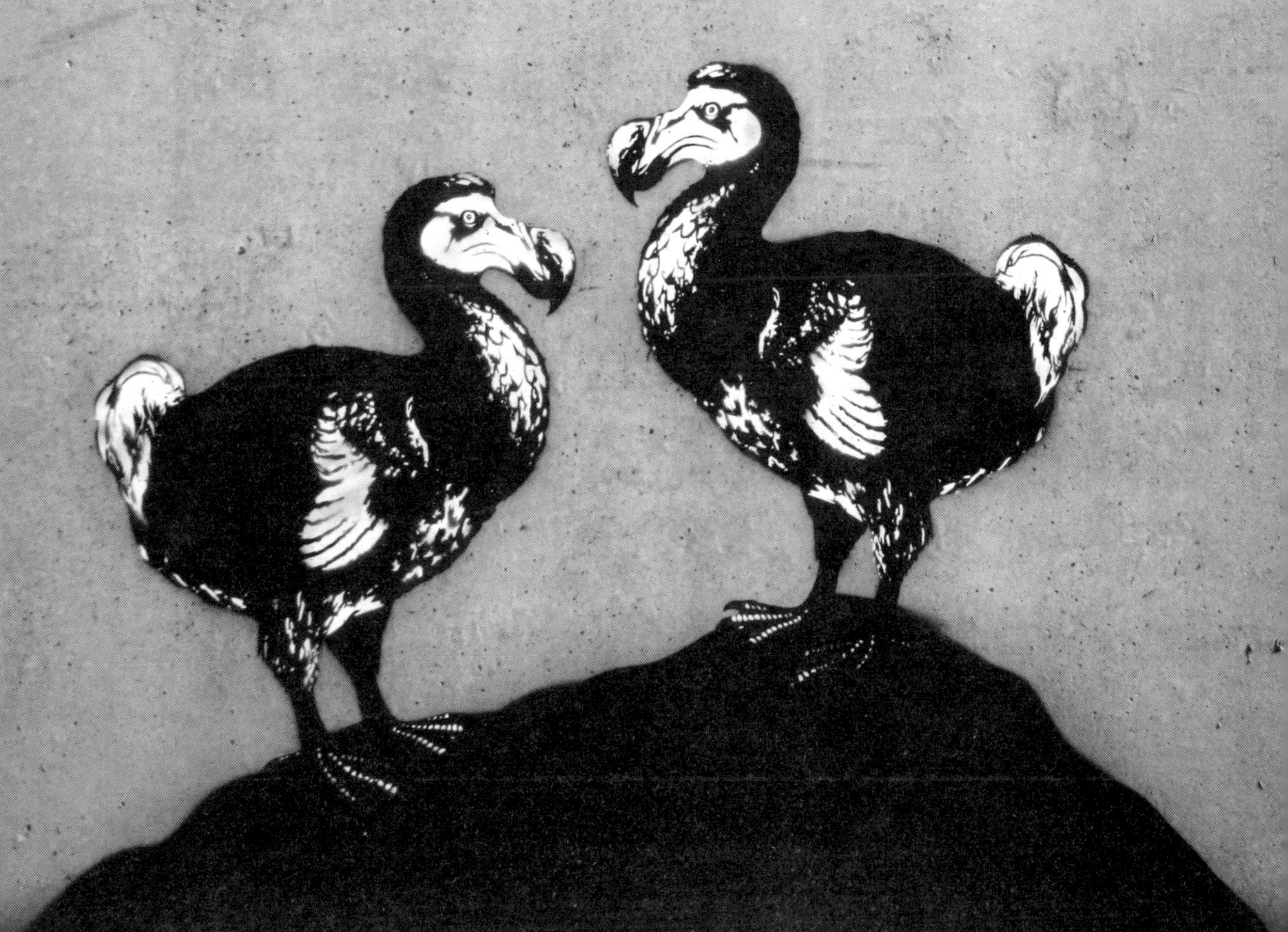

WHEATPASTE GRAFFITI

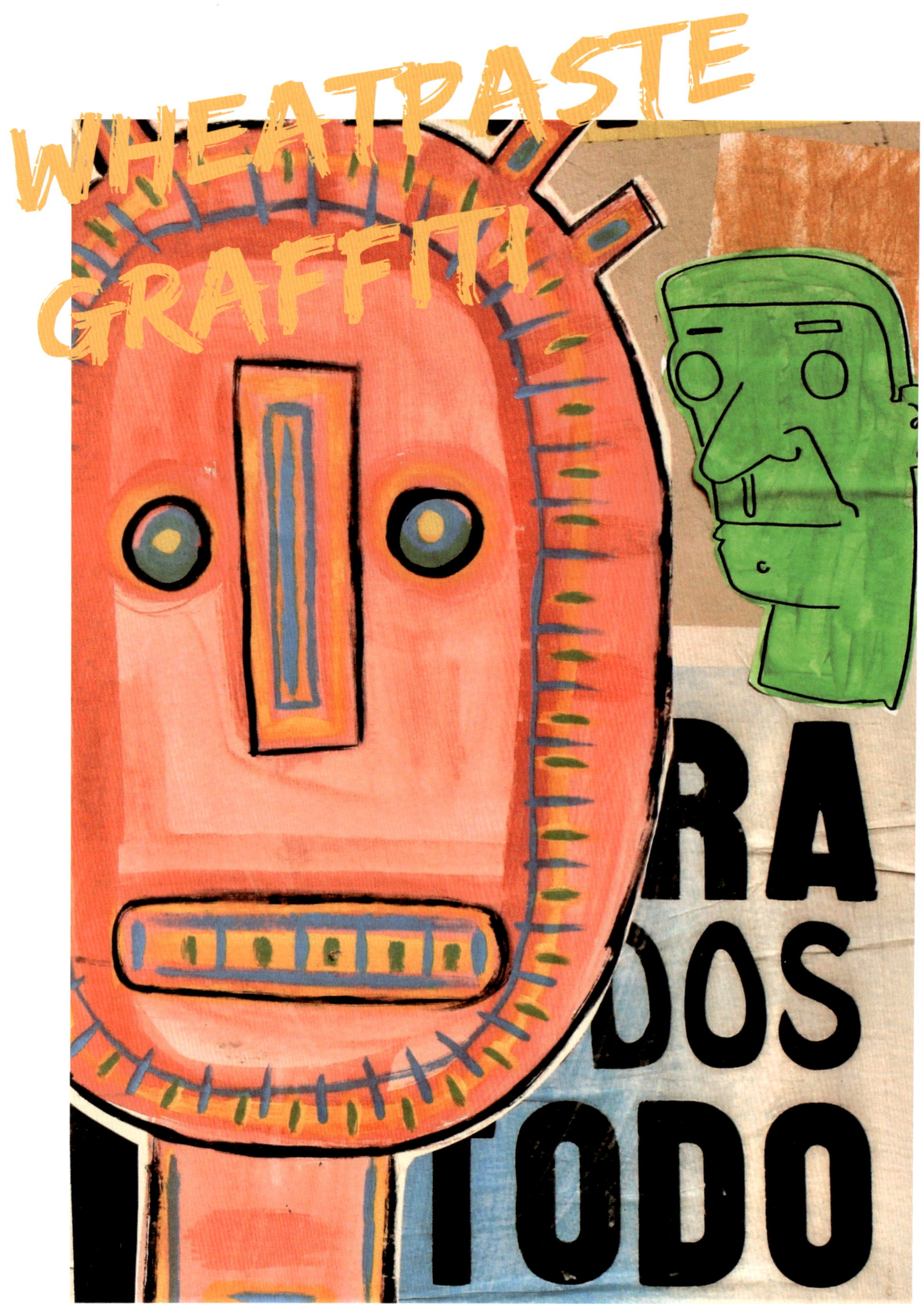

Artist/ Boxi Trixi

WHEATPASTE GRAFFITI

Stationery such as stickers, sticky labels, and Post-it notes and advertisements such as lost notices, rent ads, and posters for concerts and movie debuts are all paste-up graffiti in the broadest sense, as long as pasted without permission. In this chapter, we narrow down the definition to those paste-up works that involve creative methods such as painting, design, and collage.

WHEATPASTE GRAFFITI: GET THE MESSAGE OUT

Photographer/ Alvimann

Photo/ Morguefile

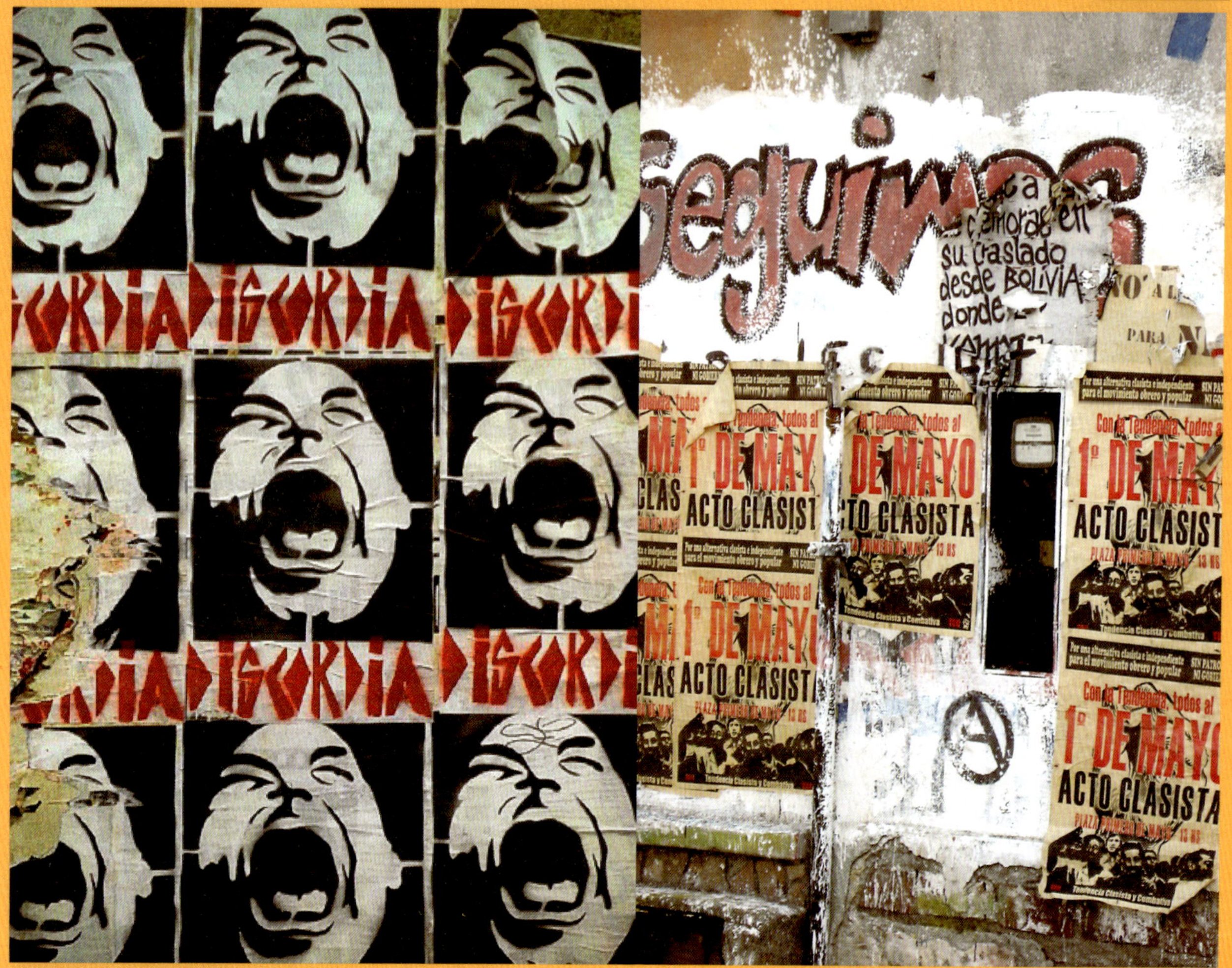

Photo/ Pedro Baesse (Flickr)

Living in the 21st-century Information Era, we are no strangers to mushrooming information. Thanks to the mobile network, the rapidity and spontaneity of message communication exceeds that of any other era. Everywhere we go, messages are flowing to you. But human brains have not evolved to match this explosion of information. Consequently services of data analysis, paid listing of search results, and "most valuable books to read" lists and the sort appear to deal with the overload and smooth people's fears of missing potentially important messages. All this is because information does matter.

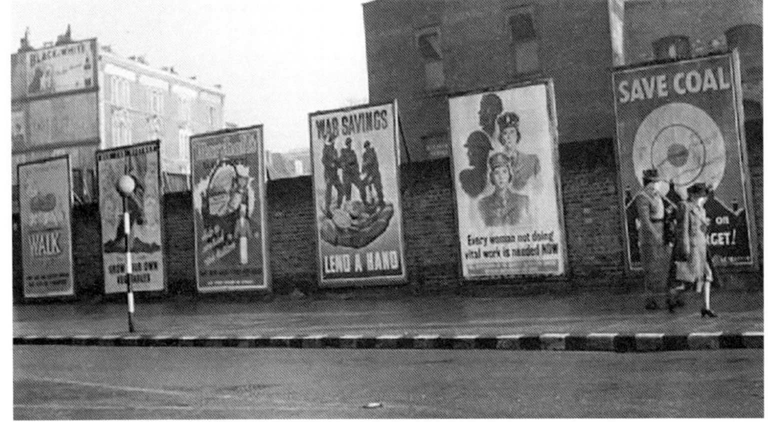

Photo/ Imperial War Museums

To trace wheatpaste graffiti's origin, one must speak of its strongest attribute: message delivering. Whether it is the papyrus, parchment, and kraft from the West, or Ba-qiao paper (灞桥纸) and Cai- hou paper (蔡侯纸) from the East, the invention and improvement of paper has increased the efficiency of sharing messages. The practice of pasting paper with messages to the public walls naturally came into use. For example, Chinese dynasties would paste up an imperial edict (皇　榜) to announce national issues, such as new emperor ascending to the throne. However, this practice offered limited applications because of the cost of production and low literacy at the time.

With the First and Second Industrial Revolutions, driven by commercial need, this practice flourished. Peasants without lands provided a labor force for industrial production. Production demands consumption, and consumption requires advertising. At the same time, mass production of paper became possible. To reach out to as many potential consumers as possible, poster advertising was born. Posters were dominated by brand names and product names with catchy slogans. To attract attention from passers-by, the posters were increased in size, and became mobile in the case of human billboards. Now, posters are widely applied everywhere imaginable.

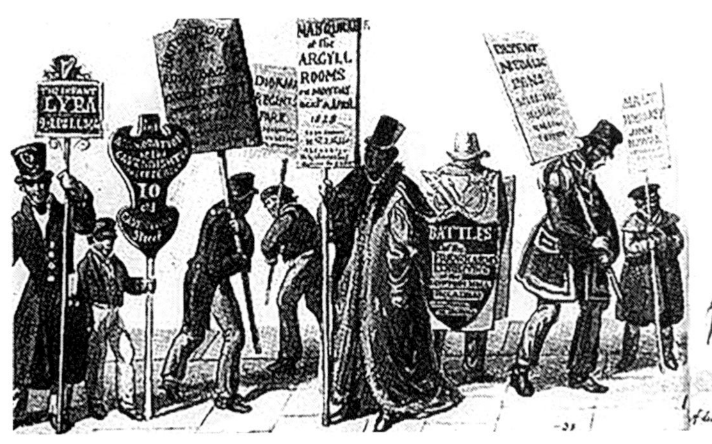

Author/ George Johann Scharf
Photo/ Wikipedia Commons

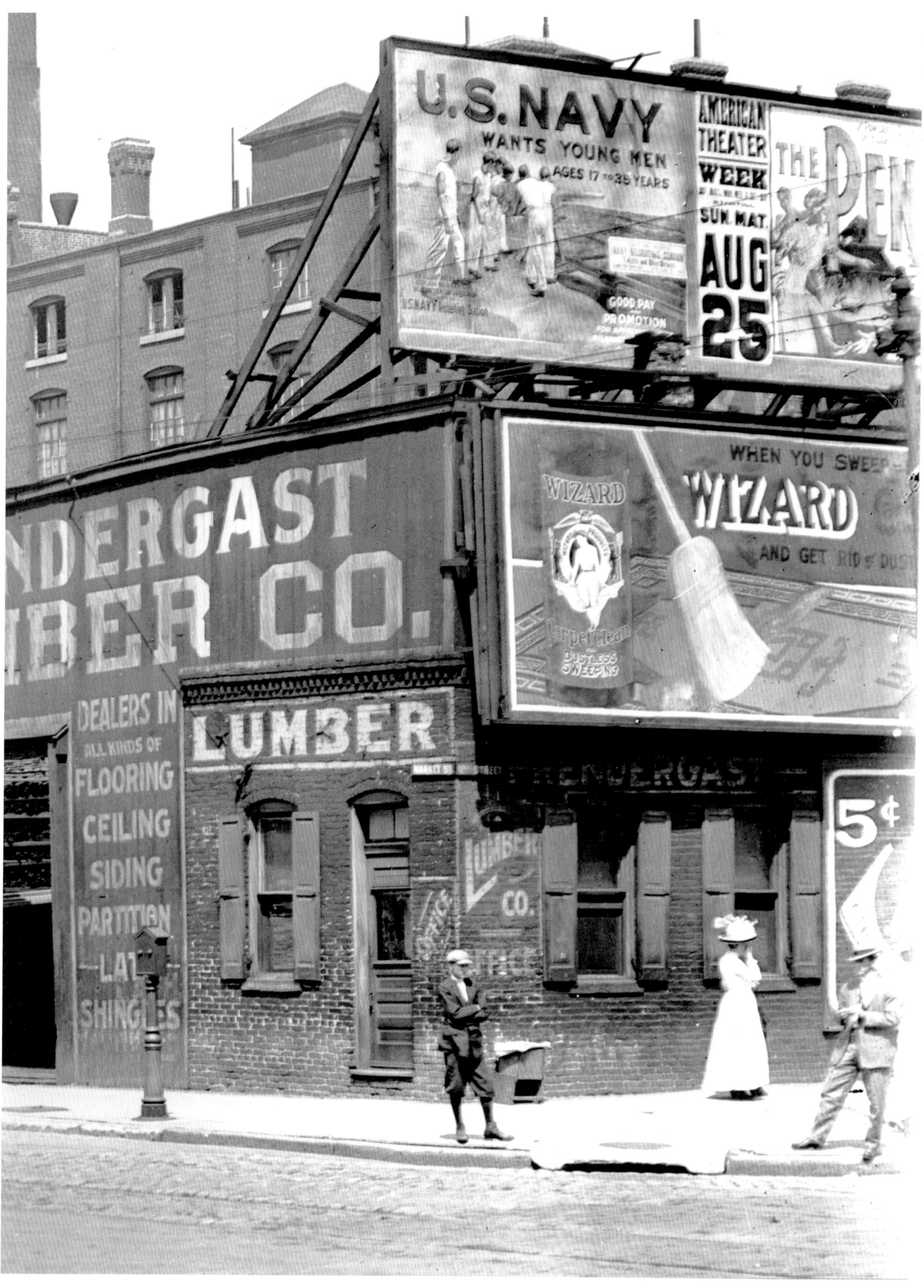

Photo/ Missouri History Museum

We can still find cities with the walls layered with posters. In the beginning, wheatpaste graffiti was no different than the annoying posters: they were mostly messy. A sheet of stickers pasted by a child would be regarded as wheatpaste graffiti. Somewhere during the 1960s, some people pasted works on the public walls just for fun, and because these works shared the creative space of street and the reputation of vandalism with text-based graffiti and stencil graffiti, this practice were considered to be graffiti as well. Also, this form often employs wheat paste as the adhesive, and thus is called "wheatpaste graffiti," or alternatively "paste-up."

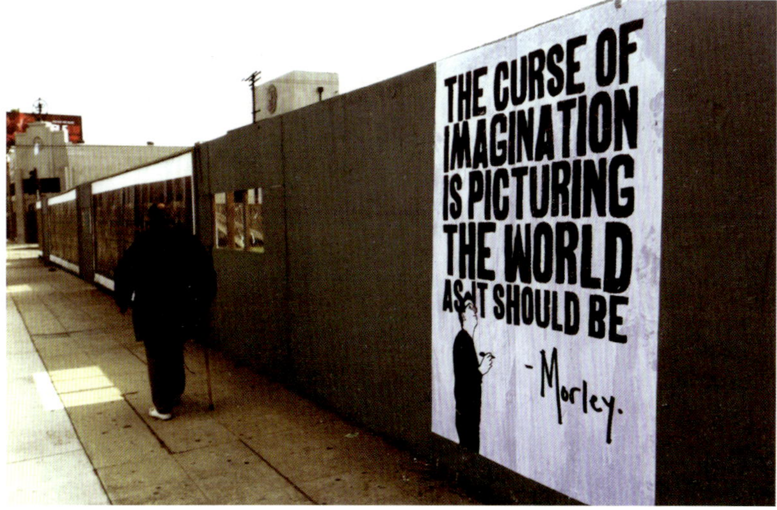

Artist/ Morley
Author/ Bedside
Photo/ Wikipedia Commons

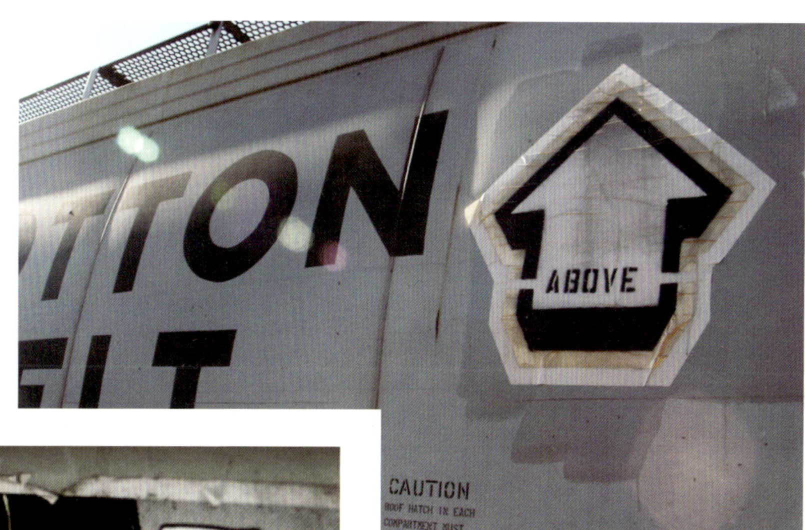

Artist/ Above
Author/ Hdepot
Photo/ Wikipedia Commons

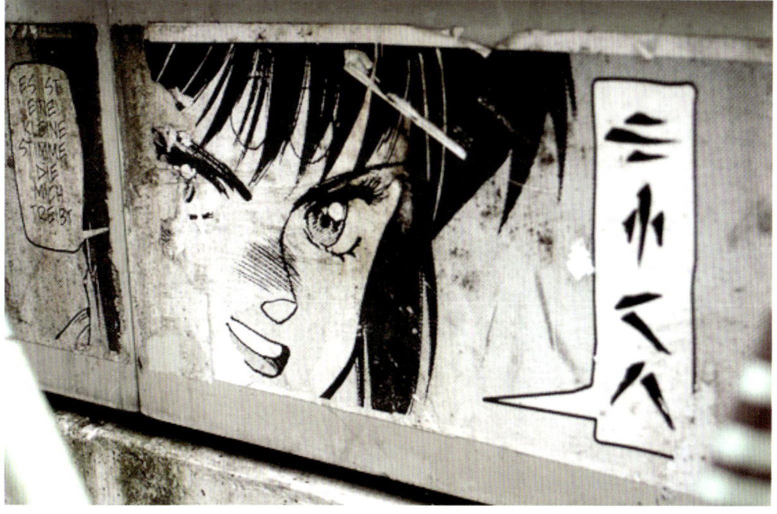

Author/ IIIIIIIII
Photo/ Wikipedia Commons

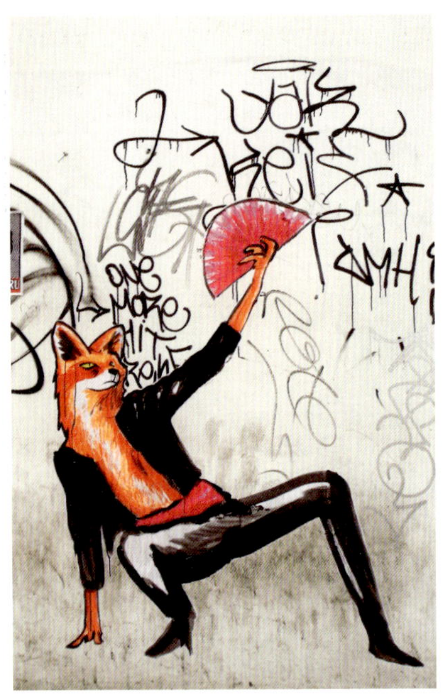

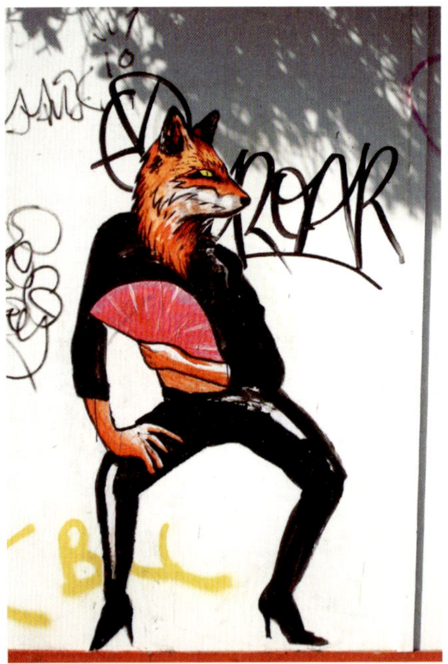

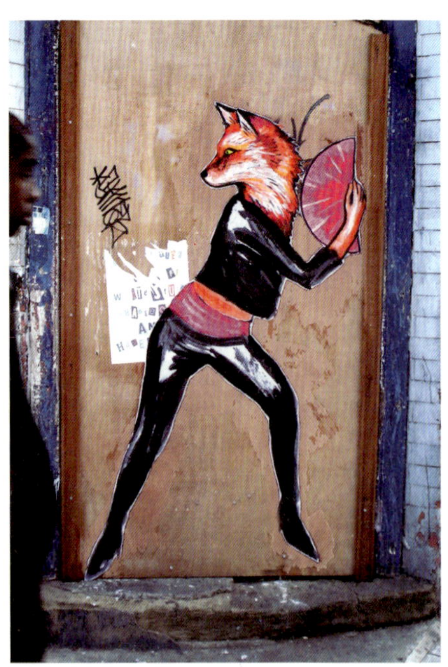

INTERVIEW WITH SURIANI

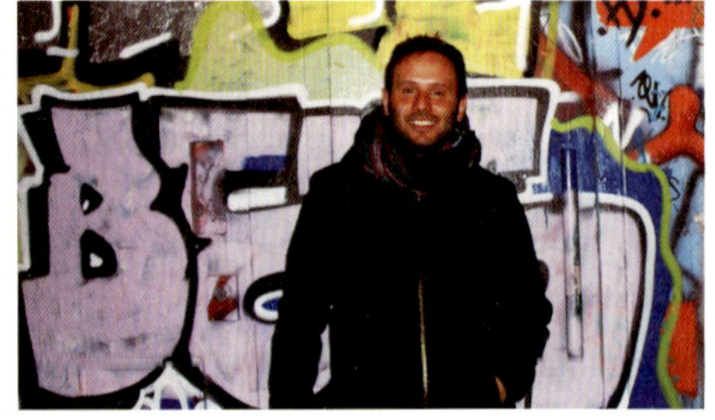

Artist/ Suriani

Q1: When did you first create street arts? Is São Paulo a city more open to street arts compared to cities of France, England, and USA?

I started in 2002, when I was still studying architecture at the University of São Paulo. I've always liked public art. At that time there was a graffiti explosion in the city, with paintings from Os Gemeos, Nina, Nunca, and many others popping up everywhere. The possibility of putting up a work on public space without needing permission or validation from anyone was very tempting. It's a free and direct way to communicate. Doing art in the streets became my new way to relate to the city.

I've worked in many different cities like São Paulo, London, Paris, Berlin, Barcelona, Istanbul, and Valparaiso. Each one is unique and has a different relation to street art. Modern and post-industrial cities like São Paulo and Berlin are the perfect context. There you can find huge industrial areas with plenty of available walls asking for art! Historical cities like Paris have a different relation with their architectural heritage, and people may easily see street art as a form of vandalism.

Q2: How does doing street arts enable you to relate to cities?

Doing street art is more than just painting on a wall. It is a way of living. To do it you need to first look and try to understand the city and its dynamics. Find the perfect spot, neighborhood, and time to paint or paste. I walk a lot in the streets with my eyes wide open to the landscape, the flow of people everywhere, the time commerce opens and closes, the use of buildings, and the possibility of getting into abandoned areas, which are great for our practice. All this strengthens my relation to the cities. It is also a great way to communicate with its inhabitants and to contribute to the local urban culture!

Q3: I know you are working on your latest series, which is inspired by drag queen culture. Why drag queens?

The political debate about equal rights has been quite active in France since 2012. I was very impressed by the mass manifestations of the conservative right and their resistance to new laws concerning gay marriage, adoption, and other gender issues. This series is the way I found to express my point of view on these issues. Drag culture spreads messages of acceptance and freedom of speech in a very amusing way! It really matches the positive vibe I have been trying to transmit with my work.

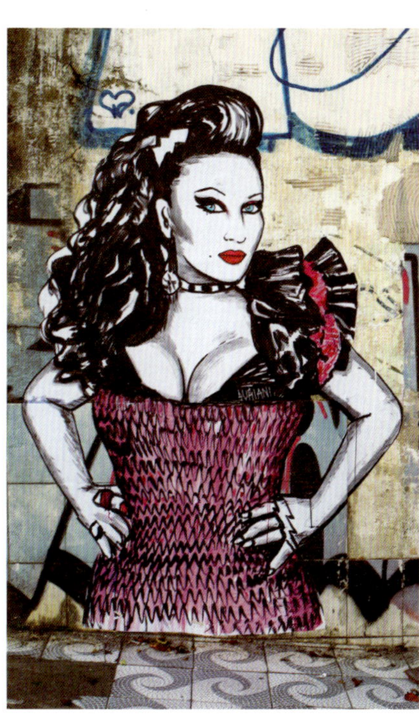

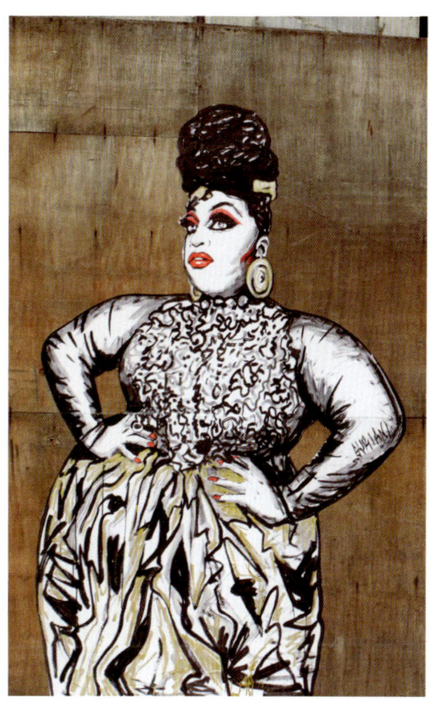

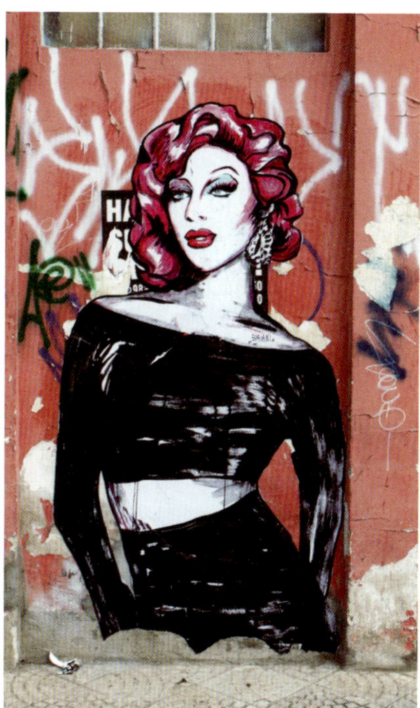

Q4: Drag is not necessarily referred to drag queens, but also drag kings. Why do you choose drag queens? Is that not "equal" to some extent?

The drag king scene is still very restraint. I am also interested in this practice in which we find very interesting androgynous artists, and I intend to do a series of drag king portraits soon. My interest for drag queens comes from my "gay boy identity" and culture, growing up in the underground São Paulo club scene of the late 1990s and early 2000s.

Q5: Many wheatepaste grafffiti are made of screen prints. Why do you choose to hand paint all of your works?

First of all because I love to paint. I only do each image once, so I don't need to use screen print, which is a manual technique of serial production and repetition.

Q6: The hybrid characters from your "Urban Jungle" and "Street Birds" projects, created by mixing animal heads to human bodies, pose in a very acrobat or Tai-chi way. This is so much fun. How did you come up with this idea?

I'm glad you think they are fun! I think so too! And I also have a lot of fun painting them. Since I was a child I've been fascinated by the animal world. In my early 20s because of the house and trance culture I have discovered relations between dance and shamanism. This took me to explore different cultures and practices that use body moves to get into altered states of mind. Tai Chi, Kung Fu and Yoga come from distant cultures and are inspired by the animal world, that's why I find it very inspiring. They help us develop our mind and achieve other levels of consciousness, like shamanic rites, where spirit animals have an important role.

Q7: I read on your website that "the mixture of animal–human anatomy explores the mythical aspects of our life experience that have been progressively lost in modern Western civilization." What do you mean by "the mythical aspects of our life experience"?

By mythical aspects of life I mean everything that cannot be explained or understood by our rational way of thinking. Through myths and rites we can get in touch with nature and the unknown. Science is incapable of explaining our universe, and modernity has taken us apart from nature. These animal–human figures appear in the production of ancient cultures all over the globe and are symbols of a different perception of mankind and its relation to the non-human.

Q8: What factors do you consider when choosing the place to put up your works?

I usually choose walls that are deteriorated or abandoned, so the work will have a longer life. Sometimes I choose a spot because it's well located and the art will be viewed by lots of people even if it is painted over in a short period of time. In São Pulo, the public service cares less about the public spaces, so this creates a good environment for street art. If you paint a wall you are doing something good to the city, which is considered by most of its inhabitants as an ugly city. The only issue around here is the confusion between street art and pixacao (local tags), but that is another subject. In Paris, people care a lot more about the public spaces, and the population is very attentive to what happens in the streets. Because a lot of buildings in central Paris are considered to be "beautiful ancient heritage," many people might think of painting a wall as vandalism.

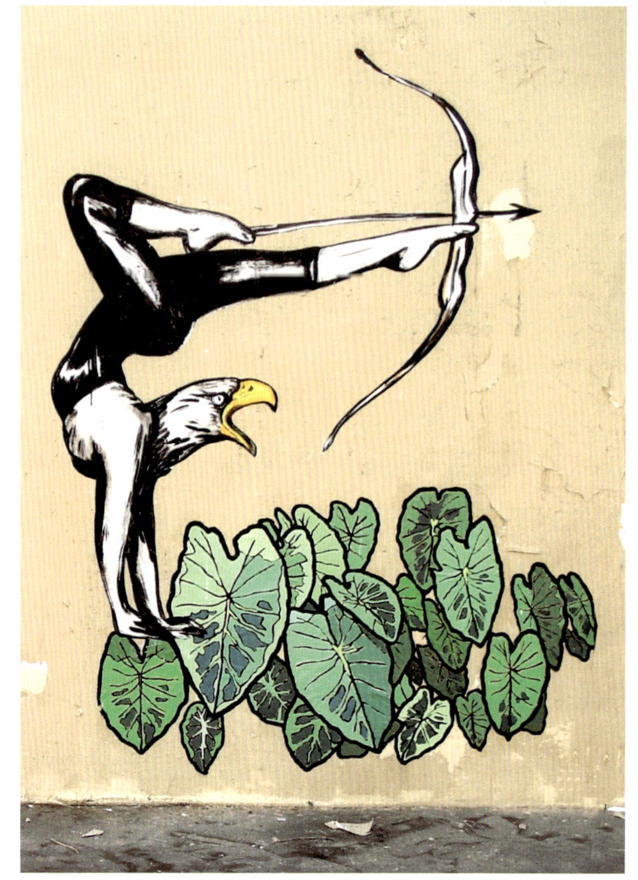

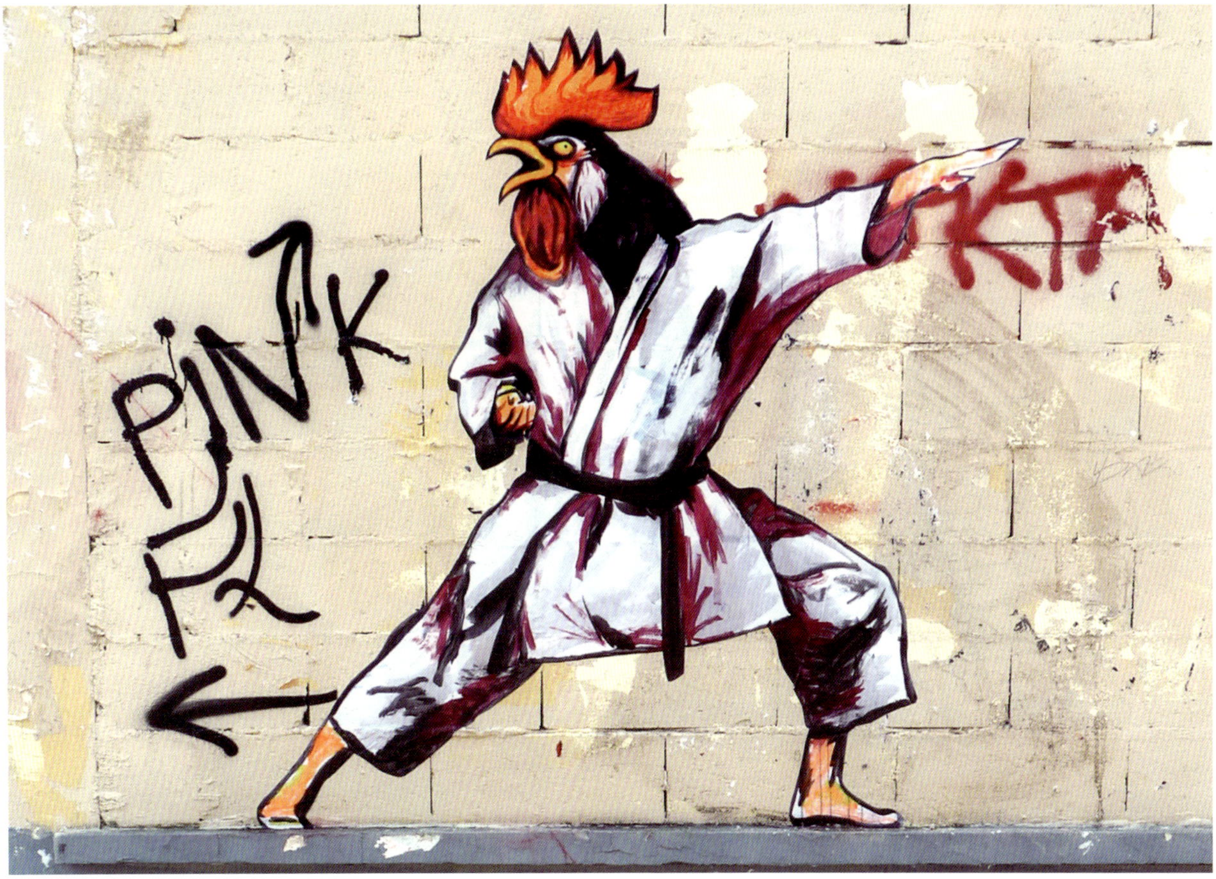

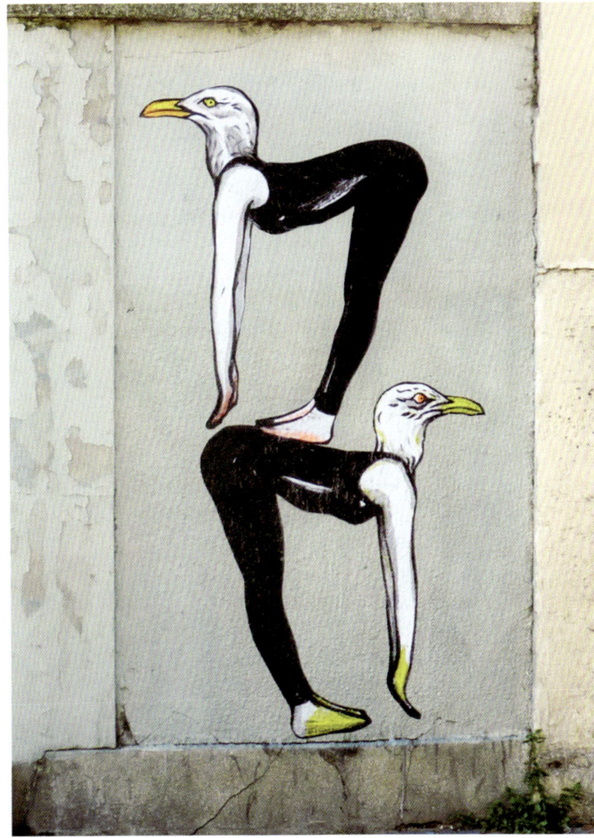

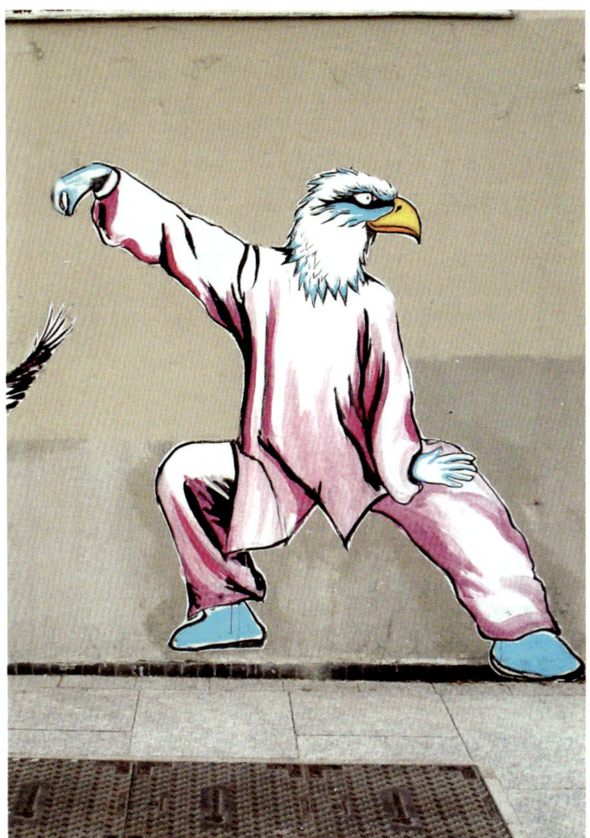

Q9: Is there any secret recipe for the wheatpaste you use? Do you mind sharing it with us?

The best one is wheat flour glue! Here you go: 7 spoons of wheat flour, 1 liter of water, and 2 spoons of vinegar. First you have to boil 3/4 of the water. In a different bowl you dissolve very well the 7 spoons of wheat in the remaining 1/4 of water. When the water is boiling, create a spin and slowly dump the water with flour inside, always swirling. Keep swirling for 5 minutes and add the vinegar only if you want to preserve it for a long time. After it gets cool, it's ready to paste! I always put paste on the wall and again over the paper.

Q10: What are your future projects?

I have moved back to São Paulo recently and I intend to spend a few years here. At the moment I'm getting in touch with the local artists to integrate into the scene again. I have also started to make larger scale murals and I want to develop this aspect of my work while I'm in Brazil. I also plan to expand my work to other forms of expression such as installation and performance. I might do this in association with other artists.

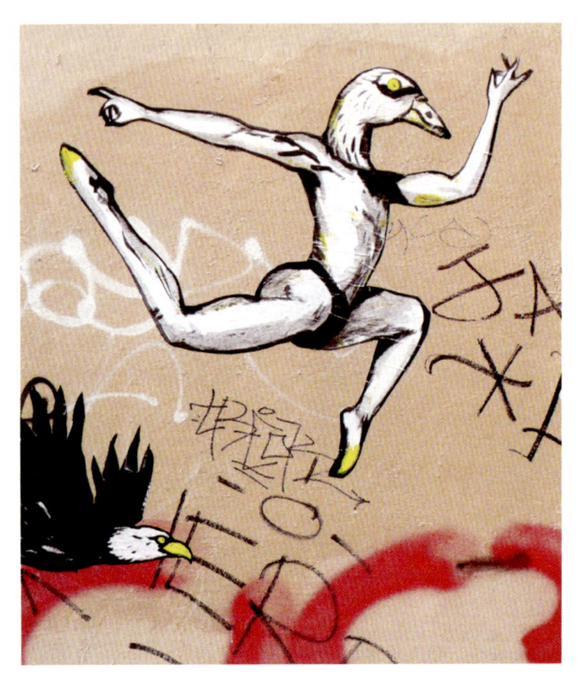

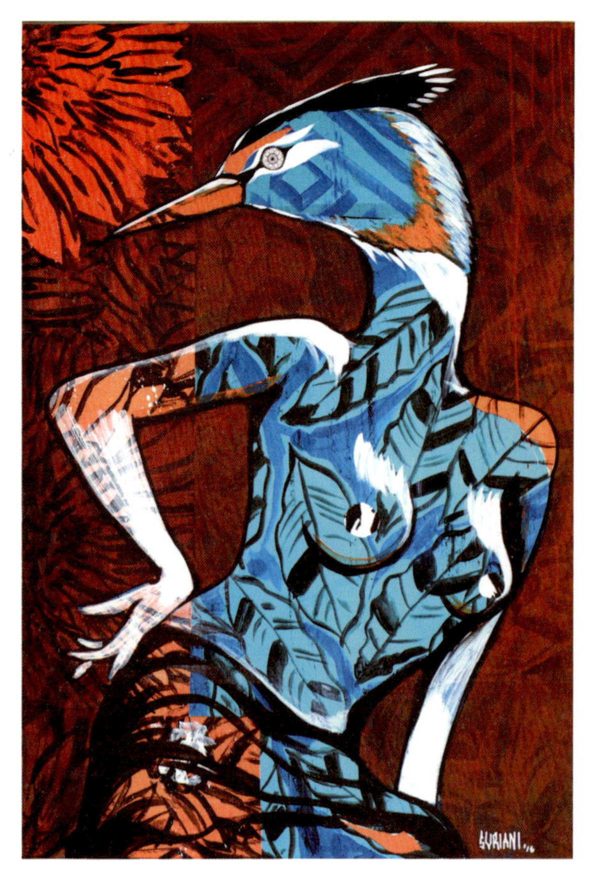

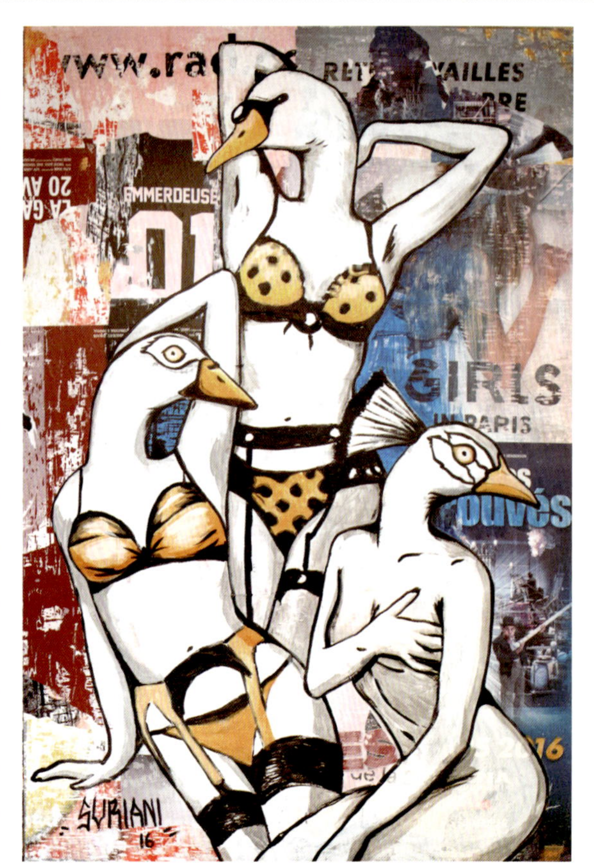

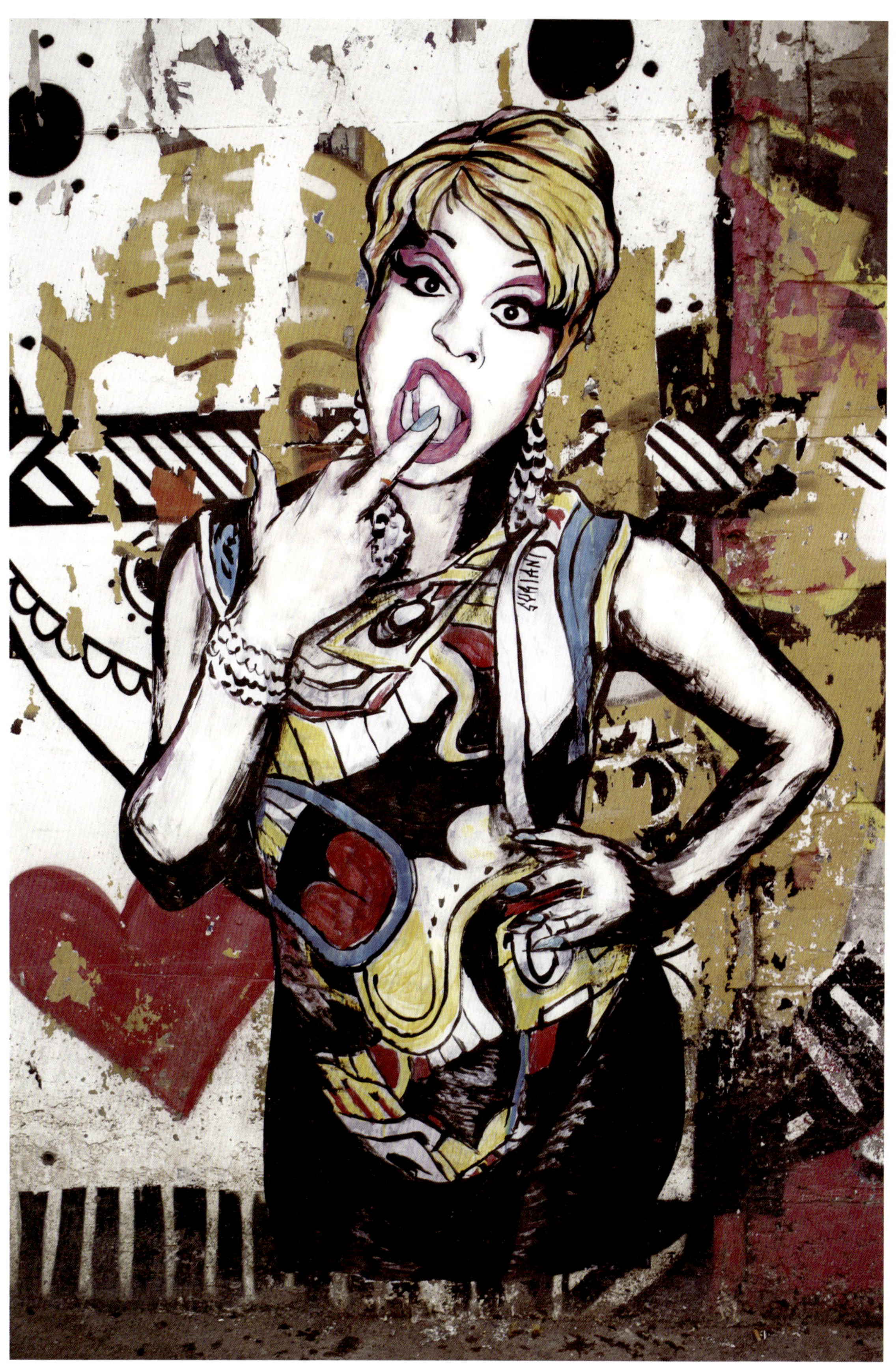

INTERVIEW WITH CAIOZZAMA

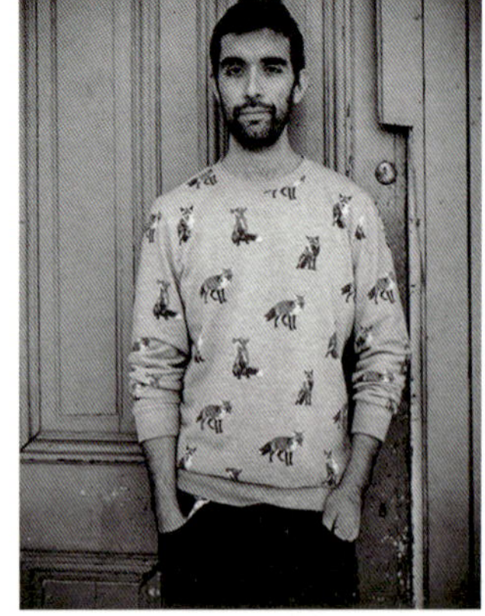

Artist/ Caiozzama

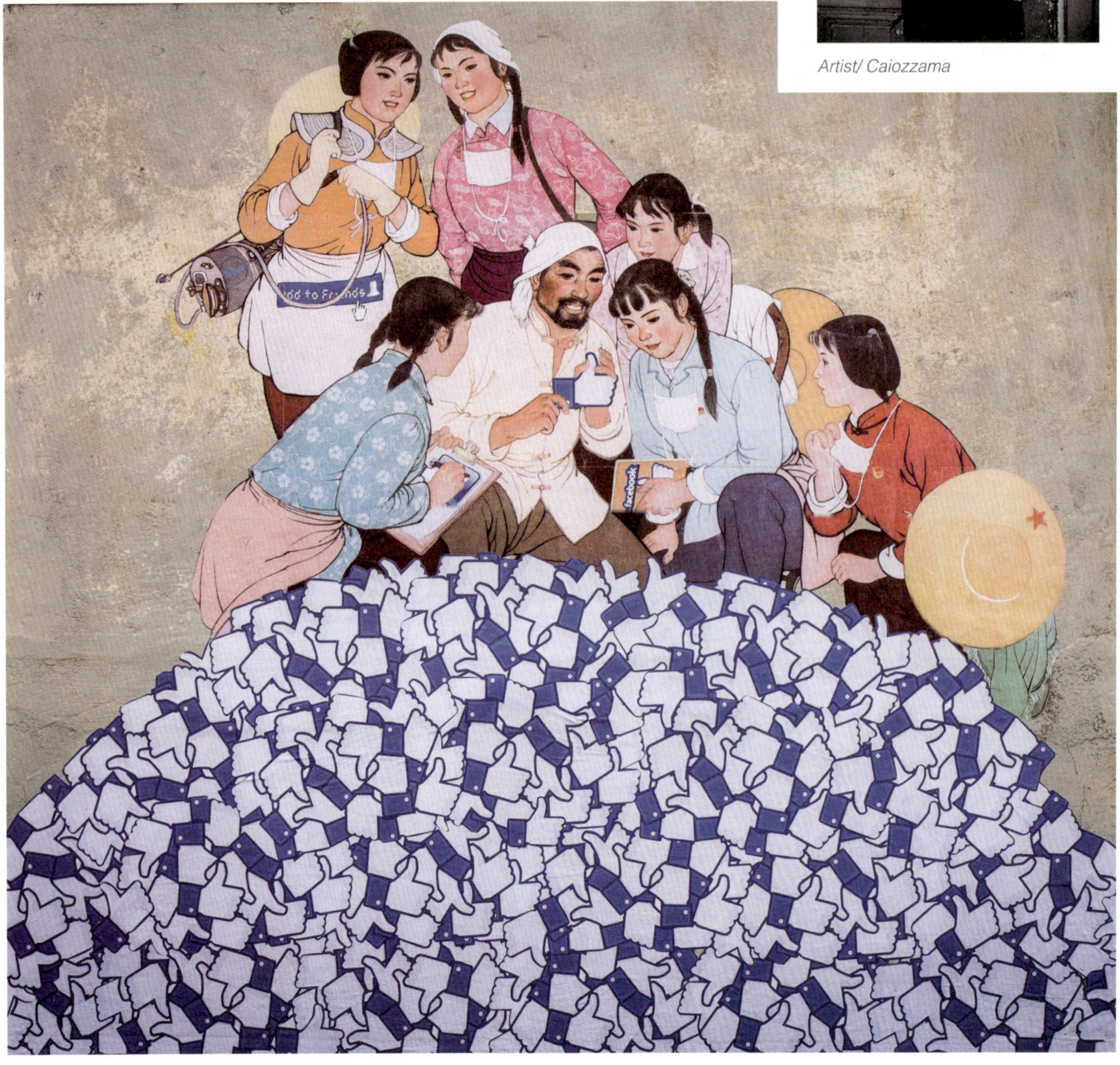

Q1: What inspired you to start making paste-ups? Street art has many forms, so why paste-ups?

I am a professional photographer, which has required me to walk around cities to collect materials. When I noticed paste-up works on the streets, it just dawned on me right away that this is for me. The more I got to know the techniques of pasting up, the more I found this art form compatible with my photography career. Through street art, the photographs I took over the years now have another dimension of life.

Q3: Your works often satirize the Internet obsession, but you never live without the Internet and WiFi yourself. What is your opinion towards Internet then?

The internet is a wonderful tool that opened a world of infinite possibilities. That's for sure, but at the same time, it has very bad sides. I consider myself an Internet addict, and it is because I am obsessed with Internet that I fully understand the positive and negative influences it has on me and almost everyone. It is also a way of mocking myself. And that's why I created works that criticize this obsession.

Q2: In other interviews you have described street art as ephemeral. Then why do you spend time checking out if they are still there and record their lifespans?

Unexpected things happen on the streets. Everyone feels they have a little say in it, and therefore have the right to intervene. I really love recording the changes of my works on the streets because people will react to my works. If they love them, they stop to feel and understand. That's great. If they don't like them, they break, scratch, tear up, or destroy them completely. That's fine as well. Watching my works interacting with others is really interesting in that it means my works are no longer just mine, they are works created by so many others.

Q4: Your works often employ the technique of collage. How did you come up with the idea of using collage?

I was on a trip to Paris once, and I found some street art using this technique. I was never good at drawing, and discovering this technique is like opening a new world for me. It is the perfect technique for me.

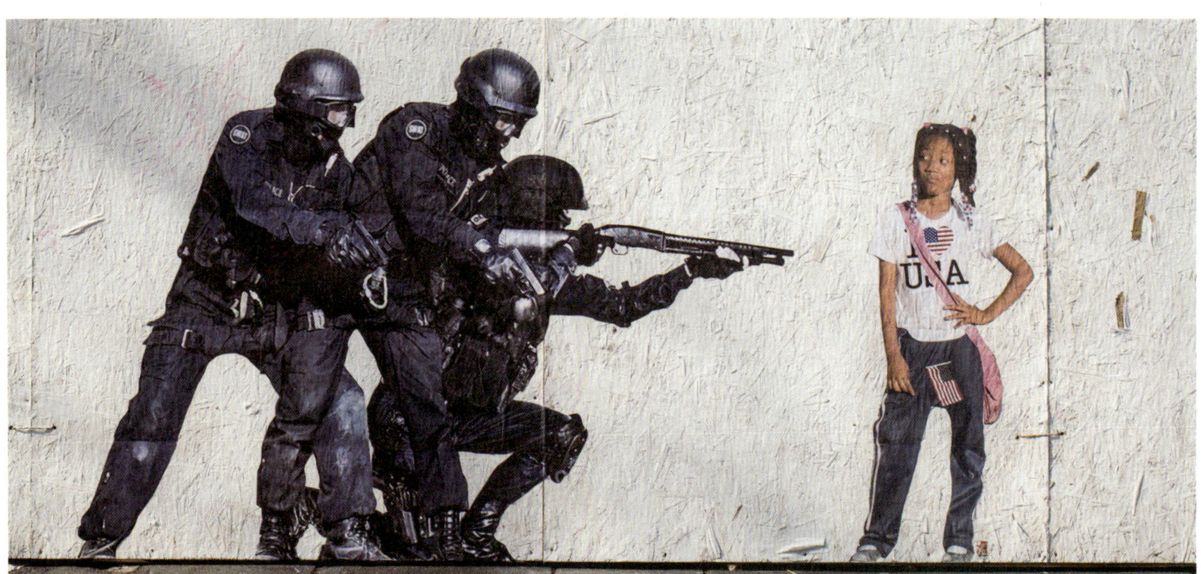

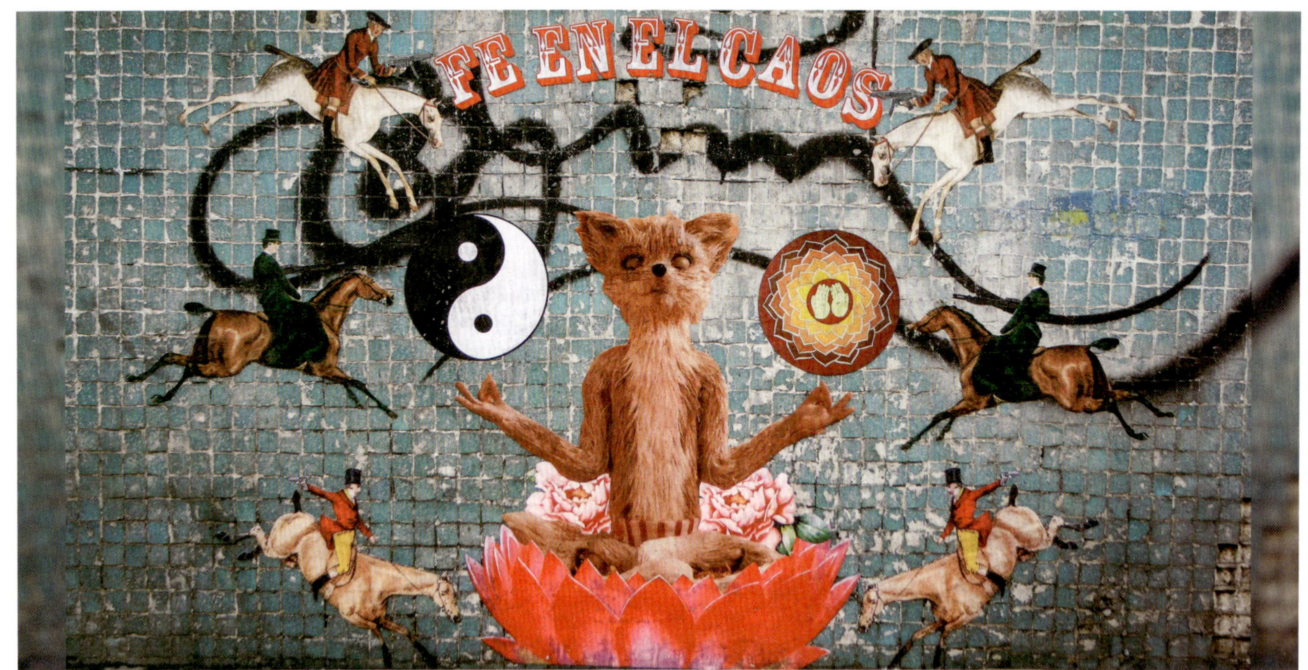

Q5: You have mentioned that you created works by adopting the point of view of the passers-by. How do you do that?

I try to make my works look real. I look for images that give the impression that they are really there from the point of view of passers-by. I guess it is an obsession that comes from my photography career.

Q6: Compared with other forms of street art, do you think paste-ups employ the least techniques of creation?

I think techniques are the least important part of the creation itself. The most important thing is what you want to say, and in what kind of form you want to present it. I was asked so many times how to create works like mine. I have no problem sharing with them, but techniques are like tools. You can have the best tools, but it doesn't mean you can create the best works. I suggest people try as many techniques as possible, and see which ones suit the idea the best.

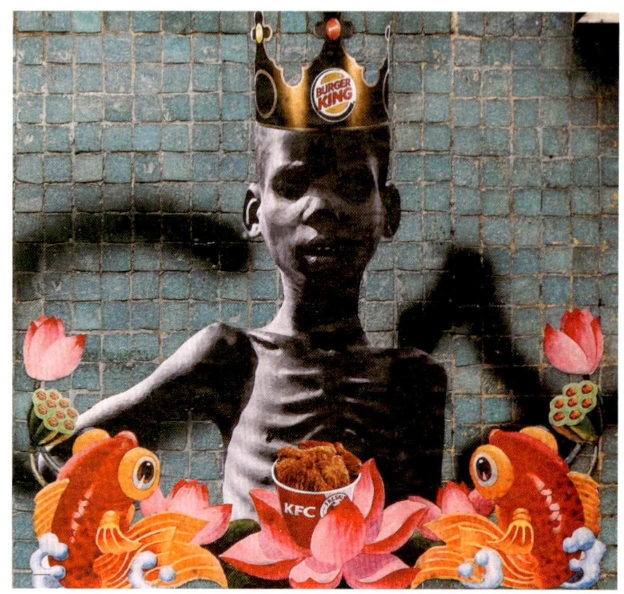

Q7: You have been to quite a few countries. Can you share with us what the street art scenes are in England, France, Chile, and China?

England has one of the best street art scenes in the world. I am a fan of Banksy myself, and I can always discover many other talented artists in the UK. In France, there are cities full of graffiti, and the styles cover a very wide range, from basic tags of early stages to amazingly complex murals. Chile has a welcoming atmosphere for street artists, and thus nurtures a large group of artists with superb techniques and awesome ideas. In China, I saw very little street art. The laws there are very strict, and works with the theme of protest and the like are hardly seen. Most works there are only for decorative purpose.

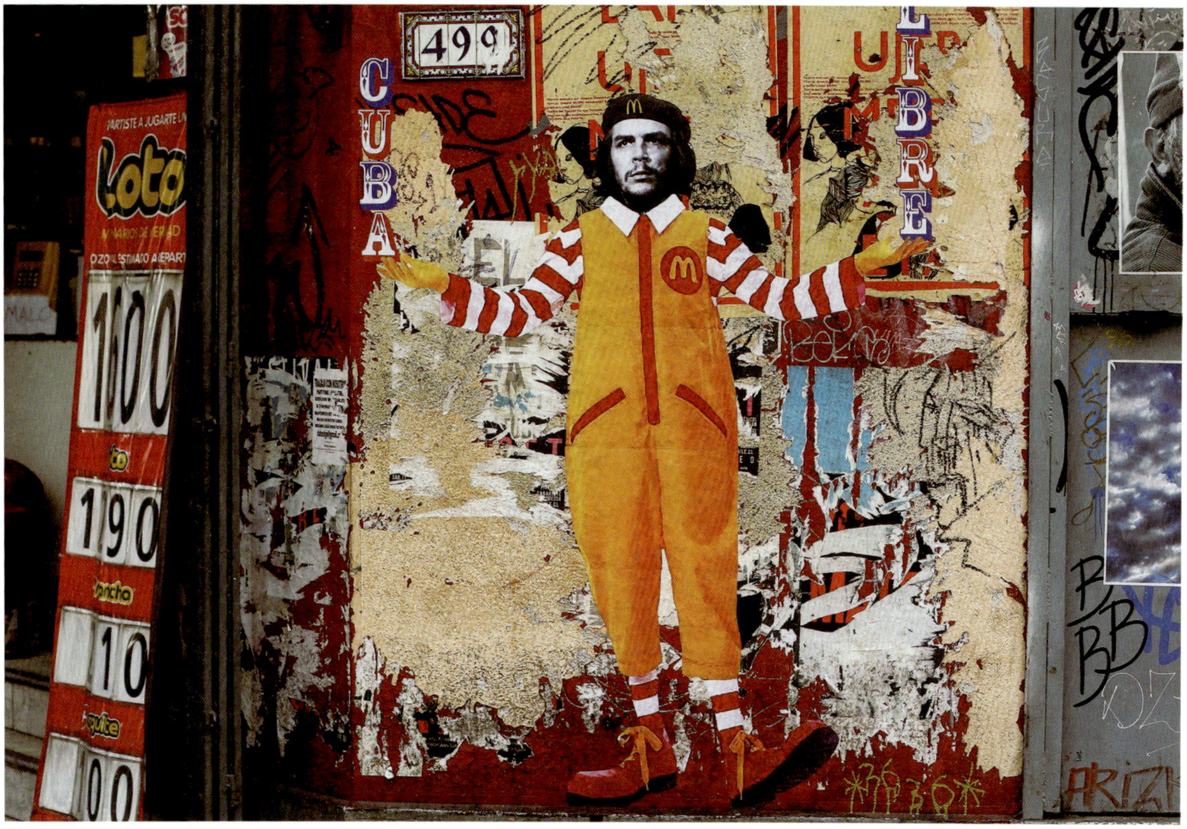

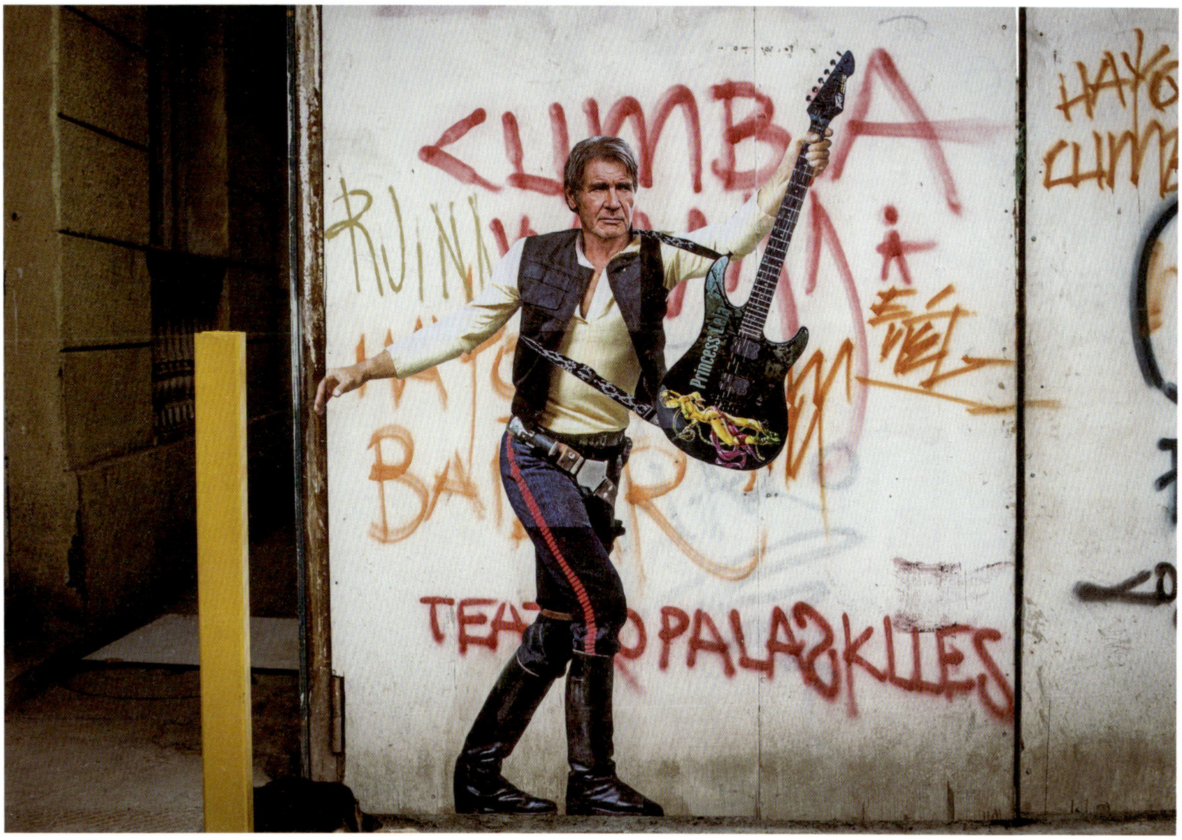

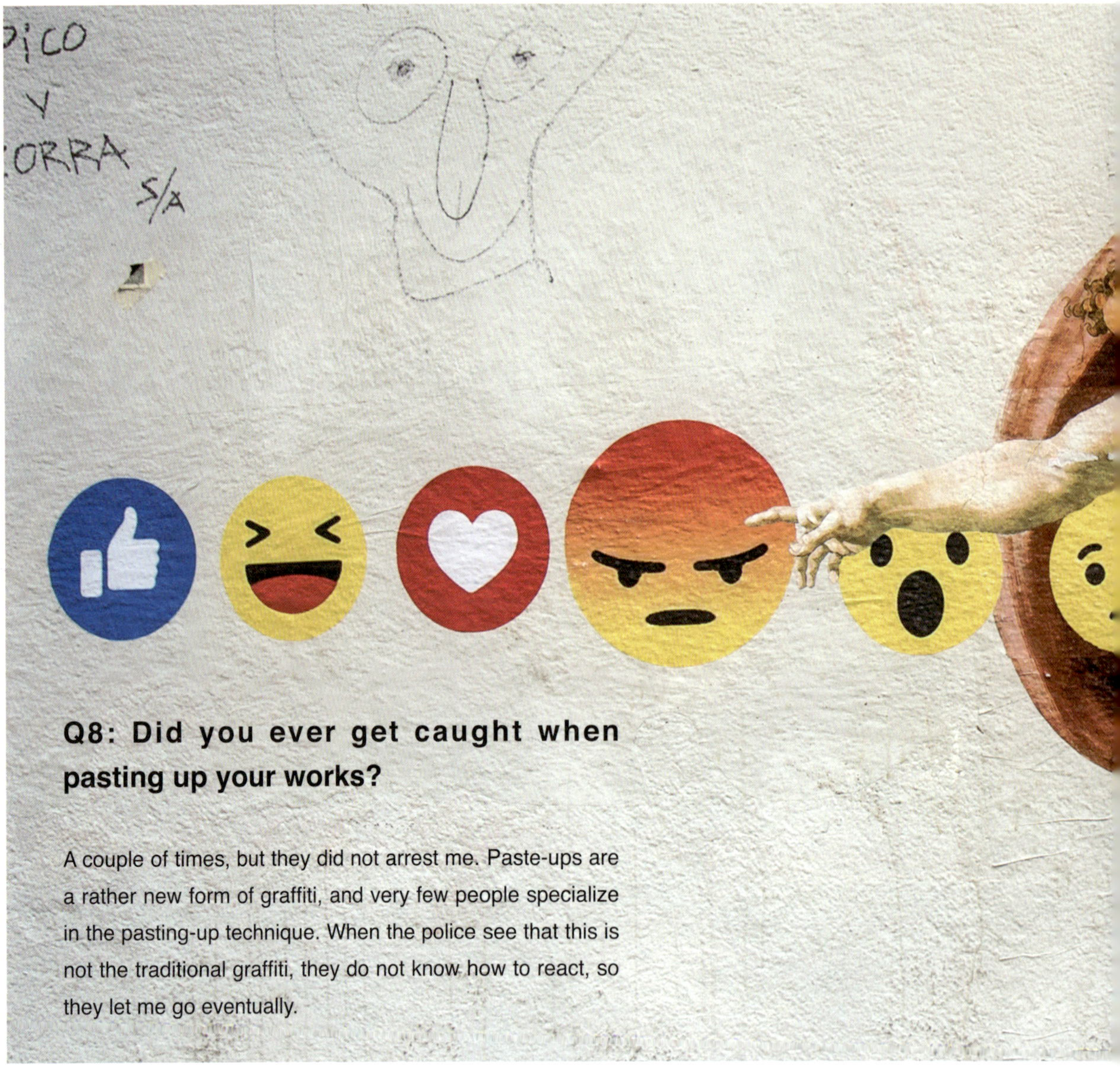

Q8: Did you ever get caught when pasting up your works?

A couple of times, but they did not arrest me. Paste-ups are a rather new form of graffiti, and very few people specialize in the pasting-up technique. When the police see that this is not the traditional graffiti, they do not know how to react, so they let me go eventually.

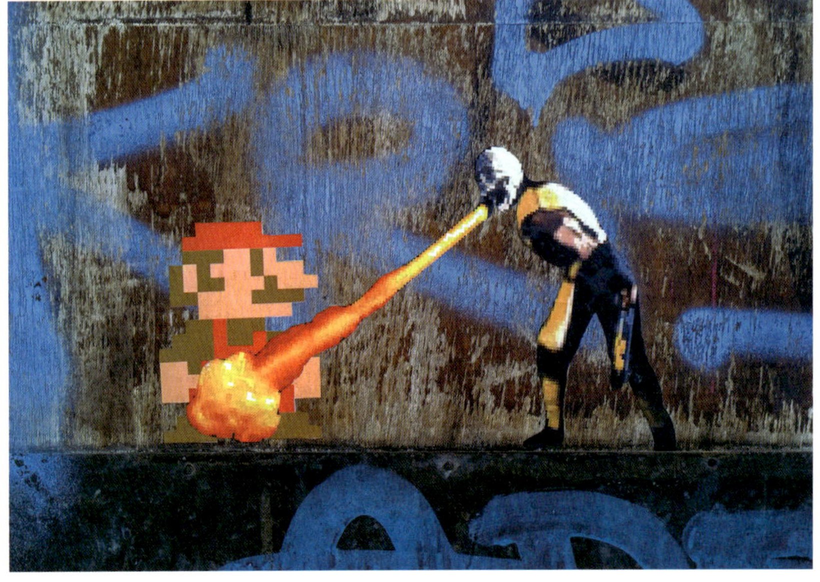

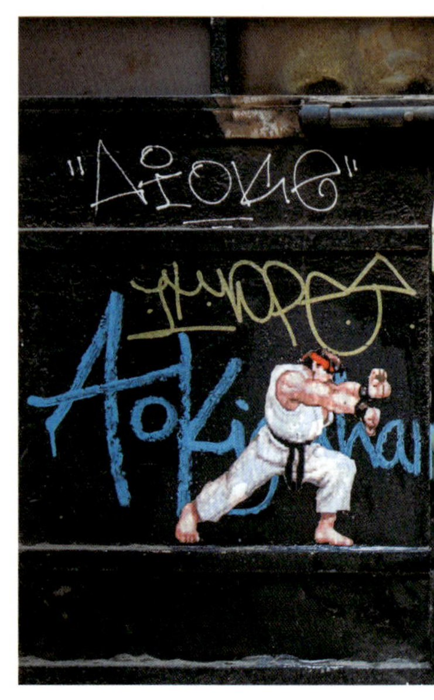

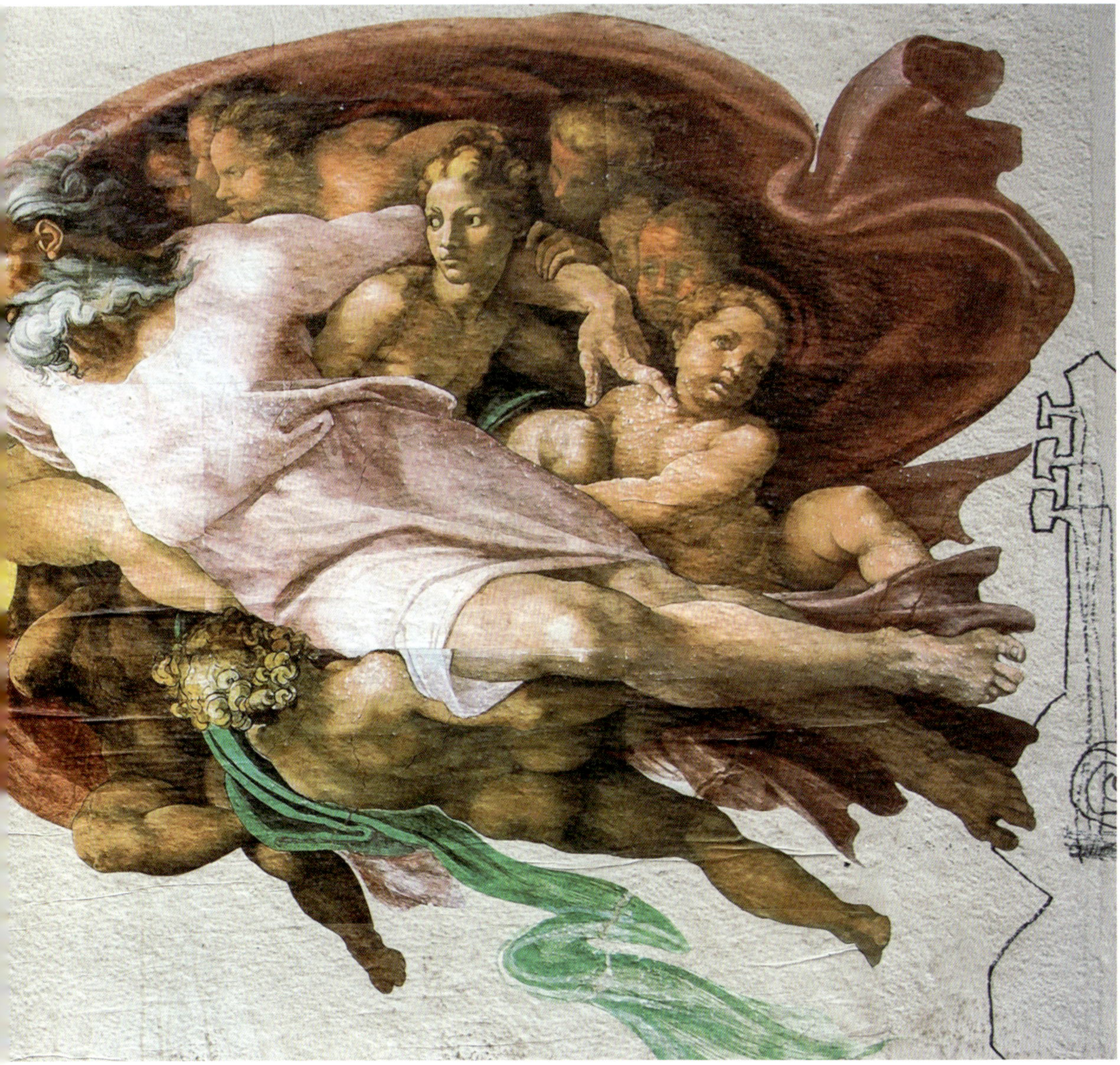

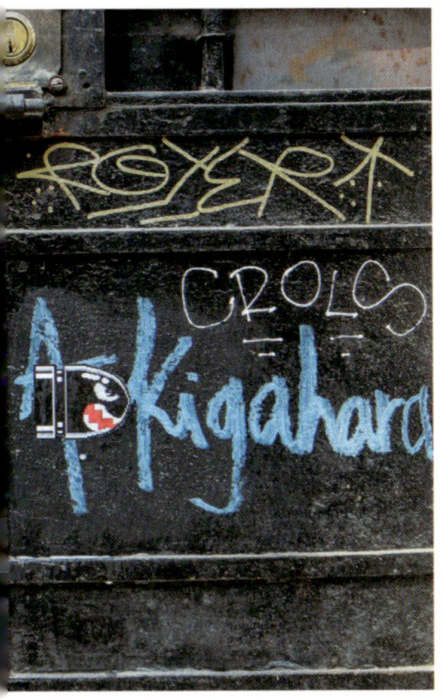

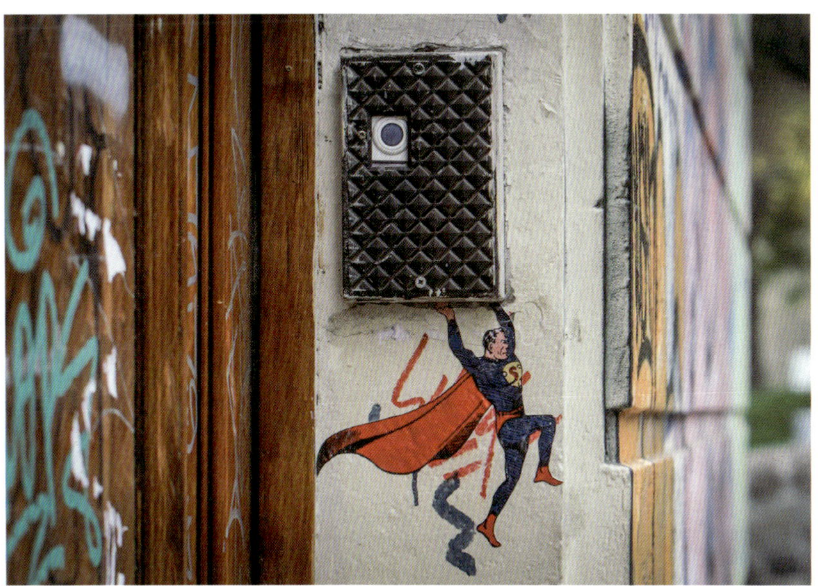

CONTEMPORARY GRAFFITI STYLES

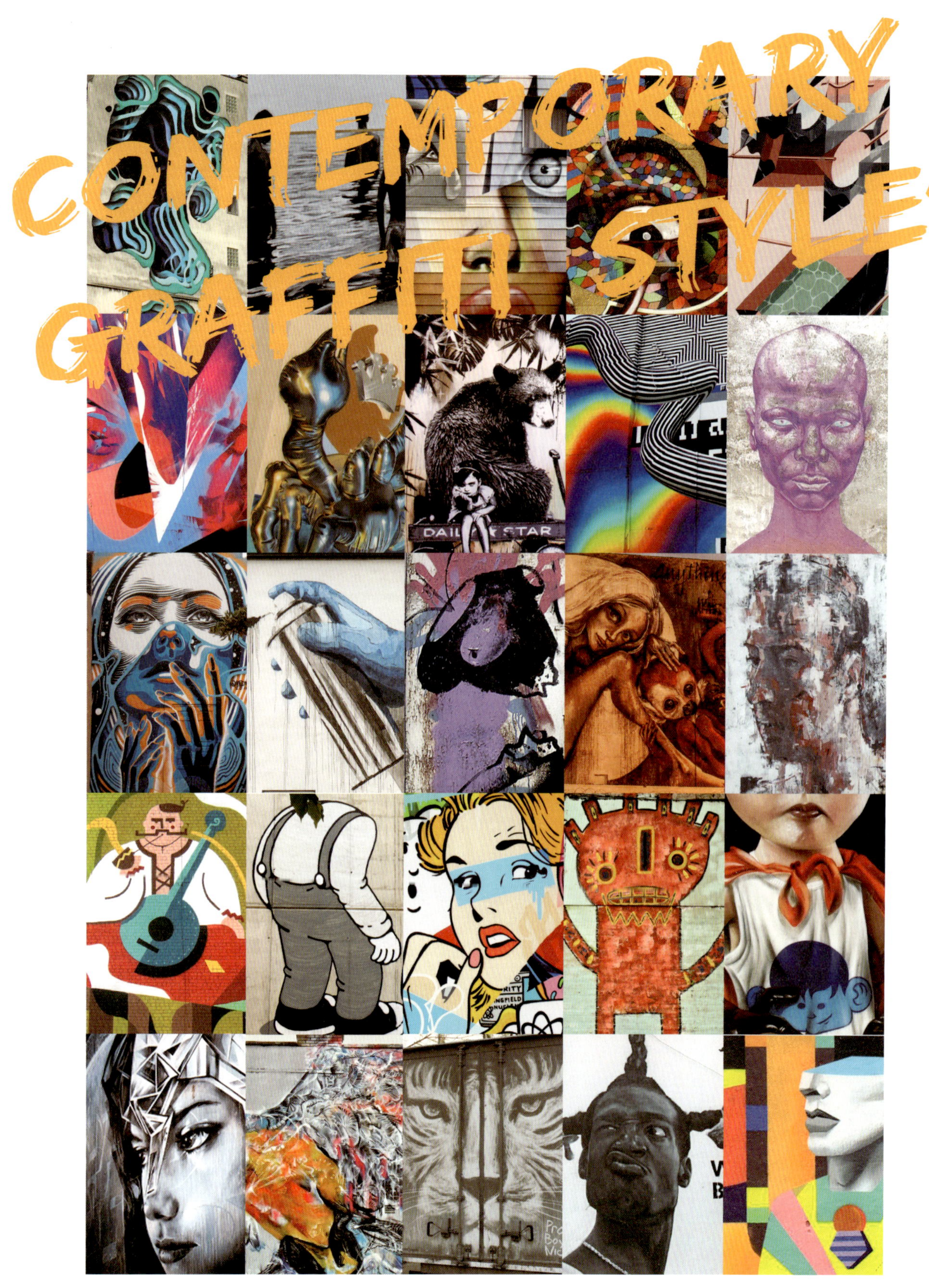

CONTEMPORARY GRAFFITI STYLES

REALISTIC CARTOON ABSTRACT

3-DIMENTIONAL REVERSE

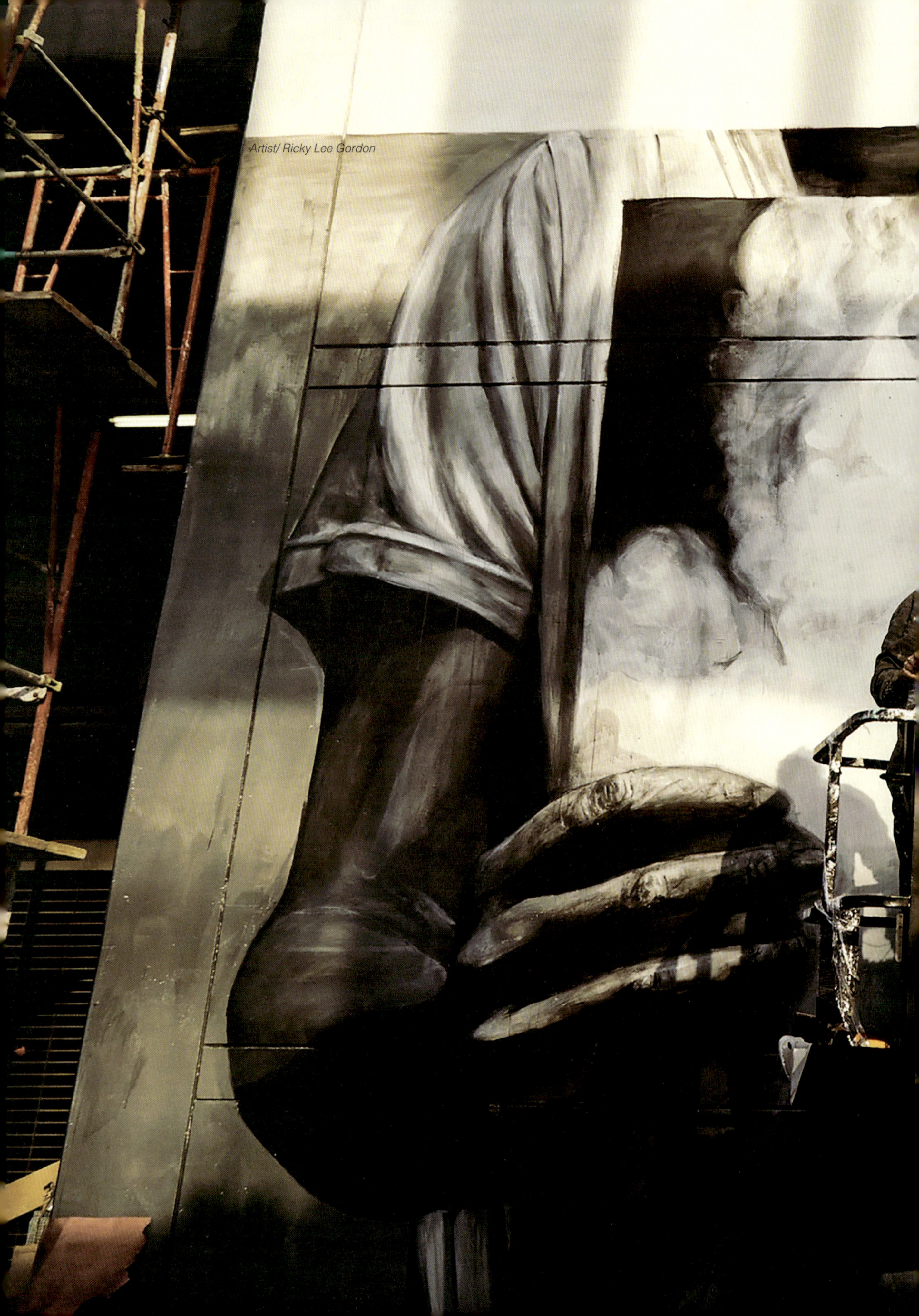

Artist/ Ricky Lee Gordon

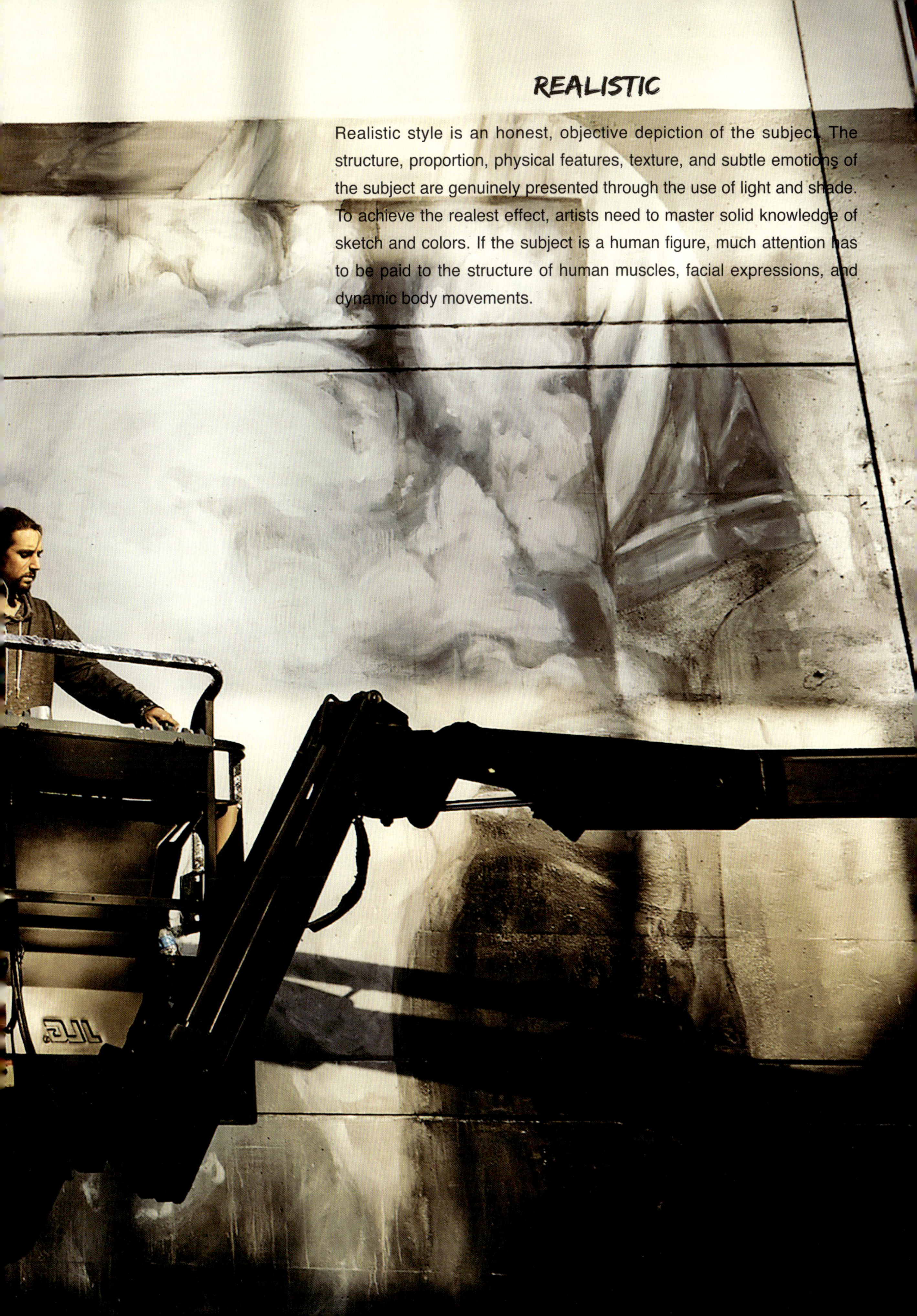

REALISTIC

Realistic style is an honest, objective depiction of the subject. The structure, proportion, physical features, texture, and subtle emotions of the subject are genuinely presented through the use of light and shade. To achieve the realest effect, artists need to master solid knowledge of sketch and colors. If the subject is a human figure, much attention has to be paid to the structure of human muscles, facial expressions, and dynamic body movements.

Inspired by his experiences in meditation and Buddhist Dharma, Ricky Lee Gordon creates street art works by exploring the nature of non-duality and interconnectedness and focusing on bringing to light relevant social issues and universal truths. His intention with his murals is to create artwork that has a connection to the people and places in which he is painting.

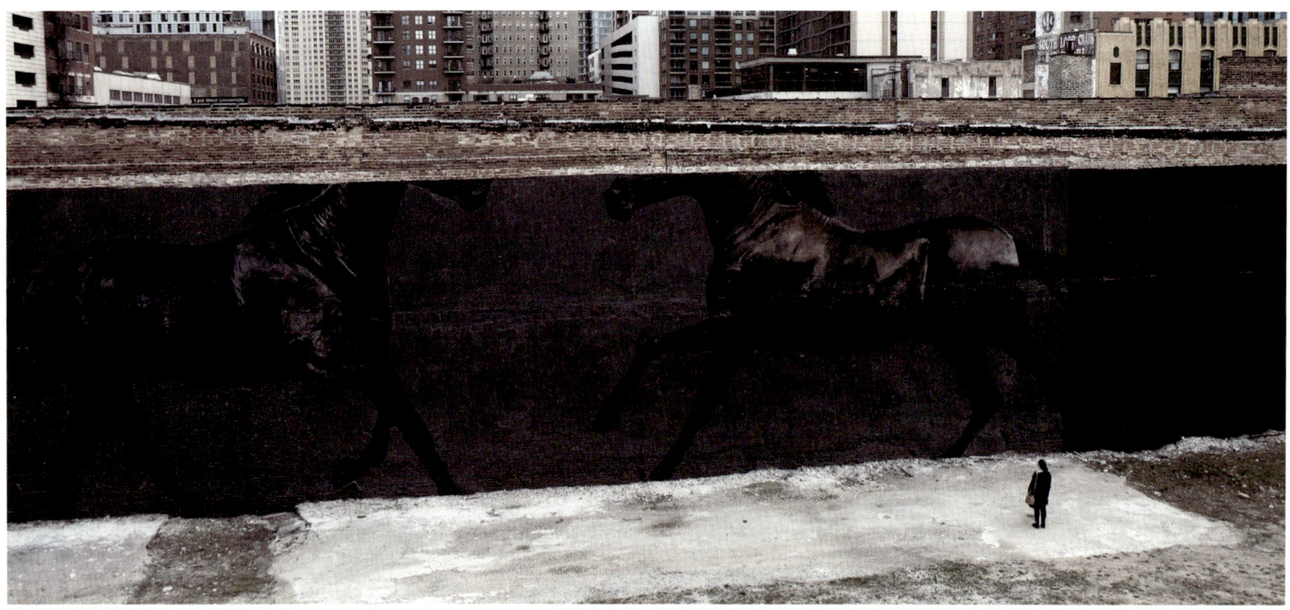

I Am You, You Are Me
@Chicago, USA 2016

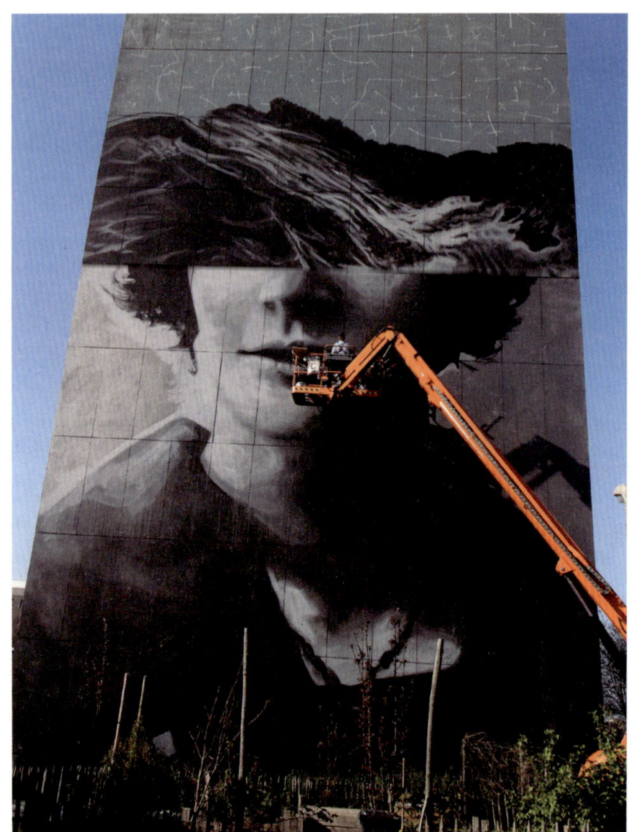

Throw A Drop Of Water Into The Sea To Prevent It From Drying Up
@Oostende, Belgium 2017 ©Sascha Bogajev

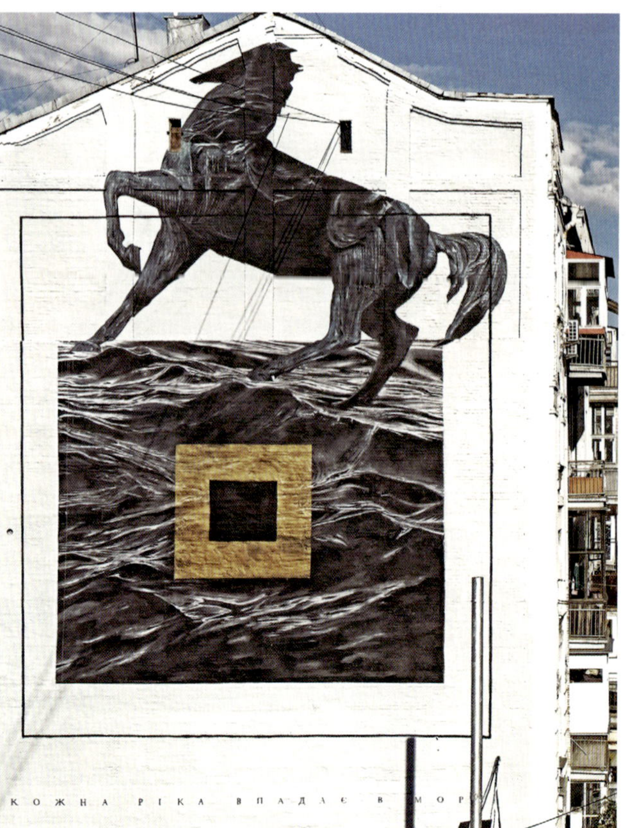

Every River Flows To The Sea
@Kiev, Ukraine 2016

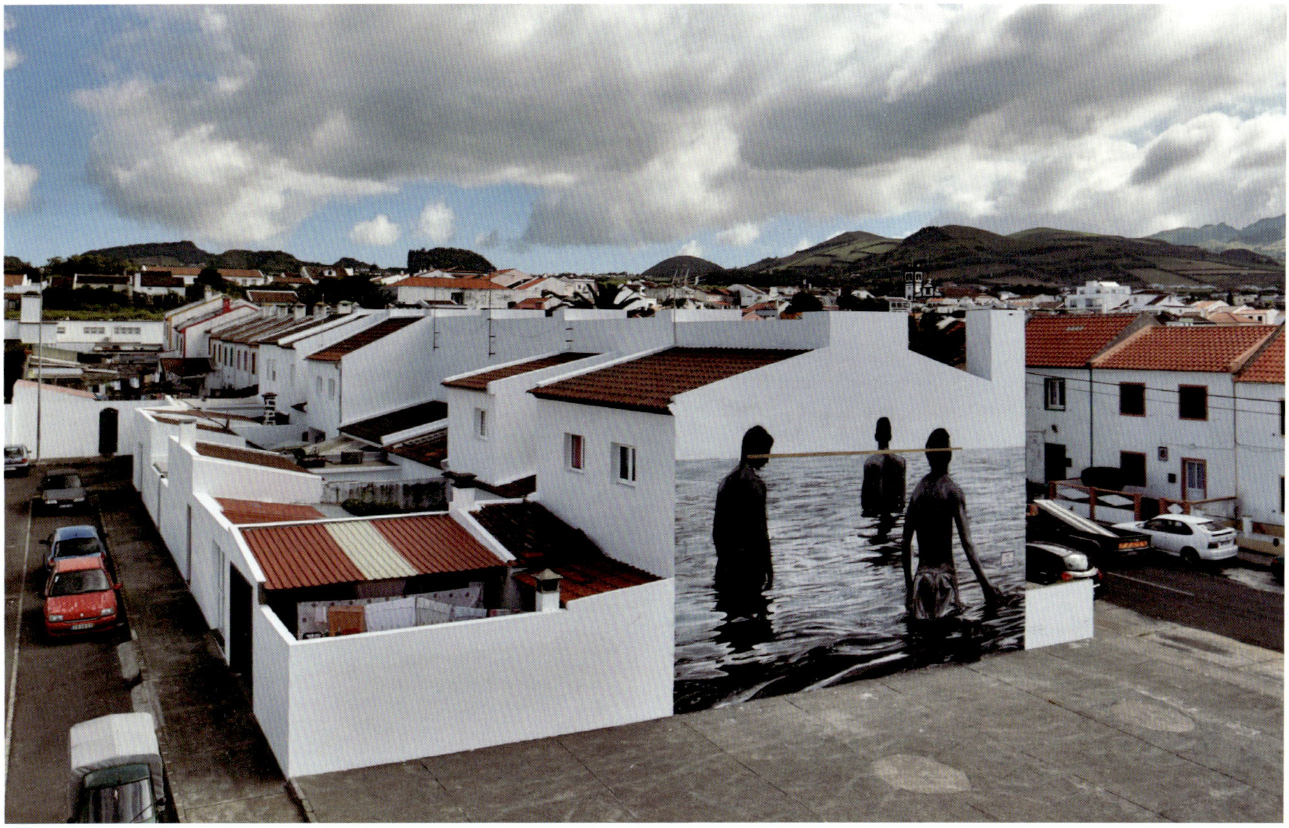

The Road of Solidarity
@Azores, Portugal 2015 *©Rui Soarez*

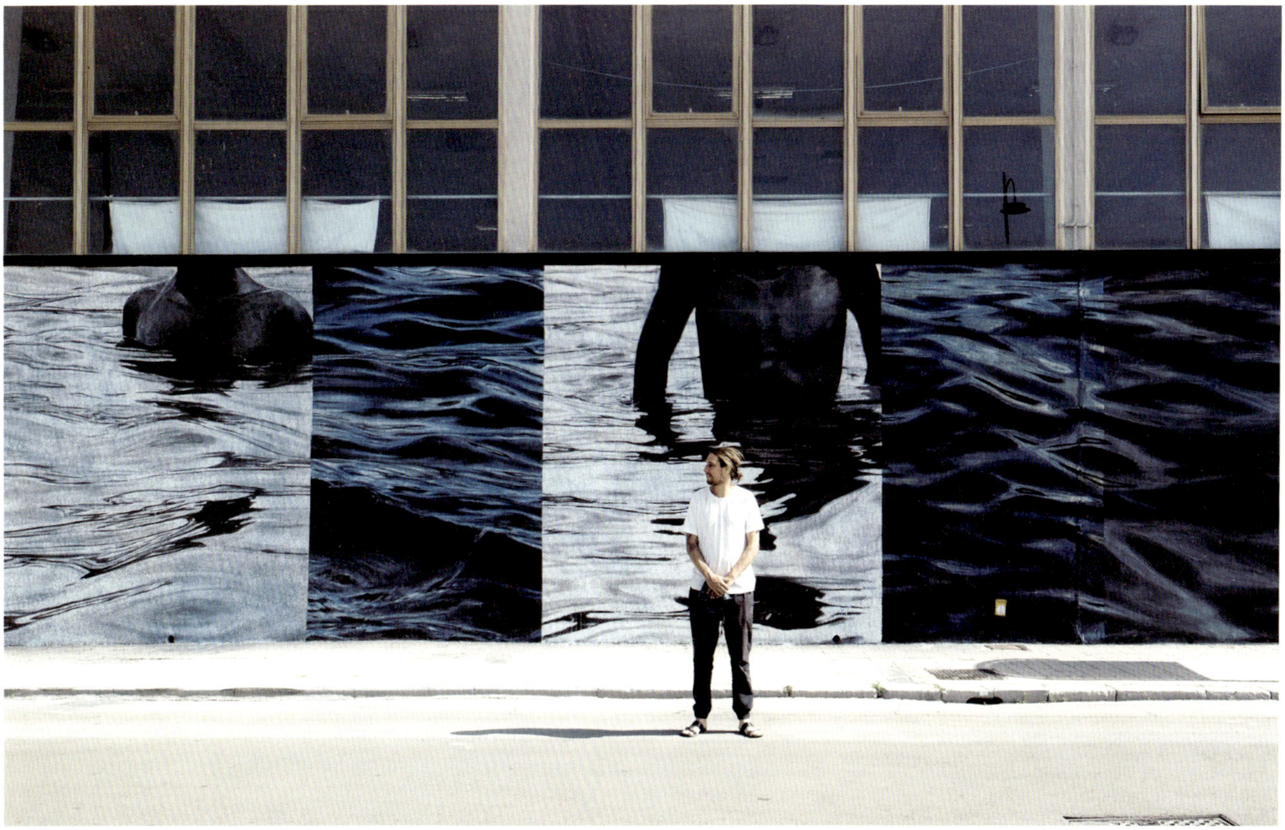

The Memory Of Water
@Gaeta, Italy 2016

Ernest Zacharevic is a Lithuanian-born artist and is based in Penang, Malaysia now. With his primary interest in the relationship between art and the urban landscape, he takes reference from artistic disciplines of oil painting, stencil and spray, installation and sculpture, and created mural works of vintage feel and naivety.

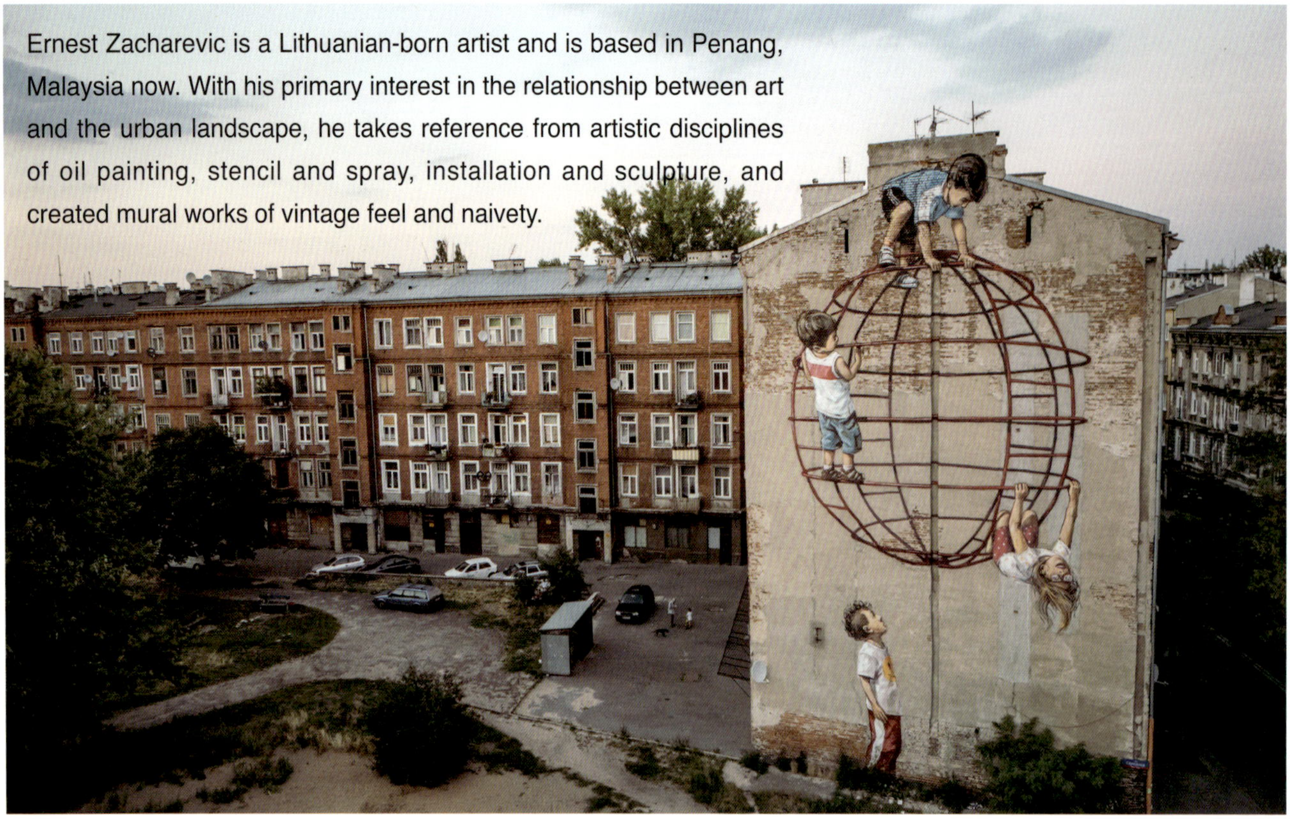

Untitled
Created for the Street Art Doping Festival
@Warsaw, Poland 2015 ©Maciej Kruger

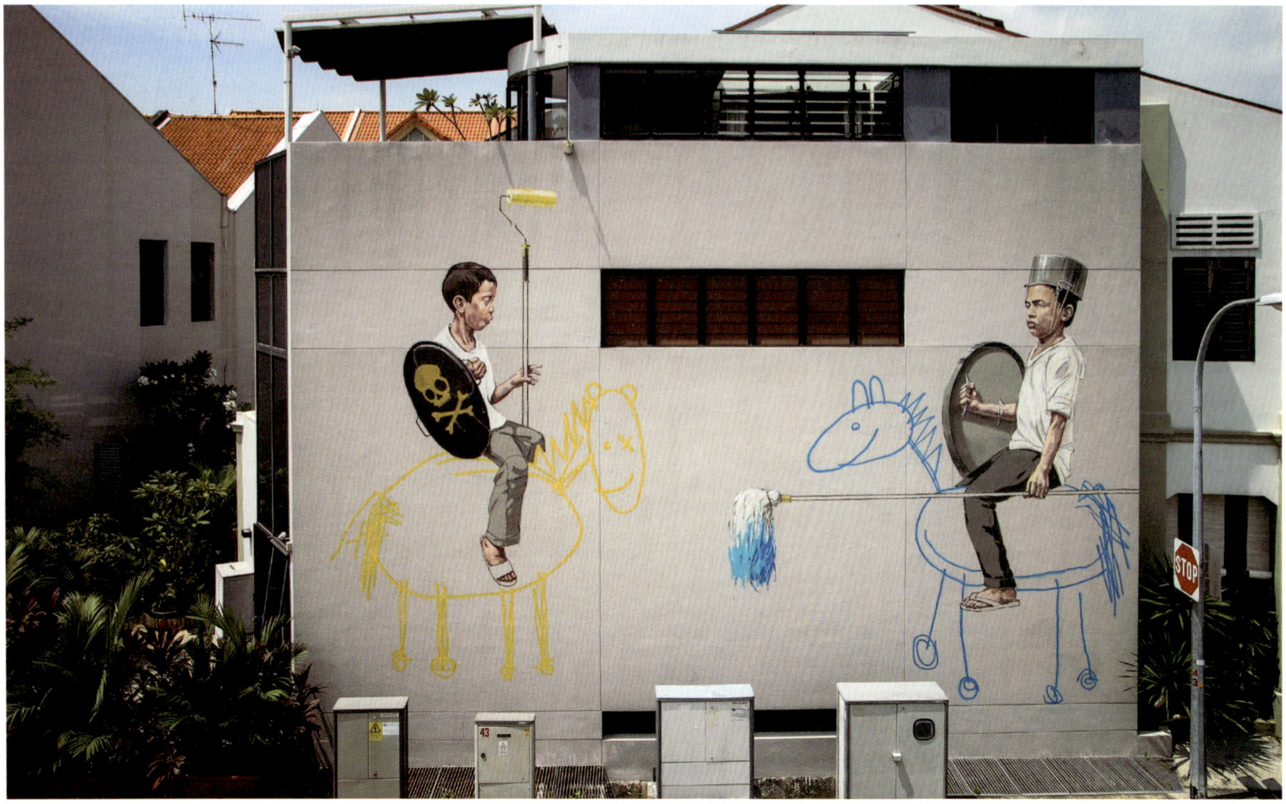

Style Wars
@Singapore 2013 ©Ernest Zacharevic

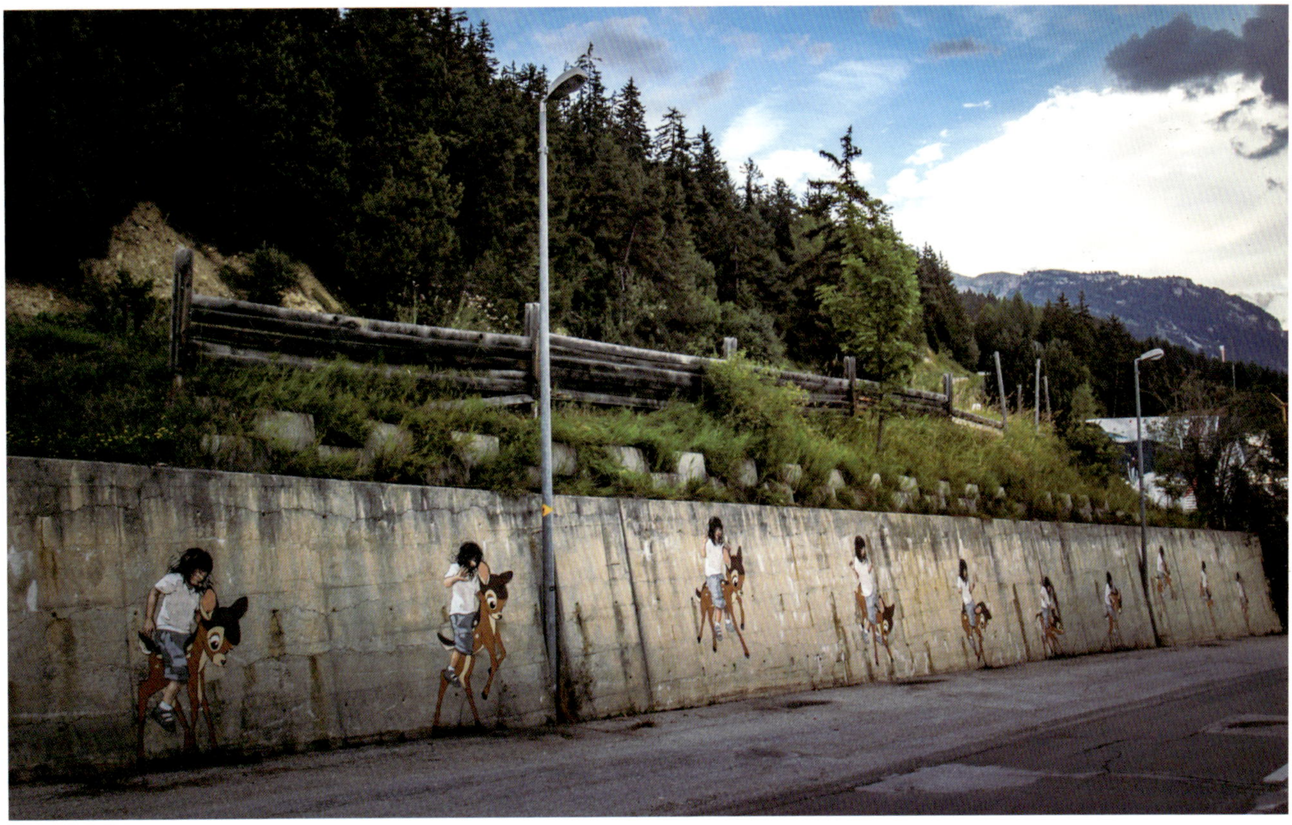

Bambi on Ice
Created for the Vision Arts Festival
@Crans-Montana, Switzerland 2016 ©Ernest Zacharevic

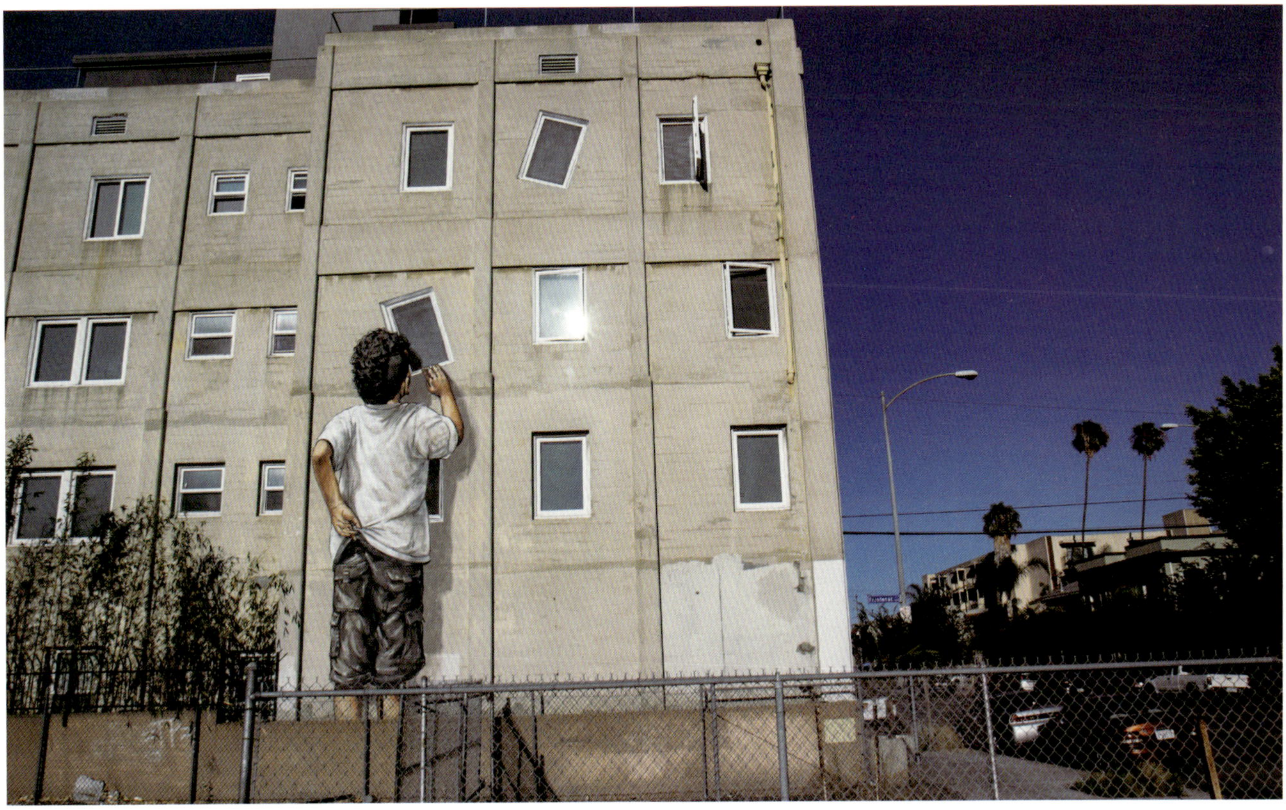

Untitled
Created for POW! WOW! Long Beach Festival
@Long Beach, USA 2016 ©Ernest Zacharevic

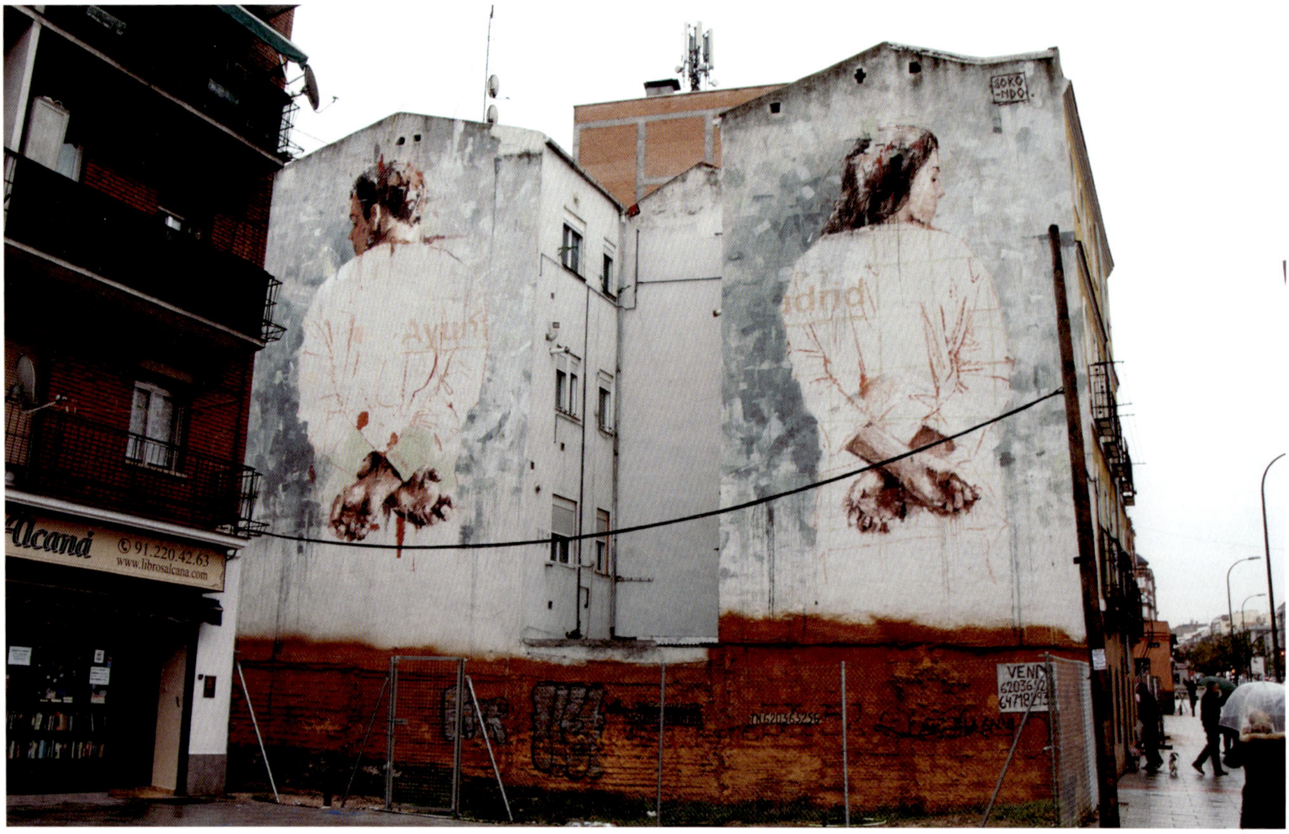

Untitled
@Madrid, Spain 2013
Created for Proyecto Paisaje Tetuàn, Madrid ©Fernando Escribano

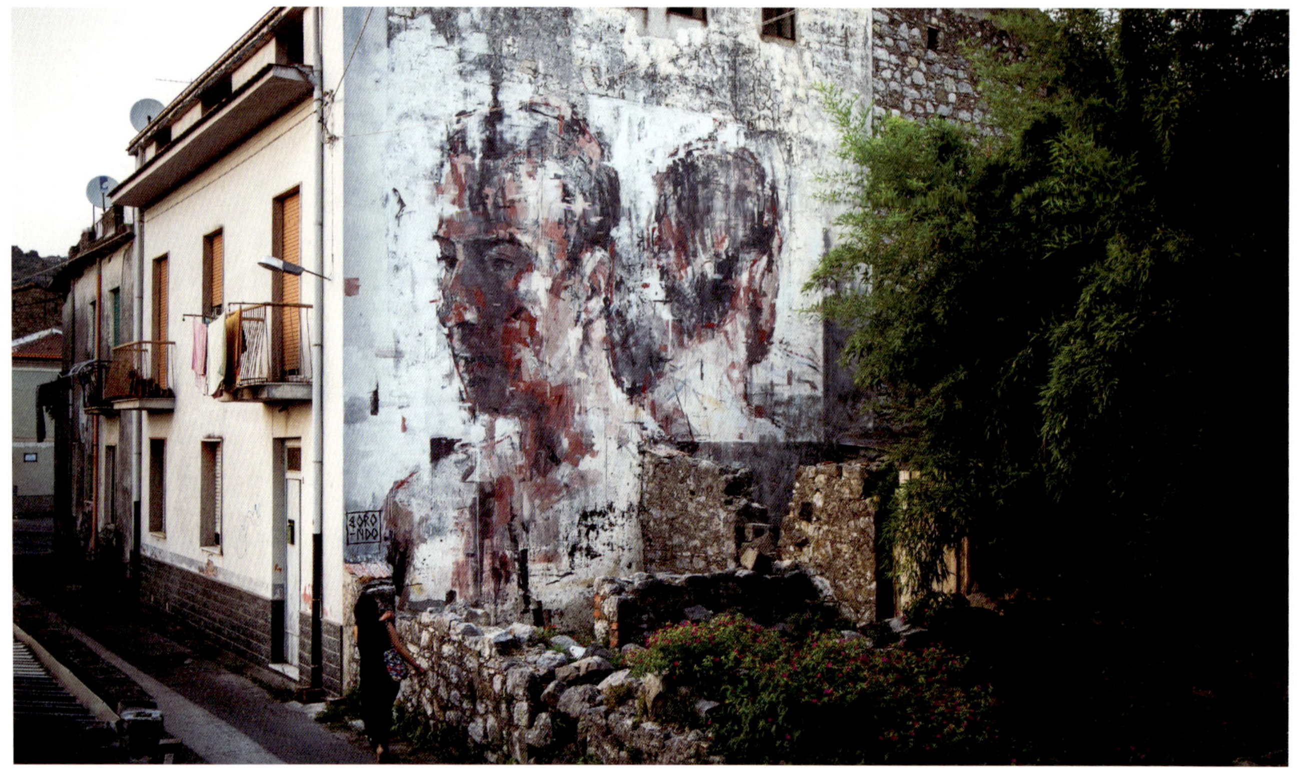

Untitled
Created for Oltre il Muro Festival, Sapri
@Sapri, Italy 2013 ©Fabiano Caputo

The notion of living in the here and now enables Gonzalo Borondo to recognize a good means of communication, take advantage of the public nature of the great walls that host his works and the surrounding space, and involve himself in the stories he tells through painting. As a result, his sincere works are always somehow reach every audience's heart.

Les Trois Ages
Created for La Nuit Blanche, Paris
@Paris, France 2014
©Jérôme Thomas

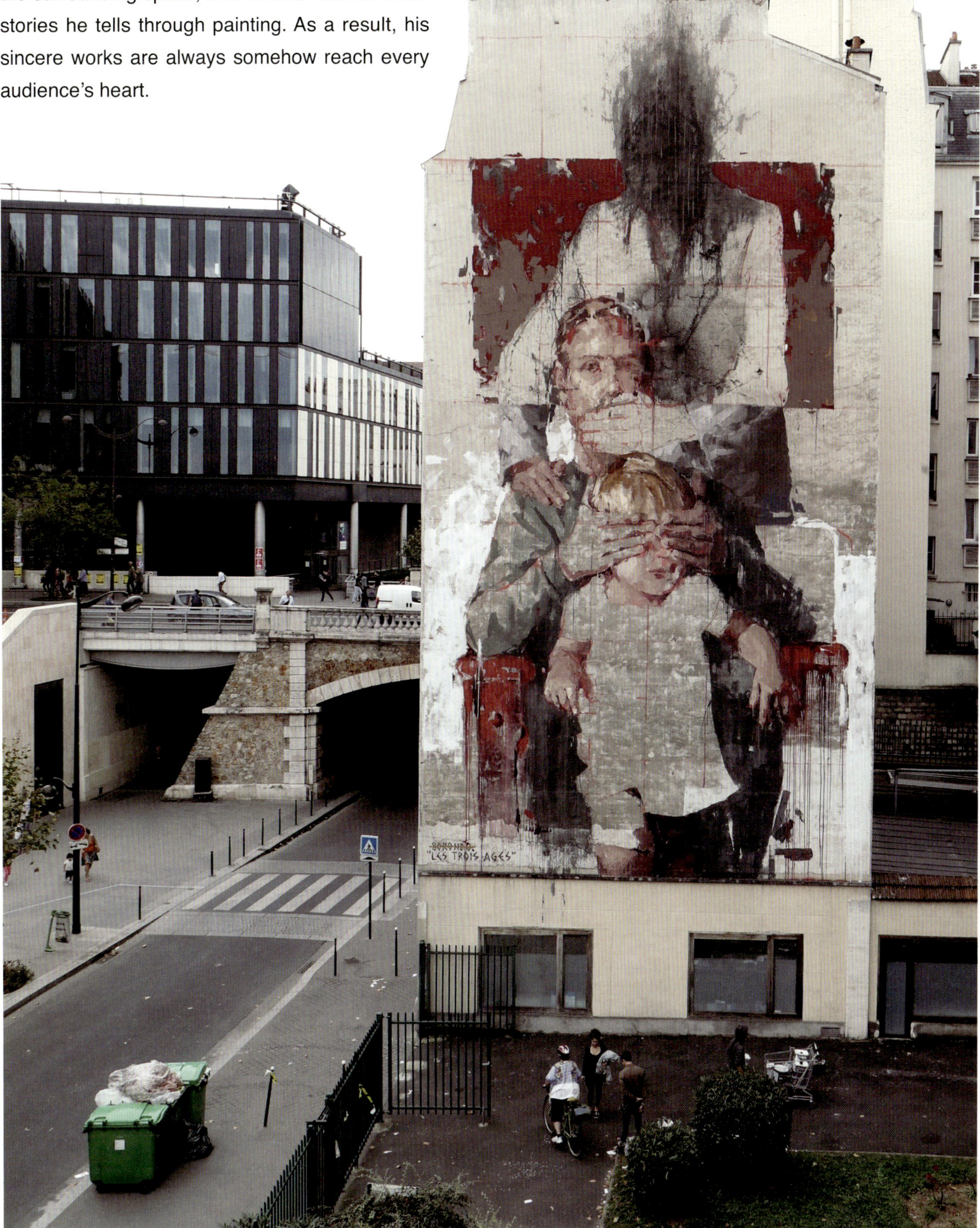

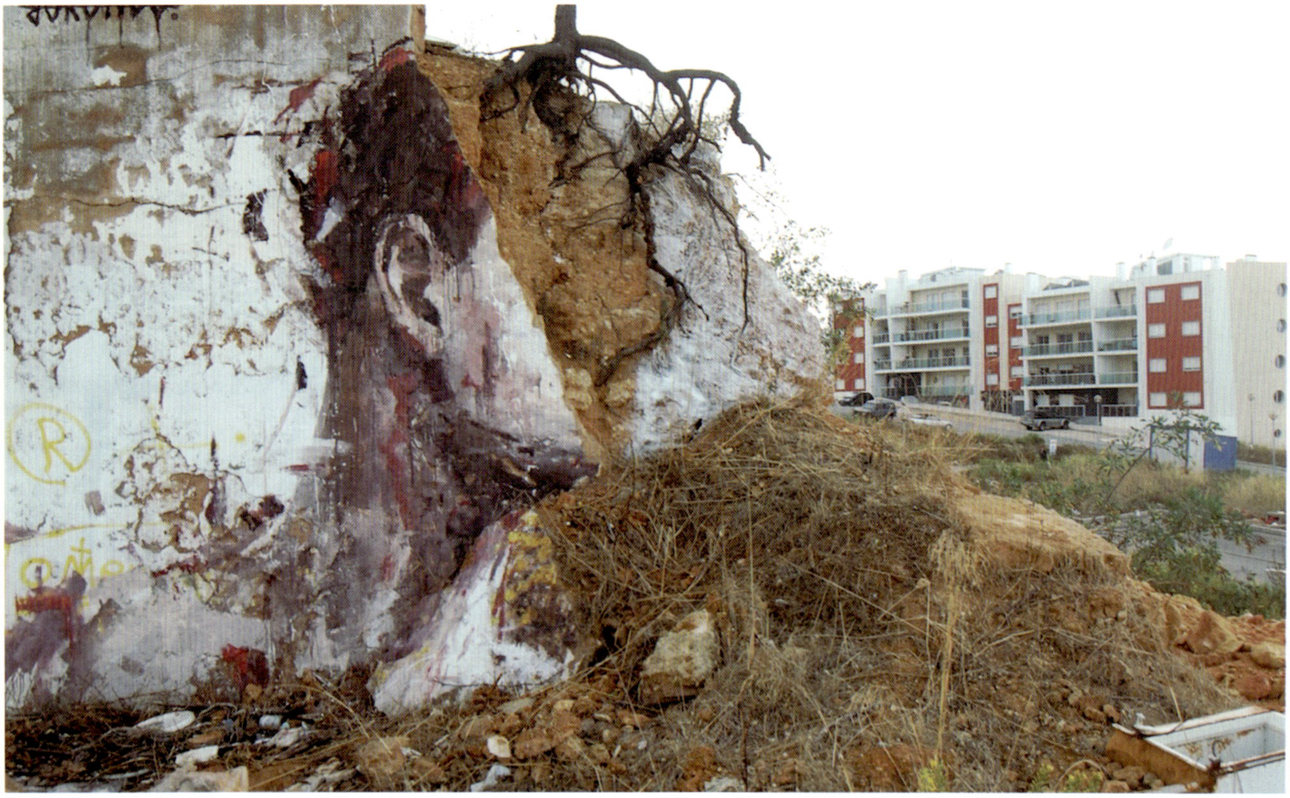

Untitled
@Lagos, Portugal 2014 ©LAC - Laboratório de Actividades Criativas

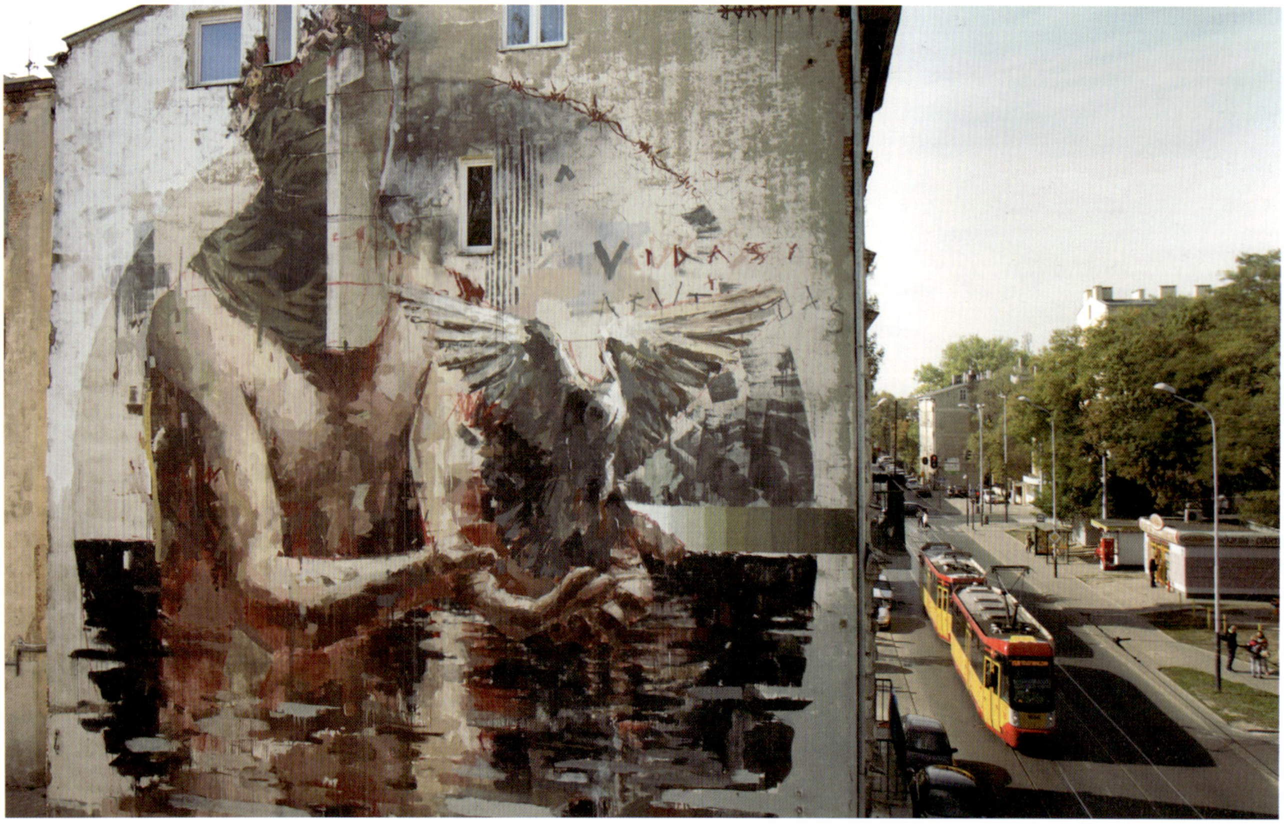

Untitled
Created for the Lodz Mural Festival
@Lodz, Poland 2015 ©Michał Bieżyński (lodzmurals)

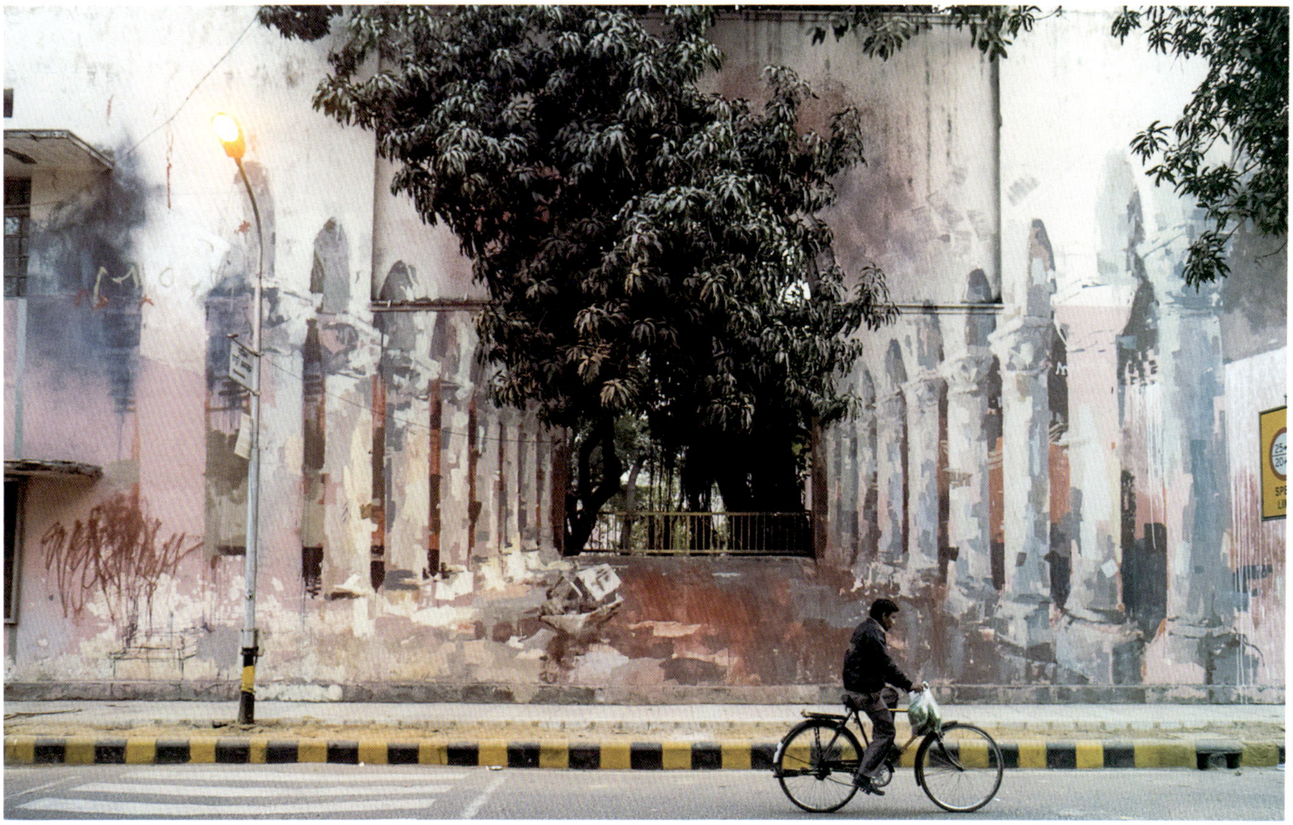

The Origin of the World
@Delhi, India 2016 ©Naman Saraiya / St+Art Festival

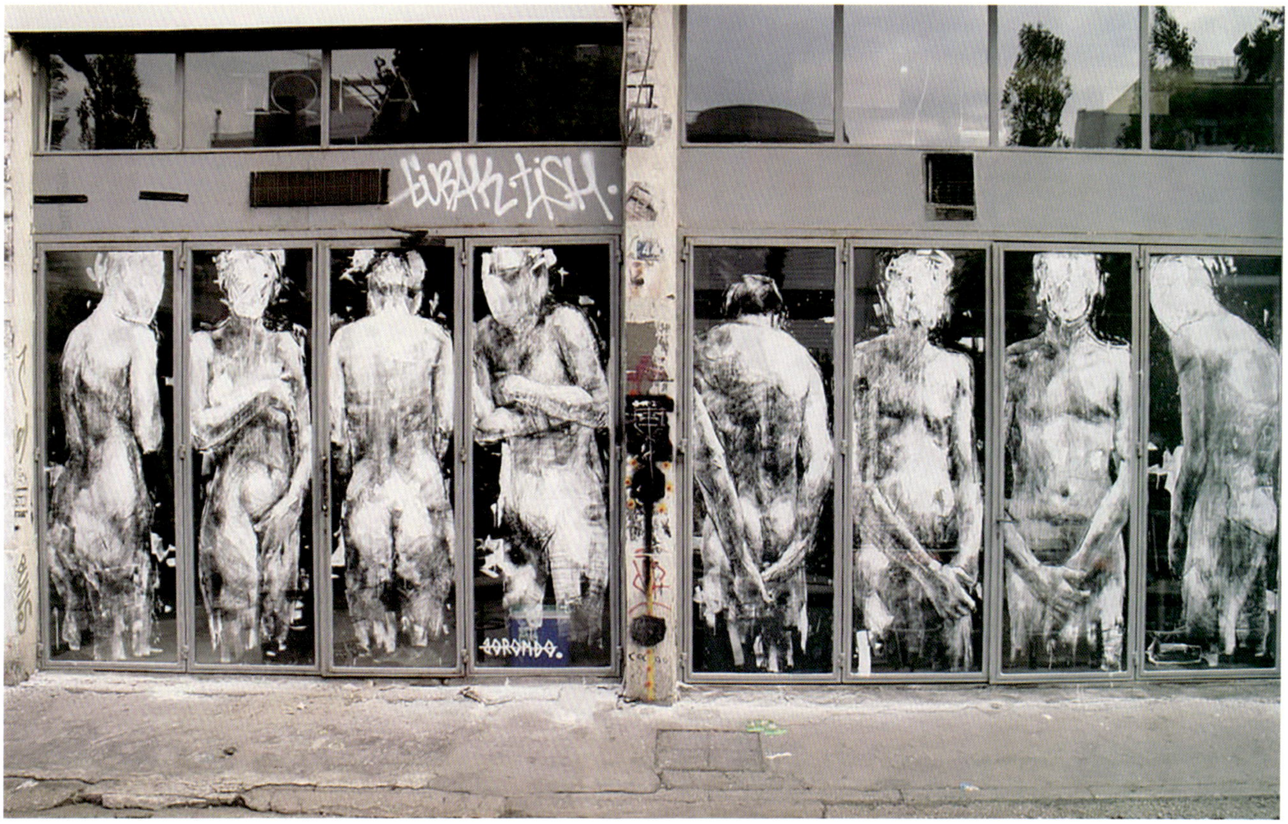

Shame
@Athens, Greece 2013 ©Gonzalo Borondo

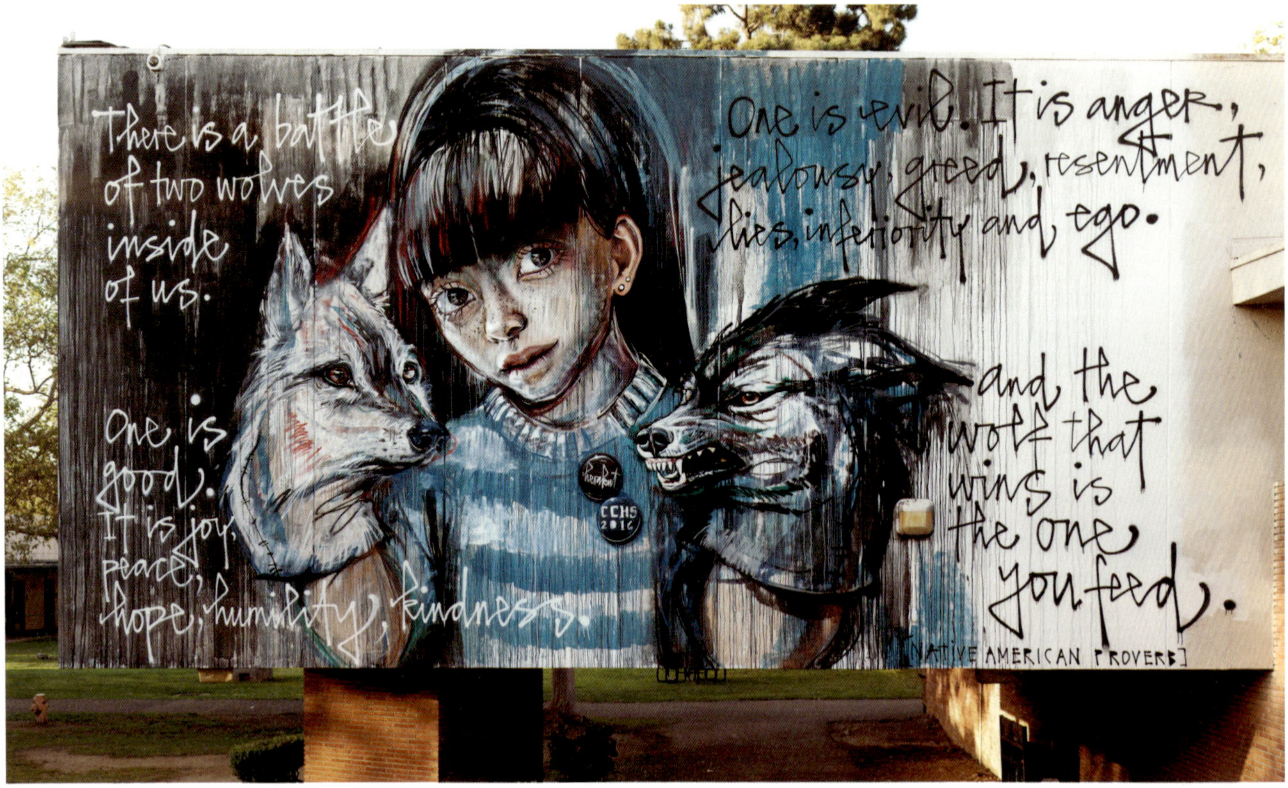

@Culver City CA, USA 2016

The German artists Hera and Akut, both with roots in the graffiti scene, joined forces in 2004 and began their collaboration under the name of Herakut. Their paintings are sensuous, savage, and sometimes lonely. Hera's expressive line-work merges with Akut's photo-realistic details, resulting in an artistic narrative of triumph, hardship, love, and humor.

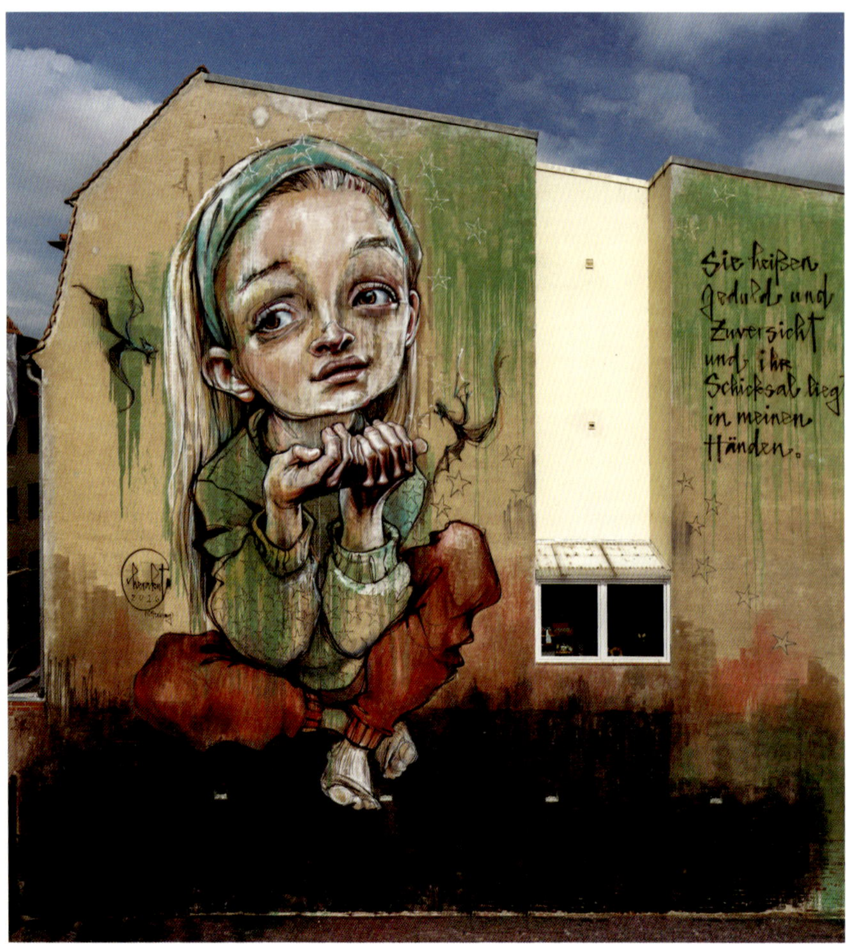

@Wittenberg, Germany 2016

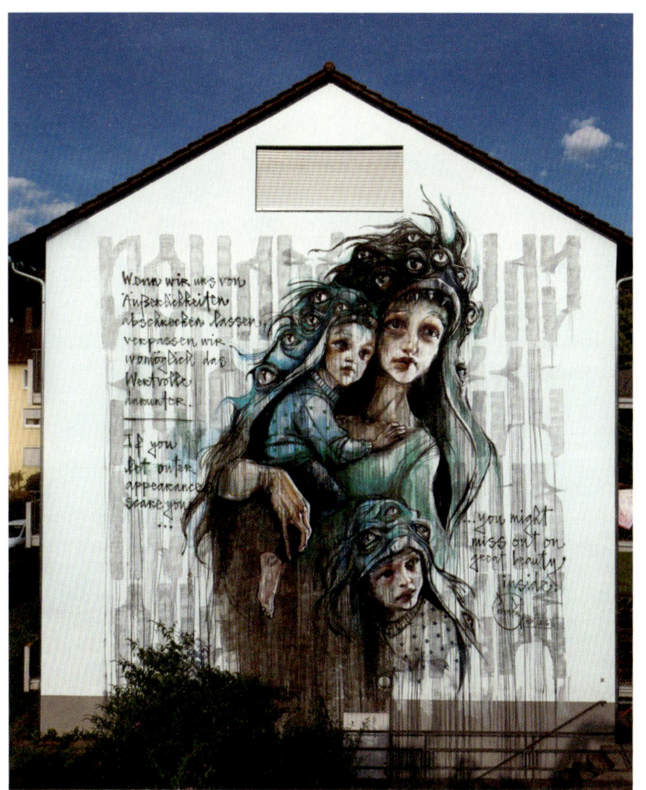

@Heidelberg, Germany 2016

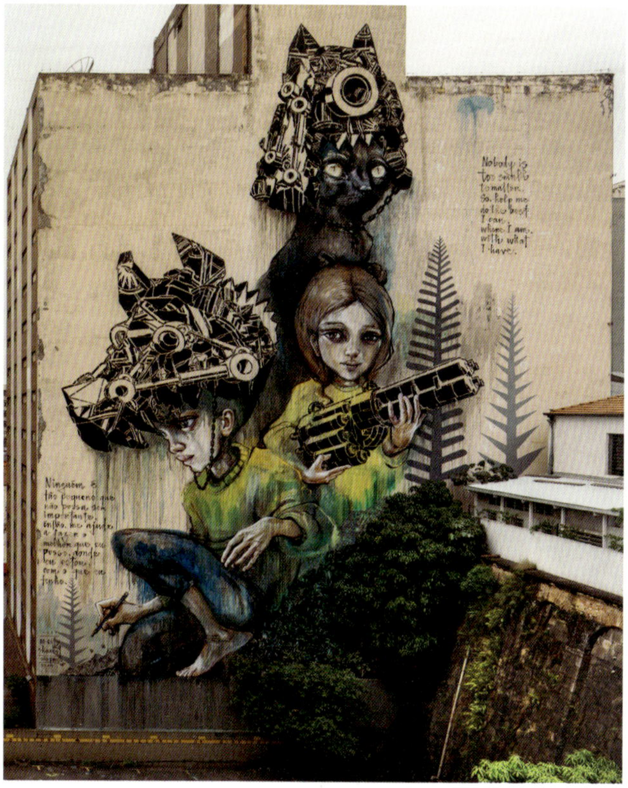

@Sao Paulo, Brazil 2015

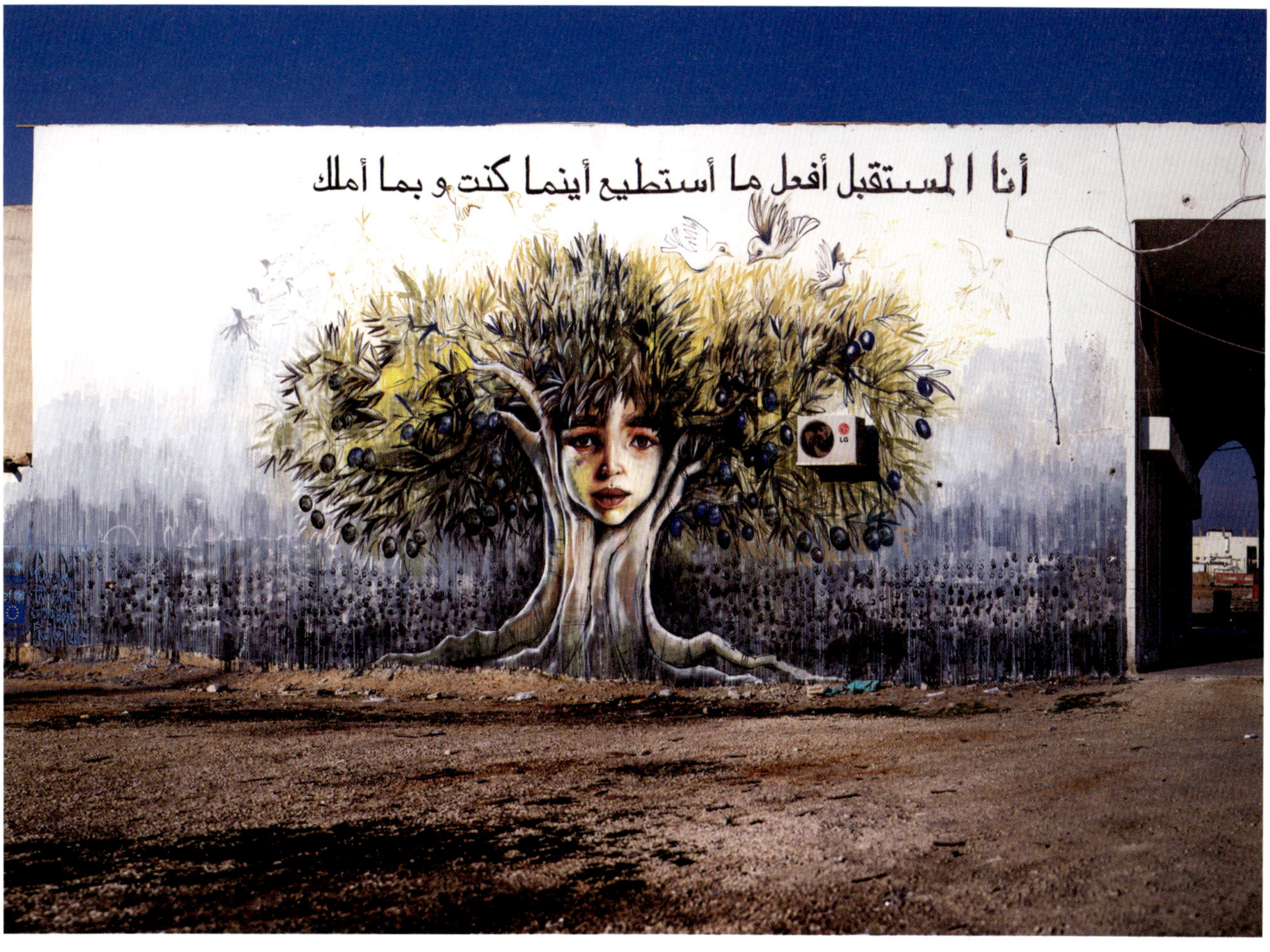

@Mafraq, Jordan 2014

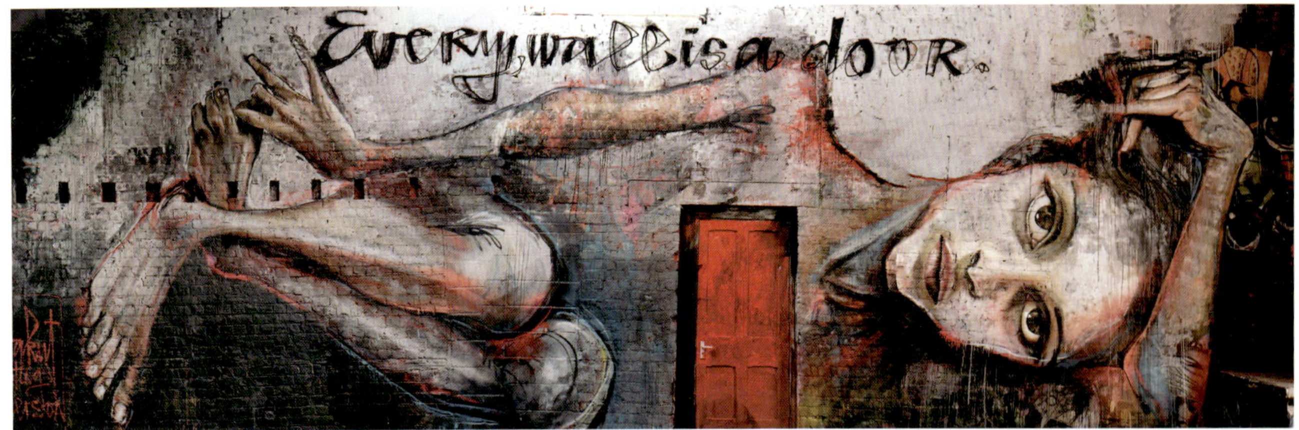

@Wittenberg, Germany 2016

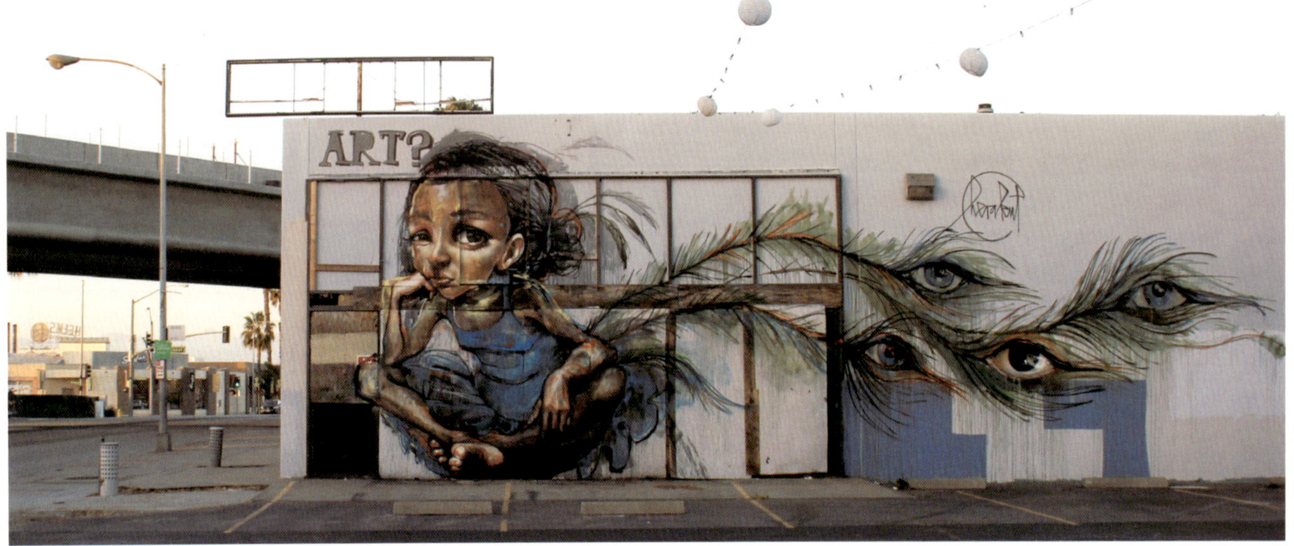

@Wittenberg, Germany 2016

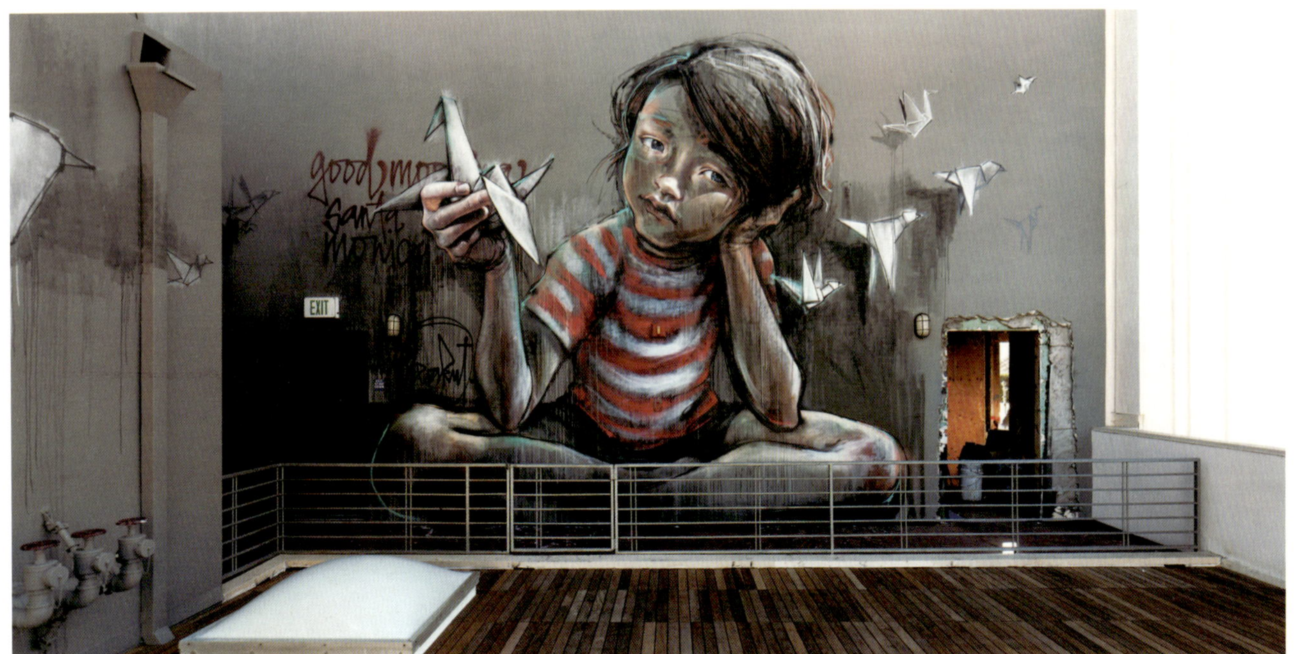

@Wittenberg, Germany 2016

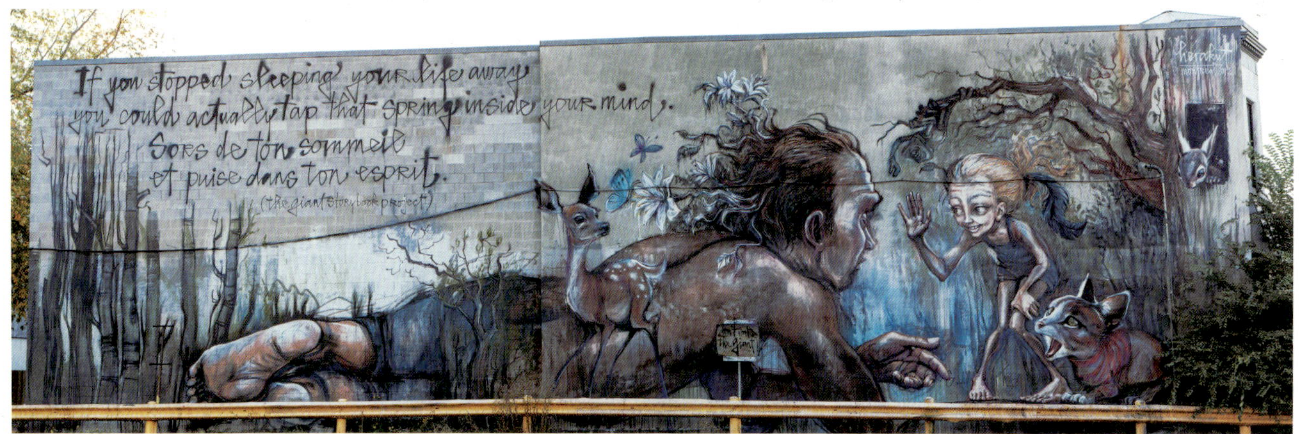

@Wittenberg, Germany 2016

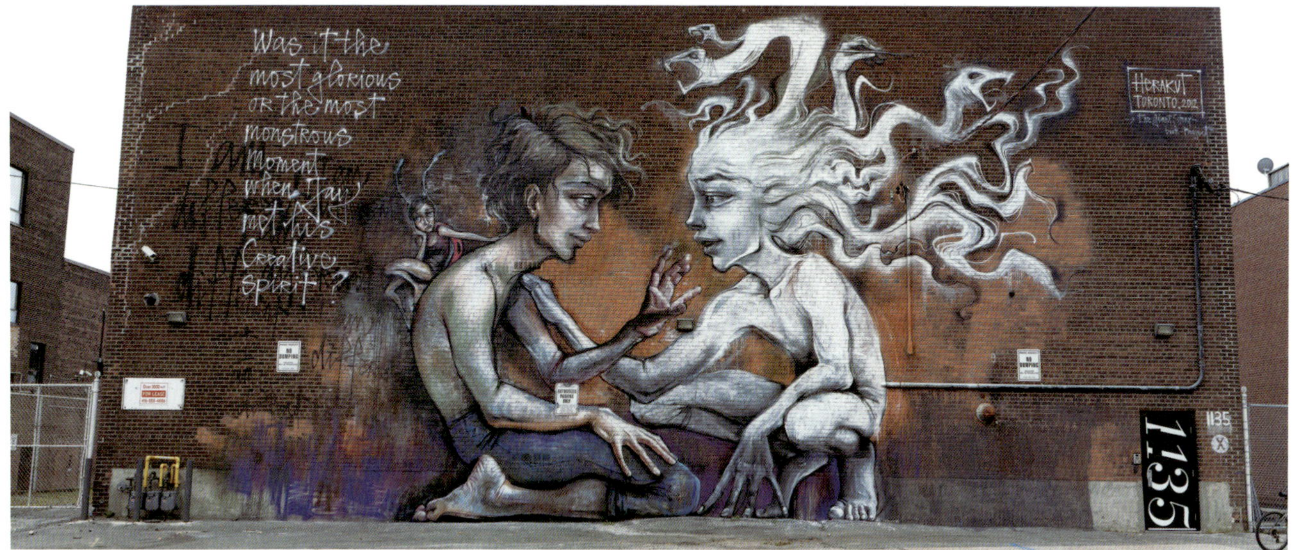

@Wittenberg, Germany 2016

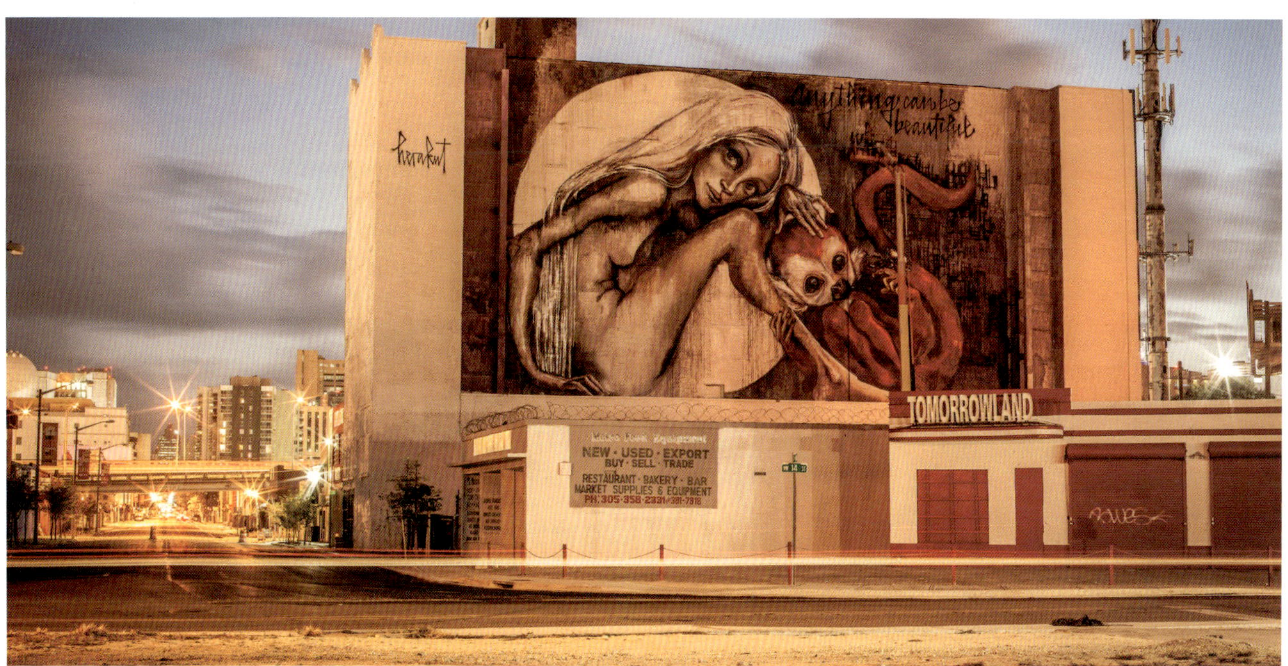

@Wittenberg, Germany 2016

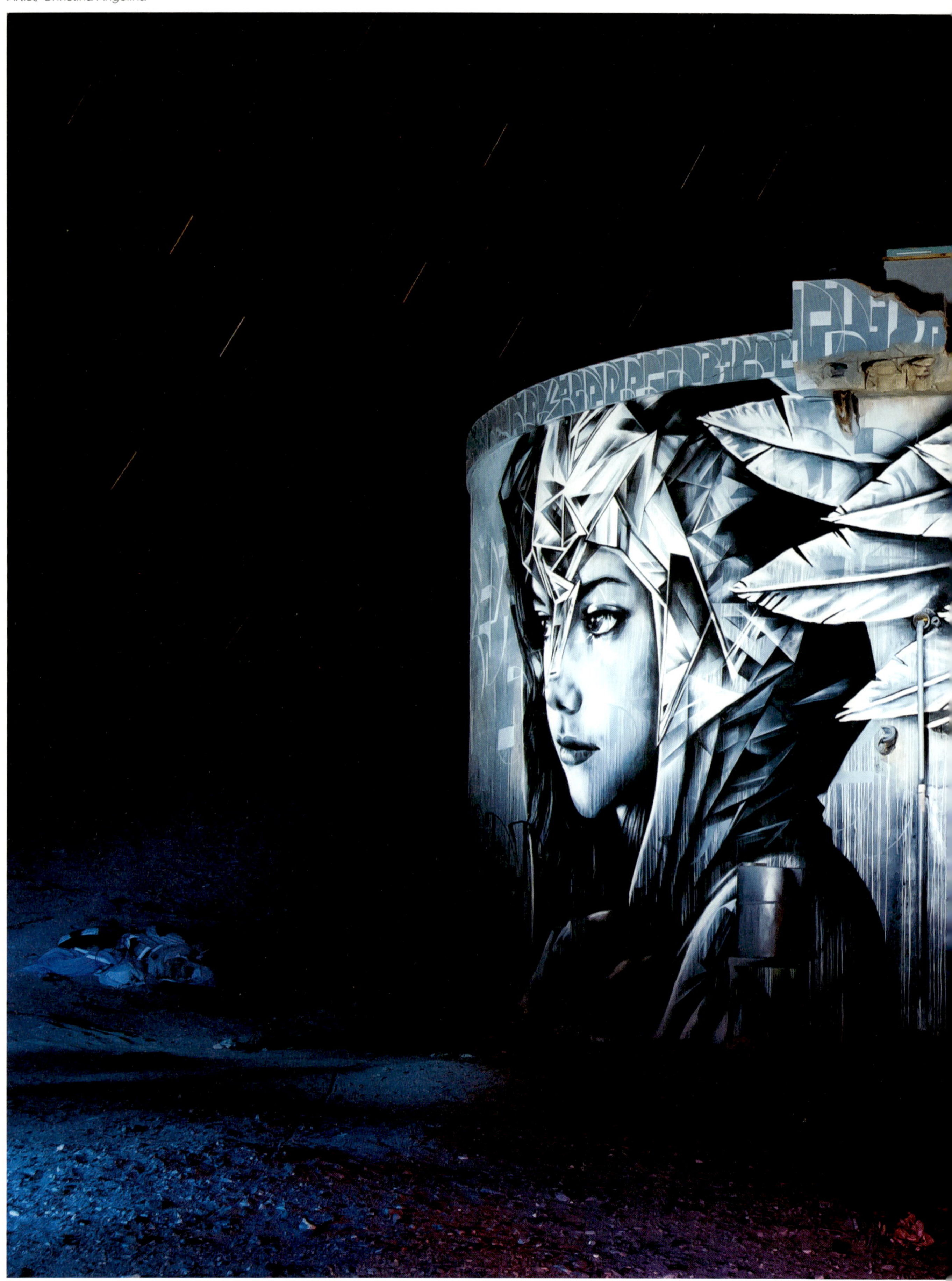

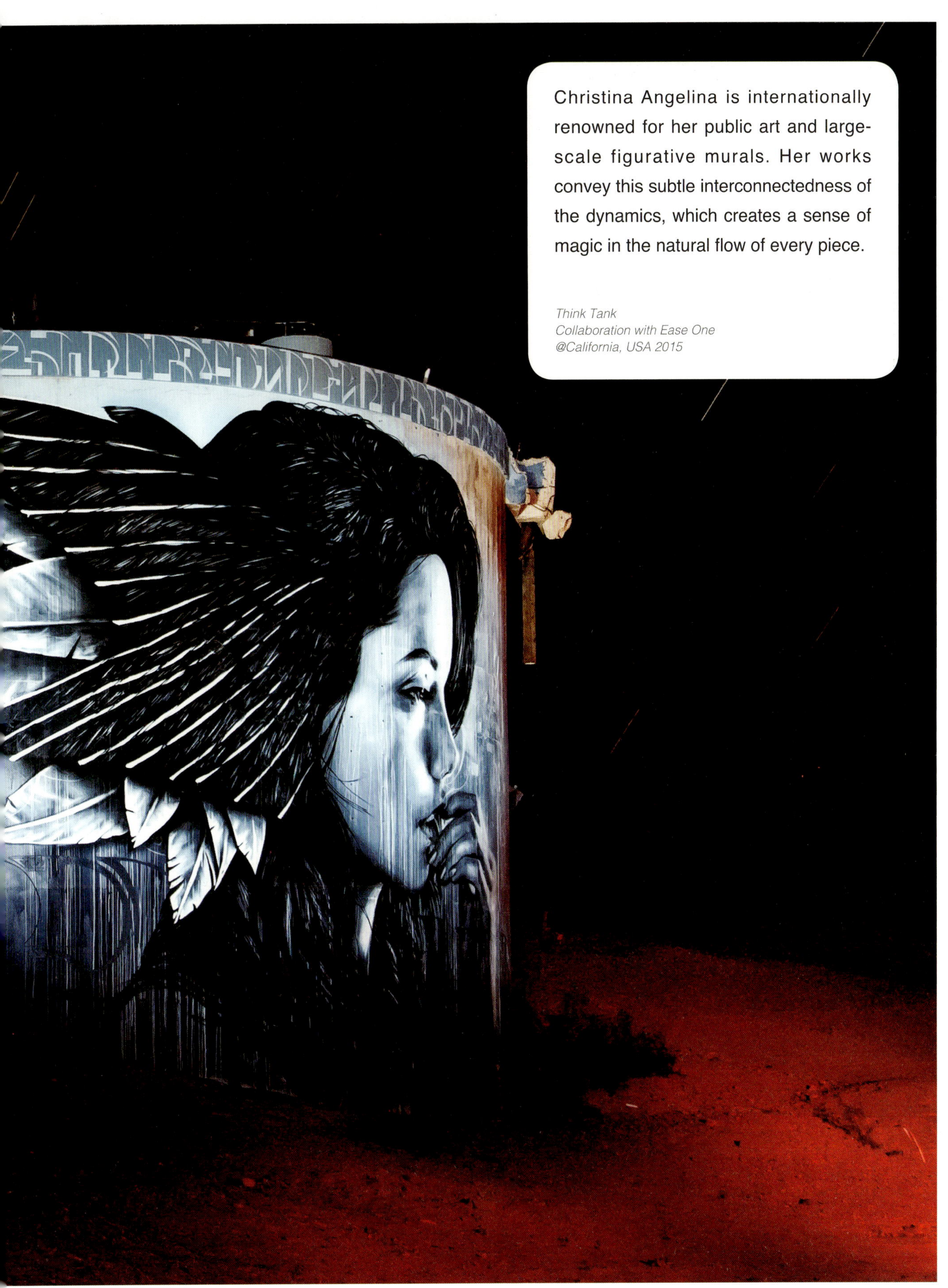

Christina Angelina is internationally renowned for her public art and large-scale figurative murals. Her works convey this subtle interconnectedness of the dynamics, which creates a sense of magic in the natural flow of every piece.

Think Tank
Collaboration with Ease One
@California, USA 2015

istina Angelina

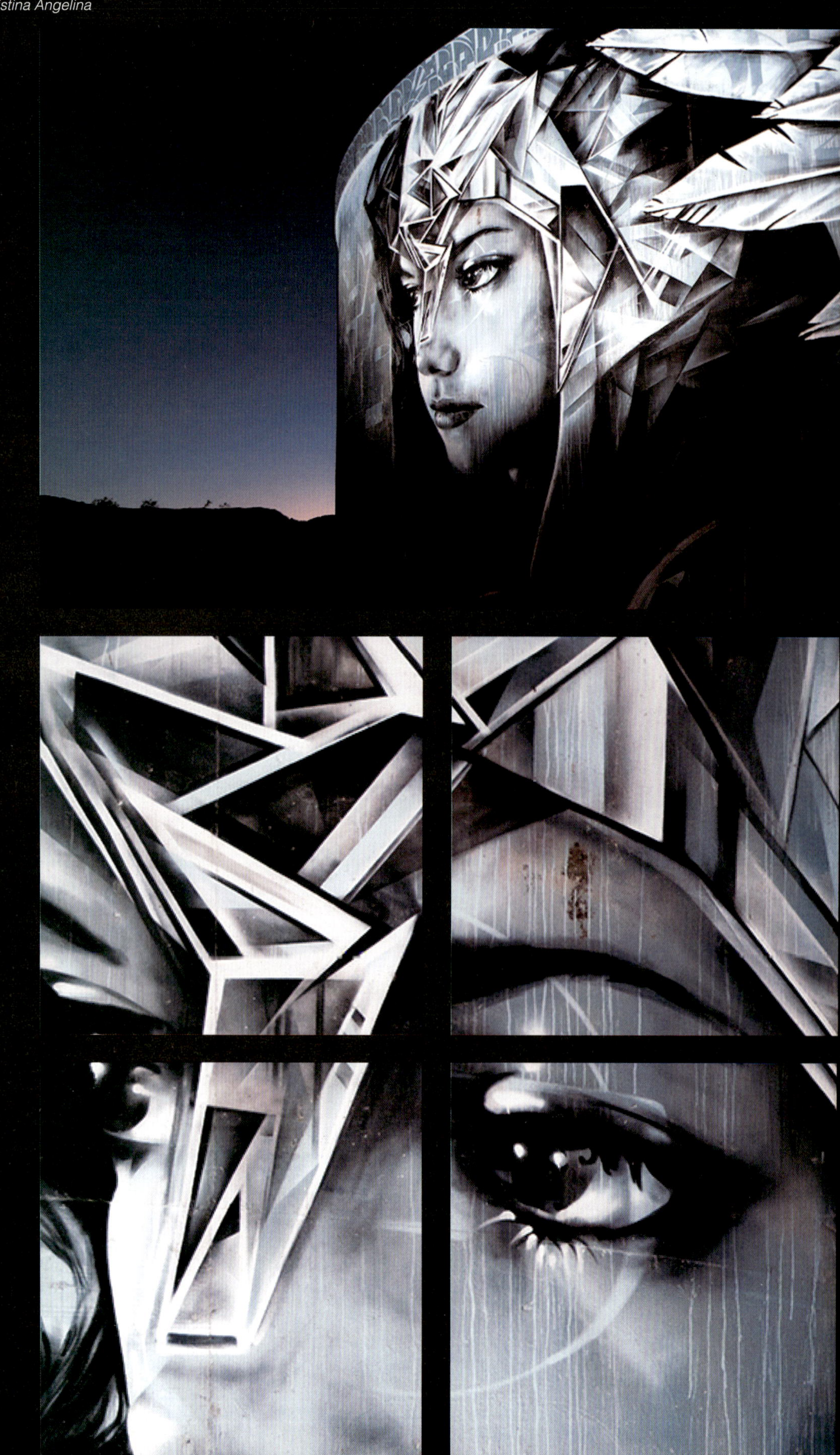

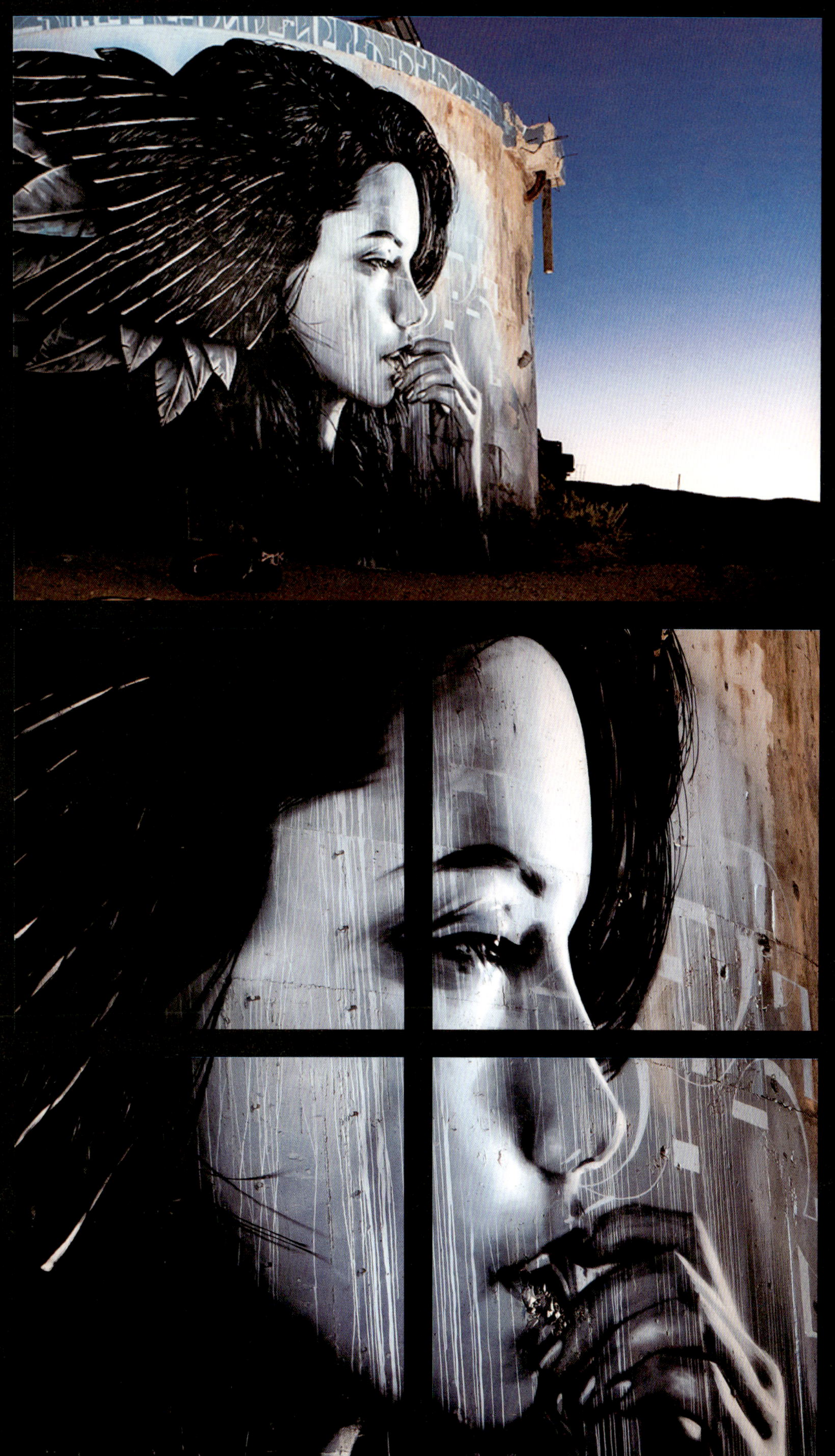

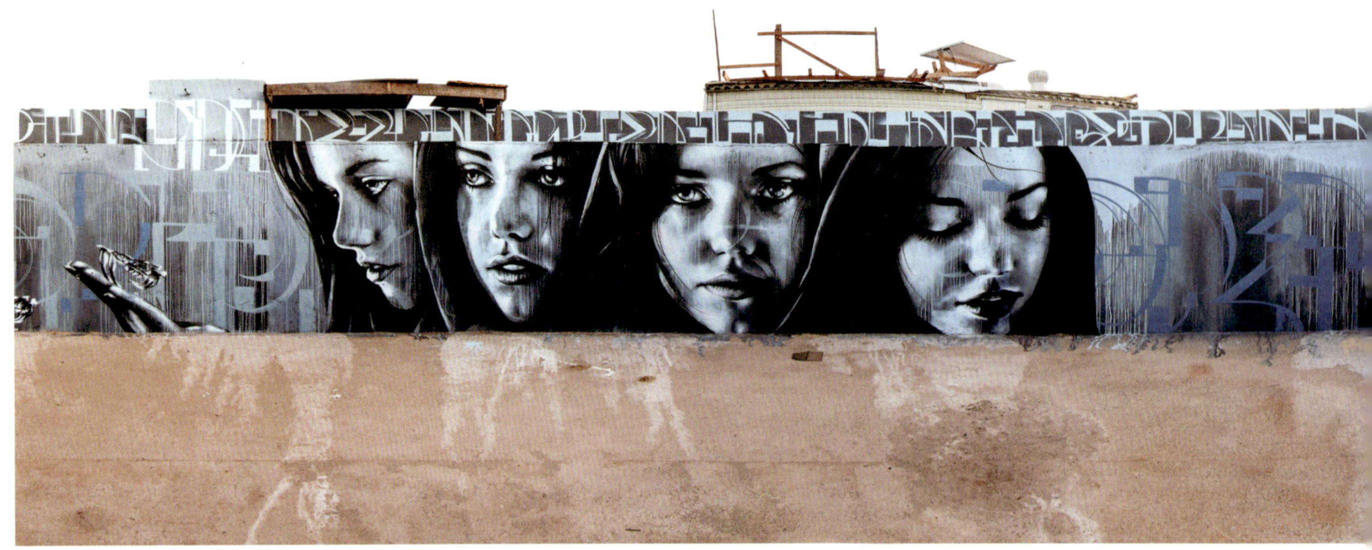

The Kinetoscope is a circular mural painted inside an abandoned water tank left over from an old military training base during WWII. Angelina has painted two sequences of fantastic, artfully rendered female faces. Each individual face embodies a specific emotion tied to a meaningful moment when Angelina trusted her intuition.

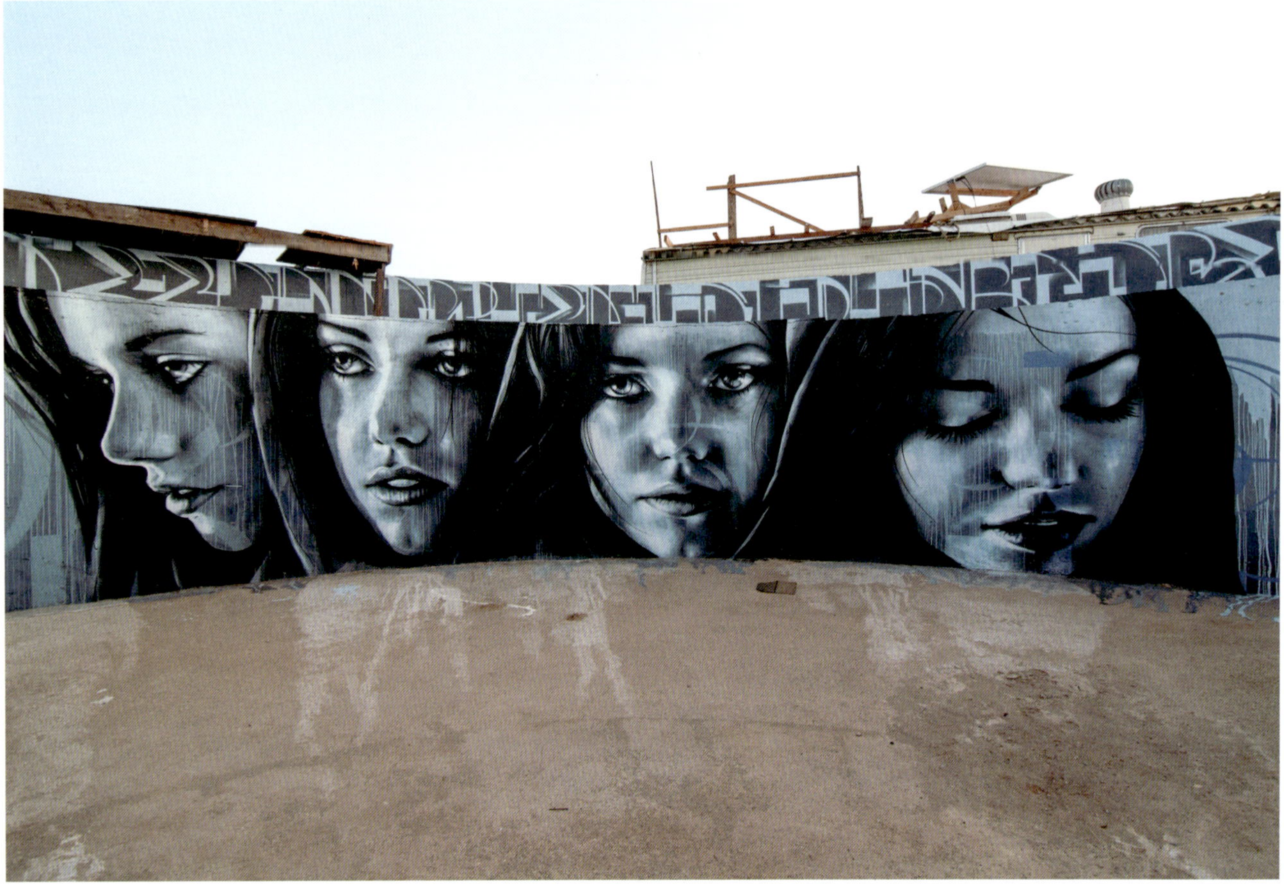

Kinetoscope
Collaboration with Ease One
@Slab City, California 2015

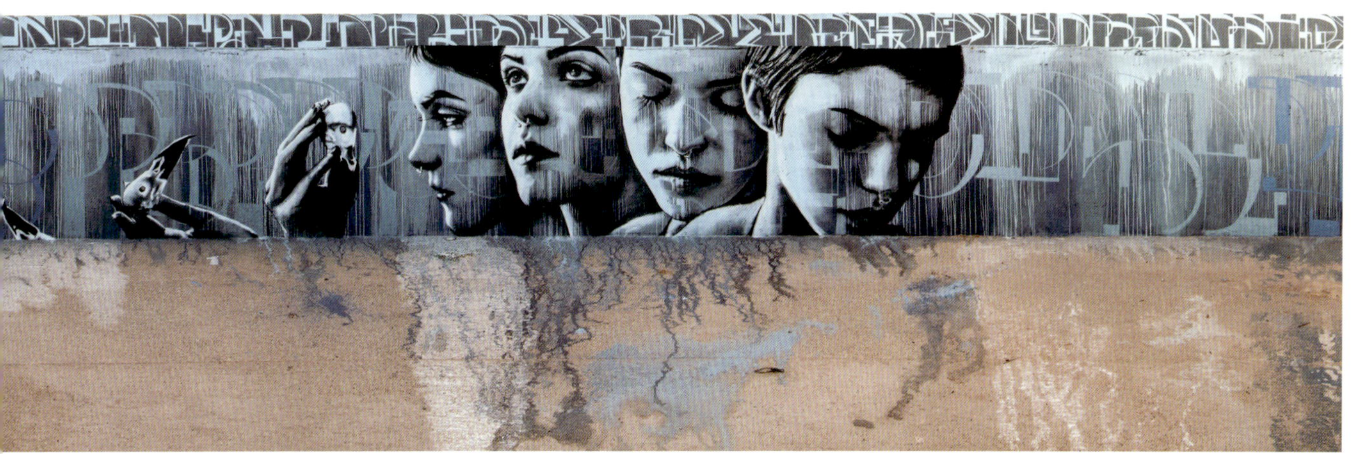

Faces sit atop a ghost-written blend of Eastern/Western writing styles by Ease One. These hidden words come from the lyrics of the song "Society" by Jerry Hannan and Eddie Vedder.

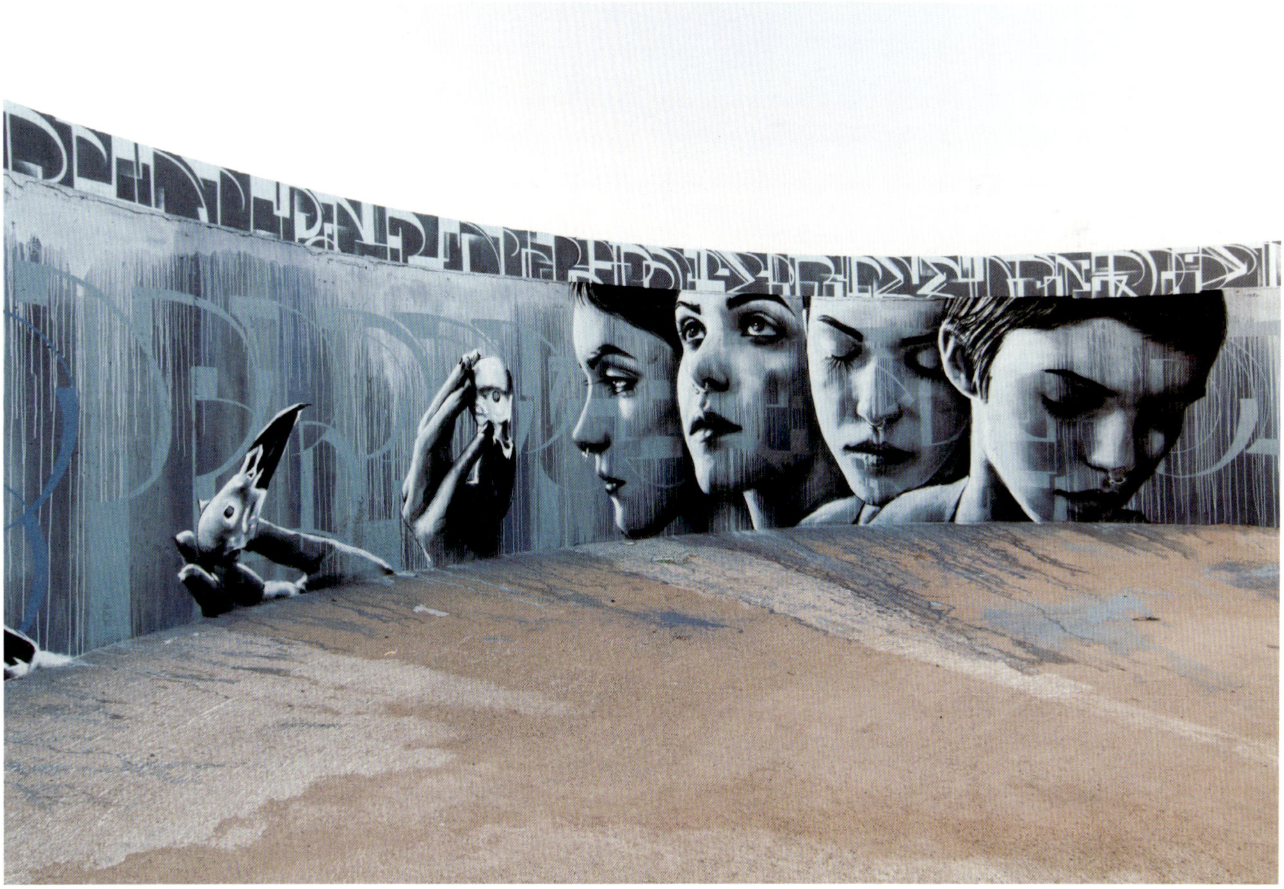

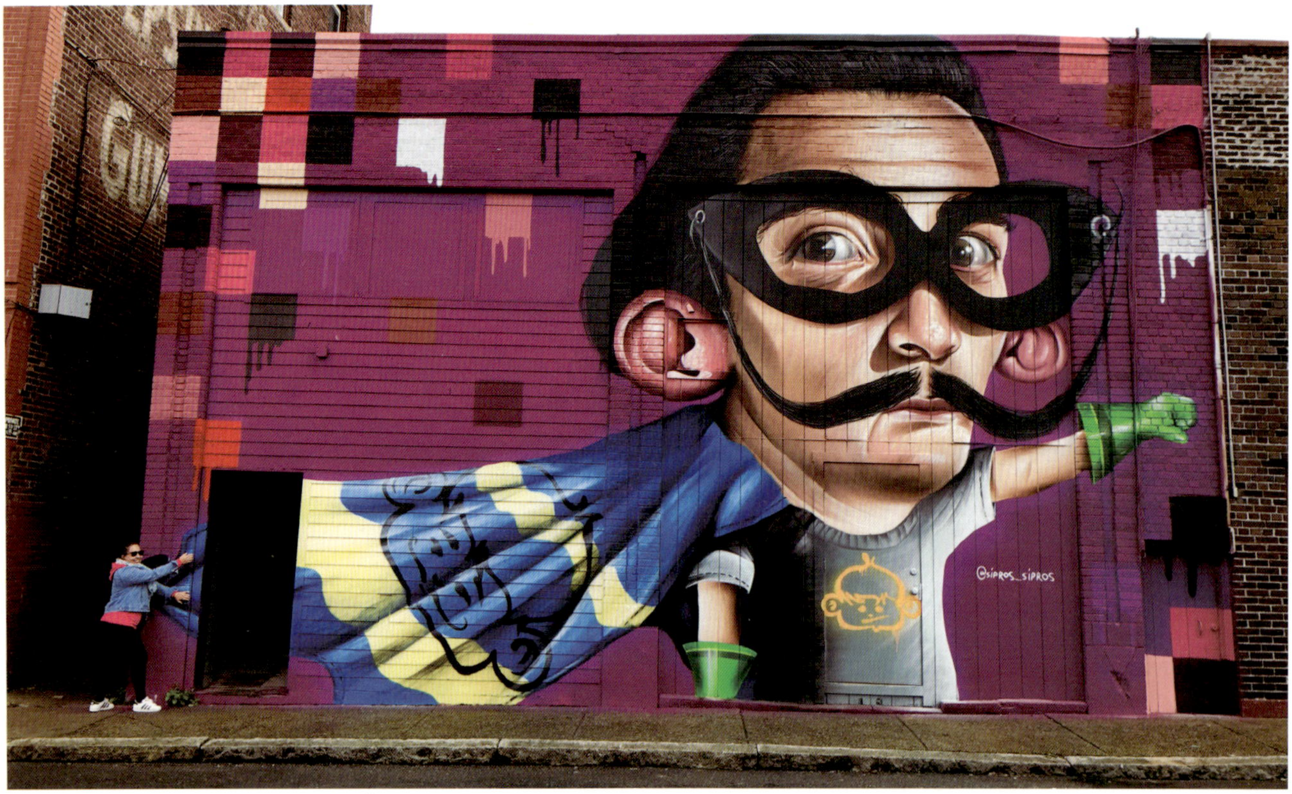

@Salem, Massachusetts, USA 2017

Sipros is a Brazilian street artist who specializes in truly fine depictions of realism. His creations are mostly of realistic characters and display a high level of imagination and personal technique. Portraits of people of all ages were recreated with amusing, exaggerated facial expressions, which generate an entertaining effect for viewers.

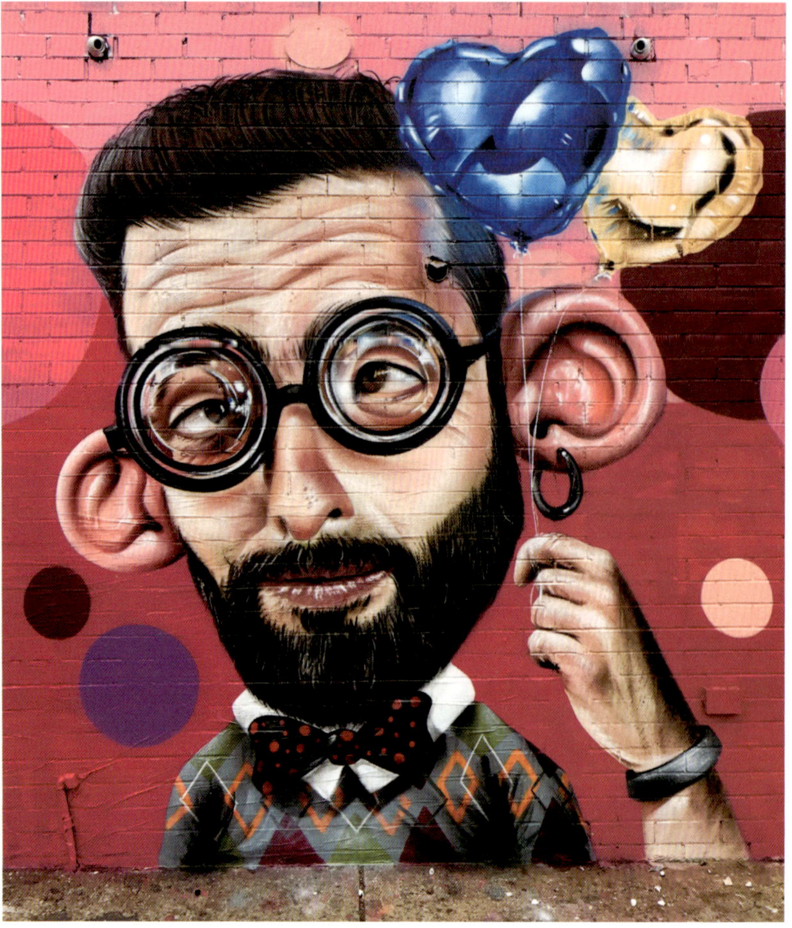

Created for the Bushwick Collective
@New York, USA 2017

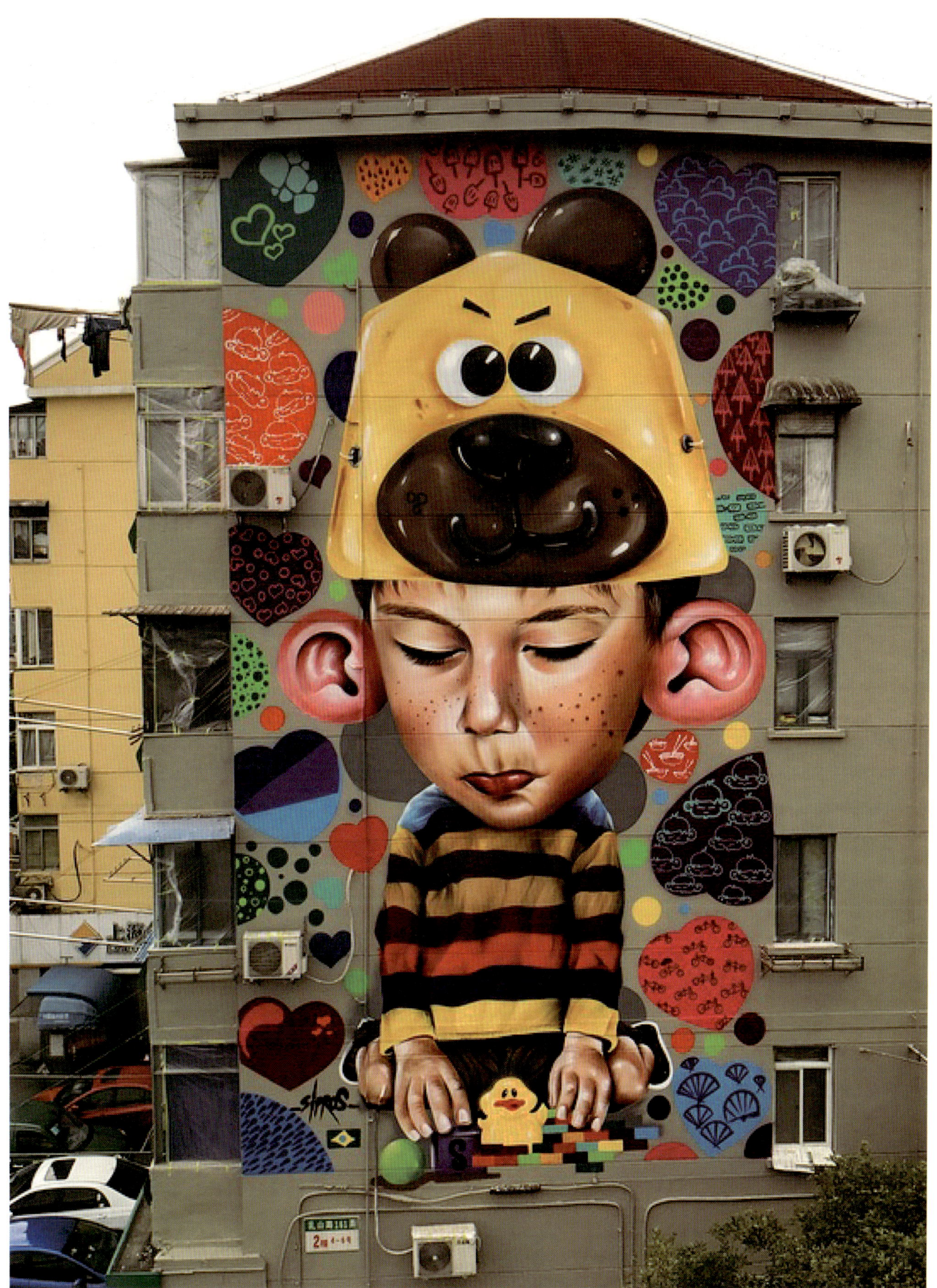

@Shanghai, China 2017

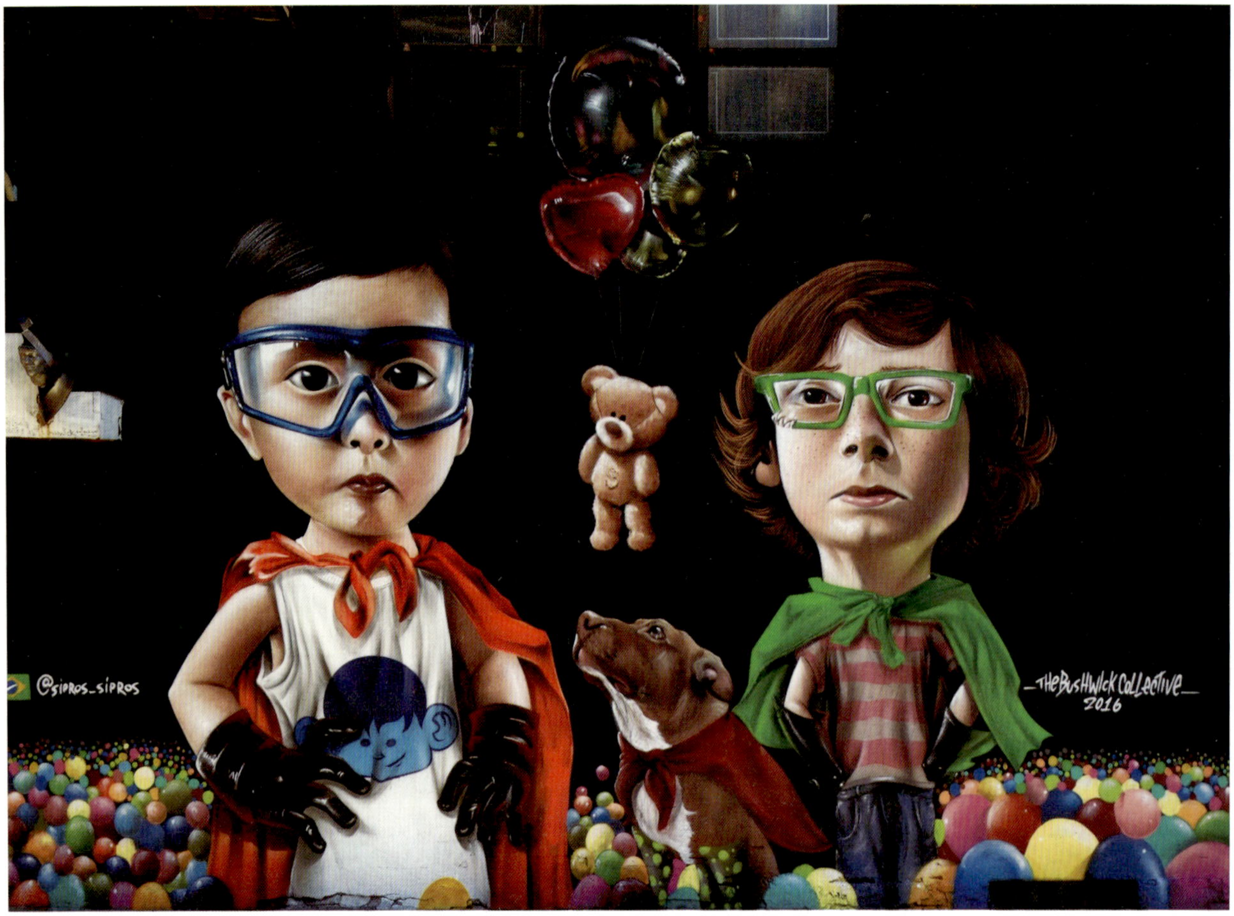

@New York, USA 2016

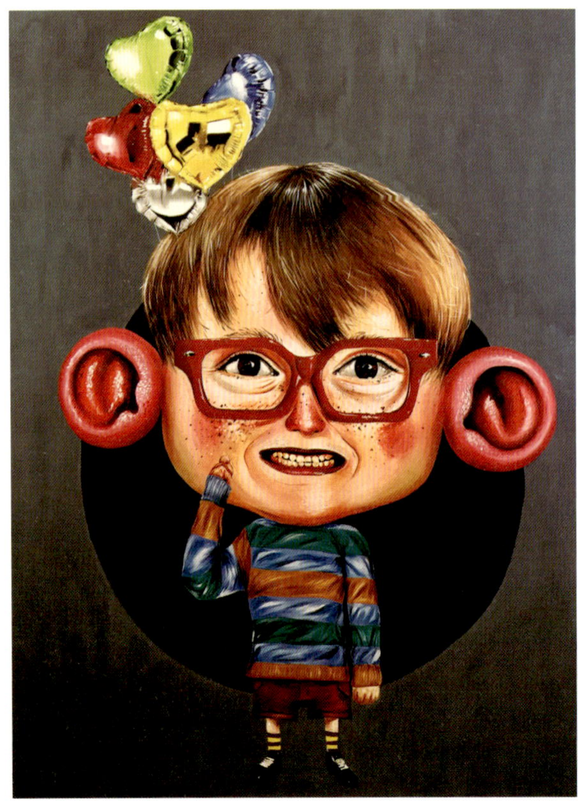

Acrylic paint on canvas

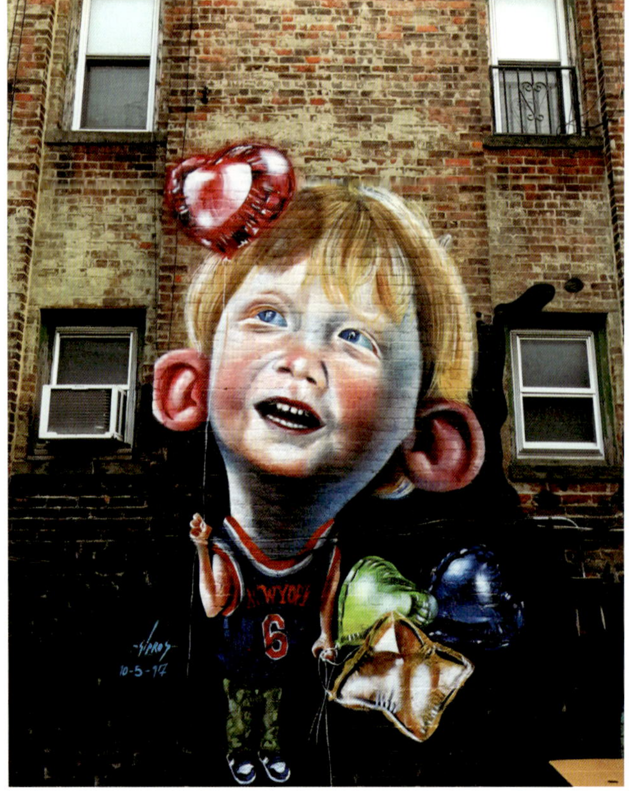

@New York, USA 2017

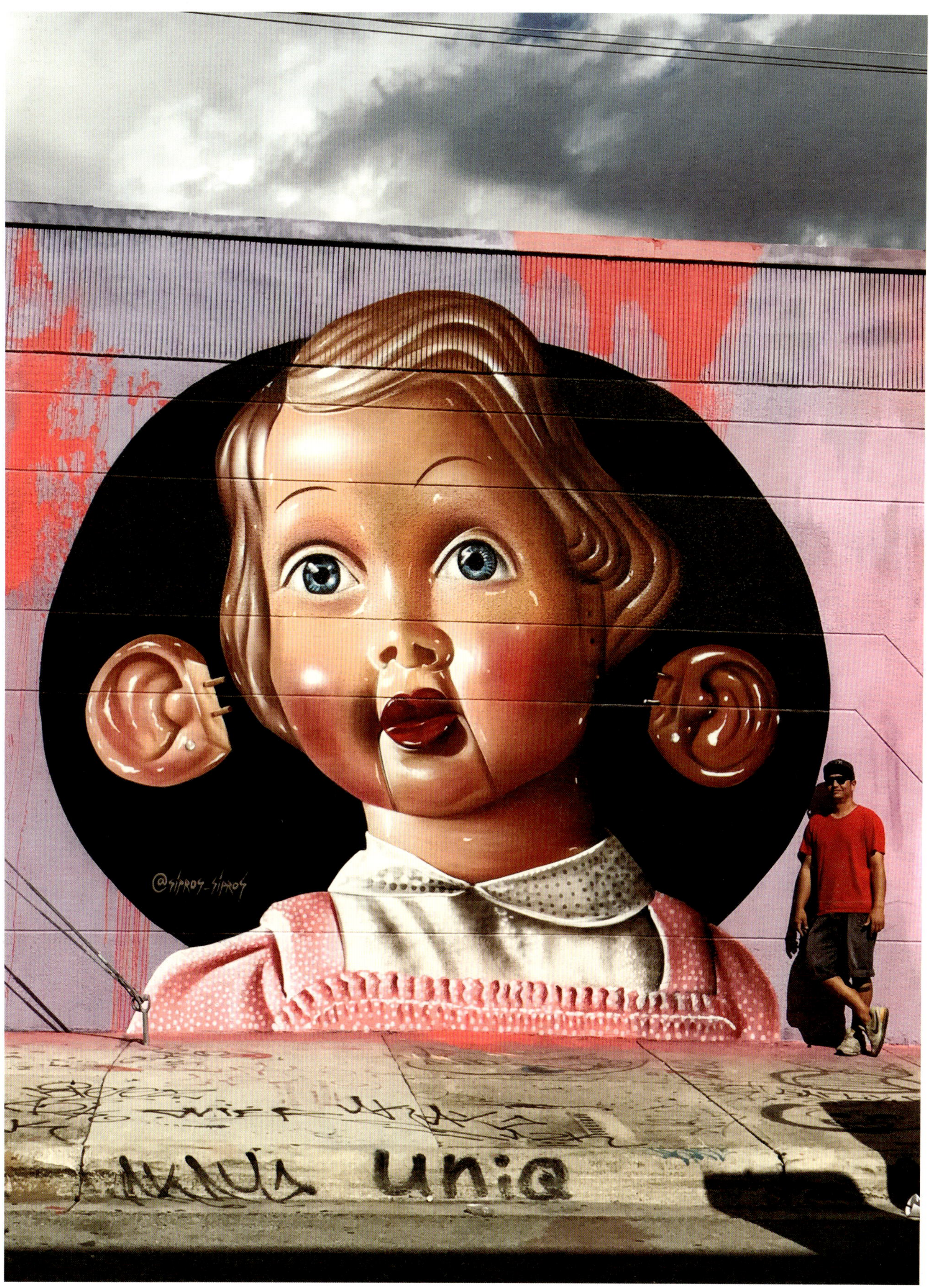

@Miami, USA 2016

GIOVA is a Chilean street artist who strives to use city walls as reflections of society, and as a way of communicating social struggles through graffiti.

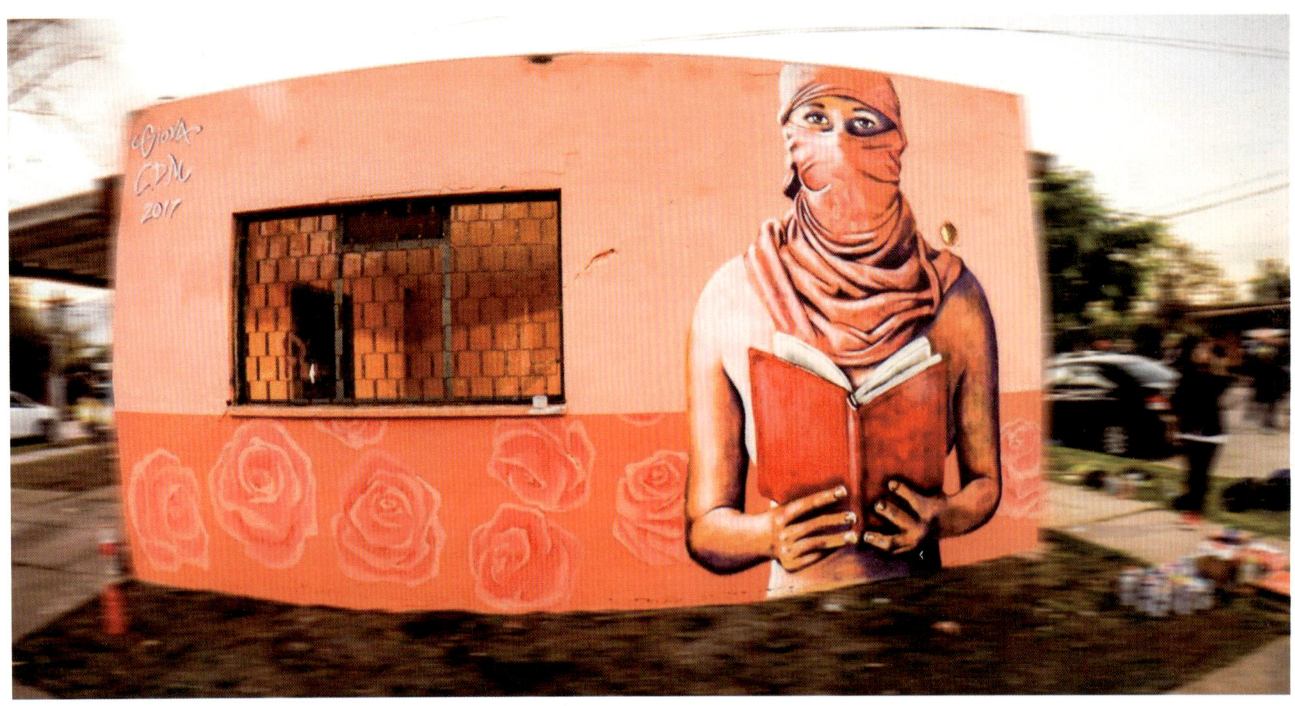

Revolution in Spring
@Valparaiso, Chile 2017

"Revolution in Spring" is about a recurrent theme in Latin America regarding the disregard for women's rights today. The hood represents the rights hidden, whereas the naked body suggests the liberation of women in a macho society.

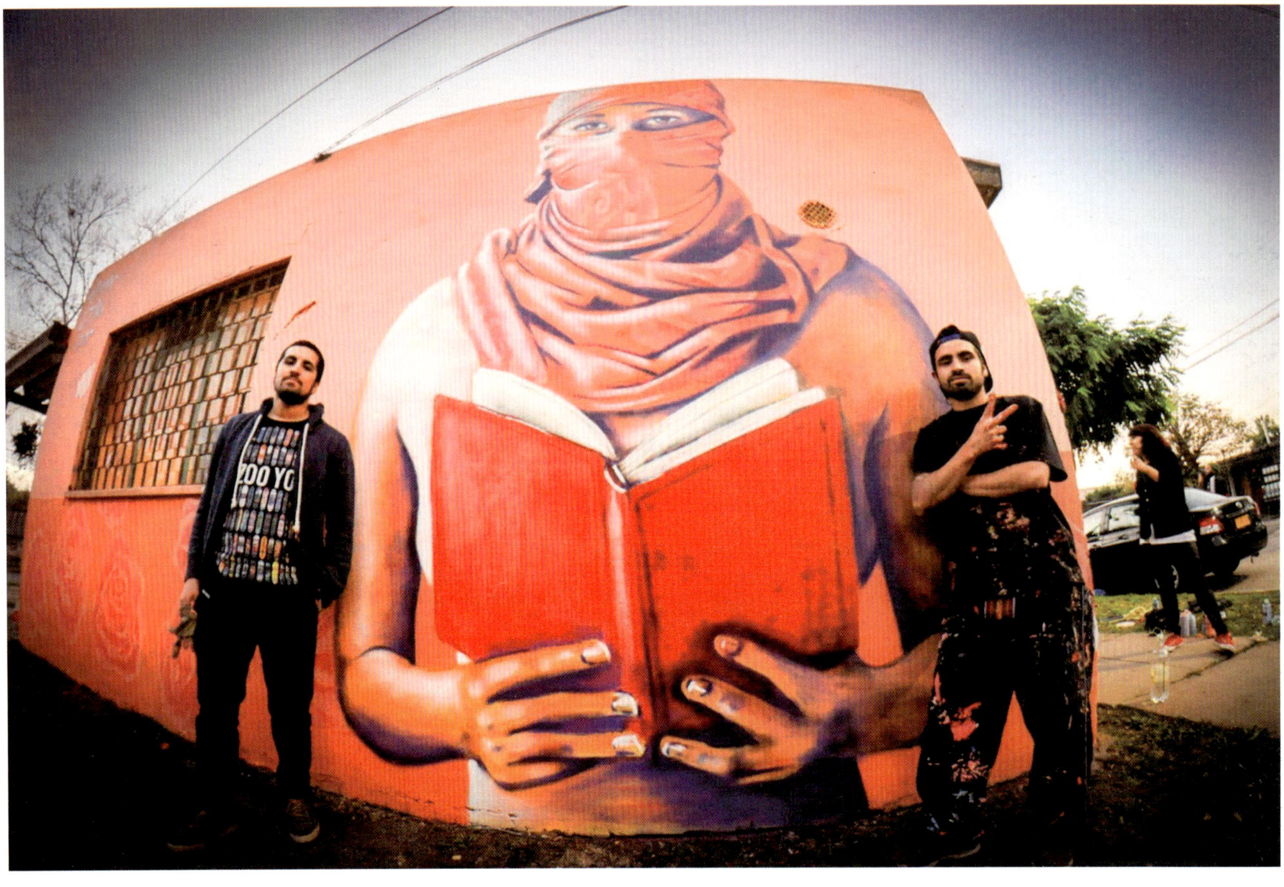

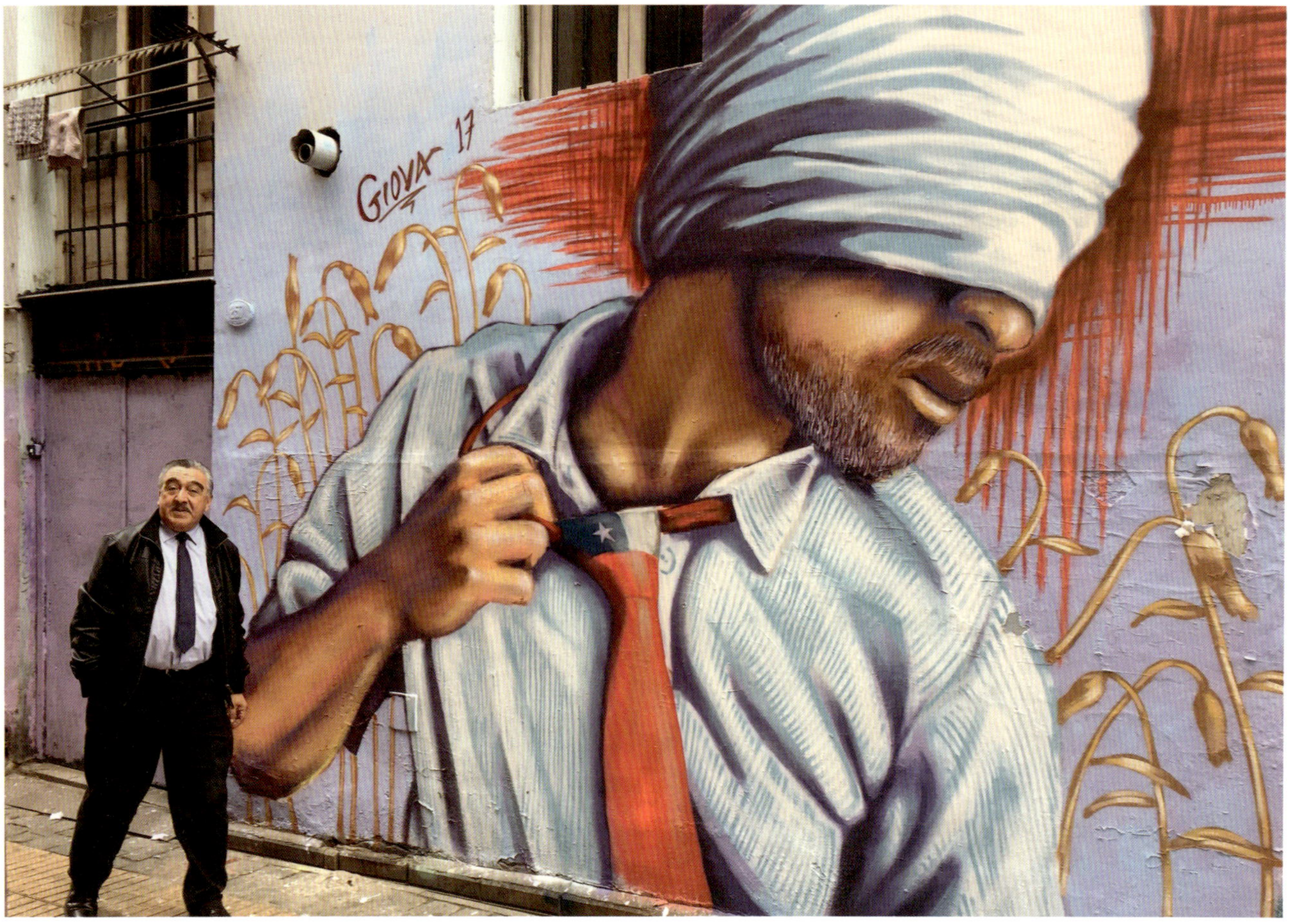

↑
The Tie
@Valparaiso, Chile 2017

"The tie"represents a reflection of the postmodern society today. The tie represents work overload, exploitation, and labor stress, and the blindfold implies unawareness of the overwhelming quality of work life.

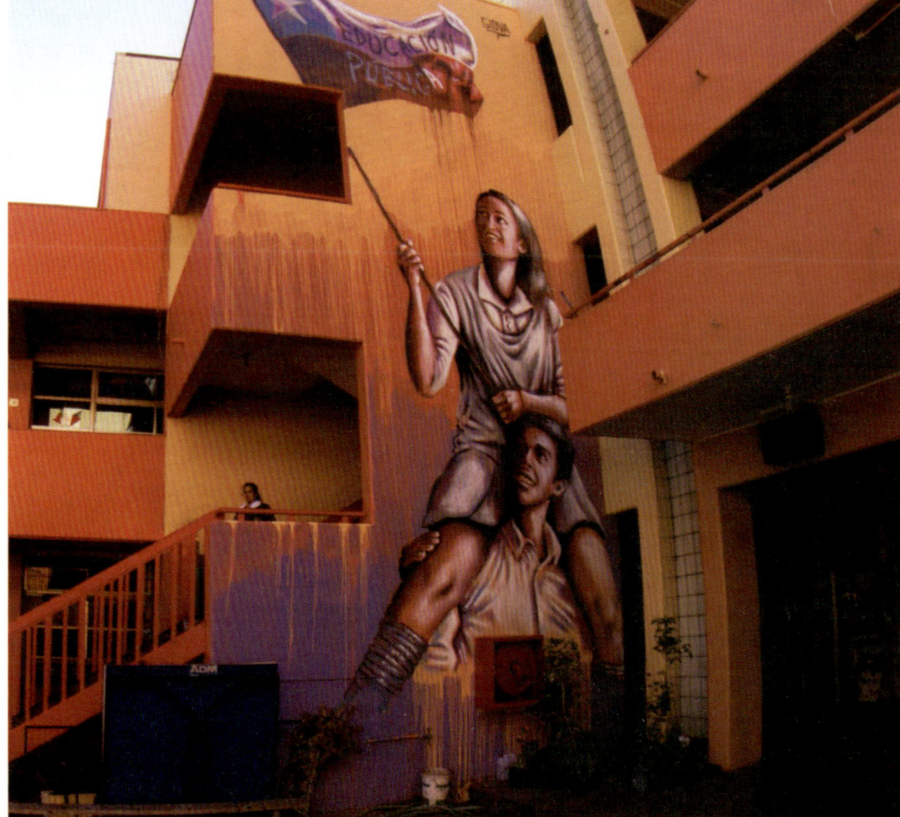

→
Chilean Students
@Valparaiso, Chile 2017

"Chilean Students" represents the struggle of the Chilean student movement since 2011, which demanded to guarantee education as a public right.

Hood Graff is a Belorussian street art duo, made up of two person, Arty Burzh and Iliya. They started in 2013 in Belorussia, where street art could only be found through the Internet and they moved to Saint-Petersburg, Russia and Bali, Indonesia later. They believe that each portrait has individual history, individual message, and gradually developed their photo-realistic style.

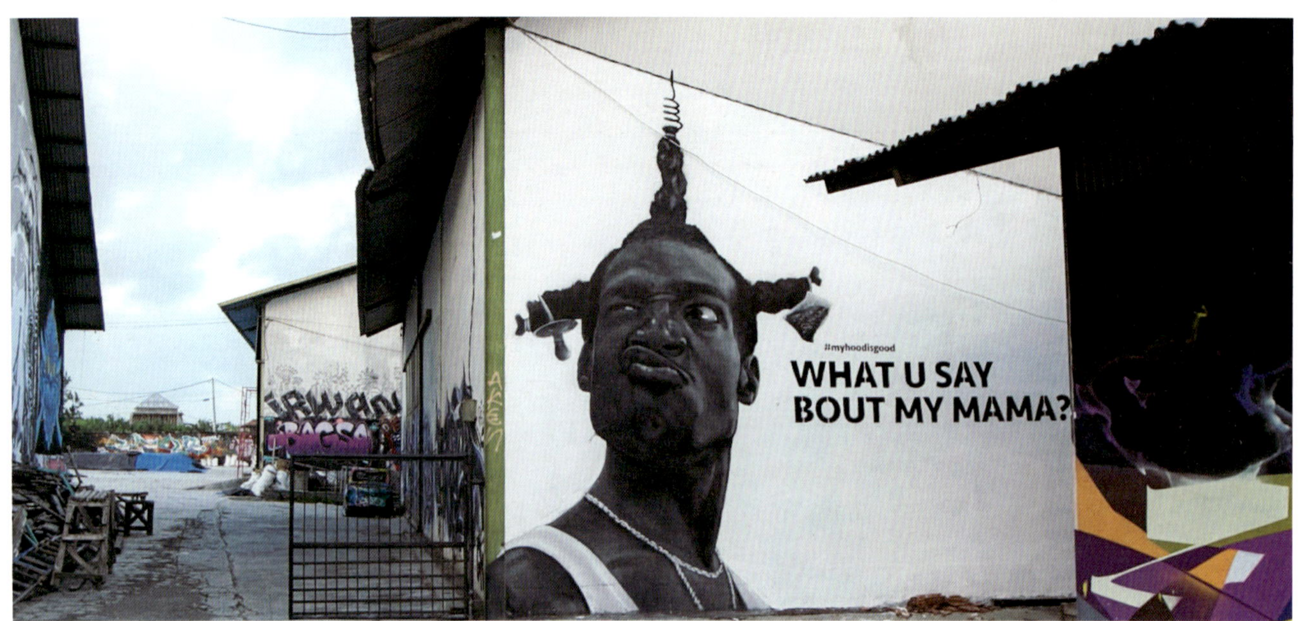

Marlon Wayans
@Bali, Indonesia 2017

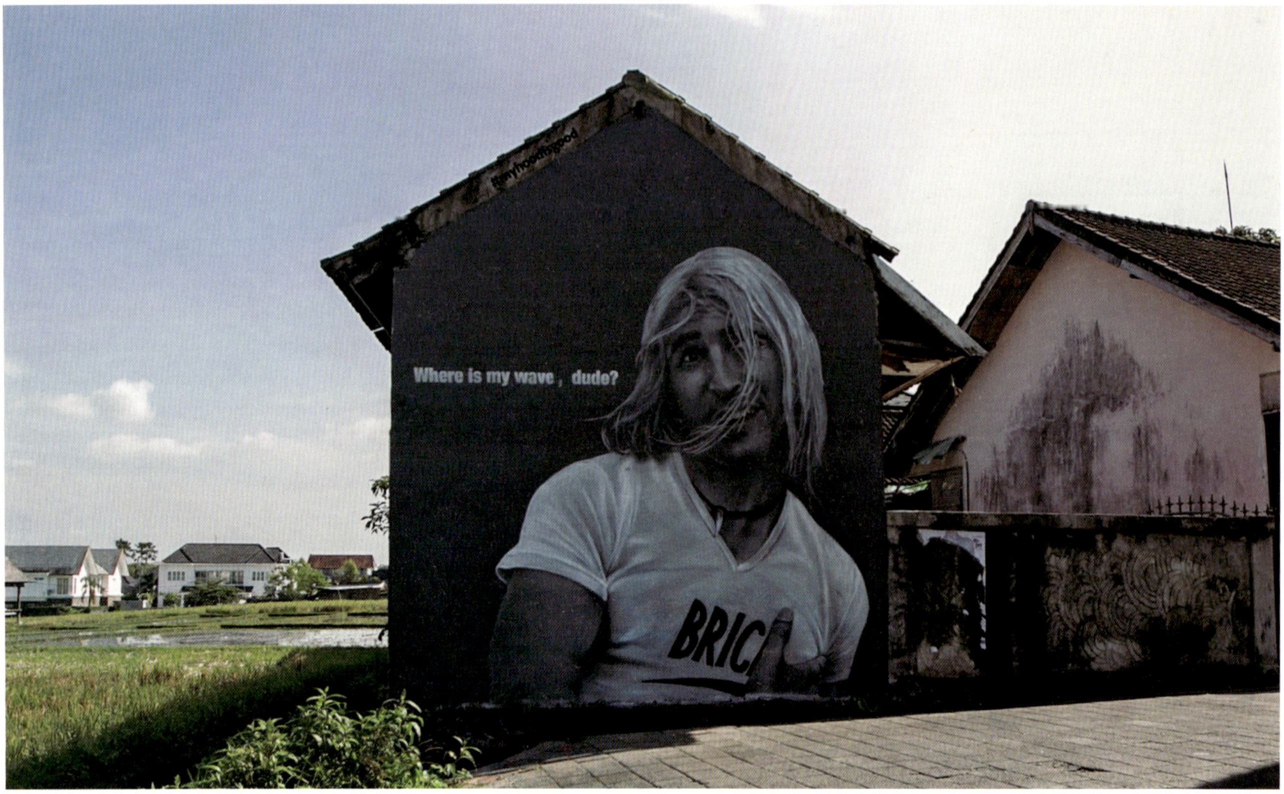

Brice de Nice
@Bali, Indonesia 2017

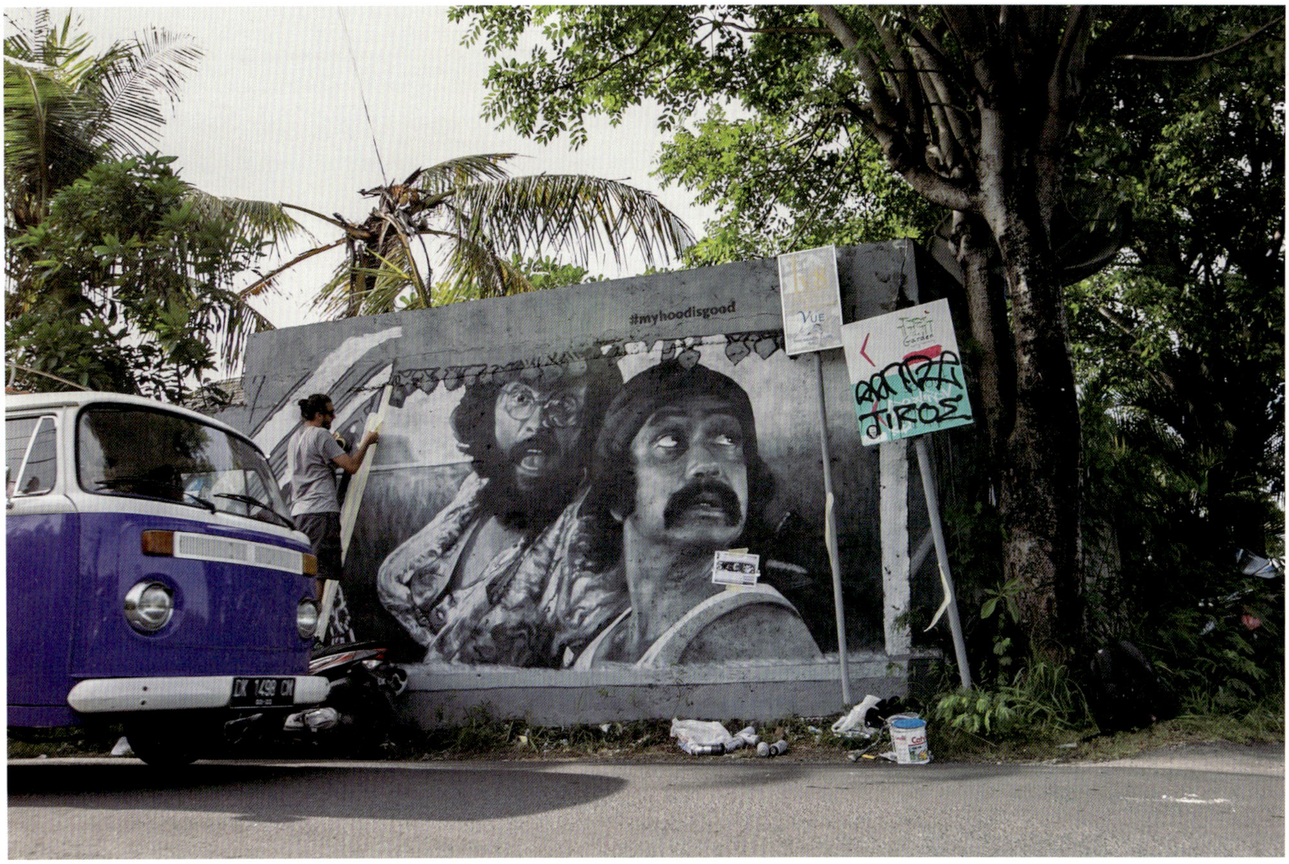

Tommy Chong & Cheech Marin
@Bali, Indonesia 2017

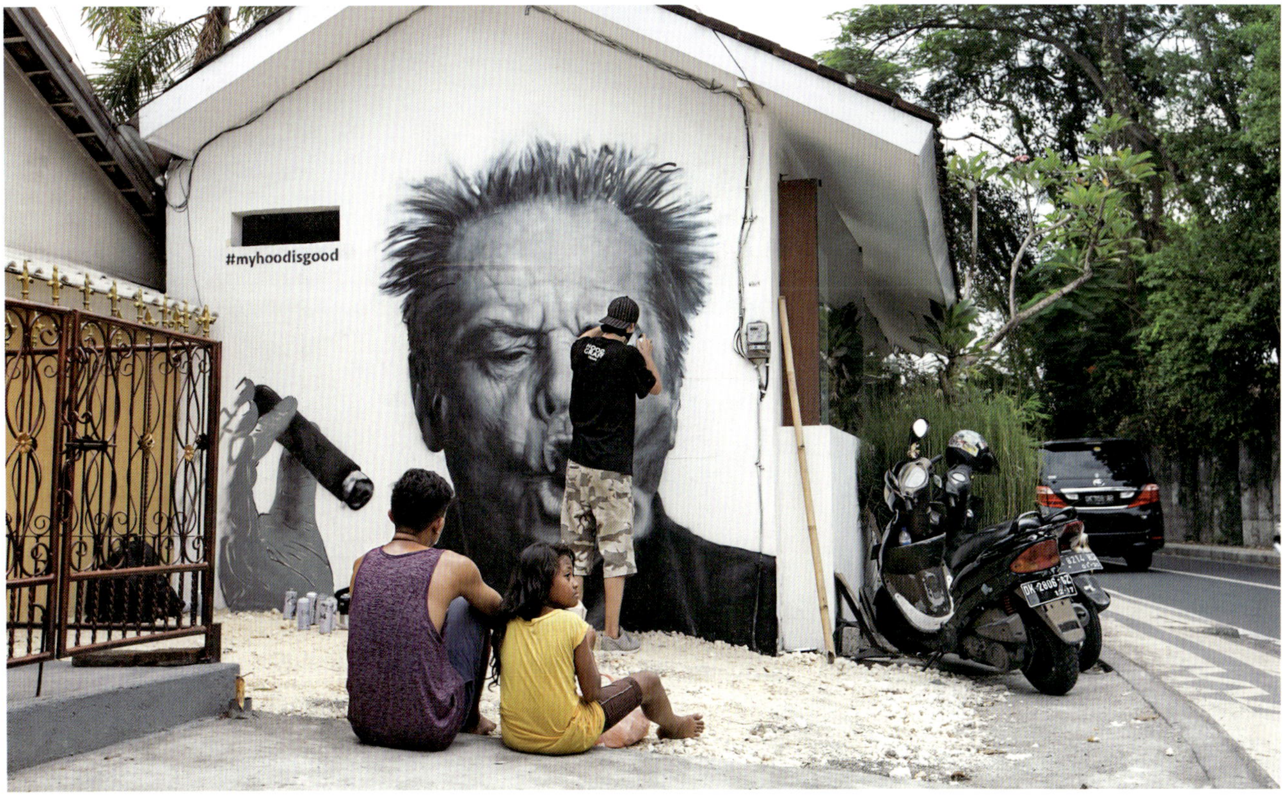

Jack Nicholson
@Bali, Indonesia 2017

Best known for his outstanding figurative murals created on a large scale, INO is one of the most internationally recognized Greek street artist. Starting off as a graffiti artist in the early 2000s, he has developed his style characterized by fragmented forms, photo-realistic elements and grayscale palette with touches of light blue, which in result, creates a dialogue between the viewer and the art.

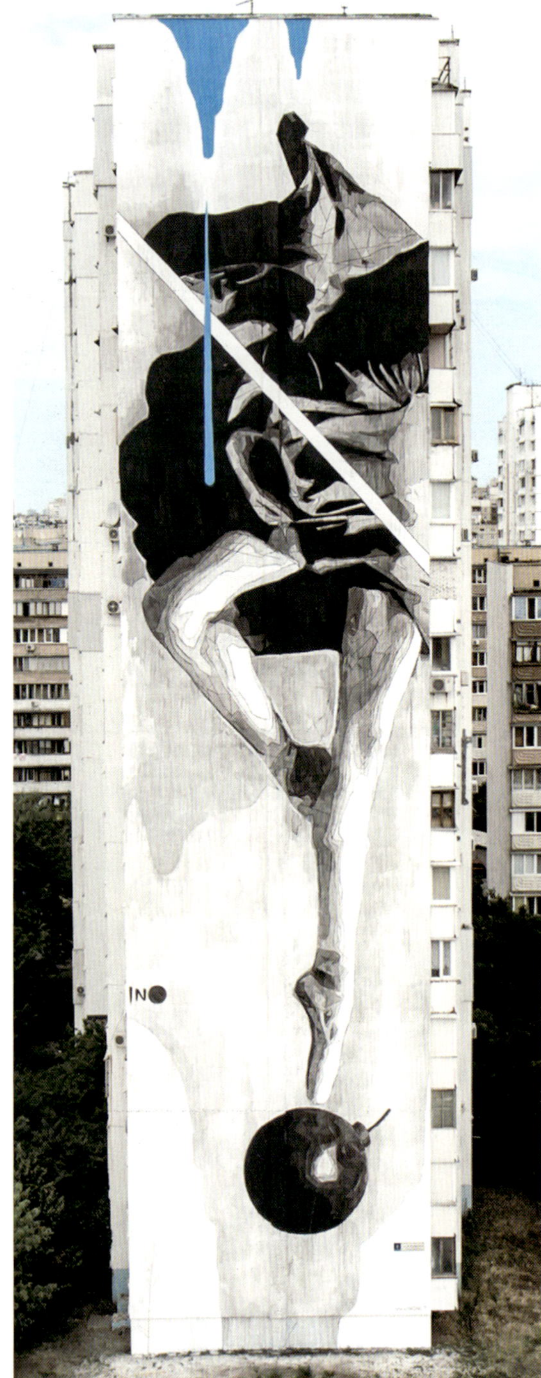

Instability
@Kiev, Ukraine 2016

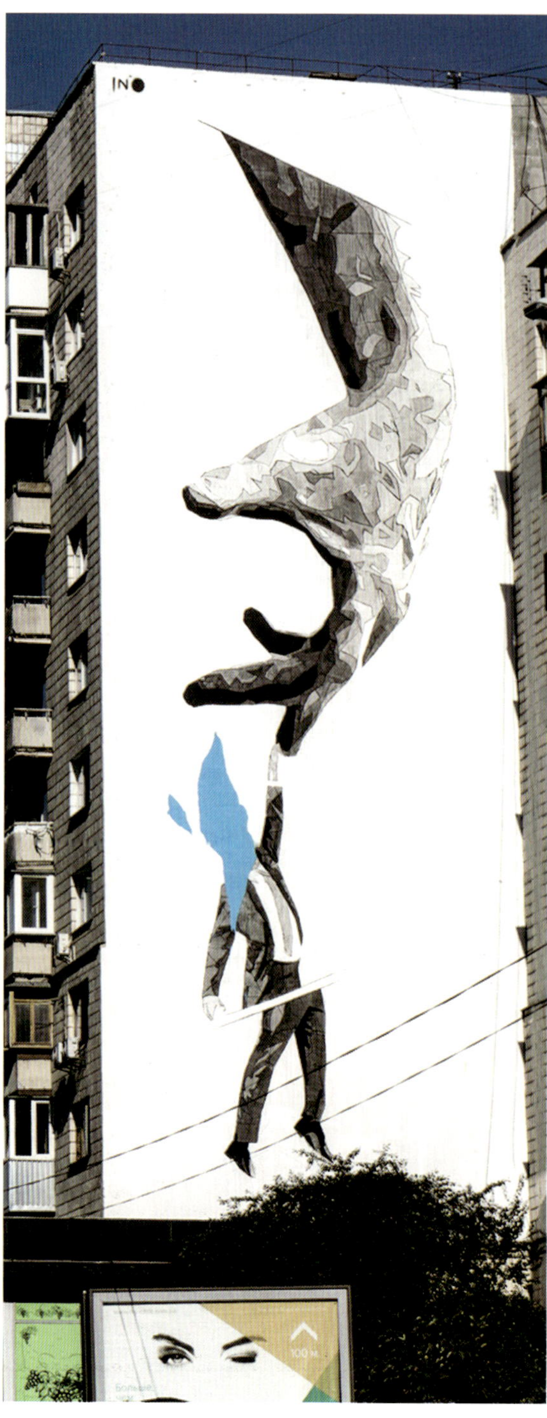

The Entrepreneur
@Kiev, Ukraine 2016

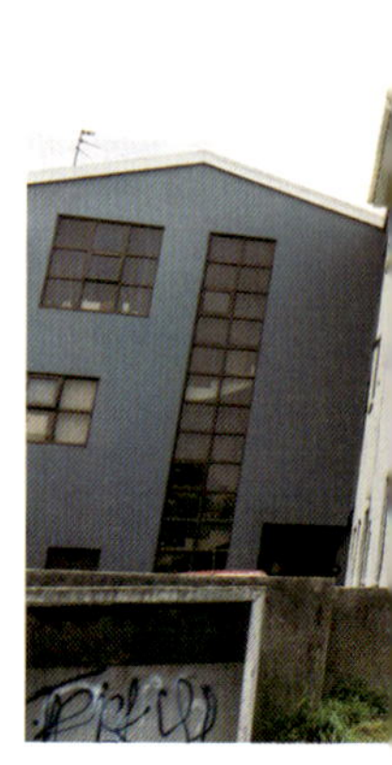

Officially Nobody
@Reykjavik, Iceland 201

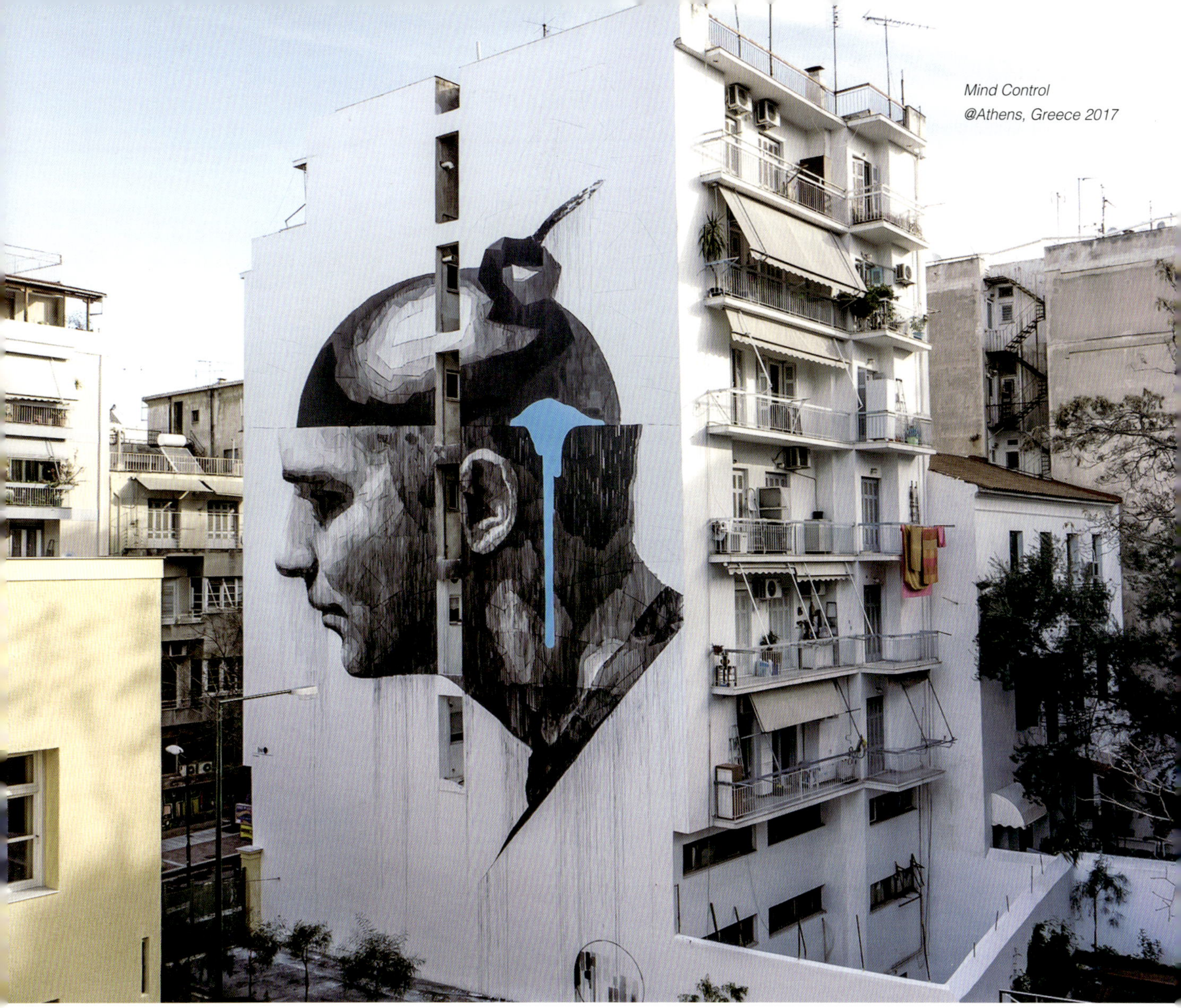

Mind Control
@Athens, Greece 2017

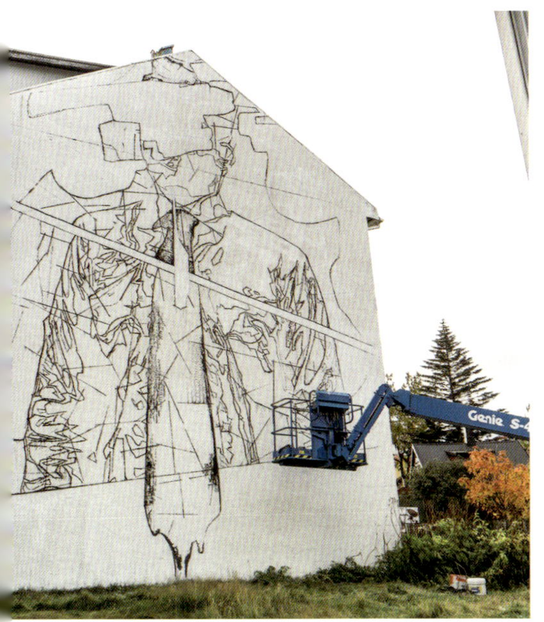

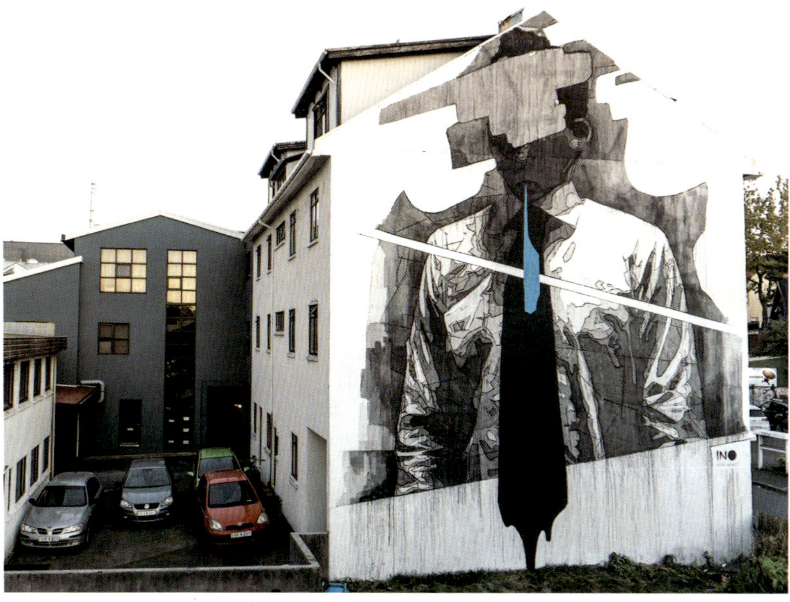

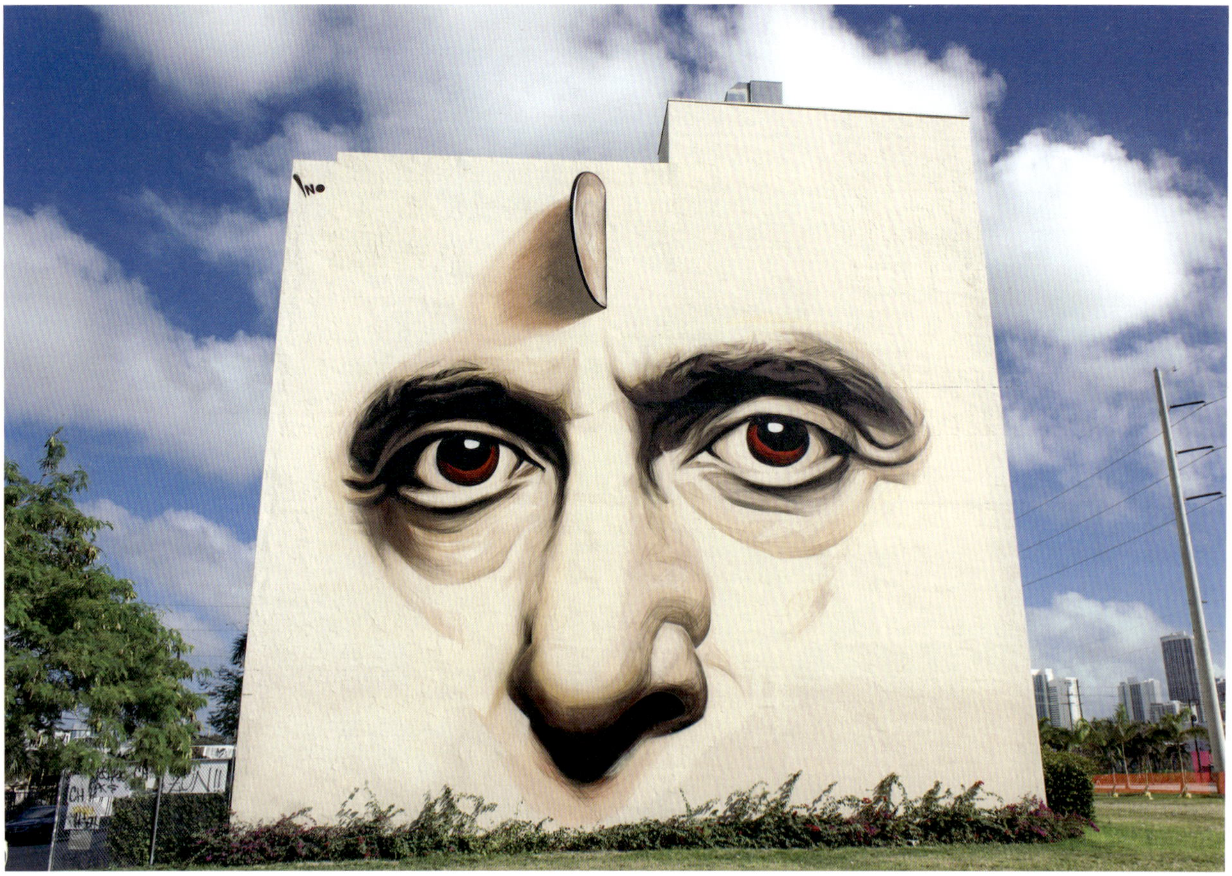

In Heaven With You
@Miami, USA 2013

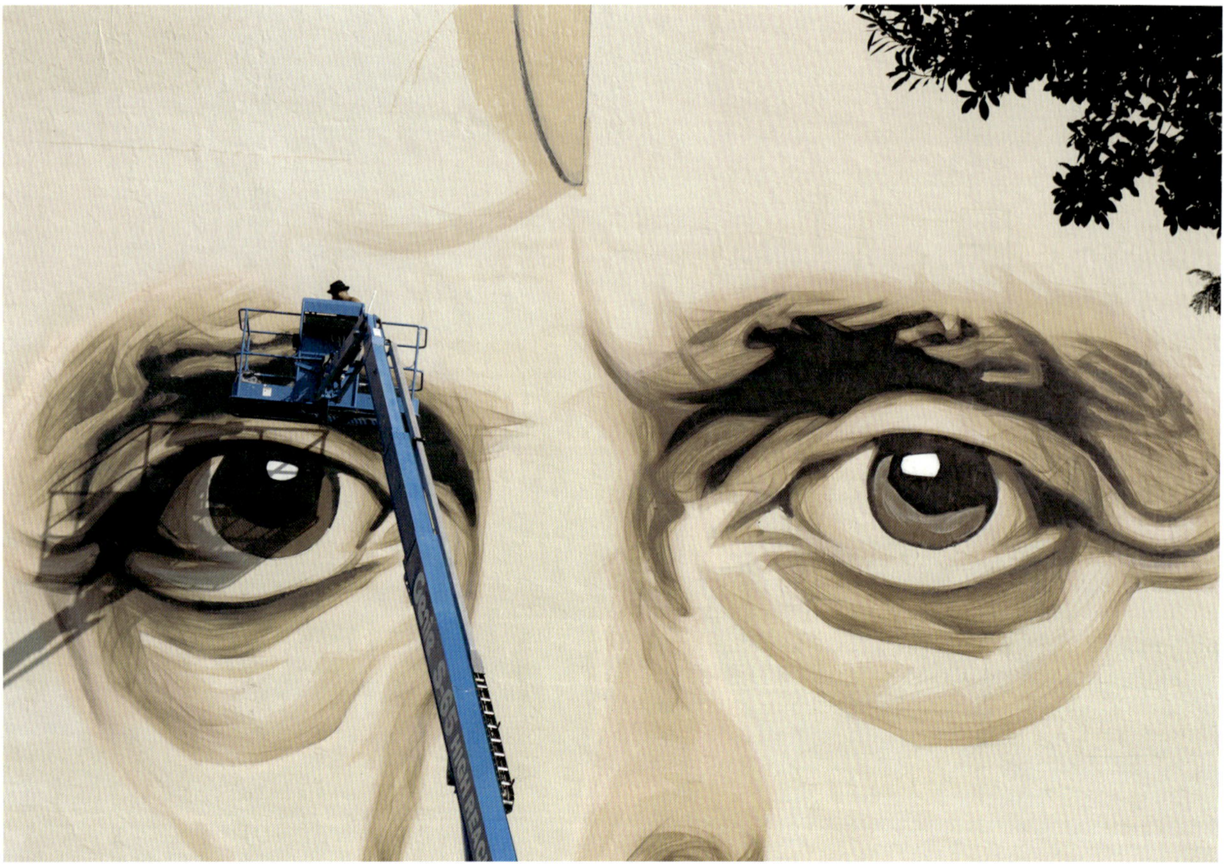

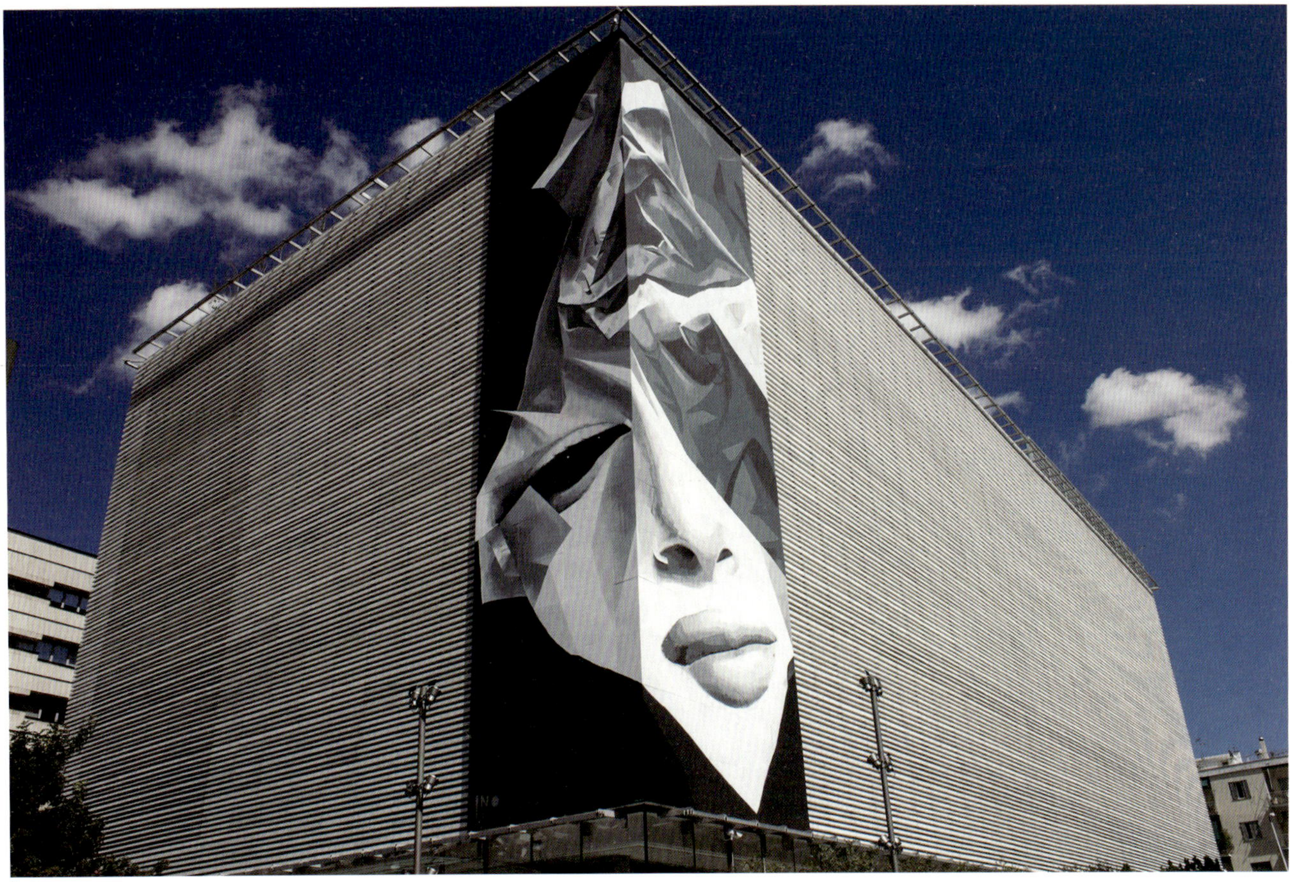

Creasing
@Athens, Greece 2014

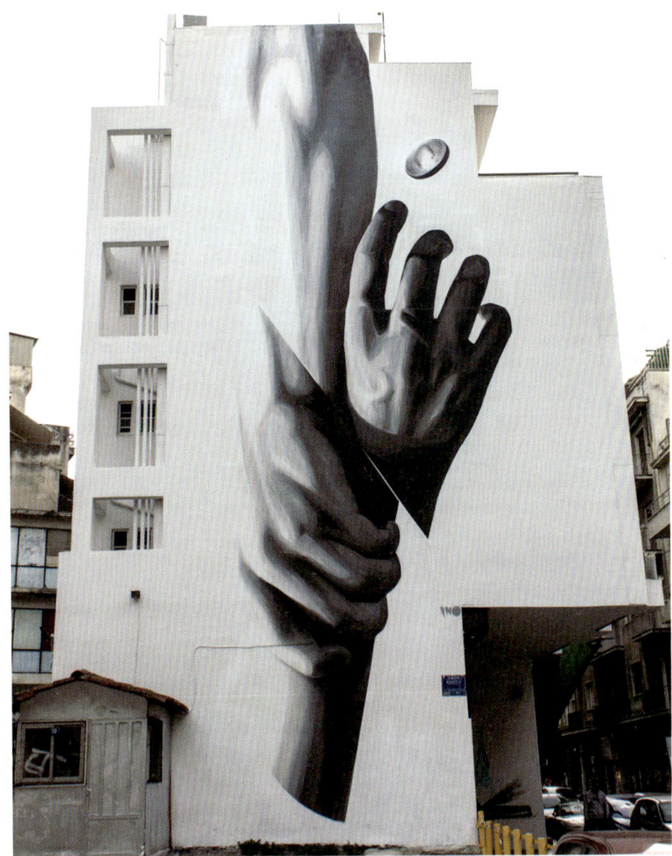

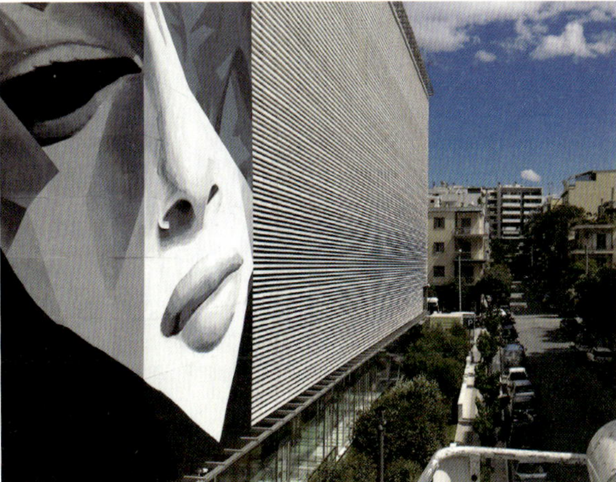

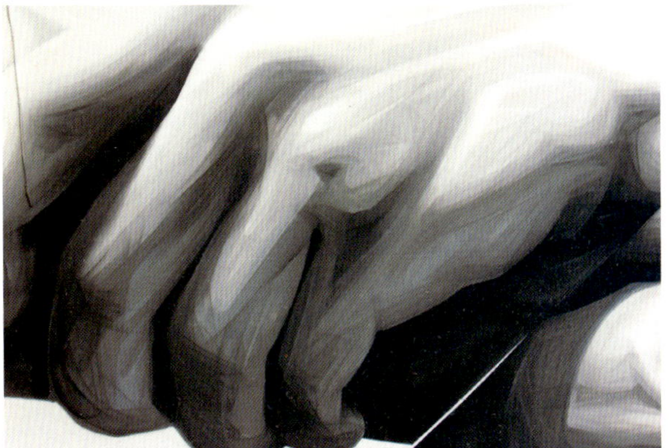

Wake Up
@Athens, Greece 2014

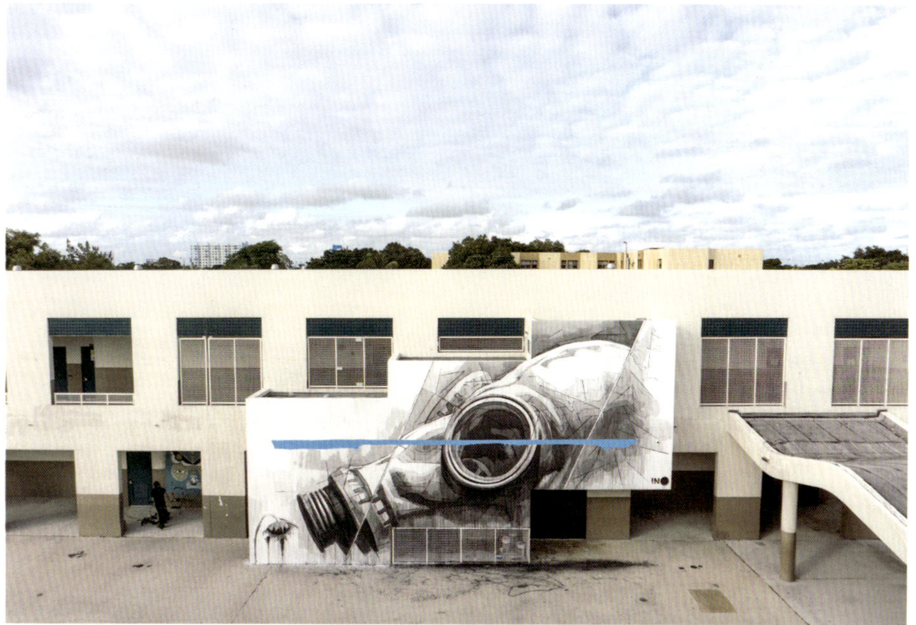

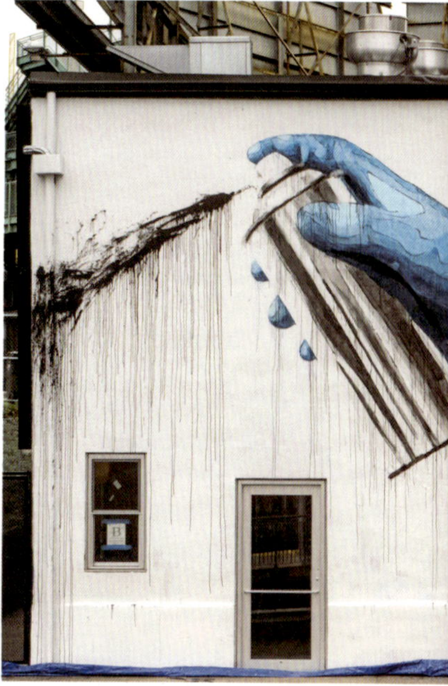

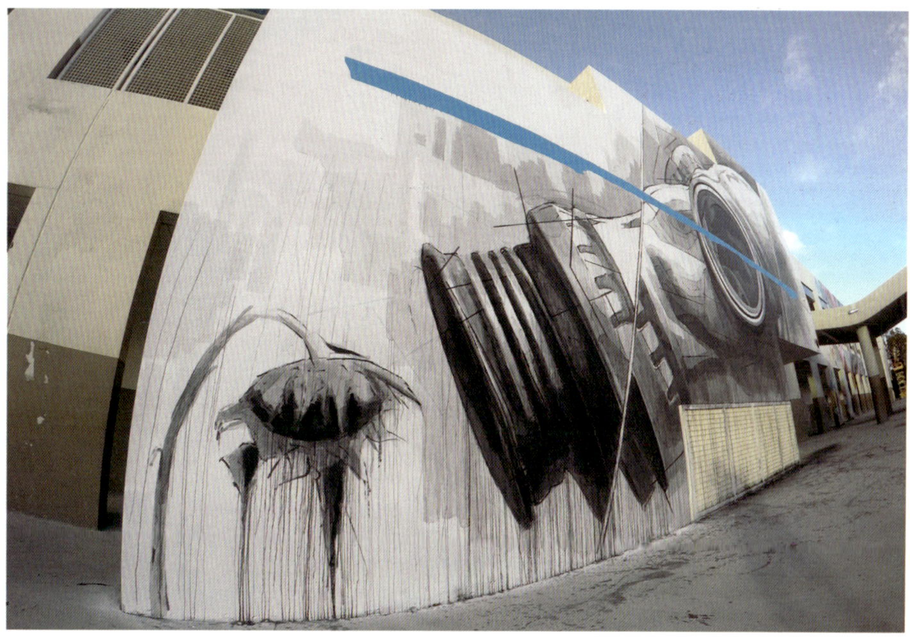

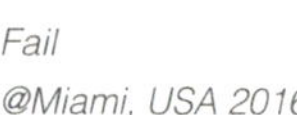

Fail
@Miami, USA 2016

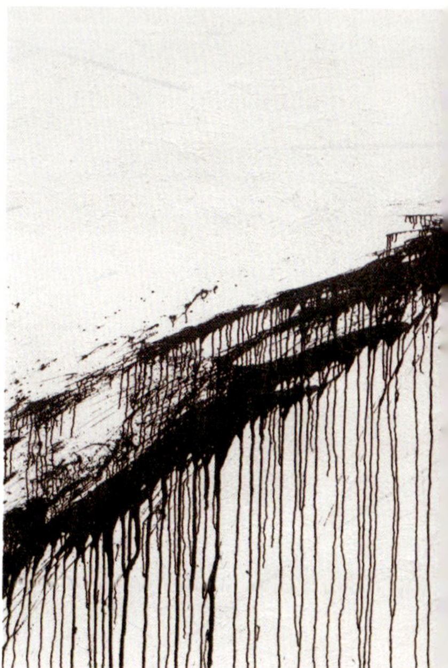

Unstoppable
@Boston, USA 2016

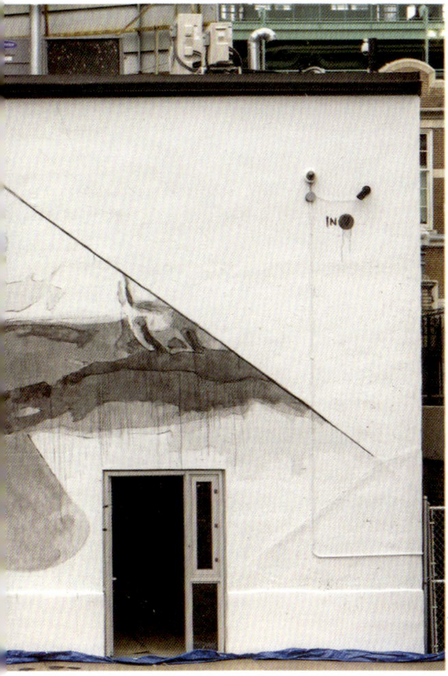

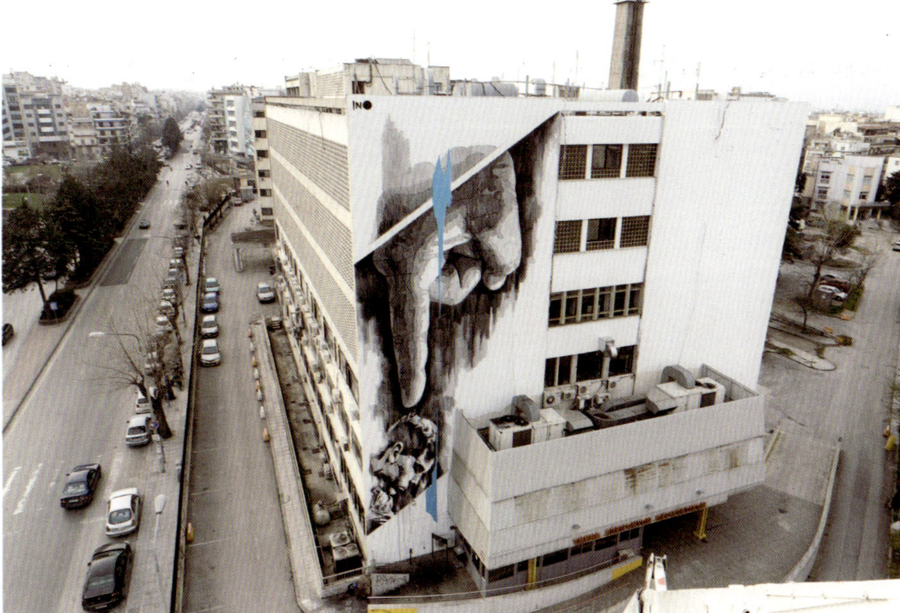

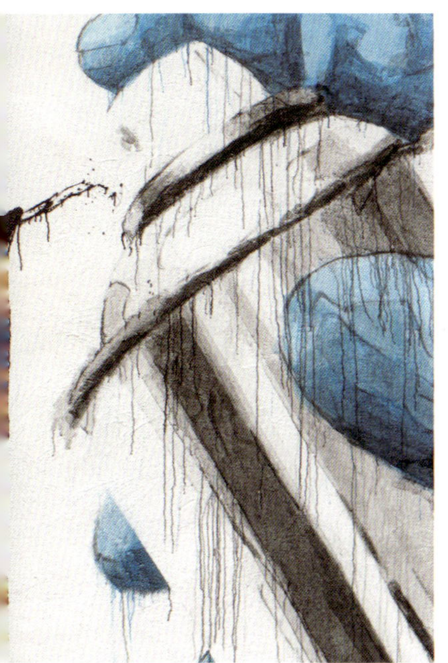

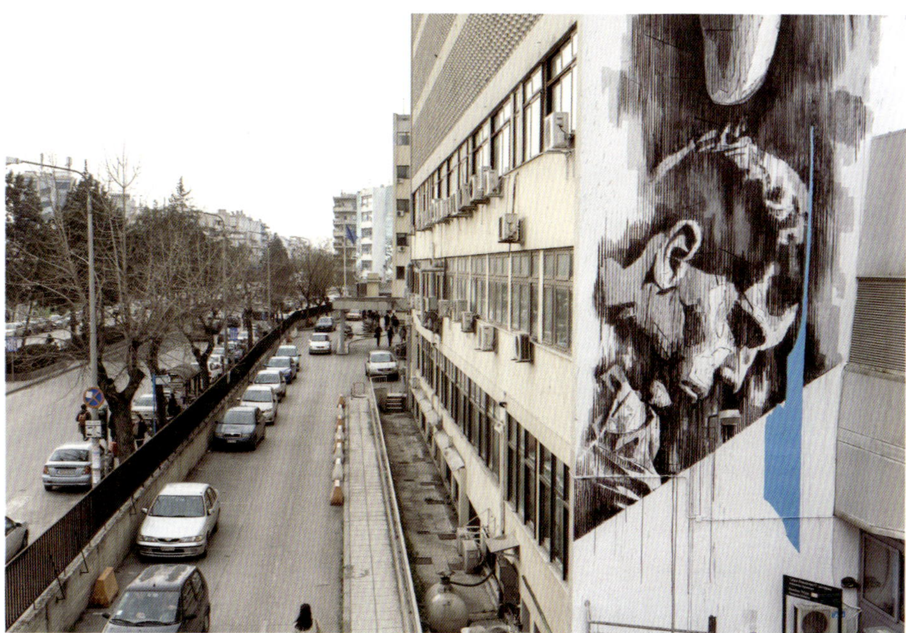

Stay Away
@Thessaloniki, Greece 2017

Marina and the Diamonds
@Budapest, Hungary 2017

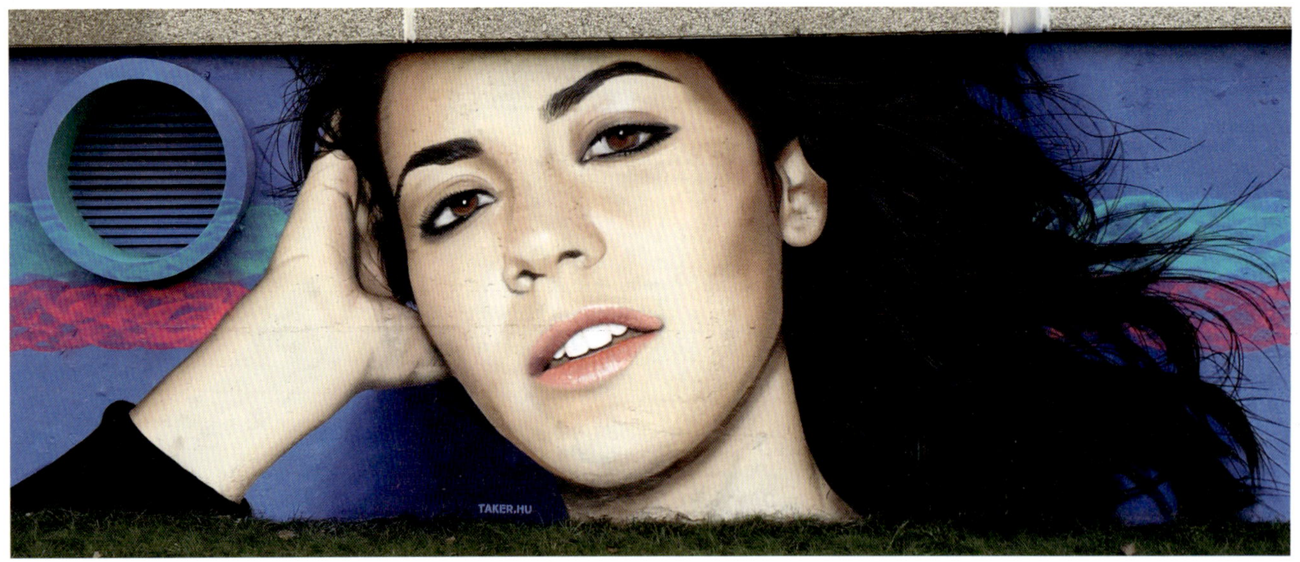

TakerOne is a photo-realistic graffiti artist from Hungary. His goal in his art is to avoid the plastic look that many photo-realistic paintings have, and go for a more natural, really photo-like result. He started to get acquainted with the world of graffiti at the end of 2001, and in 2005 he made his first photo-realistic piece on his own room's wall. Since 2006, his works have been exhibited multiple times. His works have been recognized by the media in Hungary as well as internationally many times, and can be found in multiple countries around the world, including the USA, the UK, New Zealand, Spain, Slovakia and Sri Lanka.

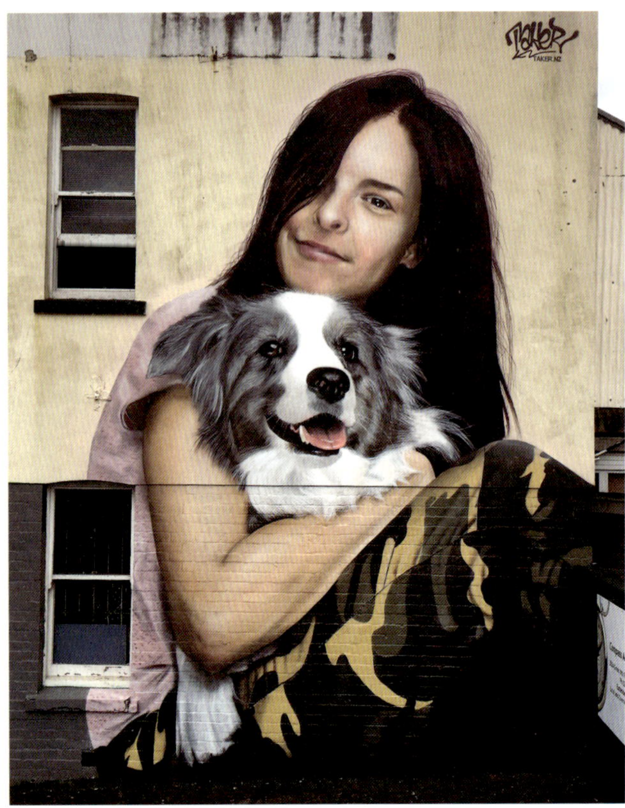

Lili and Bunny
@Auckland, New Zealand 2016

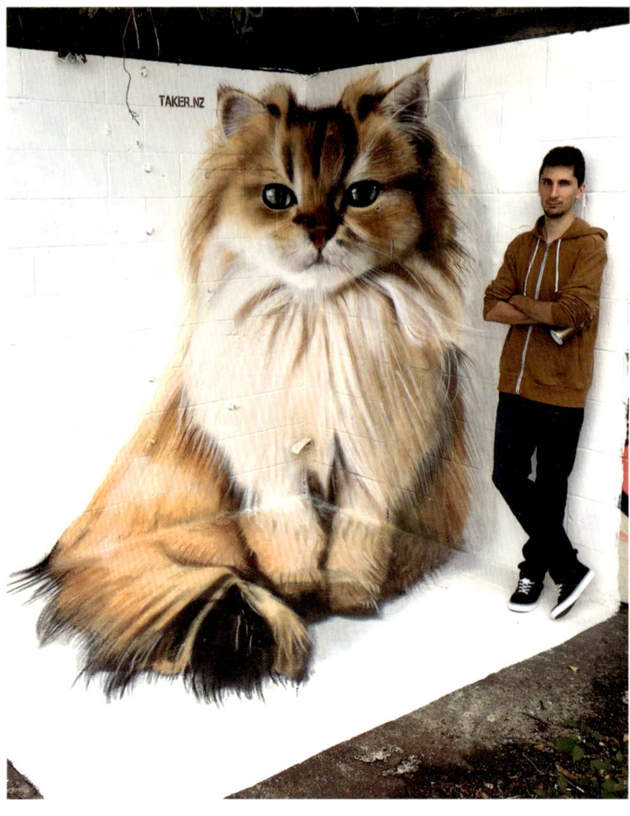

Smoothie
@Auckland, New Zealand 2017

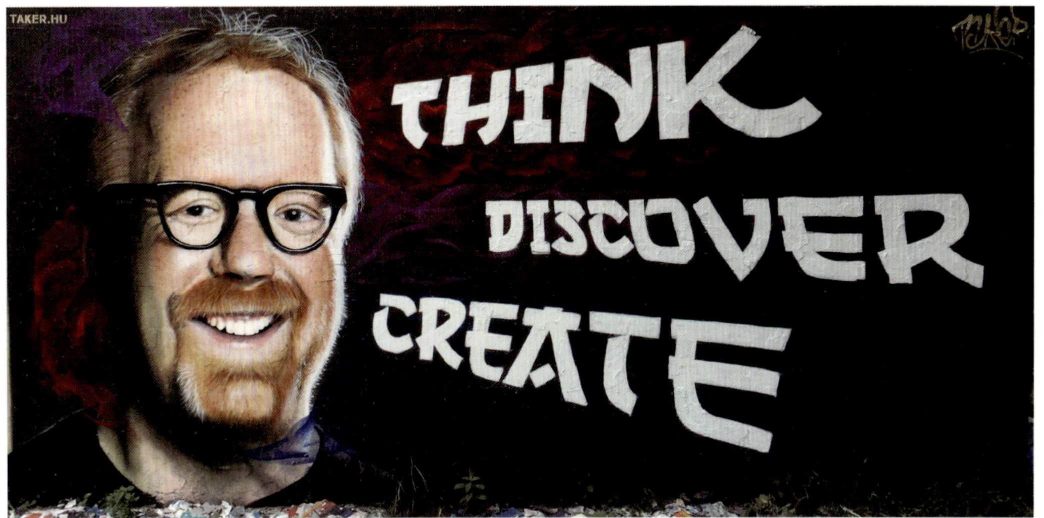

Adam Savage
@Budapest, Hungary 2016

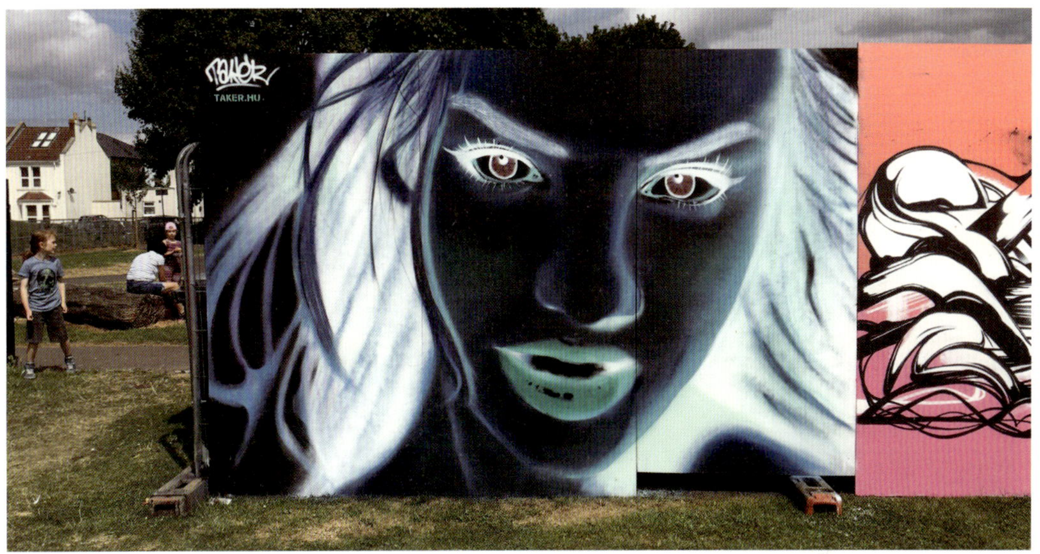

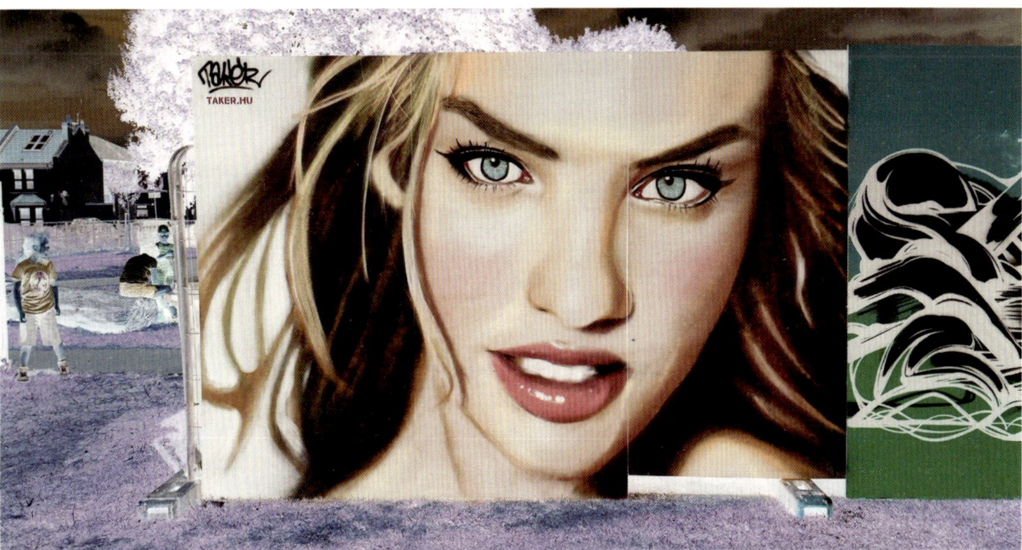

Inverse
Created for the Upfest Festival 2016
@Bristol, UK 2016

CARTOON

Cartoon characters are commonly seen in street art. Cartoons are created based on the keen observation of the subject, but instead of faithfully presenting them as the way they are, cartoons are an exaggeration of some certain characteristic of the subject, such as enlarged or shrunken arms and legs. Together with simple, clean lines, a humorous cartoon character emerges.

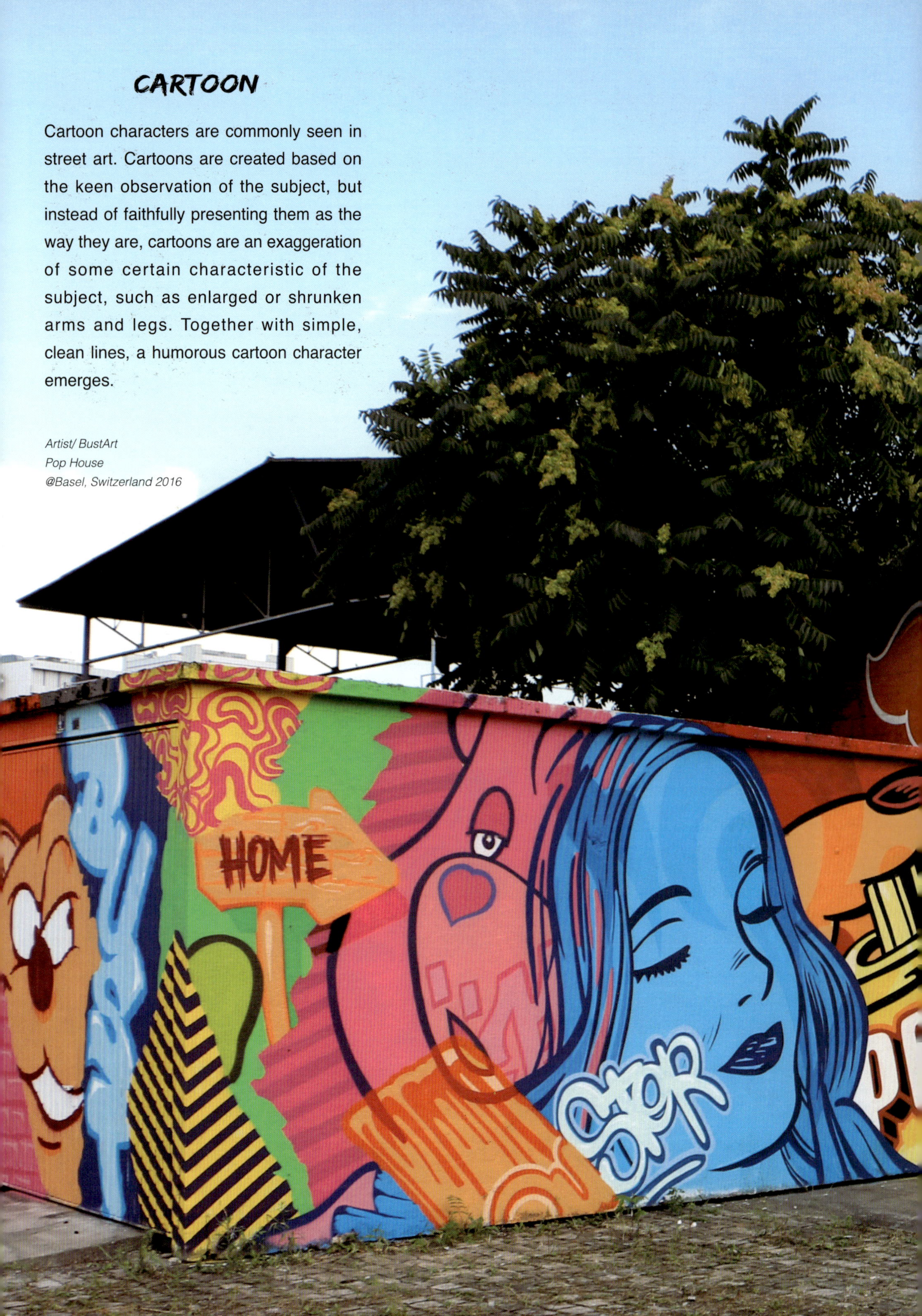

Artist/ BustArt
Pop House
@Basel, Switzerland 2016

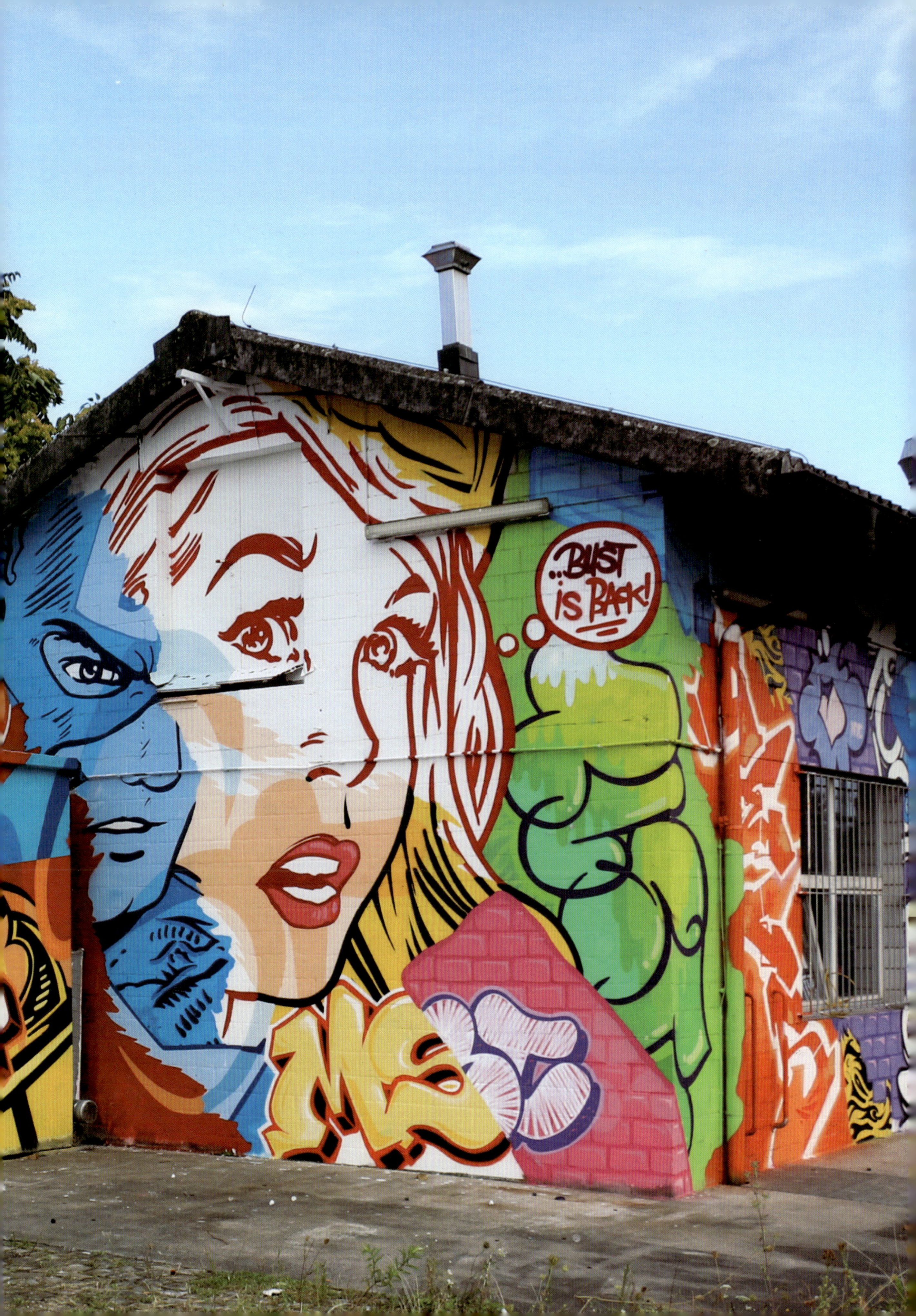
..BUST
is BACK!

Artist/ BustArt

BustArt is a neo-pop artist who tears characters and icons out of their original contexts to provide them with broader meaning. Starting with the classic graffiti in 1999, he dived deeply into the whole spectrum of graffiti art in the following years. He employed a wide range of techniques and materials, such as stencils, posters, stickers, collage to fulfill his mission to surprise passers-by, to encourage them to think, and to share the love of designing urban space.

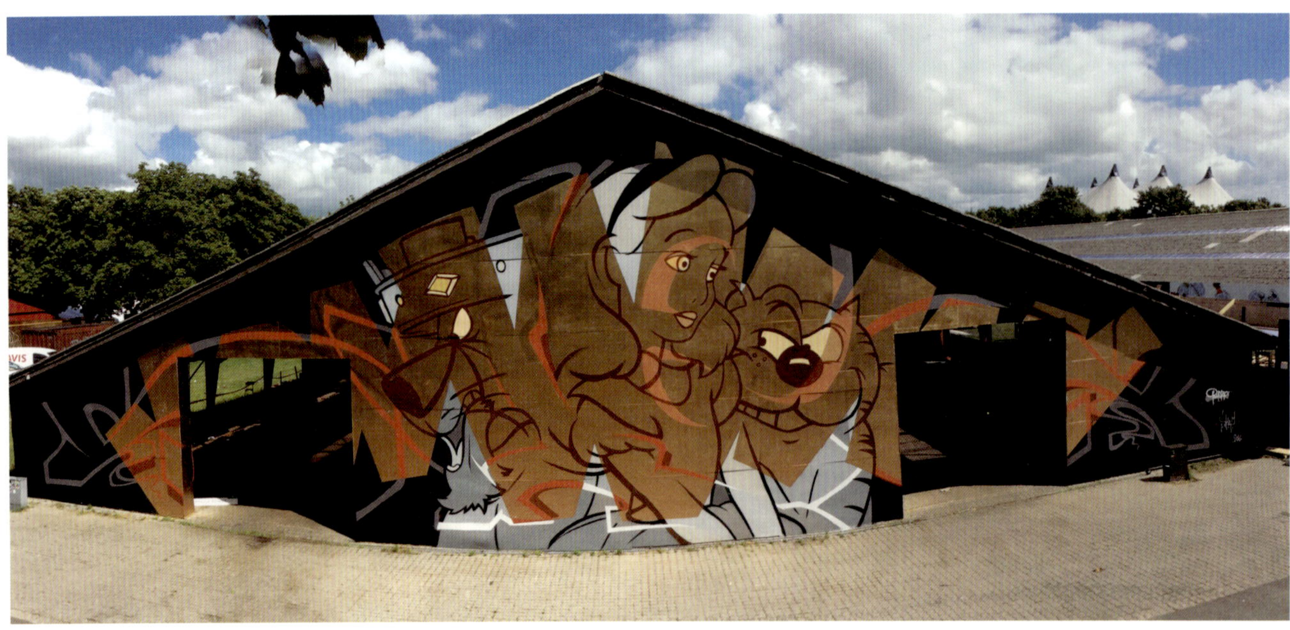

Untitled
Collaboration with Shez
@Roskilde, Denmark 2016

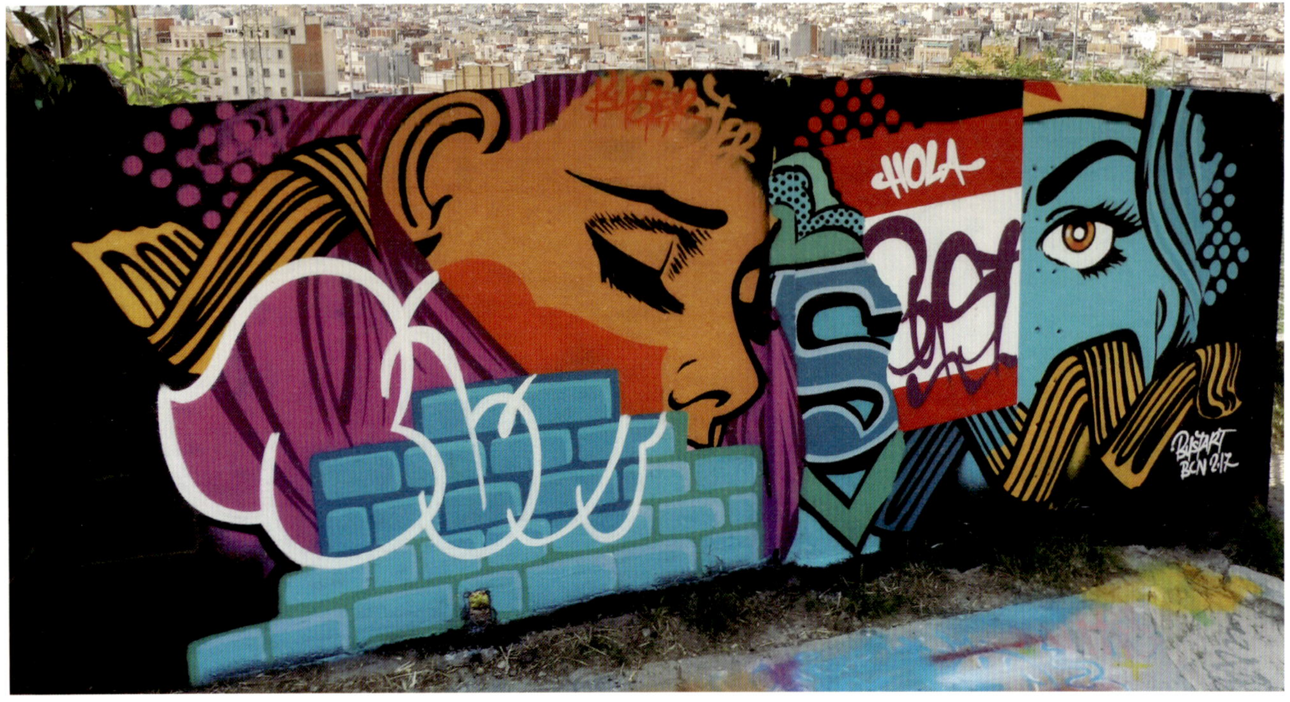

Hola!
@Barcelona, Spain 2017

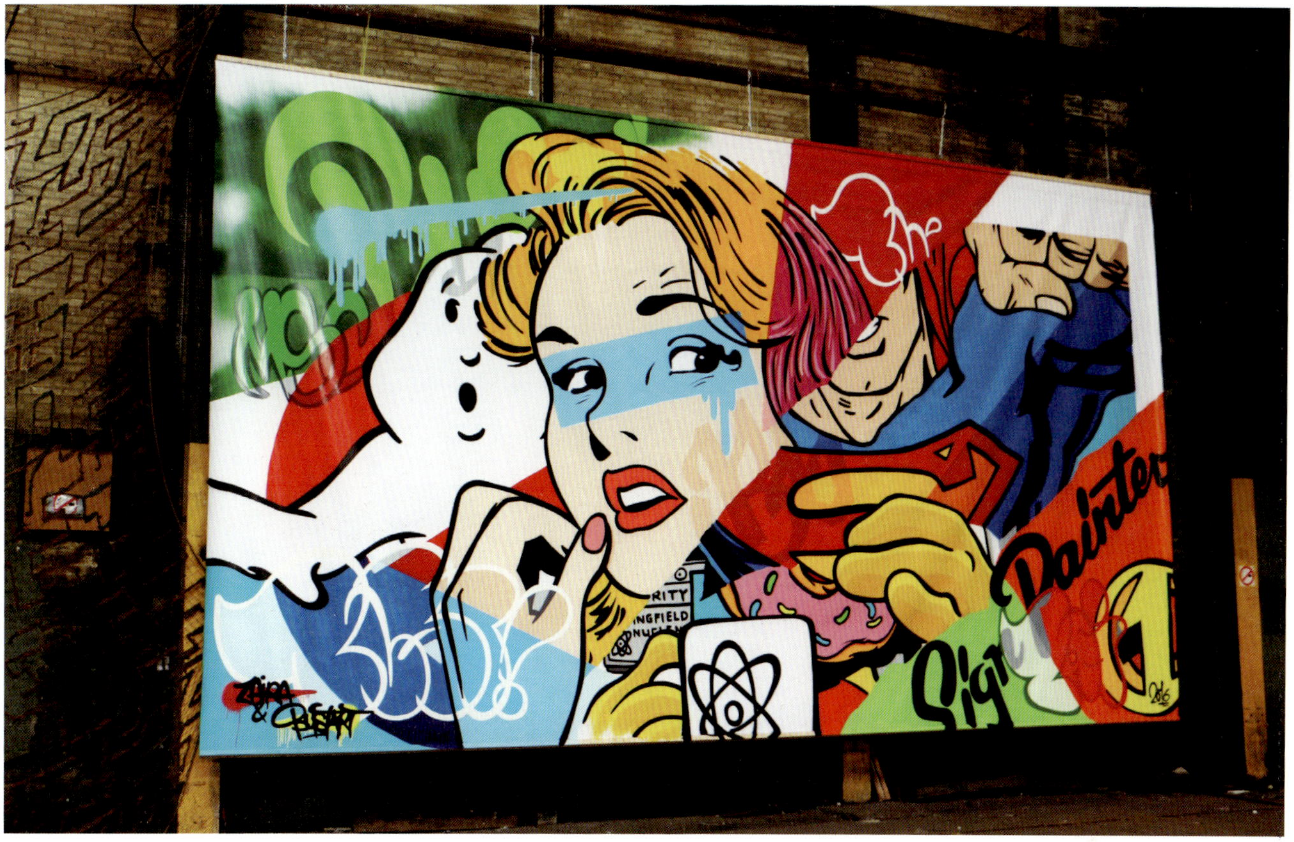

Untitled
@Amsterdam, The Netherlands 2016

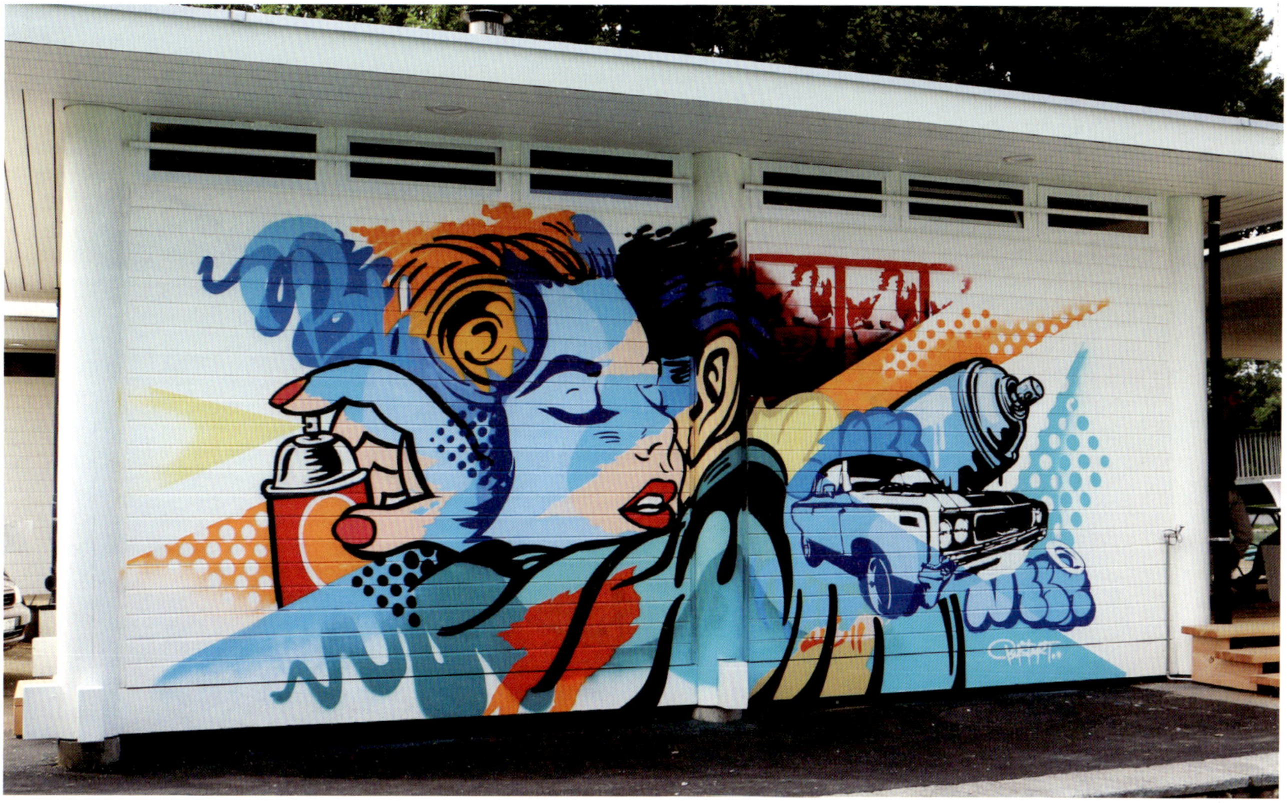

Street Pop
@Basel, Switzerland 2015

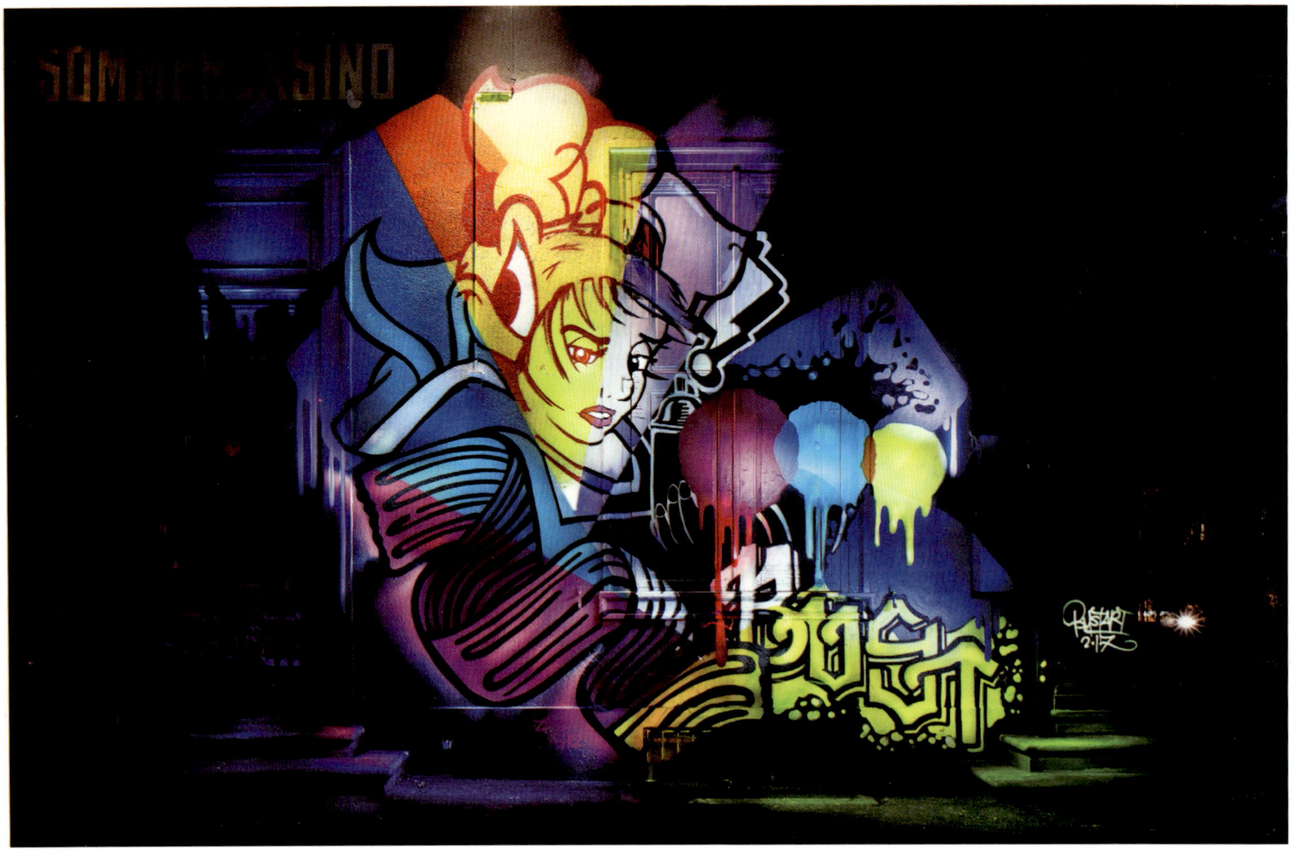

Nightlife
@Basel, Switzerland 2017
©Dedi Basel

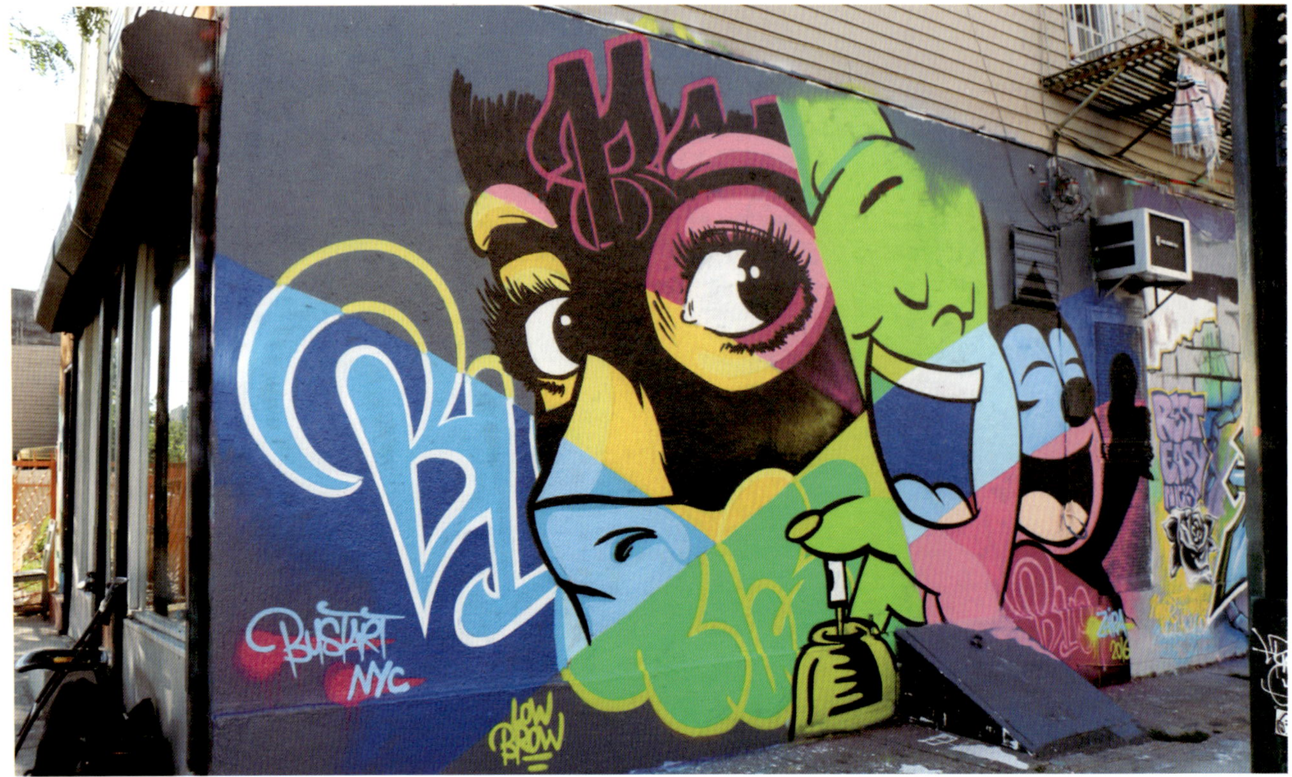

Graffitipop
@New York, USA 2016

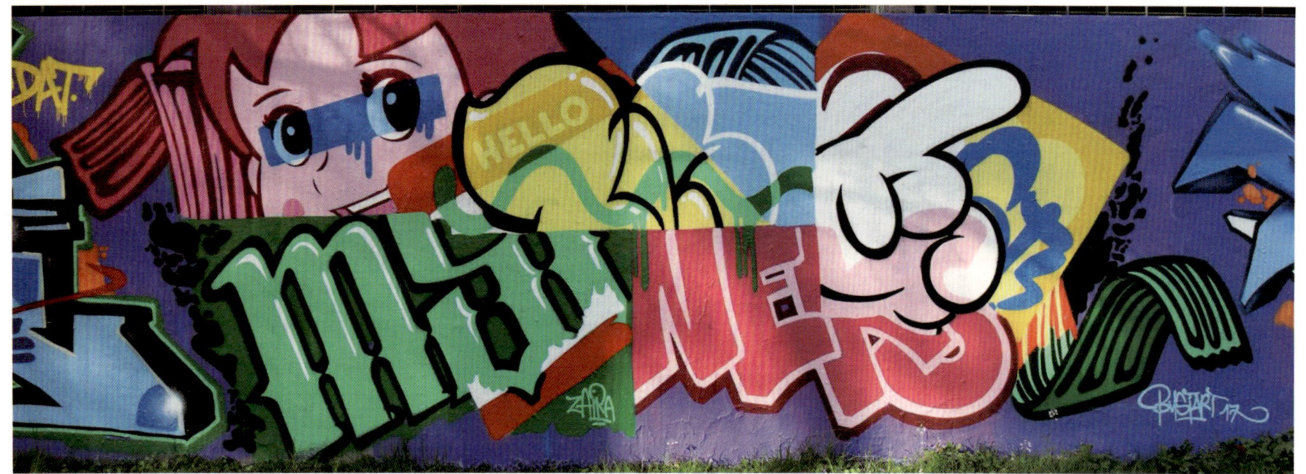

Graffitipop Madness
@Basel, Switzerland 2017

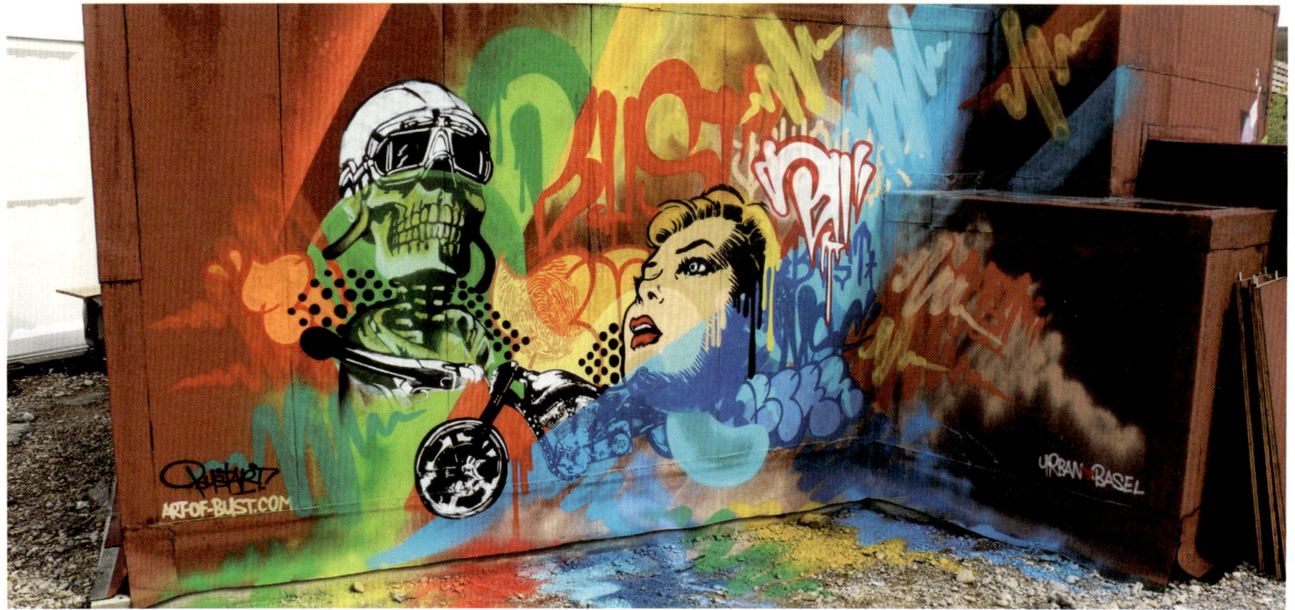

Takeover
@Basel, Switzerland 2015

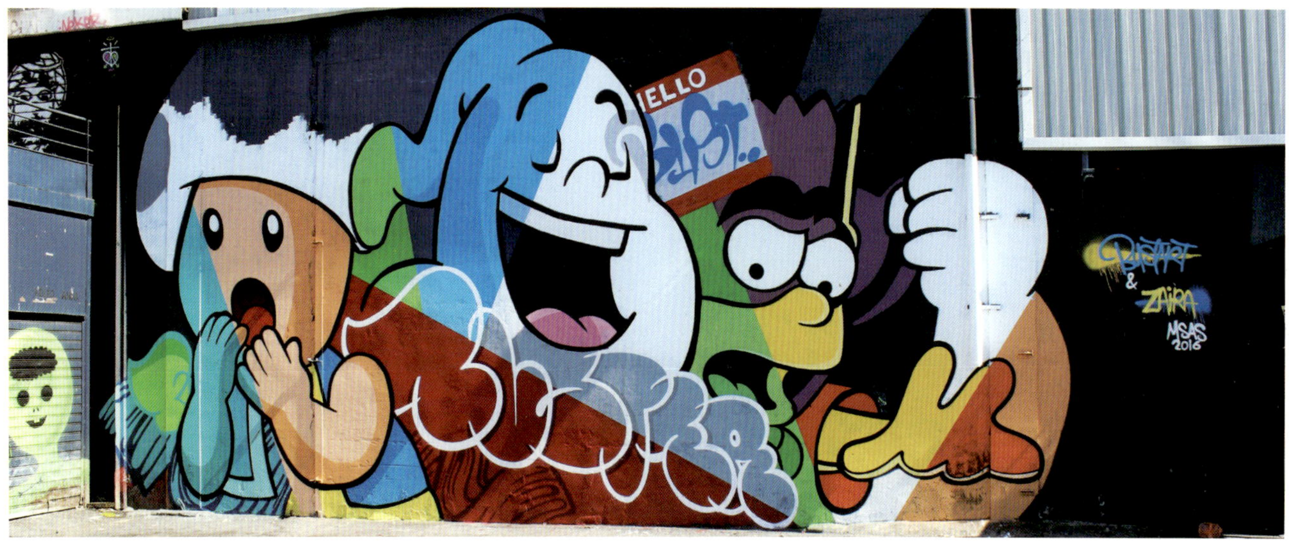

Marseille Graffitipop
@Marseille,France 2016

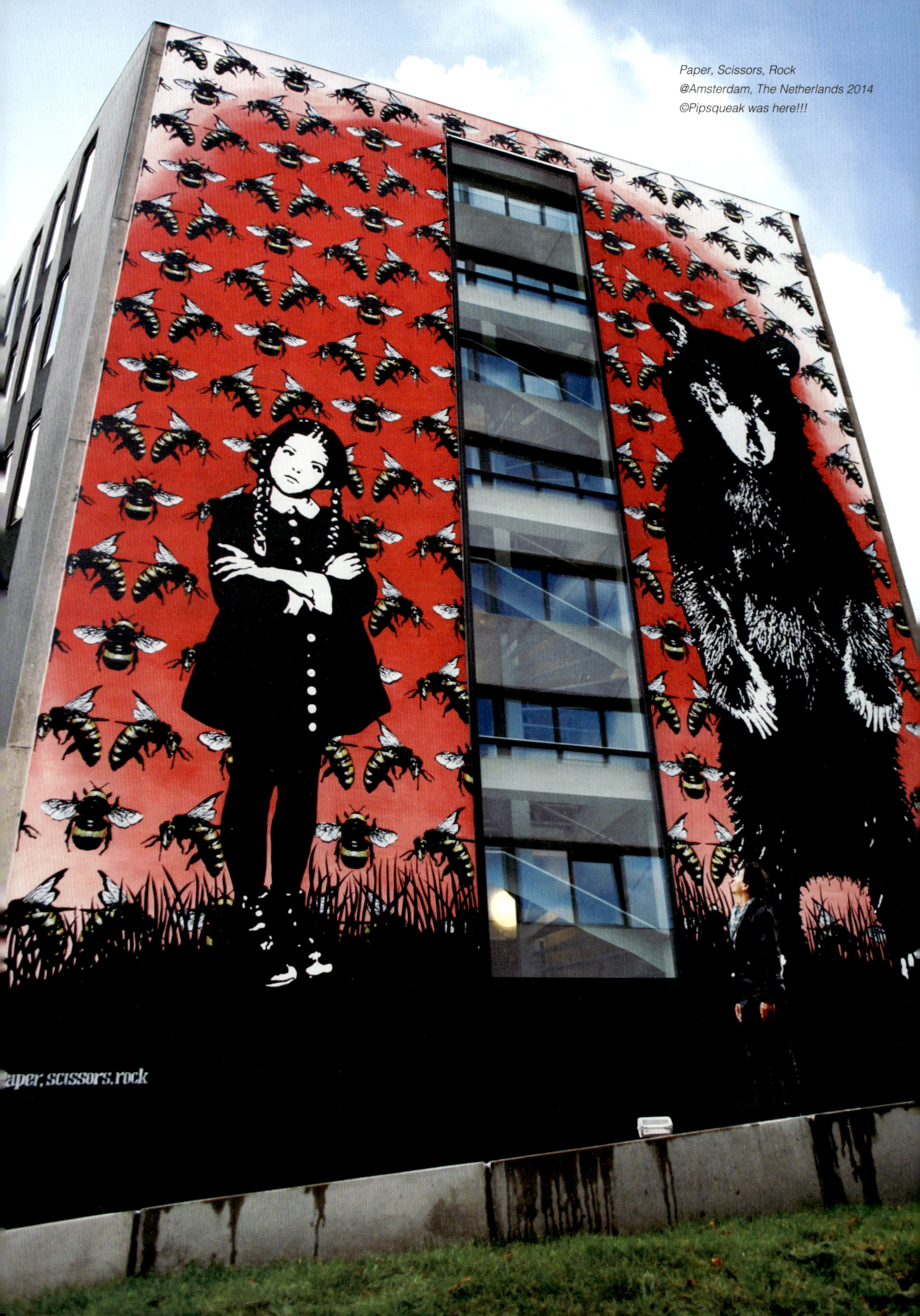

Paper, Scissors, Rock
@Amsterdam, The Netherlands 2014
©Pipsqueak was here!!!

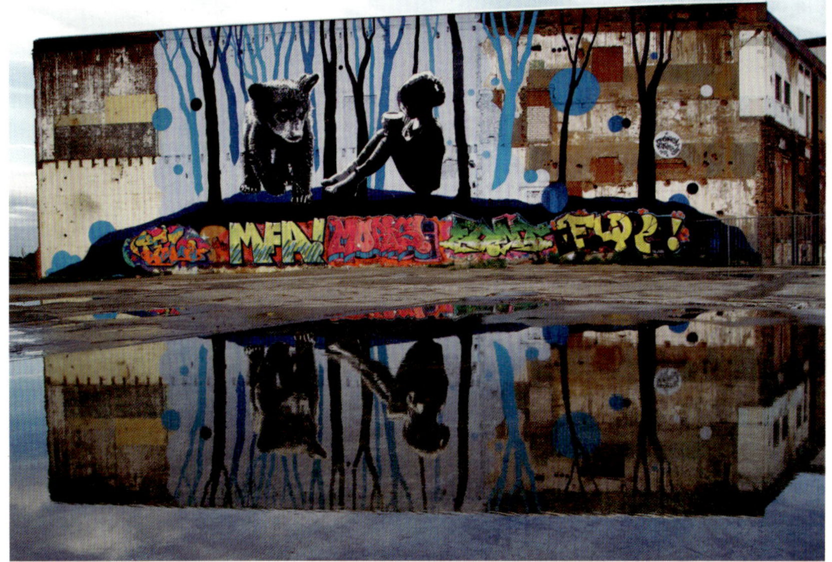

Pipsqueak Was Here!!! is an Amsterdam-based artist duo. Animals, in particular bears, are always integral components in their works, together with humans, to suggest the way humans interact with animals should be fundamentally changed as environmental worries have grown and relationships between animals and humans have become more strained.

The Bigger Picture
@Nijmegen, The Netherlands 2015
©Erik van Os

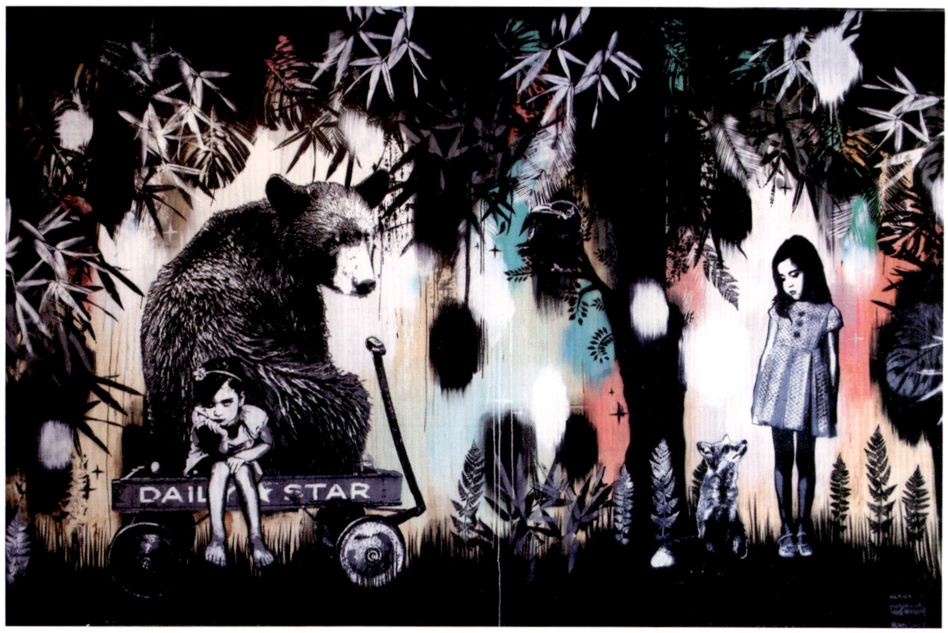

Jungle Fever
@Hengelo, The Netherlands 2017
©Pipsqueak was here!!!

Sad Bear
@Amsterdam, The Netherlands 2014
©Pipsqueak was here!!!

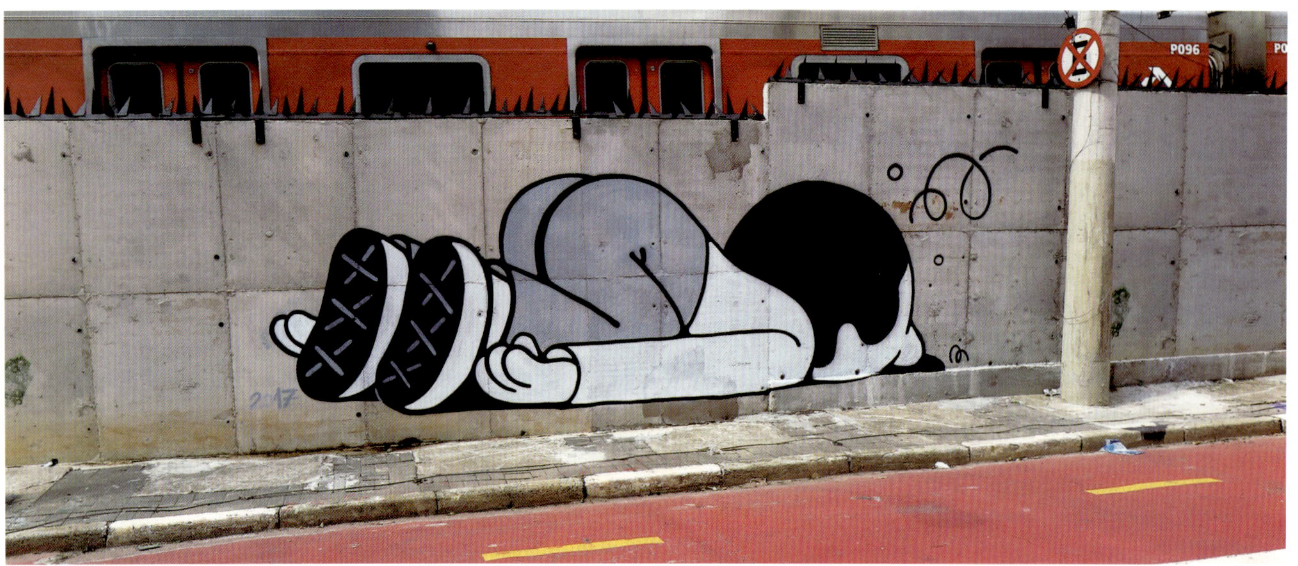

Hangover
@Sao Paulo, Brazil 2016

MURETZ (Mauro Muretz) is a Brazilian artist known mostly for his rounded, cartoon-like characters. Expelled from school at the age of 15, because of drawing, he was encouraged by friends and family to earn his living by painting. His art walks a fine line between playful and cynical, bringing a sense of humor to figures struggling with inner demons.

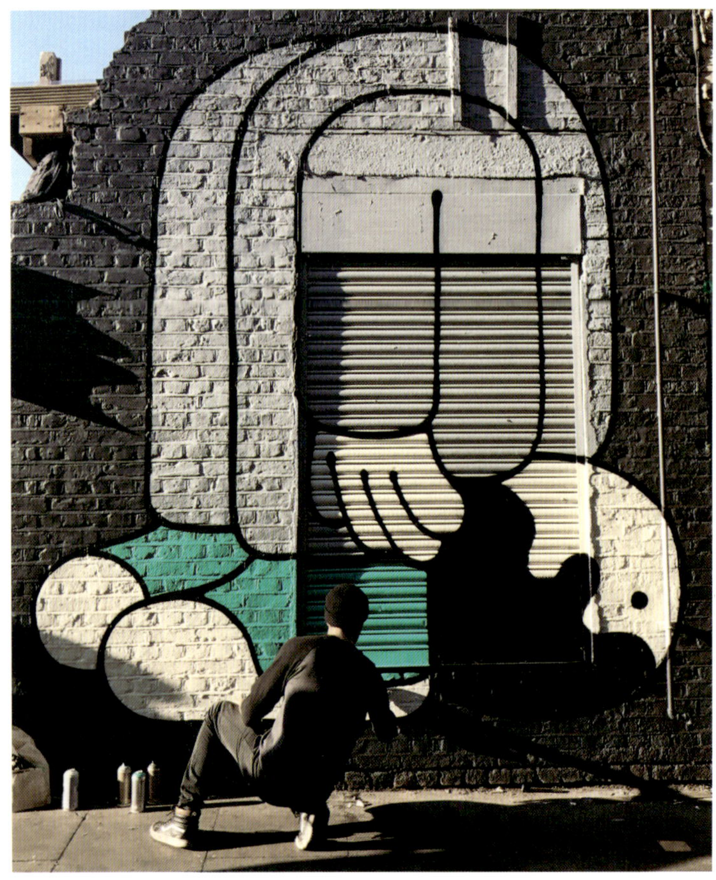

Bending Backwards
@London, UK 2017

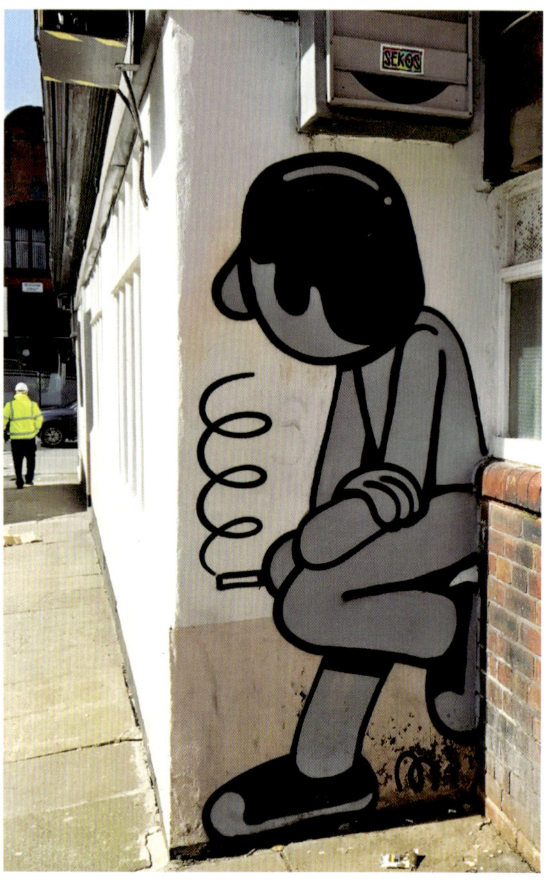

Waiting for My Bus
@Liverpool, UK 2017

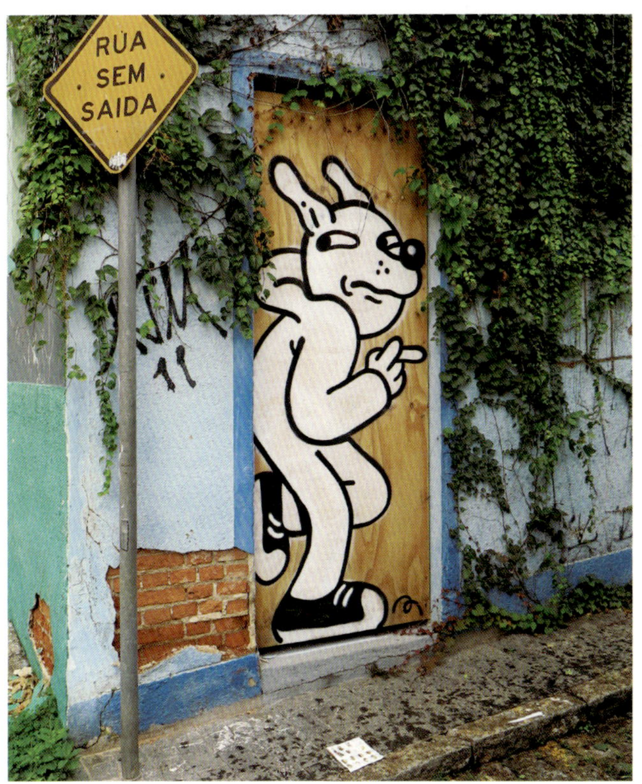

Suspicious
@São Paulo, Brazil 2016

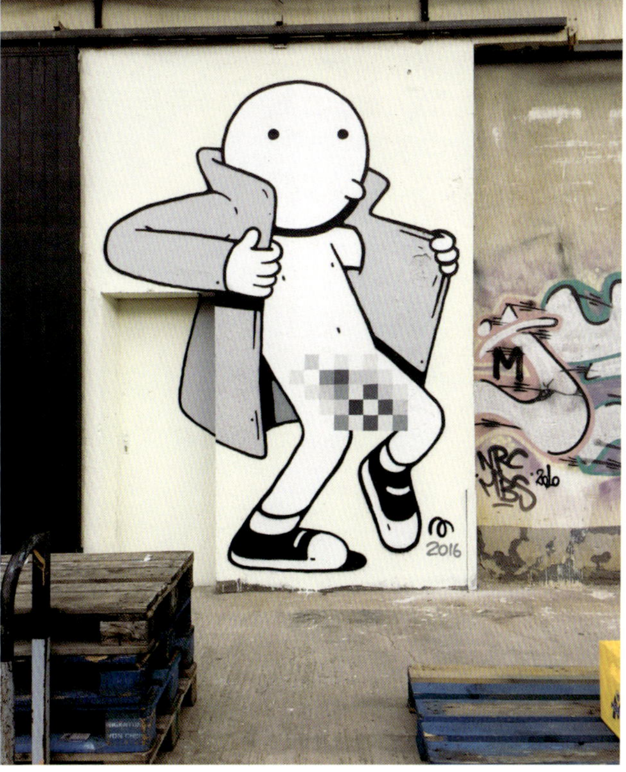

Nude
@Barcelona, Spain 2016

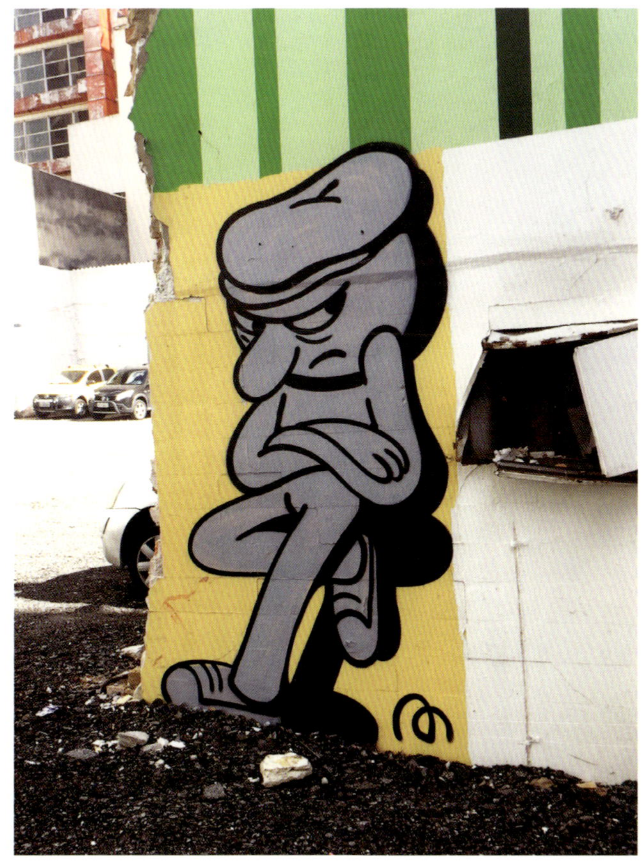

Serious Man
@São Paulo, Brazil 2016

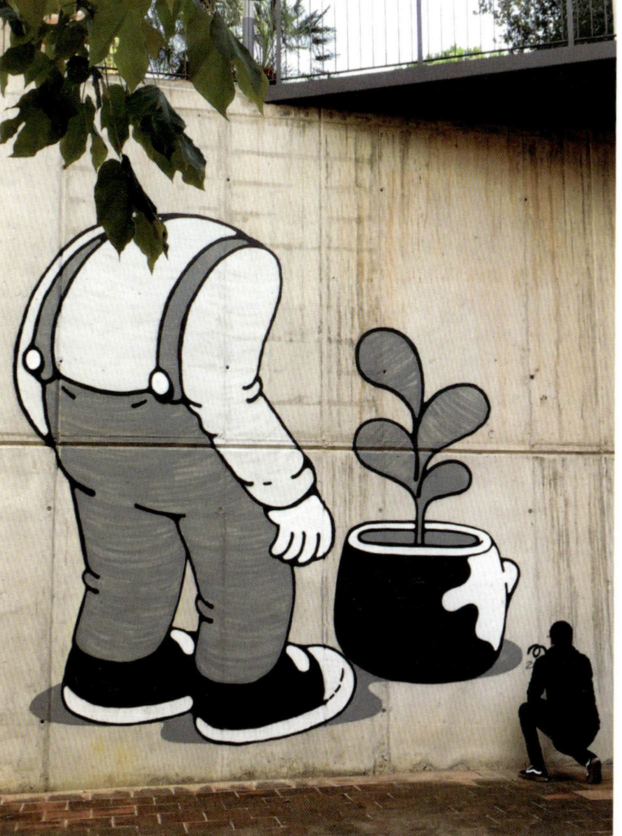

Head Plant
@Martorell, Spain 2016

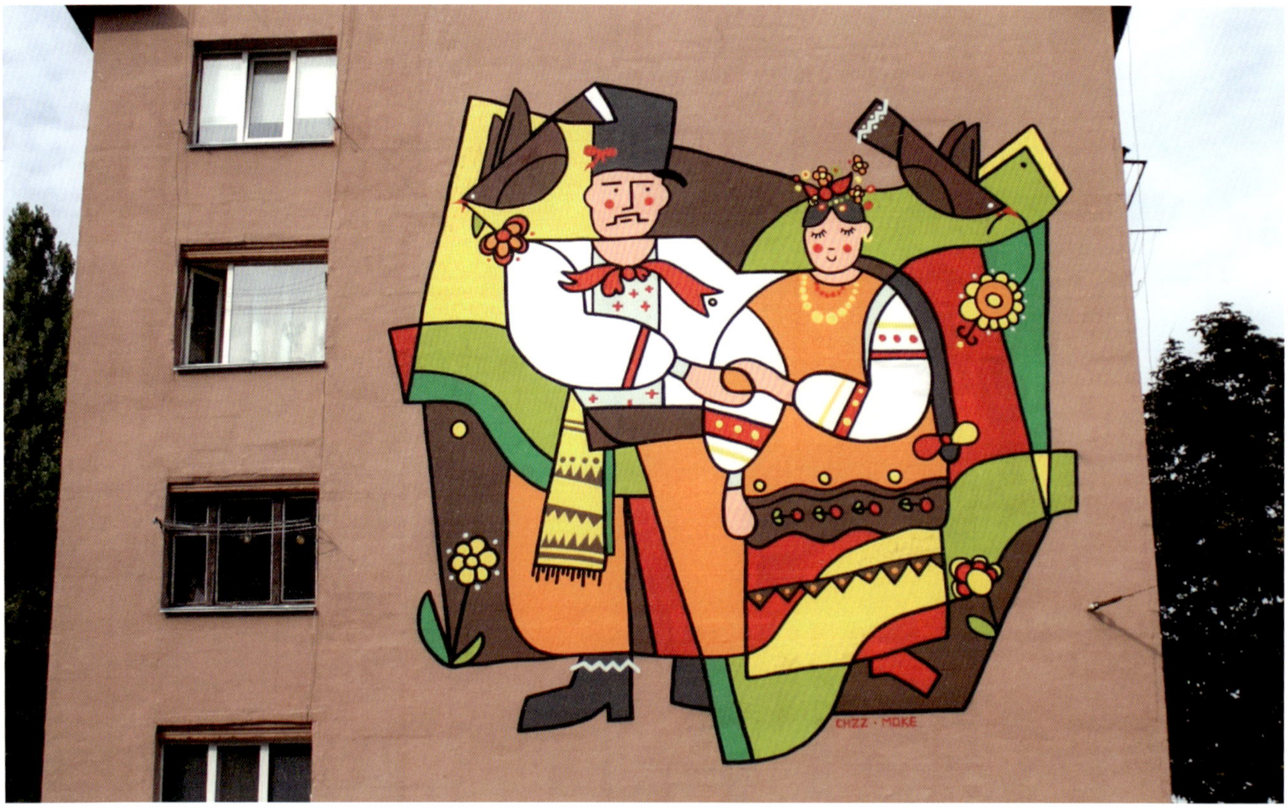

Ethno Pair
@Chernihiv, Ukraine 2016

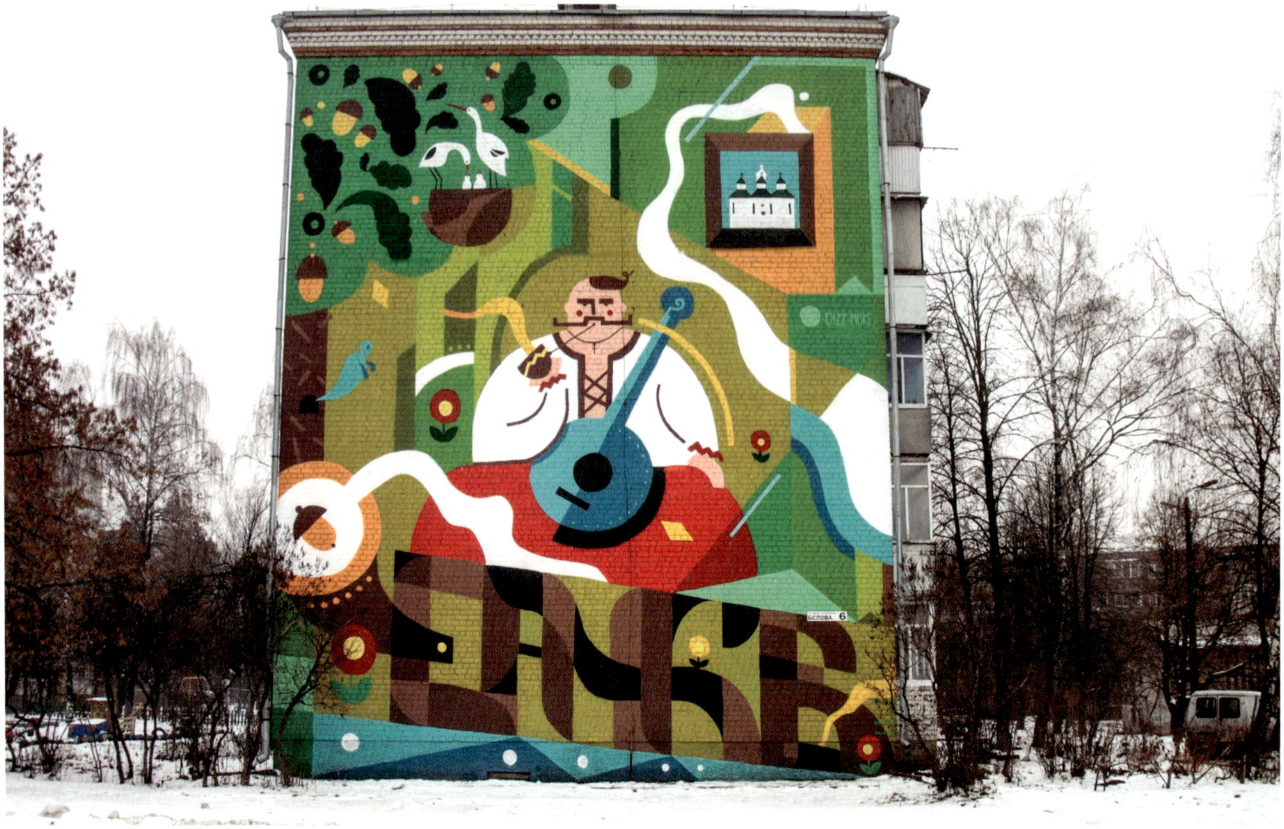

Mamay
@Chernihiv, Ukraine 2016

Chzz Zavoyovnuk is a Ukrainian visual artist. Inspired by local legends from Chernihiv, he created all the cartoon-like characters according to Ukrainian ethnic design elements, such as the style and patterns of their folk costumes.

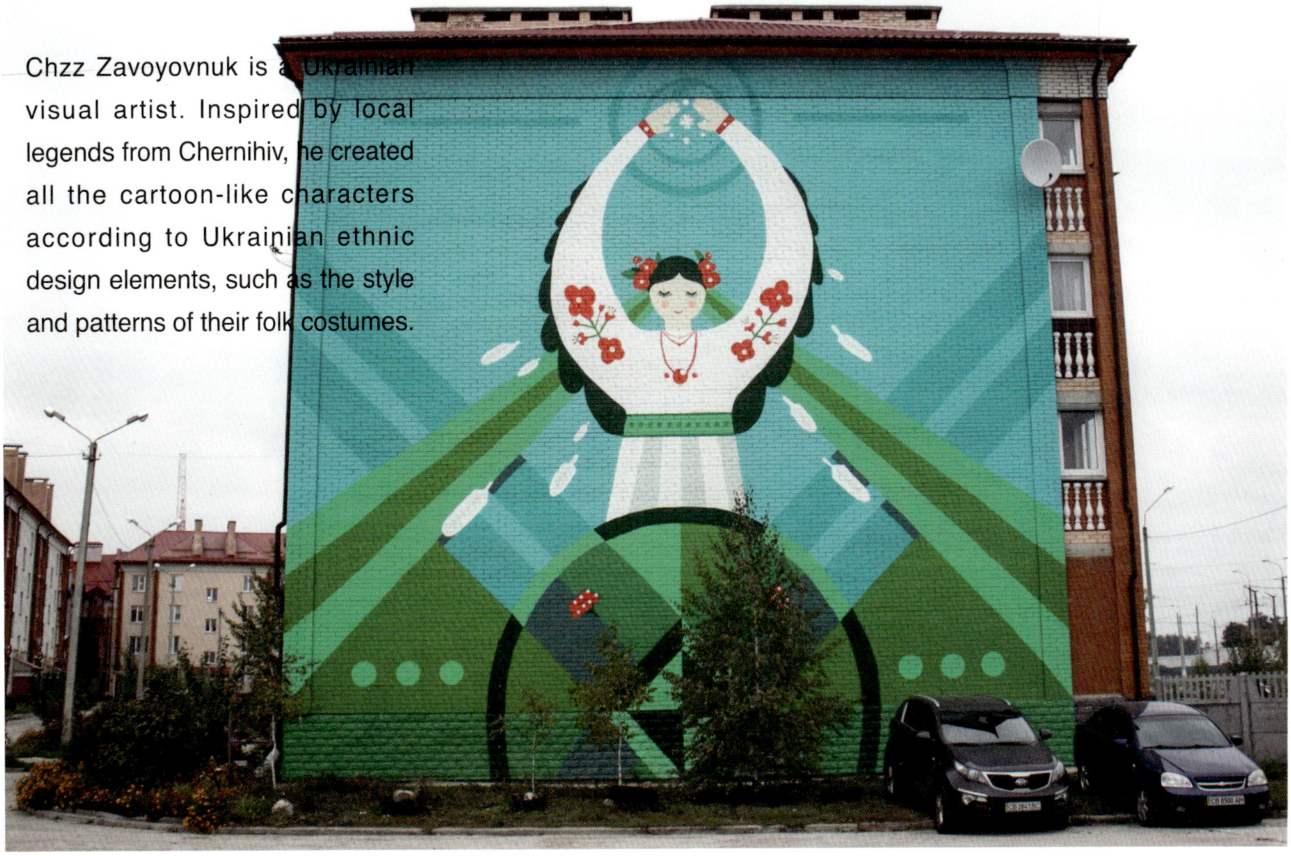

Girl Crane
@Chernihiv, Ukraine 2016

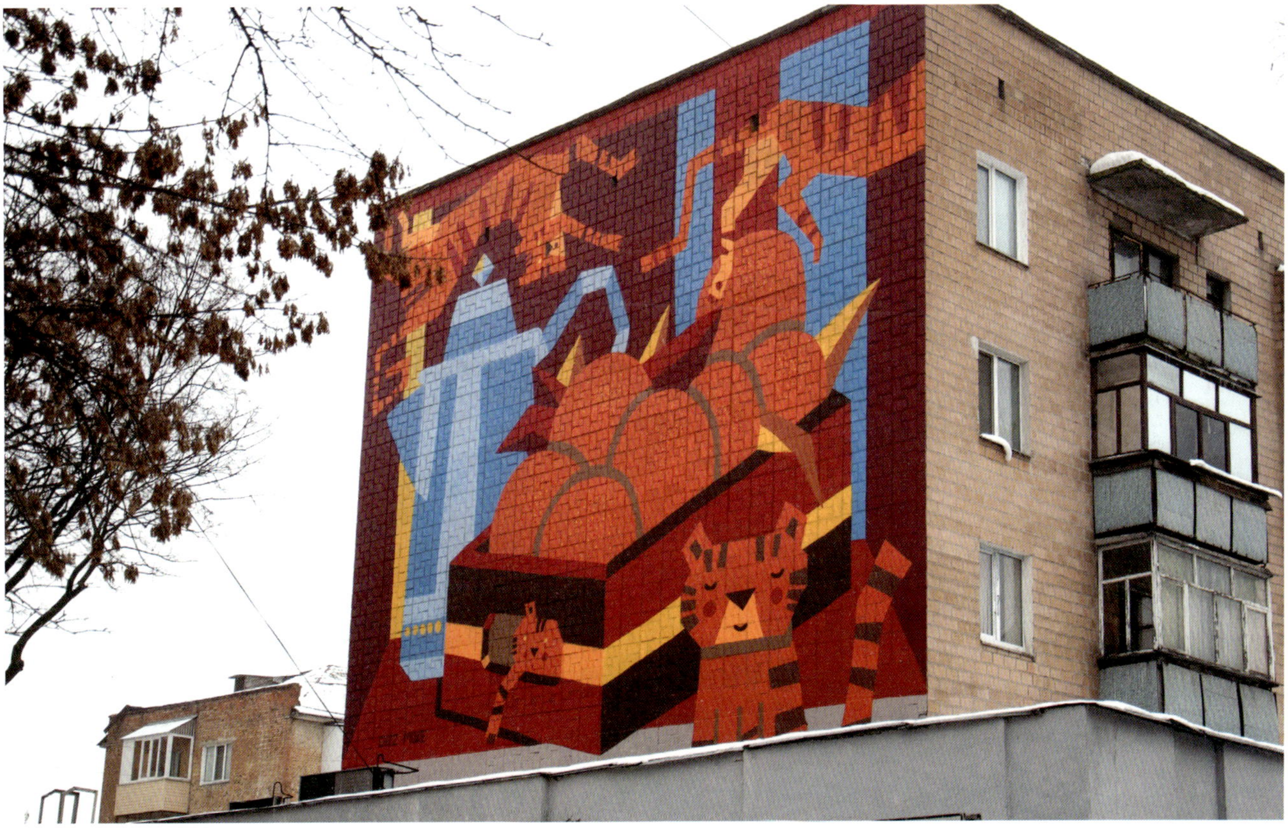

Oranges and Tigers
@Chernihiv, Ukraine 2016

Zdes Roy is an international street art and mural artist. He works with commercial murals and graffiti for different companies. His style takes roots in graphic design, 2D animation, and information design.

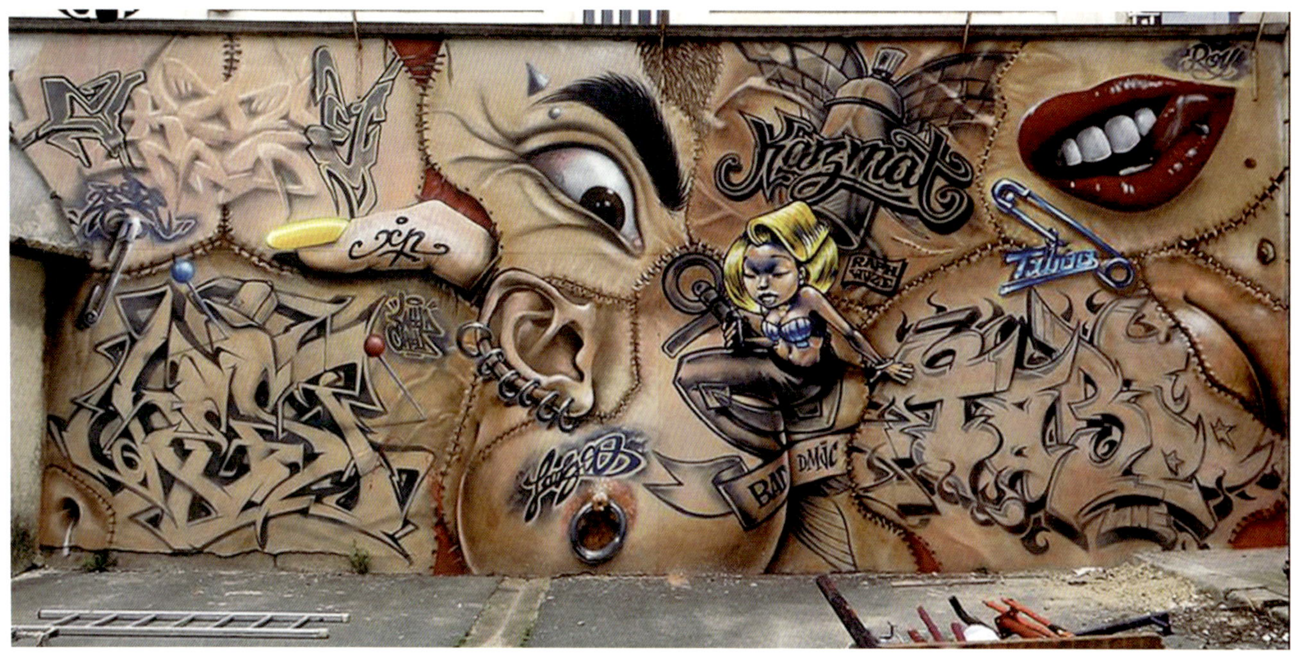

Collaboration with Francois Tworode, Wuze Fabrice, Yann Lazoo, Raphaël Simon Genty, Kaoru Tabuchi, and Nes Pounta

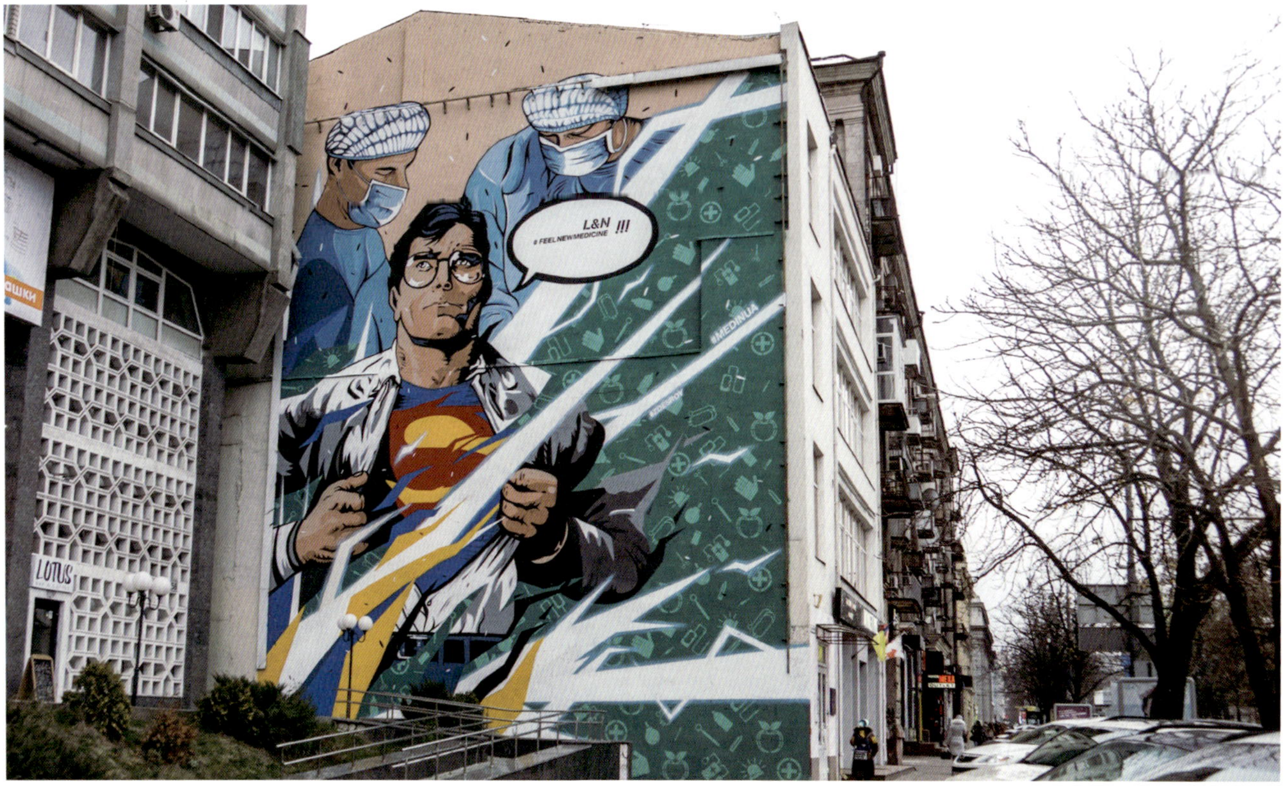

Superman
@Dnipro, Ukraine 2017

Альо! #COMFY
@Kiev, Ukraine 2016

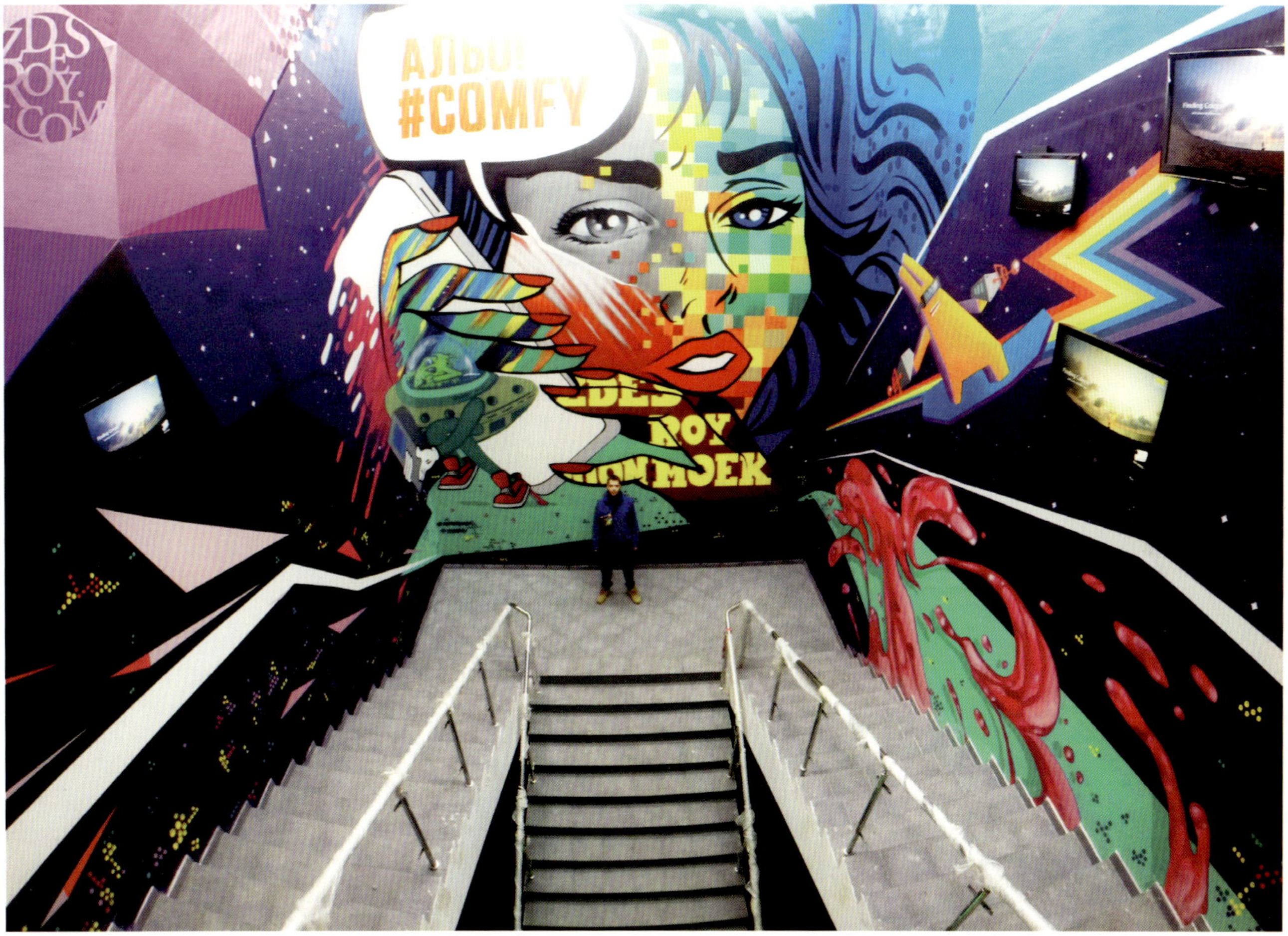

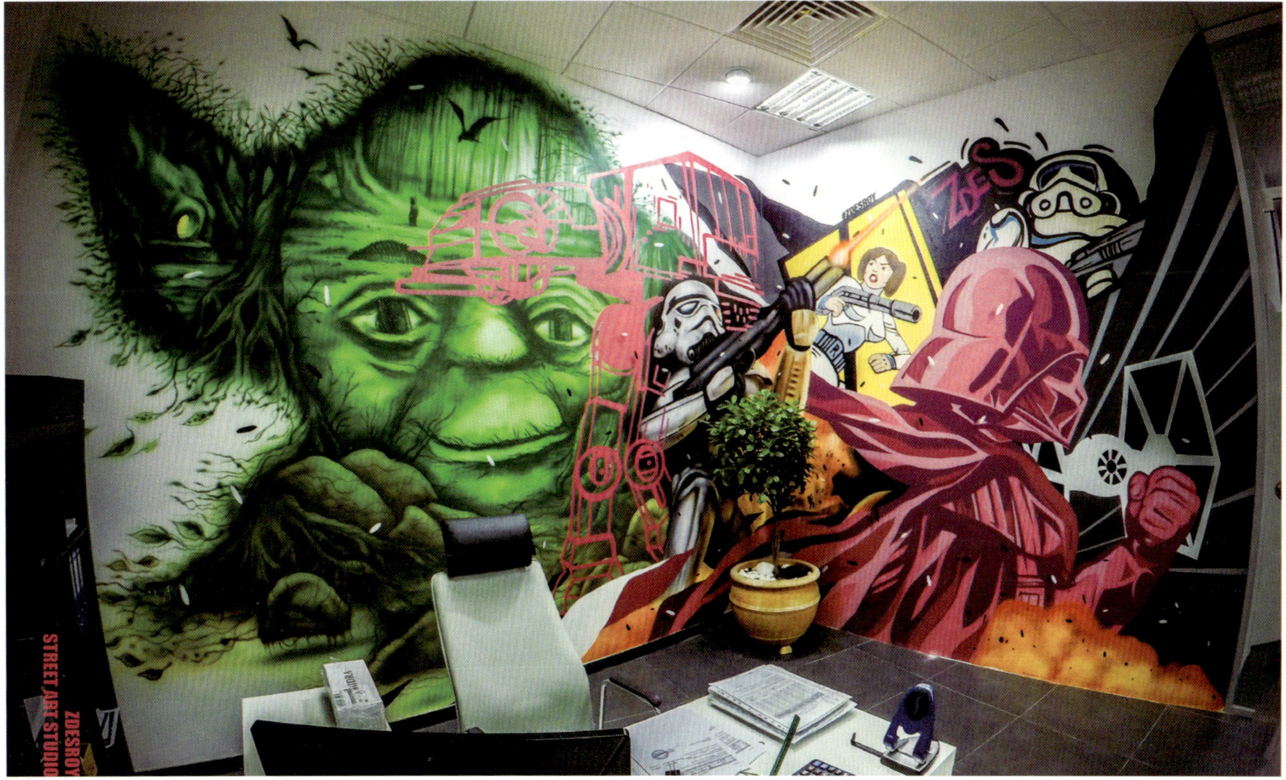

Star Wars
Created for an IT company office 2016

Art of Sool is a street art team founded in 2010, mainly formed by three Italian artists: Nick Neim, IlClod, and MATW. Their works are characterized by over-exaggerated cartoons with popping eyes, dripping effects, and crowded images.

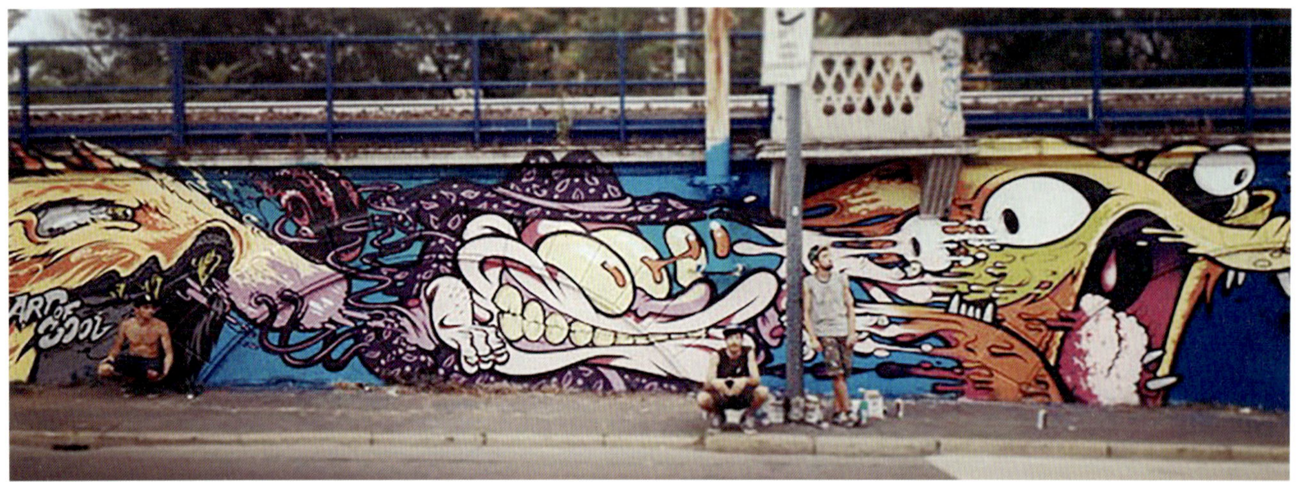

Amazing Day 2015
@Milan, Italy 2015

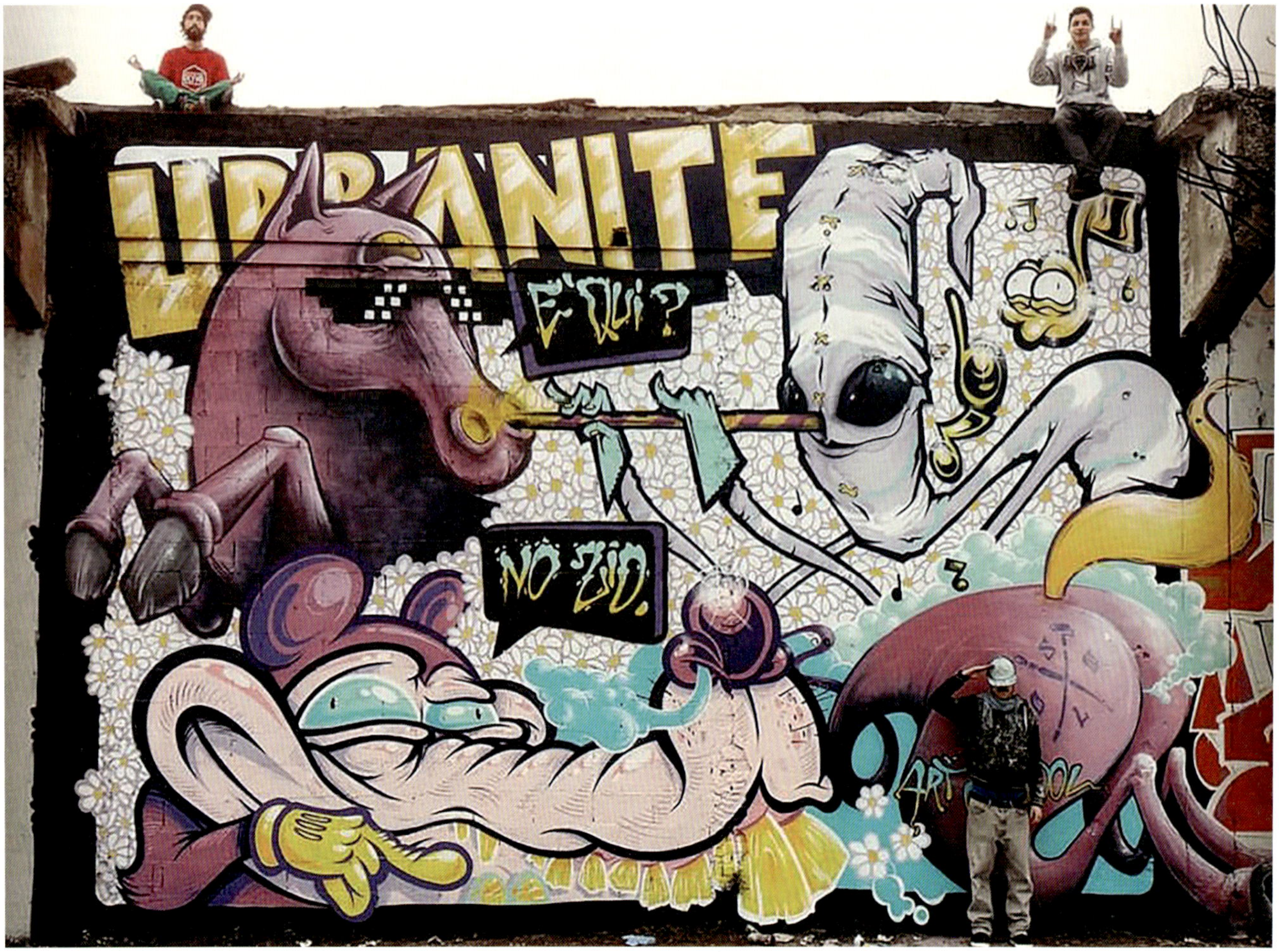

Equinozio
@Treviso, Italy 2017

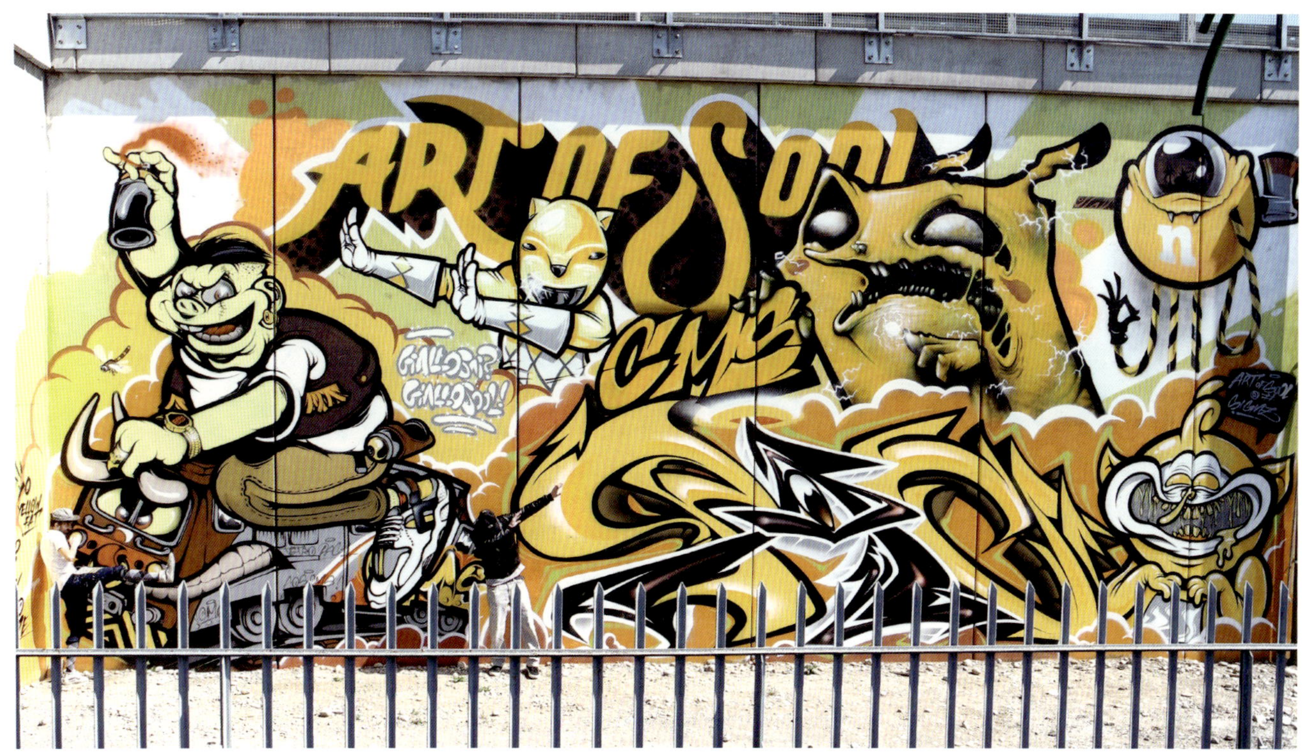

YellowJam
@Brescia, Italy 2017

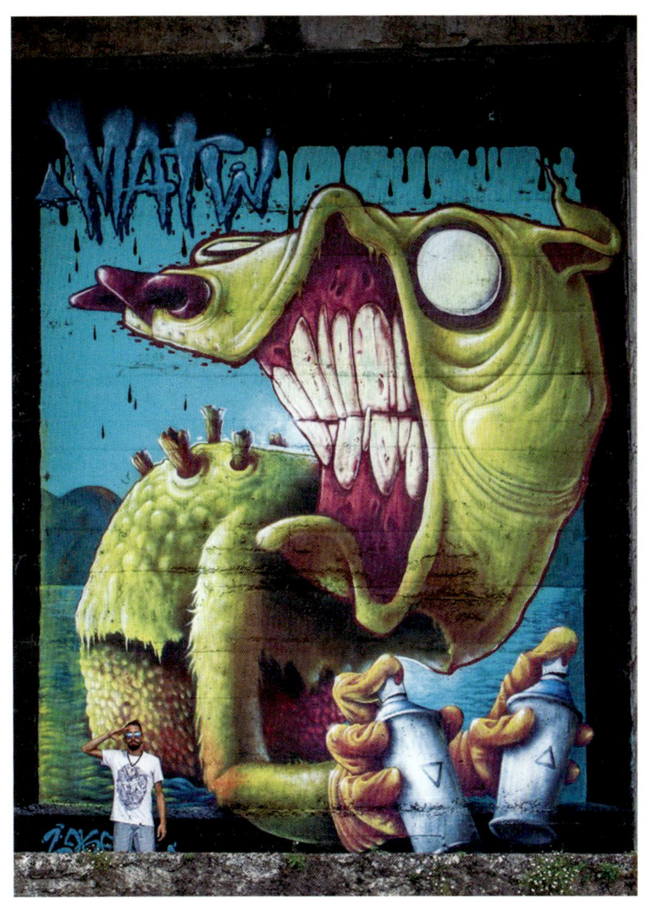

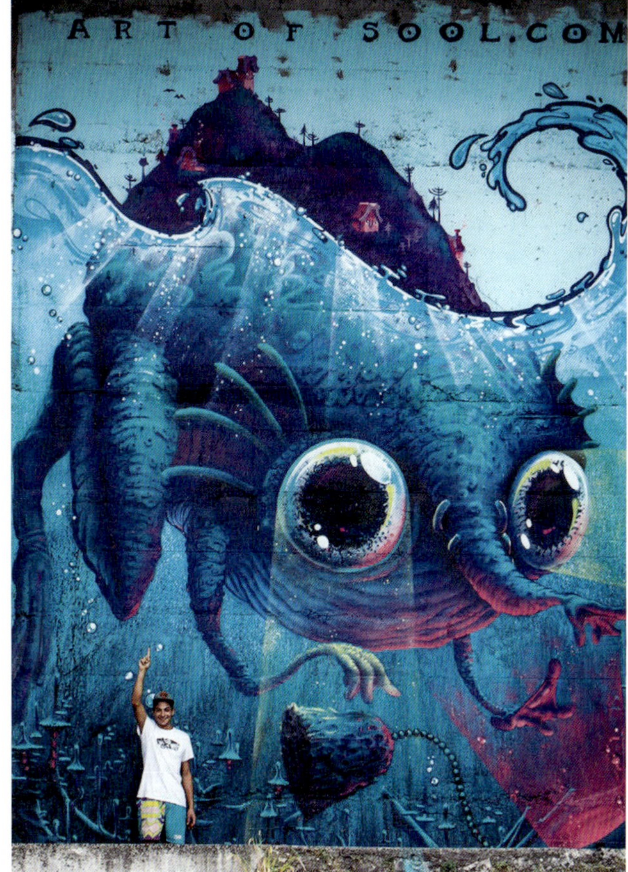

Lake Of Giants
@Val Camonica, Italy 2016

Currently based in Charleston, South Carolina, Patch Whisky is an American muralist, fine artist, and toy maker. After graduating from Art Institute of Pittsburgh in 2004, Patch Whisky continued to develop his love for mural arts. By use of aerosol and acrylics, he established a distinctive painting style of his own: a light-blue, zany character with mischievous facial expression, and a fluid and popping use of color.

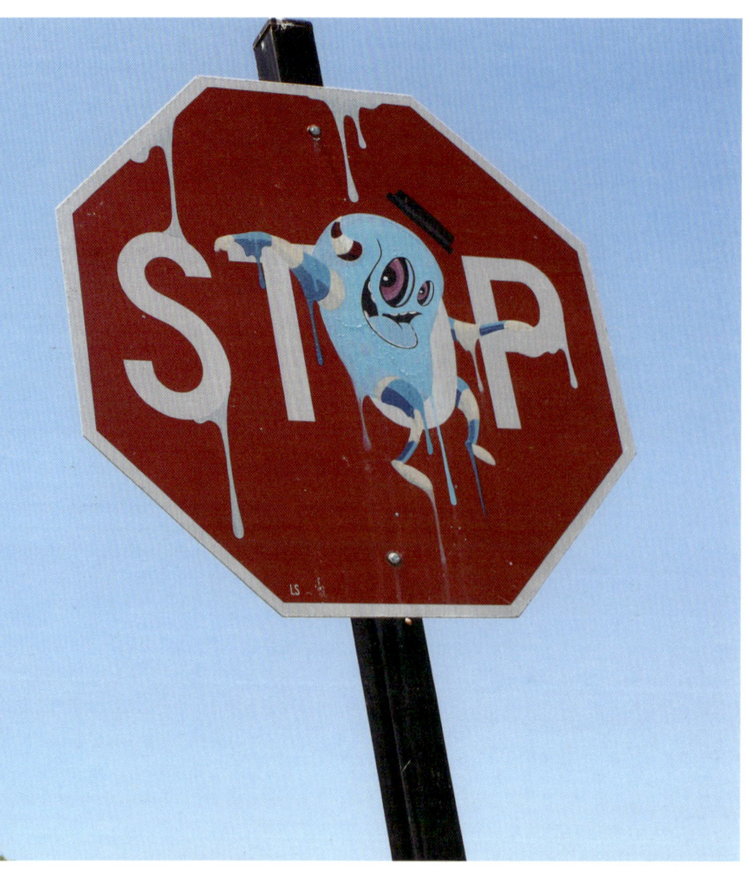

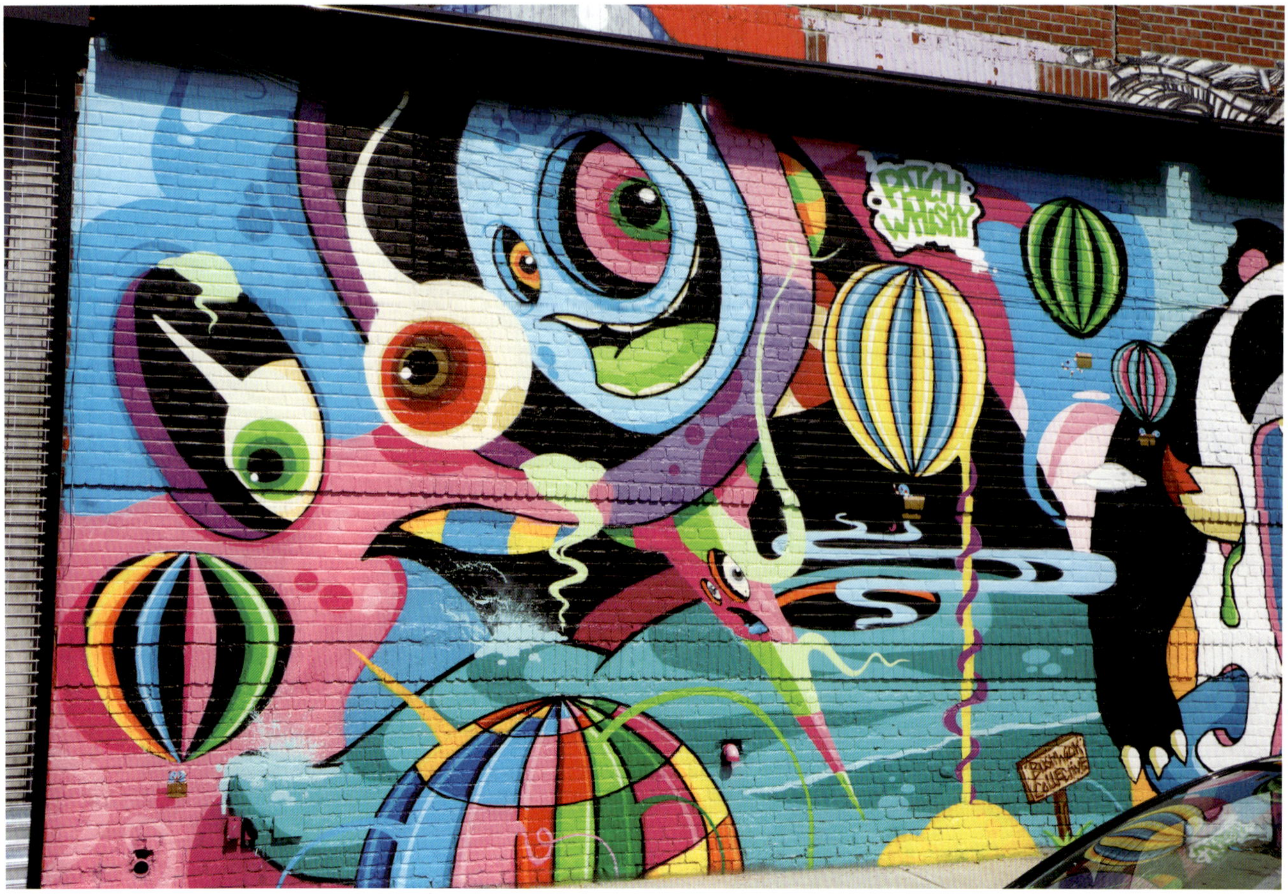

@Brooklyn NY, USA 2015

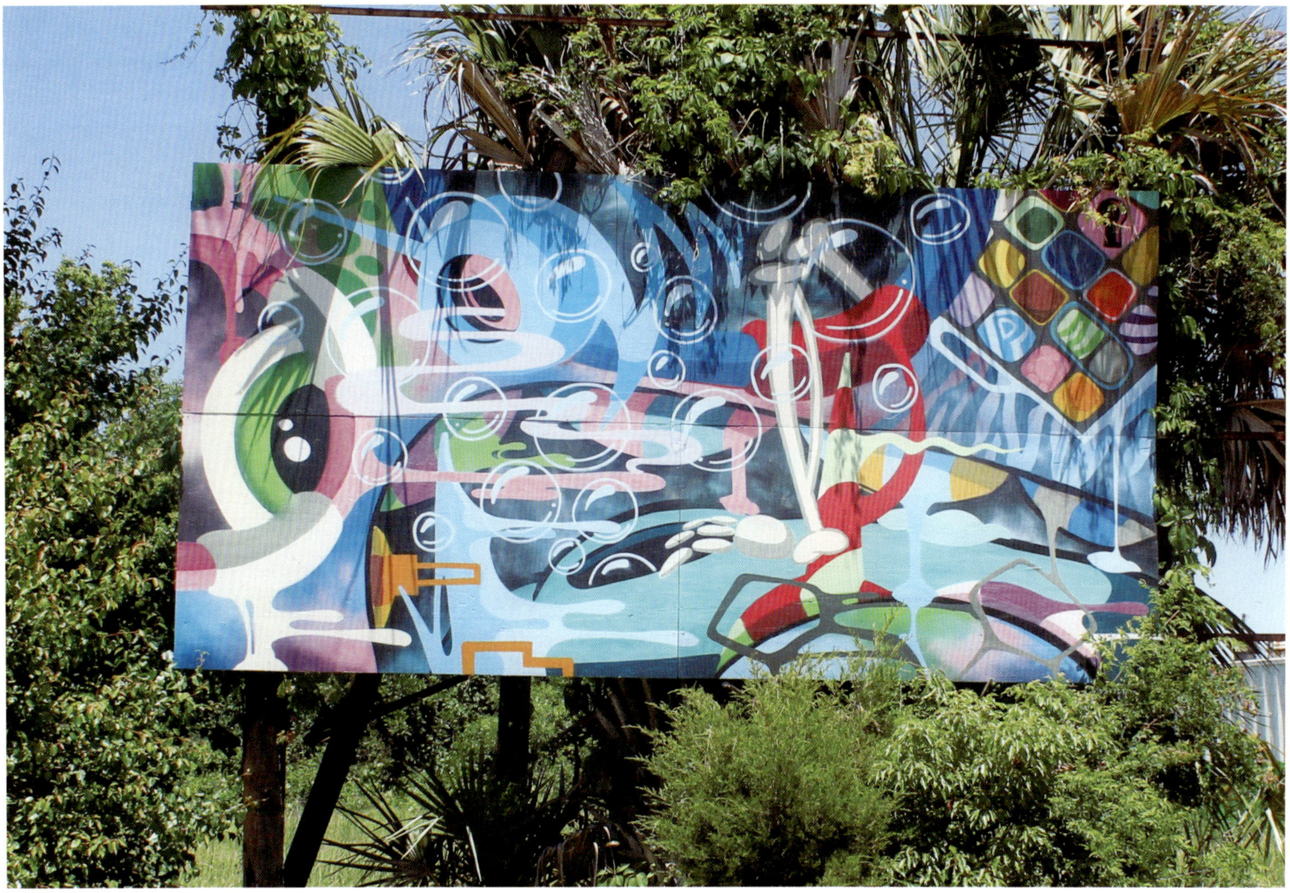

@Charleston SC, USA 2016

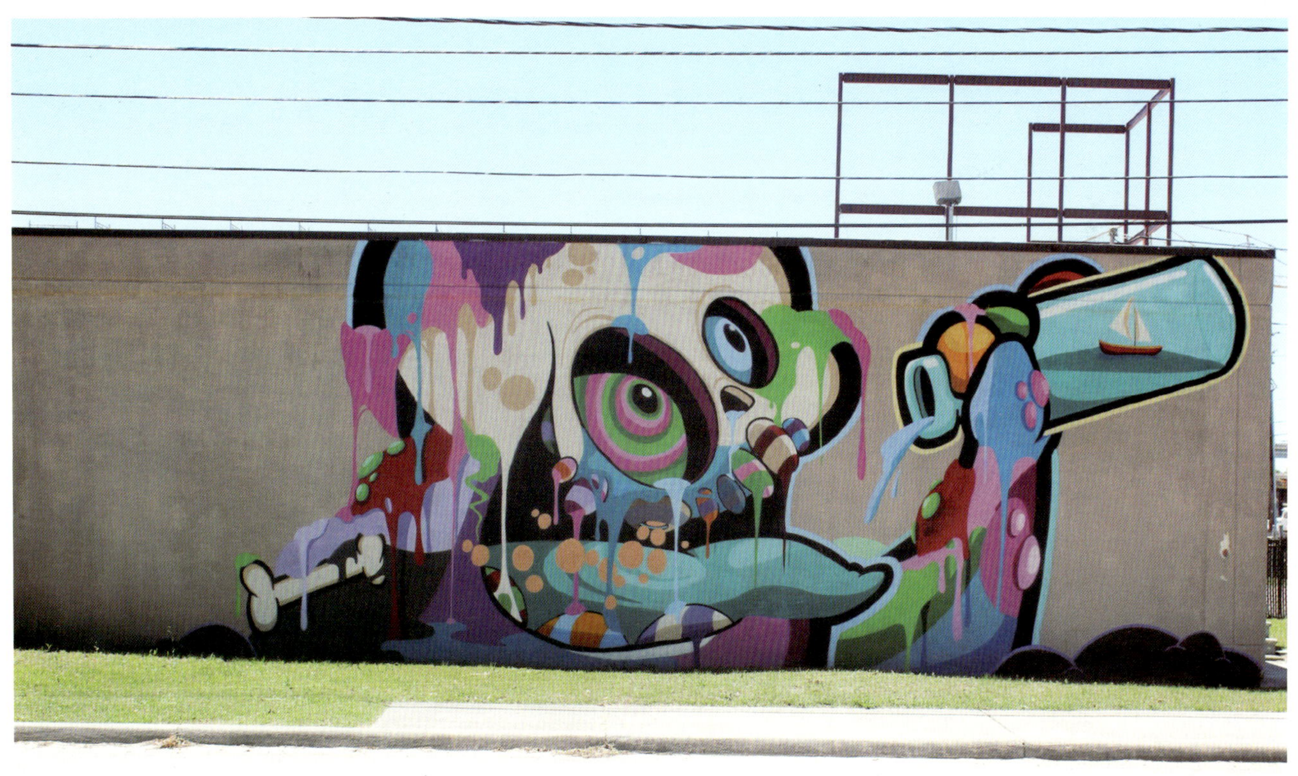

@Charleston SC, USA 2017

Artist/ Edwin Ushiro

Born in the island of Maui, Edwin Ushiro attended the Art Center College of Design, and moved to Los Angeles later. His paintings always depict childhood friends, family pets, and ghostly specters on the Hawaiian islands in a vibrant, bright tone. When the theme is dark and heavy, his use of ethereal colors magically creates an emotional tension between joy and sadness.

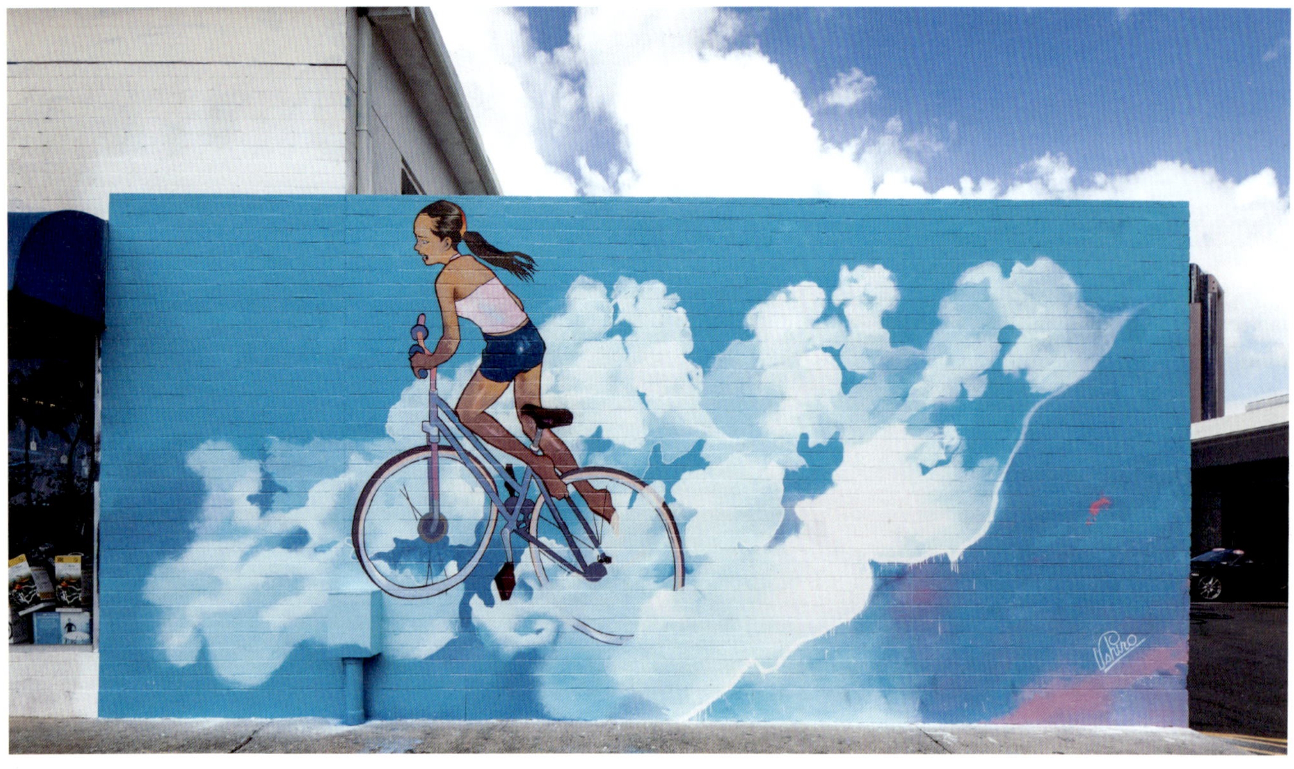

@Hawaii, USA 2016
©Brandon Shigeta

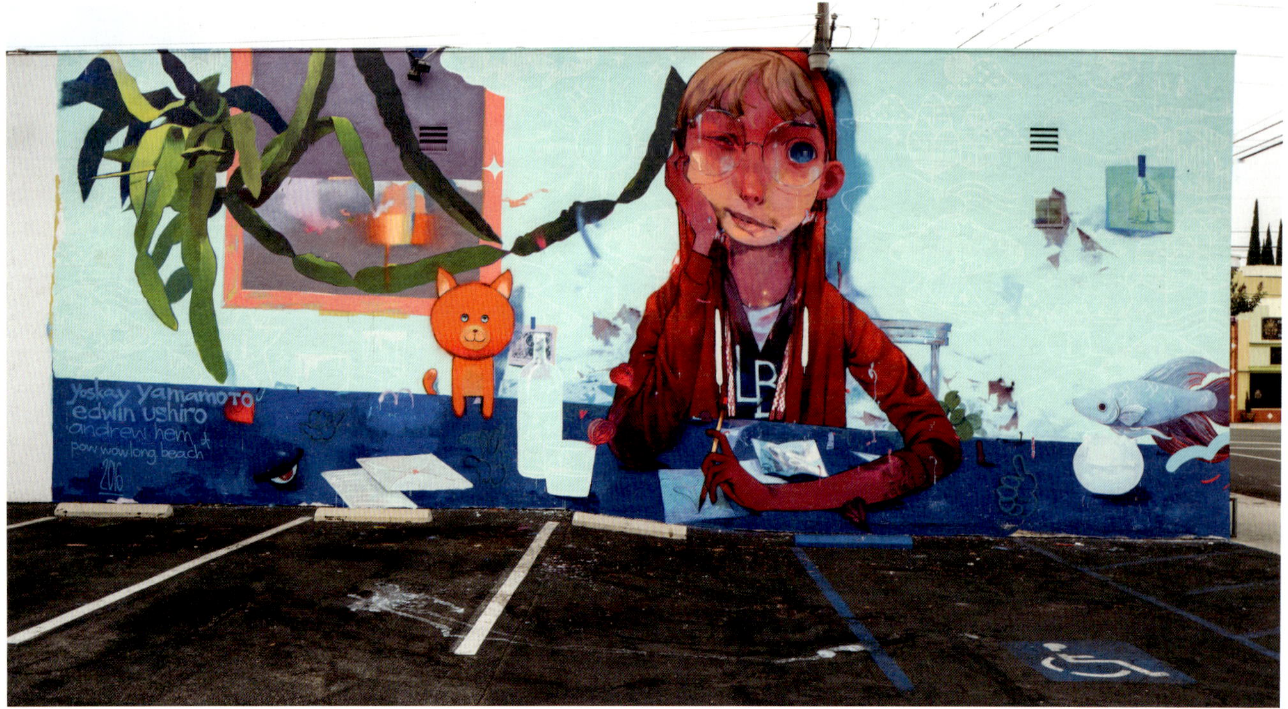

Collaboration with Andrew Hem and Yoskay Yamamoto
@California, USA 2016 ©Brandon Shigeta

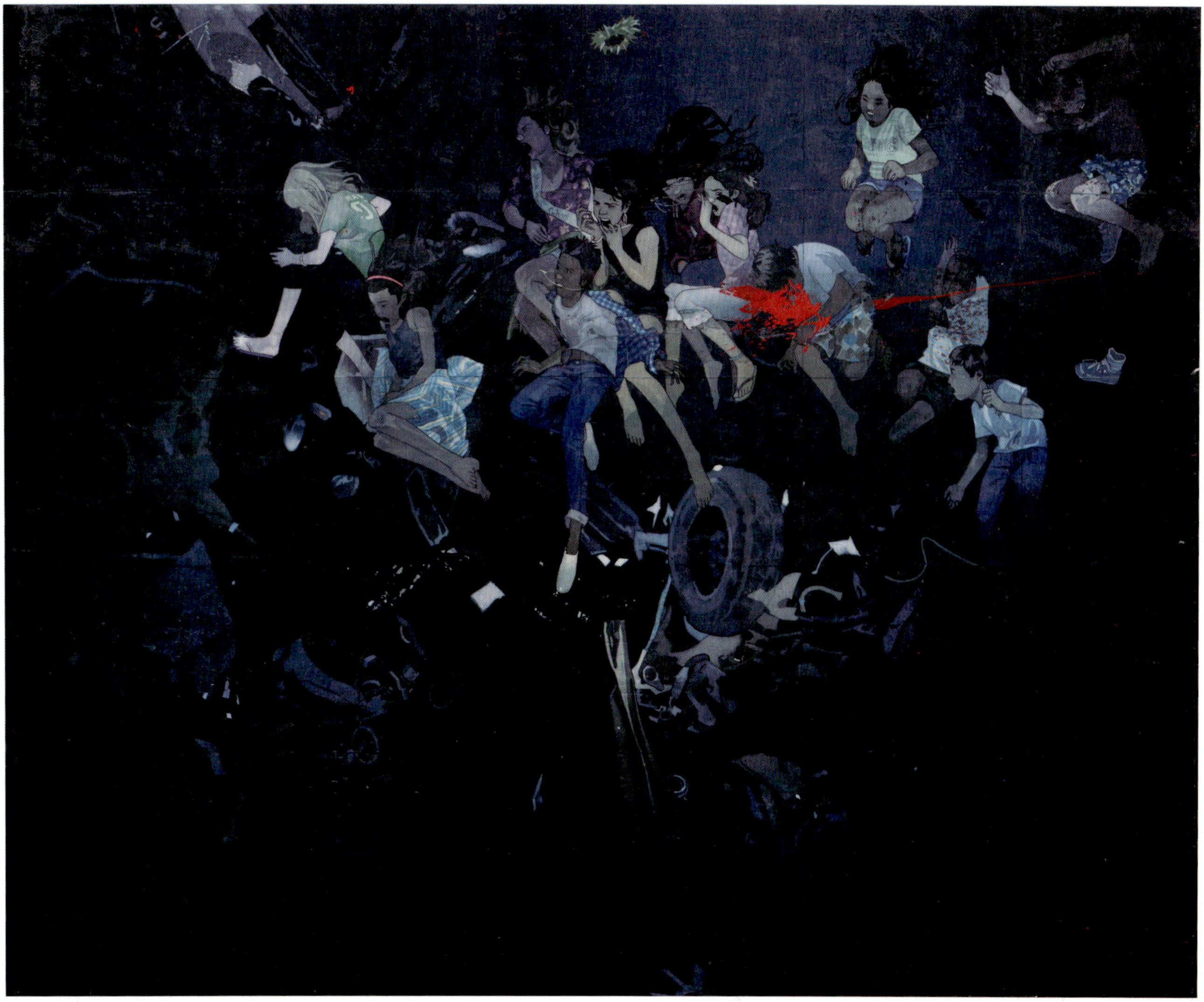

Softly Encompassing the Womb
Mixed media 2009 ©Brandon Shigeta

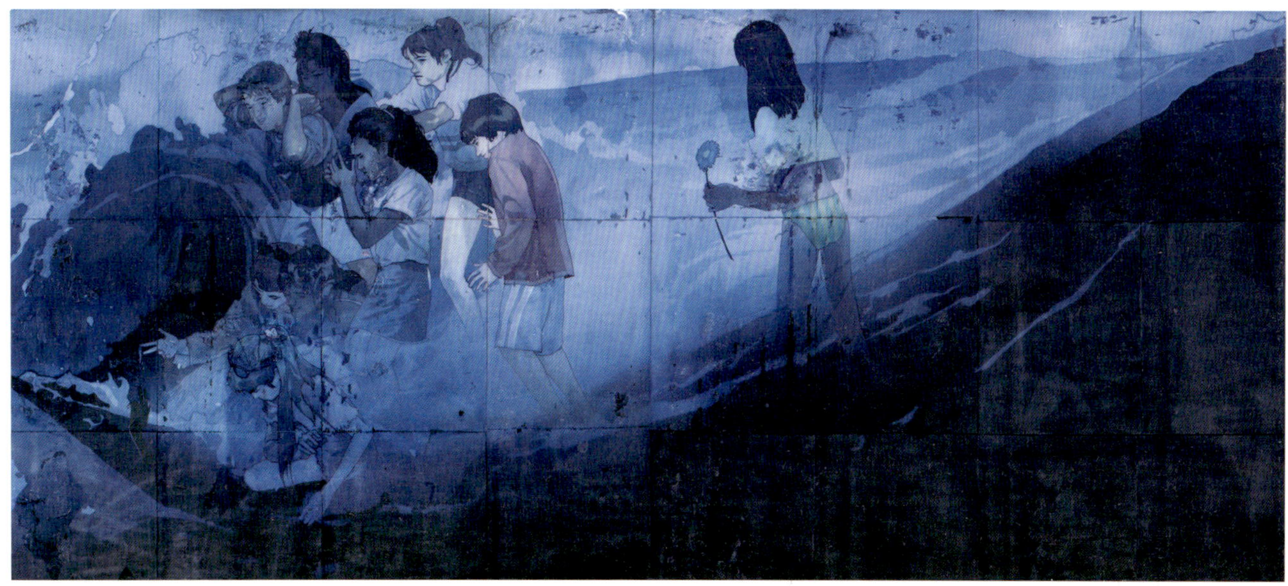

Gradiently Everything would Sparkle from the Sea to the Stars
Mixed media 2008 ©Brandon Shigeta

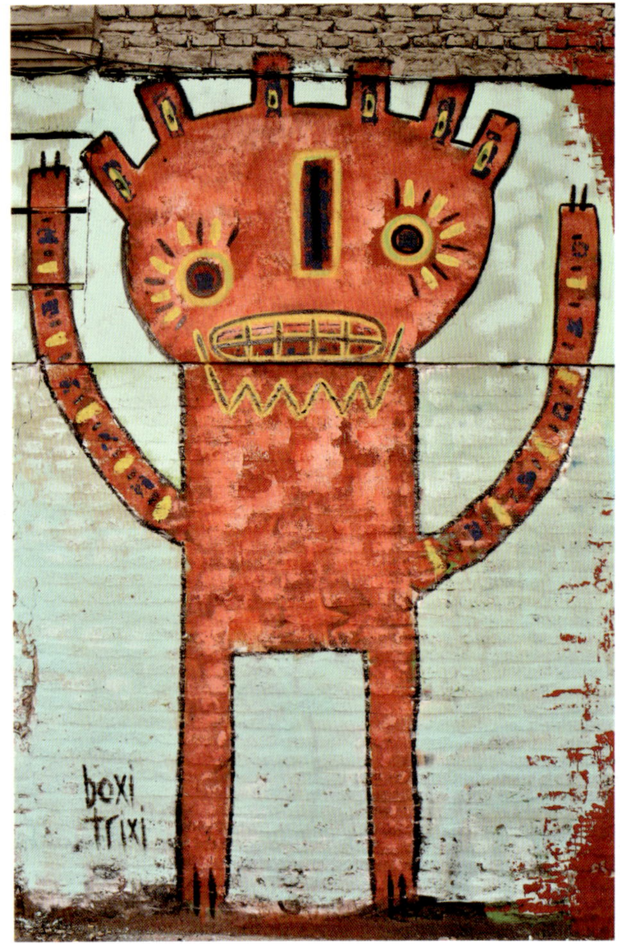
boxi
trixi

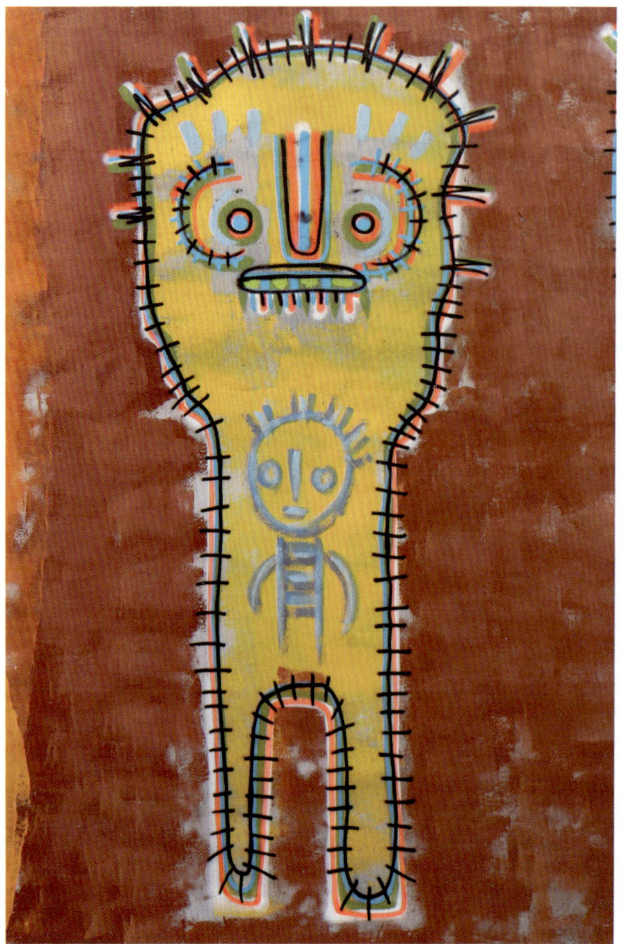

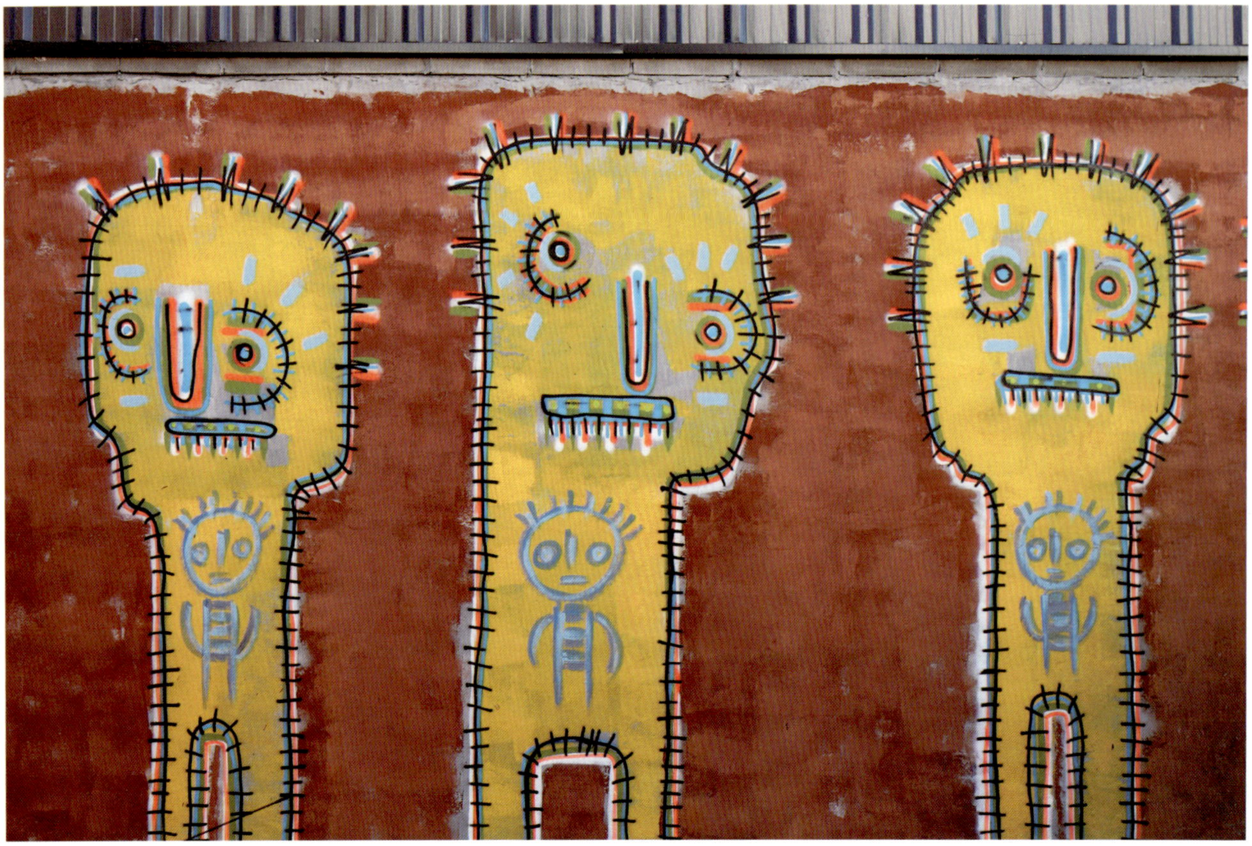

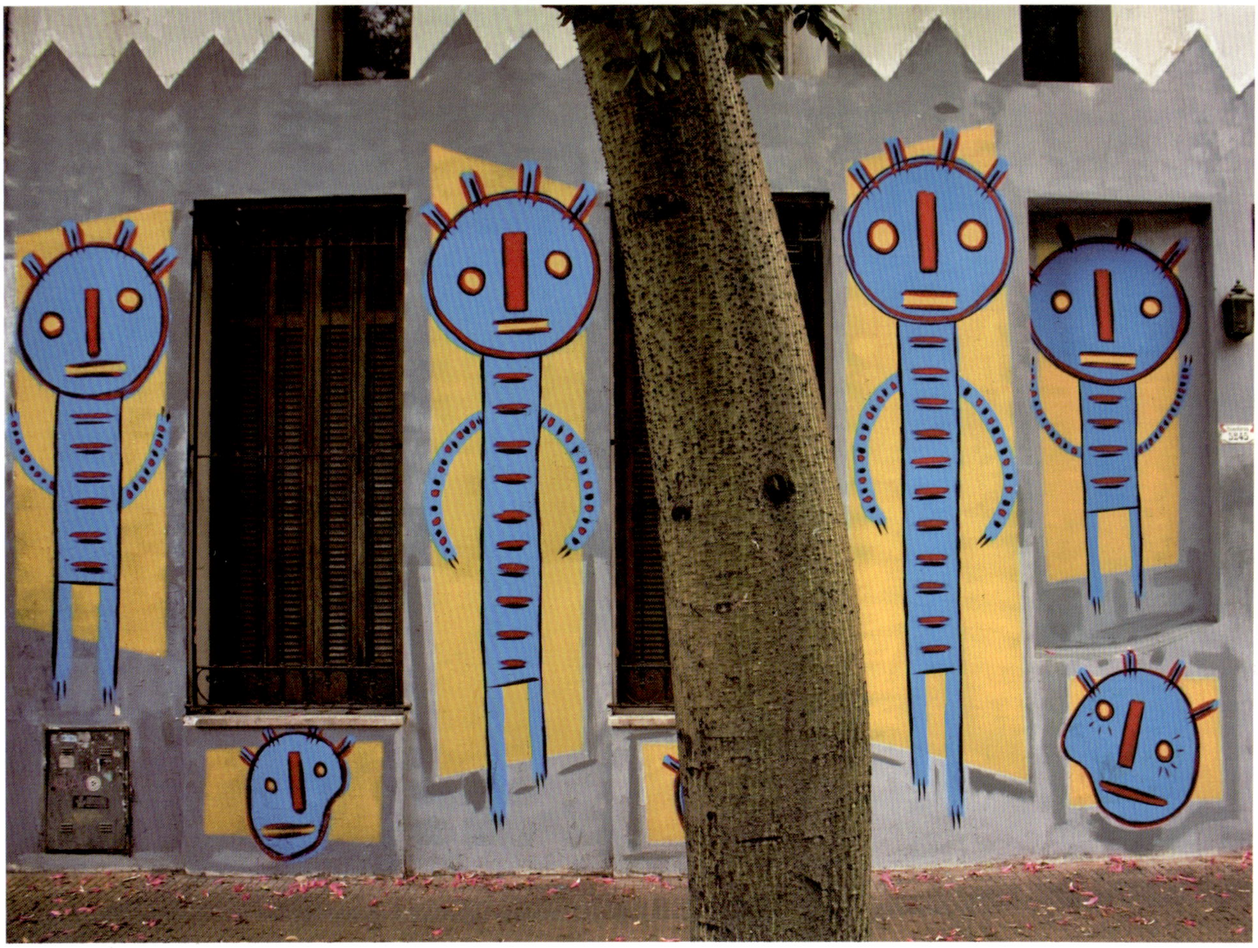

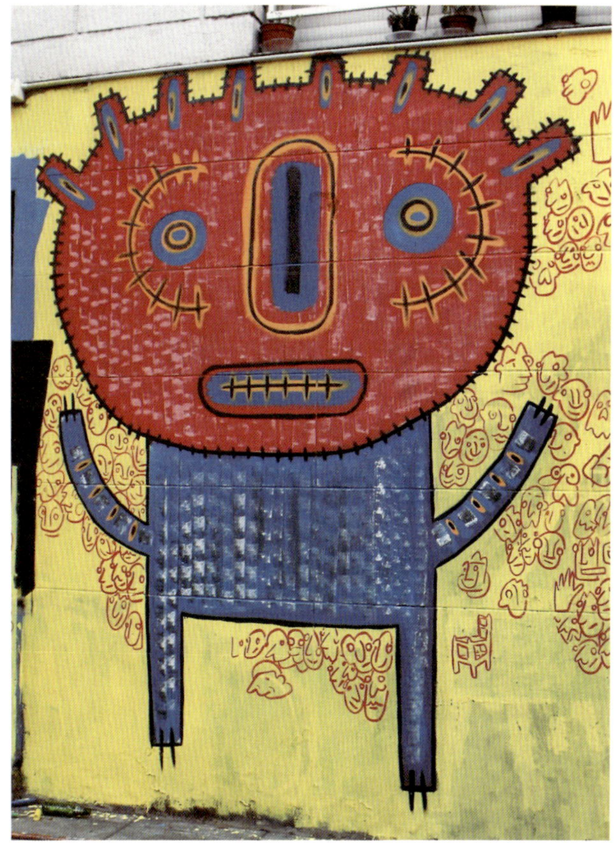

Boxi Trixi, a nickname given by his father, meaning "a box full of tricks," is an Argentinian street artist who loves travel, music, and painting. Inspired by pre-Columbian art, especially Tiahuanaco and the Legend of the Golem, he created many super interesting characters.

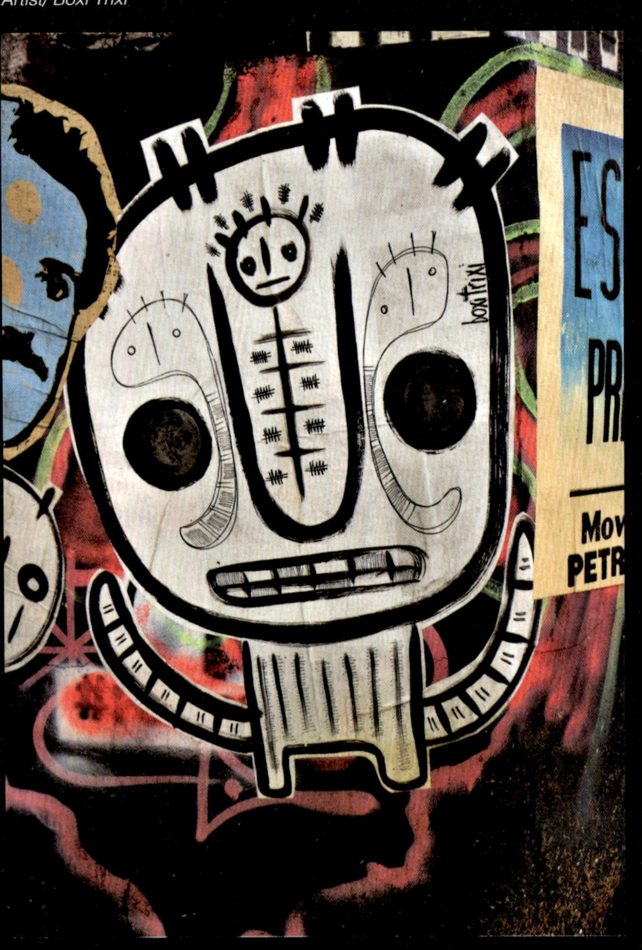

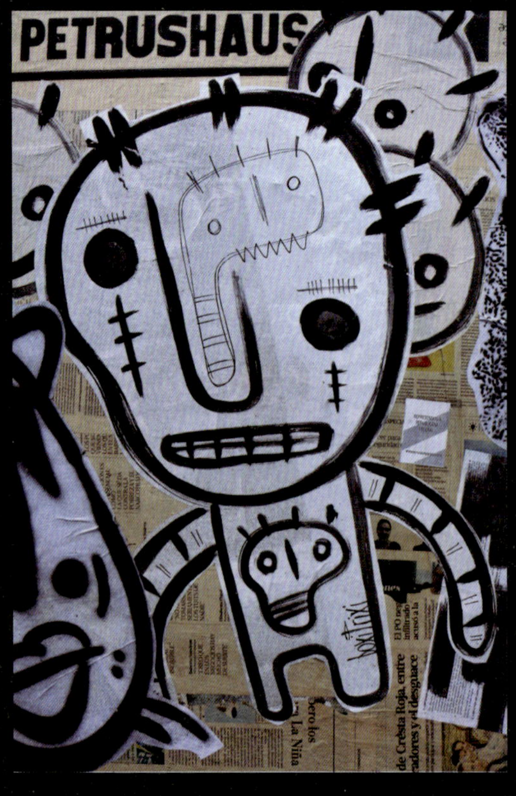
PETRUSHAUS

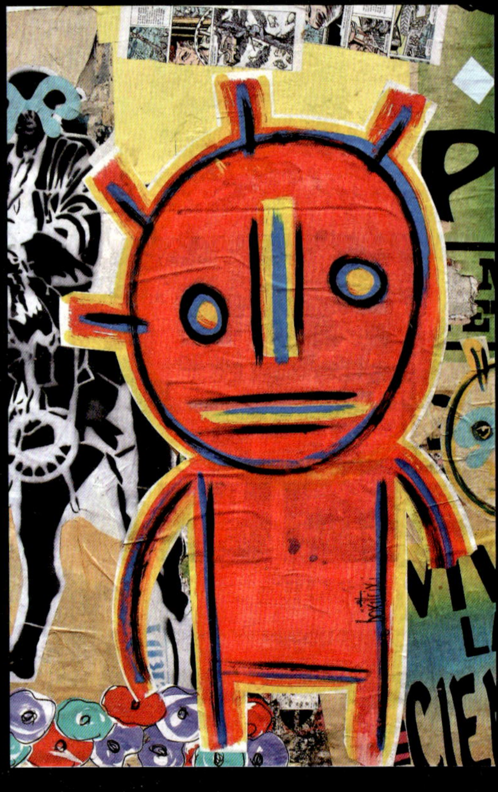

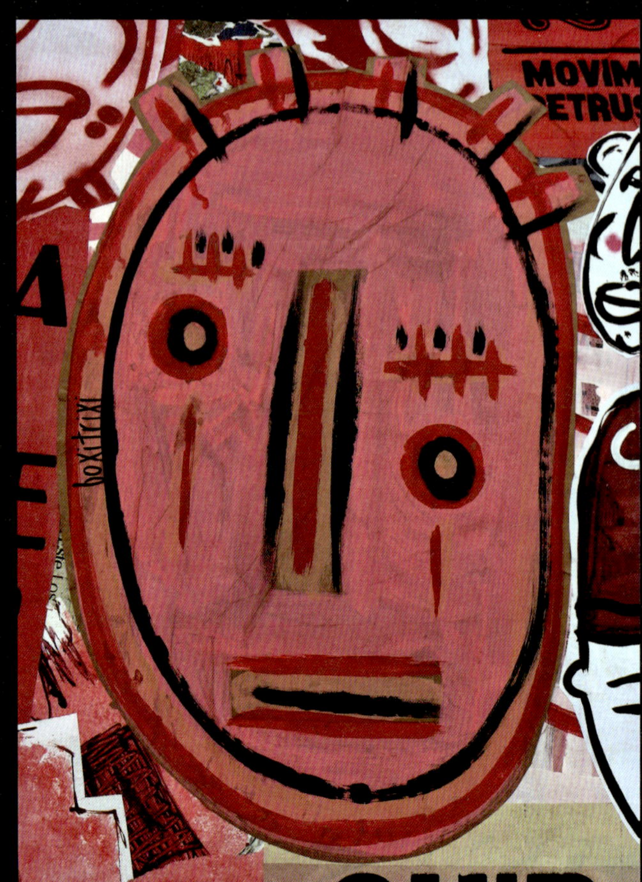

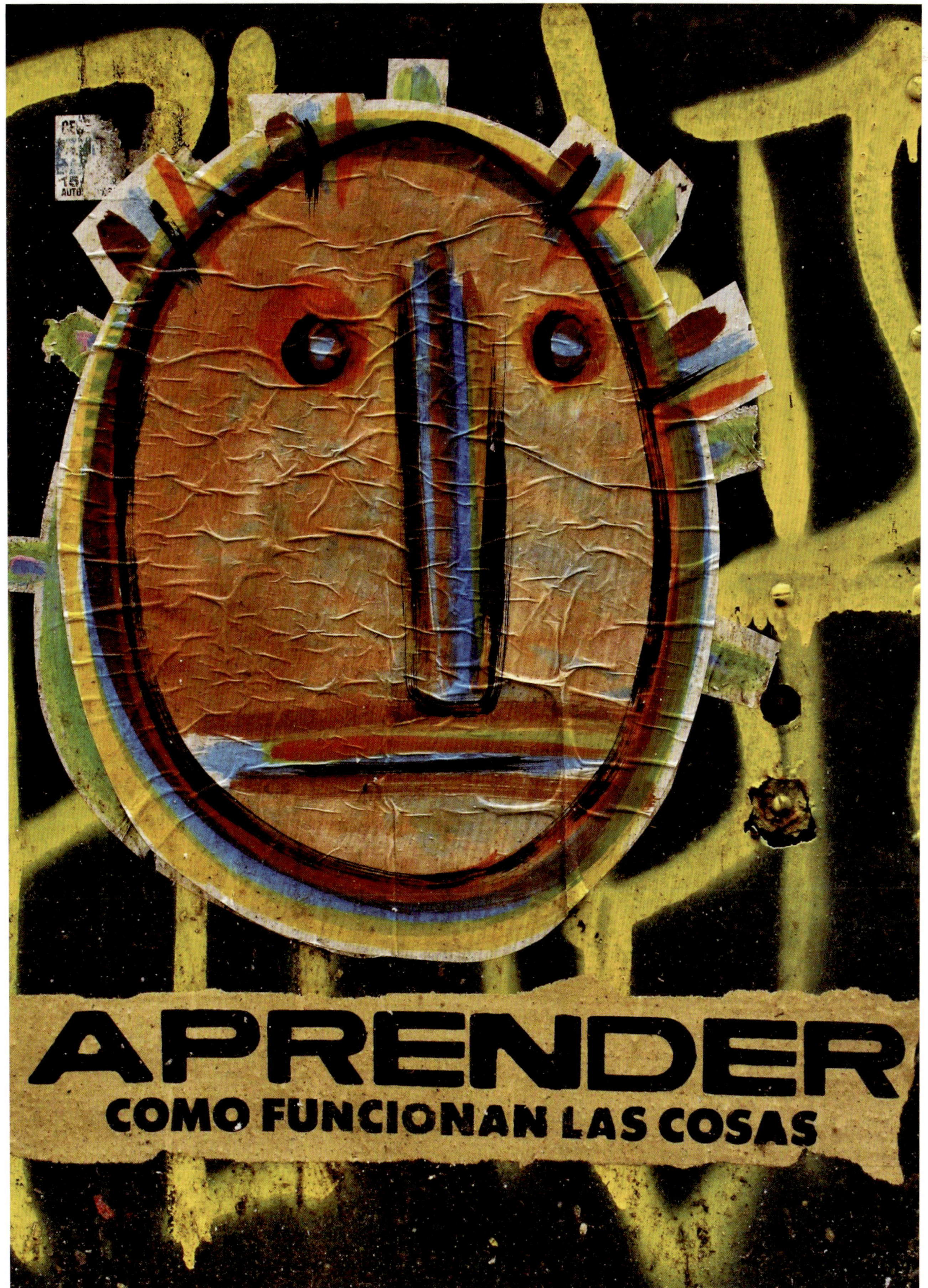
APRENDER
COMO FUNCIONAN LAS COSAS

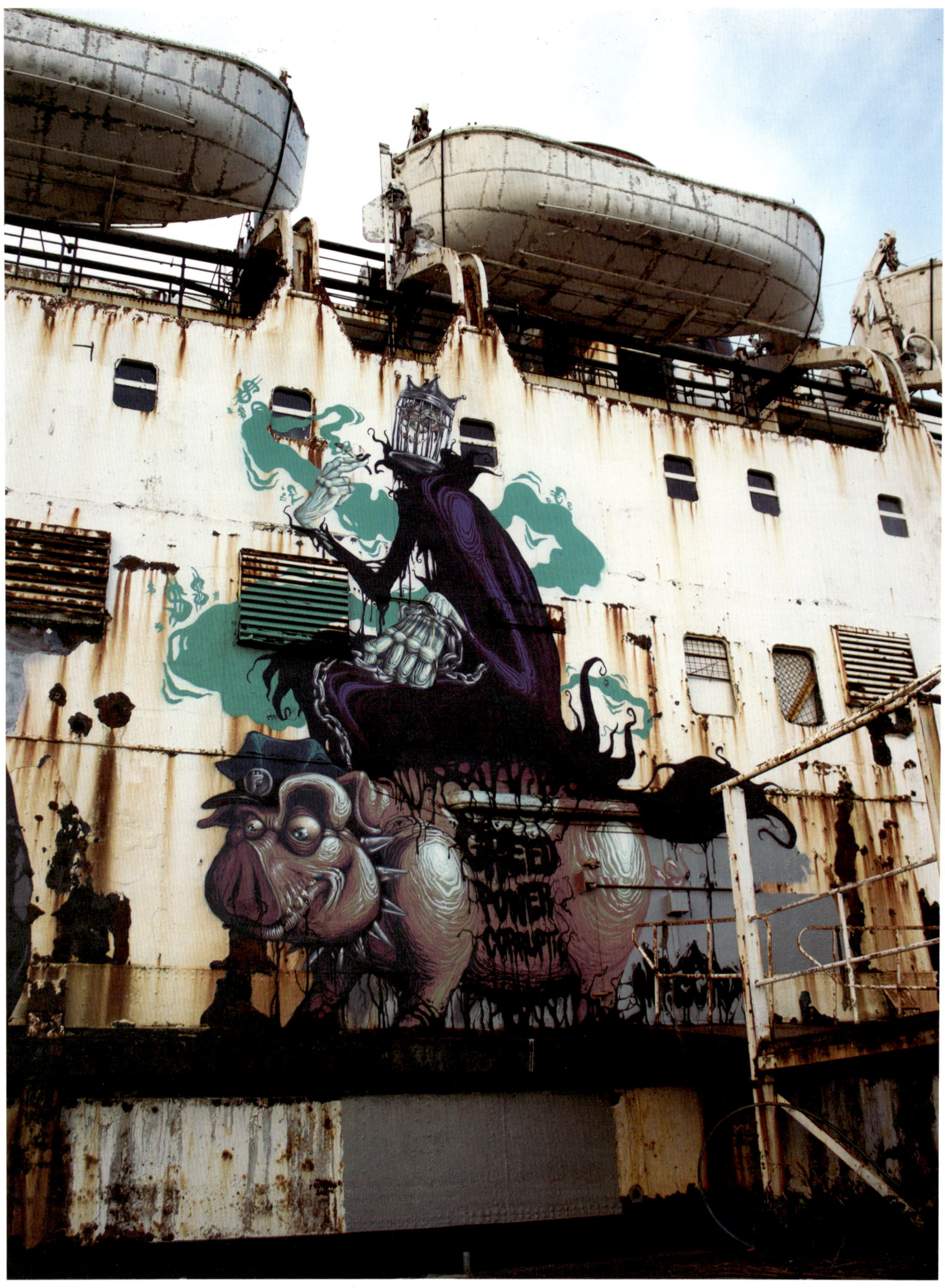

The Prophet of Profit
@North Wales, UK 2012

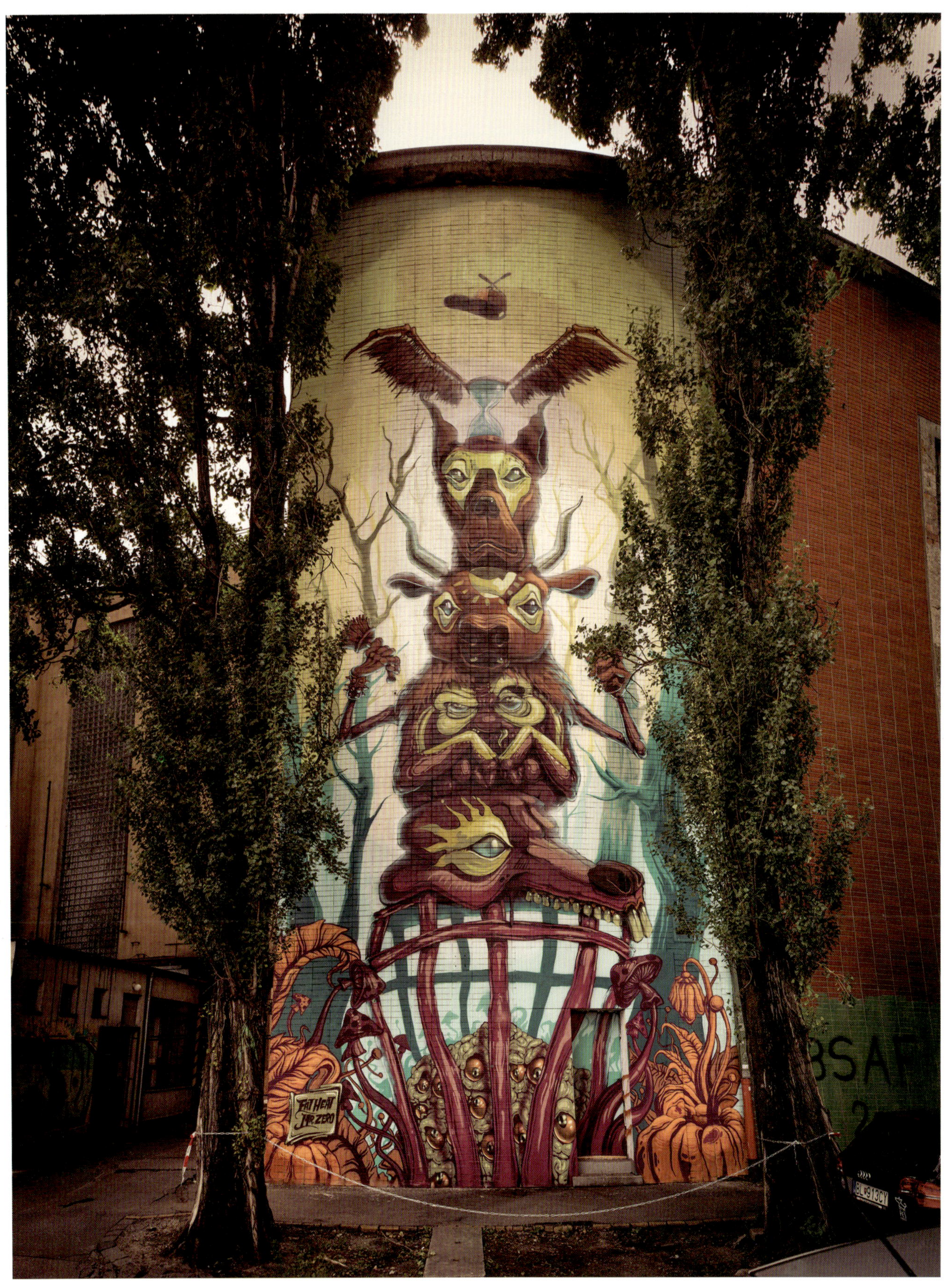

Collaboration with Fatheat
@Bratislava, Slovakia 2014

ABSTRACT

The word "abstract" means to draw away, to summarize, and to extract. Artistically, abstraction indicates a departure from reality in the depiction of imagery, or abandonment of the appearance of subjects. By the use of visual language, an artist extracts the fundamental shaping elements of the subject and reorganizes them through shape, form, color, and line, resulting in an artwork that extends spiritually.

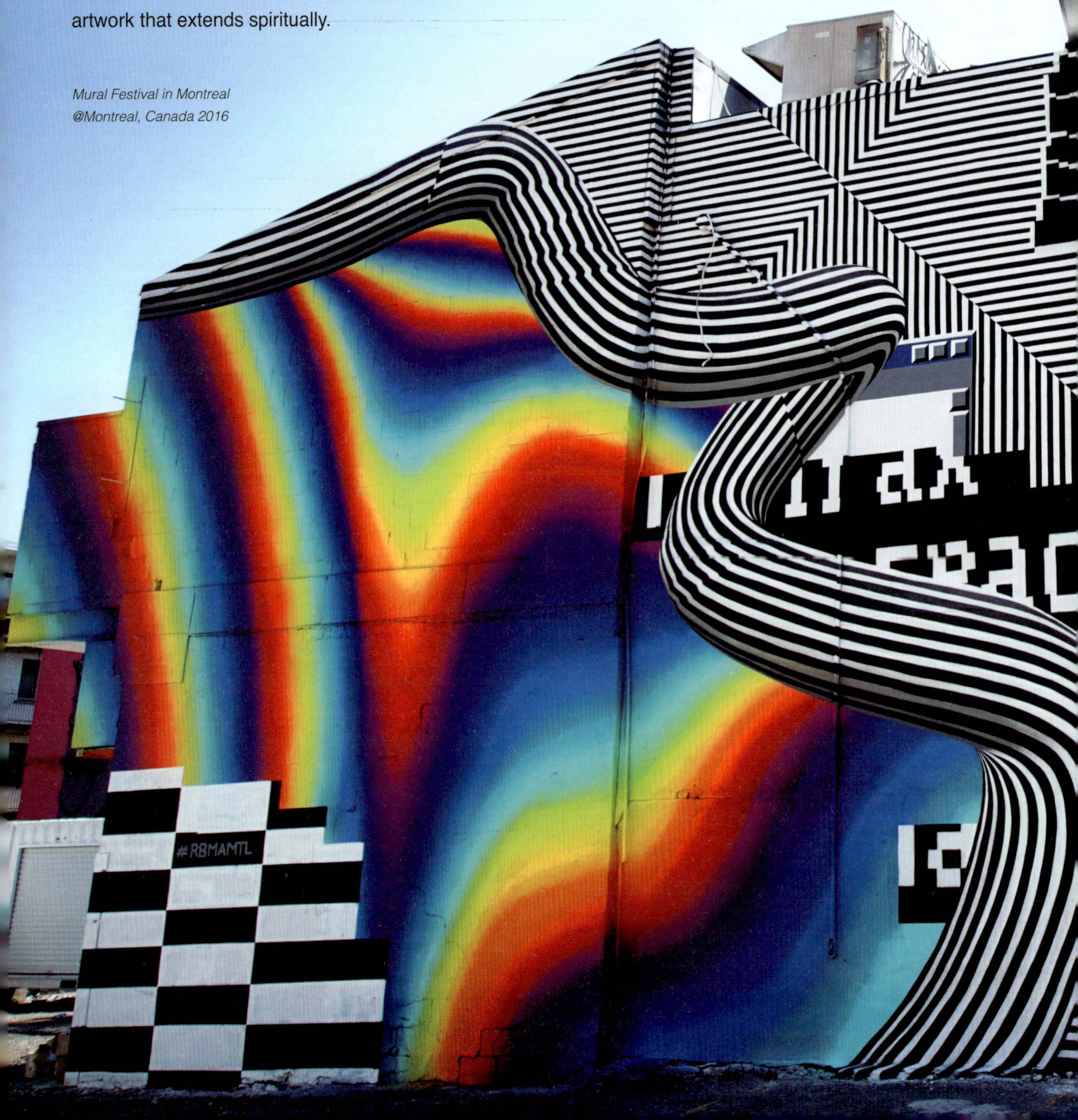

Mural Festival in Montreal
@Montreal, Canada 2016

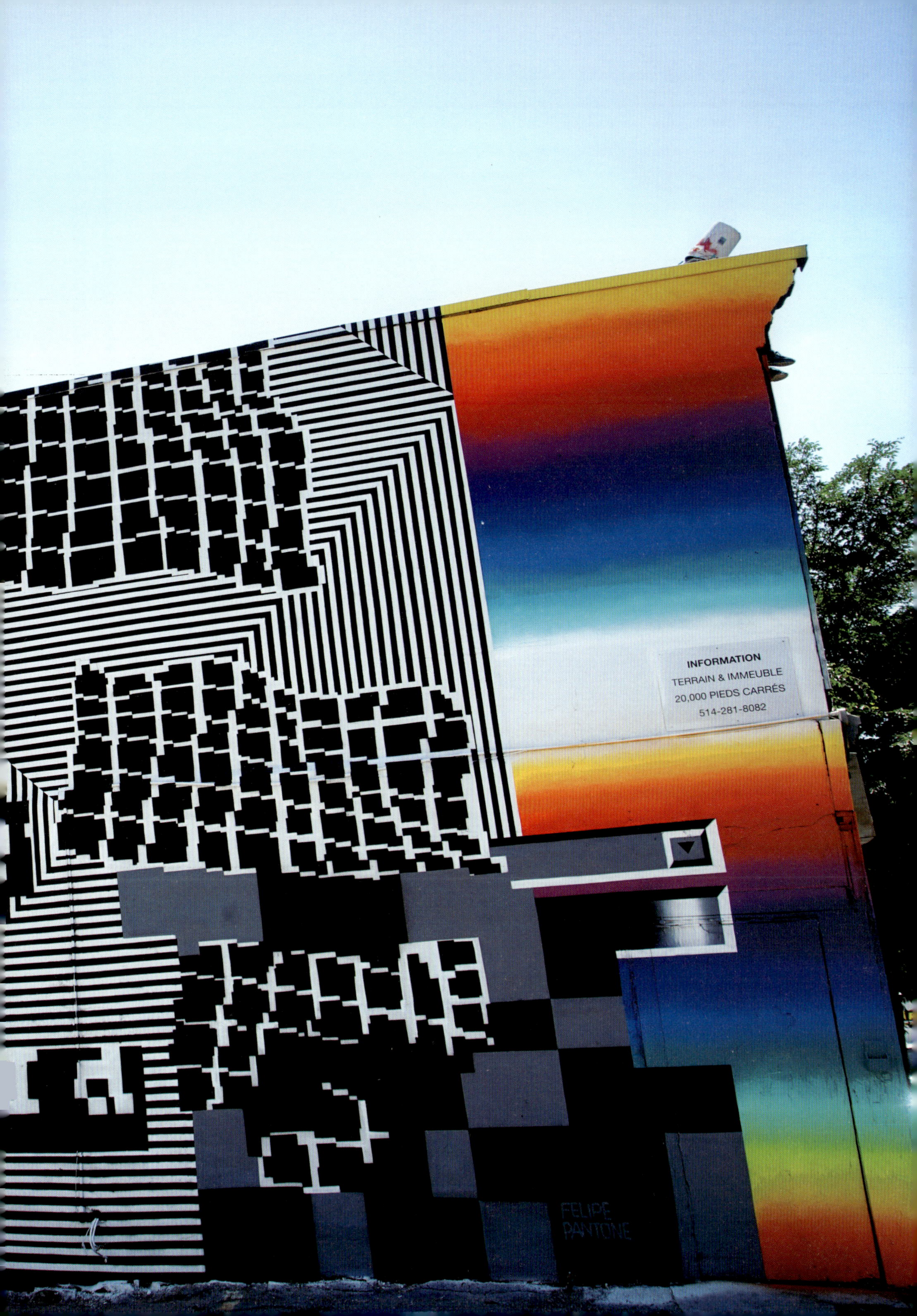
INFORMATION
TERRAIN & IMMEUBLE
20,000 PIEDS CARRÉS
514-281-8082
FELIPE
PANTONE

Felipe Pantone is an Argentinian-Spanish artist. Playing with conventional graffiti, typography, abstraction, and kinetic art, his work merges highly evolved geometric shapes with strong contrasts, and vivid colors to create a futuristic aesthetic that draws on our concerns of the digital age.

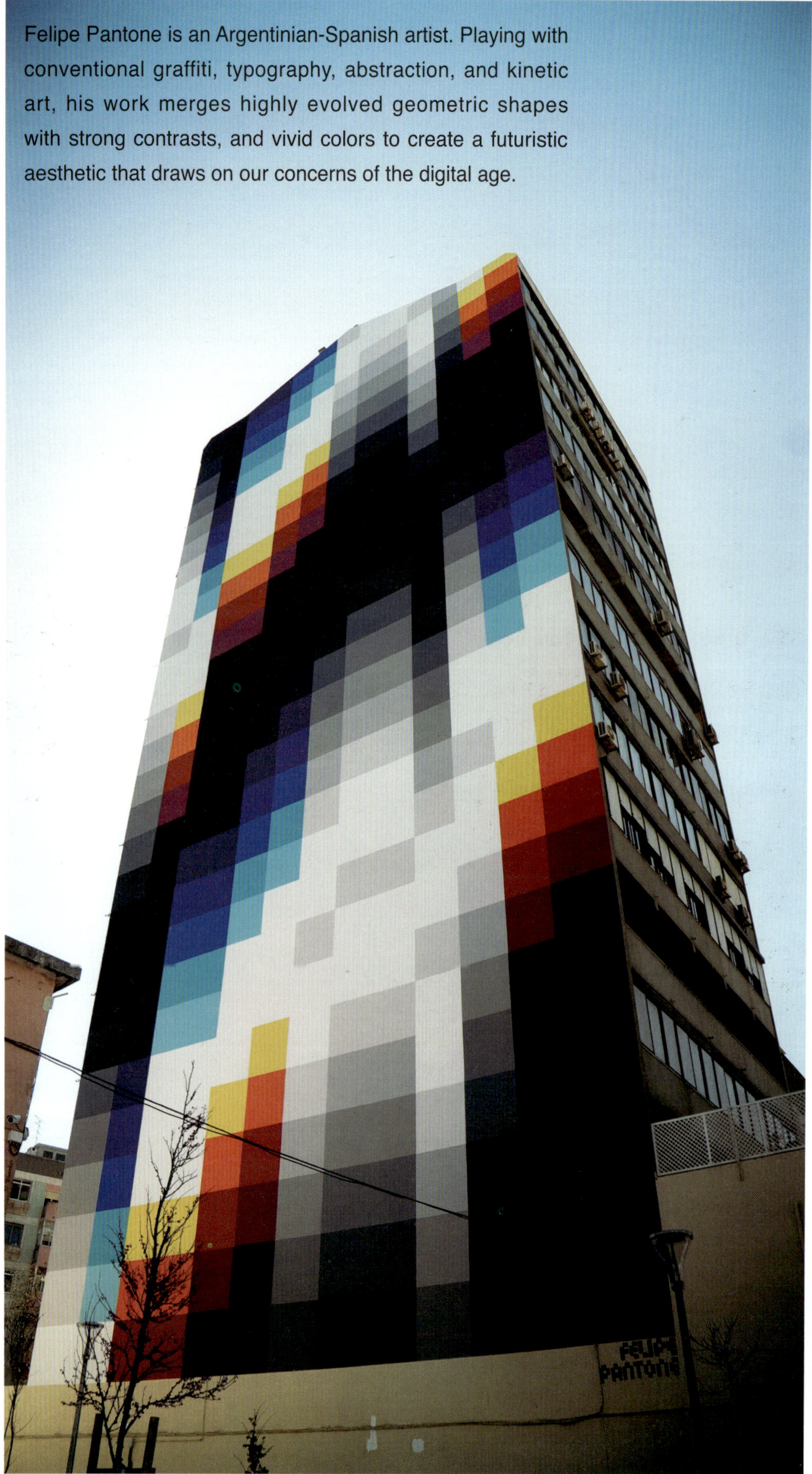

Chromadynamica for Lisbon
@Lisbon, Portugal 2016

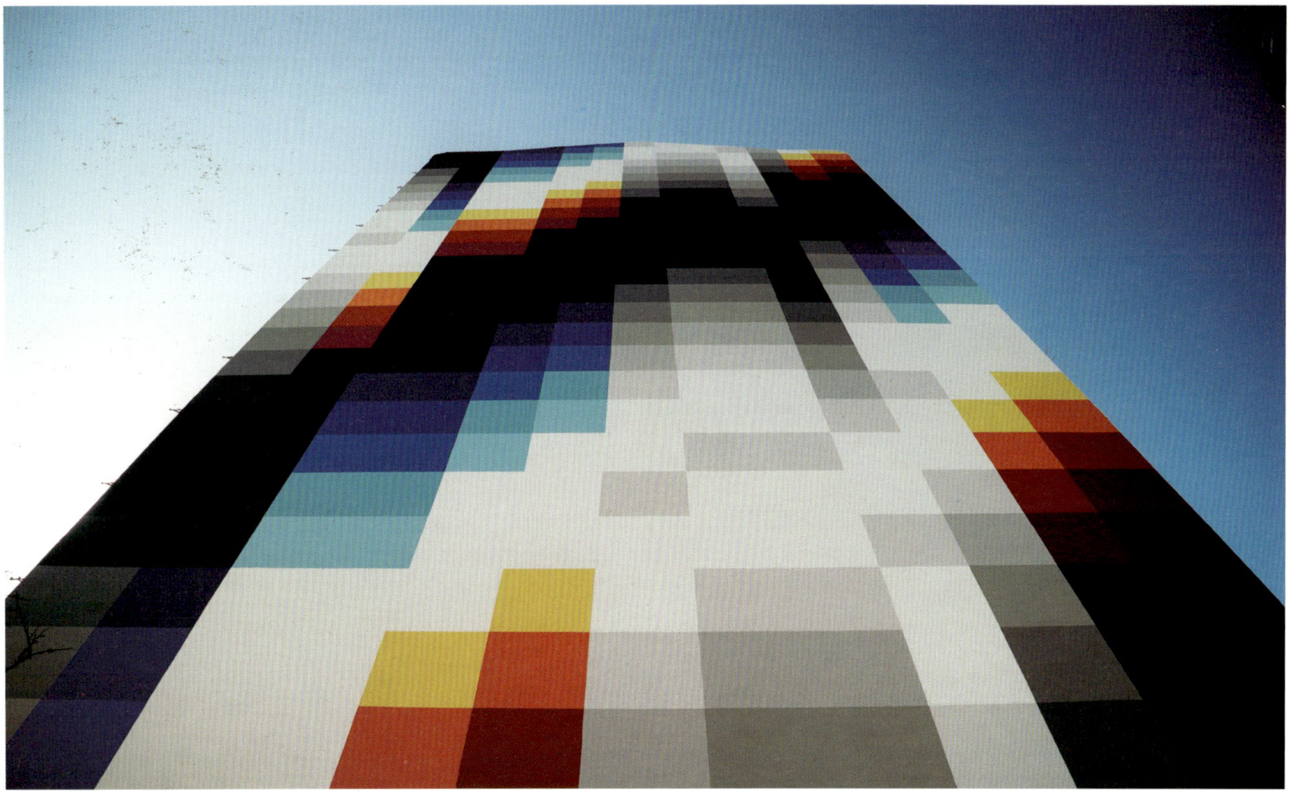

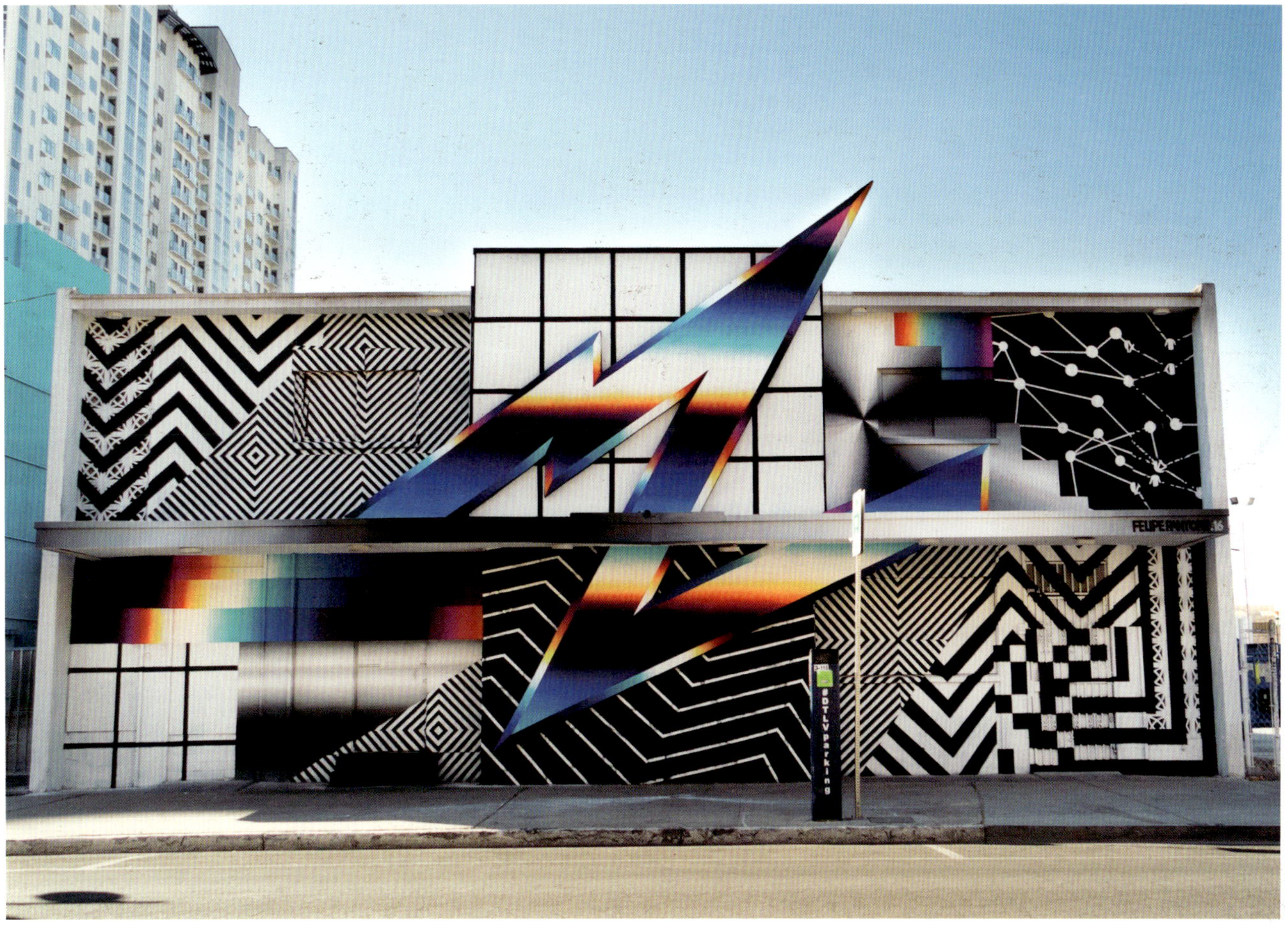

Life Is Beautiful Festival
@Las Vegas, USA 2016

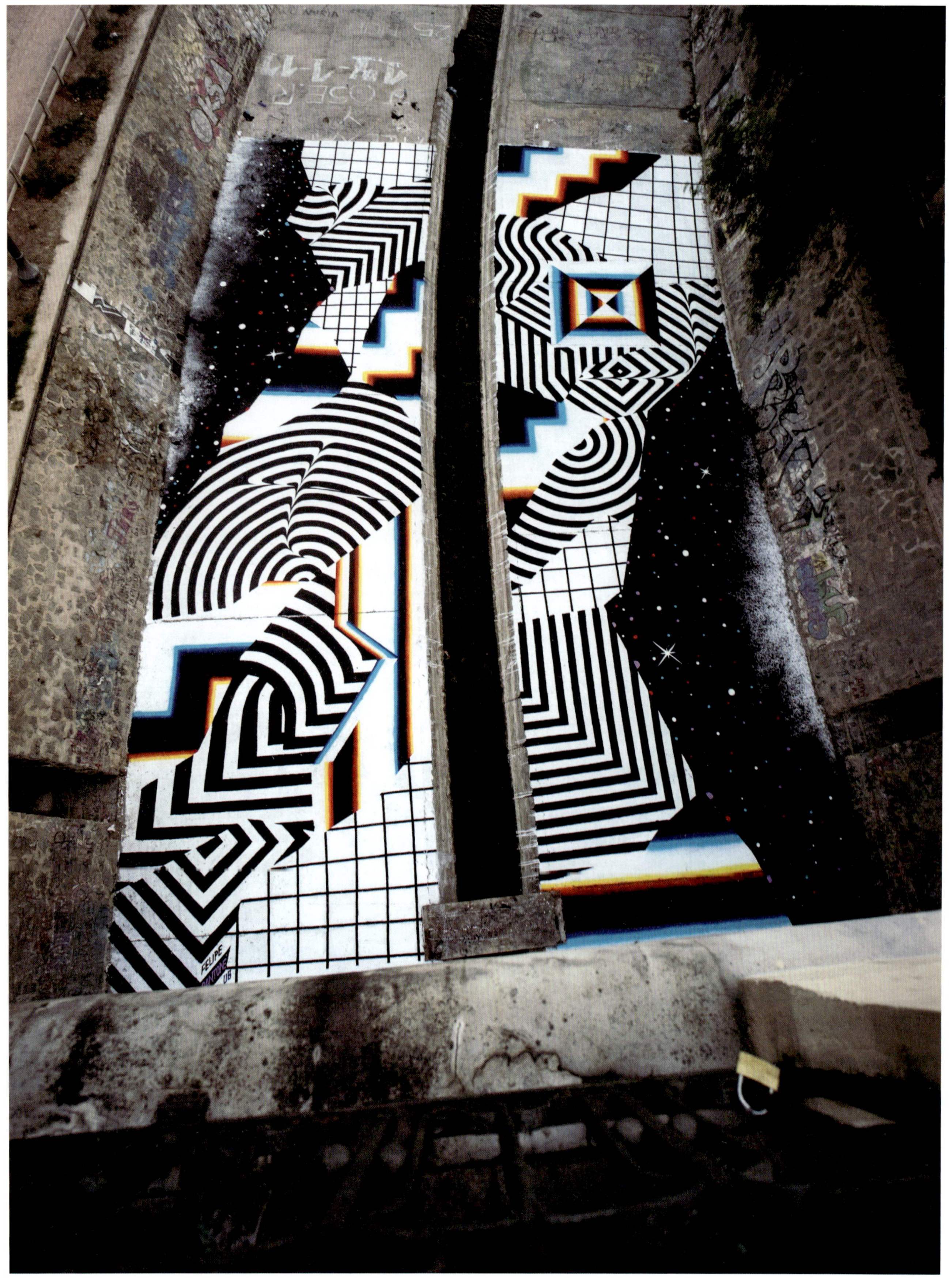

Proyecto Víbora
@Elche, Spain 2014

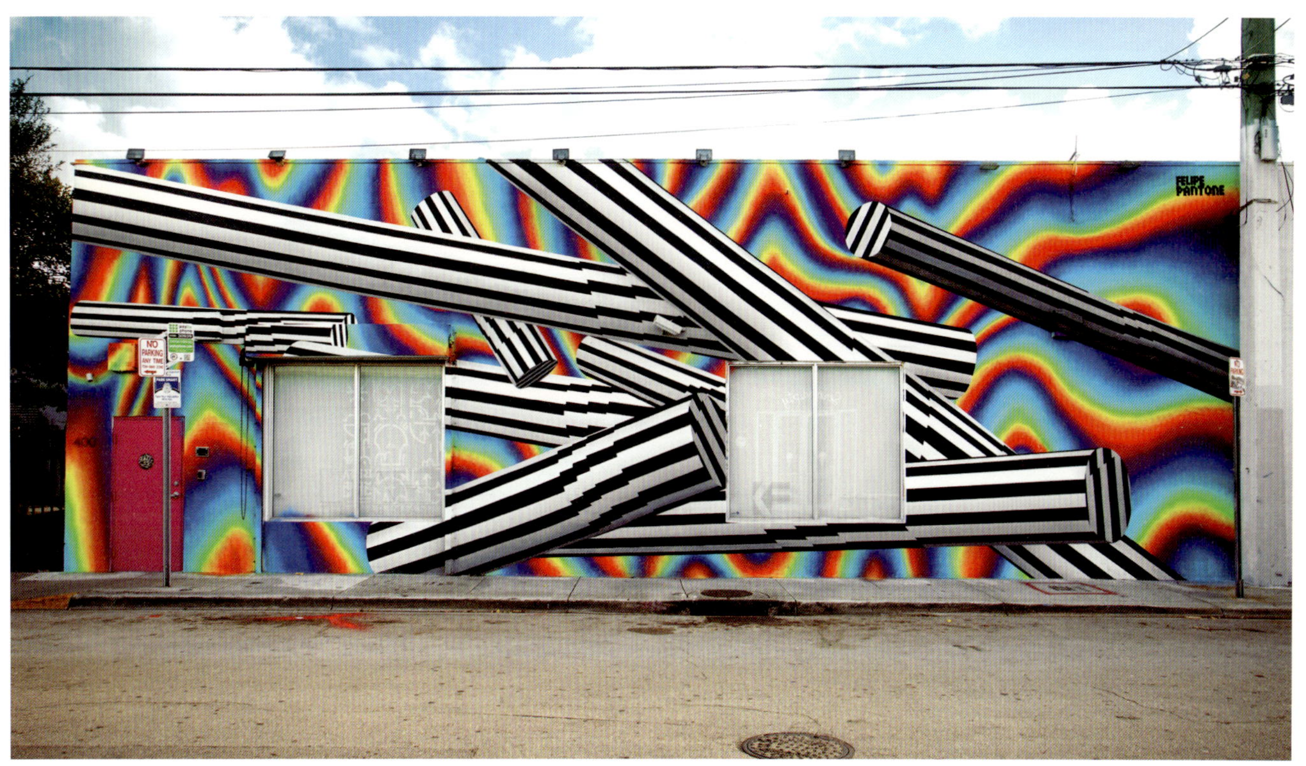

Miami Wynwood
@Miami, USA 2016

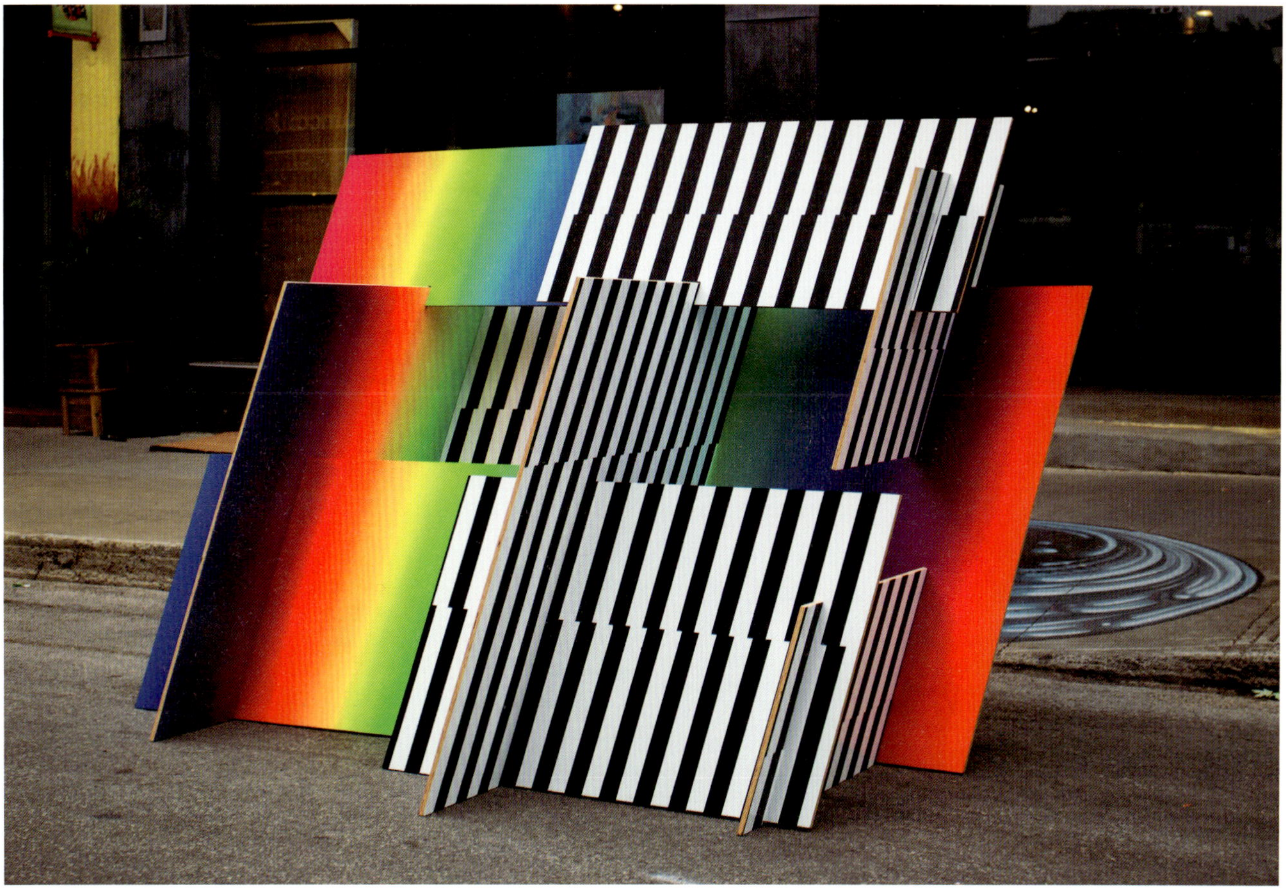

Ephemeral Sculpture For Mural Festival
@Montreal, Canada. 2016

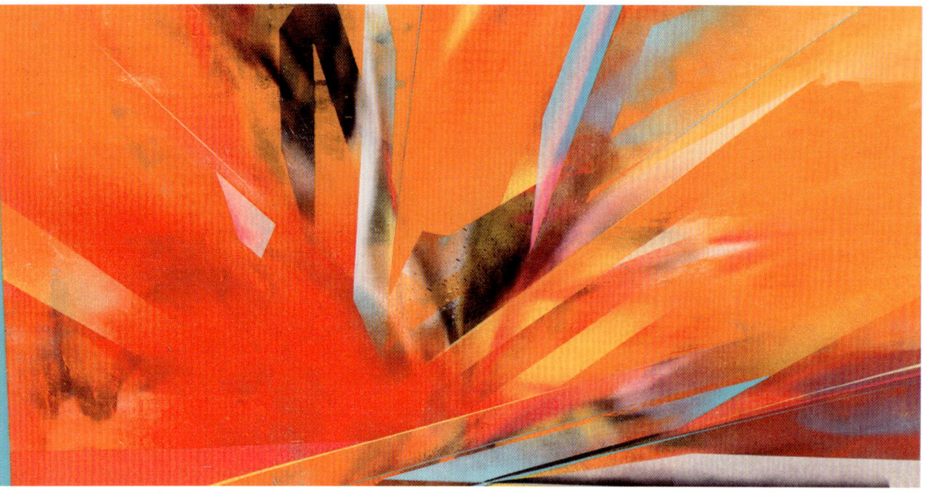

Tropic Thunder
Acrylic and spray on canvas 2017

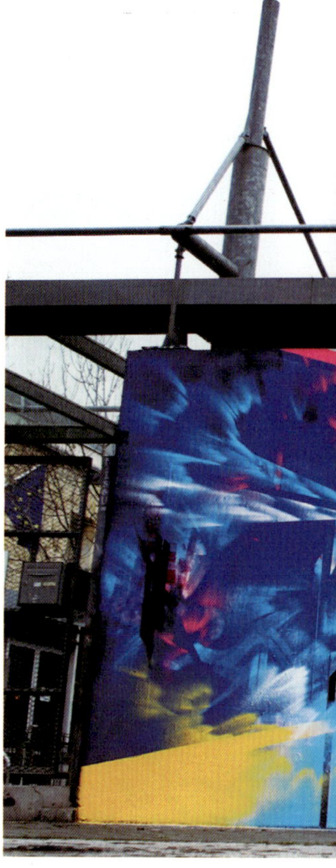

Le M.U.R Of Bordeaux
@Bordeaux, France 2016

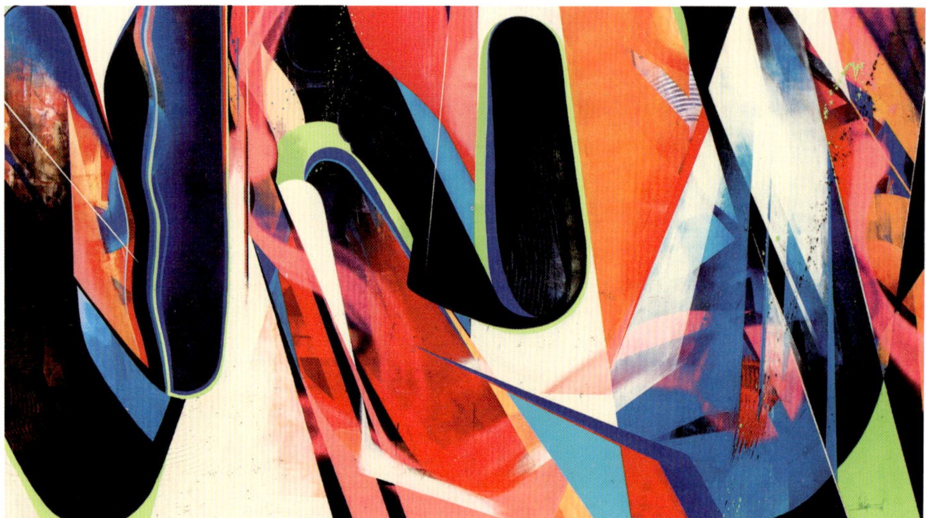

Between the Lines
Acrylic and spray on canvas 2016

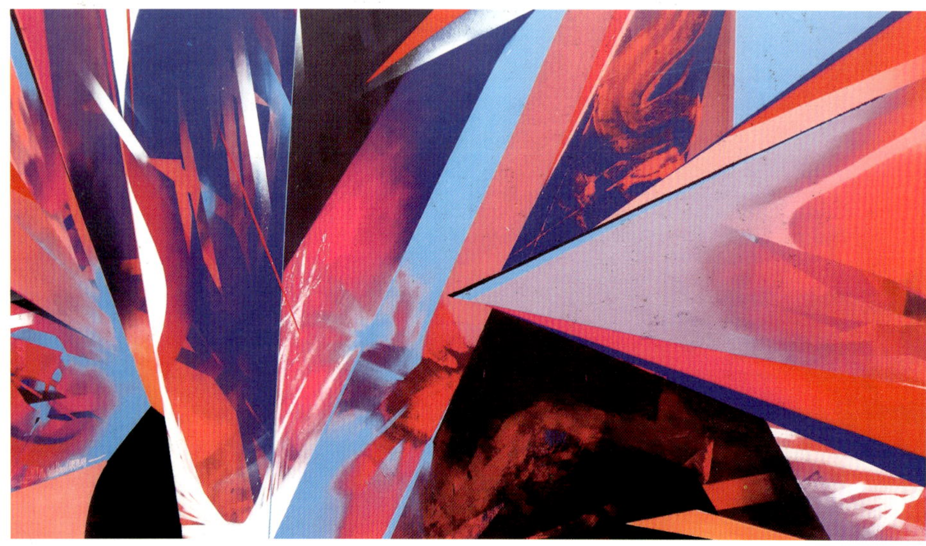

Artplay
@Moscow, Russia 2016

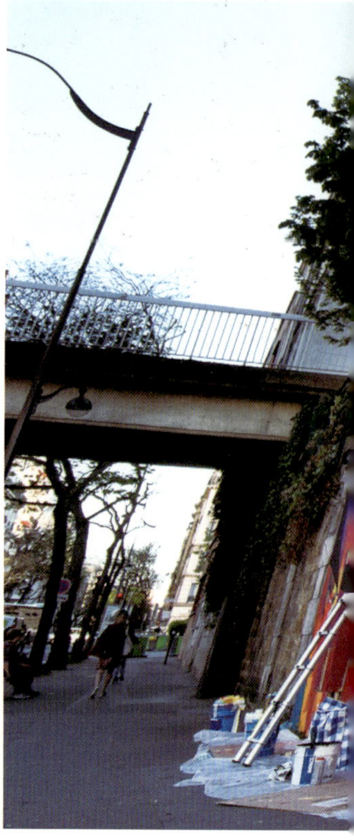

Le M.U.R XII Cicero
@Paris, France 2017 ©Jérémy Marais

Trained as a designer, Théo Lopez invested very early in an artistic approach. Since 2008, he took a decisive shift to become a painter gravitating towards abstract style. Théo Lopez conceives the paintings as a sculptor, playing with the random and causing the accident for inspiration. Multiple layers blend together, the colors dialogue, the lines vibrate and echo, the painting gains dimension of harmonies, and as a result the contrasts evoke energy flows in the audience.

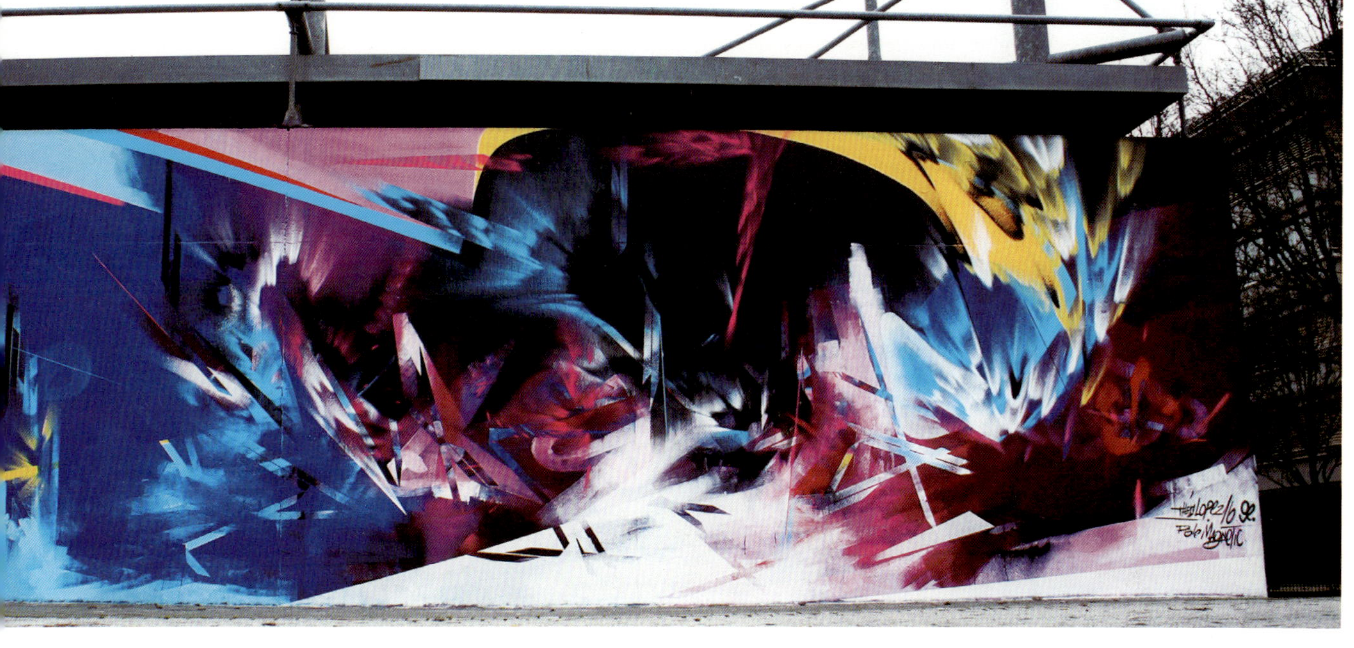

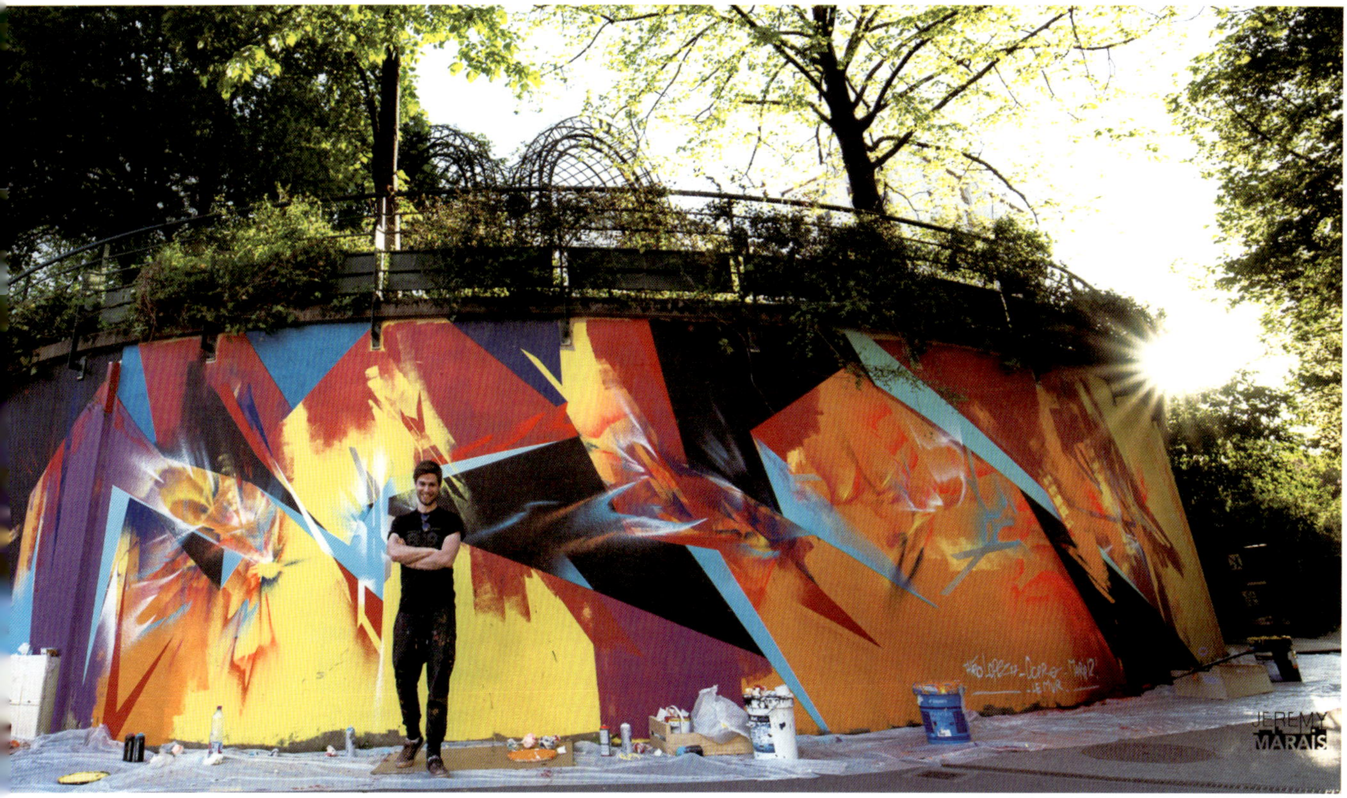

Influenced by the beauty of life and its sorrow, landscapes, and decay, L7M merges strong, bold, and striking geometric shapes with natural elements to create beautiful works that empathize with the surroundings. He captures both the blended coarseness and elegance of birds by combining stylized color puzzles with realistic elements that awaken complex and profound feelings in viewers.

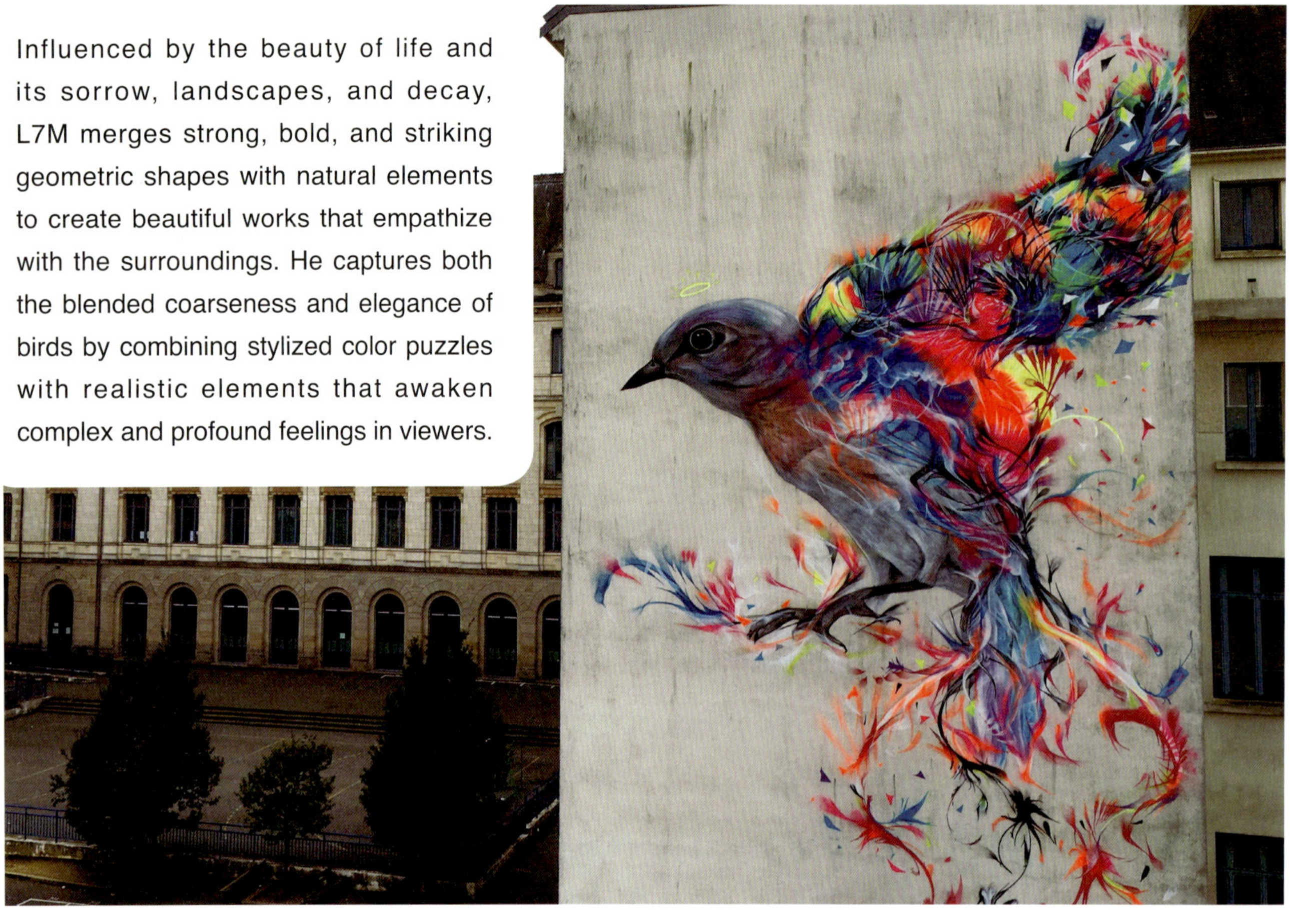

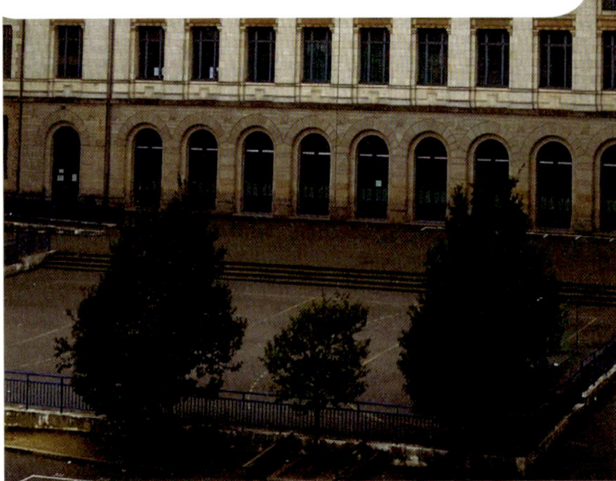

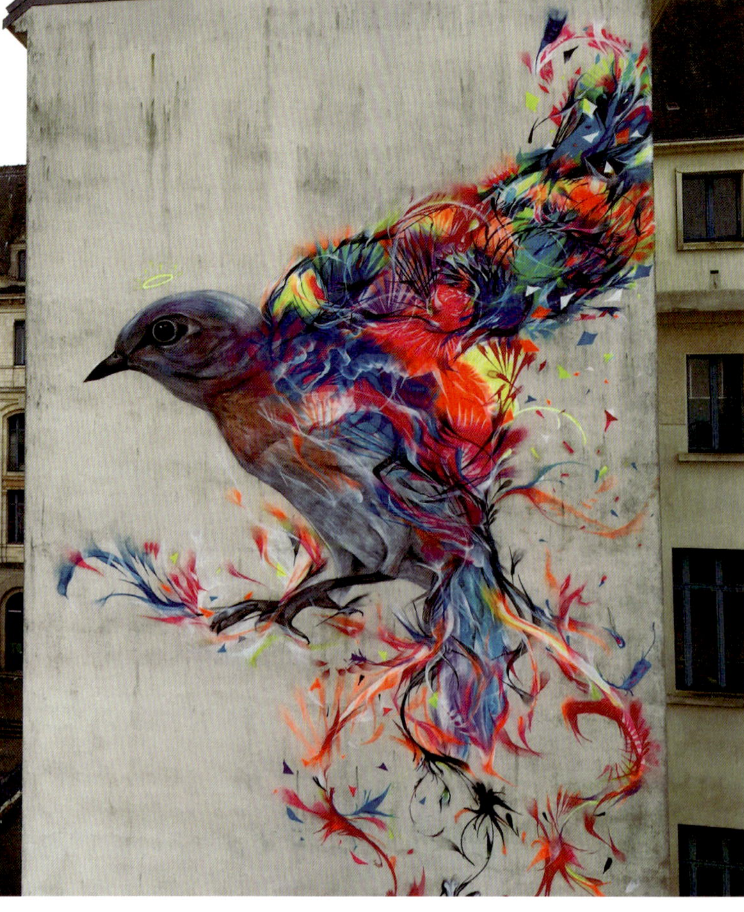

@Vannes, France 2017

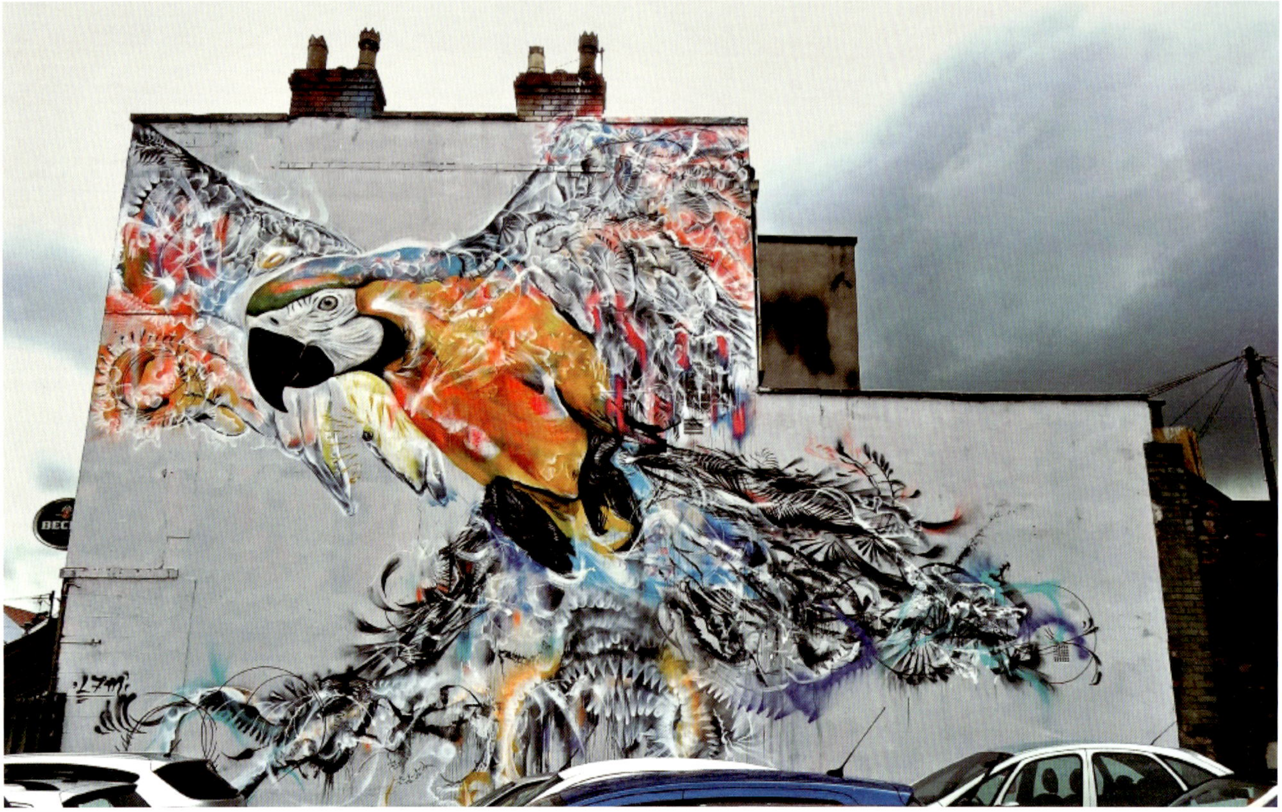

@Bristol, UK 2015

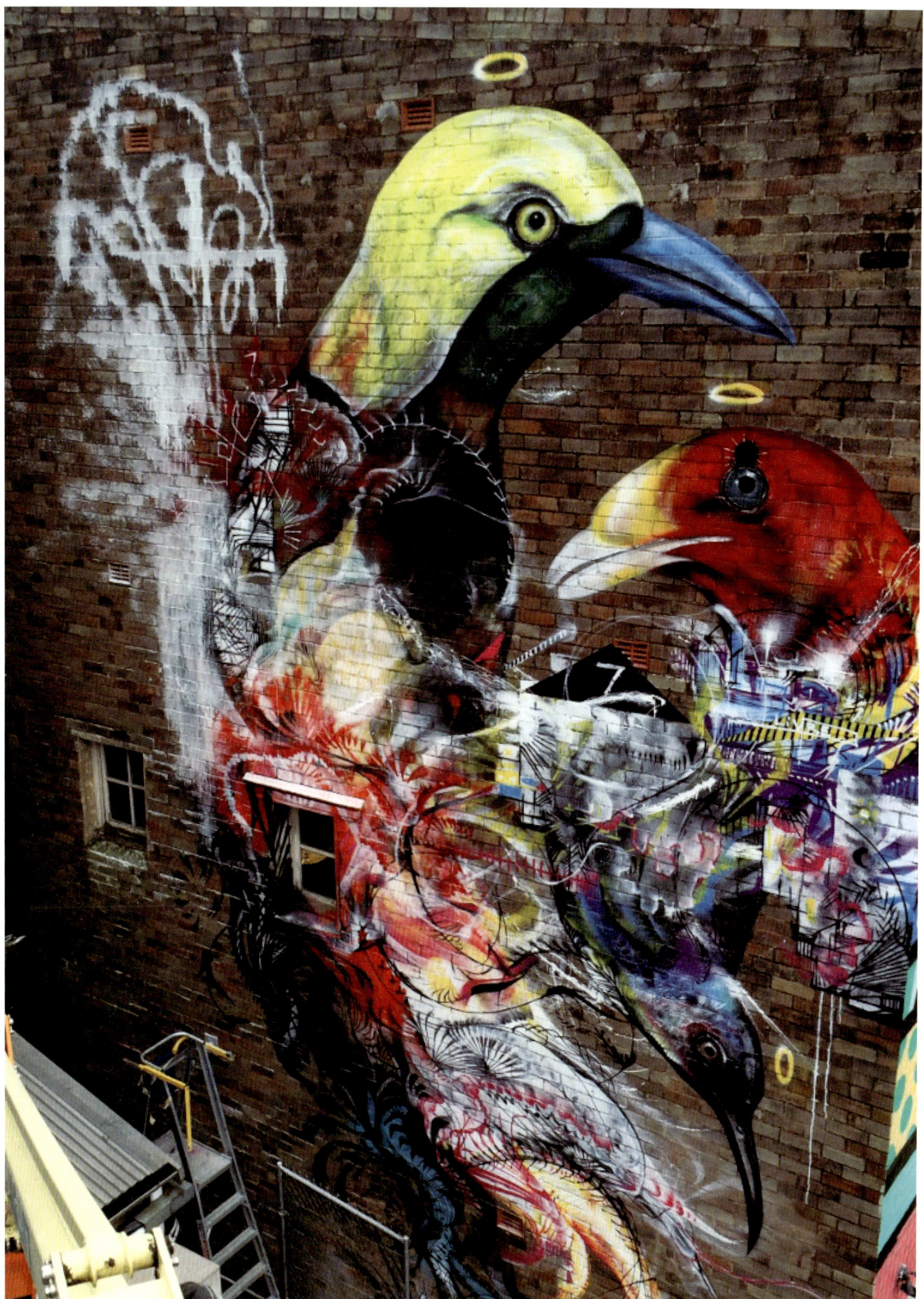

@Katoomba NSW, Australia 2015

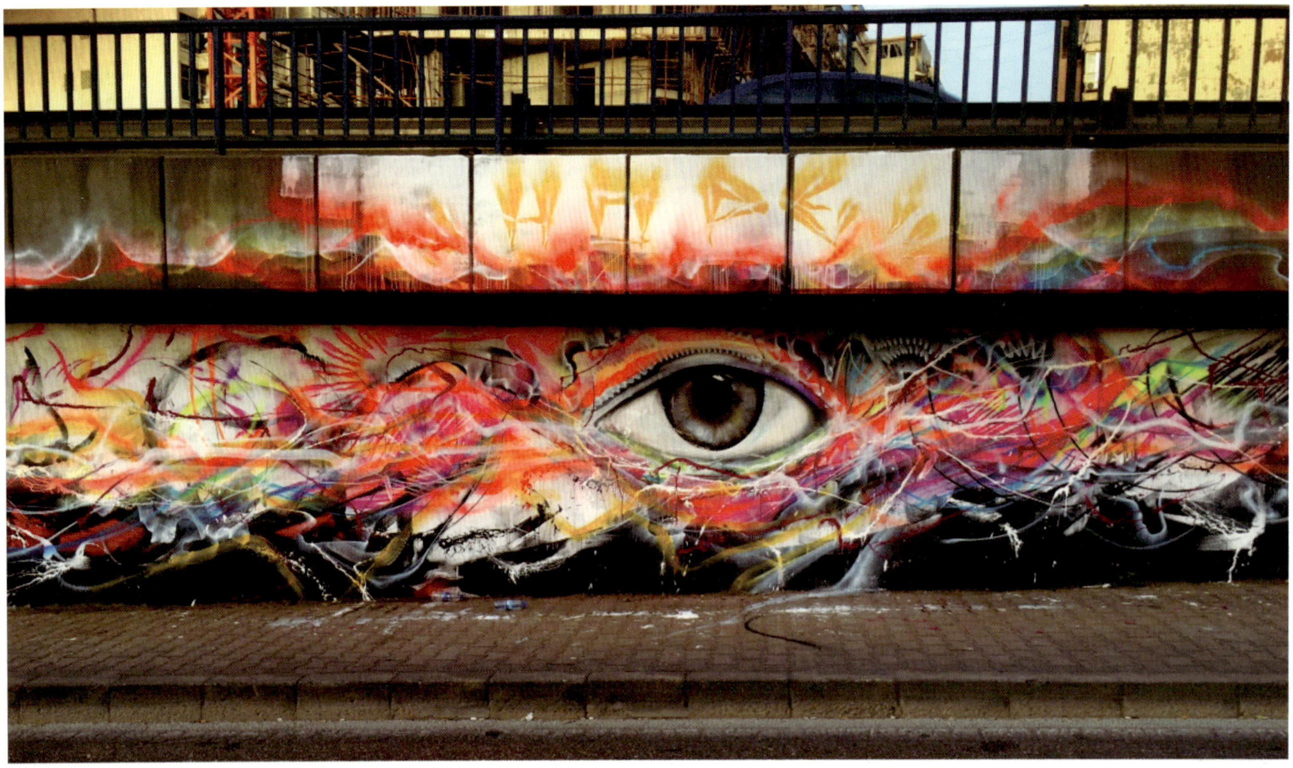

@Beirut, Lebanon 2016

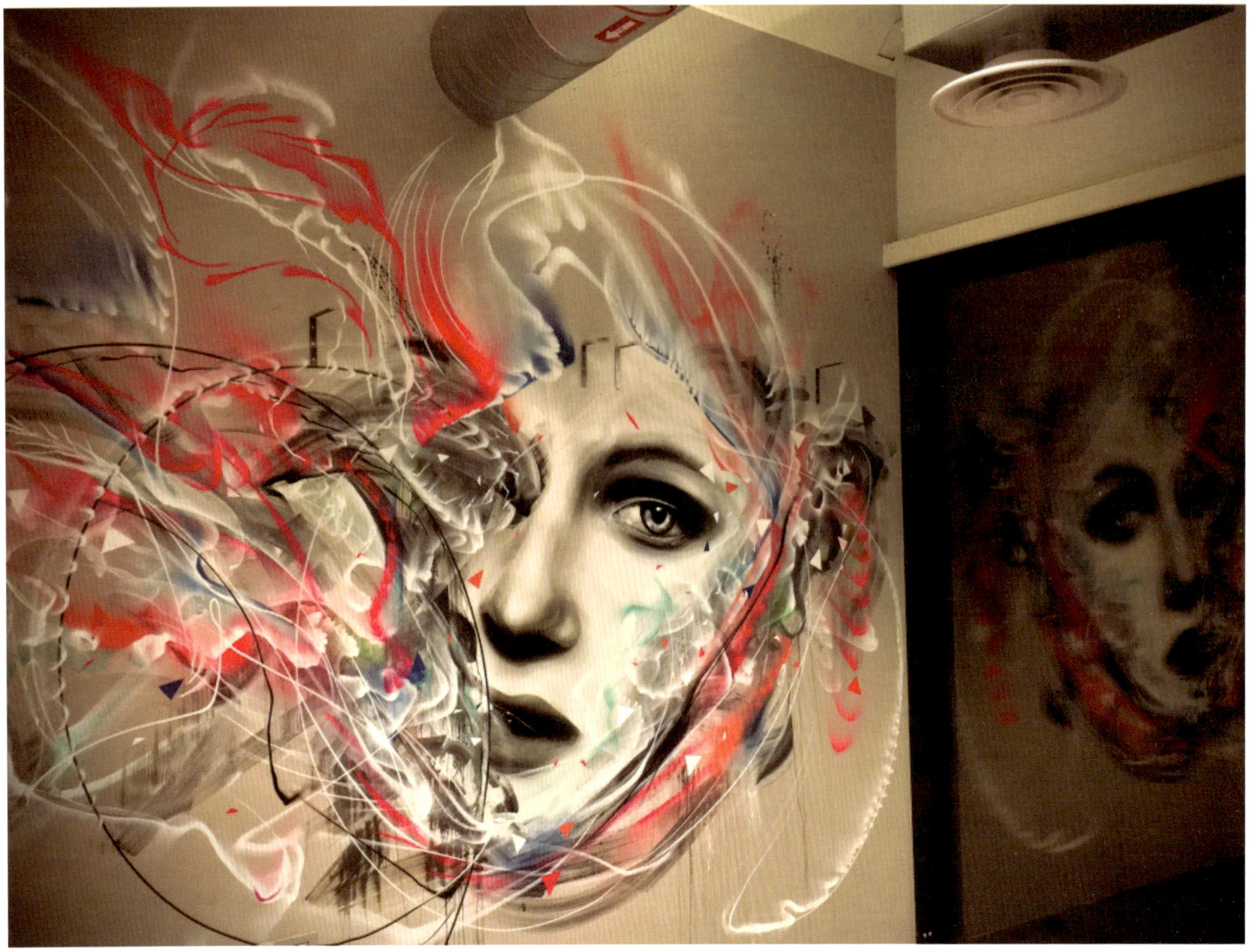

@Riga, Latvia 2016

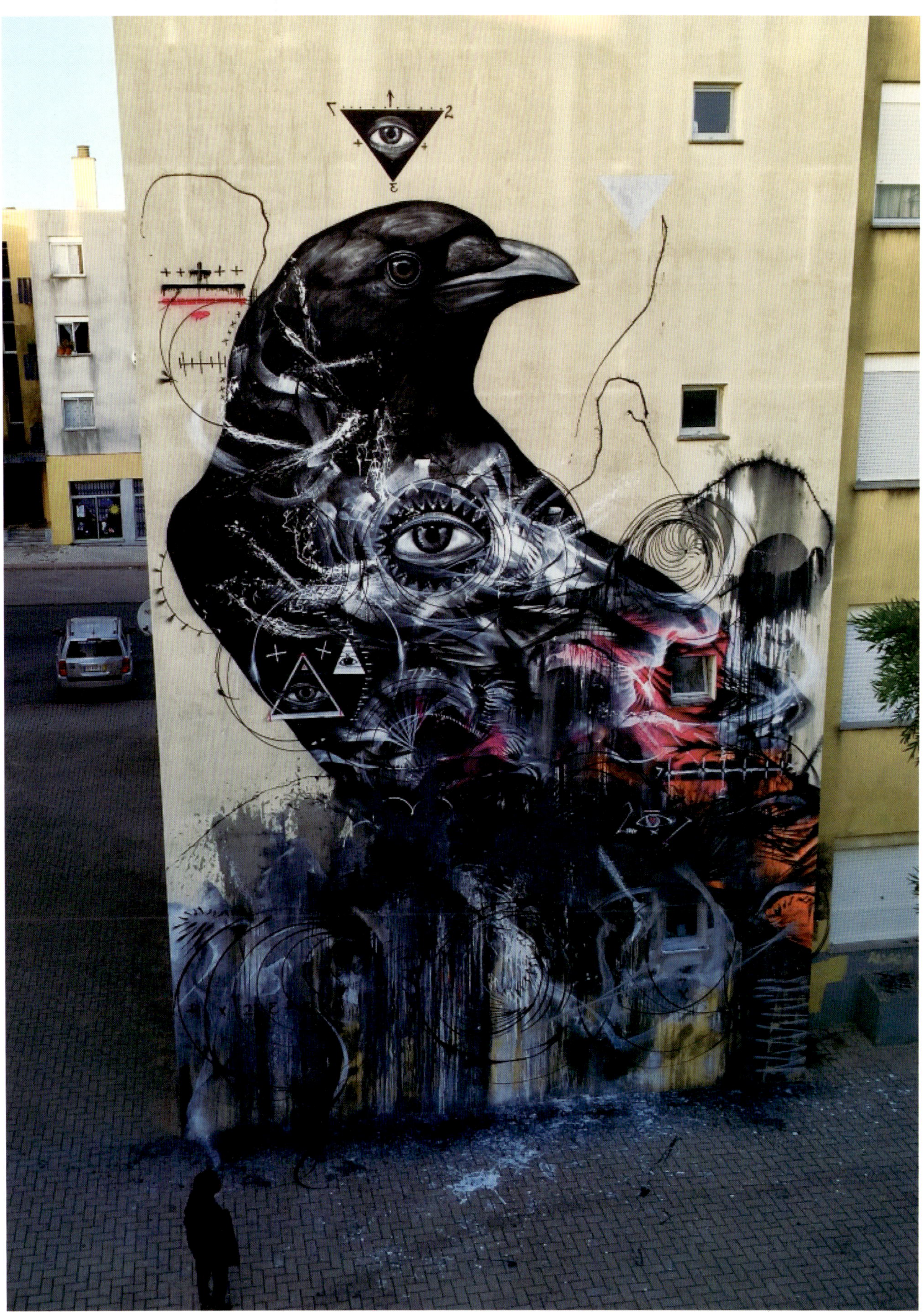

@Loures, Portugal 2015

Chor Boogie, also known as Joaquin Lamar Hailey, is a critically acclaimed spray paint artist. Chor Boogie is recognized for having achieved a groundbreaking level of technical and emotional virtuosity in the medium of spray paint. He approaches his use of color as a form of therapy and visual medicine, and has been dubbed "the color shaman" by comrades and fans. He was first nurtured by the world of street art and is primarily a self-taught artist. Through his dynamic range of artistic styles, he addresses issues of race, class, gender, neo-imperialism, corporate corruption, substance abuse, health care, drug policy reform, and the rights of indigenous peoples.

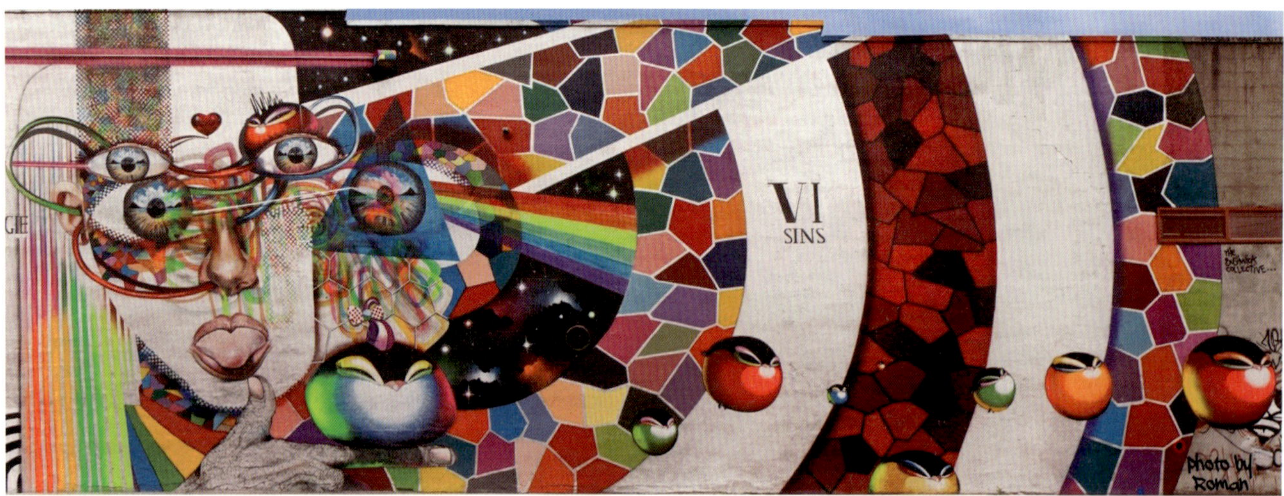

VI SINS
@New York, USA 2017

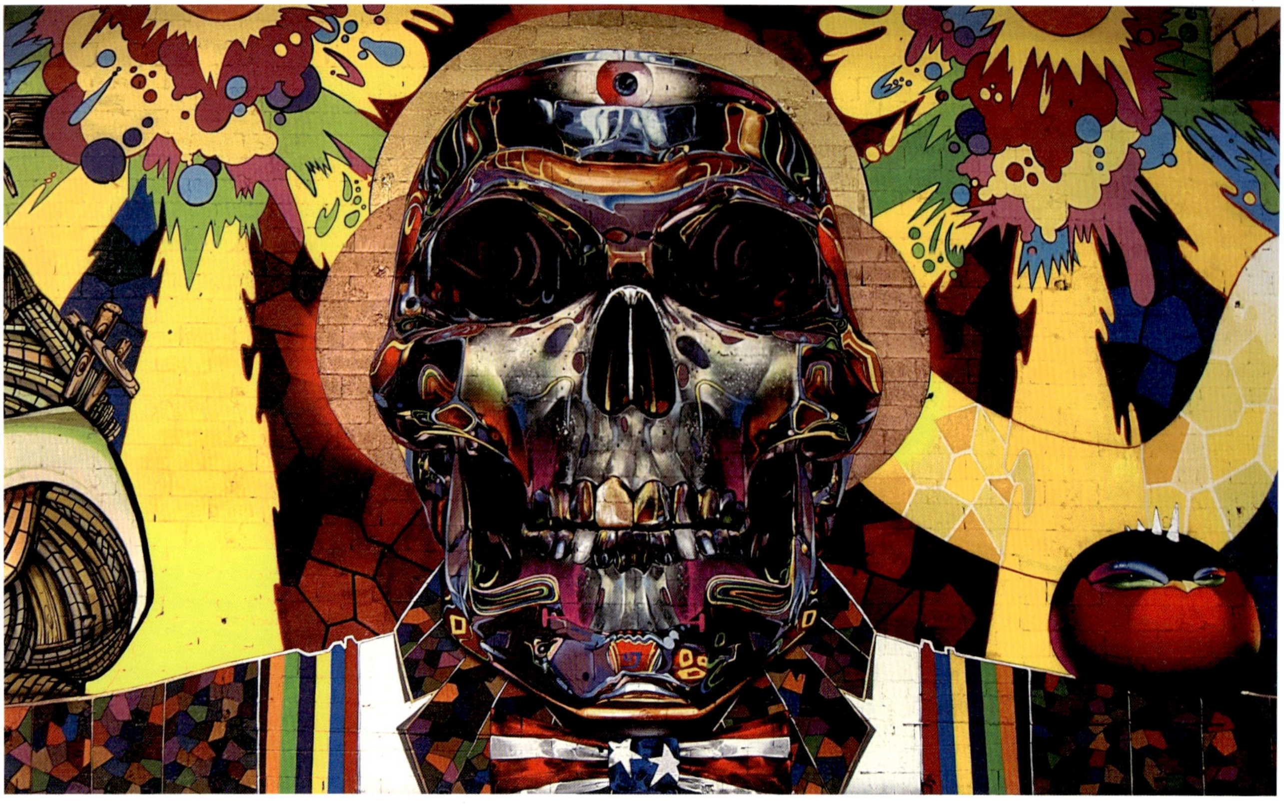

Corporate Zombies
@New York, USA 2017

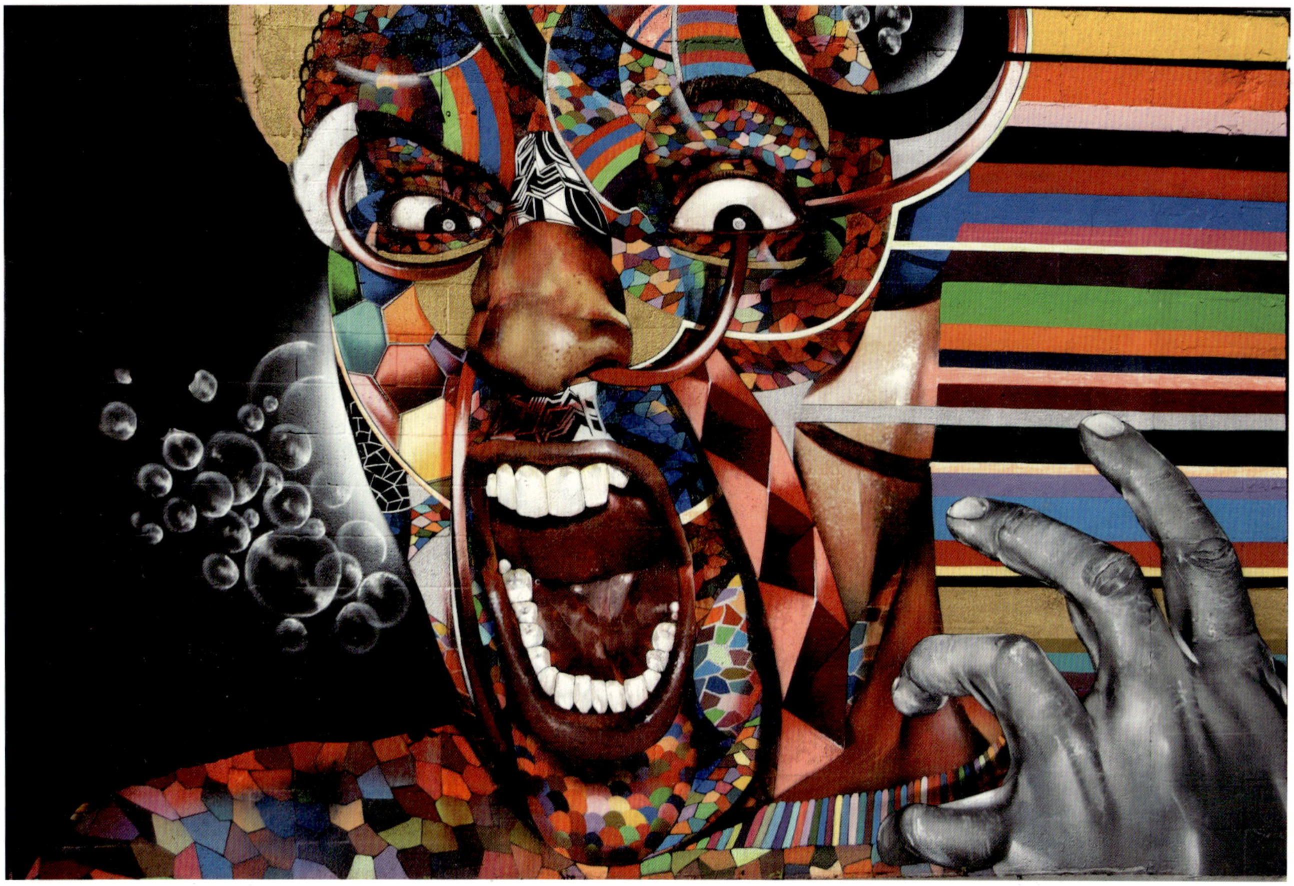

Self Portrait
@Miami, USA 2011

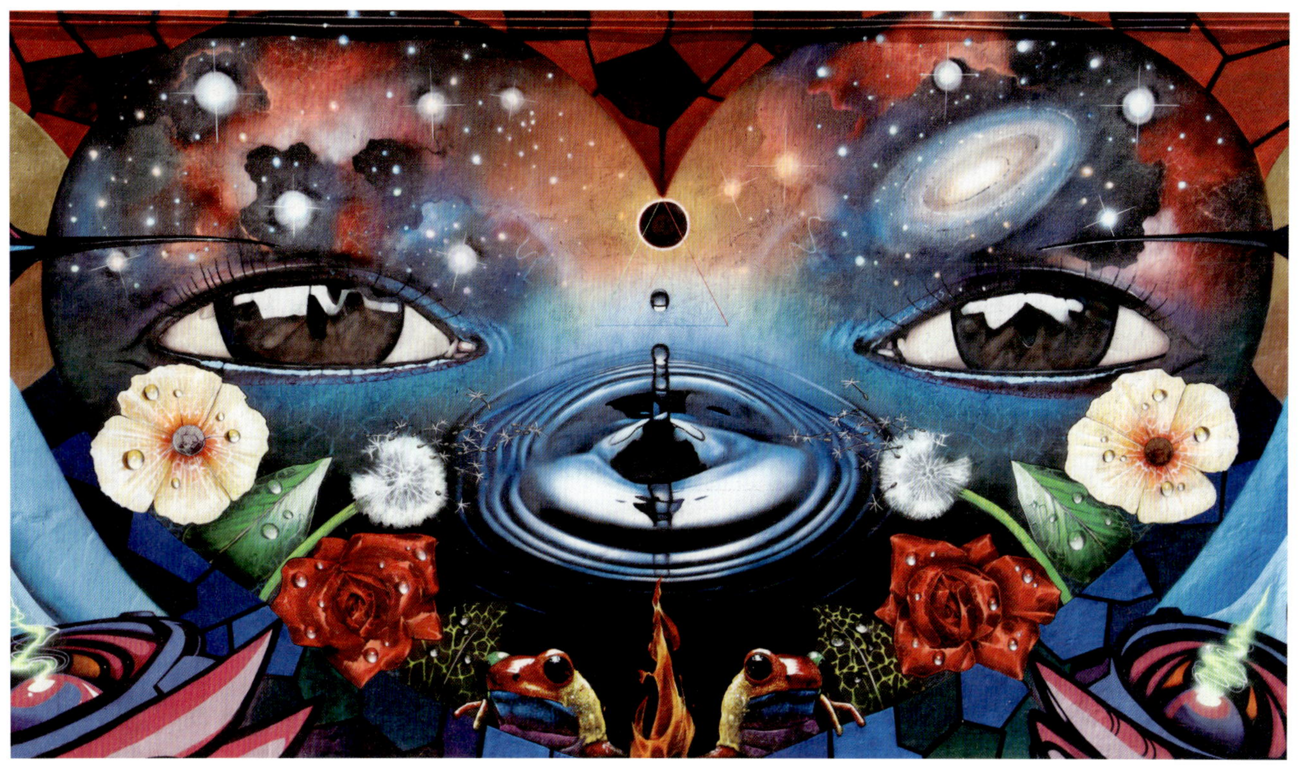

Love Your Momma
@Miami, USA 2016

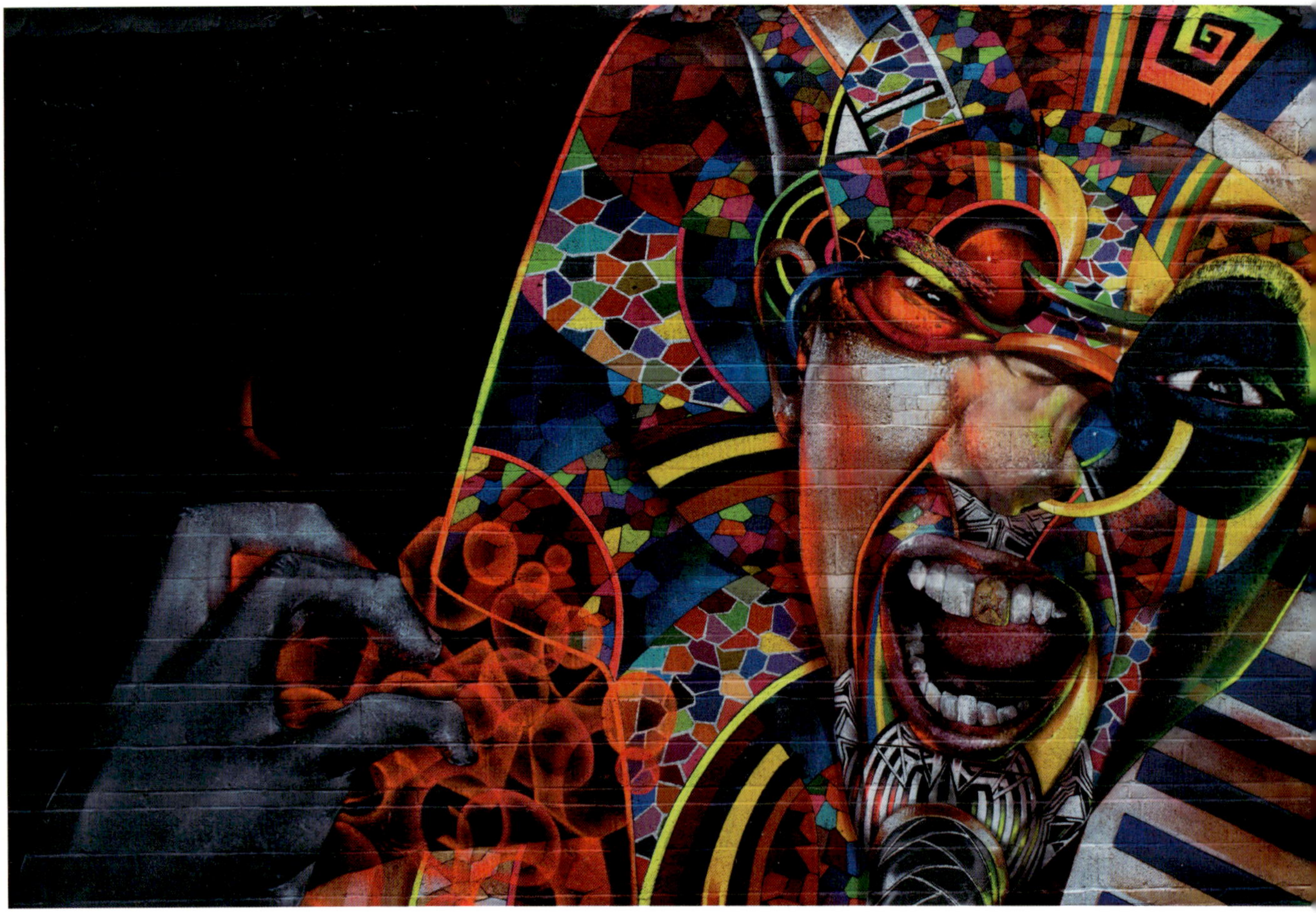

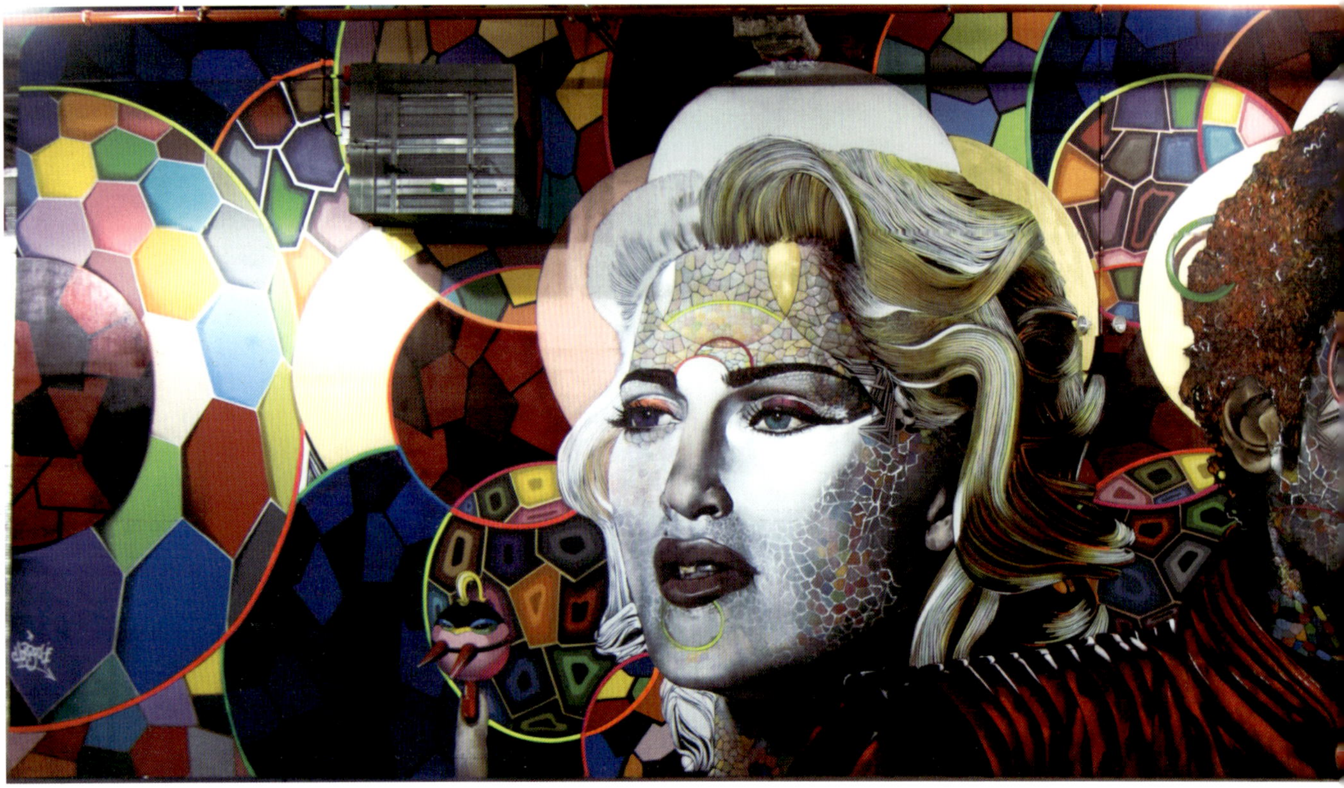

Like a Material Moonwalking Virgin
@New York, USA 2017

Modern Hieroglyphics
@Baton Rouge, Louisiana, USA 2013

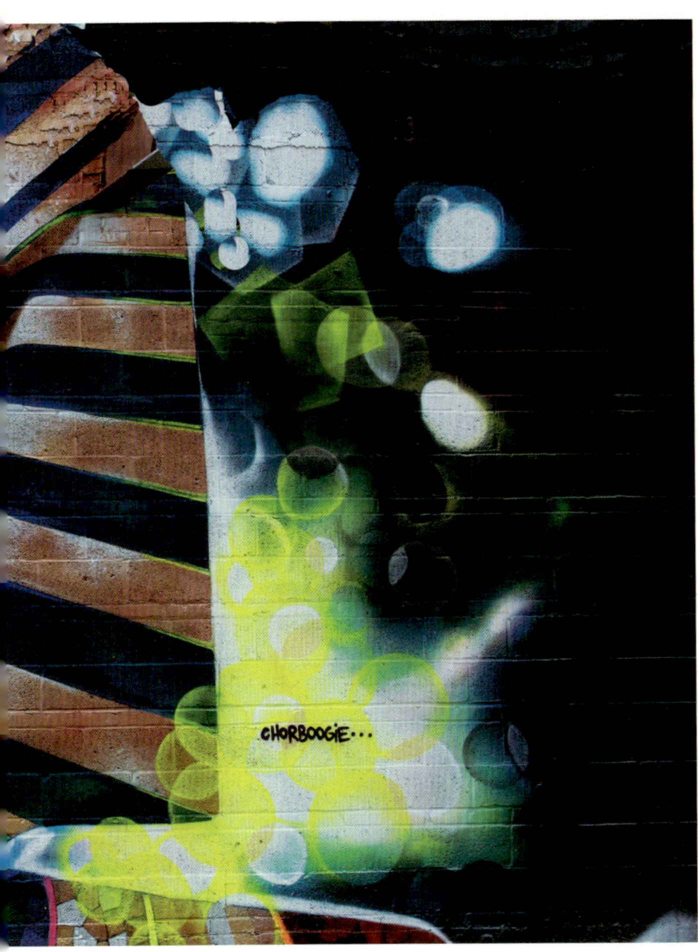

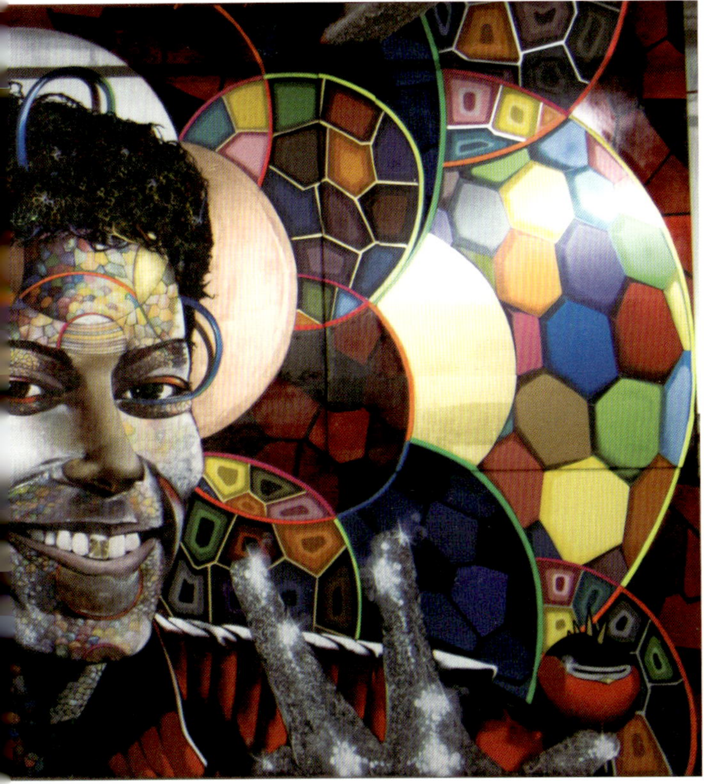

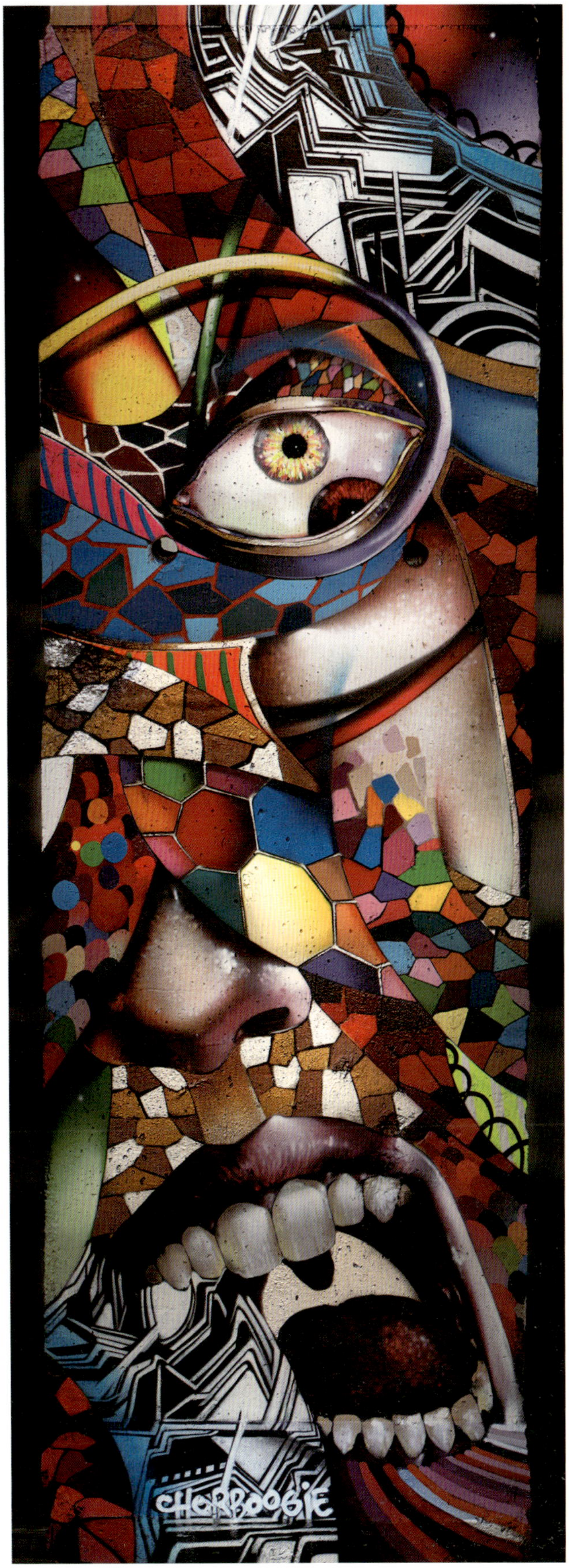

Berlin's Divide
@Berlin, Germany 2010

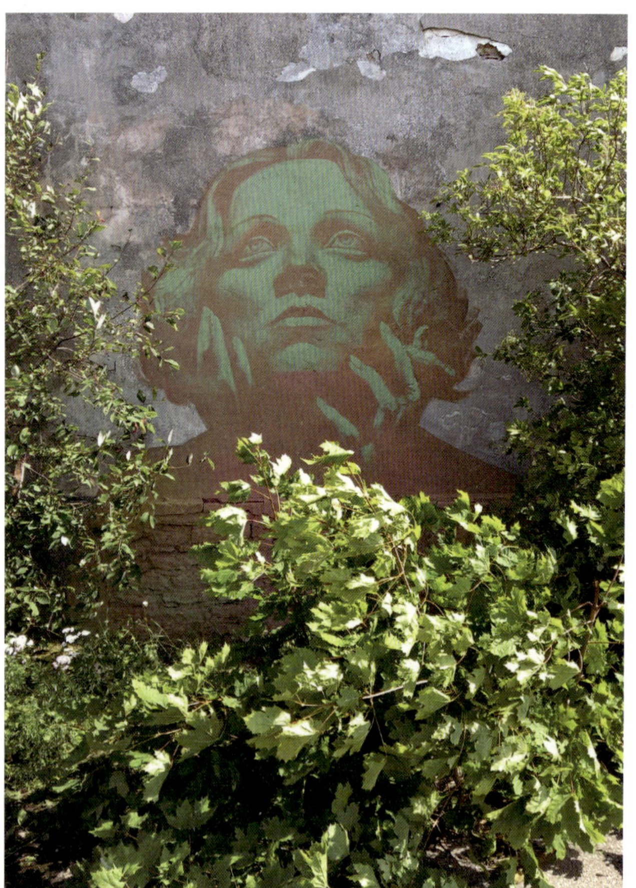

Remarqueś Muse
@Haapsalu, Estonia 2016

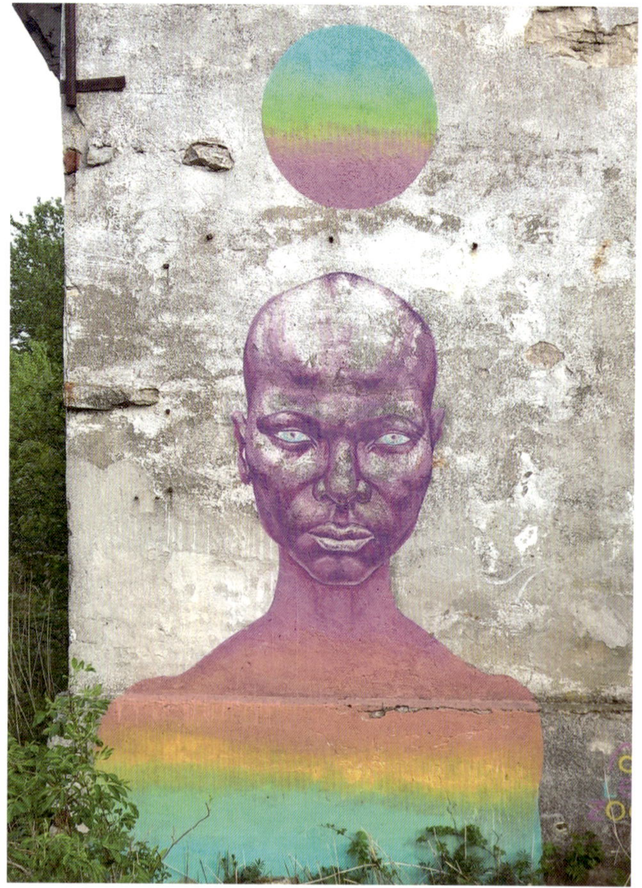

Deep Roots Africa
@Haapsalu, Estonia 2016

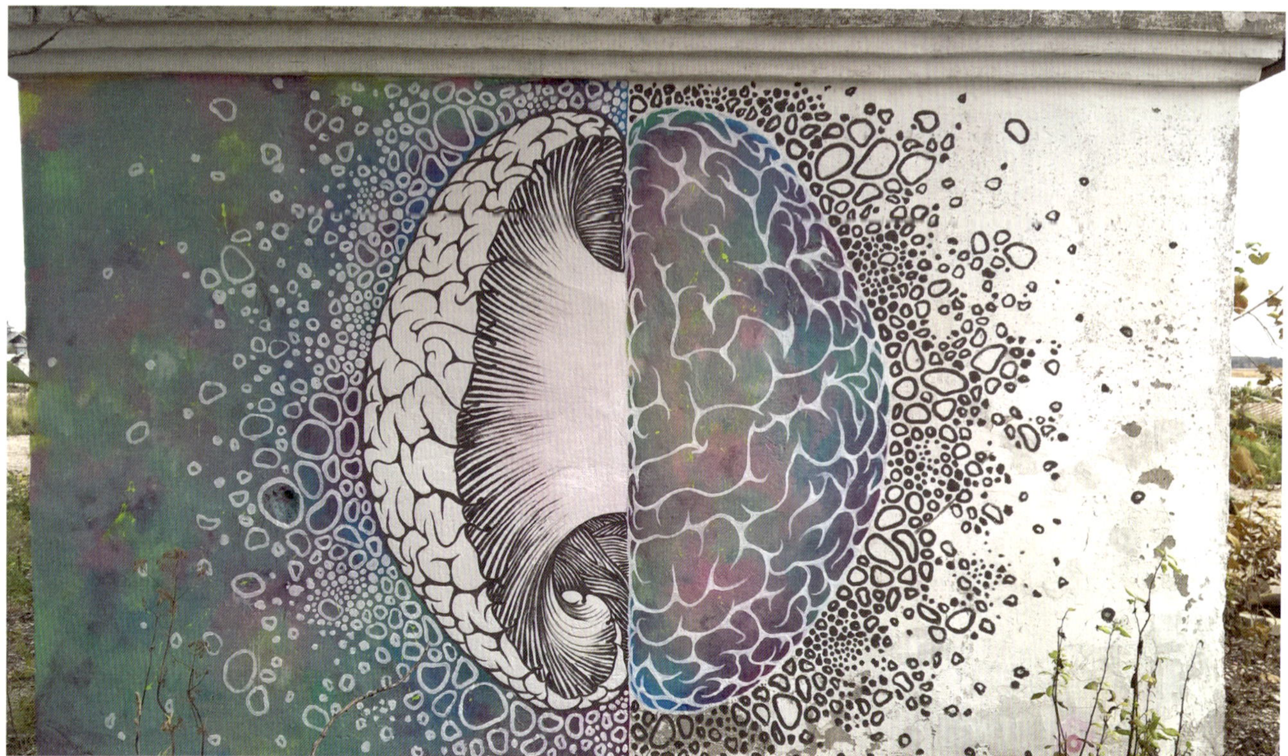

Polar Mind
@Haapsalu, Estonia 2016

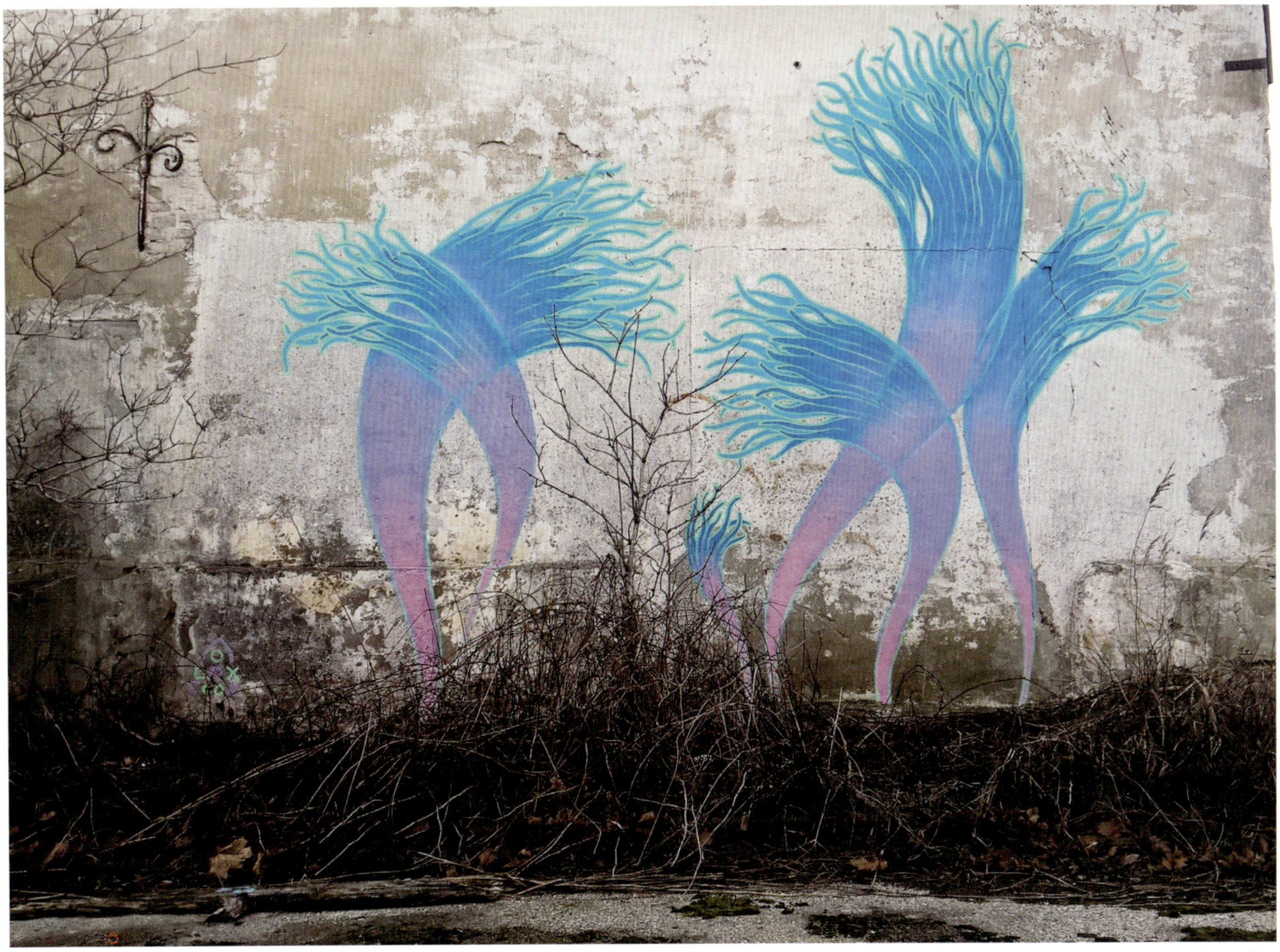

Tickling Bushes
@Haapsalu, Estonia 2016

Lex Zooz is an Estonian artist, born and living in Haapsalu town. After studying at the art department of Tallinn University and graduating from Saint Petersburg Art and Industry Academy, he now works as an urban freelancer, creating murals, stained glass, and mosaics. His works are colorful in a calm way, where the colors seem to blend in to one another like flowing water.

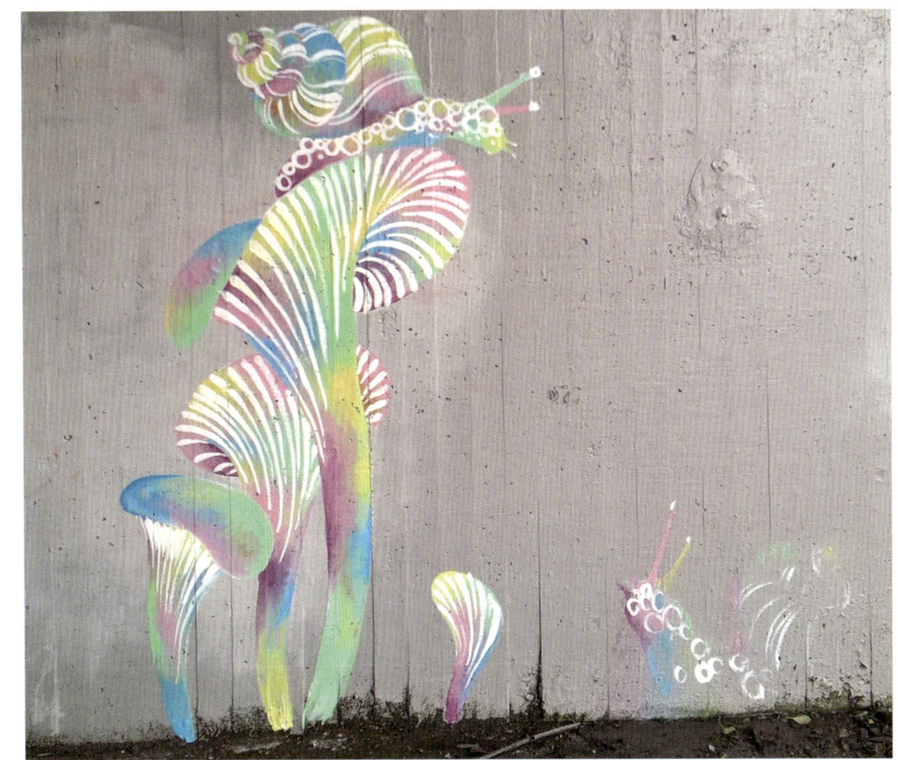

Toxic Snails
@Bergen, Norway 2016

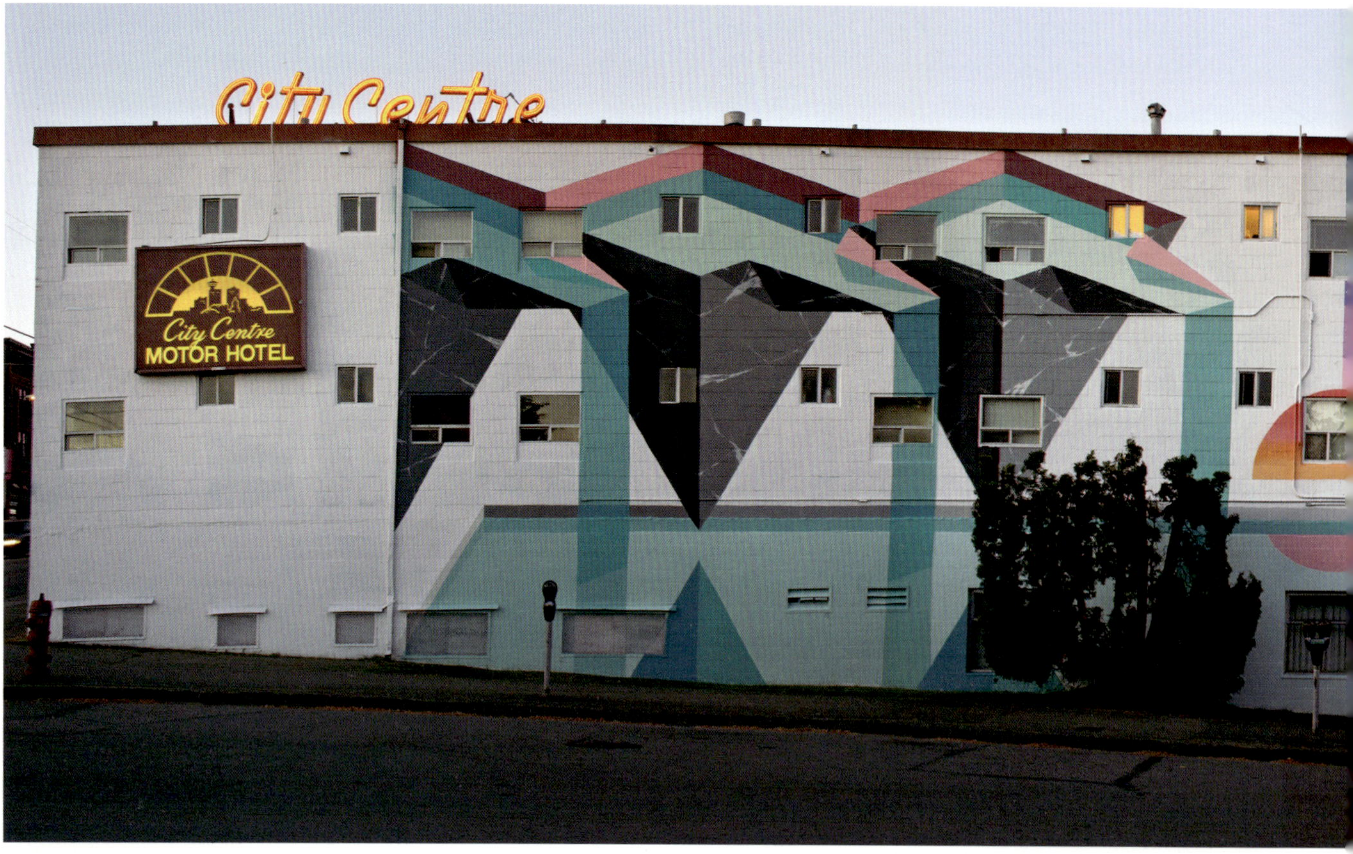

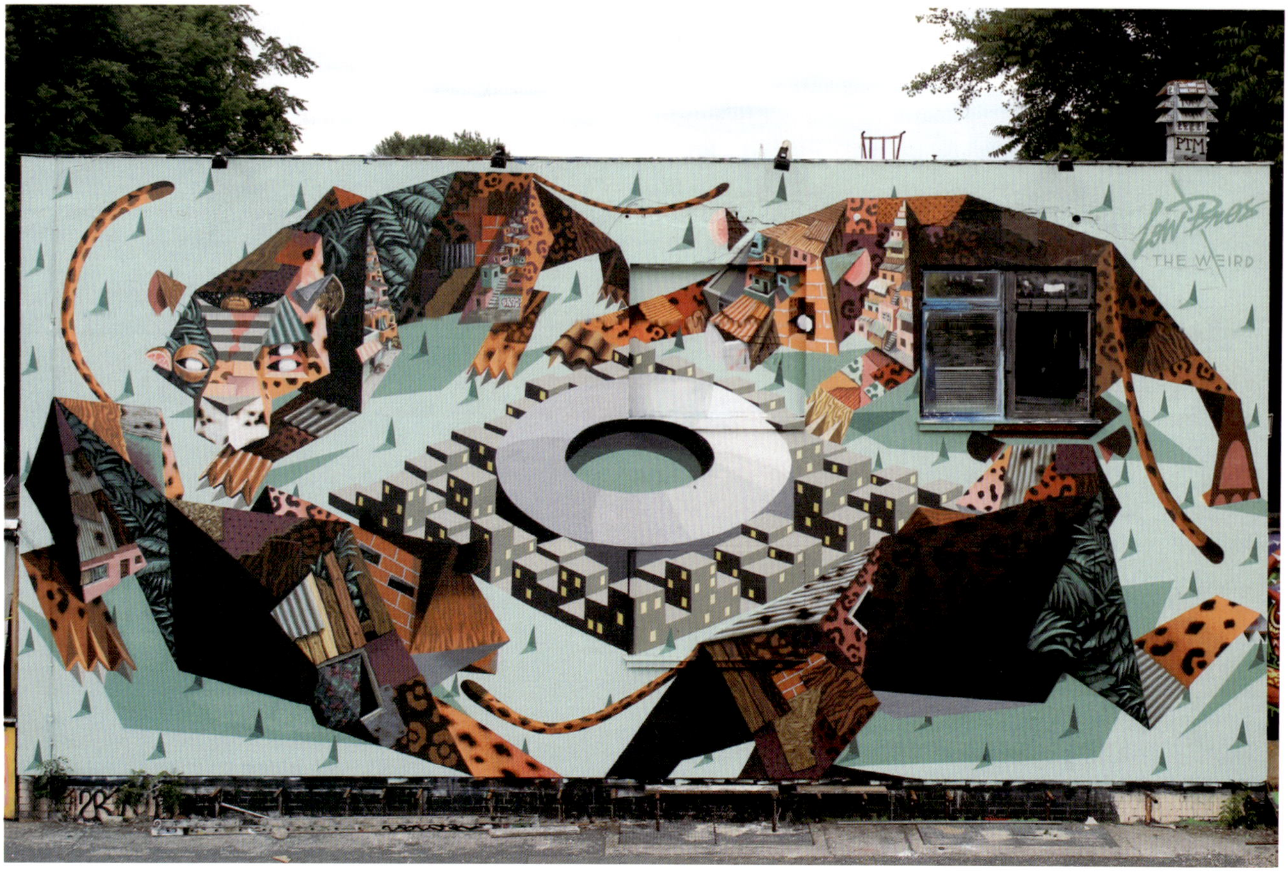

Untitled
@Berlin, Germany 2014

Untitled
@Vancouver, Canada 2016

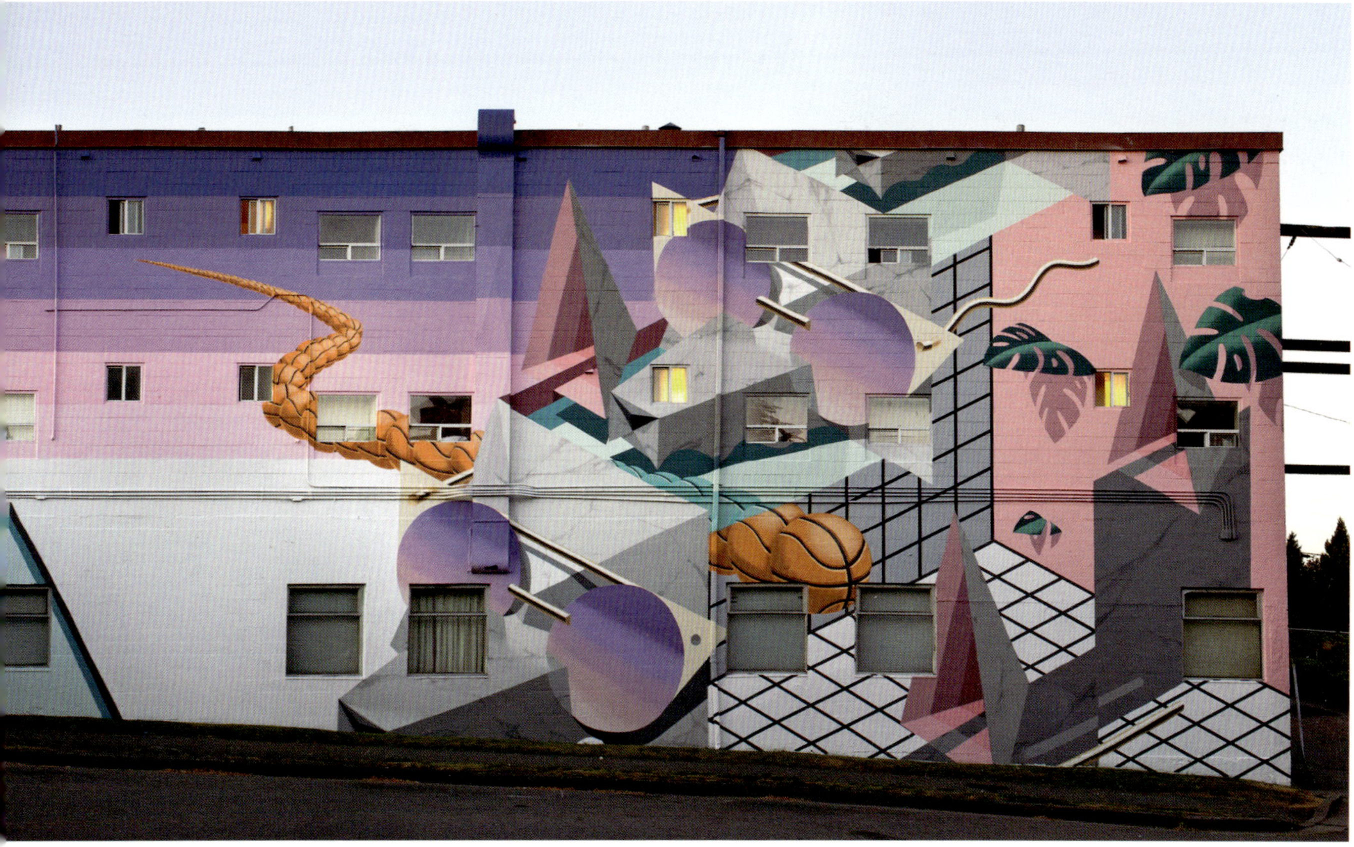

Low Bros is a retro, futuristic duo, made up of Berlin-based brothers, Christoph and Florin Schmidt. Despite the abstract nature of their meticulous painterly approach, the themes of the ambivalence of contemporary life, as well as the conflicts of progress and traditionalism are reinforced through sharp, vivid colors and atmospheric ambiguity.

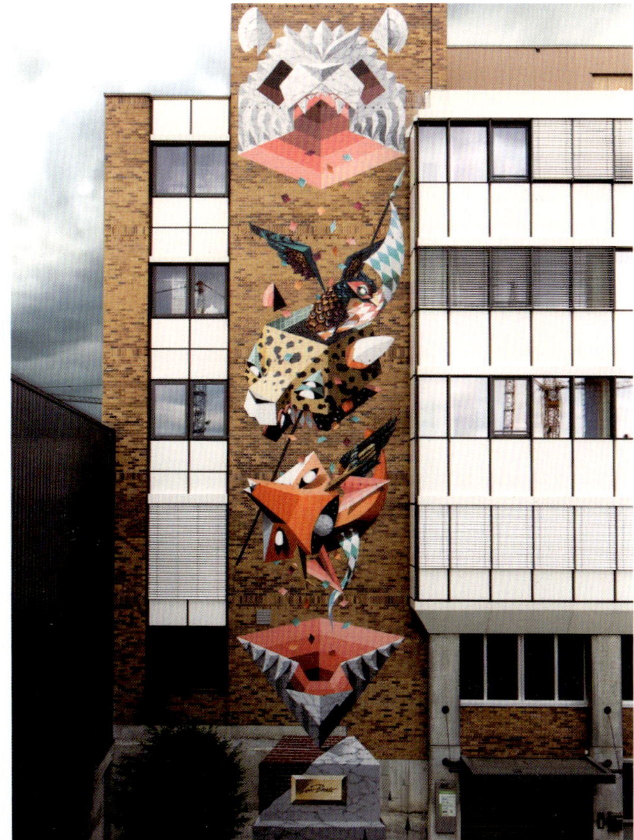

Untitled
@Munich, Germany 2014

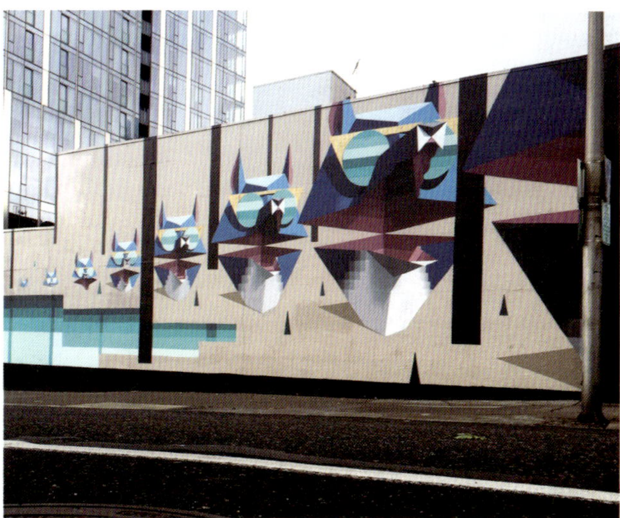

Untitled
@Portland, USA 2015

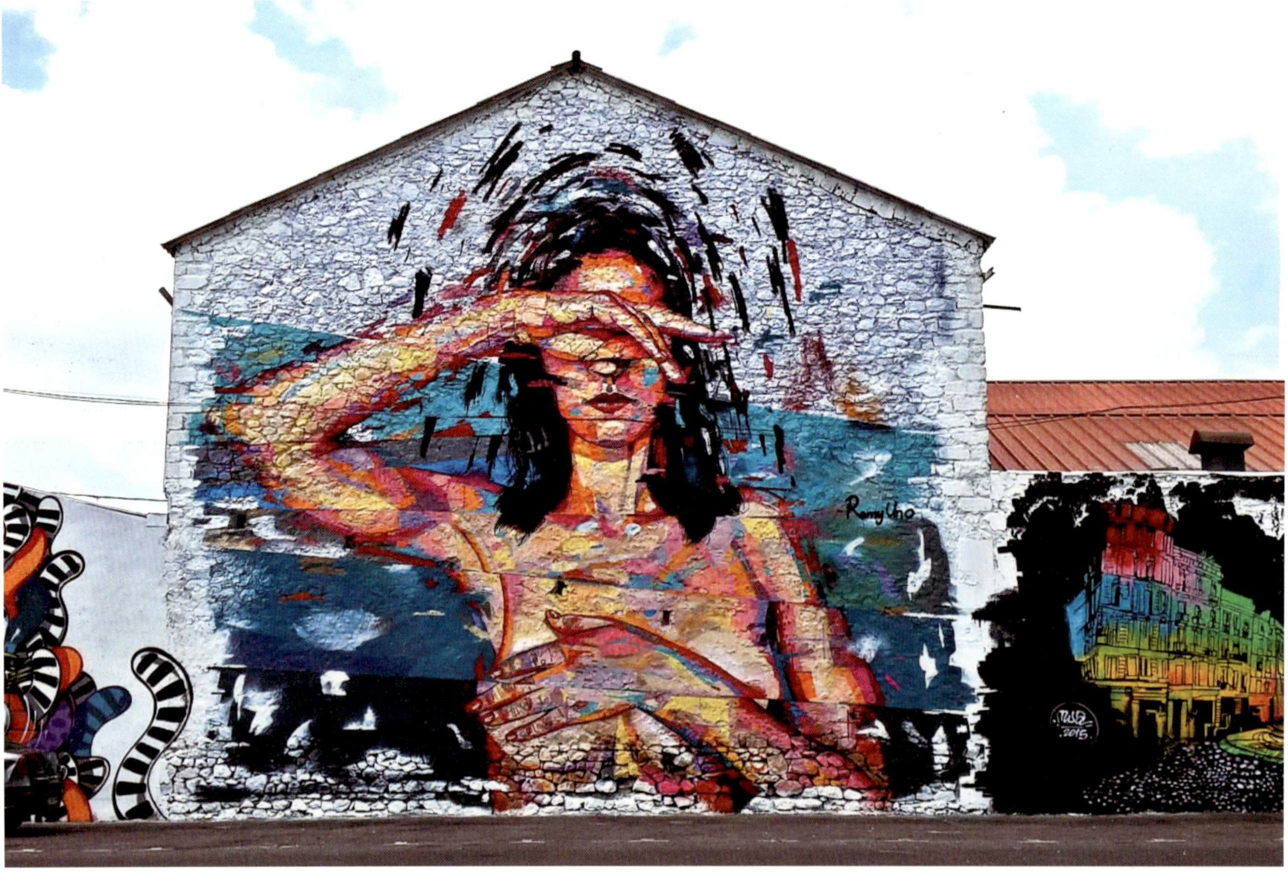

Guess Who
@Marseille, France 2015

Remy Uno is a Marseille-based artist. He started to paint his name on street walls as a game in the 1990s and attempted to form larger letters on bigger walls. Over time, a desire to paint people was born within him. Meanwhile, his graffiti left an impact on viewers who asked for works on canvas, so the partial transition from street to studio happened naturally. Portrait is the dominant theme of his works, and the notion of intimacy and relaxation is conveyed through the fragmented imagery of portraits.

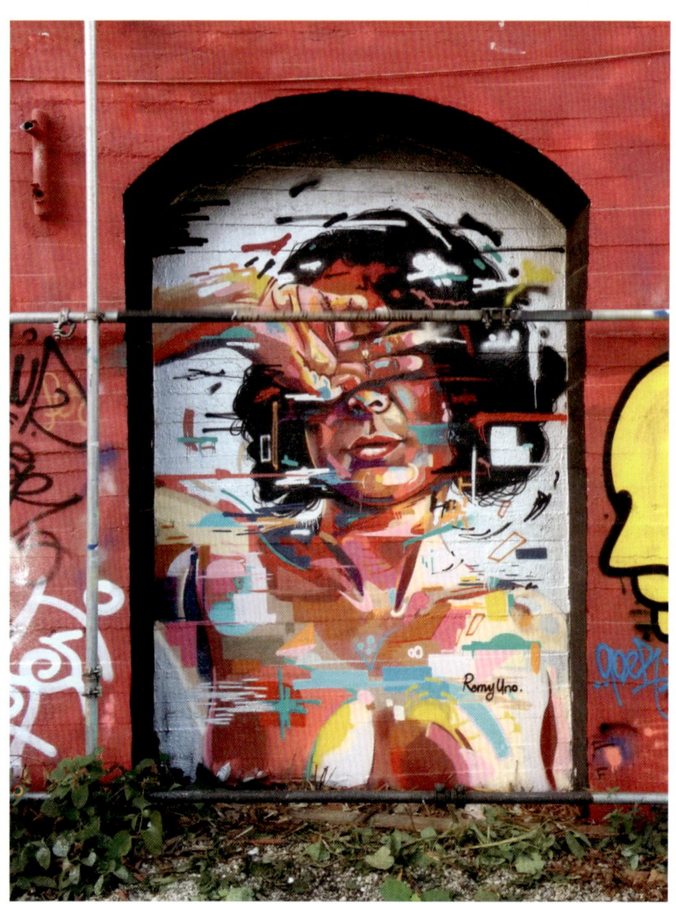

Guess Again
@Berlin, Germany 2015

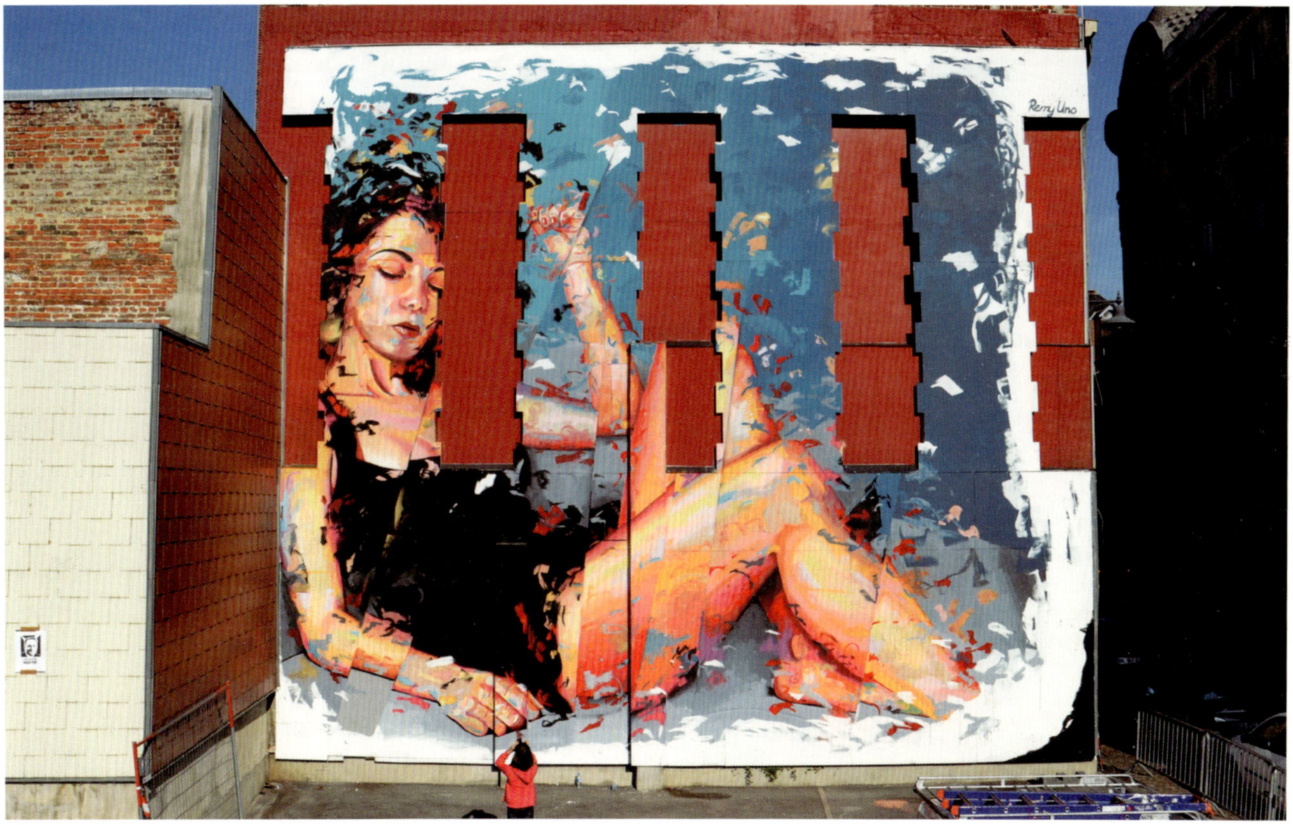

Lazy Afternoon
@Saint-Quentin, France 2015

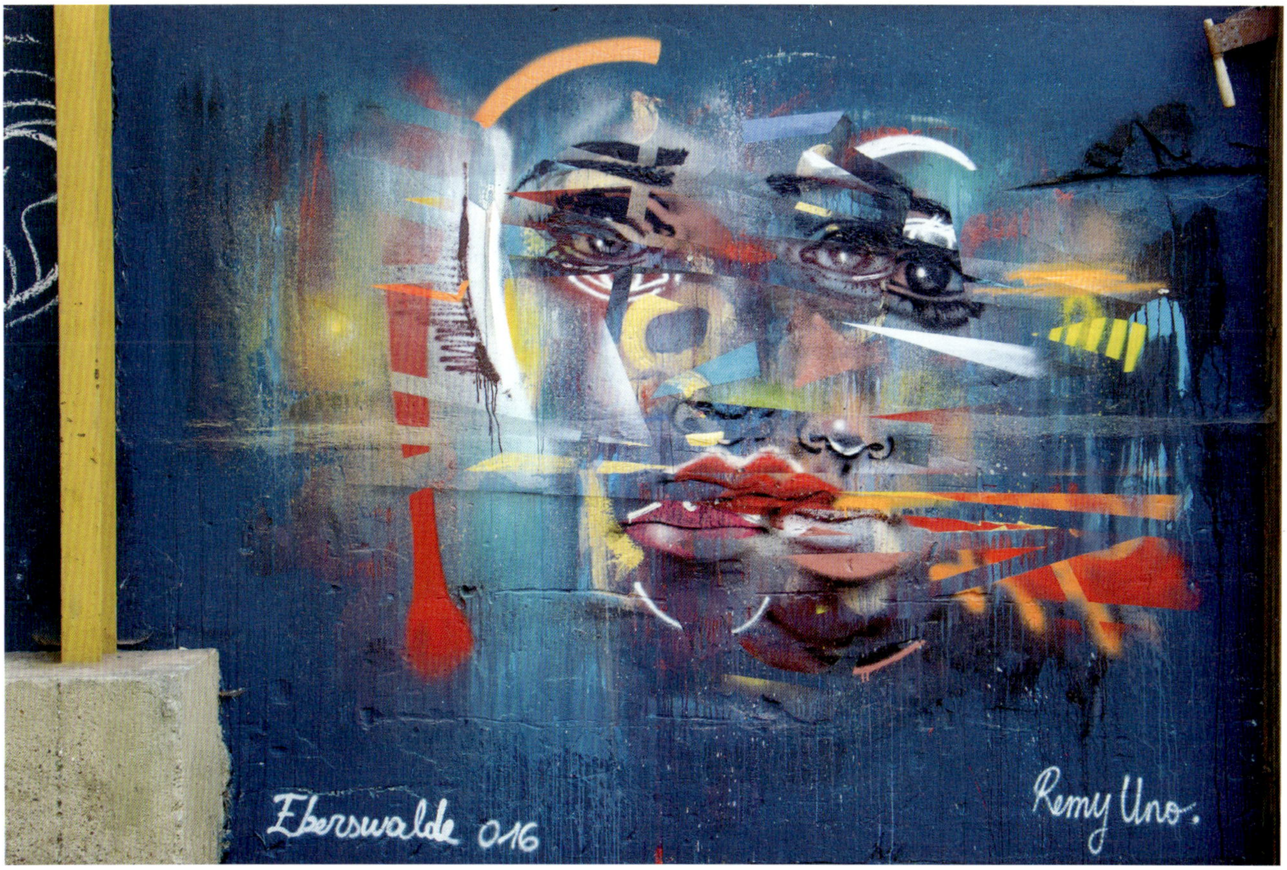

Eberwalde
@Berlin, Germany 2016

Although Elle began as an illegal graffiti artist in New York, she is now considered one of the top touring street artists. With a passion for environment and feminism, she creates street art by collaging disparate images: powerful females, flora and fauna, classical paintings juxtaposed with pop-culture and high fashion imagery, revealing purposefully designed messages of poetry for the world.

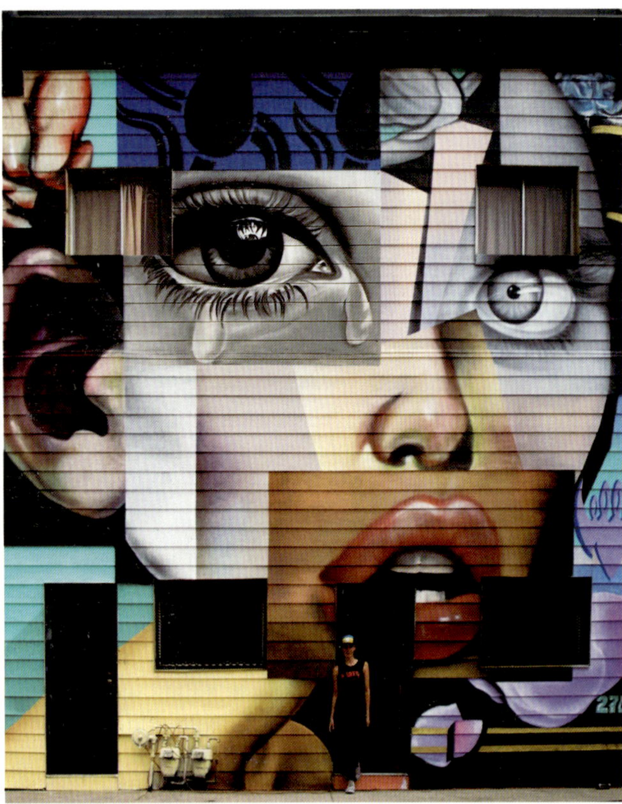

Colorado Crush
@Denver, USA 2016

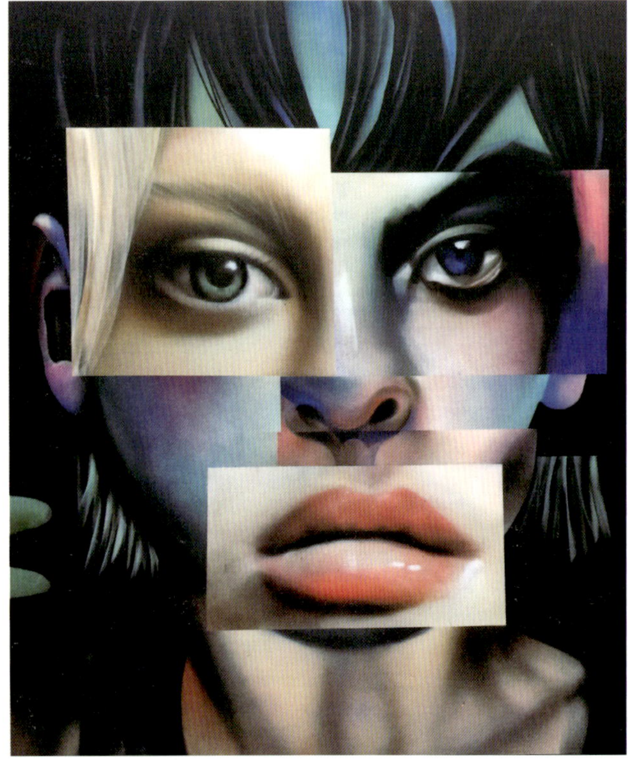

Seeing Through You
Spraypaint on Canvas 2016

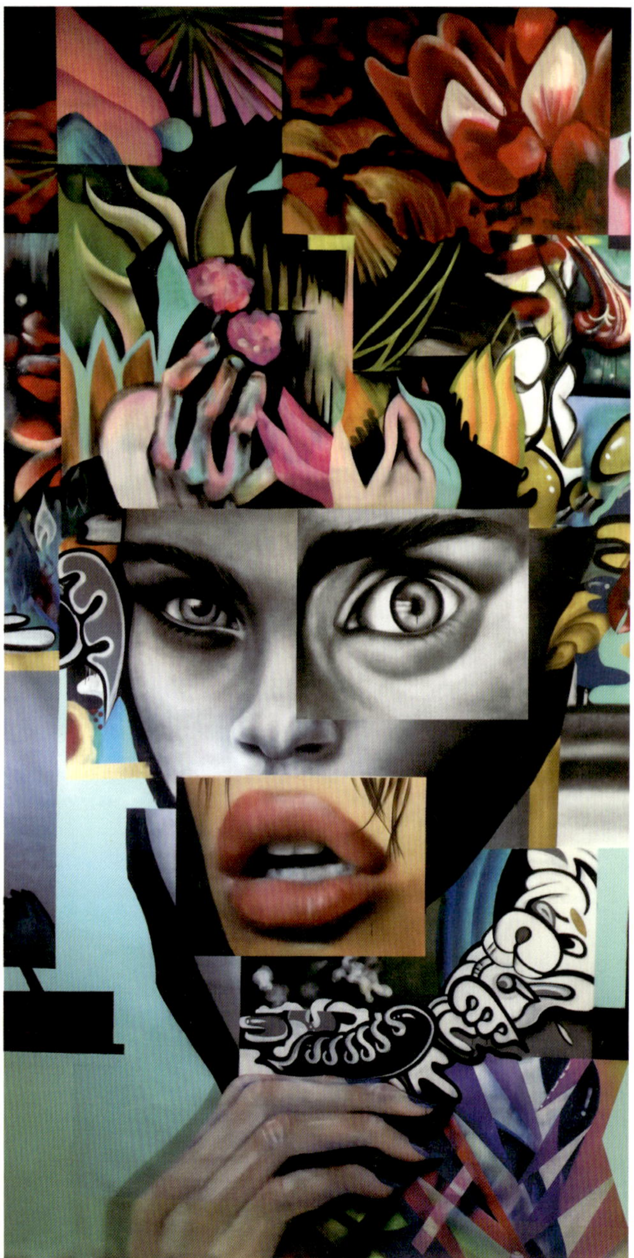

Wandering Mind
@New York, USA 2016

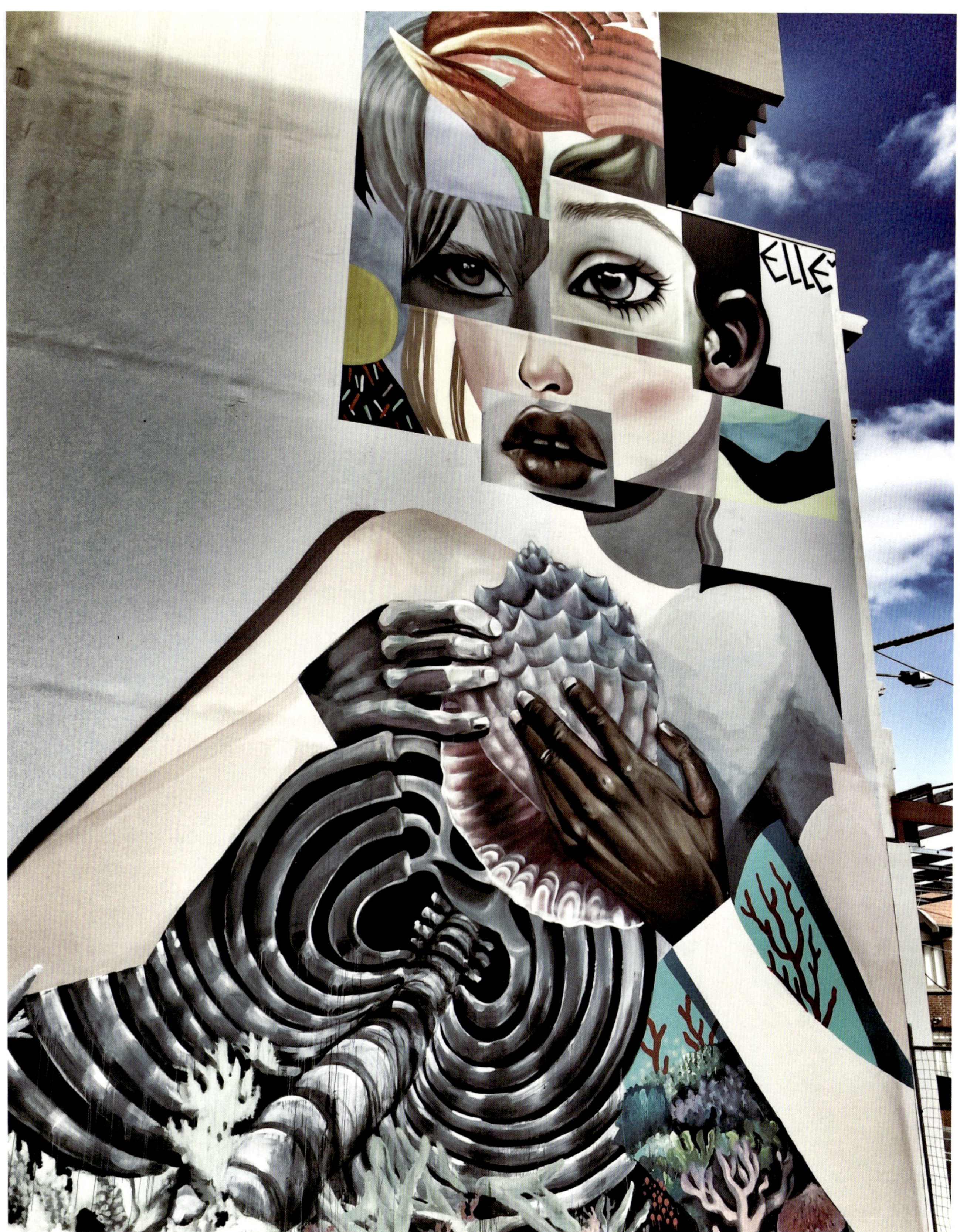

Lola
@Melbourne, Australia 2017

Magda Ćwik is a graphic designer first and foremost, but her passion to use other media has led her to engage in other disciplines, such as street arts. Her work is a blend of flowing abstract shapes and elements mixed with distinct bold colors that bring pieces to life and convey a calm, soft feel.

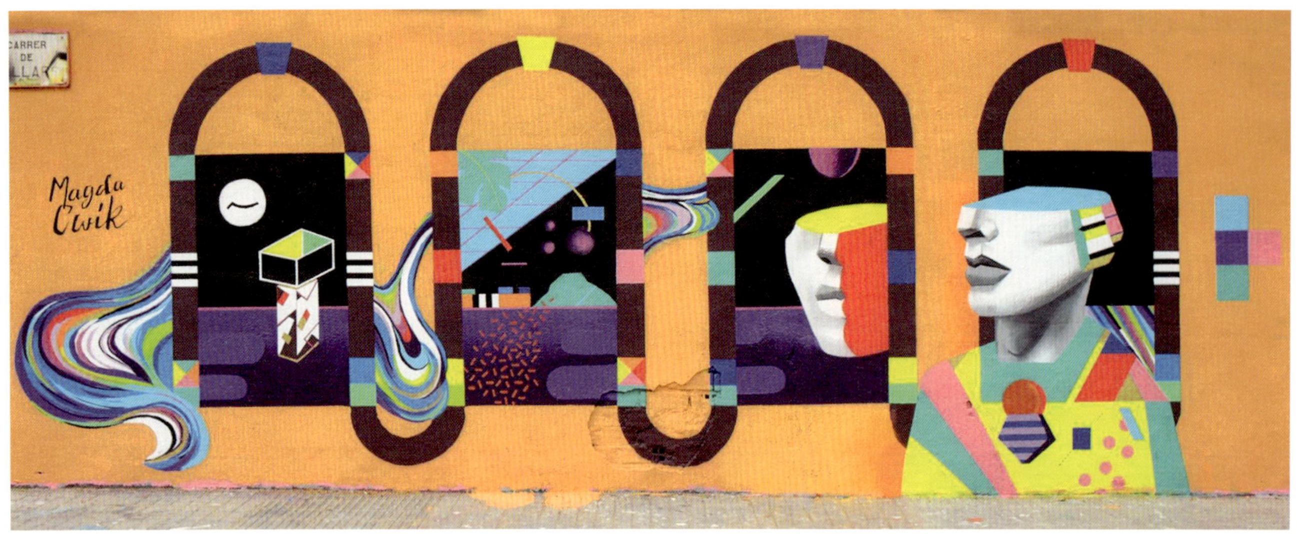

Parallel Minds
@Barcelona, Spain 2017

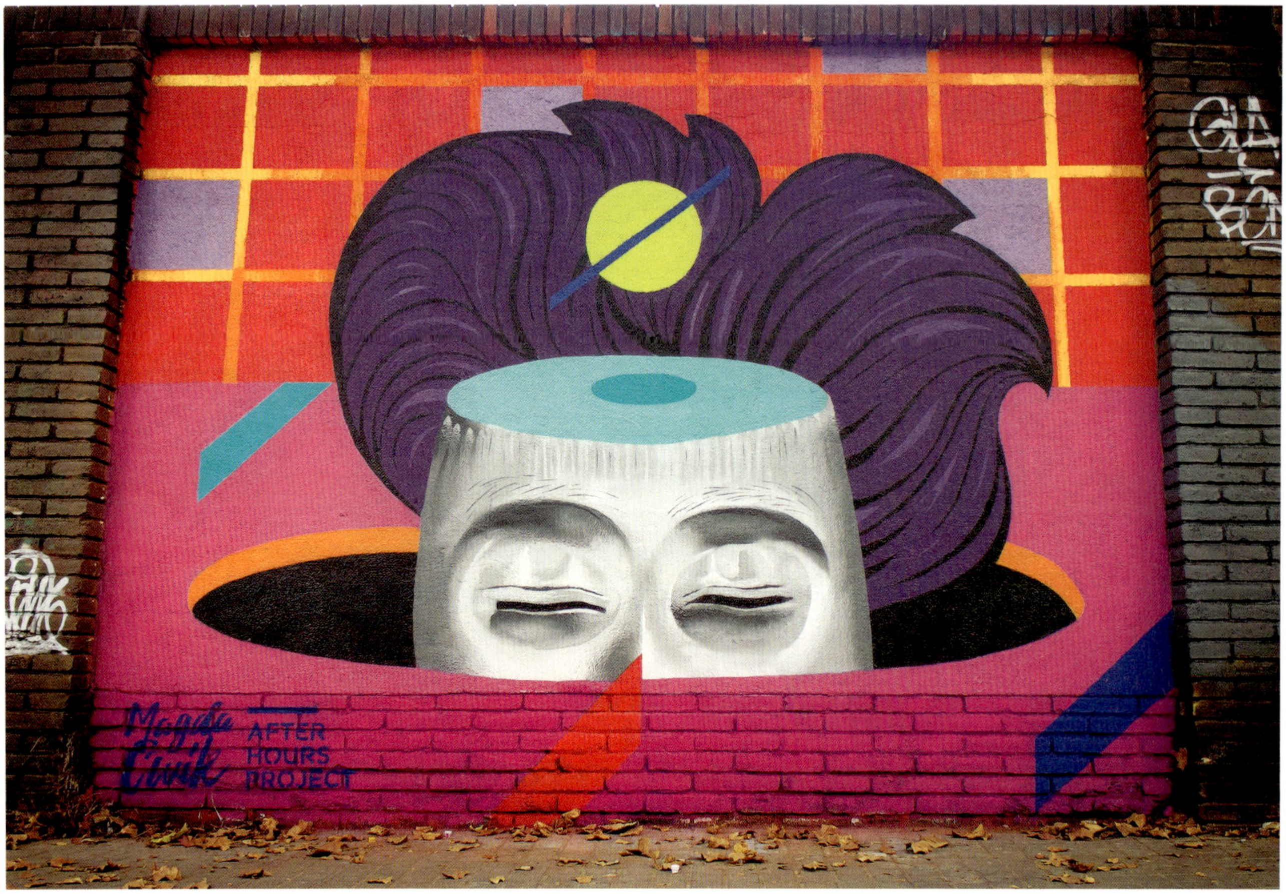

Psyched Up
@Barcelona, Spain 2017

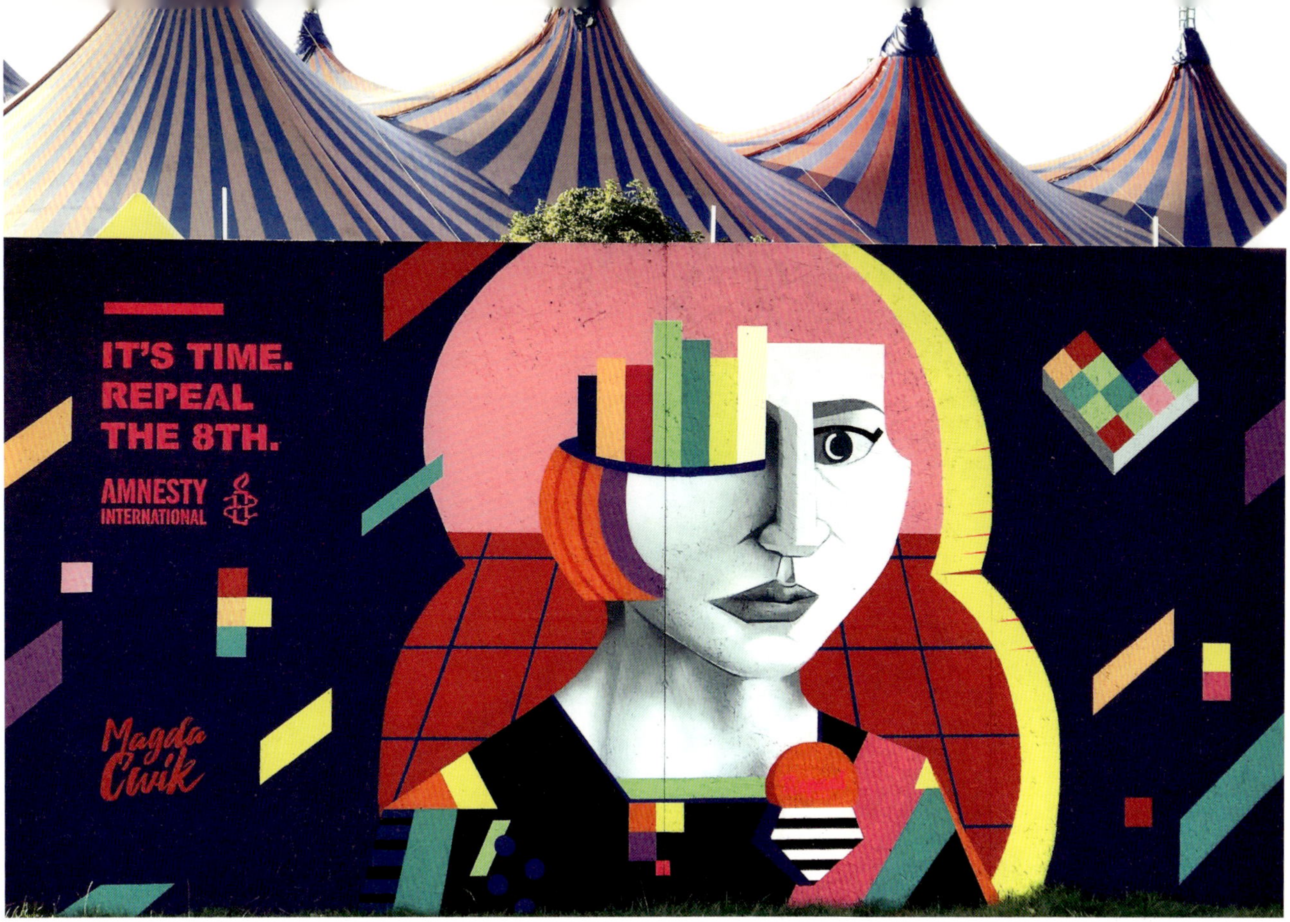

Repeal the 8th
Created for Amnesty International
@Stradbally, Ireland 2017

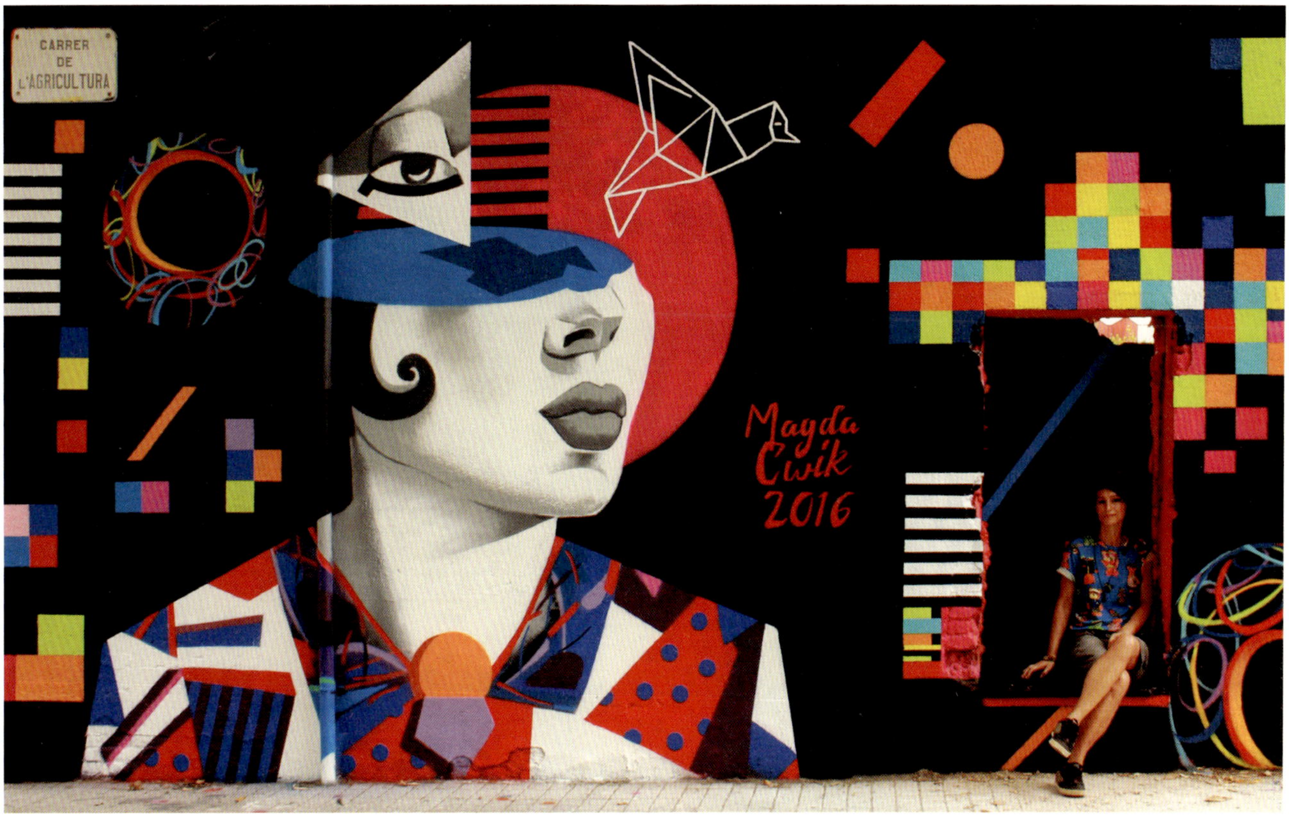

Free Your Mind
@Barcelona, Spain 2016

Sham Ptashenchuk is a Ukrainian artist and graphic designer. After graduating from South Ukrainian National Pedagogical University, he started to explore the possibilities of arts by trying street art of various styles. Accidentally spotting the painting supplies in the corner of a room one day, he improvised three masks with different looks on the wall. He believes that because a work of art is perceived subjectively, for every viewer, these symbolic masks will generate personal metaphors which are to be contemplated, but not to be interpreted. And thus, image of faces will subconsciously encourage people to contact and dialogue.

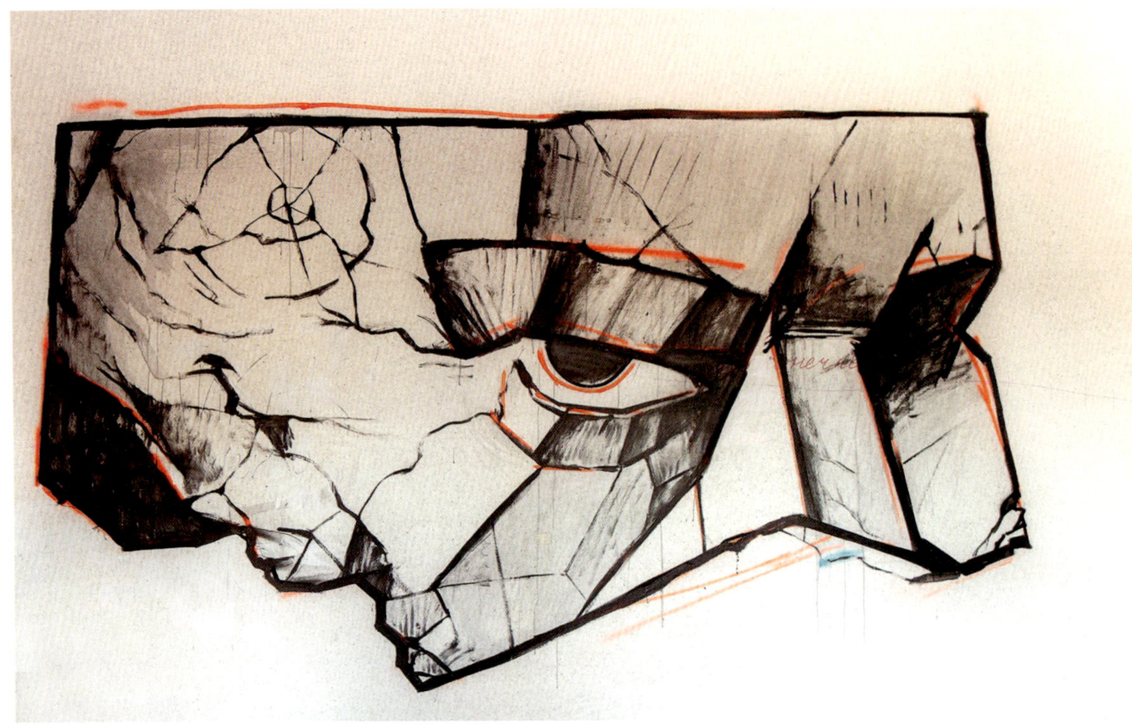

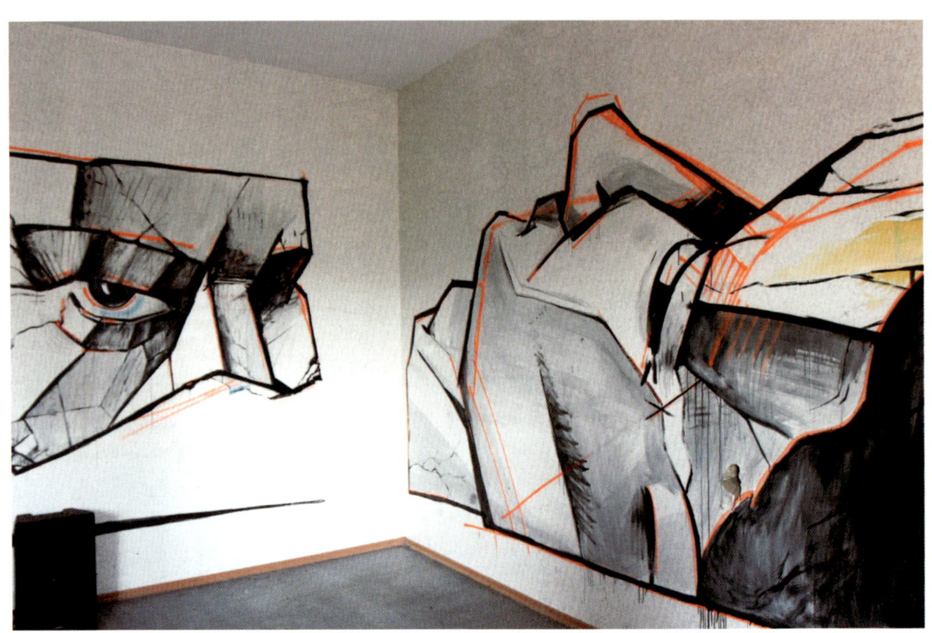

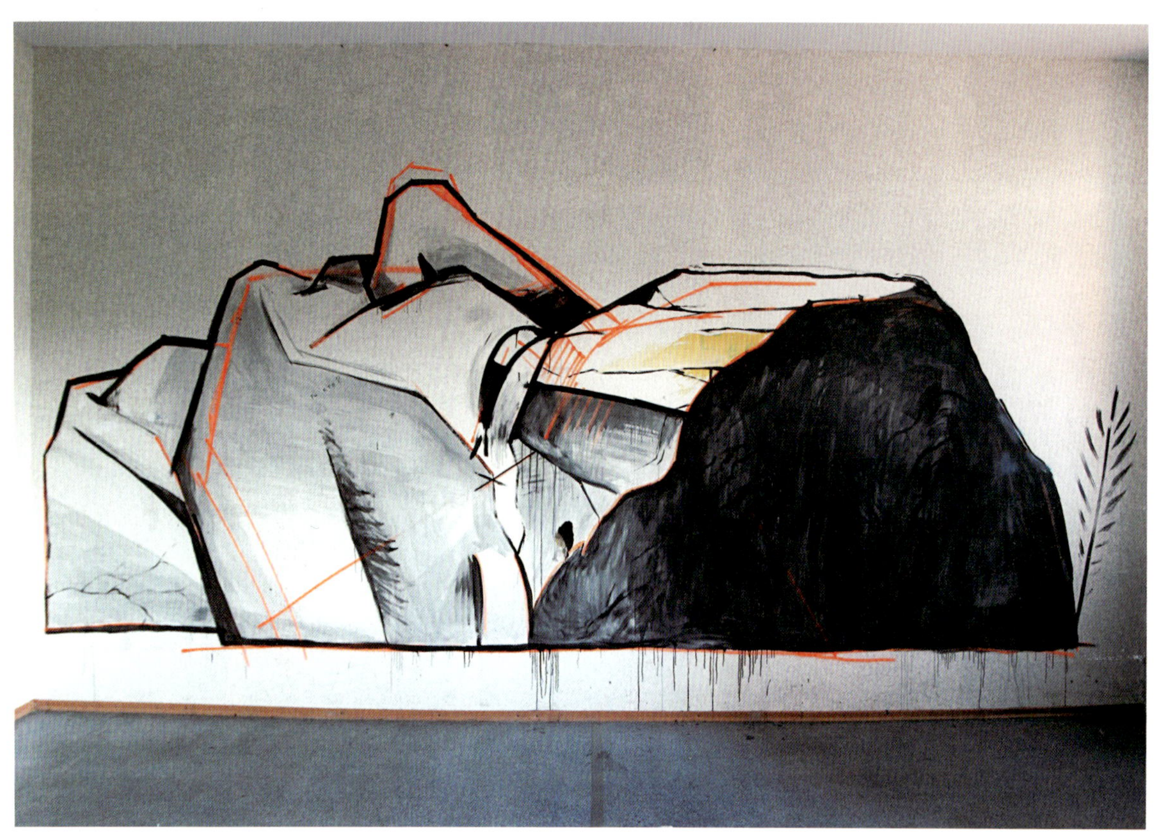

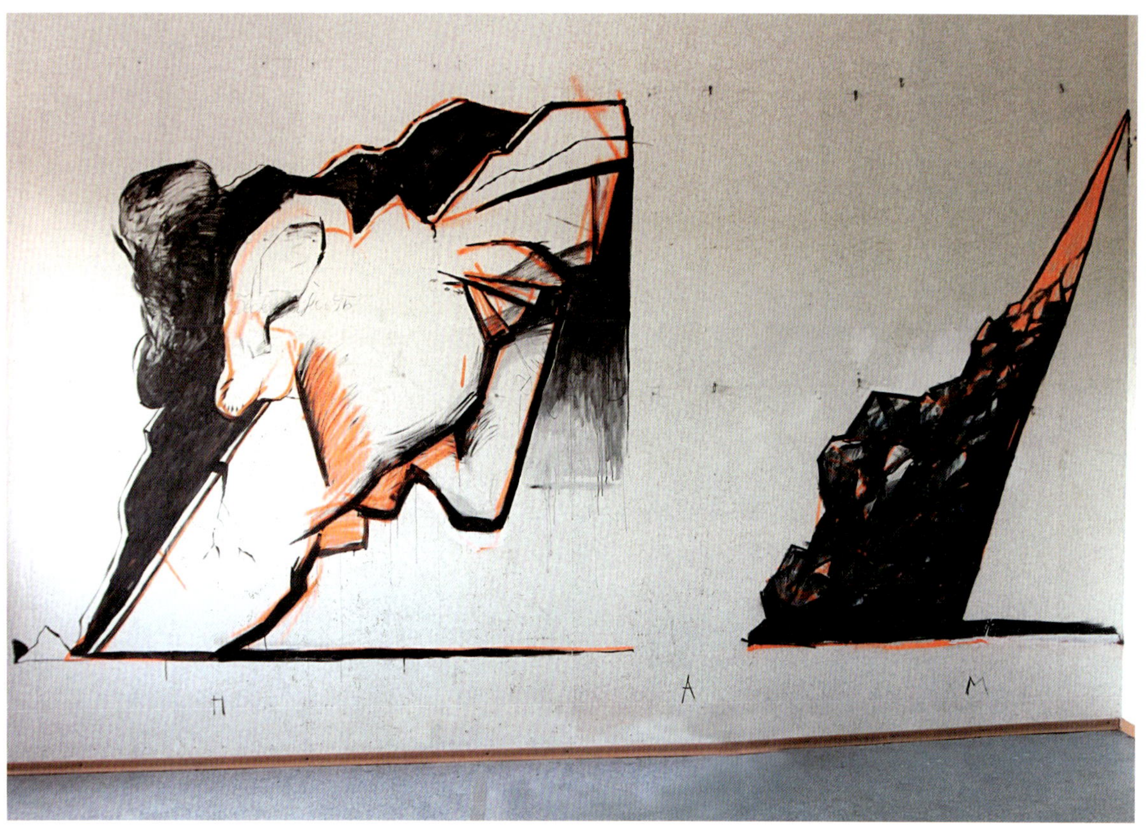

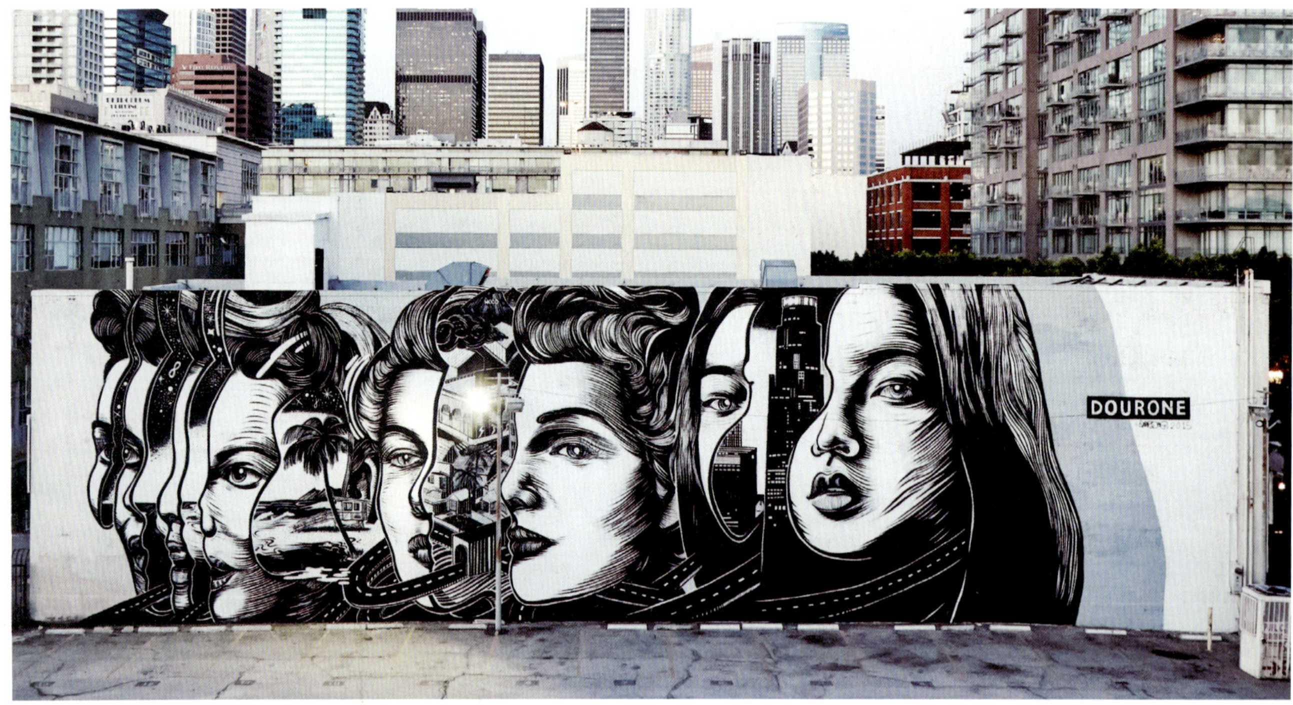

Los Angeles
@Los Angeles, USA 2015

Dourone is a philanthropic craftsman, an eclectic artist. The curves that Dourone draws and paints communicate a sense of depth. His dominant theme is elegant, feminine faces that are blended into a dreamlike setting, sometimes clear and celestial, sometimes dark and cosmic, where symbols of positivism (+), infinity (∞) and philanthropy float.

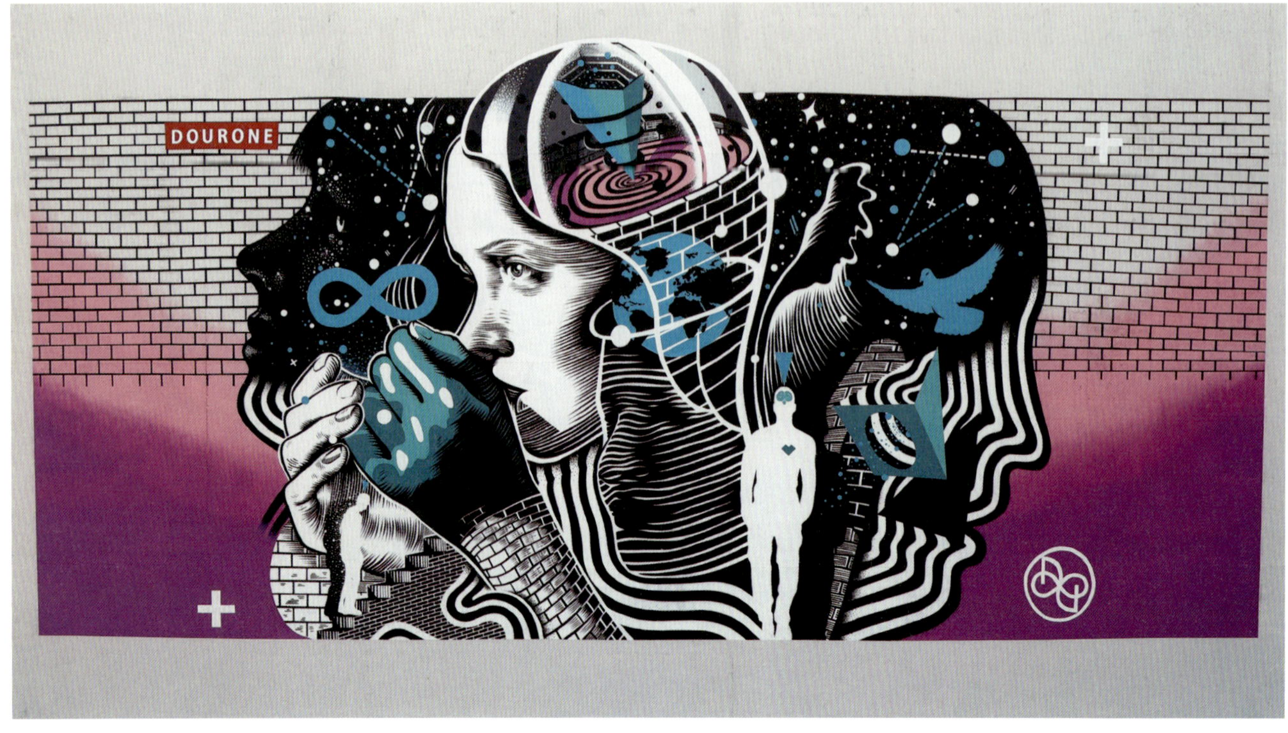

Infinita Paz Mundial
@Louvain-la-neuve, Belgium 2015

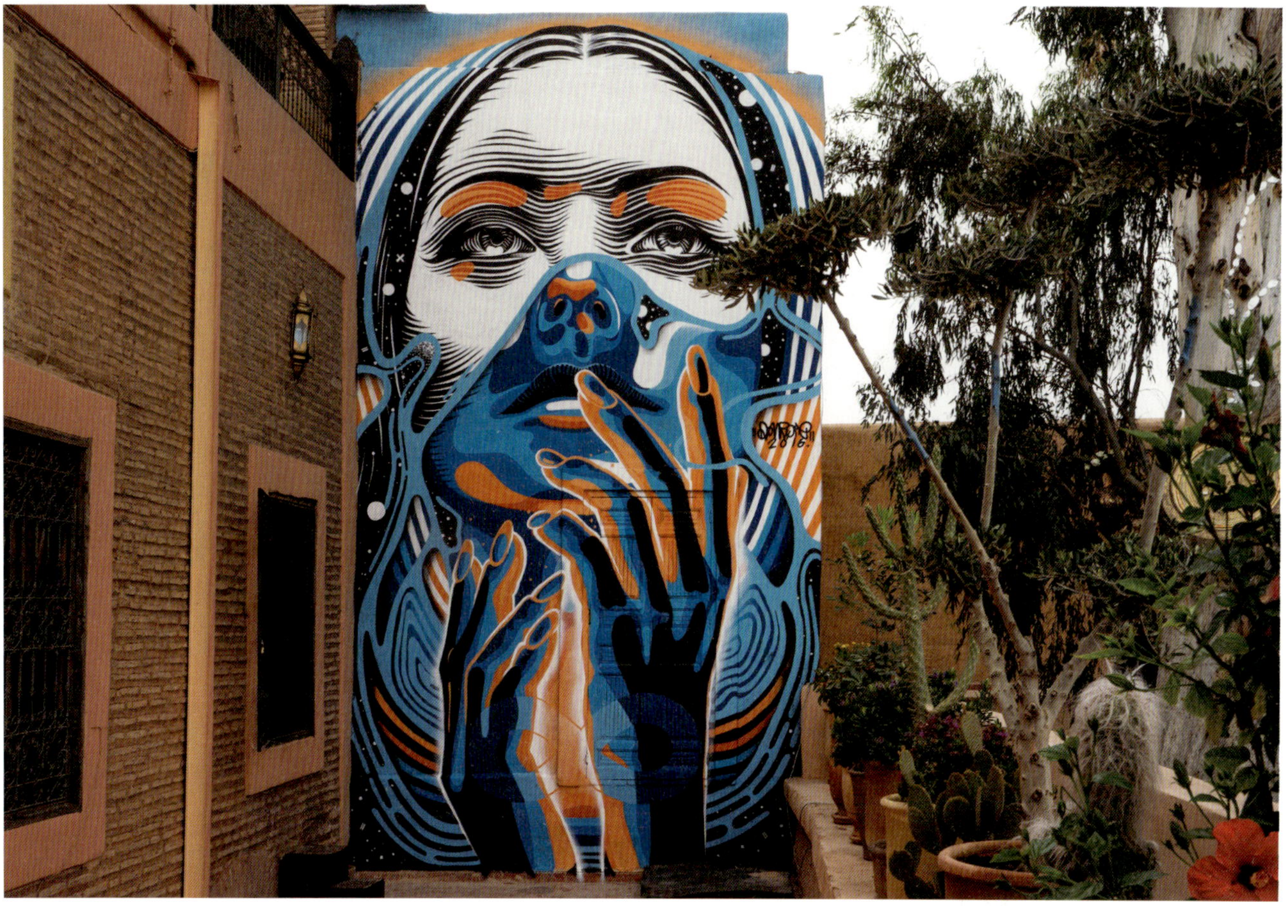

Inside Out
@Marrakesh, Morocco 2016

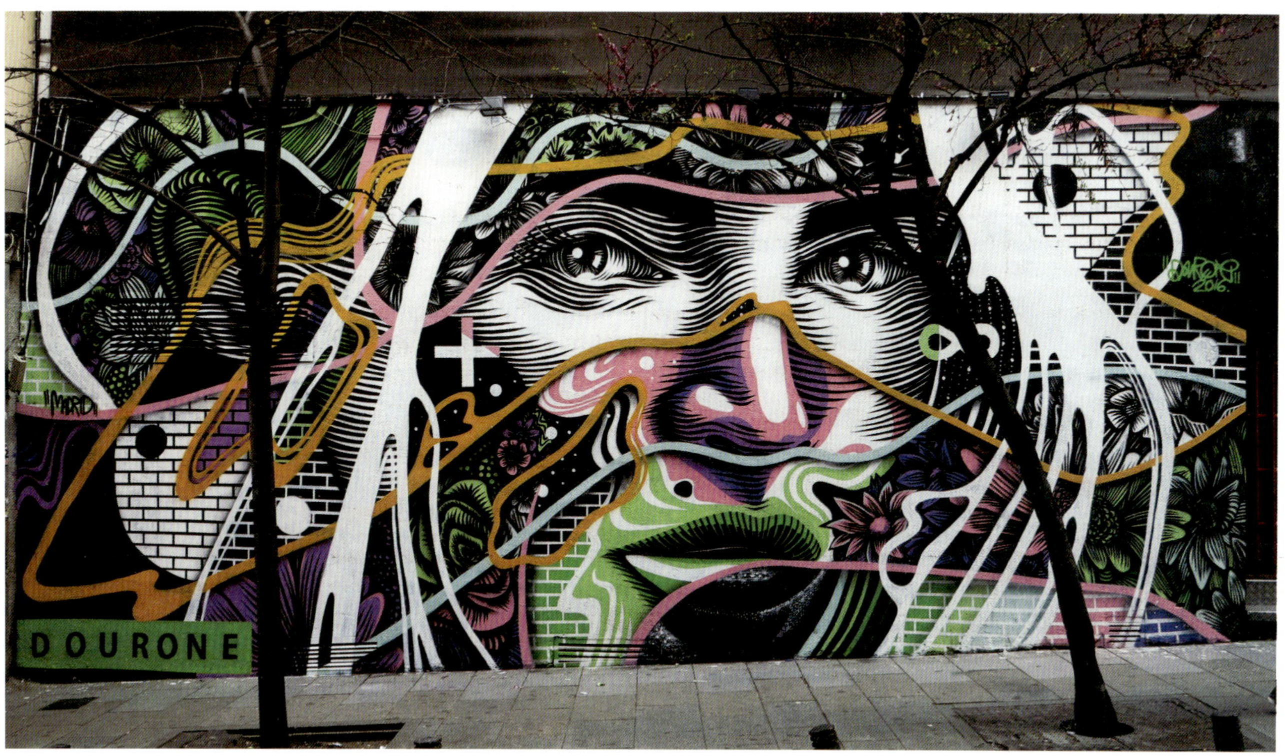

Border Line
@Madrid, Spain 2016

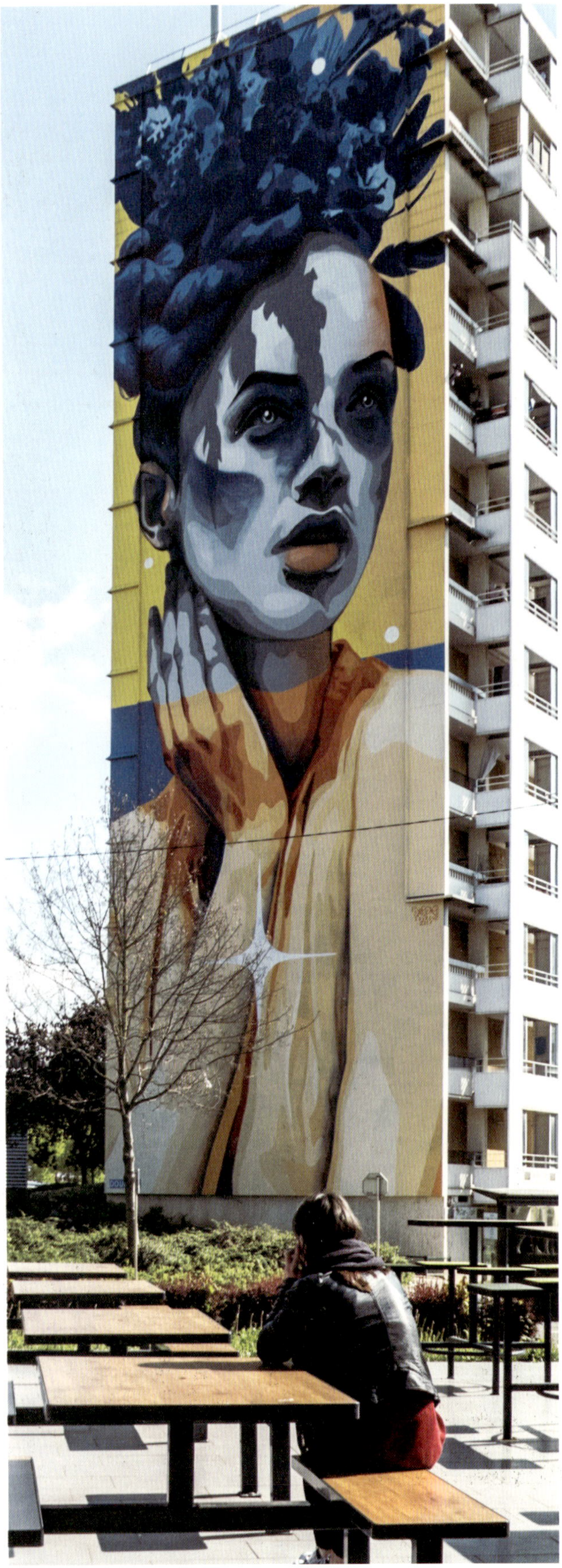

Même Composition Même Beauté
@Mulhouse, France 2017

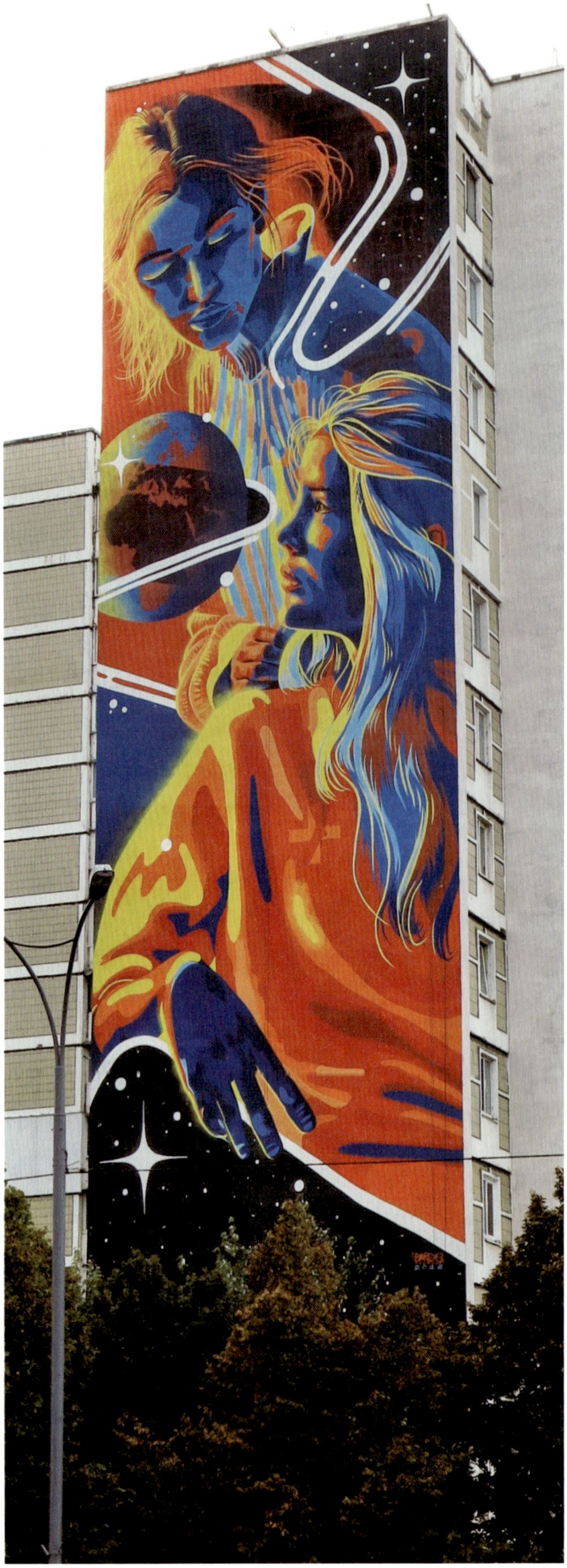

Fraternity
@Kiev, Ukraine 2016

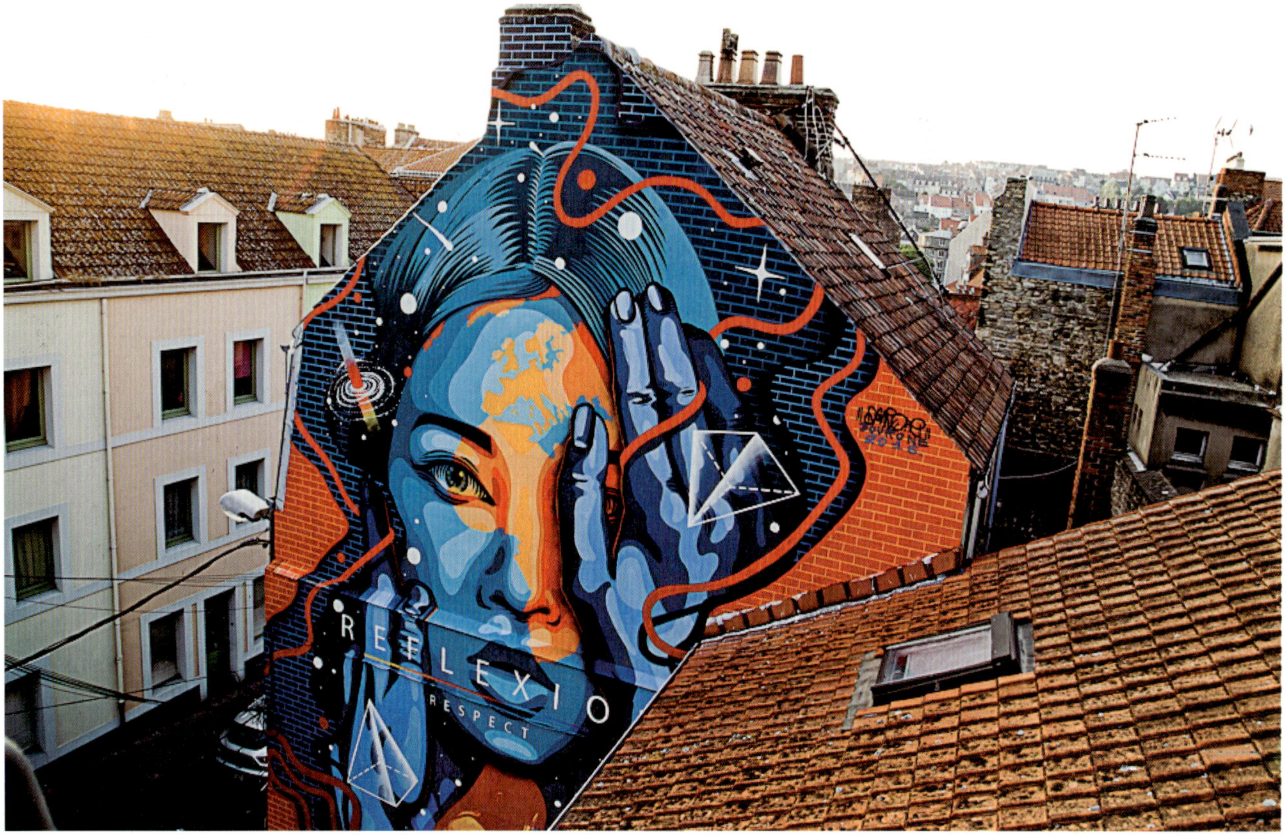

Reflexion
@Boulogne-sur-Mer, France 2016

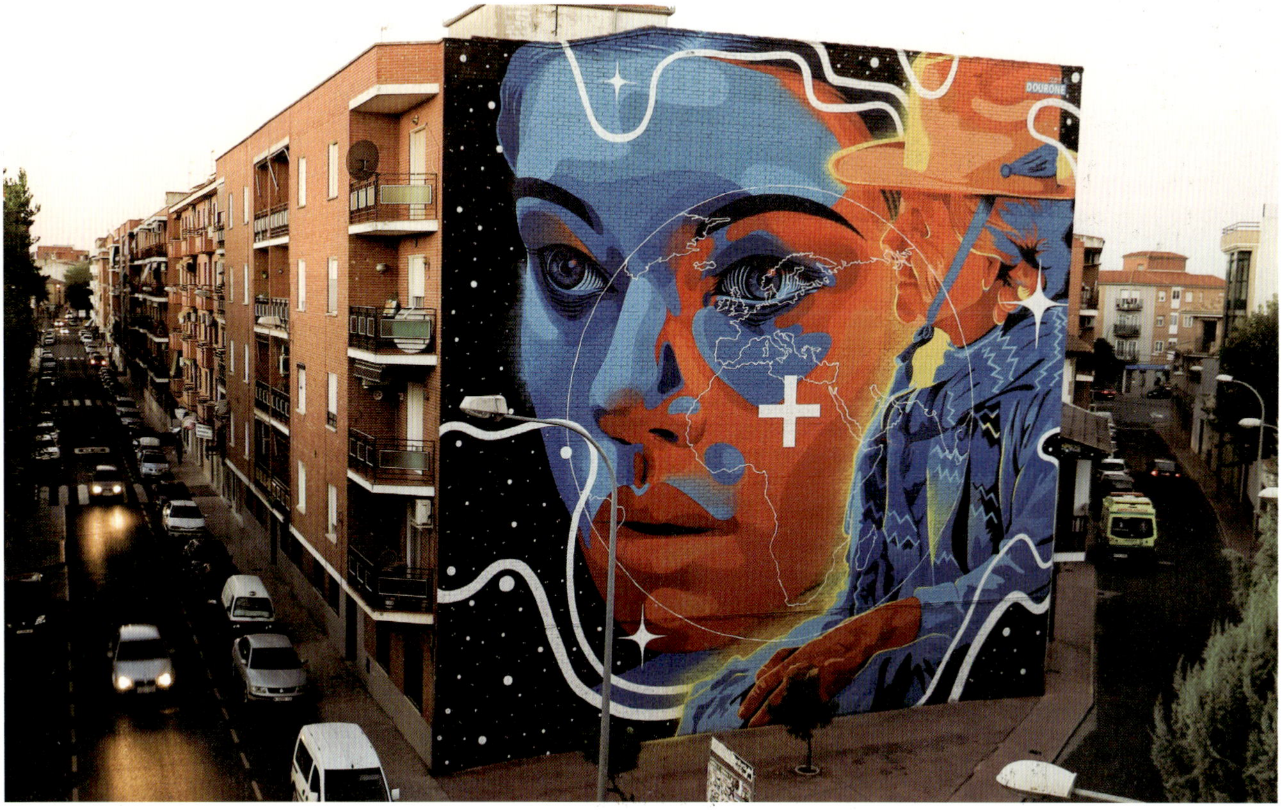

Un Mundo Posible
@Torrijos, Spain 2016

Growing up in Minsk, Key Detail has been active on the street art scene since 2000s, working consistently towards developing his unique style and his skills of street arts. Today, Key Detail is one of the best Belarusian street artists and masterly combines the fluidity of colors with the wild nature of street arts.

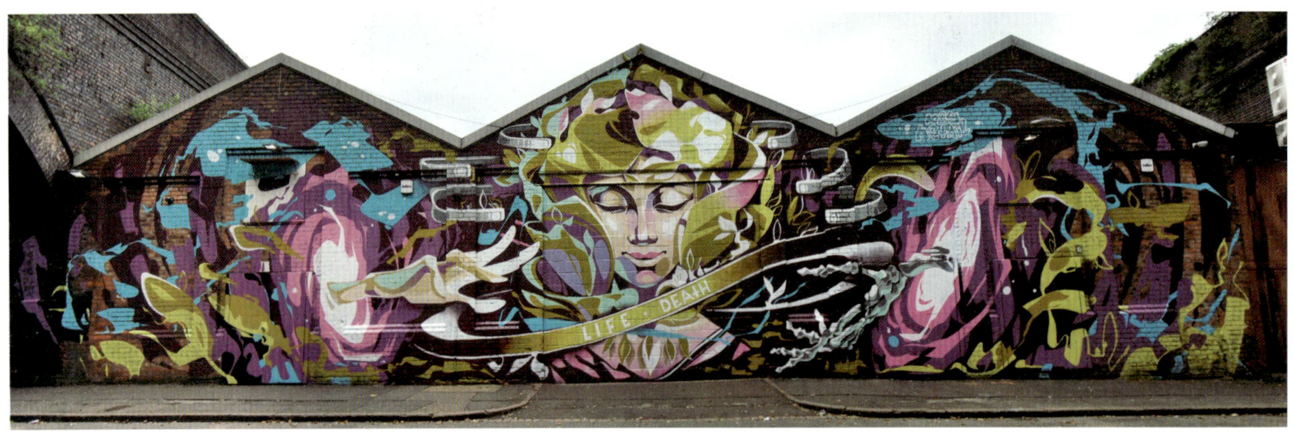

Life & Death
@Birmingham, UK 2016

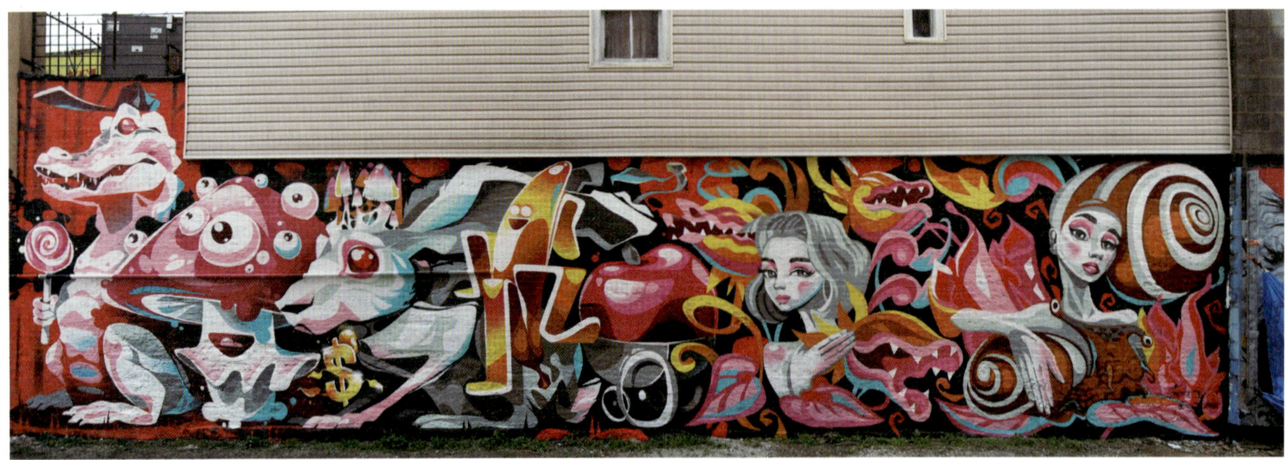

Otherwordly
Collaboration with Yu-baba
@Chicago, USA 2017

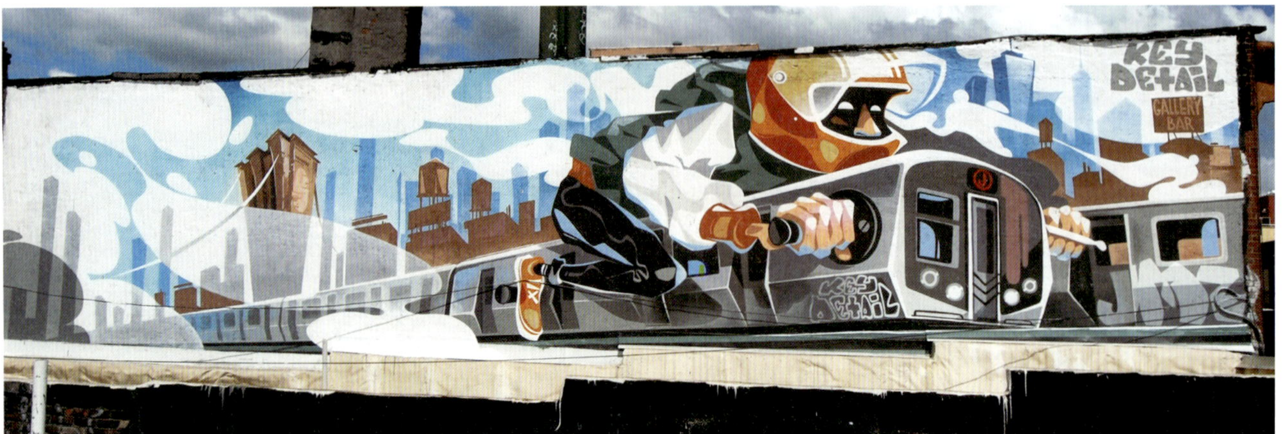

Daily Ride
@New York, USA 2016

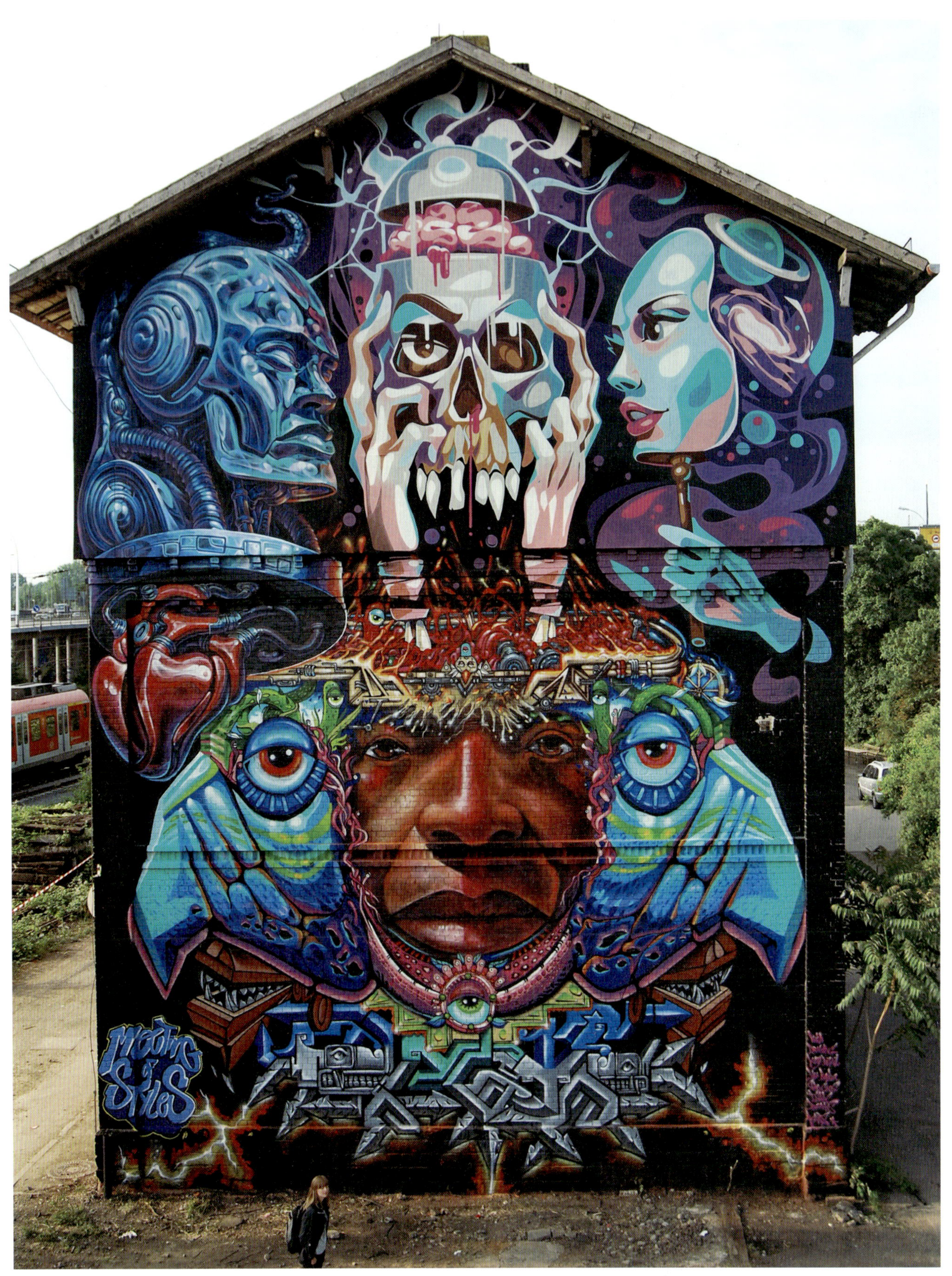

Mind Above the Matter
Collaboration with Yu-baba, WD Street Art, and DMJC Crew
@Wiesbaden, Germany 2015

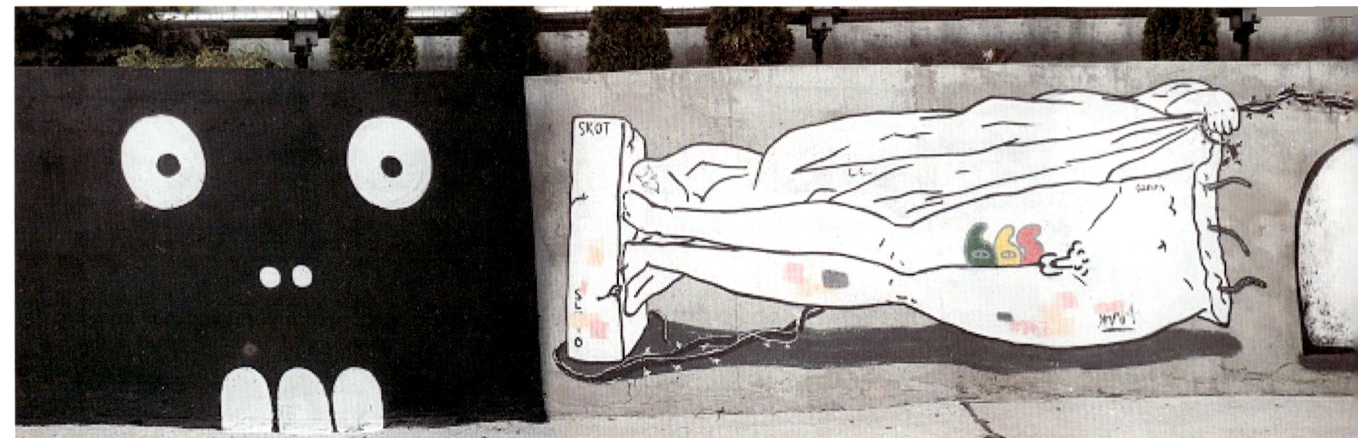

Sham·665·Canny
@Kiev, Ukraine 2016

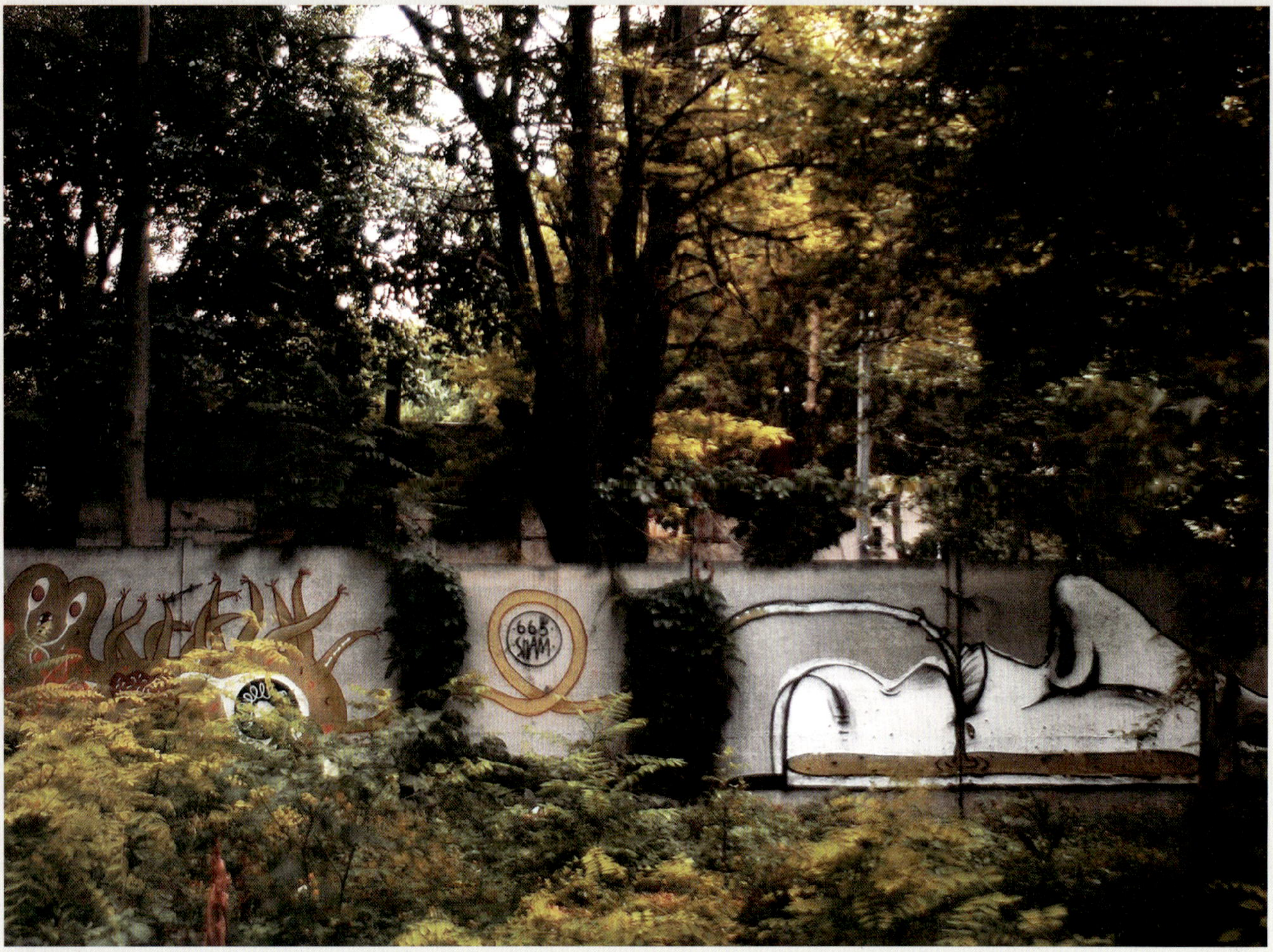

Mysterious Forest
@Odessa, Ukraine 2016

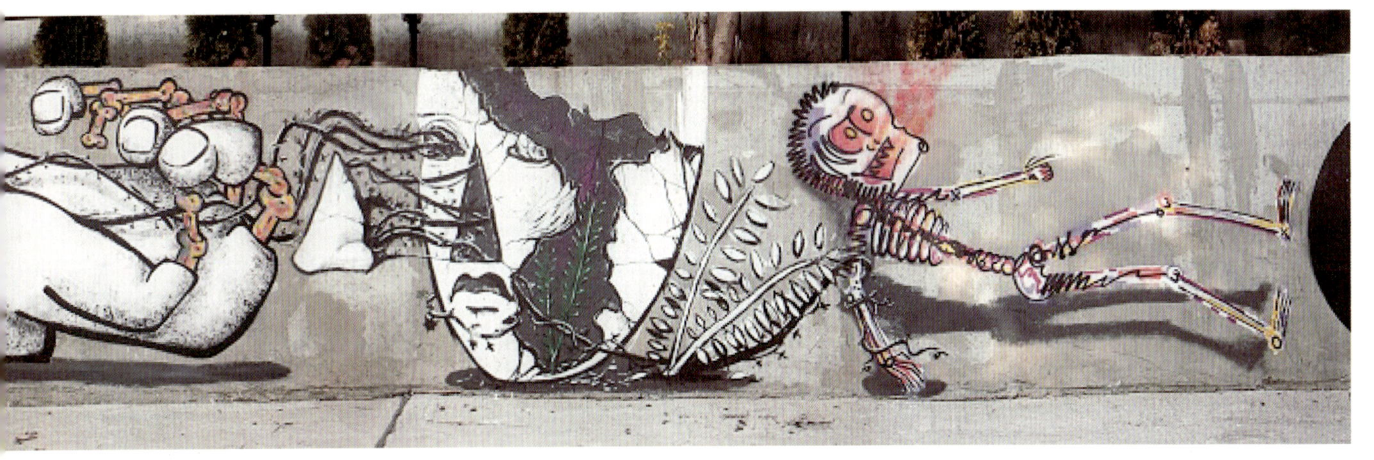

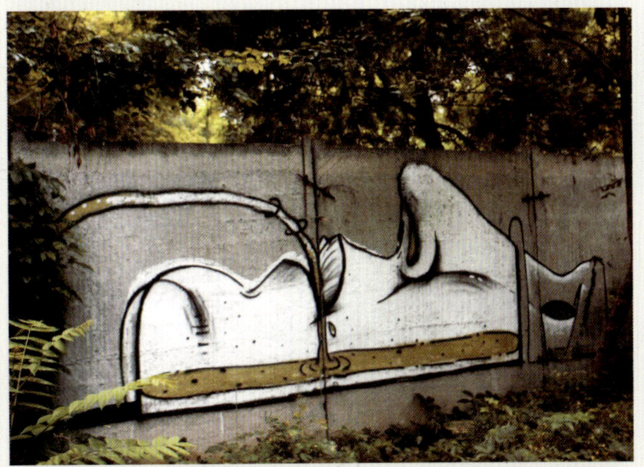

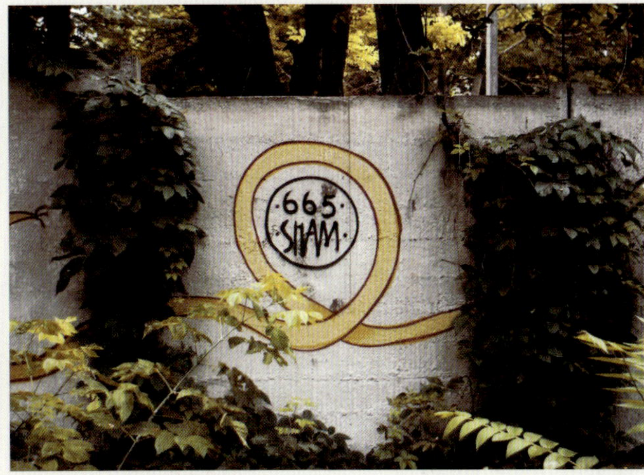

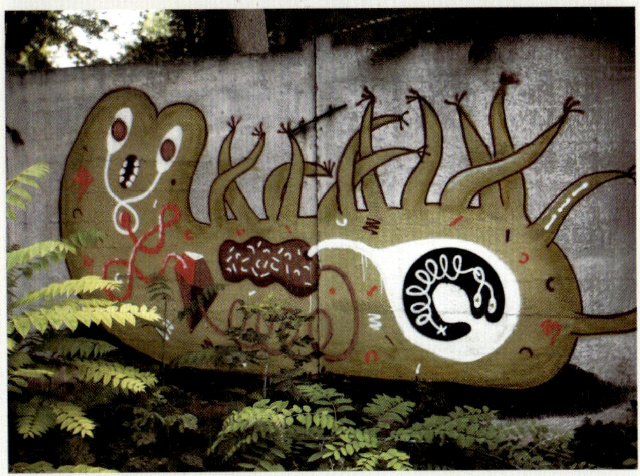

Abstract works are always confusing because the messages they send out are ambiguous. The works of Sham Ptashenchuk are the confusing type. A small fern extends its roots across a mask that is falling apart, a hand with bones exposed, and a half-cut statue, while another few roots seem to take nutrients from a skeleton. Is that a metaphor? No idea. Different from realistic works that send out clear messages by meticulous depiction, abstract works are the imaginations from our subconscious, which may mean something, or may not.

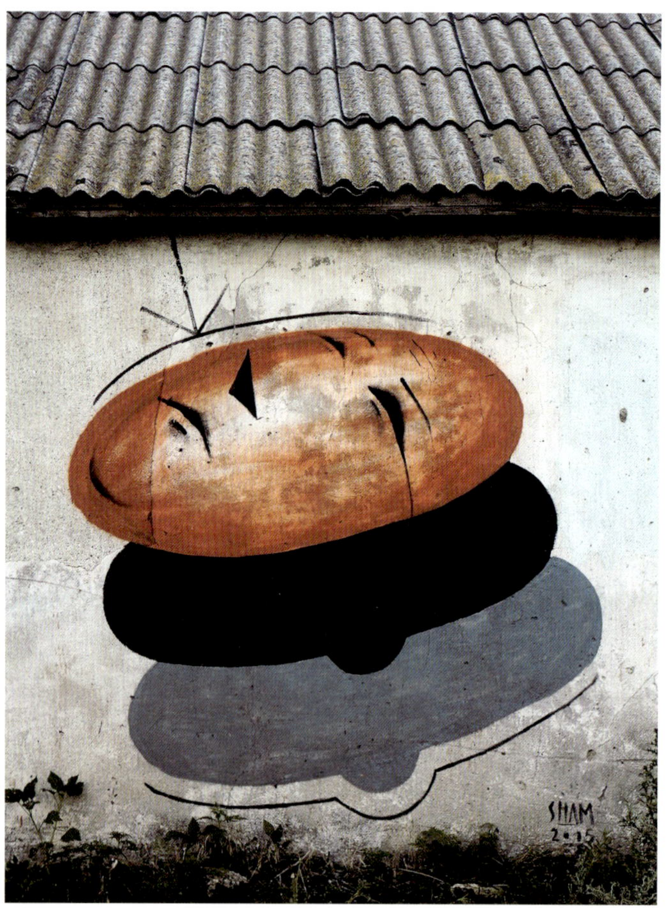

Face
@Kiev, Ukraine 2015

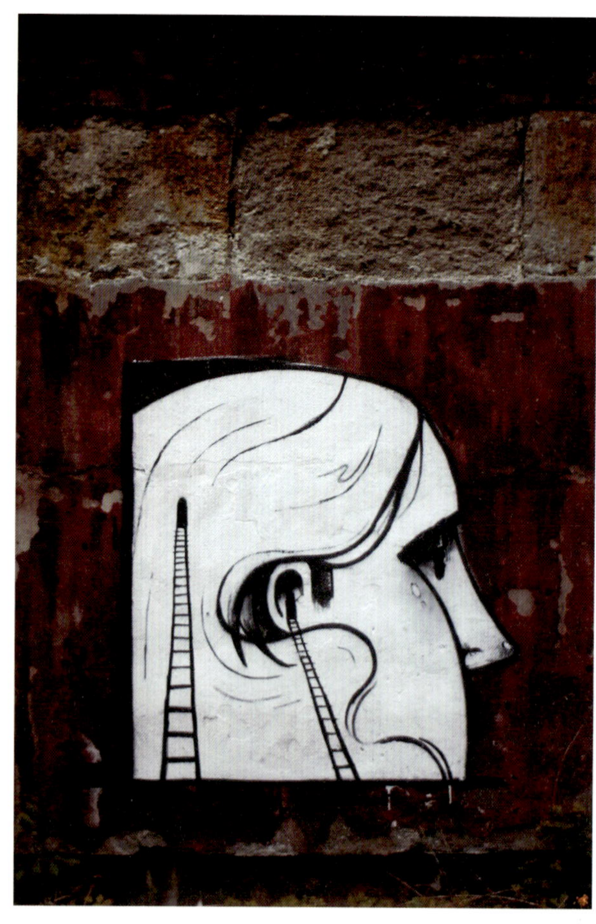

Untitled
@Odessa, Ukraine 2017

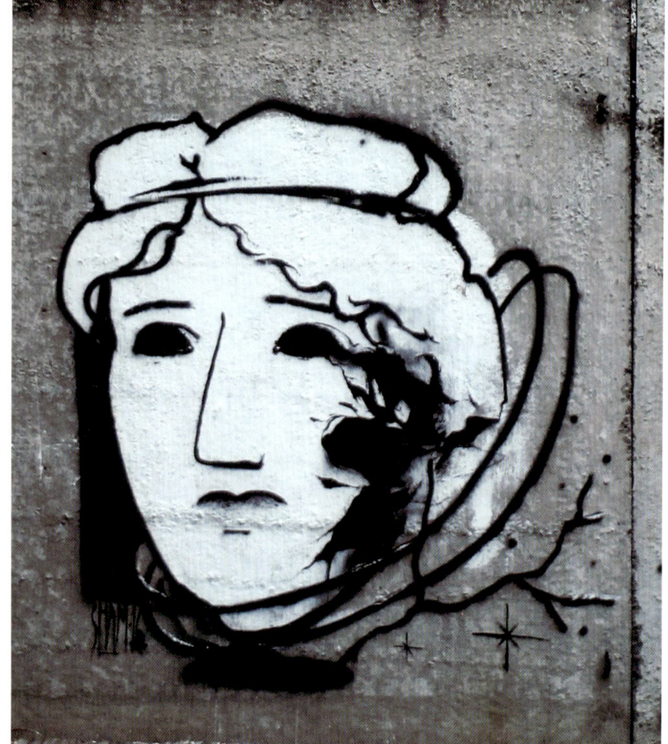

Untitled
@Odessa, Ukraine 2016

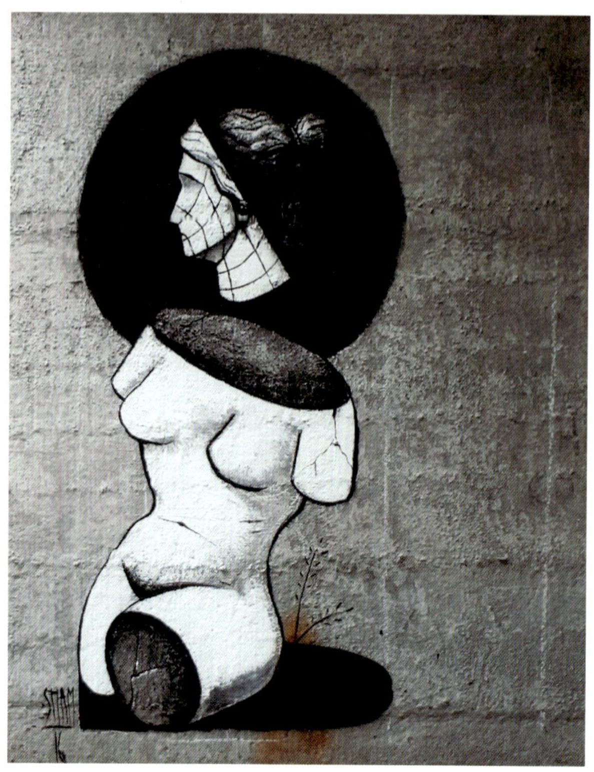

Sculpt
@Odessa, Ukraine 2016

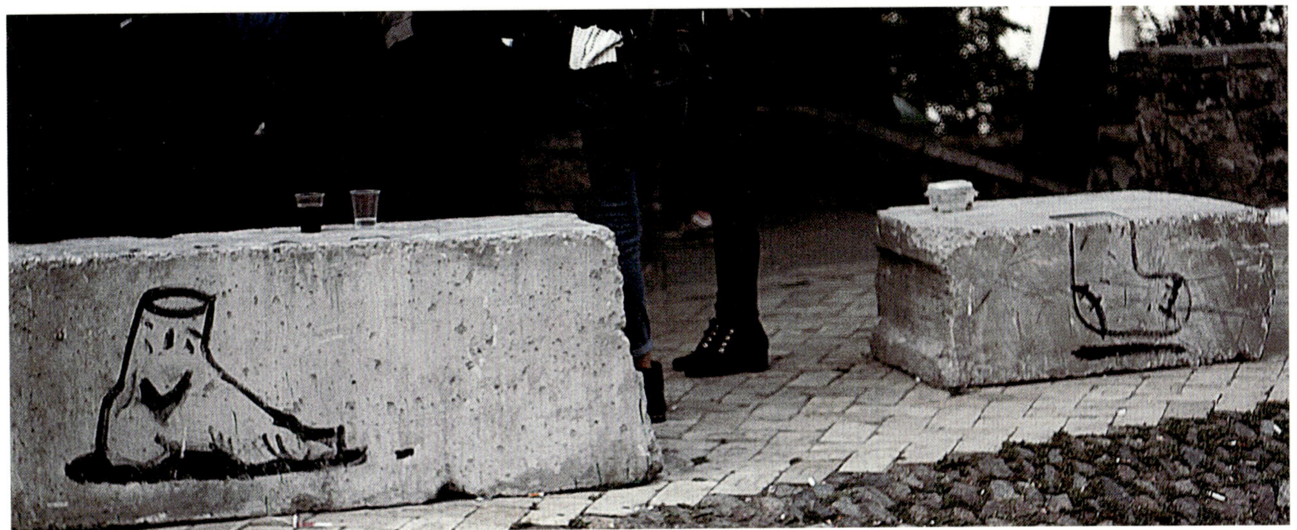

Home Coziness
@Kiev, Ukraine 2015

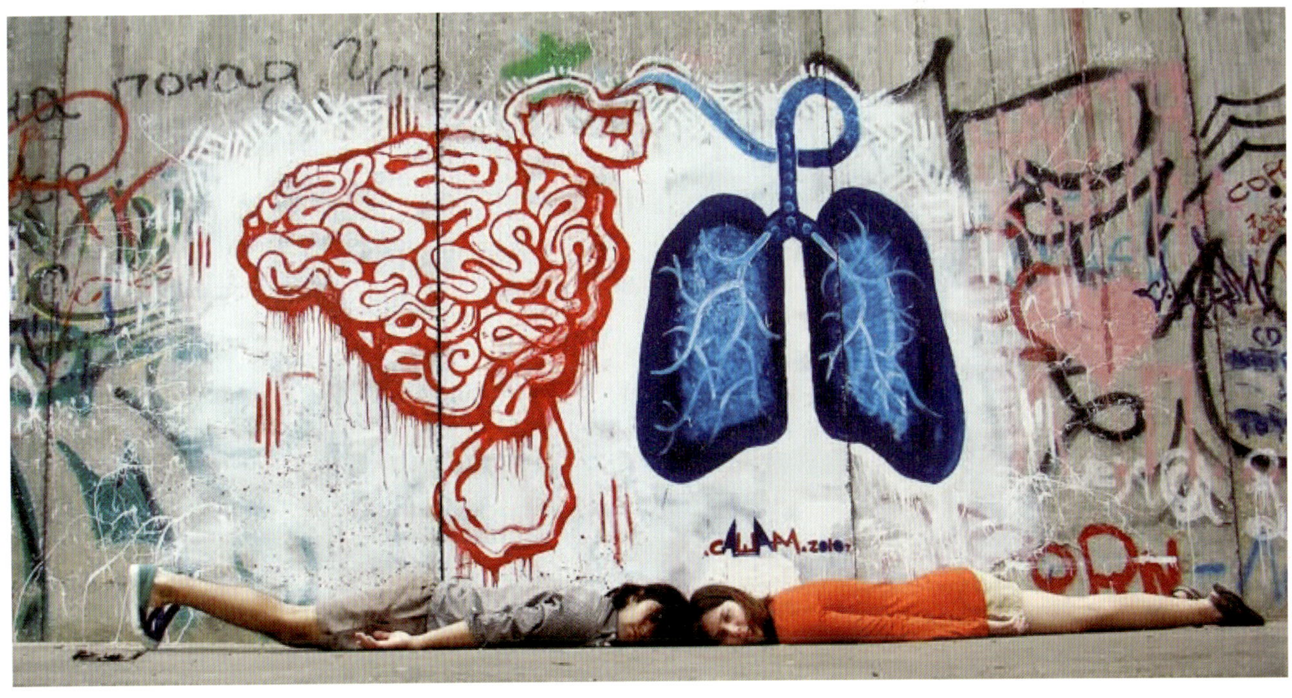

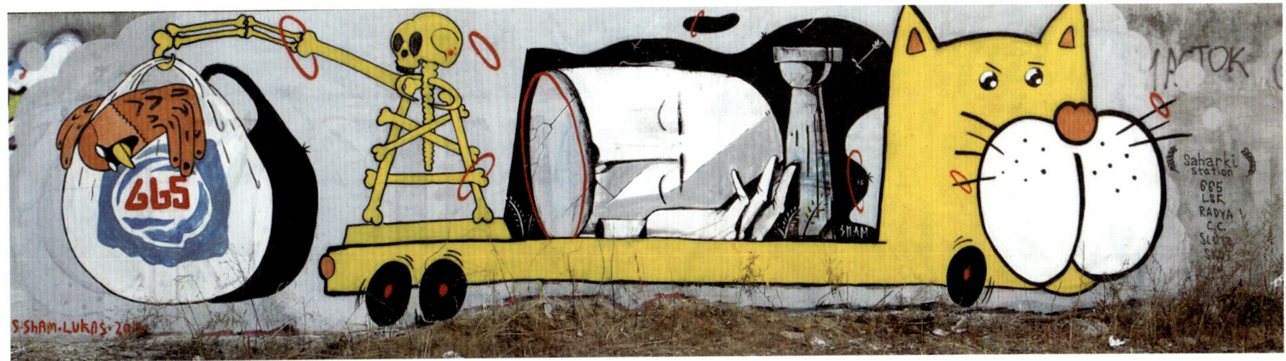

Untitled
@Kiev, Ukraine 2015

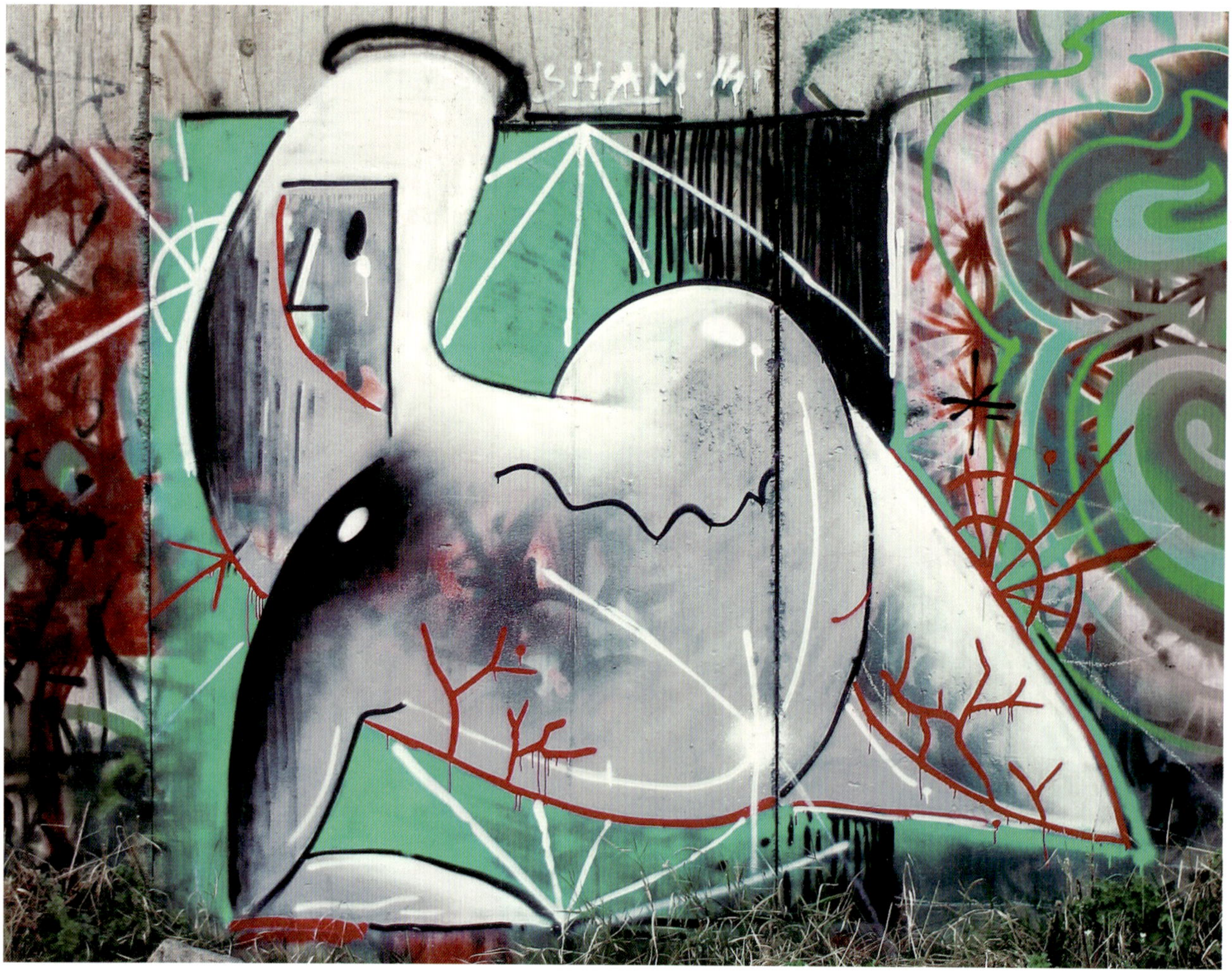

FEM.UGL
@Kiev, Ukraine 2014

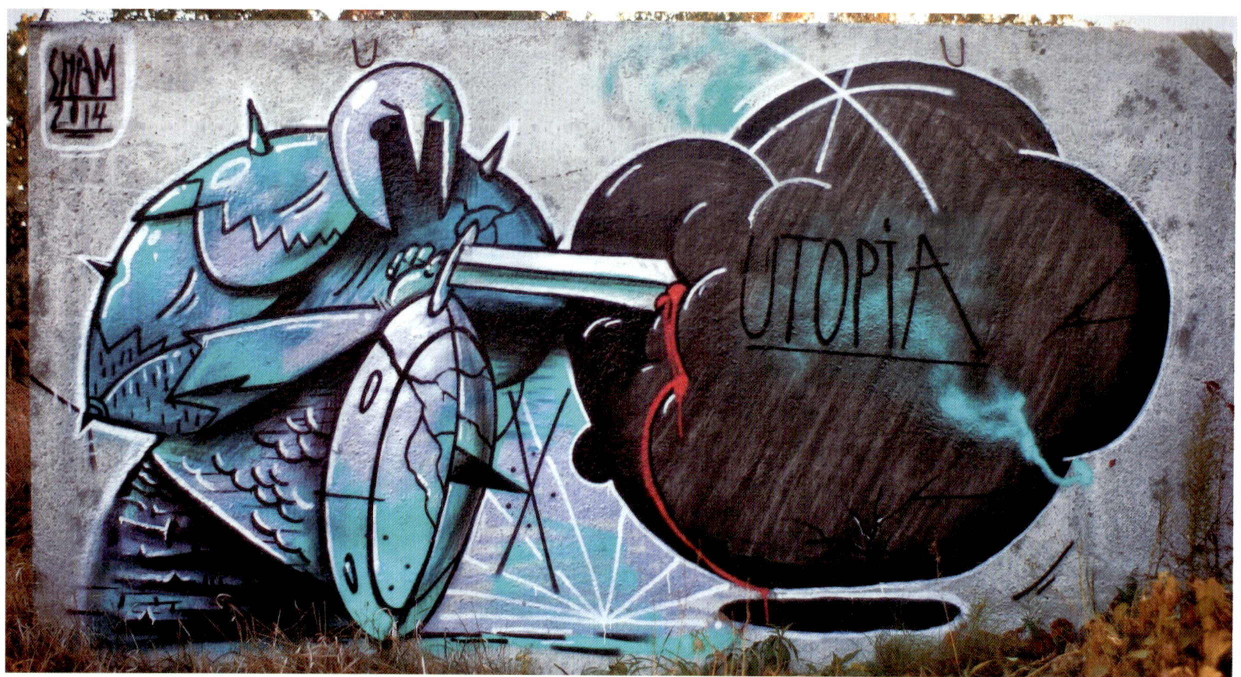

Utopia
@Kiev, Ukraine 2014

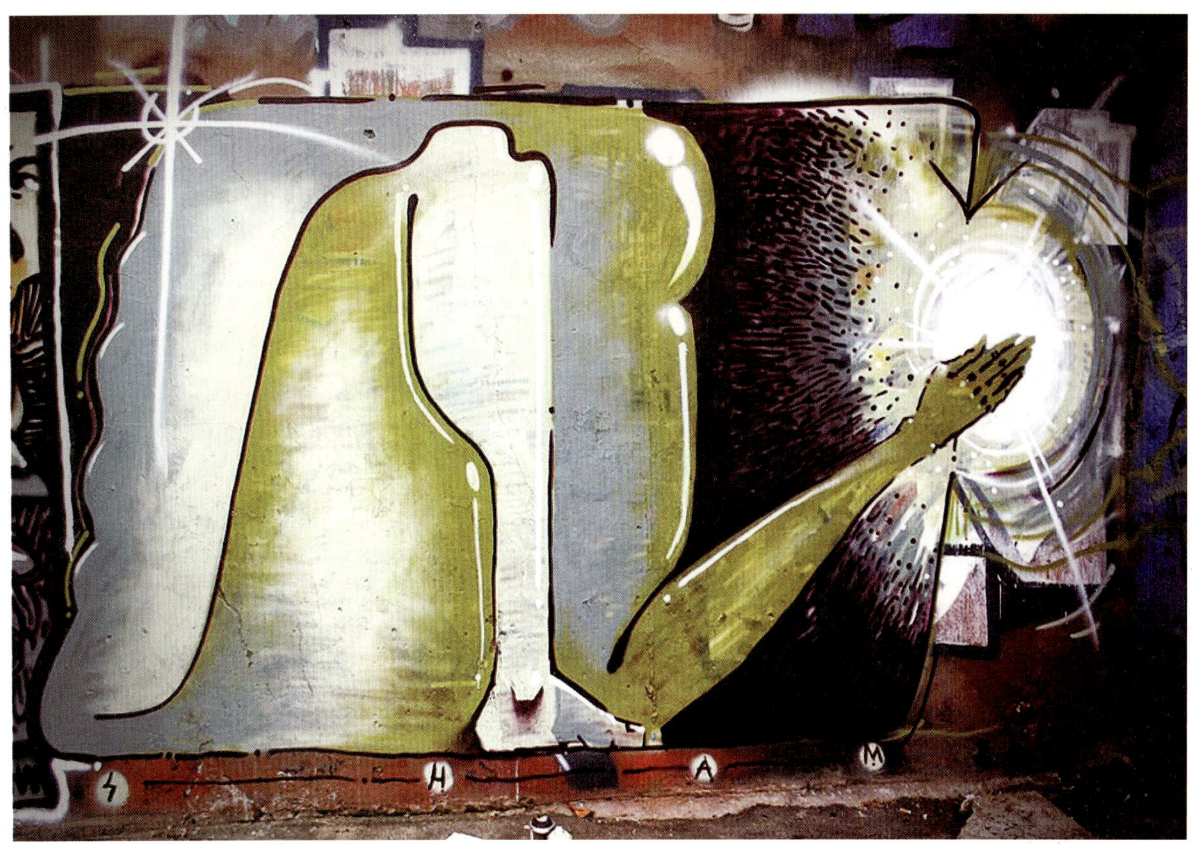

Light
@Odessa, Ukraine 2012

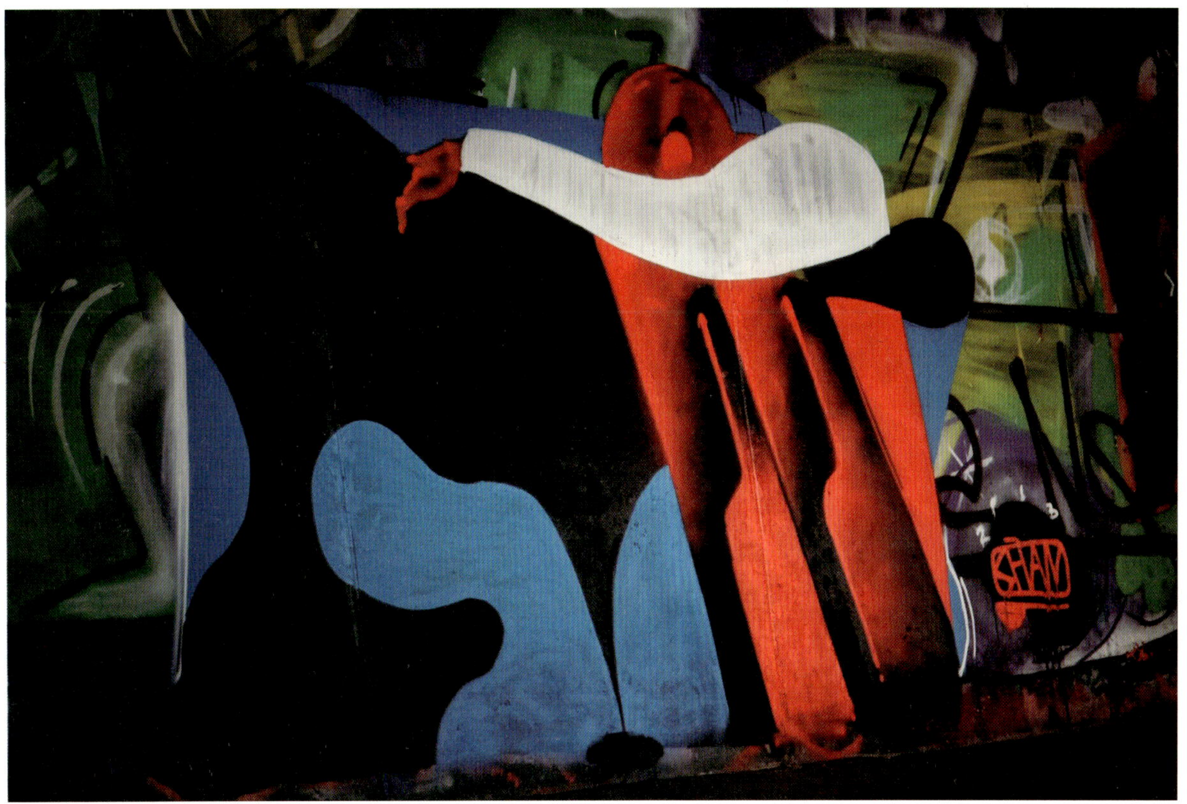

Untitled
@Kiev, Ukraine 2013

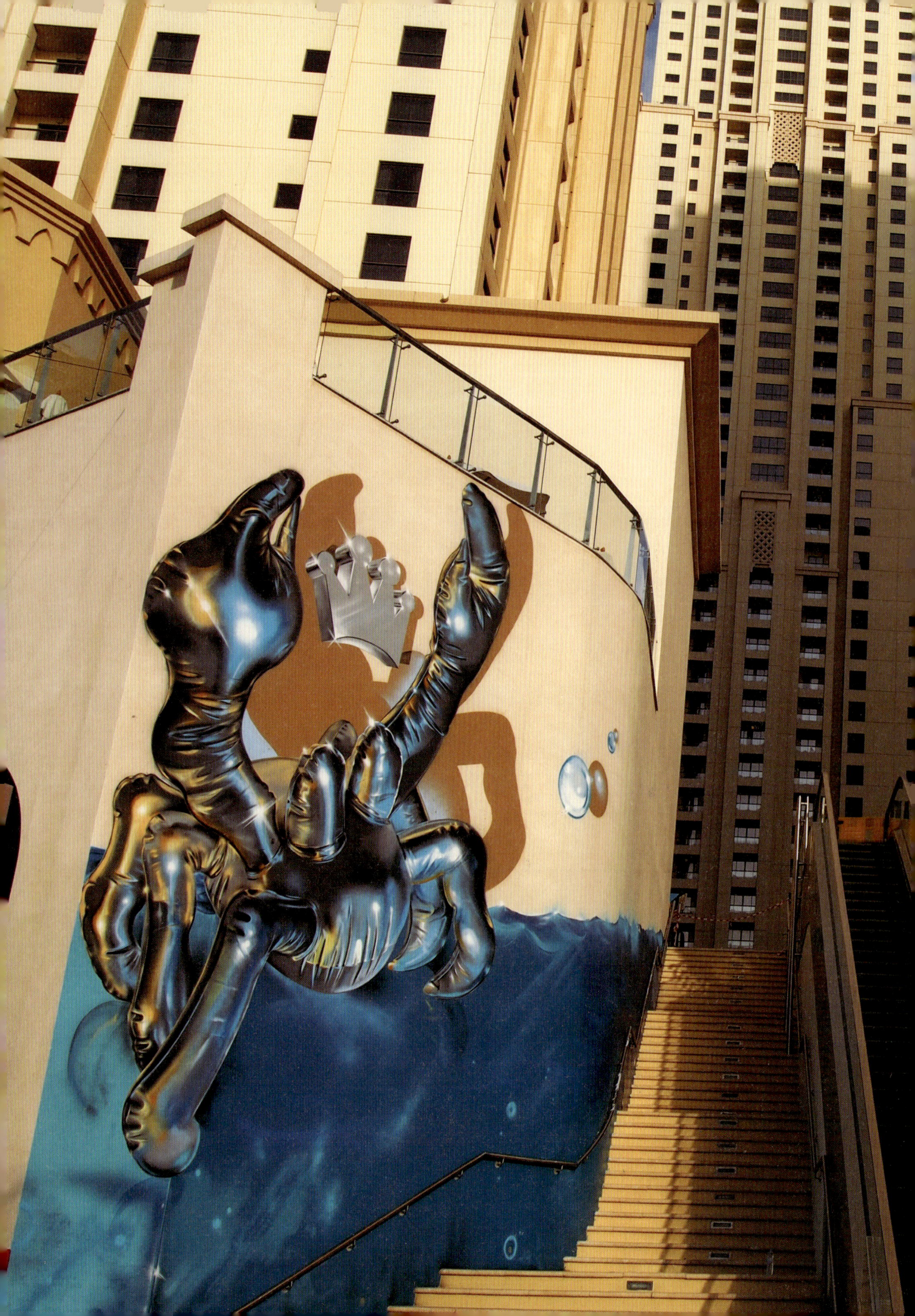

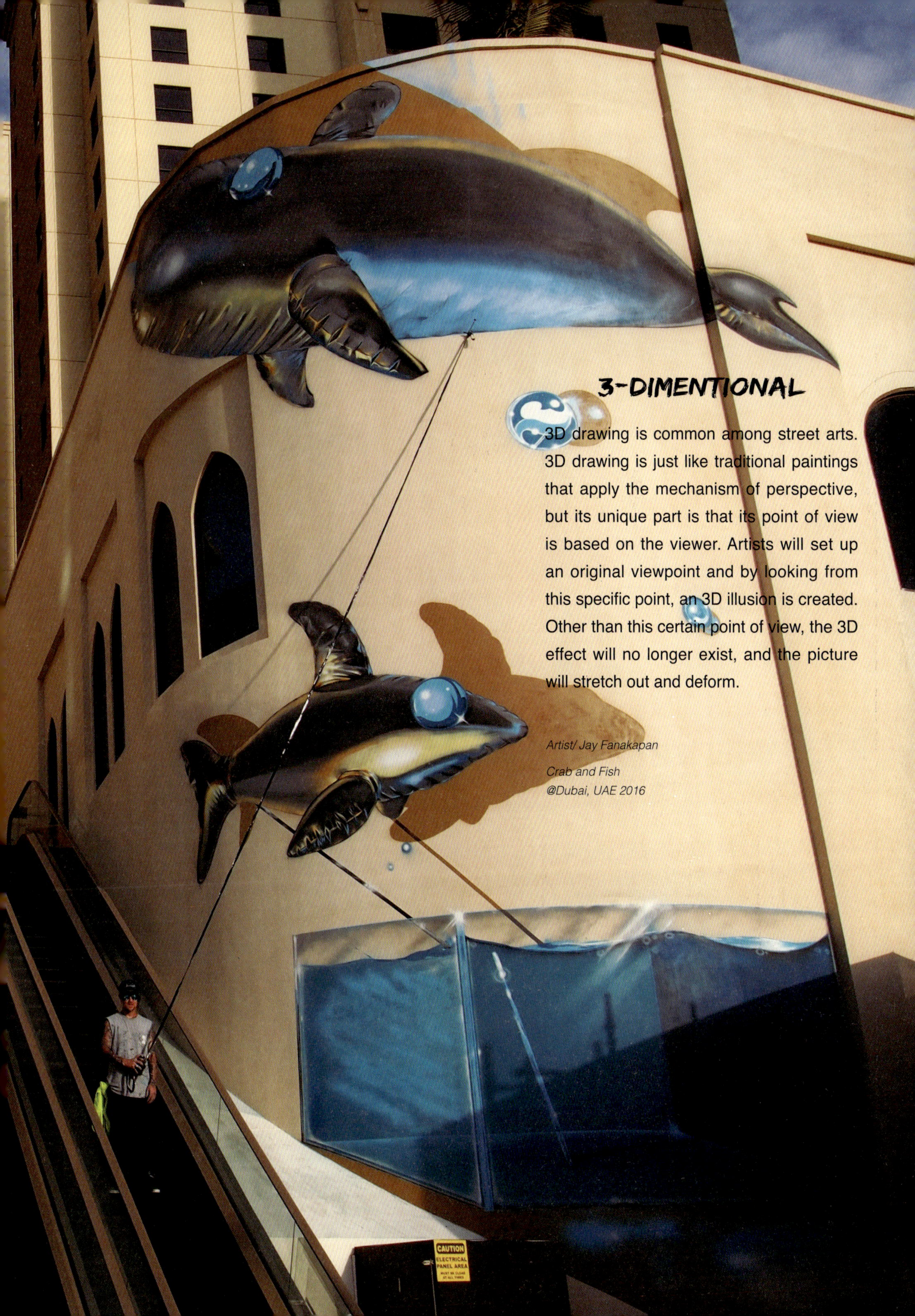

3-DIMENTIONAL

3D drawing is common among street arts. 3D drawing is just like traditional paintings that apply the mechanism of perspective, but its unique part is that its point of view is based on the viewer. Artists will set up an original viewpoint and by looking from this specific point, an 3D illusion is created. Other than this certain point of view, the 3D effect will no longer exist, and the picture will stretch out and deform.

Artist/ Jay Fanakapan

Crab and Fish
@Dubai, UAE 2016

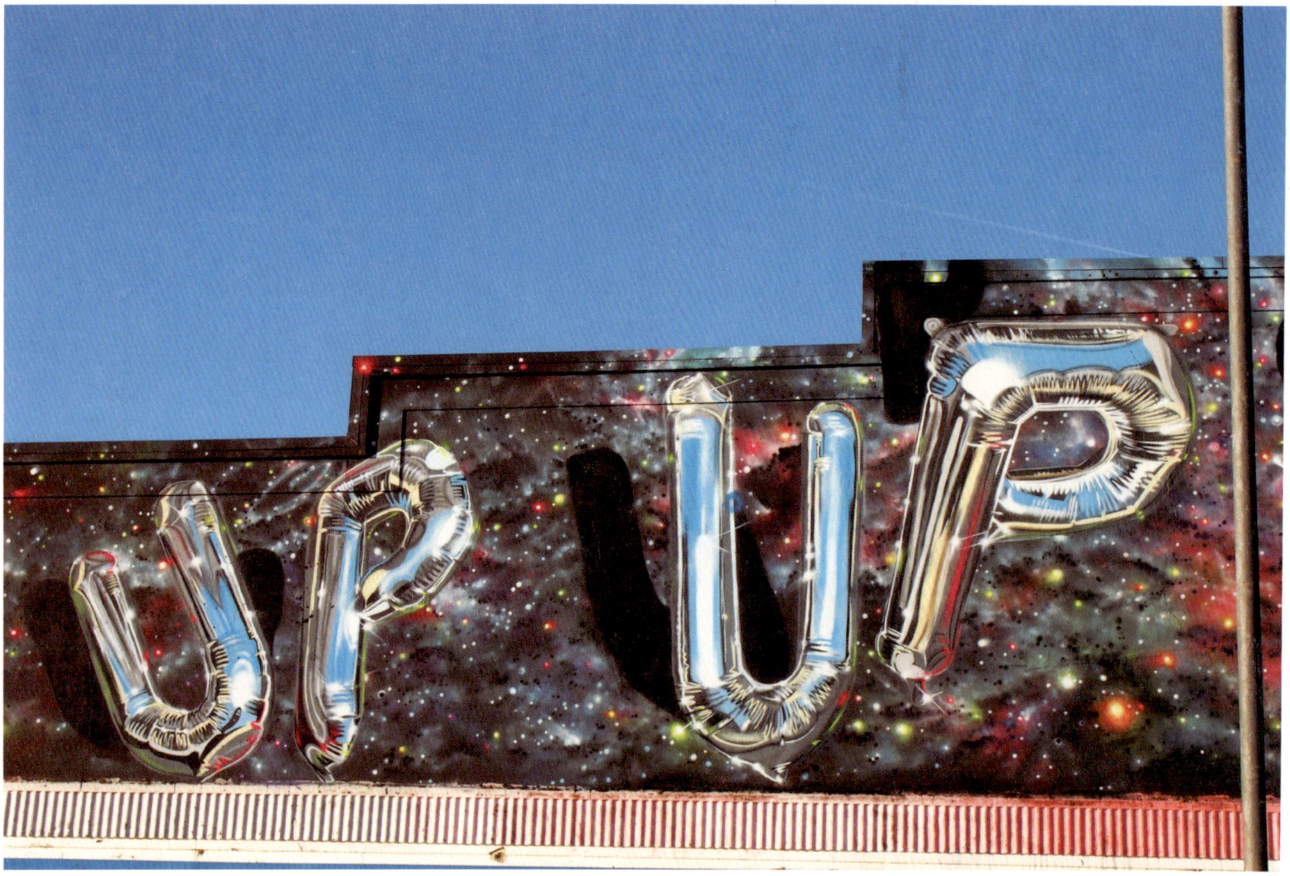

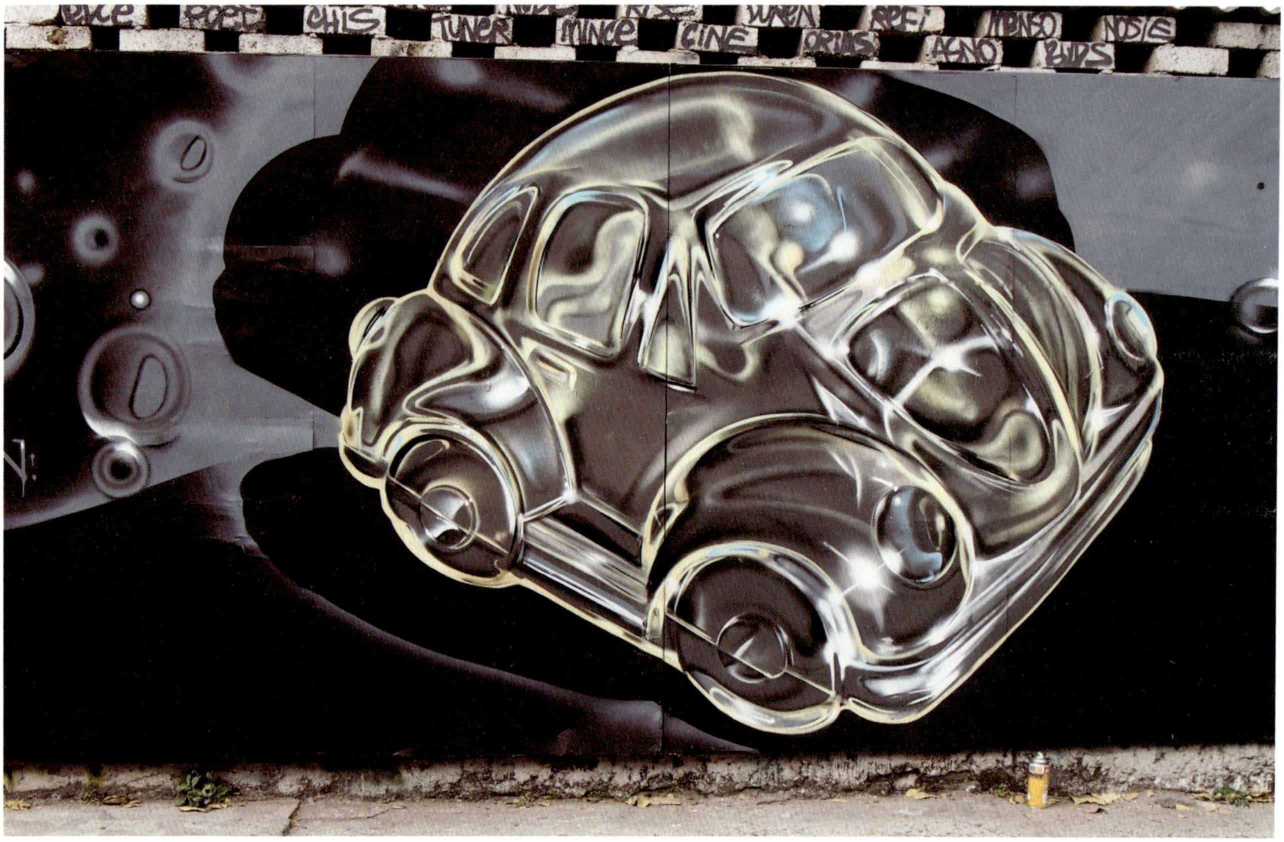

Glass Volkswagen Beetle
@Jalisco, Mexico 2017

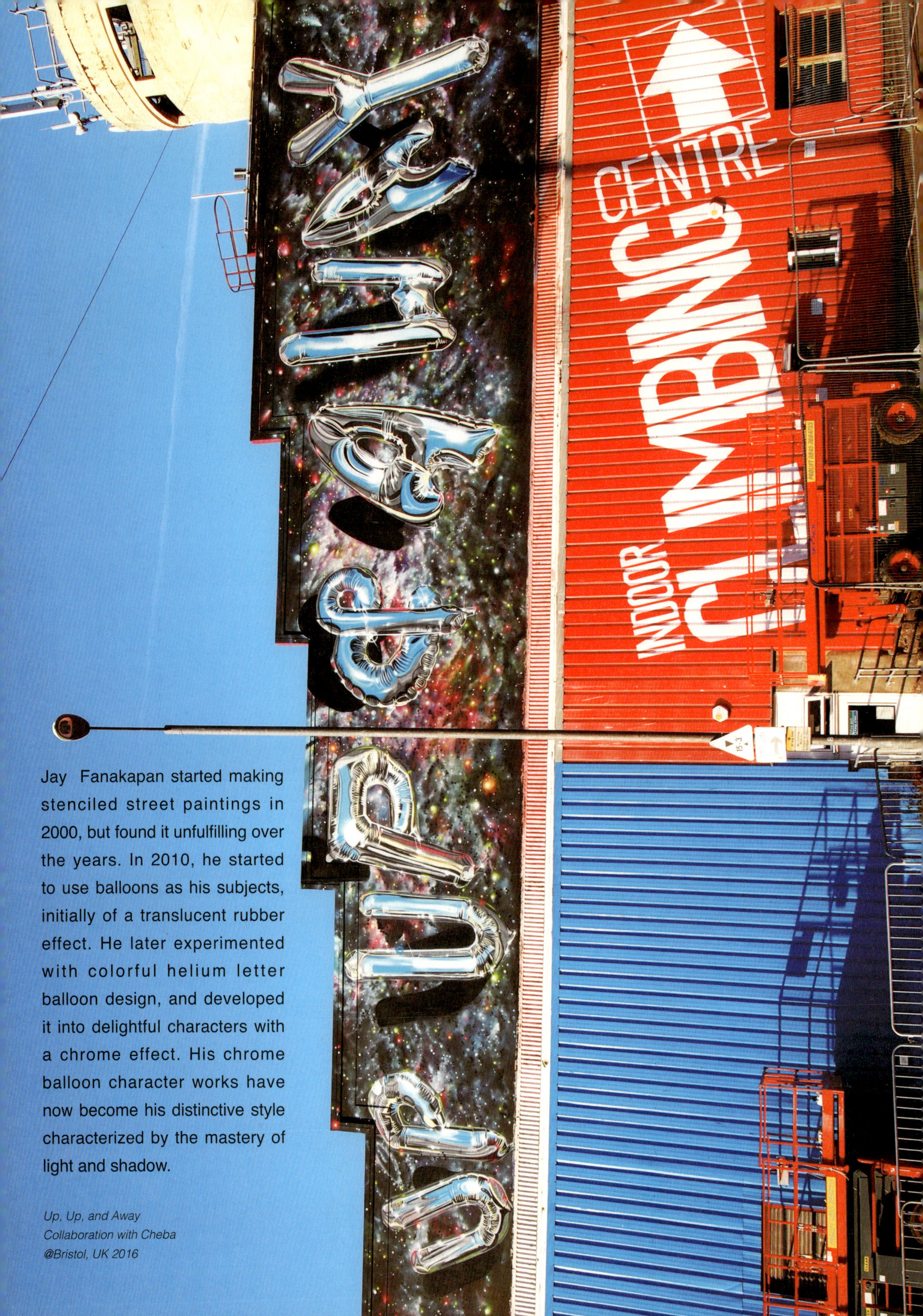

Jay Fanakapan started making stenciled street paintings in 2000, but found it unfulfilling over the years. In 2010, he started to use balloons as his subjects, initially of a translucent rubber effect. He later experimented with colorful helium letter balloon design, and developed it into delightful characters with a chrome effect. His chrome balloon character works have now become his distinctive style characterized by the mastery of light and shadow.

Up, Up, and Away
Collaboration with Cheba
@Bristol, UK 2016

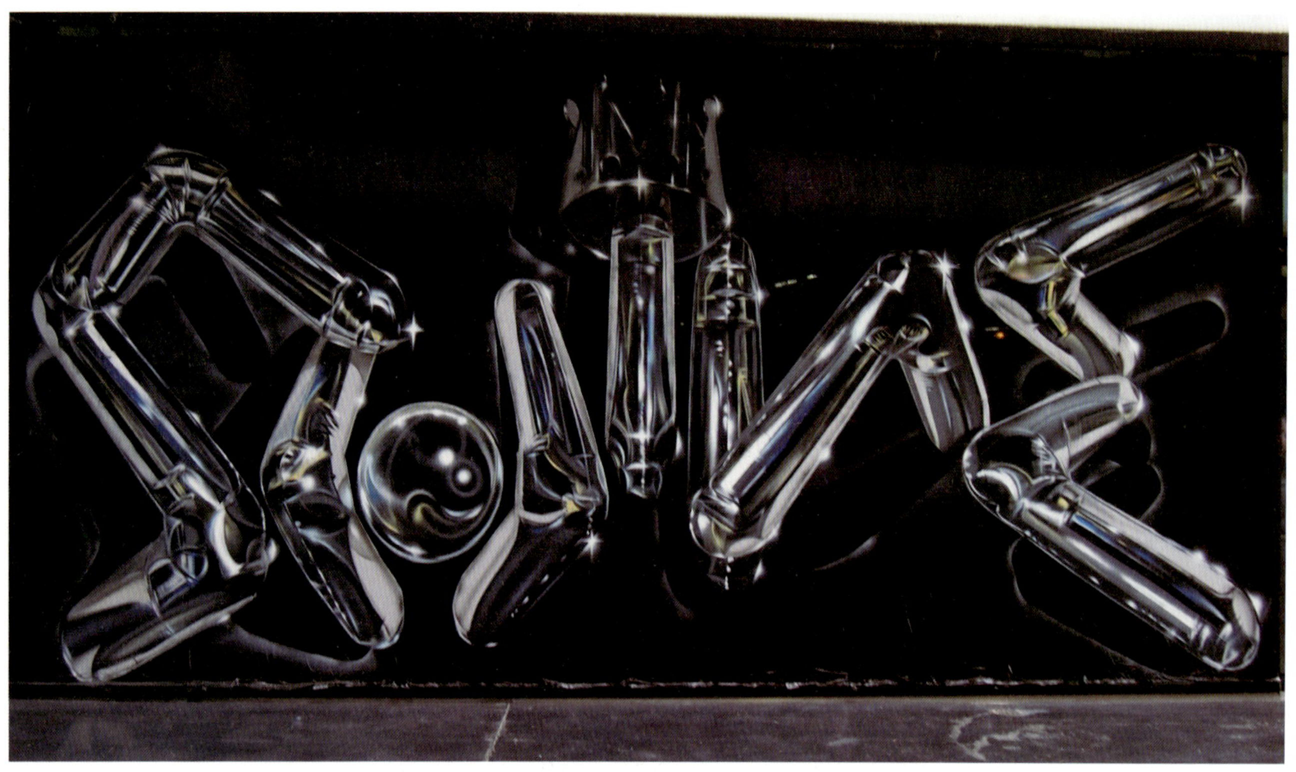

Shine
@Baden, Switzerland 2017

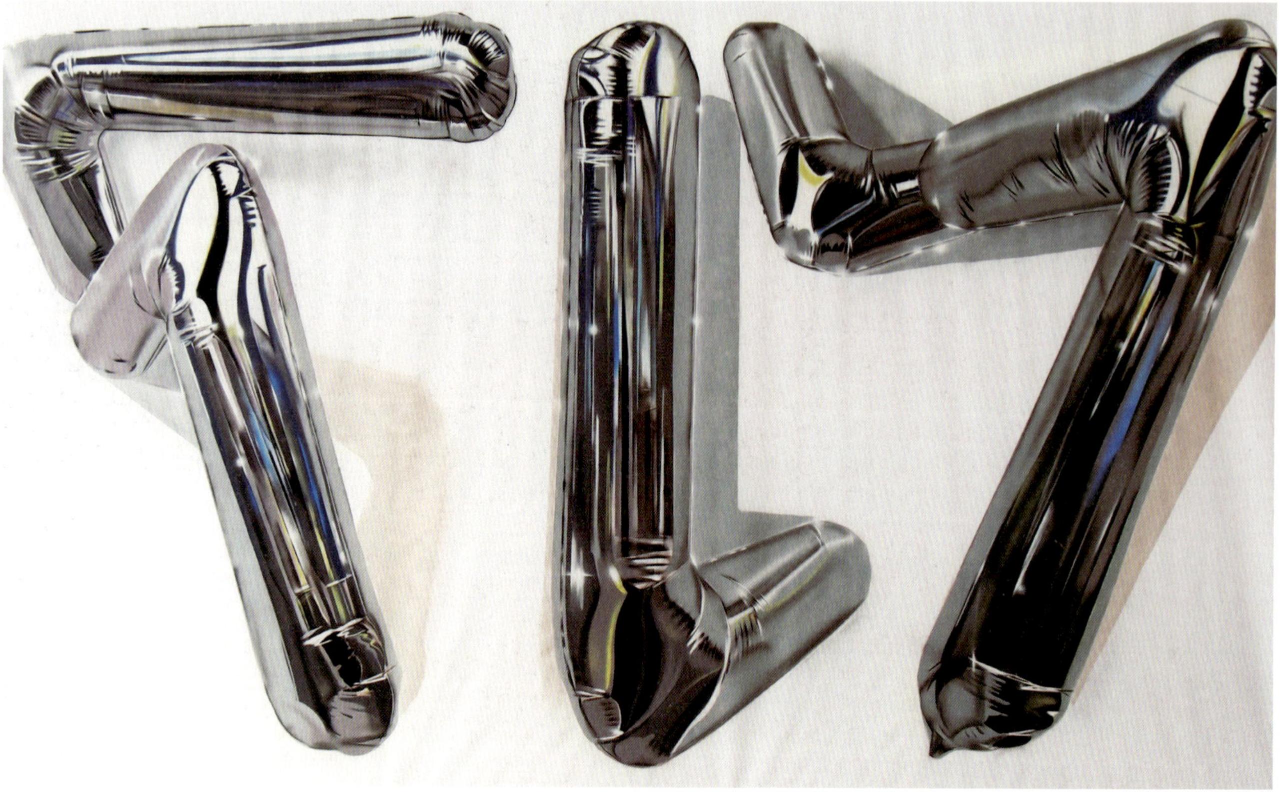

FLY
Drawing on paper 2016

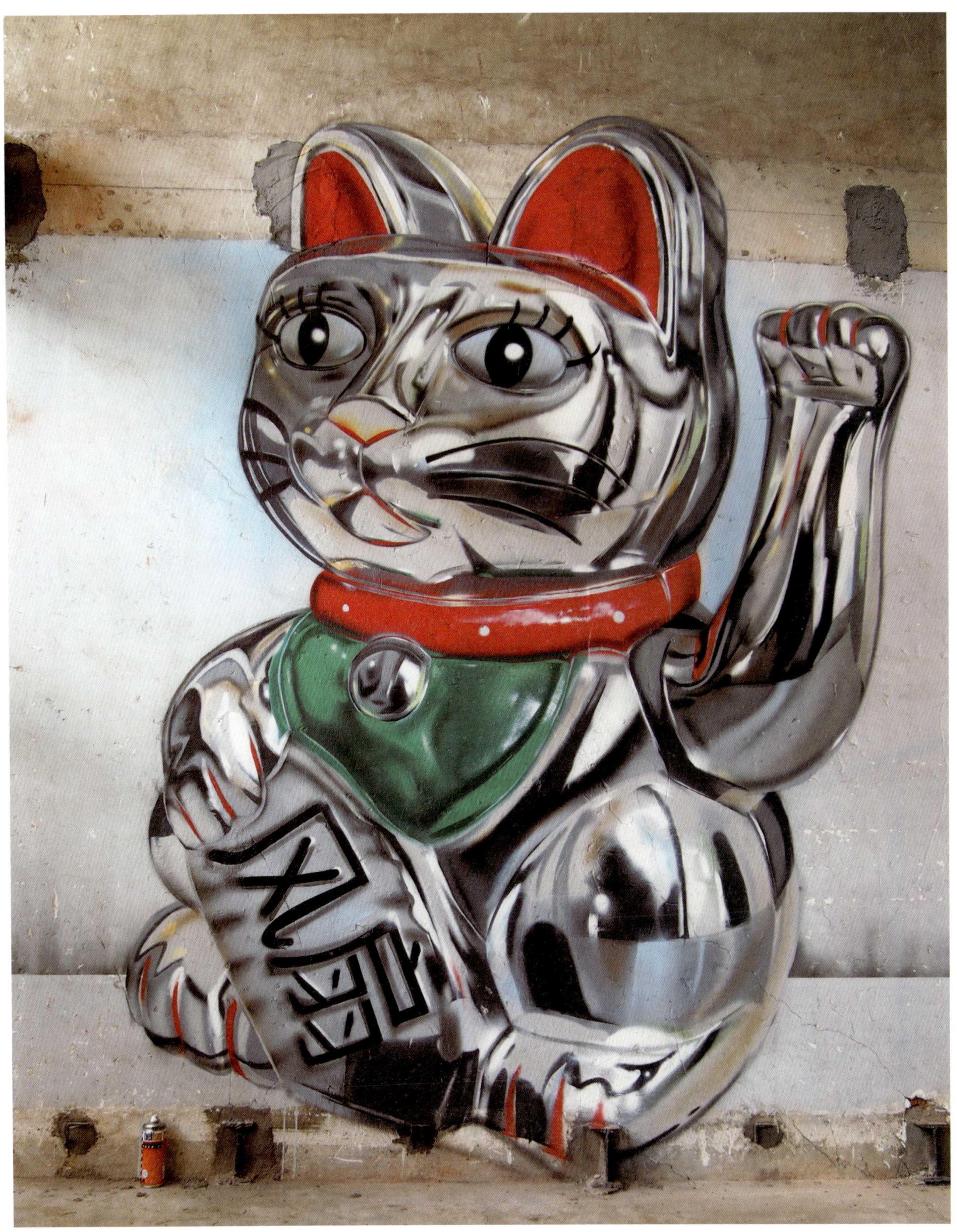

Lucky Cat
@Hong Kong, China 2016

Created for Crystal Ship Festival
@Ostend, Belgium 2016 ©David Roos

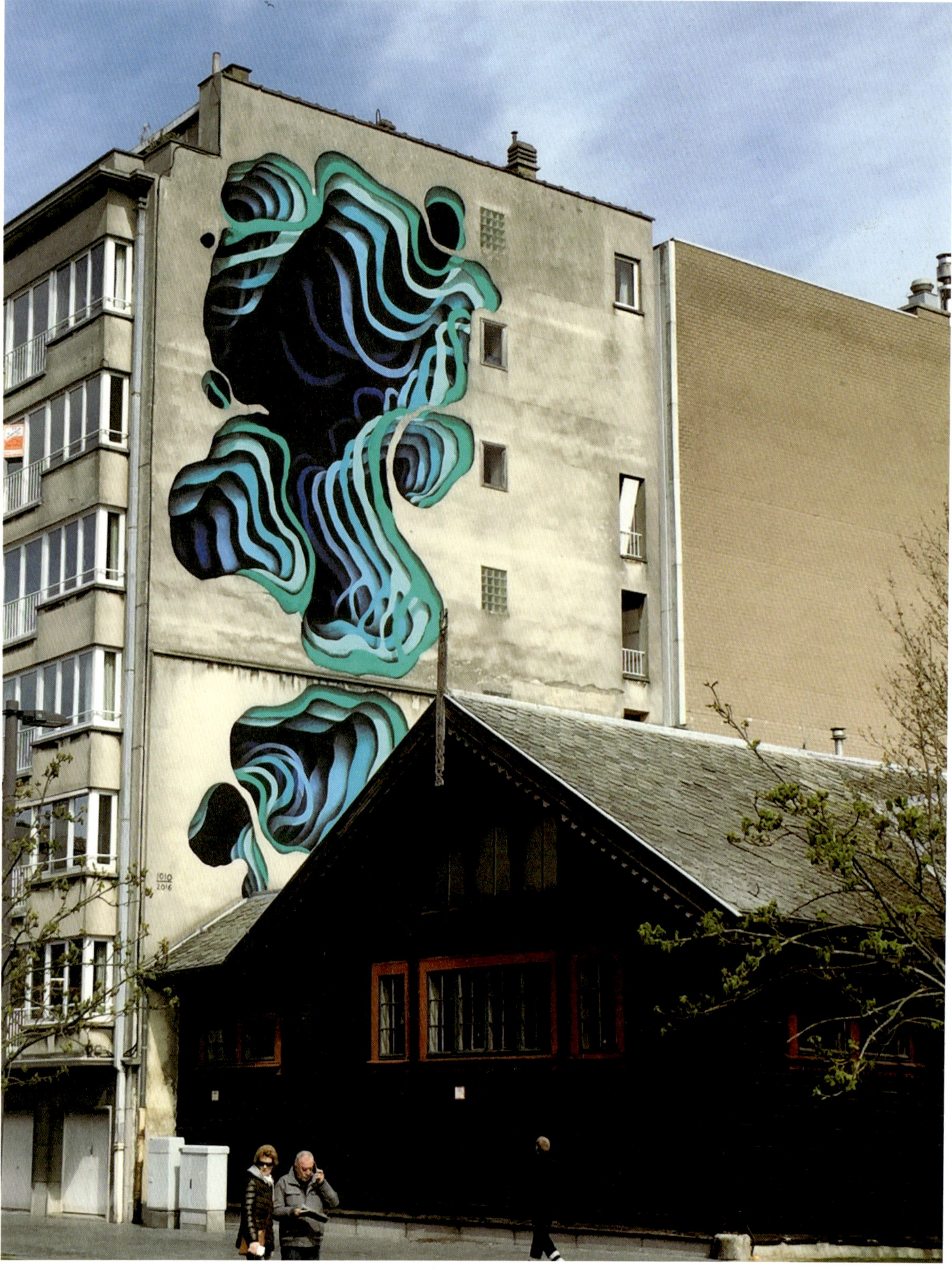

1010 is a Hamburg-based artist. His graphic outdoor paintings show illusions of portals that promise connections to other dimensions. Layers of pleasant colors and shadows lure the spectators' eyes deep into the darkness. The large scale murals seem like a painted invitation to confront the unknown and encourage unlimited imagination. Nothing is as it seems.

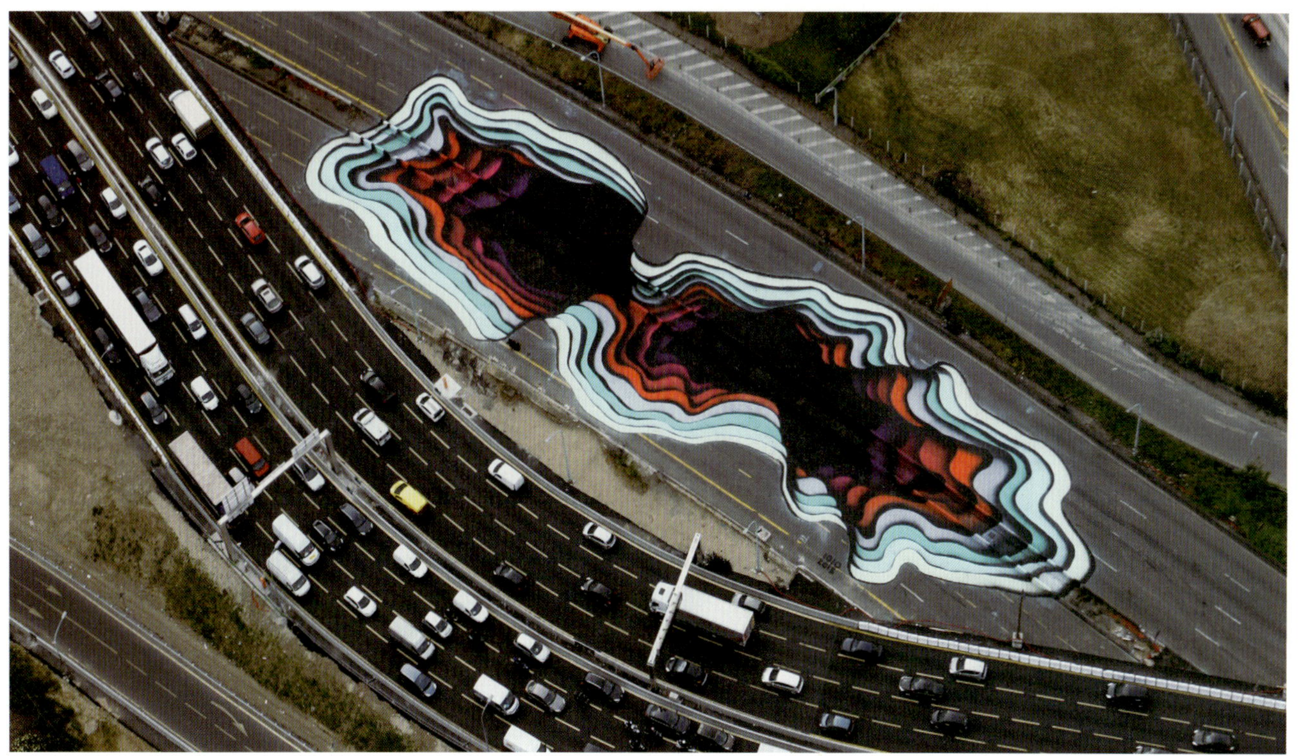

Created for Galerie Itinerrance
@Paris, France 2015 ©1010

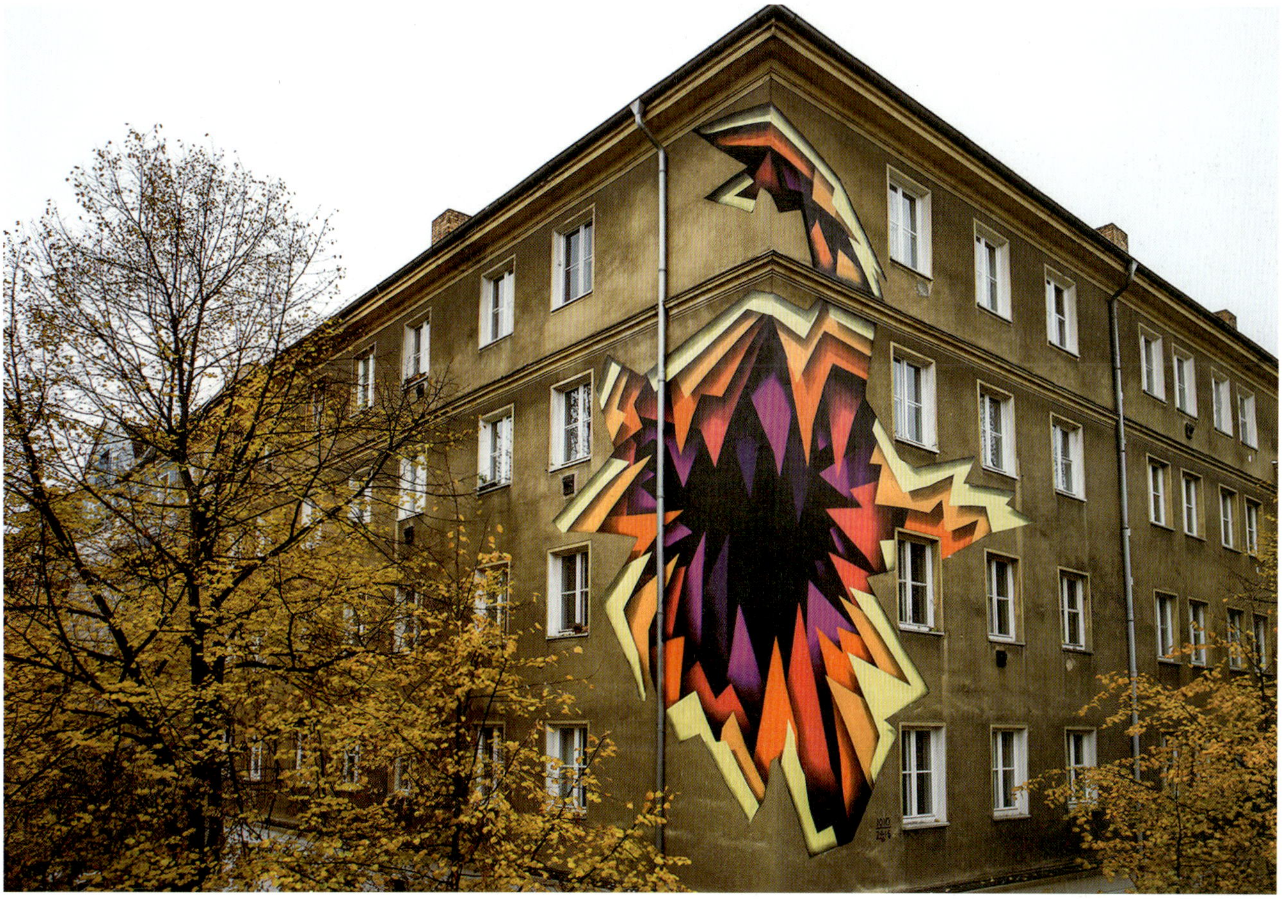

Created for Urban Nation
@Berlin, Germany 2016 ©Nika Kramer

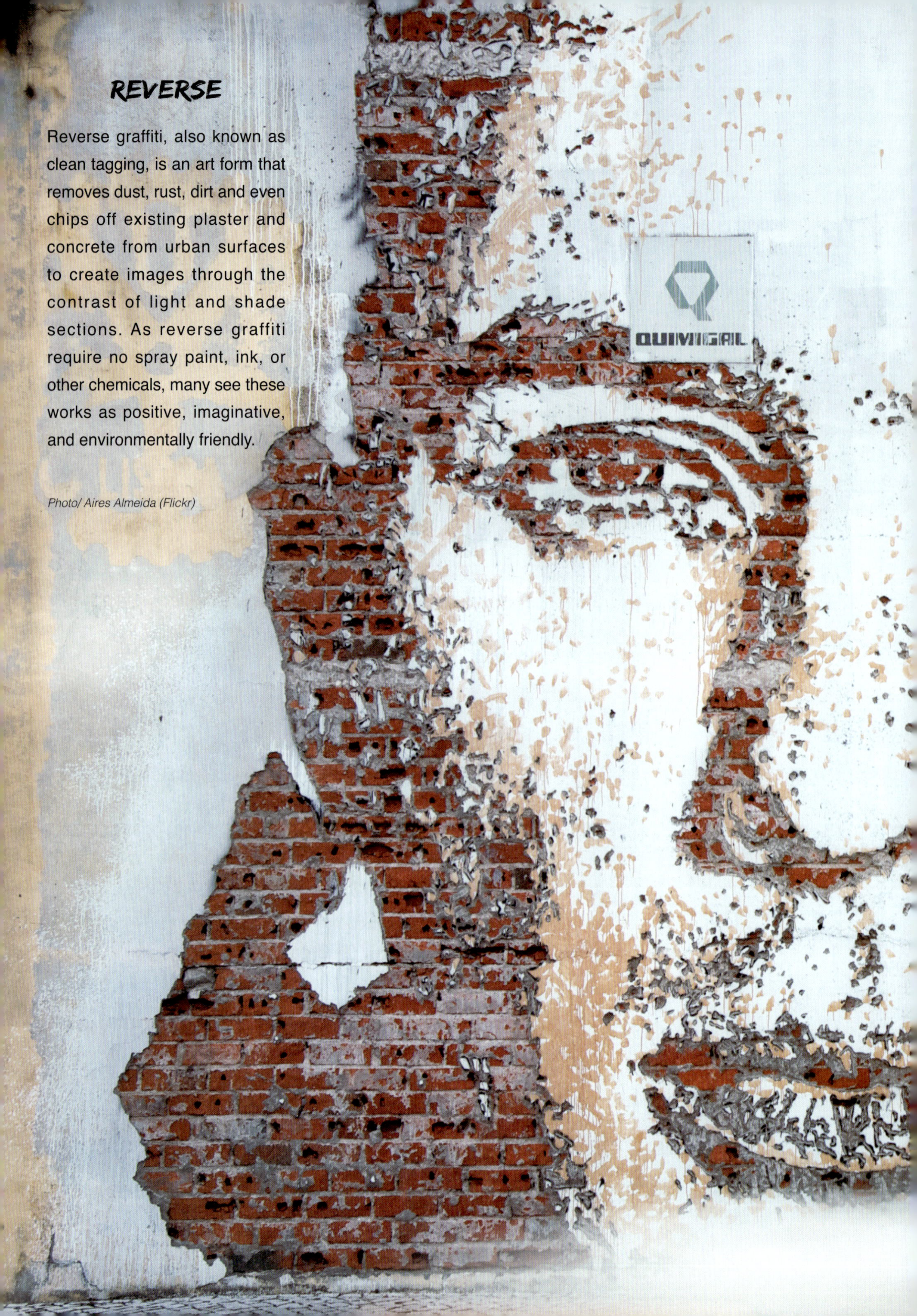

REVERSE

Reverse graffiti, also known as clean tagging, is an art form that removes dust, rust, dirt and even chips off existing plaster and concrete from urban surfaces to create images through the contrast of light and shade sections. As reverse graffiti require no spray paint, ink, or other chemicals, many see these works as positive, imaginative, and environmentally friendly.

Photo/ Aires Almeida (Flickr)

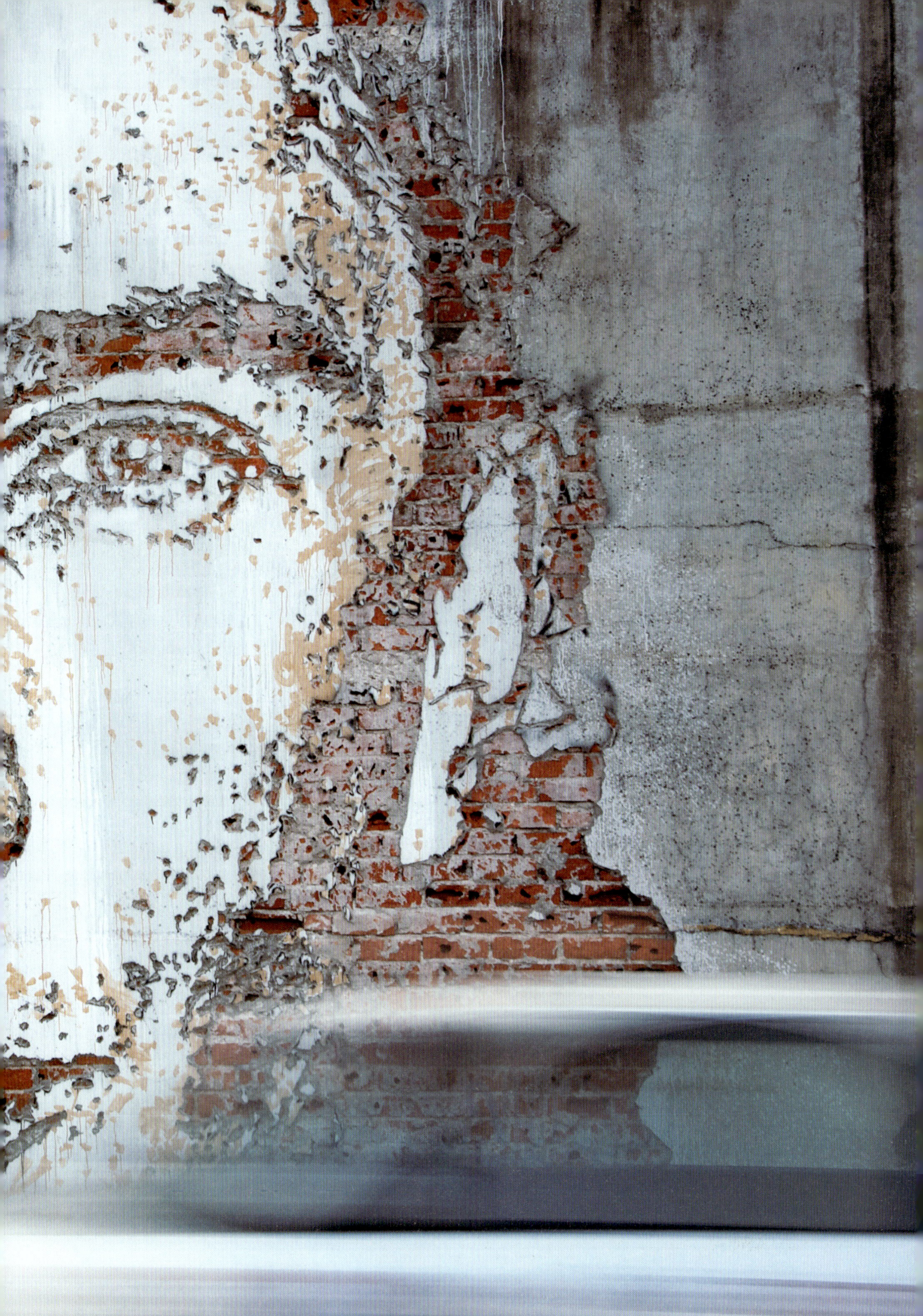

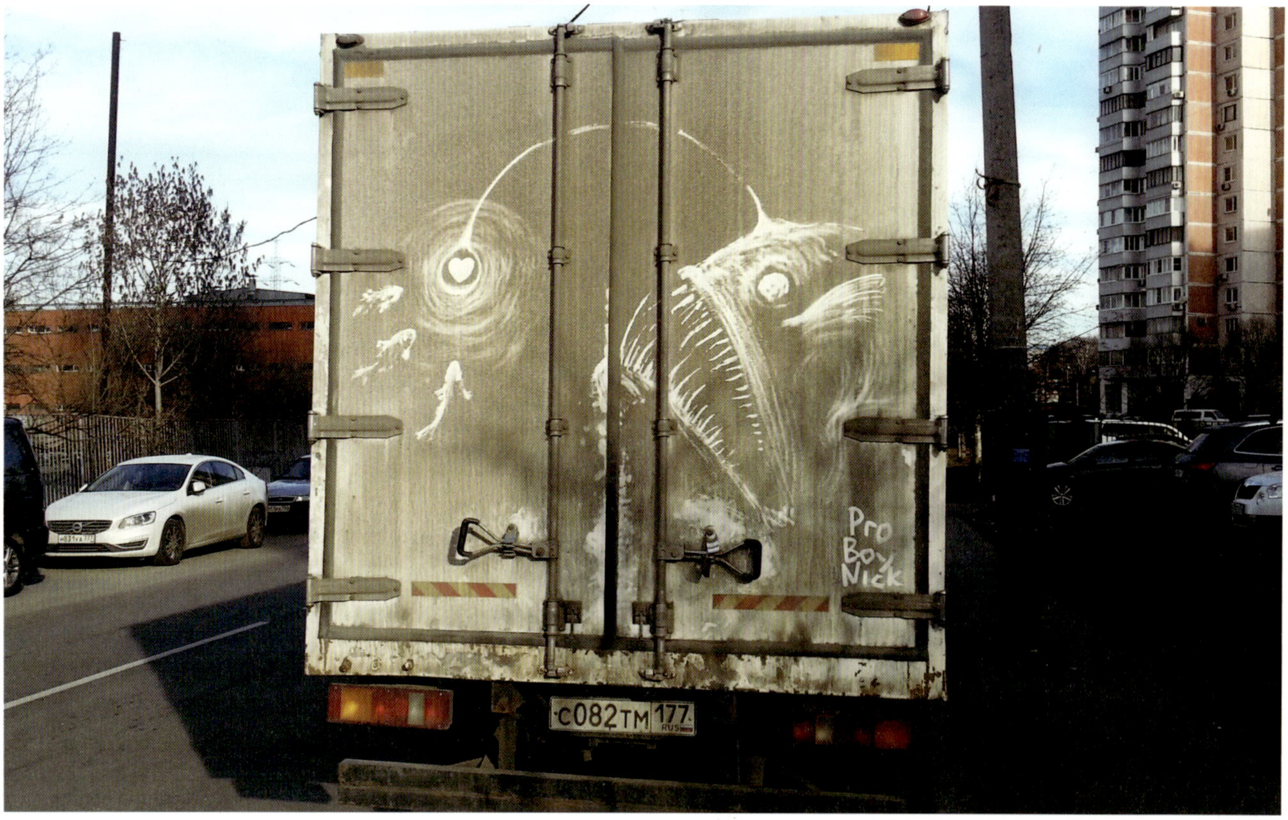

The end of every winter in Moscow is a very dirty season. Melting snow mixes with dust and covers all the cars and roads, so everything is grey. It dawned on Nikita Golubev that imagery could be created out of these large, textured surfaces by simple brushes and fingers. It started off as morning exercises for him, and now has become part of the city landscape.

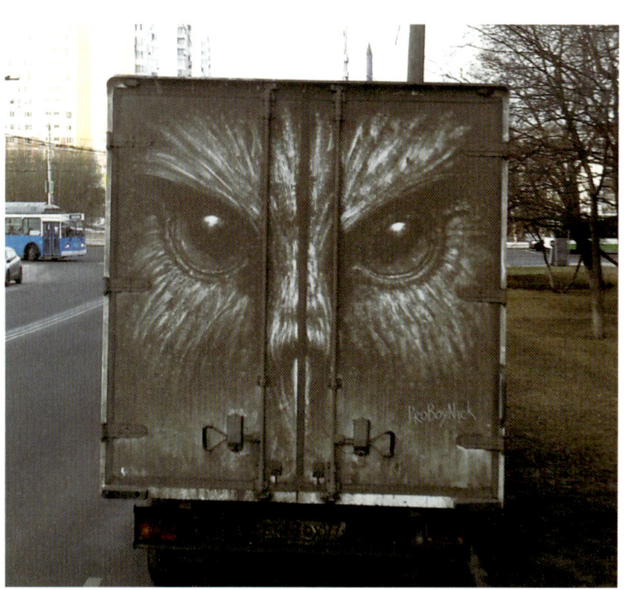

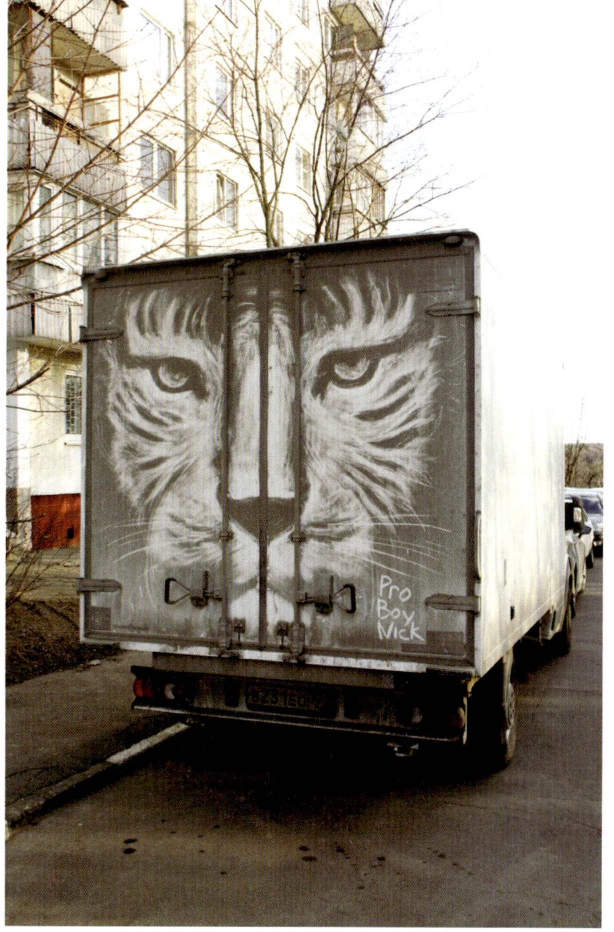

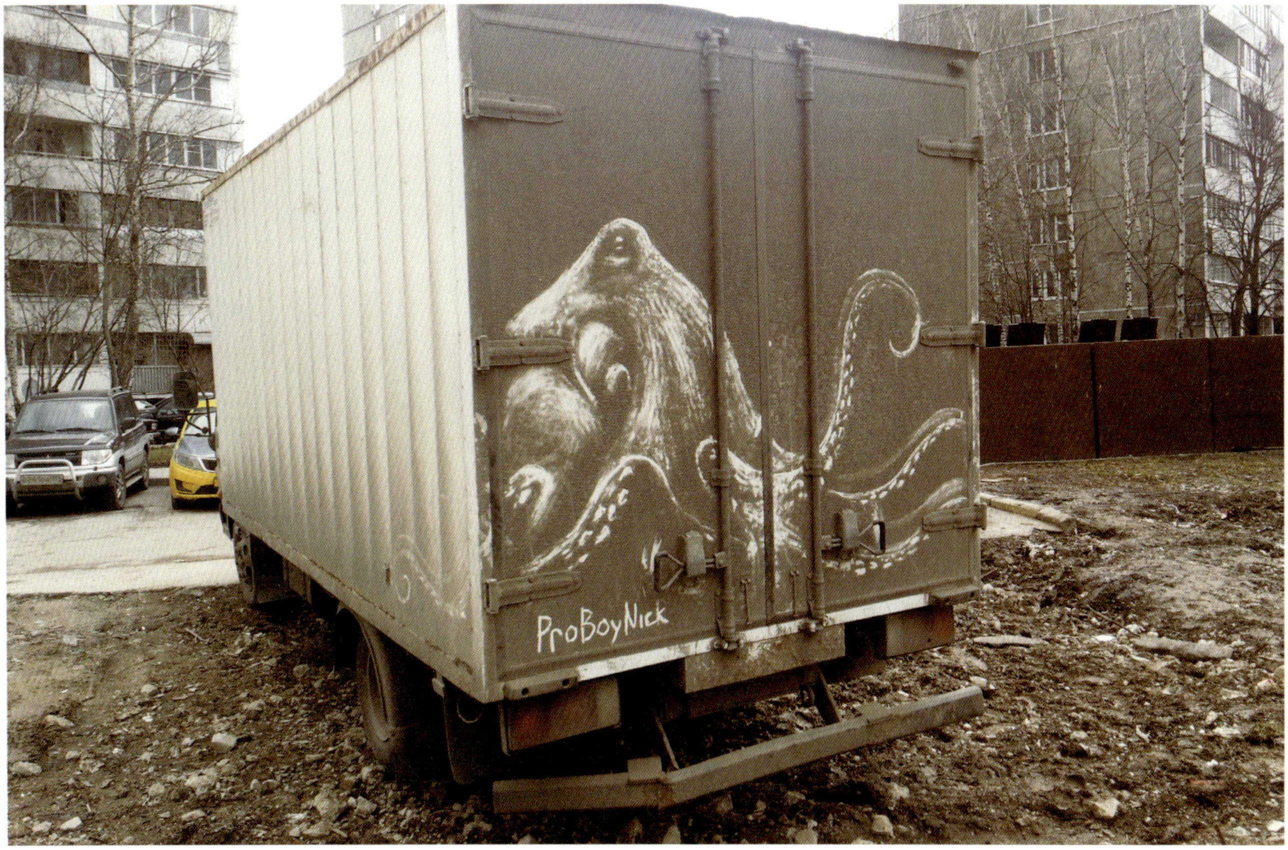
ProBoyNick

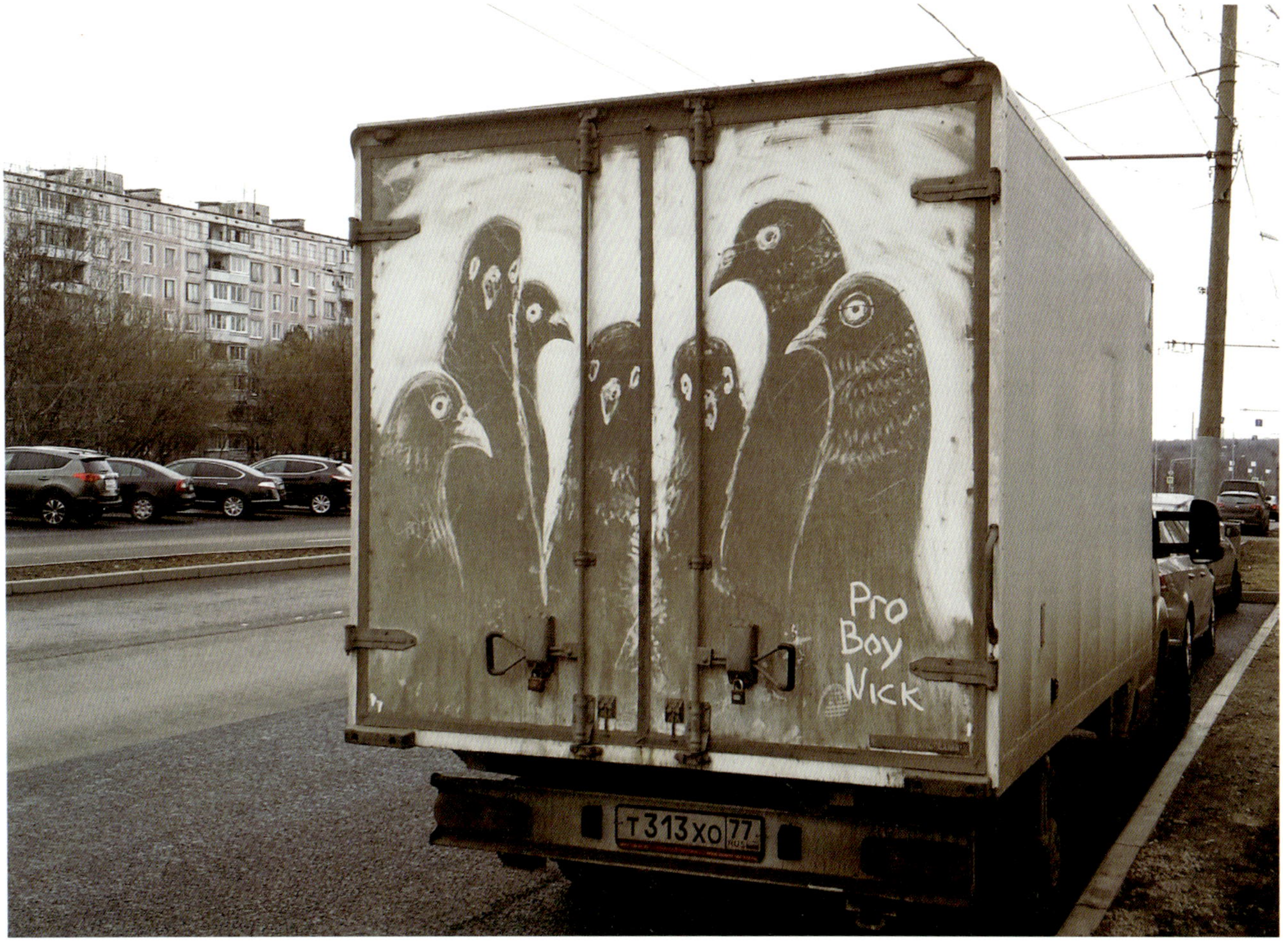
Pro
Boy
Nick
Т313ХО77

INDEX

ARTISTS

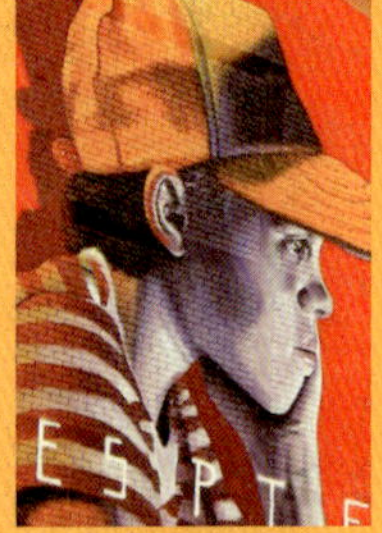

Asier
http://asier.com.es/
P002, 003, cover & back cover (top, middle)

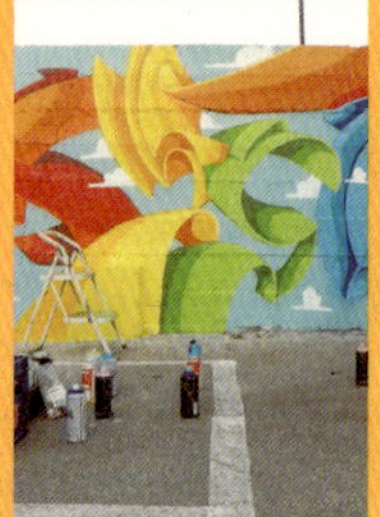

Andrea Antoni
http://www.andreaantoni.it/
P016

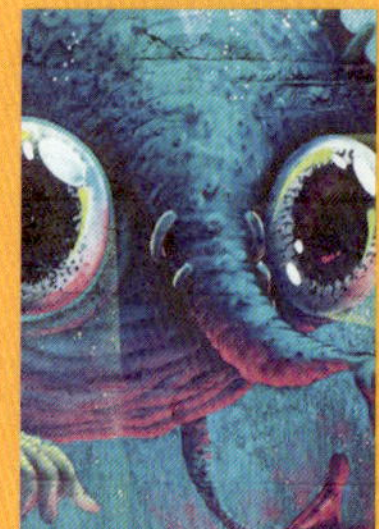

Art of Sool
http://www.artofsool.com/
P154, 155

B

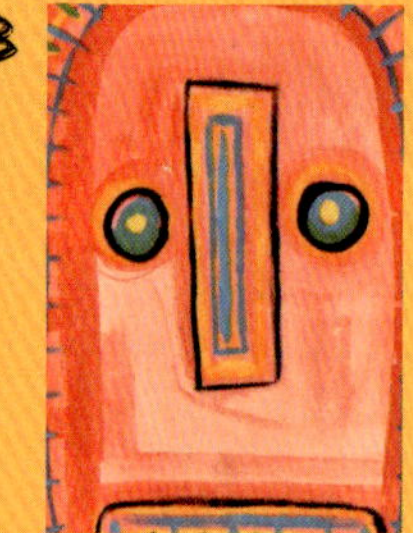

Boxi Trixi
https://www.instagram.com/boxitrixi/
P084, 160–163

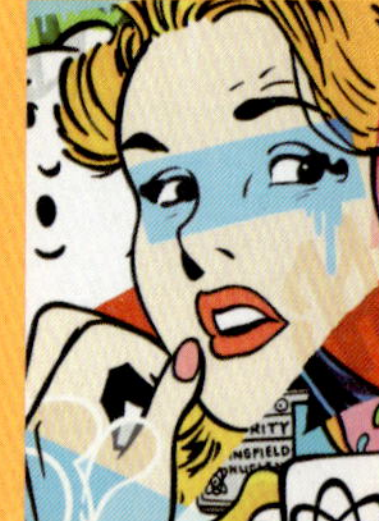

BustArt
http://www.art-of-bust.com/
P140–145

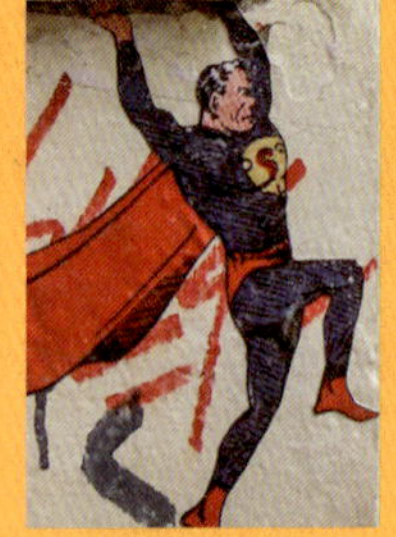

Caiozzama
https://www.caiozzama.com/
https://www.instagram.com/caiozzama/
P096–101

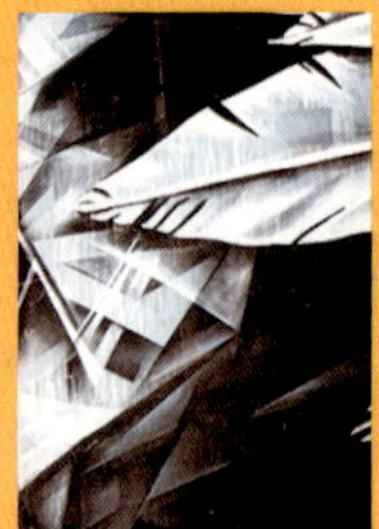

Christina Angelina
https://www.instagram.com/starfightera/
P118–123

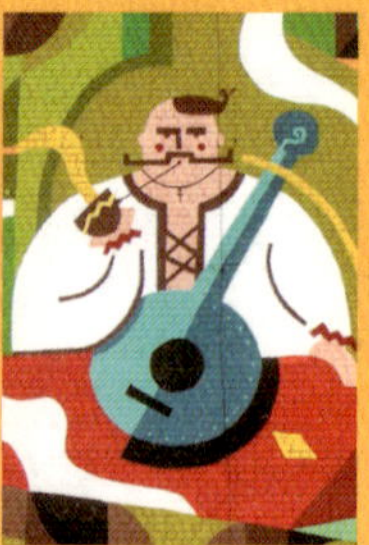

Chzz Zavoyovnuk
https://www.facebook.com/chzzavoyovnuk
P150, 151

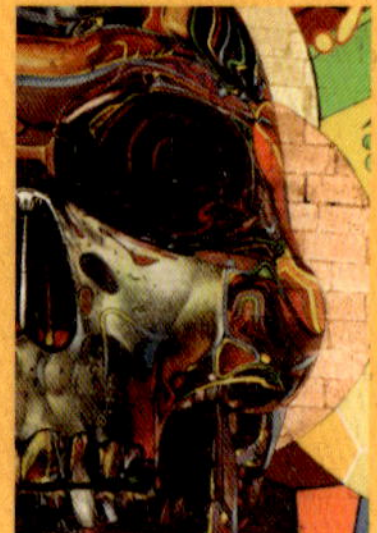

Chor Boogie
http://chorboogie.com/
https://www.instagram.com/chorboogie/
P178–181

D

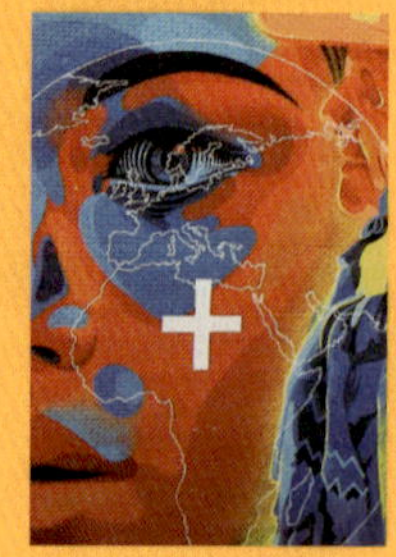

Dourone
http://dourone.com/
https://www.instagram.com/dourone/
P194–197

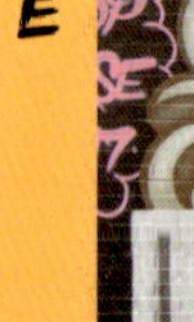

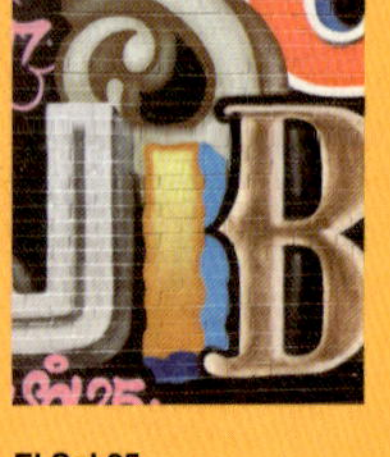

El Sol 25
https://www.instagram.com/elsol25/
P038

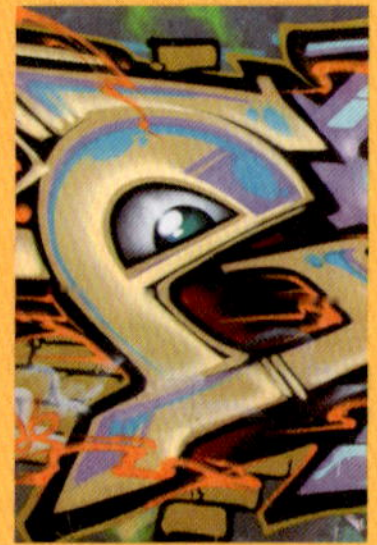

Edwin Yang
https://www.instagram.com/sdz_edwiner/
P048, 049, 052, 053

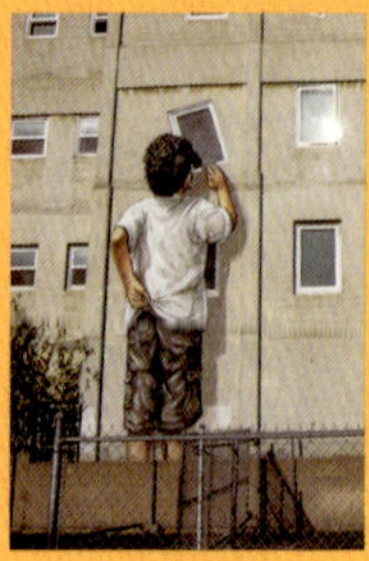

Ernest Zacharevic
http://www.ernestzacharevic.com/
P108, 109

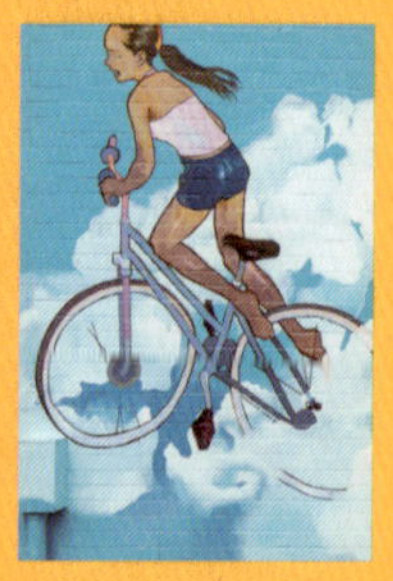

Edwin Ushiro
http://www.mrushiro.com/
https://www.instagram.com/edwinushiro/
P158, 159

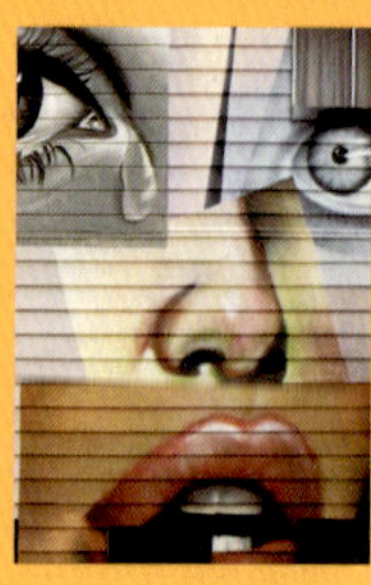

Elle
http://ellestreetart.com/
P188, 189

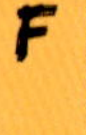

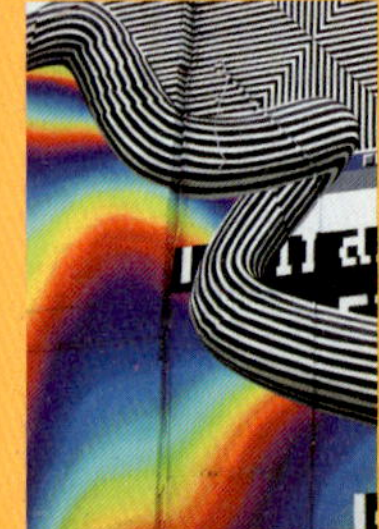

Felipe Pantone
https://www.felipepantone.com/
P166–171

G

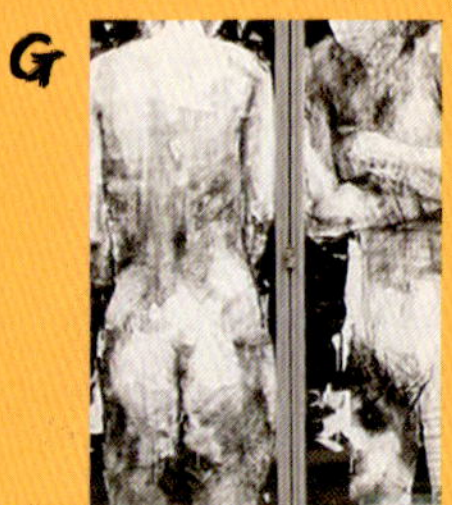

Gonzalo Borondo
http://gonzaloborondo.com/
P110–113

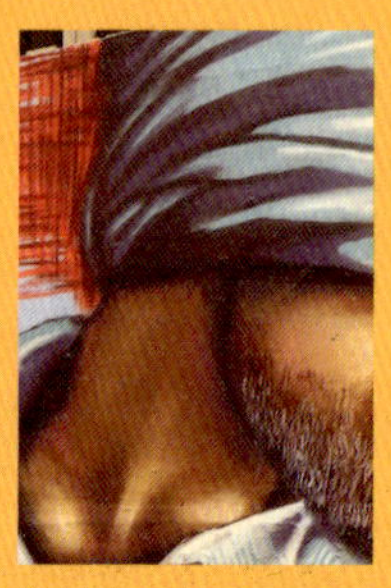

GIOVA
https://www.instagram.com/giova.graffiti/
https://www.facebook.com/giova.graffiti
P128, 129

H

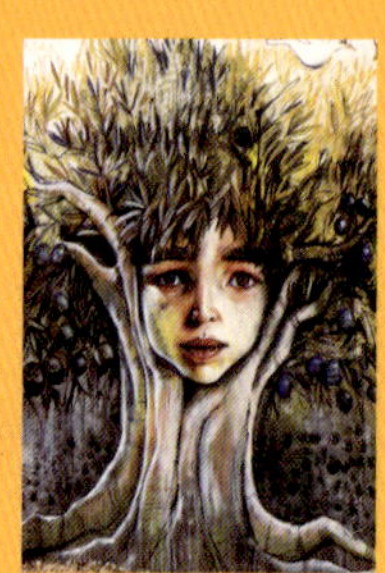

Herakut
http://www.herakut.de/
P114–117

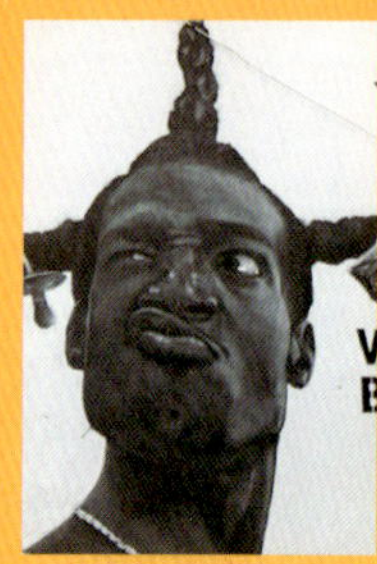

Hood Graff
https://www.instagram.com/myhoodisgood/
https://www.facebook.com/myhoodisgood
P130, 131

I

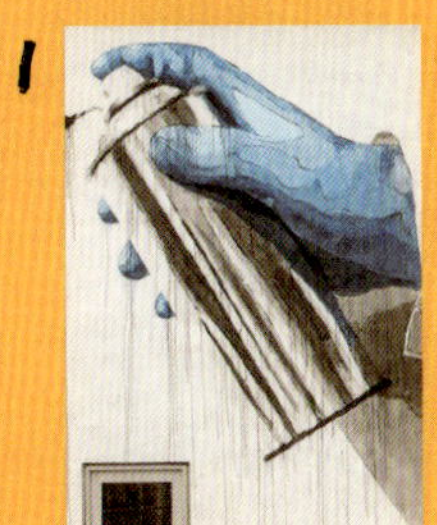

INO
http://www.ino.net/
P132–137

J

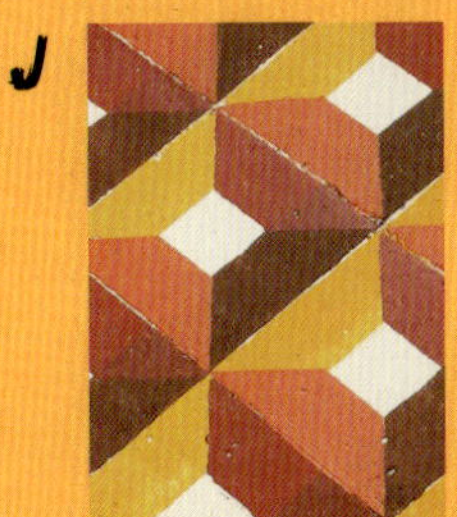

Javier de Riba
https://www.instagram.com/javierderiba/
P078–081

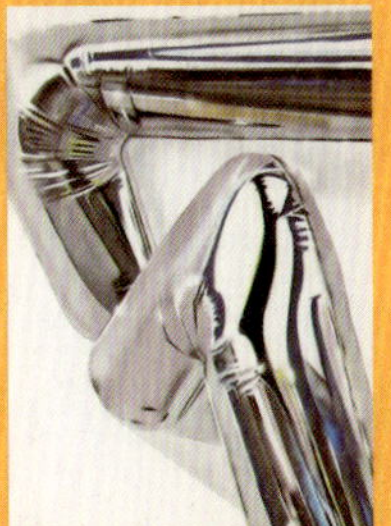

Jay Fanakapan
https://www.instagram.com/fanakapan/
P206–211

K

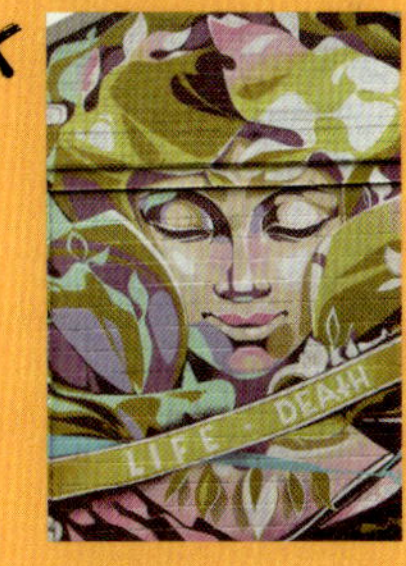

Key Detail
http://www.keydetail.org/
https://www.instagram.com/keydetail
P198, 199

L

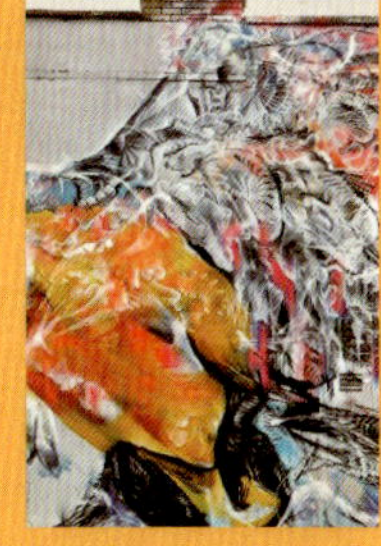

L7M
http://l7mstreetart.com/
P174–177

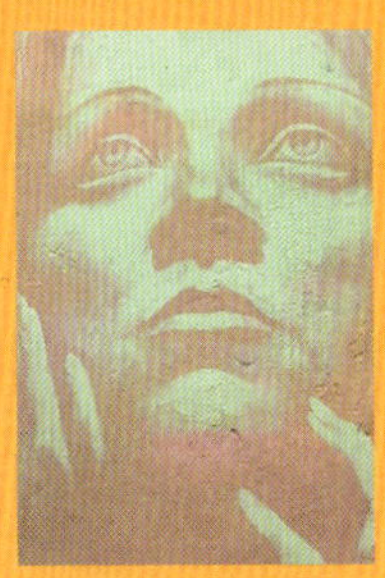

Lex Zooz
https://www.instagram.com/lexzooz/
P182, 183

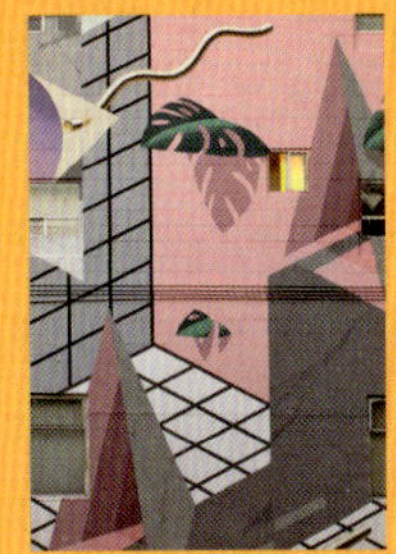

Low Bros
http://www.lowbros.de/
P184, 185

M

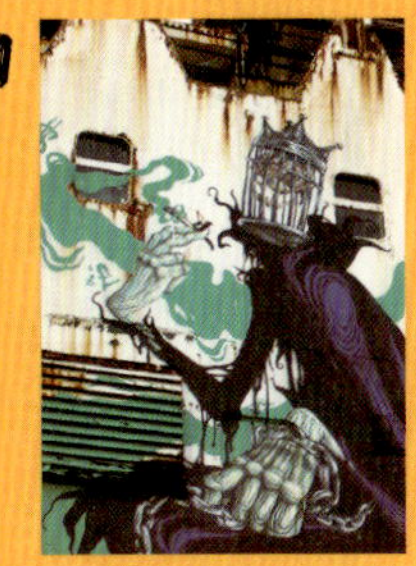

Mr. Zero
http://mr-zero.org/
P050–051, 164, 165

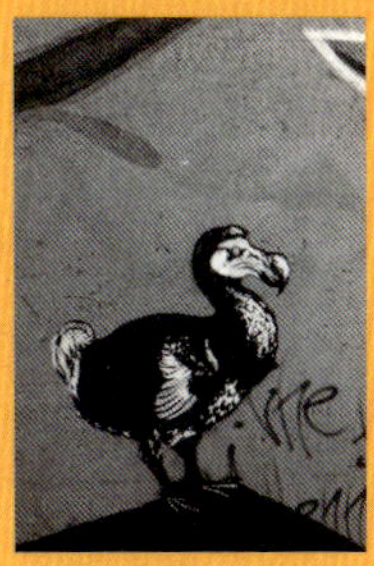

Matteo Pietra
https://www.behance.net/MatteoPietra
P082, 083

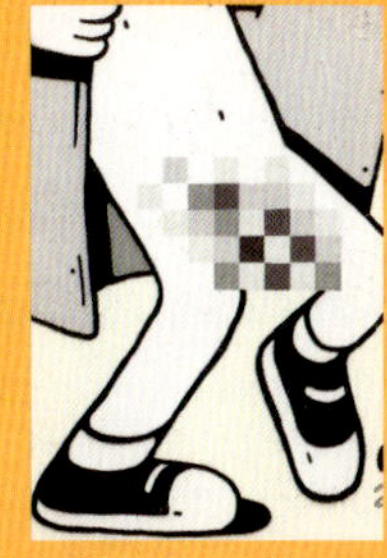

MURETZ
https://www.muretz.com/
https://www.instagram.com/muretz/
P148, 149

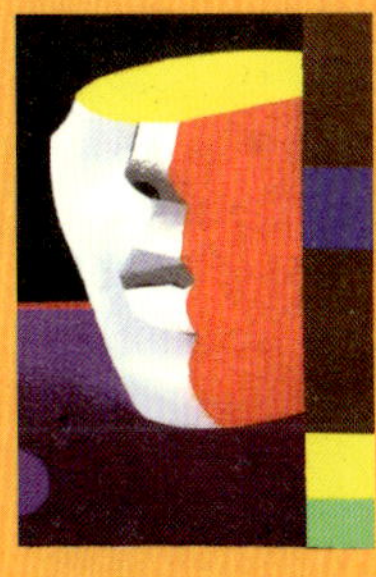

Magda Ćwik
http://www.magdacwik.com/
https://www.instagram.com/magdacwikart/
P190, 191

N

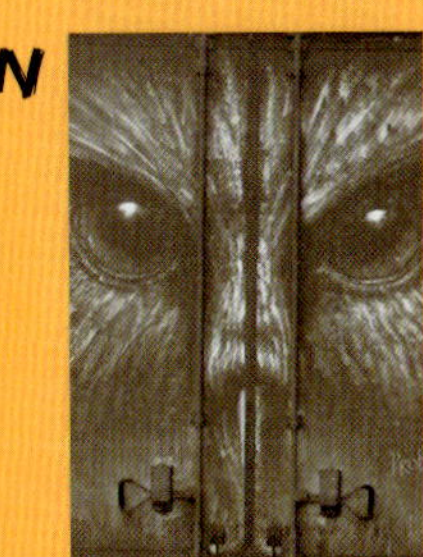

Nikita Golubev
https://www.instagram.com/proboynick/
P216, 217

P

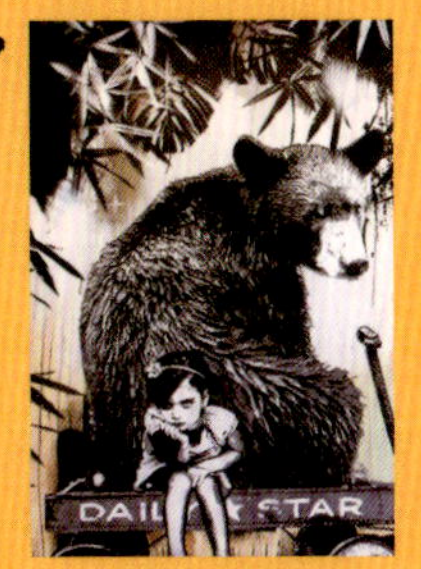

Pipsqueak Was Here!!!
http://pipsqueakwashere.com/
P014, 146, 147

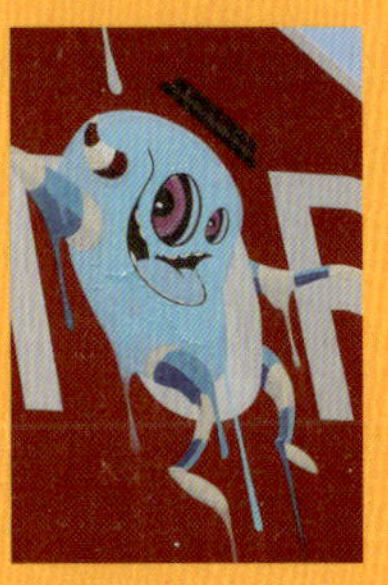

Patch Whisky
https://www.patchwhisky.com/
P156, 157

R

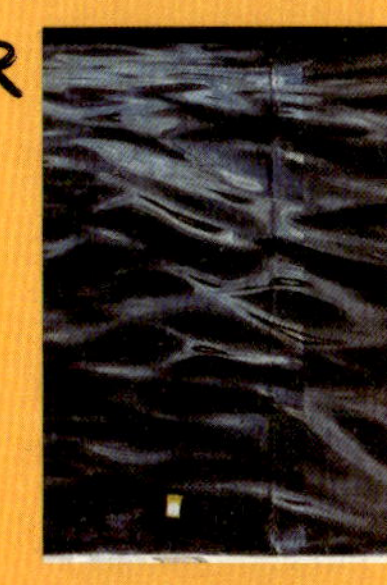

Ricky Lee Gordon
https://www.instagram.com/rickyleegordon/
P104–107

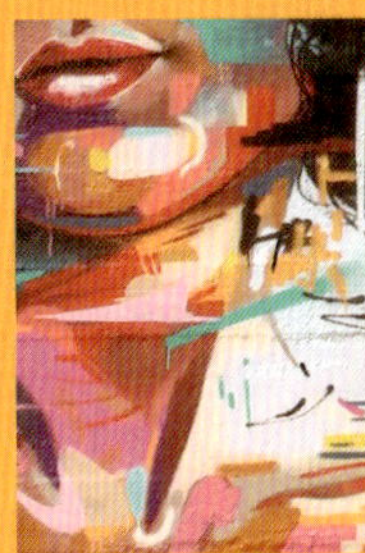

Remy Uno
http://remyuno.com/
P186, 187

S

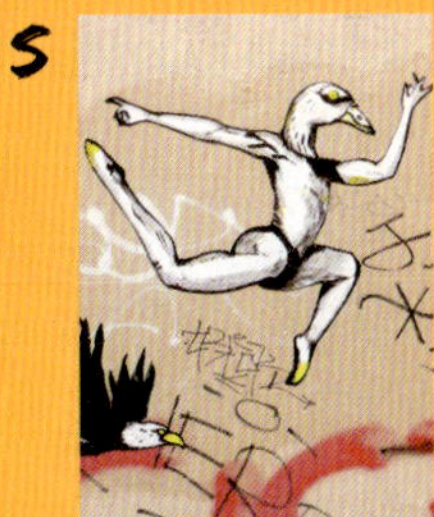

Suriani
http://www.suriani-art.com/
P090–095

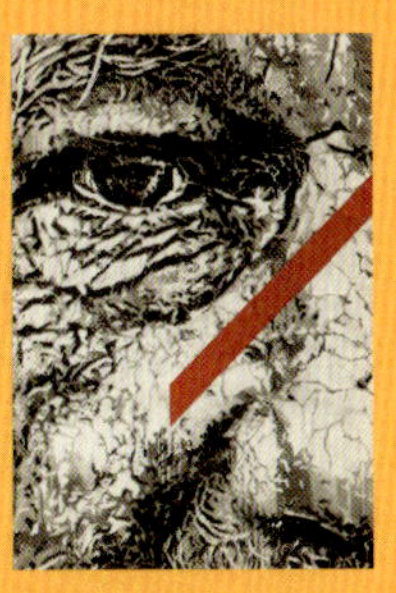

SAMINA
www.instagram.com/j_samina
www.behance.net/JSAMINA
P018, 054, 072–077

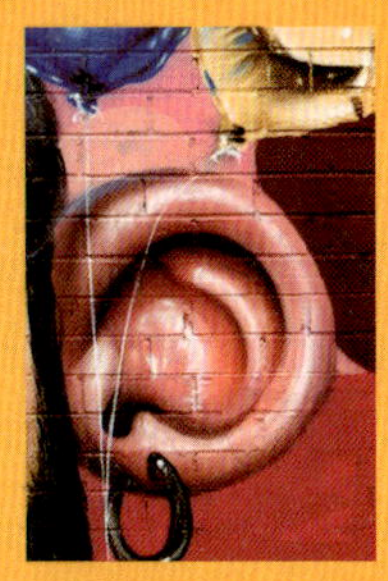

Sipros
https://www.facebook.com/siprosgraffiti/
P124–127

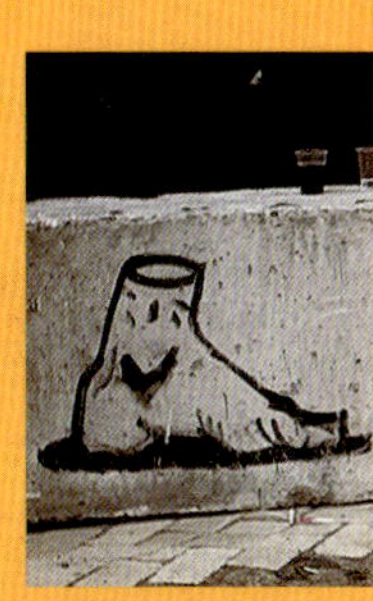

Sham Ptashenchuk
https://www.instagram.com/sham__sham__sham/
P192, 193, 200–205

T

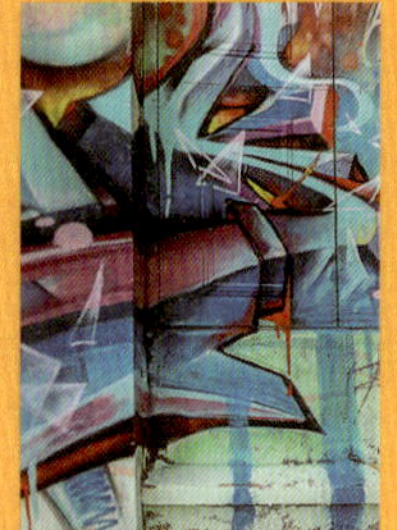

Trang Khoa
https://www.wallovers.in/
https://www.behance.net/trangkhoa
P042–045

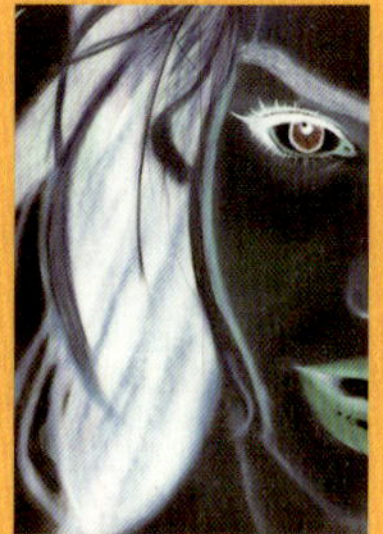

TakerOne
https://www.facebook.com/takeronegraffiti
https://www.instagram.com/takeronegraffiti/
P138, 139

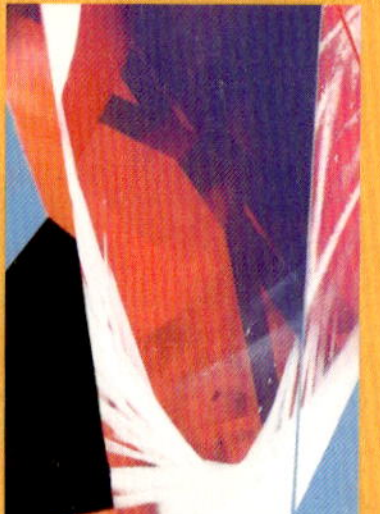

Théo Lopez
https://www.theolopez.com/
P172, 173

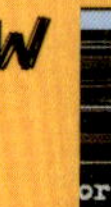

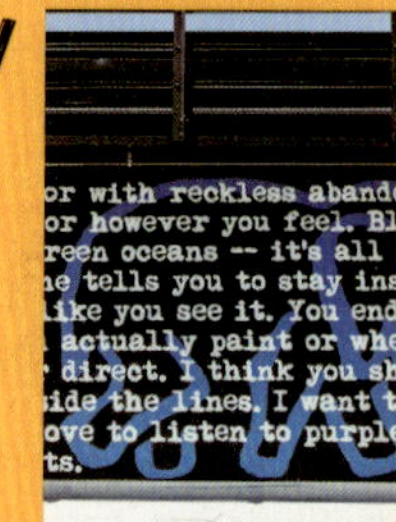

WRDSMTH
https://www.instagram.com/wrdsmth/
P015, 068–071

Z

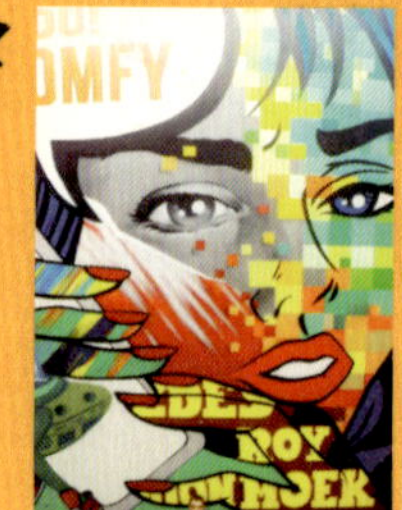

Zdes Roy
https://www.instagram.com/zdesroy/
P046–049, 152, 153

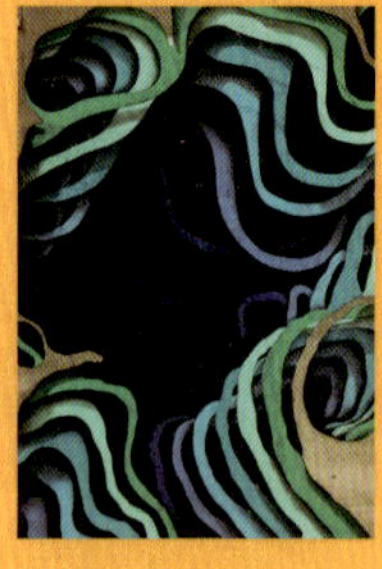

1010
https://www.instagram.com/1010zzz/
P212, 213

PHOTO CREDITS

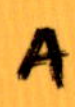

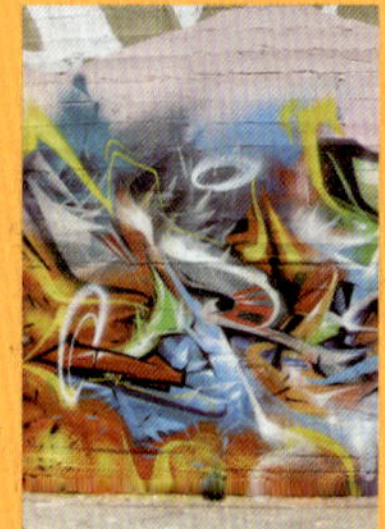

A Syn
https://www.flickr.com/photos/24293932@N00/
P039

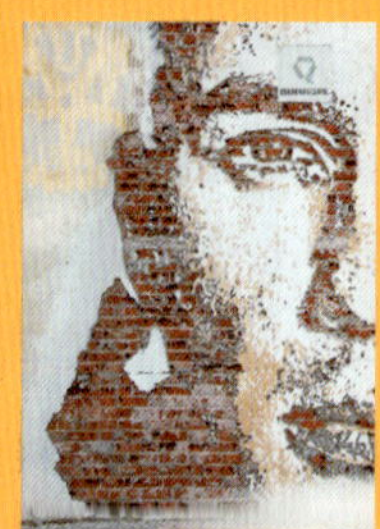

Aires Almeida
https://www.flickr.com/photos/31212180@N08/
P214–215

B

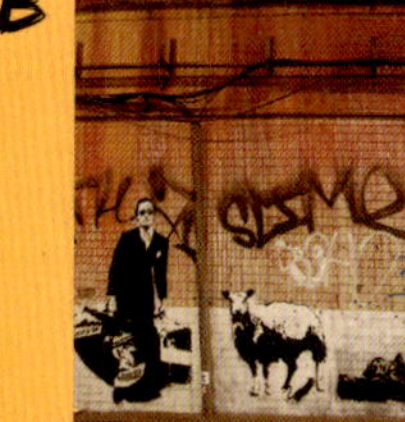

bixentro
https://www.flickr.com/photos/bixentro/
P061

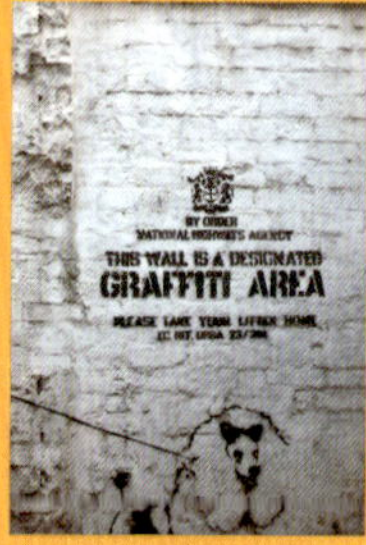

Berit Watkin
https://www.flickr.com/photos/ben124/
P067

F

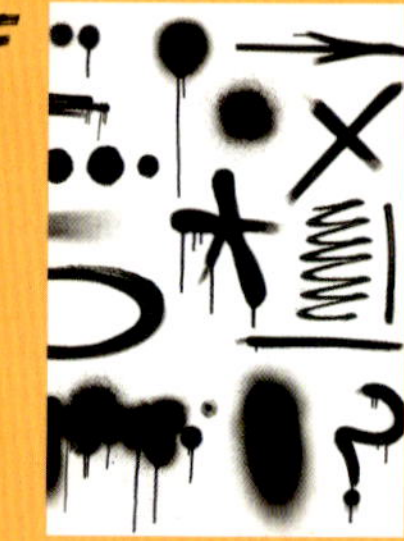

Freepik
https://www.freepik.com/
P008

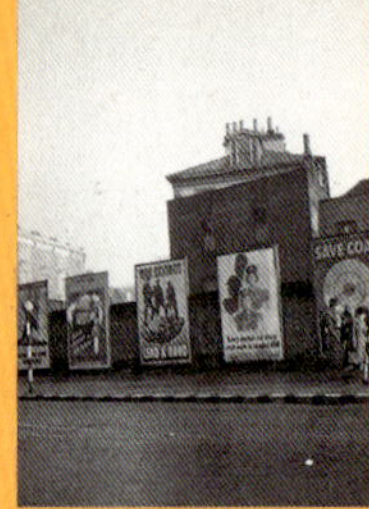

Imperial War Museums
http://www.iwm.org.uk/
P087

J

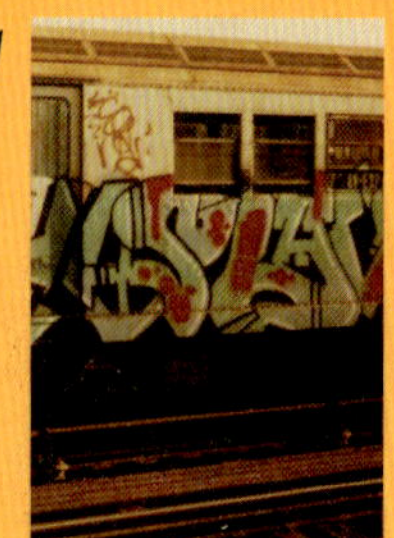

JJ & Special K
https://www.flickr.com/photos/sweet_child_of_mine/
P028, 029, 035

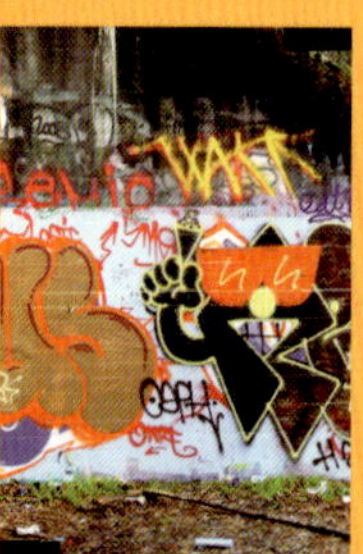

Jason Taellious
https://www.flickr.com/photos/dreamsjung/
P036

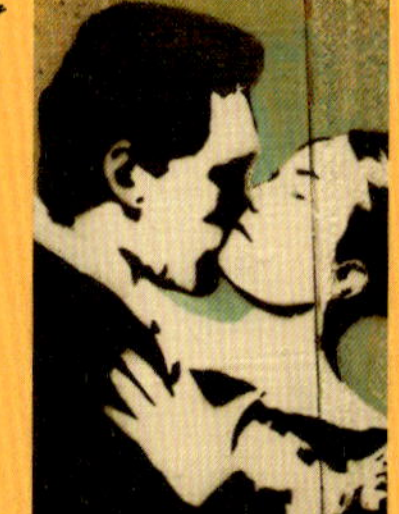

Kevin Collins
https://www.flickr.com/photos/72148272@N00/
P061

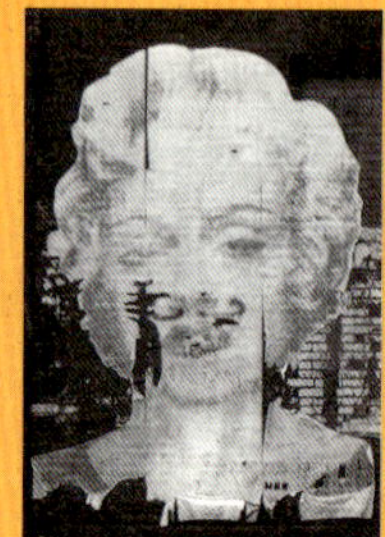

Lauren Manning
https://www.flickr.com/photos/laurenmanning/
P012

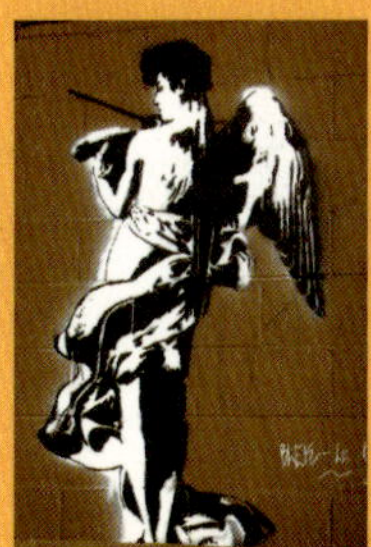

Lord Jim
https://www.flickr.com/photos/lord-jim/
P061

M

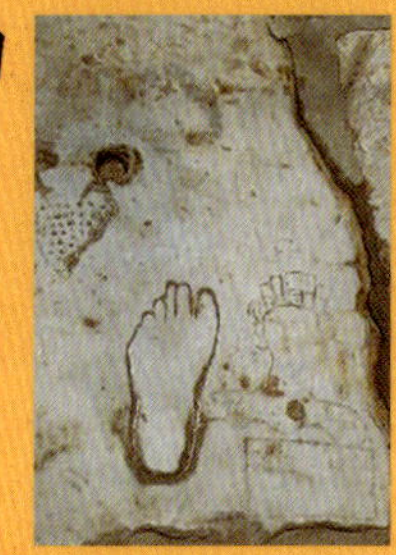

Meredith P.
https://www.flickr.com/photos/meredith/
P023

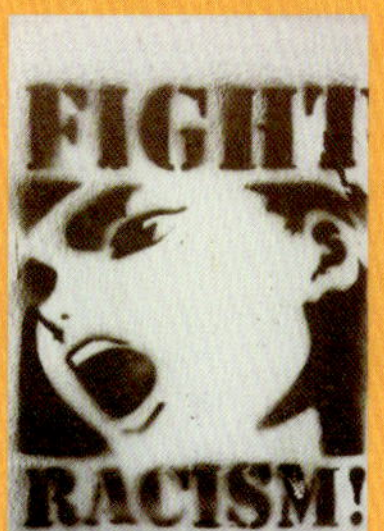

Max Pixel
http://maxpixel.freegreatpicture.com/
P065

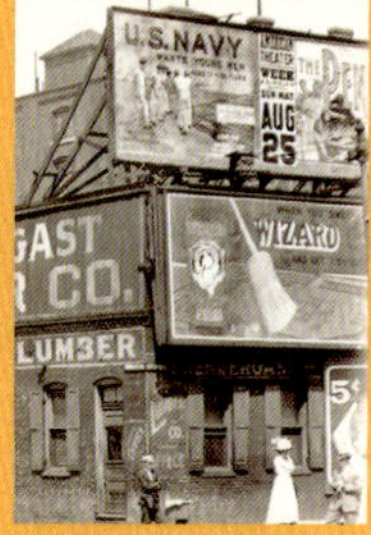

Missouri History Museum
https://www.flickr.com/photos/mohistory/
P088

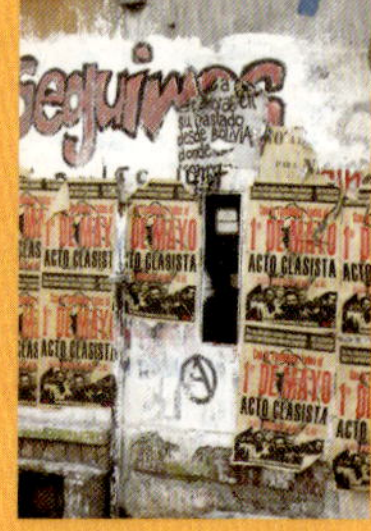

Morguefile
https://morguefile.com/
P086

N

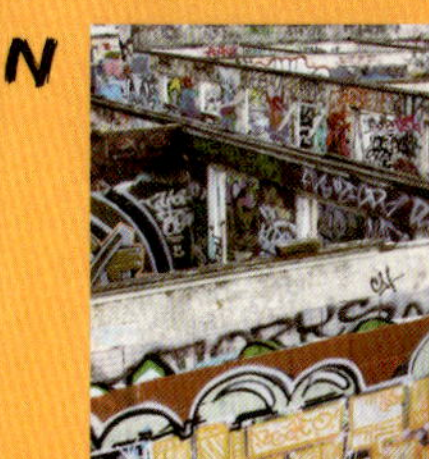

NCSphotography
https://www.flickr.com/photos/ncsphotography/
P038

O

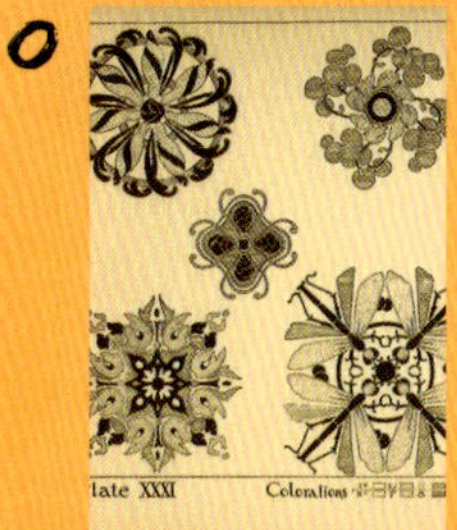

Open Library
https://openlibrary.org/
P059

P

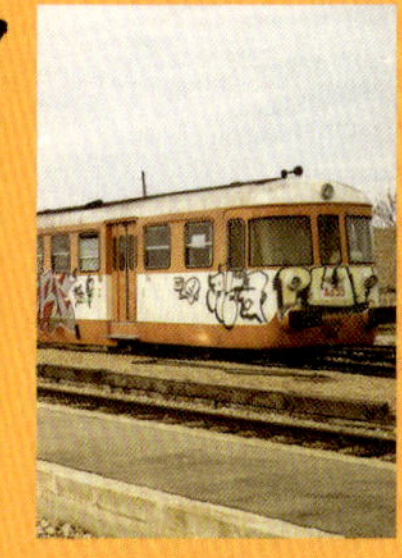

Phil Richards
https://www.flickr.com/photos/philstephenrichards/
P006

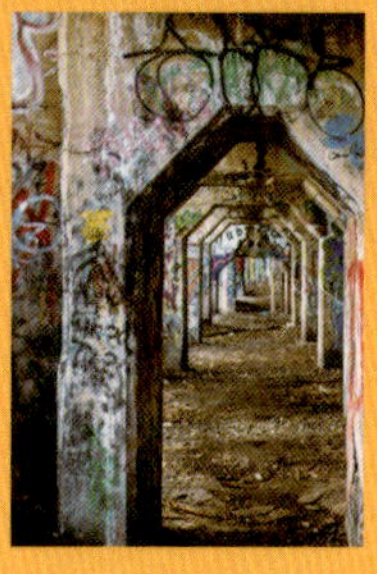

Pixabay
https://pixabay.com/
P020, 027, 038, 039, 064

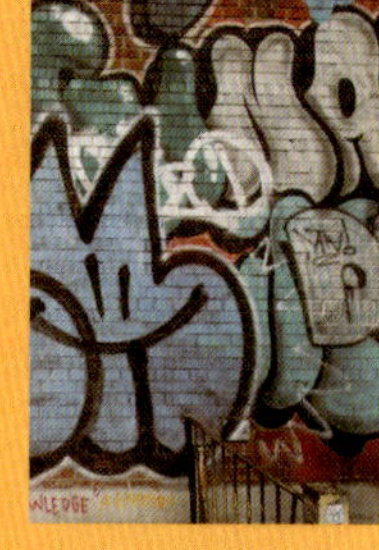

Public Domain Pictures
http://www.publicdomain-pictures.net
P037

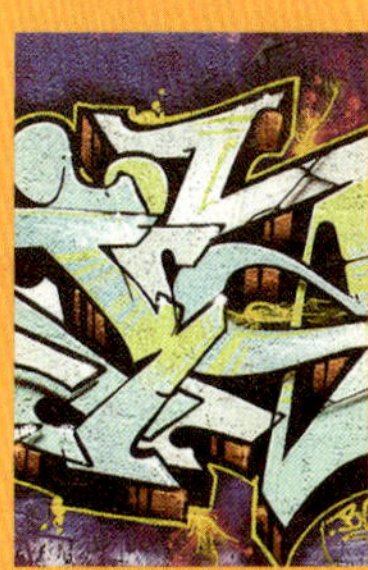

Px4u by Team Cu29
https://www.flickr.com/photos/teamcu29/
P039

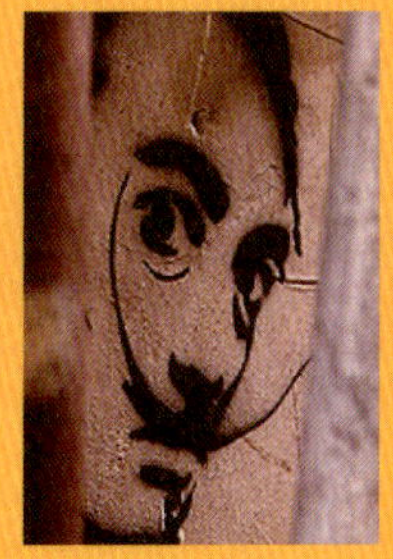

Pablo Matamoros
https://www.flickr.com/photos/pmatamoros/
P064

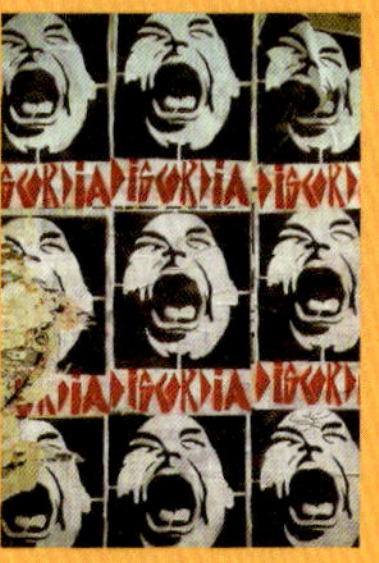

Pedro Baesse
https://www.flickr.com/photos/pbaesse/
P086

T

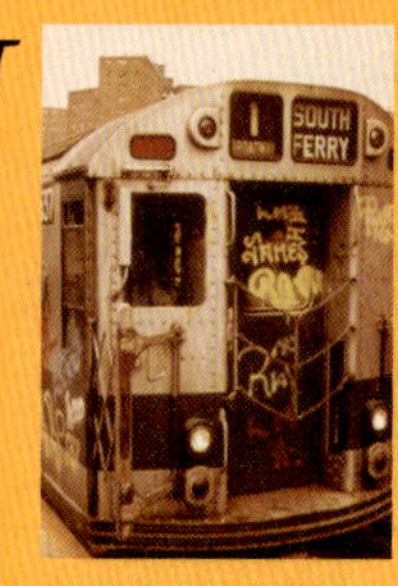

The National Archives Catalog
https://catalog.archives.gov/
P026

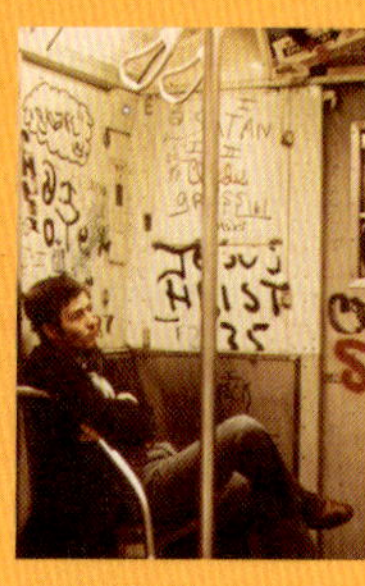

The U.S. National Archives
https://www.flickr.com/photos/usnationalarchives/
P030, 031, 033, 034

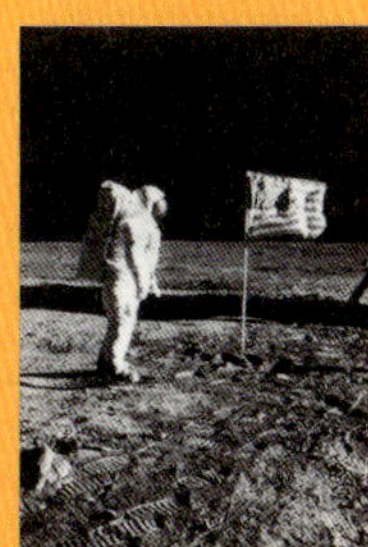

Tullio Saba
https://www.flickr.com/photos/97453745@N02/
P032

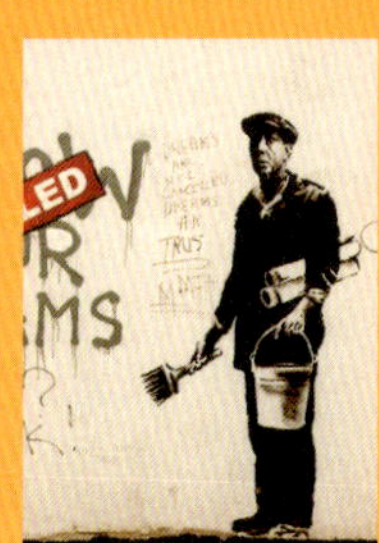

Tom Thai
https://www.flickr.com/photos/eviltomthai/
P062

W

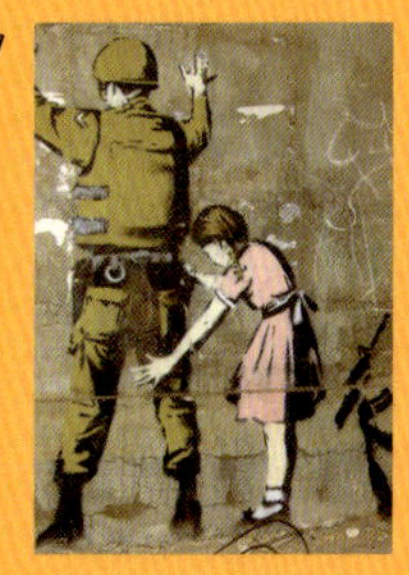

Wikimedia Commons
https://commons.wikimedia.org/
P022–025, 037, 041, 056–058, 060, 062, 063, 064, 066, 087, 089, back cover (below)

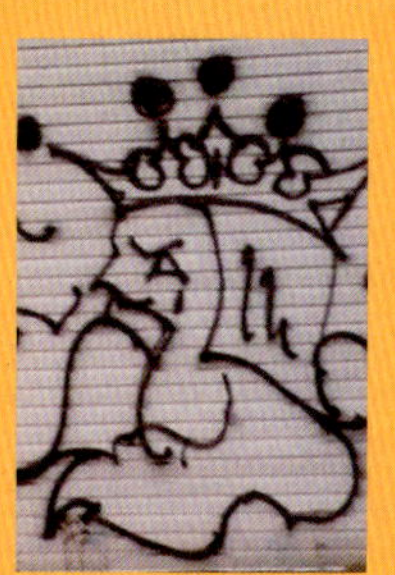

Wikipedia
https://en.wikipedia.org/wiki/Main_Page
P035, 063

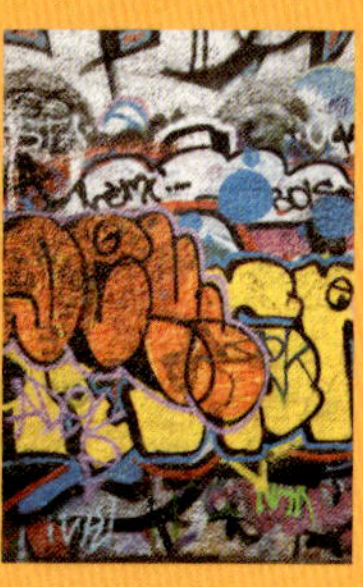

William Murphy
https://www.flickr.com/photos/infomatique/
P037

SPRAY ON WALLS — URBAN ADVENTURE OF GRAFFITI ART

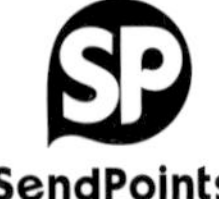

EDITED & PUBLISHED BY SendPoints Publishing Co., Ltd.
PUBLISHER: Lin Gengli
PUBLISHING DIRECTOR: Lin Shijian
CHIEF EDITOR: Lin Shijian
LEAD EDITOR: Huang Shaojun
EXECUTIVE EDITOR: Luo Yanmei
DESIGN DIRECTOR: Lin Shijian
ASSISTANT PUBLISHING DIRECTOR: Chen Ting
PROOFREADING: James N. Powell
EXECUTIVE ART EDITOR: Lin Wentao

REGISTERED ADDRESS: Room 15A Block 9 Tsui Chuk Garden, Wong Tai Sin, Kowloon, Hong Kong
TEL: +852-35832323 / **FAX:** +852-35832448
OFFICE ADDRESS: 7F, 9th Anning Street, Jinshazhou, Baiyun District, Guangzhou, China
TEL: +86-20-89095121 / **FAX:** +86-20-89095206
BEIJING OFFICE: Room 107, Floor 1, Xiyingfang Alley, Ande Road, Dongcheng District, Beijing, China
TEL: +86-10-84139071 / **FAX:** +86-10-84139071
SHANGHAI OFFICE: Room 307, Building 1, Hong Qiang Creative, Zhabei District, Shanghai, China
TEL: +86-21-63523469 / **FAX:** +86-21-63523469

SALES MANAGER: Sissi
TEL: +86-20-81007895
EMAIL: overseas01@sendpoints.cn
WEBSITE: www.sendpoints.cn / www.spbooks.cn

ISBN 978-988-78493-6-0

Printed and bound in China.

SPRAY ON WALLS

URBAN ADVENTURE OF GRAFFITI ART